The
Renaissance
New
Testament

Randolph O. Yeager

VOLUME TWELVE

Romans 9:1—16:27
I Corinthians 1:1—10:33

PELICAN PUBLISHING COMPANY

GRETNA 1983

Library of Congress Cataloging in Publication Data

Yeager, Randolph O.
   The Renaissance New Testament.

   Volumes 1-4 originally published in 1976-1978 by
Renaissance Press, Bowling Green, Ky.
      1. Bible. N.T.--Concordances, Greek. 2. Greek
language, Biblical. I. Title.
BS2302. Y4 1981   225.4'8'0321   79-28652
ISBN: 0-88289-458-7 (v. 12)

Manufactured in the United States of America

Published by Pelican Publishing Company, Inc.
1101 Monroe Street, Gretna, Louisiana 70053

The Tale of a Tub

(with apologies to Jonathan Swift)

Rub-a-dub-dub, Three men in a tub!
And who do you think they be?

Another version has it

Rub-a-dub-dub, Three men in a tub.
And how do you think they got there?

Another famous line about tubs is

While ladling butter from alternate tubs
Stubbs butters Freeman; Freeman butters Stubbs.

(W.H.Hutton, ed., *Letters of Bishop Stubbs*, 1904).

The title of this piece recalls "the custom of mariners in throwing out a tub to a whale, in order to occupy the monster's attention and divert it from an attack upon the ship - which only proves how little Swift knew of whales or sailors." (William J.Long, *English Literature*, 275).

Swift's *The Tale of a Tub* is an allegorical satire. An old man died and left a coat, which in the allegory represents Christian Truth, to each of three sons named Peter, Martin and Jack. Church historians have no difficulty identifying Peter, Martin and Jack as the Catholics, Lutherans and Calvinists. Each son accepted his coat and remodeled it to suit his fancy. Swift, with tongue in cheek, purported to be defending the Anglicans but "that institution fares perhaps worse than the others; for nothing is left to her but a thin cloak of custom under which to hide her alleged hypocrisy." (*Ibid.*).

The Mother Goose nursery rhyme goes on to identify the three men in the tub as the butcher, the baker and the candlestick maker and then dares to assert that they are "knaves all three" - an unsupported stereotype which is less than kind to such eminent gentlemen.

Bishop William Stubbs and Edward Freeman, along with John R. Green comprised the Oxford School of English history. Stubbs' area of special competence was constitutional history of Medieval England while "Freeman is equally at home in Athens and Rome, Aachen and Constantinople, Rouen and Winchester." (G.P.Gooch, *History and Historians in the Nineteenth Century*, 318-323, *et passim*). John R.Green's *History of the English People* is a masterpiece in social and intellectual history.

Freeman was slightly older than Stubbs but he regarded him as his master. Green deferred to both Stubbs and Freeman and dedicated his most popular work to "my masters in English history." "Stubbs and Freeman differed widely in temperament. Stubbs was cool and reserved, Freeman a hero-worshipper and propagandist. Stubbs was concise, Freeman diffuse. Stubbs was an extreme conservative; Freeman was a militant radical." (*Ibid.*). Yet they complemented each other. As Stubbs said, he buttered Freeman and Freeman buttered him.

The three men in the tub and Stubbs and Freeman in the same history department speak of unity in diversity. I suggest that the three hermeneutical men in the tub, who butter each other, are so diverse, each from the other two, that few will suspect them. I will put the hyper-emotional charismatics (as distinct from the true charismatics), the Quakers and the German schools of Higher and Lower Criticism into the same tub and suggest that they are "knaves all three." I will then suggest that my reader and I should also have a look to see if we also are in the same tub. If so, why and if not, why not?

Fanatics at football games who throw away fifty dollars hats because some jock crosses a goal line carrying a football do not thereby lose face. They are only enthusiastic supporters of dear old Siwash, their hallowed Alma Mater, who have told the coach how to run the game and have contributed their money to buy the jock who just scored a sports car. We have developed a euphemism. We call them "fans" and forget for the moment that if they had more in the attic they would behave more rationally at the Homecoming game.

But let a Christian get excited at church about his supernatural encounter with the Son of God and you have a fanatic on your hands. An old man who had "good religion" indulged the indiscretion of saying, "Amen" in a worship service where any visible or audible evidence of personal approbation for Christianity was considered in bad taste and therefore *verboten*. Whereupon an usher donned his ice skates, skated down the aisle to the happy old man and whispered that he should contain himself. The old man apologized and explained that he "had religion." The usher replied, "Very good, but you didn't get it here, so Shut Up!"

That is one exteme.

Here is another.

A delightful old maid, a Methodist, now retired from her long and successful tenure as a Professor of English in a state university, who knows the Lord and has the proper mix of intellect, will and emotion told me this:

In a tent meeting the preacher and the choir occupied a high platform, equipped with an additional railing across the front to approximate a total height of perhaps five feet about the sawdust flood. During the sermon a man in the choir, whose intellectual elevator did not go much above the mezzanine, was suddenly attacked by something that the preacher called the Holy Spirit. Whereupon he arose, leaped over the railing and ran down the center aisle. The preacher followed in hot pursuit. After two or three circumnavigations around the tent they ended up playing "dog and bear" around the center pole of the tent. The man "faked the preacher out," ran back to the front and tried to leap over the rail to his place in the choir. He didn't make it, but caught his foot on the railing, fell back and hit his head on a front seat. Those nearest him rushed to his rescue, only to be told by the preacher, "Leave him lay where Jesus flang him!"

That is the other extreme.

In the former case it was all nerves and no glands; in the latter all glands and no nerves. Man is both soul and spirit - both emotion and intellect. Neither can be brought into subjection to Christ without a surrender of the will. The cold intellectual who appreciates the Word of God only because of a thorough knowledge of the text, etymological, grammatical and syntactical, is no better than the religious enthusiast who doesn't care what the Bible teaches as long as he feels good.

The proper mix of intellect, will and emotion will yield a humble search of the mind for the true and total message of the Word of God, a surrender of the will and a set of emotional responses that flow from the fruits of the Holy Spirit - "love, joy, peace, longsuffering, gentleness, goodness, faith, meekness, and temperance." No regulation has yet been devised to contain a man like that, but jumping off a platform and running around a tent as a witness for Jesus is not listed as a fruit of the Spirit.

Those who jump too high or fail to jump high enough, as in the case of the man who had "to lay where Jesus flang him" seldom walk straight when they come down.

How does it happen that Peter, Martin and Jack, not to mention the rest of us, have chosen to remodel the coat which the Greek New Testament handed down to us? Why the hermeneutical chaos? Why are we in danger of being doomed by what Carl F.H.Henry has called "Hermeneutical Nihilism"? ("The Interpretation of the Scriptures: Are we Doomed to Hermeneutical Nihilism?" *The Review and Expositor*, Vol.LXXI, #2, Spring, 1974, 197-215).

Before we examine the hermeneutical philosophy of the three knaves in the tub to determine why, like Stubbs and Freeman, they butter each other, we should recall that they had a predecessor who set the Church up to housekeeping in the method of Biblical interpretation which produces heretics. His name was Origen. I have paid my respects to him and included the opinion of Mosheim, the great Lutheran church historian previously. (*The Renaissance New Testament*, 9, viii-x). Like their notorious predecessor of the Patristic period, modern tubmen are unwilling to allow the Bible to teach anything to which they object and offer instead the teachings which they "feel" are true.

The coat of Christian Truth has passed through a great many hands since the Greek New Testament literature was perfected at the close of the first century. Peter, Martin and Jack are not the only ones who have tried to remodel its style and change its color. Some have modified it, as Swift accused the Anglicans, until there is little left except a rag that covers nothing and attracts no one but tired old men and women who have nothing better to command their attention.

There has been a spate of spin-offs from Peter's transubstantiation, Martin's consubstantiation and Jack's predestination. A charismatic women in England had "revealed" to her an eschatalogical detail about the rapture of the church which was not revealed to any student of the Scriptures before, mainly because it is not there. As a result during the past one hundred and fifty years the footnotes in the Schofield Reference Bible are regarded by some as inerrant as the text printed above the line. Thus while some leap off the platform and run around the tent others see visions and dream dreams. The coat of Christian Truth has been modified in keeping with the personality constructs of the modifiers who felt inclined to remodel it because they didn't like its original design. They range all the way from the fanatic who depends upon the emotions that result from undue glandular stimulii to those who conduct the formal liturgical service, eschew emotion and fancy themselves to be intellectual. Few there are who find in the New Testament the challenge to surrender the human will and commit it to the will of God (John 17:7), an experiential knowledge of the "joy of the Lord" (Neh.8:10), the "peace that passes understanding" (Phil.4:7) and the non-conformity to the world that comes only by "the renewing of the mind" (Rom. 12: 1-2).

Unless the entire personality is conformed to the divine image, we have got another "Tale of a Tub." The Renaissance Christian knows God and His Word only when he has faith, reason and experience in proper balance.

The first man in the tub if we view them in chronological sequence in modern times was George Fox (1624-1691), the founder of the Society of Friends.

The second is a composite man, representing the schools of German Lower and Higher Criticism. Names like Friedrich Ernst Daniel Schleiermacher, Adolf Harnack, Karl Barth, Wilhelm Dilthey, Hans-Georg Gadamer, Martin Heidigger and Rudolph Bultmann come to mind. They have carried on a concerted subjective attack upon objective presuppositional exegesis and hermeneutics for the past two hundred years, with varying degrees of offense to evangelicals, Barth perhaps being the least offensive and Heidegger and Bultmann, whose names are anathema to those of us who believe that the divine revelation is located in the text, not in the subjective impression of the reader. This is not to say that we do not ask the Holy Spirit to subject us to what is said in the text, once we have determined what the text says. It is to say that the determination of the message of the text is made on a basis of historical exegesis and this means diction, grammar, syntax, context and *zeitgeist*.

The third knave in the tub is the superglandular "charismatic" fanatic who lacks the synaptic structure needed to bring thought and feeling into proper balance. These are the people who, for all of their sincere desire to understand the Bible and serve the Lord, believe that the way to serve Him best is to talk gibberish and jabberwocky at church or play "dog and bear" with the preacher in a tent meeting. It is virtually useless to point out to these people what the New Testament has to say about their behavior. If they listen at all to your remarks they are also reflecting upon the fact that they are "spiritual" and since you do not agree with them, you are not. For them only "spiritual" people are able to tell what the Scripture means by what it says. Thus they give higher marks to subjective impression than to objective exegesis and hermeneutics.

Misery, politics and poverty are all said "to make strange bedfellows." (William Shakespeare, *The Tempest,* II, 2; C.E.Warner, *My Summer in a Garden*, XV; English proverb, first recorded in 1849). Add to the list the desire to make the Bible teach what one wishes it had, instead of what it does.

Who would have thought that the fanatics in the modern charismatic movement (so designated to distinguish them from the *true* charismatics) would ever be found in bed with the Quakers and the German school of rationalism? George Fox, if he were alive and the Holy Roller choir member in the tent meeting who was left to "lay where Jesus flang him" would be certain to castigate Bultmann and Heidegger and even Barth perhaps for their work in laying the ground for Modernism. Yet Fox, with his subjective extra-scriptural impressions and the recent crop of "apostles" who claim to possess gifts of prophecy, special knowledge which is unavailable to ordinary mortals and glossalalia, are making the same mistake that Schleirmacher, Barth, Dilthey, Gadamer, Heidegger and Bultmann made. And the result is that their disciples are no longer interested in what the Bible *says* because they know what it *means*. It is much easier to watch television and be told what is true than to make the intellectual effort to be a Berean and "search the scriptures daily whether those things were so." (Acts 17:11). A man and his wife who boasted that they were constantly chasing horizons in their world-wide evangelistic ministry, complained of jet lag, but predicted that they expected the Lord to "rapture" them from the United States to India and thus prevent the jet lag which they suffered when they flew on a 747. To which prediction the host on the program remarked that it was his view that he, his evangelist guests and others who appeared on his show were twentieth century Peters, Pauls, James's, Johns and Philips - especially endowed Apostles and Deacons with the same powers which their first century counterparts possessed. The reader will forgive my skepticism, but I intend to doubt that until someone with a bottle of oil grows arms and legs on a Vietnam war veteran who lost his, or until someone of these self-appointed Apostles raises from the dead a modern Eutychus who went to sleep on him and fell out of a window and broke his neck.

There can be no doubt that God raptured Enoch and Elijah, but their destination was heaven, not India. To be sure Philip enjoyed a quick trip to Azotus, which was too far up the coast for him to walk. If TWA had flown from Gaza to Azotus in Philip's day, it is likely that Philip would have used his American Express gold card. Thus there is no doubt that God can do whatever he wishes in His sovereign wisdom to do, and who of us is to say Him nay, but God does not normally perform miracles if there is an alternative way to accomplish his purpose. The way to avoid jet lag on a long flight from here to there is to sleep on the plane or leave a day early and catch up on your sleep when you arrive. Surely the audience in India can wait an extra day while the Apostle recovers from the rigors of the flight.

The men in the tub, - "knaves all three" - have one thing in common. Thus they butter each other as Stubbs buttered Freeman and Freeman buttered Stubbs. For them, the revelation is not in the text, but in their own personal subjective encounter with the text. Thus the same text could mean different, perhaps even opposite, things to two people, and the text could mean one thing to a reader one moment and something different to the same reader a moment later. This is because we are constantly subjected to the influence of our environments. Millions of sensory stimulii bombard us every day, some of which we ignore and to others of which we respond. But every man's environment is different from that of every other. Every person has been conditioned with a different cultural construct. Now if it is the culture that interprets the text instead of the diction, grammar, syntax, context and *zeitgeist*, as these matters are viewed objectively, in the light of historical research, the bottom line is the subjective impression, not the text, and the Bible can only mean what ten thousand butchers, bakers and candlestick makers say it means. And what it says to each of these knaves is going to be different from what it says to the others. This amounts to saying that the Bible says nothing significant to anyone.

The Existentialists are not afraid to go that far. In fact they are proud of what they preach. Martin Heidegger insisted that anything written two thousand years ago could convey nothing to him who reads it two thousand years later. Why? Because language is a form of communication, but language is the child of the culture in which it currently exists, having been evolved by the evolving culture of the past. For example the word "prop" means a stick under the clothes line, placed there to prevent the sagging line from dragging the white sheets in the mud, only to your grandmother who still does the laundry like everyone did one hundred years ago. Those with automatic clothes washers and dryers no long use props. Pilots who fly jet-propelled airplanes may soon forget what is meant by "prop" at an out-of-date airport. And neither your grandmother nor the jet pilot understands the word as it is used backstage in a theatre. As language, in terms of diction ("prop" - "propeller" - "property"), grammar and syntax, changes with the culture which uses it for communication, the writer of the 18th century, who was a child of 18th century culture can write significant material and communicate with perspicuity and perspicacity only to a reader who is also a child of the 18th century culture. It follows that nobody today really knows what Thomas Jefferson meant in the Declaration of Independence. And if we cannot understand Jefferson who wrote in 1776, how can we understand Paul who wrote in the first century?

The existentialists go even further. For time is not the only factor that separates writer from reader. So does cultural conditioning for two people who though contemporary are products of differing backgrounds. No one says that communication is easy, but evangelical Christians will insist that it is not impossible.

That problems in communication exist, between those separated by time as well as contemporaries who are separated by culture, can be illustrated by the following: Indian students from Bacone College in Muskogee, Oklahoma were given an IQ test which students in New York take. They did poorly and New Yorkers leaped to the false conclusion that Indians are not as smart as kids from the Bowery, the Bronx and Flatbush, until New Yorkers were given the IQ test given to Indians of the same age in Muskogee. They did less well than the Indians. The difference was not in the native intelligence but in the cultural conditioning.

Italian children were asked to supply the missing item on a door that had no doorknob. They pencilled in a crucifix. Everyone who has been to Italy knows that there are few doors with doorknobs but none without a crucifix.

Thus there is evidence that as cultural backgrounds differ problems of communication are exacerbated. While evangelical Christians recognize this fact, deplore it and struggle to overcome the difficulties which it presents, extreme existentialists rejoice that it is true and develop their philosophy that there is really no cause and result connection between the present moment and any other, past or future. If John Locke, David Hume and George Berkeley were correct that there is nothing in the intellect except that which was first in the senses, then it follows that all knowledge is grounded in sensation. And since we experience our environment which is always changing on a momentary basis and know only what we sense, it follows that what I know now is other than what I knew a moment ago. It requires time to "think" about what we have "sensed" but in the time required to think about it, the environment has changed and receded into the past which cannot be recalled. By the time we have followed Kant's method and seen the progress from stimulus to sensation to perception to concept to law to knowledge, the world has gone away and left us and it is not true any longer. In order to observe we must stop the world, but if we stop it there is nothing to observe. Thus radical existentialism. Intelligent communication is impossible since there is no birfurcation between subject and object, Rene

DesCartes to the contrary notwithstanding.

If object and subject are the same then he who speaks or writes can communicate only to himself. As subject he speaks to himself as object since he is the only person in the universe who has been conditioned by his cultural background. Even his identical twin, according to this view, cannot understand what he is saying. Though genetically identical they have not received idential sensory experiences. One went to the football game while the other went to the theatre. The speaker at Emory University was a religion professor from Duke. After roundly damning DesCartes, who gave us differential calculus (!) for saying that subject and object are different entities, he spent forty minutes trying to communicate to us that communication between persons is impossible! In the discussion period that followed I asked him why, if it were true that he could not communicate to us, he took up forty minutes of our time. The audience applauded my question, but the professor from Duke did not understand it! Cratylus would have told him that he should not even have tried to make signs. As Henry wells says, "The theory of historicity of understanding cannot in fact be true unless it is false, else nobody could communicate it intelligbly to anyone else." (Henry, *Hermeneutical Nihilism*, 205).

Martin Buber explains the same nihilism is terms of his "I and Thou" formula. One cannot call it a concept, not at least a concept that can be communicated, since I am I and Thou art Thou and never the twain shall meet.

It was Wilhelm Dilthey who first attacked the rigid epistemological formula of Hegel. Even though thesis and antithesis are contemporary and move contemporaniously through time to synthesis, which in turn becomes a new thesis which attracts a new antithesis which must move across time to a second more valid synthesis, yet in the process both thesis and synthesis are influenced by environmental forces which are different from those encountered by the opposition. Dilthey thought that Hegel overlooked this and Dilthey reminded the Hegelians that cultural diversity makes communication impossible. Dilthey, of course, labored under the illusion that he understood Hegel! When Hegel said "Only one man understands me and he does not" he was not speaking of Dilthey. "In Italy, Benedetto Croce took up Dilthey's ideas and offered a kind of modified Hegelianism that proved must seductive. The Italian philosopher insisted that history recorded the progress of the spirit, or, more specifically, of human liberty. All genuine history is contemporary history — because 'however remote in time events there recounted may seem to be, the history in reality refers to present needs and present situations wherein those events vibrate.' And notion of necessity, 'causal or transcendent' is flatly rejected. . . . Croce saw man as a product of the past, 'immersed in the past.' Yet at the same time he was obliged to move toward a future. The only way he could do this was to write history. This was 'the one way of way of (*sic*) getting rid of the past,' by making the past serve the present. Historical thought, Croce wrote, 'transforms (the past) into its own material and transfigures it into its object . . . .'. . . . Liberty is 'on the one hand the explanatory principle of the course of history, and on the other the moral idea of humanity.' Whether the age was 'propitious or unfavourable, liberty appeared as abiding purely and invincibly and even consciously only in a few spirits.' "

(Benedetto Croce, *History as the Story of Liberty*, 17,18, as cited in Page Smith, *The Historian and History*, 81-83, *et passim*).

"When Croce declared that 'history is in all of us and . . . its sources are in our own breasts,' he made the critical point that history is not something 'objective,' something 'out there,' about which we speculate and about which we reach certain scientific conclusions. His writings on history gave new life to nineteenth-century Hegelianism *and to its stepchild, historical relativism.*" *(*Yeager's emphasis). *(Ibid.)*.

Thus the trend in philosophy during the last two hundred years reflects doubt about ontology and therefore doubts about metaphysics, epistemology, logic, axiology and aesthetics. If one cannot be sure about what is real how can he have an opinion about the transcendent, or what to believe, or how to think, or what is valuable or beautiful? If all alike has equal value, if equally both true and false, equally beautiful and ugly, then communication is not only impossible but totally unnecessary. In fact speech is a rude intrusion upon the consciousness of all those within hearing distance. One speaker cannot tell a listener anything, even though speaking and listening take place at the same time. So why does not everyone shut up?

Perhaps the hermit in his cave is smarter than the rest of us.

Maybe that is why the Holy Rollers speak in "tongues." Nobdy is going to understand it anyway.

Paul told the loquacious, multi-lingual Corinthians that if the language they spoke was not understood by the audience they were to remain silent. But fanatics are compulsive personalities, who are deluded into thinking that they are divinely chosen mouthpieces for the Holy Spirit. And they wish to be heard, even though not understood. If the speaker is fluent both in French and English and I understand nothing but English, why should he not speak to me in English? Perhaps he is compulsive because he is insecure and wishes to demonstrate to me what a skilled linguist he is. He makes an impression upon me but it is not the impression which he so fondly imagines. I see him not as one qualified to interpret at the United Nations but as a boor and a bore. Paul reminded the Corinthians that such childish display was not love and that it did nothing to edify the Body of Christ.

Modern Quakers may object to what we say about their founder, George Fox. Did he know the Bible or not? Did he believe it or not? If he knew and believed it why did he depend upon "inner light" in a subjective sense rather than the light to be derived from historical exegesis of the text itself in the objective sense?

There can be no doubt that Fox read the Bible. "It is plain from all his writings and from what he tells of his practice that he was steeped in the Scriptures. One critic indeed asserted that Fox wrote nothing but a string of texts." (W.D.Niven, *George Fox and the Scriptures*, "The Expositor", Ninth Series, No.7, July, 1924, 47). That was an unfair exaggeration but "the same glance will reveal that for every statement Fox makes, unless it be pure narrative, he adduces support from the Scriptures. He uses throughout Biblical language. He read the Bible diligently before he came to the light. He used it as constantly afterward. Whatever else the Spirit revealed, He certainly gave Fox great openings in the Scriptures. . . . His encouragement of Friends, his warning of sinners, his denunciation of enemies of the Truth, his criticism of 'priests' and their 'worships' were all based on Scripture, and expressed in the very terms of Scripture." (*Ibid,* 47,48).

Fox proved his points by the Bible and challenged his enemies to show from the Bible that he was wrong. In his Journal he wrote, "We laid it upon him to prove all his charges against us by Scripture," and again "If the Scriptures of Truth would not bear us out in our principles, doctrines and practices, then let us fall with shame." (George Fox, *Journal,* ii, 217,218 as cited in *Ibid.,* 48).

Passages such as these are typical. When someone said that women have no souls, Fox pointed them to Mary's words, "My soul doth magnify the Lord." (Sewell, *History of the Quakers,* i, 19). That Fox was begging the question is not the point. The point is that he believed what Luke 1:46 says.

Fox and the early Friends carried on their outreach work with "Bible in hand." (Barclay, *Inner Life of Religious Societies of the Commonwealth,* 401, as cited in *Ibid.*). He did not agree with the Seekers, who held that the reading of Scripture to a mixed congregation is dangerous. (*Ibid.*) That the Seekers were mystics is clear from the strange objection to Bible reading in public to mixed audiences. (R.M.Jones, *Studies in Mystical Religion,* 457, as cited in *Ibid.*).

When Fox died however public Scripture reading was abandoned. (D.Phillips, *Vindiciae Veritatis,* 203-206, as cited in *Ibid.*). The Friends explained their aversion to the Bible as a fear that it would prove a "fettering of the Spirit." Yet they did not object to reading it at home! As a preacher spoke from a text he was admonished to be careful that what he said was not premeditated. (Barclay, *Apology,* "Exposition of Prop.," xi, as cited in *Ibid.,* 49). Fox declared that expository preaching was "a vanity of priests." (*Journal,* i, 73, as cited in *Ibid.*). It is interesting that a so-called charismatic evangelist whose ministry takes him among Pentecostal and Assembly of God churches said the same thing about *The Renaissance New Testament* since our work teaches Christians to "Study to show (themselves) approved unto God . . ." (2 Tim.2:15). He spoke as though those who study the Greek New Testament first before they preach thereby disqualify themselves as mouthpieces of the Holy Spirit. It is true that a careful exposition of the Greek New Testament will go far to reveal how unscriptural much is that is preached by those who, like this evangelist, depend upon the immediate inspiration of the Holy Spirit, and not upon what the Holy Spirit has written into the text. This is the same mistake that George Fox and the Seekers, Schleirmacher, Harnack, Dilthey, Croce, Heidgegger and, to a lesser extent, Barth made.

Fox, the fanatics in the charismatic movement and the German Rationalists, who are the three knaves in the tub, imagine that they have a "Bible within the Bible." "He takes from one part of Scripture a text that lends support to his views, and finds reasons for setting aside any that seems to contradict them."

(*Ibid.*). Before we criticize him too much, let us face the question as to whether or not we have ever done as much? When Origen did not like what the Bible clearly says, he changed the meaning of the words! Bultmann got rid of the supernatural by the process which he called demythologizing. Eric Rust says that the Old Testament writers described the cosmos as they did because everyone in their day thought that the world was flat. The Holy Rollers will speak in "tongues" despite what Paul wrote in 1 Corinthians 12-14. They refuse even to listen to an exposition of these chapters. This is because they exalt experience above reason - emotion above thought - glands above nerves. The Arminian will ignore Acts 13:48 and Calvinists agonize over Matthew 24:13. Pentecostalists prepare their tar and feathers when they are told that Mark 16:9-20 is not a part of the inspired text. The textual critics, however honest, scholarly, objective and dedicated they may be and however committed to the virgin birth, blood atonement, bodily resurrection and second coming, are nevertheless infidels if they take away snake handling, poison drinking, baptismal regeneration and signs following.

Fox was by no means alone in his tendency to select texts which supported his preconceived views and to reject texts which opposed him. "There is in practice for everybody a Scripture within the Scripture. . . . The general bearing of many views is plain and acceptable; but press them into details or to their logical conclusions, and seemingly unanswerable questions immediately emerge. Most men . . . especially in the sphere of religion and politics, are apt to demand in the views of their opponents a degree of explicitness and consistency which it would puzzle them to exhibit in their own (*Ibid.,* 46).

Let us all freely admit that the Scriptures present us with what seem to us to be polarities, and let us be the first to rejoice that we are not Gnostics. God's thoughts are still high above our own, despite our prowess as exegetes. But that kind of intellectual humility is a far cry from the view that what the reader "feels" to be the revelation is the truth which is to be regarded above what the text clearly says. If God's revelation is immediate let us renounce exegesis and let us deplore as the evangelist referred to above did, the approach to New Testament study represented for example by A.T.Robertson, *The Greek New Testament in the Light of Historical Research.* Why slave over the meaning of the aorist tense, as distinct from the imperfect, or the difference between the subjunctive and the optative modes if a high school dropout can distill divine wisdom out of thin air? This is not to say that God has not used many high school dropouts in the ministry, some of them with greater effectiveness than the Ph.D.'s, but those whom He used in preaching His gospel got their message from a book that they could never have read in the original Greek and can scarcely read in English.

If divine revelation is unfinished at this point and available on an immediate and subjective basis then *The Renaissance New Testament,*the result of more than fifty years of work is a classic waste of time. A country preacher in Arkansas ridiculed preachers who had taken the time and expended the effort and wealth to get the Ph.D. degree. He had no degrees, he added, not even a high school diploma, but he announced that he would have conferred upon him a Ph.D. "in a moment, in the twinkling of an eye, at the last trump" when the rapture occurred. No Bible taught, Holy Spirit directed Ph.D. is going to say that God cannot use this misguided brother, as long as he gets his message from the text. Neither should he have boasted about his ignorance, condemned other members of the Body of Christ who are more educated than he, felt so confident that he was able to discern the total revelation of God, inasmuch as he could read no Greek and very little English. Nor should he have assumed that a graduate degree was available at the rapture. Born again Ph.D.'s are looking for something better than that when the Lord returns.

Fox said that Christ is the *Word* and the Bible are the *words*. (*Journal*, i, 105; ii, 200, as cited in *Ibid*, 51). But he supported every statement from the Bible and demanded that his critics do the same. His apologist, Barclay, held that immediate revelation conveys not new truth, but imparts anew the old truths set forth in Scripture. He added that whatever contradicts is false. No Presbyterian was going to argue with that for that is precisely what they meant by saying, "Scripture is the Rule of Faith." But by "Rule of Faith" Fox and Barclay meant something individual and subjective.

So if you want to know how the three men in the tub got there, the answer is by their efforts, not to rewrite the Bible, but to interpret it to conform to what to them seems reasonable and fulfilling to believe. Those of us who are still outside the tub are still trying to fathom what the Presbyterians in Fox's day meant by saying that "Scripture is the Rule of Faith." Indeed it is the rule of faith but what does it say when it is approached in terms of historical and objective exegesis? The current evangelical exegete need not shrink from agreeing with Croce that the problem of historicity is present, but he need not agree with Croce that it is insoluble. To be sure it is difficult to achieve von Ranke's *zeitgeist*. Koine Greek written by and to products of a culture which has now receded two thousand years into the past requires much knowledge of the history of the evolution of cultures with their folkways and mores, their understanding of the meaning of words and of grammatical and syntactical constructions, but the goal is not unattainable and the rewards for success are beyond computation. With Karl Barth we must think *after* the writer (*nachdenken*), then we must think *with* him (*mitdenken)* and finally we are able to identify with him completely (*selberdenken*). (Henry, *Hermeneutical Nihilism*, 203). It is a great challenge. We will not meet it successfully if we ignore the warning implicit in Barth's dogma that no man can be totally objective. He used it against Harnack and Bultmann and asserted that they could not find a supernatural Jesus in the New Testament because they were convinced when they began the search that He was not supernatural. For Barth objectivity leads to supernaturalism in the person and work of our Lord. If Harnack and Bultmann were indulging a prejudicial eisegesis when they concluded that theism is not taught in the New Testament, is it not possible that those who see Jesus as the supernatural Son of God, incarnate in human flesh, can yield to prejudices in other areas of doctrine and practice? Why should charismatics ignore what 1 Corinthians 13:8 clearly says about the gifts of prophecy and knowledge? Yet they do and continue to insist that they possess the gifts which Paul said were phased out ($\kappa\alpha\tau\alpha\rho\gamma\epsilon\omega$) when the revelation of the New Testament became complete ($\tau\epsilon\lambda\epsilon\iota\sigma\varsigma$). Why should pretribulation rapture teachers read their doctrine into 1 Thessalonians 4:13-18?

No exegete saw this view in the New Testament before the 19th century.

We have identified the three men in the tub - "knaves all three." Each has taken the coat which he inherited and altered it to suit his fancy. And as they ladled the butter they also buttered each other.

How shall we stay out of the tub?

First, we must recognize the danger of prejudice. Karl Barth was correct when he doubted the ability of any man to approach the Greek New Testament with a determination to believe all that it teaches and only what it teaches, without regard to what he has previously thought and taught to be the truth. The flesh is the source of human pride. It is so easy for us to believe that what we believe is true, if for no other reason than that we have always believed it. It is so easy for us to rearrange our prejudices when we are confronted with material which disproves our position. Rationalization is a vicious psychological disease. To be rid of it is the desire of every true Bible student.

As we guard against our own prejudices, let us look carefully at the meaning of the words in the passage, not as Homer used them, nor as the Attic writers, nor the early Hellenists, nor the patristic or Medieval writers used them, not as our nextdoor neighbour who is Greek uses them, but as they were used and understood by writers and readers in the first century.

Once we have established word meanings, we must pay careful attention to the grammar. Again we are interested in the grammar of the writer in the first century, not in that of a writer of any other era.

The same care must be given to syntax and context. If we succeed in solving the etymology, grammar, syntax and context problems we are true exegetes only if we have not allowed our own prejudicial wishes to dictate to us what we are going to prove by the passage before us.

The question now becomes one of hermeneutics. If I know precisely what the passage says, all that it says and only that which it says, what does it mean to me? And this can be answered only by determining what it meant to the author who wrote it and to his audience who first read it. Paul did not realize that he was writing for an audience that would live two thousand years after he died. If he had he could have done nothing about it, since he could not have known how we, in the 20th century have been culturally conditioned by two thousand years of social evolution. Therefore since he could not write for us, we must interpret what he wrote in the light of his culture. This is *zeitgeist* - "the spirit of the times."

Let us assume that we have been successful thus far in our exegesis and hermeneutics. Aware of the danger involved in our subjective prejudices, we have succeeded in escaping them. We know what the words meant to the author and his readers; we know how he used and how they understood his grammar and syntax; we have given due regard to the context and *zeitgeist*. Up to this point we have escaped fellowship with the three knaves in the tub. But we are faced with the problem of polarities in the Scriptures.

That there are what we, in our poor, mortal human wisdom must regard as polarities in Scripture there can be no doubt. Thus Calvinists are convinced that there are contexts which support the TULIP and other passages which *seem* to contradict it. Arminians build their theology on passages that for them teach against the TULIP, but honestly face passages which support it in all of its five points. Is man depraved in will, intellect and emotion or not? Perhaps as the Thomists and the Jesuits teach in will and emotion but not in intellect. Is God's choice of His elect conditioned on human merit or is it unconditional? Is the atonement limited or unlimited and if limited is the limitation one of quantity or quality? Did Christ on the cross make salvation possible for all or certain for some? Or perhaps there are no limitations upon what He did for us, either quantitatively or qualitatively. If He actually secured for those for whom He died release from the law and if He did this for all of Adam's fallen race, then we are driven to Universalism. But in this case, we are confronted with the passages that teach eternal punishment for some.

There is one more tool which the exegete has in his kit, which he can employ. It is inherent in the jigsaw puzzle analogy. We begin by affirming *a priori* that the Holy Spirit wrote the Bible and that He is God and has made no mistakes. If this is true He certainly has not contradicted Himself in any portion of the message which He wishes to reveal to us. Armed with these *a priori* assumptions we note that Peter said that no Scripture is of its own interpretation (2 Peter 1:20). This must mean that every passage, objectively exegeted and interpreted, fits into its *unique* place in the puzzle, in perfect harmony with all of its neighbours. This must also mean that no scripture teaches anything until the light of all of the other scriptures which are germane to the point have been allowed to shine their light upon it. This also means that if any scripture is forced by eisegesis, whether because of faulty etymology, grammar, syntax, context or *zeitgeist*, into a place in the puzzle where it does not belong, the entire puzzle is to some degree contorted. If the reader doubts this try putting a single piece of a jigsaw puzzle into a spot where it does not belong and see what happens. True exegesis is rewarded by the experience of seeing every part of the puzzle fitting with perfect harmony into its place, shedding its light here and there and enriching every concept to which it is designed to have addressed itself. All of this stems from our two *a priori* assumptions that the Holy Spirit wrote the Bible and that He does not make mistakes and contradict Himself.

If we do all of this and the polarities still persist (and they will) we turn to Isaiah 55:8,9 and humbly rejoice that we are not Gnostics who know as much as God. If we knew it all now and had our Biblical jigsaw puzzle put together perfectly there would be nothing left for us to learn when we get to heaven.

But what do we do in the meantime? We admit that polarities exist. While we are sure that there are no contradictions we confess that in the light of our current imperfect knowledge they seem to exist and we cannot resolve the difficulty. This is the humility that always results when we try to think God's thoughts after Him. And then we decide on the basis of the preponderance of the evidence what the Word of God teaches. And we are tolerant of those who decide the issue in some other way. Thus we stay out of the tub.

God's Election of Israel

(Romans 9:1-18)

Romans 9:1 - *"I say the truth in Christ, I lie not, my conscience also bearing me witness in the Holy Ghost."*

  Ἀλήθειαν λέγω ἐν Χριστῷ, οὐ ψεύδομαι, συμμαρτυρούσης μοι τῆς συνειδήσεώς μου ἐν πνεύματι ἁγίῳ,

"I am speaking the truth in Christ, I am not lying; my conscience bears me witness in the Holy Spirit, . . . " . . . RSV

  Ἀλήθειαν (acc.sing.fem.of ἀλήθεια, direct object of λέγω) 1416.
  λέγω (1st.per.sing.pres.act.ind.of λέγω, aoristic) 66.
  ἐν (preposition with the locative, association) 80.
  Χριστῷ (loc.sing.masc.of Χριστός, association) 4.
  οὐ (negative conjunction with the indicative) 130.
  ψεύδομαι (1st.per.sing.pres.mid.ind.of ψεύδομαι, aoristic) 439.
  συμμαρτυρούσης (pres.act.part.gen.sing.fem.of συμμαρτυρέω, genitive absolute) 3844.
  μοι (dat.sing.masc.of ἐγώ, indirect object of συμμαρτυρούσης) 123.
  τῆς (gen.sing.fem.of the article in agreement with συνειδήσεώς) 9.
  συνειδήσεώς (gen.sing.fem.of συνείδησις, gen.absolute) 3590.
  μου (gen.sing.masc.of ἐγώ, possession) 123.
  ἐν (preposition with the locative, association) 80.
  πνεύματι (loc.sing.neut.of πνεῦμα, association) 83.
  ἁγίῳ (loc.sing.neut.of ἅγιος, in agreement with πνεύματι) 84.

Translation - "I am telling the truth in association with Christ. I am not lying. My conscience bears witness to me in association with the Holy Spirit."

Comment: Often the grammarian finds it possible to give more than one grammatically correct translation. When neither grammar nor syntax can provide the final guide for translation we must translate in keeping with the context, as we take care not to contradict any other clear statement in the New Testament. It is an inerrant communicant of the total message which the Holy Spirit wishes us to have. It cannot contradict itself. Thus when diction, grammar and syntax do not lead us with precision the context of the total New Testament does. So there is really no problem. The phrases ἐν Χριστῷ and ἐν πνεύματι ἁγίῳ speak of the mystical union of Christ, the believer and the Holy Spirit. We are "in Christ" and the Holy Spirit is in us (1 Cor.6:19). This great truth is precious to the saint, if utterly incomprehensible to the unregenerate. The work of Adolph Deissmann, *Die Neutestimentliche Formel "in Christo Jesu" (1892)* is the classic discussion. *Cf.* 1 Cor.9:1; Rom.6:11,23; John 15:4; Col.1:16; 3:3; Rom.9:1; 14:14; Phil.3:9; Eph.4:21. Goodspeed and Weymouth translate - "I am telling the truth as a Christian" (Goodspeed) and "I am telling you the truth as a Christian" (Weymouth). This is not wrong and it may very well be what Paul meant, which is not greatly different from our locative, (for the instrumental of association) idea or indeed for the dative of personal advantage - "I am telling the truth for the advantage (the glory) of Christ." The Deissmann idea is also expressed by the instrumental. The phrase ἐν πνεύματι ἁγίῳ recalls Rom.8:16.

All of this protestation of veracity, which may appear to some as honesty on parade, indicates that what he is about to say would not normally be believed. His declaration, announced in verse 1, follows ὅτι in verses 2 and 3. In view of the Jewish persecution heaped upon Paul and his sufferings at their hands, with his full knowledge that soon after writing this, he would go to Jerusalem to be arrested and tried for a capital crime (which would ultimately result in his death), it is not unreasonable to suppose that Paul would have no tears for Israel.

On the contrary we note the indirect discourse of his statement in

Verse 2 - "That I have great heaviness and continual sorrow in my heart."

ὅτι λύπη μοί ἐστιν μεγάλη καὶ ἀδιάλειπτος ὀδύνη τῇ καρδίᾳ μου.

". . . that I have great sorrow and unceasing anguish in my heart." . . . RSV

ὅτι (conjunction introducing an object clause in indirect discourse) 211.
λύπη (nom.sing.fem.of λύπη, subject of ἐστιν) 2788.
μοί (dat.sing.masc.of ἐγώ, possession) 123.
ἐστιν (3d.per.sing.pres.ind.of εἰμί, aoristic) 86.
μεγάλη (nom.sing.fem.of μέγας, in agreement with λύπη) 184.
καὶ (adjunctive conjunction joining nouns) 14.

#3956 ἀδιάλειπτος (nom.sing.fem.of ἀδιάλειπτος, in agreement with ὀδύνη).

King James Version

continual - Rom.9:2.
without ceasing - 2 Tim.1:3.

Revised Standard Version

unceasing - Rom.9:2.
constantly - 2 Tim.1:3.

Meaning: Cf. ἀδιάλειπτως (#3786). α privative plus διά (#118) plus λείπω (#2636). διαλείπω means "to lack totally," hence ἀδιάλειπτος means "not ever to lack totally." Hence, always, continuously, unintermittently. With reference to Paul's sorrow for Israel - Rom.9:2. With reference to Paul's prayers for Timothy - 2 Tim.1:3.

#3957 ὀδύνη (nom.sing.fem.of ὀδύνη, subject of ἐστιν).

King James Version

sorrow - Rom.9:2; 1 Tim.6:10.

Revised Standard Version

anguish - Rom.9:2.
pangs - 1 Tim.6:10.

Meaning: Cf. ὀδυνάω, (#1920). Consuming grief; pain, sorrow. For the lost condition of Israel - Rom.9:2. The sorrows that result from apostasy caused by the love of money - 1 Tim.6:10.

τῇ (loc.sing.fem.of the article in agreement with καρδίᾳ) 9.
καρδίᾳ (loc.sing.fem.of καρδία, place) 432.
μου (gen.sing.masc.of ἐγώ, possession) 123.

Translation - ". . . that I have great sorrow and continuous anguish in my heart."

Comment: ὅτι introduces the object clause in indirect declaration. Note the dative of possession in μοι - "great sorrow is to me" or "is mine." This is one of the best descriptions of what most Christians glibly refer to as "a burden for the lost." Paul really had it.

Verse 3 - "For I could wish that myself were accursed from Christ for my brethren, my kinsmen according to the flesh."

ηὐχόμην γὰρ ἀνάθεμα εἶναι αὐτὸς ἐγὼ ἀπὸ τοῦ Χριστοῦ ὑπὲρ τῶν ἀδελφῶν μου τῶν συγγενῶν μου κατὰ σάρκα.

"For I could wish that I myself were accursed and cut off from Christ for the sake of my brethren, my kinsmen by race." . . . RSV

ηὐχόμην (1st.per.sing.imp.mid.ind.of εὔχομαι, potential) 3670.
γὰρ (causal conjunction) 105.
ἀνάθεμα (nom.sing.neut.of ἀνάθεμα, predicate adjective) 3597.
εἶναι (pres.inf.of εἰμί, noun use, object of ηὐχόμην) 86.
αὐτὸς (nom.sing.masc.of αὐτός, intensive) 16.

ἐγώ (nom.sing.masc.of ʼεγώ, subject of ηὐχόμην) 123.

ἀπό (preposition with the ablative of separation) 70.

τοῦ (abl.sing.masc.of the article in agreement with Χριστοῦ) 9.

Χριστοῦ (abl.sing.masc.of Χριστός, separation) 4.

ὑπέρ (preposition with the ablative "in behalf of") 545.

τῶν (abl.pl.masc.of the article in agreement with ἀδελφῶν) 9.

ἀδελφῶν (abl.pl.masc.of ἀδελφός, "in behalf of") 15.

μου (gen.sing.masc.of ἐγώ, relationship) 123.

τῶν (abl.pl.fem.of the article in agreement with συγγενῶν) 9.

συγγενῶν (abl.pl.fem.of συγγενής, apposition) 1815.

μου (gen.sing.masc.of ἐγώ, relationship) 123.

κατά (preposition with the accusative, standard) 98.

σάρκα (acc.sing.fem.of σάρξ, standard) 1202.

Translation - "Because I myself almost wished to be cut off from Christ in behalf of my brothers, my blood relatives."

Comment: Paul's great burden of verse 2 is manifest by his feelings of verse 3. γὰρ is causal. ηὐχόμην is a "potential" imperfect, ". . . a peculiar use of the tense for present time, where the present indicative fails to meet the requirement of the situation." (Robertson, *Grammar*, 885). If Paul had said εὔχομαι - "I wish," the statement would be too strong, since for Paul to have wished what follows would be to assert his own will against the will of God. This is tantamount to suggesting that God had made a mistake when He saved him. He was a Christian and an Apostle by the will of God (Gal.1:1), and to say that he wished that he might be "set aside and marked for death" (#3597) would have been morally wrong.

In English when we wish to say something better left unsaid, we say, "I was about to say . . . " or "I was on the point of saying. . . " thus saying it but apologizing for doing so. Paul did not really wish to say that God made a mistake and saved him when He should have damned him; he is only saying that his burden for the lost sheep of the House of Israel is so great that the thought had crossed his mind that perhaps it would be better for him to be lost, if, in the exchange, his national brothers could be saved. Robertson adds that rather than "express(es) a moral wrong . . . he holds himself back from the abyss by the tense" (*Ibid.*,886). Again "Here the indicative is used for direct assertion, but the statement is thrown into the past tense, though the present time is contemplated." (*Ibid.*, 919).

The apposition τῶν συγγενῶν μου κατὰ σάρκα is added to make clear that Paul is not talking about his Christian brothers in Christ, but his national brothers, genetically united to him in Abraham's flesh and blood. He further identifies these people and lists their national advantages in verse 4.

Paul's concern for the unregenerate Jews recalls Moses' prayer of Exodus 32:32 in which he prays that God will blot out his own name from the book of life, if by doing so, God can save the Jews who had aroused the divine anger. Paul's request, if he had in fact made it, would have been rejected on the same ground on which God rejected Moses' suggestion. Neither Moses nor Paul were qualified to offer themselves in the court of divine justice in expiation for the sins of another. Had Moses or Paul or any other transgressor died as a result of the heavenly sentence, he would have died for his own sins, not for those of others.

Verse 4 - "Who are Israelites; to whom pertaineth the adoption, and the glory, and the covenants, and the giving of the law, and the service of God, and the promises;"

οἵτινές εἰσιν Ἰσραηλῖται, ὧν ἡ υἱοθεσία καὶ ἡ δόξα καὶ αἱ διαθῆκαι καὶ ἡ νομοθεσία καὶ ἡ λατρεία καὶ αἱ ἐπαγγελίαι,

"They are Israelites, and to them belong the sonship, the glory, the covenants, the giving of the law, the worship, and the promises;" . . . *RSV*

οἵτινές (nom.pl.masc.of ὅστις, indefinite relative, subject of εἰσιν) 163.
εἰσιν (3d.per.pl.pres.ind.of εἰμί, aoristic) 86.
Ἰσραηλῖται (nom.pl.masc.of Ἰσραηλείτης, predicate nomintive) 1967.
ὧν (gen.pl.masc.of ὅς, relative pronoun, possession) 65.
ἡ (nom.sing.fem.of the article in agreement with υἱοθεσία) 9.
υἱοθεσία (nom.sing.fem.of υἱοθεσία, subject of the verb understood, and so with all of the substantives in verse 4) 3934.
καὶ (adjunctive conjunction joining nouns) 14.
ἡ (nom.sing.fem.of the article in agreement with δόξα) 9.
δόξα (nom.sing.fem.of δόξα) 361.
καὶ (adjunctive conjunction joining nouns) 14.
αἱ (nom.pl.fem.of the article in agreement with διαθῆκαι) 9.
διαθῆκαι (nom.pl.fem.of διαθήκη) 1575.
καὶ (adjunctive conjunction joining nouns) 14.
ἡ (nom.sing.fem.of the article in agreement with νομοθεσία) 9.

#3958 νομοθεσία (nom.sing.fem.of νομοθεσία).

King James Version

giving of the law - Rom.9:4.

Revised Standard Version

giving of the law - Rom.9:4.

Meaning: A combination of νόμος (#464) and τίθημι (#455). Hence, law giving; legislation. With reference to Israel at Sinai - Rom.9:4.

καὶ (adjunctive conjunction joining nouns) 14.
ἡ (nom.sing.fem.of the article in agreement with λατρεία) 9.
λατρεία (nom.sing.fem.of λατρεία) 2787.
καὶ (adjunctive conjunction joining nouns) 14.
αἱ (nom.pl.fem.of the article in agreement with ἐπαγγελίαι) 9.
ἐπαγγελίαι (nom.pl.fem.of ἐπαγγελία) 2929.

Translation - "Who are Israelites, to whom belong the adoption and the glory and the covenants and the administration of law and the temple service and the promises, . . . "

Comment: οἵτινές, the indefinite relative pronoun has ἀδελφῶν as its antecedent. Here is a list of the advantages enjoyed by the Jews to which Paul alluded in Romans 3:1-2, where he placed τὰ λόγια τοῦ θεοῦ at the head of the list. Here he places υἱοθεσία at the head of the list. God has adopted (υἱοθεσία, #3934) the nation Israel as well as the elect members of the body of Christ. This does not mean that every Jew will be saved because he is a genetic descendant of Abraham, as Paul is soon to point out in verses 6-13. But it does mean that the eternal future of Israel *as a nation* is assured in the economy of God, as will become clear in Romans 10-11. No other nation can include in its history the experience of having seen the Shekinah. God has entered into covenant relationships with no other nation in history. But God made two unconditional covenants with Israel - the first with Abraham in Genesis 15 and 17 and the other with David in 2 Samuel 7:10-17. He also entered into a conditional covenant in Exodus 20*ff*, on the basis of which He is under no obligation, since Israel failed to live up to its conditions. His reason for giving the covenant of the law is explained in Galatians 3:19*ff*. A textual variant has ἡ διαθήκη (singular number). Metzger's explanation is interesting: "Although the reading ἡ διαθήκη is strongly supported (p46 B Dgr it61vid? copsa,bo mss eth *al), the plural* αἱ διαθῆκαι (Sinaiticus C K Ψ 33 81 614 1739 *Byz Lect* itd,g vg syrp,h,hgr copbo goth arm *al*) was preferred on the grounds that (*a*) copyists would have been likely to assimilate the plural to the pattern of instances of the singular number in the series, and (*b*) plural covenants may have appeared to involve theological difficulties, and therefore the expression was converted to the singular number. Certainly there is no good reason why the singular, if original, should have been altered to the plural." (Metzger, *A Textual Commentary on the Greek New Testament*, 519).

If Paul had written ἡ διαθήκη, instead of αἱ διαθῆκαι the exegete would have never known which of the covenants he had in mind. The context indicates that, in addition to the law covenant, Paul meant also the Abrahamic covenant (verses 9-9). That he also meant the law covenant is clear from ἡ λατρεία, which were given in the Mosaic covenant. God gave the Decalogue to Israel but in the same covenant He included instructions for the temple order of worship.

Israel's history is unique. No other nation can say that God revealed Himself in the Shekinah; no other nation was given a moral and legal code as a guide to public administration; no other nation worshipped God in a tent with accouterments which were made according to specifications, on a schedule which was ordered and in specific ways that were dictated. And it was only to Israel that God sent the prophets with all of their promises. Paul will conclude that with all of these advantages, God must have a future for the physical seed of Abraham.

The greatest distinction which the nation of Israel enjoys is that she was called out from among other nations for the specific purpose of producing the Messiah, Who would be their King and the Saviour of the world. This we learn in

Verse 5 - "Whose are the fathers, and of whom as concerning the flesh Christ

came, who is over all, God blessed forever. Amen."

ὧν οἱ πατέρες, καὶ ἐξ ὧν ὁ Χριστὸς τὸ κατὰ σάρκα, ὁ ὢν ἐπὶ πάντων θεὸς εὐλογητὸς εἰς τοὺς αἰῶνος, ἀμήν.

"to them belong the patriarchs, and of their race, according to the flesh, is the Christ. God who is over all be blessed for ever. Amen."

ὧν (gen.pl.masc.of ὅς, relative pronoun, relationship) 65.

οἱ (nom.pl.masc.of the article in agreement with πατέρες) 9.

πατέρες (nom.pl.masc.of πατήρ, subject of verb understood) 238.

καὶ (adjunctive conjunction joining relative clauses) 14.

ἐξ (preposition with the ablative of source) 19.

ὧν (abl.pl.masc.of ὅς, relative pronoun, source) 65.

ὁ (nom.sing.masc.of the article in agreement with Χριστὸς) 9.

Χριστὸς (nom.sing.masc.of Χριστός, subject of the verb understood) 4.

τὸ (acc.sing.neut.of the article, adverbial accusative) 9.

κατὰ (preposition with the accusative, standard) 98.

σάρκα (acc.sing.fem.of σάρξ, standard) 1202.

ὁ (nom.sing.masc.of the article in agreement with ὢν) 9.

ὢν (pres.part.nom.sing.masc.of εἰμί, substantival, in apposition with Χριστὸς) 86.

ἐπὶ (preposition with the genitive, place description) 47.

πάντων (gen.pl.masc.of πᾶς, place description) 67.

θεὸς (nom.sing.masc.of θεός, in apposition with Χριστὸς) 124.

εὐλογητὸς (nom.sing.masc.of εὐλογητός, predicate adjective) 1849.

εἰς (preposition with the accusative of time extent) 140.

τοὺς (acc.pl.masc.of the article in agreement with αἰῶνας) 9.

αἰῶνας (acc.pl.masc.of αἰών, time extent) 1002.

ἀμήν (explicative) 466.

Translation - "To whom the fathers belong, and from whom came Messiah in His incarnation, the One Who is sovereign over all, God blessed forever. Amen."

Comment: The list of advantages for Israel includes two more items. The patriarchs, Abraham, Isaac, Jacob, Judah and David were Israelites and from this line in His human incarnation came the Messiah, who is called God, the One Who is designated as sovereign over all. (Mt.28:18; Eph.1:19-23; Phil.2:9-11; Rev.19:16 *et al*). *Cf.*#47 for ἐπί and the gentitive in the same sense. The doxology ends Paul's song of praise.

Everyone can trace his line back to a patriarch - a head of his clan or tribe. The difference is that the Jews are the only people who can trace their line back to a patriarch to whom God made an unconditional covenant that relates to a political role in the eternal kingdom over which Messiah will reign.

Everyone can trace his line back to Adam to whom God gave an unconditional covenant to the effect that from the family of Adam and Eve the "serpent bruiser" would come (Gen.3:15). This does not mean that everyone in Adam's family will be included in the blessings of the Adamic covenant, any ιore than the Abrahamic covenant means that every Jew, descended from Abraham, is to be included in God's promise to Abraham.

Paul is not speaking to the Jews here as individuals, but he is speaking about the nation Israel. Not all sons and daughters of Israel will be saved by virtue of the fact that they have Abraham's blood in their veins. Some will; others will not. But the nation, *as a nation* has a future. The responsibility for the murder of the Son of God on a cross cannot be charged against every Jew - only against those who perpetrated it. God's promise to Abraham, which was confirmed to Isaac, Jacob, Judah and David, can never be abrogated because of Israel's sins, since it was unconditional. The fulfillment of it is not contingent upon faithfulness on the party of the second part.

Paul now begins to distinguish between those children of the flesh of Abraham who are also destined to become the children of the promise, and those who are not. This is a matter of election.

Verse 6 - "Not as though the word of God hath taken none effect. For they are not all Israel which are of Israel."

Οὐχ οἷον δὲ ὅτι ἐκπέπτωκεν ὁ λόγος τοῦ θεοῦ. οὐ γὰρ πάντες οἱ ἐξ'Ισραήλ, οὗτοι'Ισραήλ.

"But it is not as though the word of God had failed. For not all who are descended from Israel belong to Israel."

Οὐχ (negative conjunction with the indicative) 130.
οἷον (acc.sing.neut.of οἷος, relative pronoun, adverbial) 1496.
δὲ (adversative conjunction) 11.
ὅτι (conjunction introducing an epexegetic clause) 211.
ἐκπέπτωκεν (3d.per.sing.perf.act.ind.of ἐκπίπτω, intensive) 3247.
ὁ (nom.sing.masc.of the article in agreement with λόγος) 9.
λόγος (nom.sing.masc.of λόγος, subject of ἐκπέπτωκεν) 510.
τοῦ (gen.sing.masc.of the article in agreement with θεοῦ) 9.
θεοῦ (gen.sing.masc.of θεός, designation) 124.
οὐ (negative conjunction with the indicative) 130.
γὰρ (causal conjunction) 105.
πάντες (nom.pl.masc.of πᾶς, subject of ἐστιν understood) 67.
οἱ (nom.pl.masc.of the article in agreement with πάντες) 9.
ἐξ (preposition with the ablative of source) 19.
'Ισραήλ (abl.sing.masc.of'Ισραήλ, source) 165.
οὗτοι (nom.pl.masc.of οὗτος, resumptive) 93.
'Ισραήλ (nom.sing.masc.of'Ισραήλ, predicate nominative) 165.

Translation - "But it is not as if the word of God is not currently effective, because not all of those of Israel's flesh are of Israel's faith."

Comment: Literally it reads, "Not all those of Israel,these are of Israel." The distinction is that of physical descent from Abraham, as opposed to spiritual participation with Abraham in saving faith. Note that ἐκπέπτωκεν is perfect, pointing both to God's promise in Abraham's day (preterite punctiliar) and in

Paul's (durative current). God's promise was fulfilled then as well as now. This is to forestall the superficial conclusion drawn from verses 4,5 that since (a) Israel was the recipient of all the assets listed in verses 4,5 and (b) were nevertheless lost, God's promise had failed. It has not failed, but it has been, and is being applied selectively. This becomes clear in verses 7-13. οὗτοι is clearly resumptive.

Verse 7 - "Neither, because they are the seed of Abraham are they all children: but, in Isaac shall thy seed be called."

οὐδ' ὅτι εἰσὶν σπέρμα' Ἀβραάμ, πάντες τέκνα, ἀλλ', 'Ἐν Ἰσαὰκ κληθήσεταί σοι σπέρμα.

". . . and not all are children of Abraham because they are his descendants; but 'Through Isaac shall your descendants be named.' " . . . RSV

οὐδ' (disjunctive particle) 452.
ὅτι (conjunction introducing a subordinate causal clause) 211.
εἰσὶν (3d.per.pl.pres.ind.of εἰμί, static) 86.
σπέρμα (nom.sing.fem.of σπέρμα, predicate nominative) 1056.
Ἀβραάμ (nom.sing.masc.of Ἀβραάμ, relationship) 7.
πάντες (nom.pl.masc.of πᾶς, subject of εἰσὶν) 67.
τέκνα (nom.pl.neut.of τέκνον, predicate nominative) 229.
ἀλλ' (adversative conjunction) 342.
ἐν (preposition with the locative of sphere) 80.
Ἰσαὰκ (loc.sing.masc.of Ἰσαάκ, sphere) 10.
κληθήσεται (3d.per.sing.fut.pass.ind.of καλέω, predictive) 107.
σοι (dat.sing.masc.of σύ, possession) 104.
σπέρμα (nom.sing.fem.of σπέρμα, subject of κληθήσεται) 1056.

Translation - "Nor that all the descendants of Abraham are children, but in Isaac your children will be designated."

Comment: οὐ of verse 6 is correlative with οὐδ' of verse 7. Paul is arguing against the false conclusion that since the Jews of verses 1-3 are lost, a fact because of which he has a great burden, even though they were given all of the blessings listed in verse 4-6, God's promise has failed. His argument is based upon his statement that not all of physical Israel will be counted in the number of regenerate Israel, and also upon the statement of verse 7 (which is really repetitive) that not everyone who descended from Abraham is to be counted among his children for purposes of fulfillment of God's promise. Some will; others will not.

To be more specific, Ishmael was a physical son of Abraham (τέκνον - "born one" in the biological sense). But he was not a τέκνον in the sense of John 1:12; Rom.8:16. And so also with the entire Arab world - a tribe of men who would never have existed but for Abraham's folly in doubting God's promise to the point that he married Hagar. This is not to say that an Arab is predestined to be damned because Ishmael's blood flows in his veins, any more that it is to say that a Jew is predestined to be saved because Isaac's blood flows in his veins. The distinction is between physical and spiritual sonship. But it is to assert that the Arab world, as an ethnic group, has no special place in the economy of God, while the Jewish race is indeed to come in for special blessing in the eternal kingdom of the heavens, due to God's promise to Abraham (Gen.12:1-3; 2 Samuel 7:10-17). Note that 144,000 Jews will be sealed for preservation (Rev.7:1-8) and that these are descendants of Isaac through Jacob and his twelve sons, rather than through Ishmael. Thus, in a physical sense, a remnant shall be called in Isaac.

Nor does this say that only those 144,000 Jews will be saved. Anyone, be he Arab, Jew or Gentile who has Abraham's faith is "a child of Abraham" in the spiritual (τέκνον) sense (Gal.3:7-9). The divine election is according to grace (Eph.2:8,9) and God's selective process in which the Holy Spirit effectually calls those for whom Christ died, transcends all boundary lines of blood, clan, tribe, people, nation and language (Rev.5:9). There will be some of each as members of the Body of Christ. But the Lord Jesus Christ, Who is the only Man, born of a women (Gal.4:4) who has any legal right to sit upon David's throne and occupy it forever, will come again and take His place on that throne in the greatest coronation of time and eternity, and when He does He will exercise His suzerainty over all the nations (Micah 4:1-5). But He will implement His administration through His chosen nation Israel, the first members of which will be the 144,000 - chosen, 12,000 from each of twelve tribes. The twelve Apostles are destined to preside in a judiciary capacity over the twelve tribes of Israel (Mt.19:28; Lk.22:30).

Paul's quotation of Gen.21:12 is interpreted in the light of Abraham's experience across fourteen years (Gen.15-21). See Paul's discussion of it in Romans 4:13-25 and our comments *en loc.* κληθήσεται is to be taken in the sense of a summons primarily, although it can also be taken in the sense of a designation. It is "calling" in the sense of Romans 8:30. When God calls a sinner to justification, it is in the sphere of supernatural faith in a supernatural God who does superrational things solely because He wishes to do them. Of course those who are summoned to be the children of God are also properly given the name "child of God" which is proper. Thus the RSV is not wrong, although it misses the primary point.

Isaac, not Ishmael, was the child of promise and thus he was the seed of Abraham through whom God was to keep His promise to the patriarch. And this involved a miracle. This was no problem for God although it has created a great deal of difficulty for the antisupernaturalists with their dogma of evolutionary uniformitarianism. If NeoDarwinism is in fact scientific, then there is no room for miracles and if we do not have room for miracles we do not need God. Thus has arisen, especially in America the dogmas of secular humanism, defended by the high priests of Herbert Spencer with a fanatical zeal and vigor in comparison to which the Spanish Inquisition pales into insignificance. As we listen to the gospel of "No good news, because no God" we are reminded of the forensic notes pencilled in the margin of the preacher's manuscript which said, "Argument weak here. Yell and wave arms."

Verse 8 - "That is, They which are the children of the flesh, these are not the children of God: but the children of the promise are counted for the seed."

τοῦτ᾽ ἔστιν, οὐ τὰ τέκνα τῆς σαρκὸς ταῦτα τέκνα τοῦ θεοῦ, ἀλλὰ τὰ τέκνα τῆς ἐπαγγελίας λογίζεται εἰς σπέρμα.

"This means that it is not the children of the flesh who are the children of God, but the children of the promise are reckoned as descendants." . . . RSV

τοῦτ᾽ (nom.sing.neut.of οὗτος, subject of ἔστιν, epexegetic) 93.
ἔστιν (3d.per.sing.pres.ind.of εἰμί, static) 86.
οὐ (negative conjunction with the indicative) 130.
τὰ (nom.pl.neut.of the article in agreement with τέκνα) 9.
τέκνα (nom.pl.neut.of τέκνον, subject of λογίζεται) 229.
τῆς (abl.sing.fem.of the article in agreement with σαρκὸς) 9.
σαρκὸς (abl.sing.fem.of σάρξ, source) 1202.
ταῦτα (nom.pl.neut.of οὗτος, subject of λογίζεται, resumptive) 93.
τέκνα (nom.pl.neut.of τέκνον, predicate nominative) 229.
τοῦ (gen.sing.masc.of the article in agreement with θεοῦ) 9.
θεοῦ (gen.sing.masc.of θεός, relationship) 124.
ἀλλὰ (alternative conjunction) 342.
τὰ (nom.pl.neut.of the article in agreement with τέκνα) 9.
τέκνα (nom.pl.neut.of τέκνον, subject of λογίζεται) 229.
τῆς (abl.sing.fem.of the article in agreement with ἐπαγγελίας) 9.
ἐπαγγελίας (abl.sing.fem.of ἐπαγγελία, source) 2929.
λογίζεται (3d.per.sing.pres.mid.ind.of λογίζομαι, static) 2611.
εἰς (preposition with the accusative, adverbial reference) 140.
σπέρμα (acc.sing.neut.of σπέρμα, adverbial accusative) 1056.

Translation - *"That is, these, not the children of the flesh, but the children of the promise, are the children of God, who are declared to be the real children."*

Comment: τοῦτ᾽ ἔστιν is epexegetical, as Paul explains the Genesis quotation of verse 7. οὐ . . . σαρκὸς is emphasized. "Not . . . κ.τ.λ. but (ἀλλὰ) τὰ τέκνα . . . κ.τ.λ." The two categories are set over against each other in contrast by οὐ . . . ἀλλὰ. Ishmael and his descendants are children of the flesh. These (resumptive ταῦτα) are not to be considered the true seed of Abraham. There was nothing supernatural about the birth of Ishamal. Abraham's faith was not involved - only his knowledge of gynecology and obstetrics. Anyone could do what he did, with or without the direction of almighty God. Only those who are the descendants of Abraham as a result of God's promise to him and to Sarah that Sarah (not Hagar) should have a son. That excludes Ishmael, but includes Isaac, the miracle baby, his son Jacob and his twelve sons who became tribal heads of the nation Israel. Of the twelve Judah was chosen and it is of this line that Messiah came (Gen.49:8-12; Rev.5:5; Mt.1:1-16; Lk.3:23-31). And it is also from these lines that the Jewish remnant will be selected (Rev.7:1-8).

In the sphere of personal, as distinct from national salvation, only those whose faith is like that of Abraham with reference to God's promise (Rom.4:24,25) are regenerate, and, as such, spiritual children of Abraham (Gal.3:7,9).

Verse 9 - "For this is the word of promise, At this time will I come, and Sarah shall have a son."

ἐπαγγελίας γὰρ ὁ λόγος οὗτος, Κατὰ τὸν καιρὸν τοῦτον ἐλεύσομαι καὶ ἔσται τῇ Σάρρᾳ υἱός.

"For this is what the promise said, 'About this time I will return and Sarah shall have a son.' " . . . RSV

ἐπαγγελίας (gen.sing.fem.of ἐπαγγελία, description) 2929.
γὰρ (causal conjunction) 105.
ὁ (nom.sing.masc.of the article in agreement with λόγος) 9.
λόγος (nom.sing.masc.of λόγος, subject of ἐστιν understood) 510.
οὗτος (nom.sing.masc.of οὗτος, predicate nominative) 93.
Κατὰ (preposition with the accusative, standard) 98.
τὸν (acc.sing.masc.of the article in agreement with καιρὸν) 9.
καιρὸν (acc.sing.masc.of καιρός, standard) 767.
τοῦτον (acc.sing.masc.of οὗτος, in agreement with καιρὸν) 93.
ἐλεύσομαι (1st.per.sing.fut.mid.ind.of ἔρχομαι, predictive) 146.
καὶ (continuative conjunction) 14.
ἔσται (3d.per.sing.fut.ind.of εἰμί, predictive) 86.
τῇ (dat.sing.fem.of the article in agreement with Σάρρᾳ) 9.
Σάρρᾳ (dat.sing.fem.of Σάρρα, possession) 3894.
υἱός (nom.sing.masc.of υἱός, subject of ἔσται) 5.

Translation - "Because the message of promise was this - at this same time I will come and Sarah will have a son."

Comment: The quotation is from Genesis 18:10,14. We supply ἐστιν as the verb with ὁ λόγος while οὗτος is deictic, as a predicate nominative. It introduces the direct quotation. The dative of possession is found in Genesis 18:14 while in Genesis 18:10 we have καὶ ἕξει υἱὸν Σάρρα ἡ γονή σου - "Sarah, your wife will have a son." After God's statement to Abraham in Genesis 18:10, Sarah, who overheard the promise, expressed some reasonable doubts about it. So God repeated the promise with language that could not be misunderstood. The dative of possession of Gen.18:10 could be construed to mean that Ishmael, Hagar's son, who at that time was thirteen years old, would be to Sarah's advantage. But there was no way to misconstrue what God said in verse 14.

The true "seed of Abraham" are those who have faith in God's willingness and ability to do what He promises, all scientifically rational arguments to the contrary notwithstanding. The God of the regenerate is Creator. He is able to raise the dead (Rom.4:17-25). He is able to perform the miracle of restored youth to a man who was ninety-nine and to his wife who was eighty-nine. Thus, one year later, Isaac, the miracle baby was born. It had been Abraham's lapse in faith, fourteen years before, that resulted in his affair with Hagar and in Ishmael's birth. But God could not be deterred from His purpose. "Let God be true but every man a liar" (Romans 3:4). Even Abraham! The "seed" recognized by God was the miracle baby, born to Sarah. God would work through him, and in each subsequent generation through the child He selected, to produce the Messiah. And why is it important that God should have produced the incarnate Messiah? If He had not, God's promise to Adam (Gen.3:15) would never have been fulfilled and Lucifer would have dominated all of God's creation. If He had not, His promise to Abraham would never have been fulfilled and Israel's future as a nation would never have been secured. If He had not there would have been no "seed of the woman" (Gen.3:15), "born of a woman, born under the law" (Gal.4:4), "to redeem them that are under the law" and we, for whom He paid the redemption price would never have received "the adoption of sons."

Christian theology depends upon three miraculous births. This is not to say that in order to be saved, the sinner must confess his faith in three miraculous births. Successful soul winners do not catechize repentant sinners who "come to the mourner's bench." If they did the prospects, in most cases would not know what the preacher was talking about. All we need is positive answers to two questions: (1) Do you realize that you are lost? and (2) Do you accept Jesus Christ as your Saviour? But, if the issue is raised and the sinner has been made to think about it, his confession of faith must include his willingness to accept three miracle births. God performed a miracle when Sarah had a baby. If He had not, Sarah would have had no child; there would never have been an Isaac, nor a Jacob, nor a Judah, nor a David, nor a Nathan nor a young woman in Nazareth, named Mary. Nor would there have been a Jesus.

God performed another miracle when Mary had a baby without benefit of husband. One does not ask a sinner, who comes weeping to the altar if he believes in the Virgin Birth. But if the weeping sinner, without being asked, says that he does not believe in the Virgin Birth of Jesus, then he should be told to go back to his seat and think about it, and not to come back until he is willing to believe in a God of miracles.

There is a third miracle birth which is essential to Christianity. That is the miracle of the new birth "from above" (John 3:3,7; 1 Pet.1:23), without which we "cannot see the kingdom of God."

Satan, Dean of the Graduate School of Synthetic Error, teaches a course in which the student is taught how to explain Isaac, Jesus and the new birth on scientific grounds. There was no miracle when Isaac was born. Abraham's body was not dead for purposes of paternity, as Paul said. (Rom.4:19). Nor was the womb of Sarah dead. Sick, maybe, but they each took a dose of Geritol! Mary was not really a virgin and her conception of Jesus really means that she "conceived the idea of God." Her baby was not a miracle, but her idea about God was. And as for the "new birth" it is easy to explain that away by describing the experience as moral reformation, graduation from Alcoholics Anonymous or a membership ceremony in the Boy Scouts.

To repeat, if God had not performed the miracle of restoring to Abraham and Sarah their youth, if God had not performed the miracle of fertilizing the female gamete of the virgin Mary, and if God, the Holy Spirit does not perform the miracle of a "birth from above" as He baptizes us into the body of Christ (1 Cor.12:13), then Christians have nothing to offer the world which is in any essential respect unique. Preachers who lead their congregations to repudiate the essential elements of the Christian faith, in the name of "scholarship" and "sophistication" are reducing their institutions to the status normally described as social, economic, political, cultural or eleemosynary. As such they are, in most cases, unable to compete with other secular institutions which are designed solely for the purposes indicated. The average Modernist church does not enjoy the social status of the country club, nor the intellectual sophistication which highly intelligent persons seek. Nor is it able to relieve poverty with the cost efficiency of the welfare state. If we turn to cultural offerings, who, unless he is tone-deaf would prefer the cacophonies of the village choir to the Metropolitan Opera or the ham acting of the local thespian society to what is available on or off Broadway, or even in summer stock?

The promise to Abraham, that he would be the father of Messiah and heir of the world, would have passed down to his firstborn son, Isaac, according to the ancient rule of primogeniture if Abraham had not allowed his own depraved human reason to dictate policy. Because of his liaison with Hagar and the illegitimate son who resulted, he forced God to set aside primogeniture and designate the second son instead. *Secundogeniture* seems to be God's plan. It was not Cain but Abel; it was not Ishmael but Isaac; it was not Esau but Jacob. Similarly, it is not the first birth "of water" (John 3:5a), but the second "of the Spirit" (John 3:5b) that God recognizes.

This *secundogeniture* principle is seen, not only in the case of Abraham, Sarah and Isaac, but also in Isaac, Rebecca and Jacob.

Verse 10 - "And not only this; but when Rebecca also had conceived by one, even by our father Isaac."

οὐ μόνον δέ, ἀλλὰ καὶ Ῥεβέκκα ἐξ ἑνὸς κοίτην ἔχουσα, Ἰσαὰκ τοῦ πατρὸς ἡμῶν,

"And not only so, but also when Rebecca had conceived children by one man, our forefather Isaac, . . . " . . . RSV

οὐ (negative conjunction with the indicative) 130.
μόνον (acc.sing.neut.of μόνος, adverbial) 339.
δέ (continuative conjunction) 11.
ἀλλὰ (adversative conjunction) 342.
καὶ (adjunctive conjunction joining substantives) 14.

#3959 Ῥεβέκκα (nom.sing.fem.of Ῥεβέκκα suspended subject).

King James Version

Rebecca - Romans 9:10.

Revised Standard Version

Rebecca - Romans 9:10.

Meaning: From *Reenqah*, from *Ranaq* - not found in Hebrew, but in Arabic - "to bind" or "to fashion." Hence, one who ensnares men by her beauty. The wife of Isaac - Romans 9:10.

ἐξ (preposition with the ablative of source) 19.
ἑνὸς (abl.sing.masc.of εἷς, source) 469.
κοίτην (acc.sing.fem.of κοίτη, direct object of ἔχουσα) 2448.
ἔχουσα (pres.act.part.nom.sing.fem.of ἔχω, adverbial,temporal) 82.
'Ισαὰκ (abl.sing.masc.of 'Ισαάκ, in apposition with ἑνὸς) 10.
τοῦ (abl.sing.masc.of the article in agreement with πατρὸς) 9.
πατρὸς (abl.sing.masc.of πατήρ, apposition) 238.
ἡμῶν (gen.pl.masc.of ἐγώ, relationship) 123.

Translation - "And that is not all. For when Rebecca also became pregnant by one, our forefather, Isaac . . . "

Comment: οὐ μόνον . . . ἀλλὰ καὶ - "not only . . . but also." The participle ἔχουσα is a temporal adverb, modifying the verb ἐρρέθη of verse 12. It is present tense, thus indicating the time when God told Rebecca that Esau, the firstborn would be subservient to Jacob, who was born last. God told her before, not at the time when the twins were born. This is confirmed by Genesis 25:23, and stated in

Verse 11 - ("For the children being not yet born, neither having done any good or evil, that the purpose of God according to election might stand, not of works, but of him that calleth;)"

#3960 μήπω (temporal adverb).

King James Version

not yet - Rom.9:11; Heb.9:8.

Revised Standard Version

not yet - Rom.9:11; Heb.9:8.

Meaning: A combination of μή (#87) and πω, an enclitic particle. A temporal adverb - with the participle - Rom.9:11; with an accusative and the infinitive - Heb.9:8.

γὰρ (causal conjunction) 105.
γεννηθέντως (1st.aor.pass.part.gen.pl.masc.of γεννάω, genitive absolute) 8.
μηδὲ (negative continuative particle) 612.
πραξάντων (aor.act.part.gen.pl.masc.of πράσσω, genitive absolute) 1943.
τι (acc.sing.neut.of τις, indefinite pronoun, direct object of πραξάντων) 486.
ἀγαθὸν (acc.sing.neut.of ἀγαθός, in agreement with τι) 547.
ἤ (disjunctive particle) 465.
φαῦλον (acc.sing.neut.of φαῦλος, in agreement with τι) 1990.
ἵνα (conjunction introducing a sub-final clause) 114.
ἡ (nom.sing.fem.of the article in agreement with πρόθεσις) 9.

κατ' (preposition with the accusative, standard) 98.

ἐκλογὴν (acc.sing.fem.of ἐκλογή, standard) 3189.

πρόθεσις (nom.sing.fem.of πρόθεσις, subject of μένῃ) 968.

τοῦ (gen.sing.masc.of the article in agreement with θεοῦ) 9.

θεοῦ (gen.sing.masc.of θεός, designation) 124.

μένῃ (3d.per.sing.pres.act.subj.of μένω, purpose/result) 864.

Translation - "Because, although they were not yet born nor had they done anything good or evil, in order (and with the result) that the purpose of God in keeping with election might prevail . . . "

Comment: γὰρ is causal. The participles γεννηθέντων and πραξάντων are concessive. God announced the destinies of the two sons of Rebecca before they were born and thus before either could have done anything either for or against God's law. Why was it thus? The ἵνα clause with the subjunctive μένῃ is sub-final. It expresses both the divine purpose and the divine result, since divine purposes always result in keeping with the purpose. The sovereign purpose of God will prevail. The noun πρόθεσις is modified by the prepositional phrase κατ' ἐκλογὴν in the attributive position (between the article and the noun). It is "the according to election purpose of God."

Paul is facing squarely, refuting boldly and answering decisively the objections to the doctine of divine decrees. God announced to Abraham His purpose (Gen.15:6), and said that it would be implemented by Isaac's birth. God was not deterred from His purpose by Abraham's stratagem that resulted in the birth of Ishmael. "In Isaac" (not in Ishmael) "shall thy seed be called." (Gen.21:12). Now, so that there will be no mistake about it, God is about to announce to Rebecca, who is experiencing an unusual amount of prenatal activity and who is praying about it, that she is going to be the mother of twins, the descendants of each of whom will become national groups. Esau's children will be the Edomites and Isaac's children the Israelites. The further announcement is that the second son born, not the first born, has been selected in advance to carry forward God's purpose, while the first born would be forever subservient to his younger brother.

This announcement came to Rebecca before Esau was born to live nobly as he did, albeit with scant regard for the spiritual blessings which could have been his as owner of the birthright,and also before Jacob was born, to live as deceptively as he did. For all of Jacob's perfidy he was given the gift of faith to see that God would keep His promise to his grandfather Abraham and his father Isaac and thus he was determined to gain the place in which he could share in the honor of having fathered the line that would produce the Serpent Bruising Messiah.

The philosophy of legalism dictates that God should have waited until the twins were born and had grown up in order to grade their respective performances, thus to reward the good and punish the evil. Had this been done, Esau would have gained the prize and Jacob would have been rejected. But the legalist is not making the decisions. Almighty God is.

Verse 12 - "It was said unto her, The elder shall serve the younger."

οὐκ ἐξ ἔργων ἀλλ' ἐκ τοῦ καλοῦντος, ἐρρέθη αὐτῇ ὅτι Ὁ μείζων δουλεύσει τῷ ἐλάσσονι.

". . . she was told, 'The elder will serve the younger.' " . . . RSV

οὐκ (negative conjunction with the subjunctive) 130.
ἐξ (preposition with the ablative of source) 19.
ἔργων (abl.pl.neut.of ἔργον, source) 460.
ἀλλ' (alternative conjunction) 342.
ἐκ (preposition with the ablative of source) 19.
τοῦ (abl.sing.masc.of the article in agreement with καλοῦντος) 9.
καλοῦντος (pres.act.part.abl.sing.masc.of καλέω, substantival, source) 107.
ἐρρέθη (3d.per.sing.aor.pass.ind.of ῥέω, culminative) 116.
αὐτῇ (dat.sing.fem.of αὐτός, indirect object of ἐρρέθη) 16.
ὅτι (recitative) 211.
ὁ (nom.sing.masc.of the article in agreement with μείζων) 9.
μείζων (nom.sing.masc.of μείζων, subject of δουλεύσει) 916.
δουλεύσει (3d.per.sing.fut.act.ind.of δουλεύω, predictive) 604.
τῷ (dat.sing.masc.of the article in agreement with ἐλάσσονι) 9.
ἐλάσσονι (dat.sing.masc.of ἐλάσσων, personal advantage) 1977.

Translation - ". . . not from works but because of the One Who is calling, it was said to her, 'The older will serve the younger.' "

Comment: The division of verses in the KJV is not the same as that in the Greek text, οὐκ ἐξ ἔργων ἀλλ' ἐκ τοῦ καλοῦντος being translated as a part of verse 11. God's purpose stands. It is not determined on the basis of human works, but it is a function of Him Who calls men to salvation and assigns them to certain destinies (Eph.2:10). Good works are very much a part of the lives of the elect after they are called and justified, since now the Holy Spirit is indwelling them and producing His fruits (Gal.5:22,23; Eph.2:10; 2 Tim.4:7, *et al*). But human good works which are performed before God calls have nothing to do with whom He calls. His is the prerogative of the calling and His purpose in calling is κατὰ ἐκλογή (verse 11). God told Rebecca that she would bear twins and that Esau, the firstborn would be subordinate to Jacob who was born second. The quotation is from Genesis 25:23. Rebecca's two sons, Esau and Jacob became the heads of two nations - the Edomites and Israel.

Verse 13 - "As it is written, Jacob have I loved, but Esau have I hated."

καθὼς γέγραπται, Τὸν Ἰακὼβ ἠγάπησα, τὸν δὲ Ἡσαῦ ἐμίσησα.

"As it is written, 'Jacob I loved, but Esau I hated.' " . . . RSV

καθὼς (particle introducing a comparative clause) 1348.
γέγραπται (3d.per.sing.perf.pass.ind.of γράφω, intensive) 156.
Τὸν (acc.sing.masc.of the article in agreement with Ἰακώβ) 9.
Ἰακὼβ (acc.sing.masc.of Ἰακώβ, direct object of ἠγάπησα) 12.

ἠγάπησα (1st.per.sing.aor.act.ind.of ἀγαπάω, constative) 540.
τὸν (acc.sing.masc.of the article in agreement with Ἡσαῦ) 9.
δὲ (adversative conjunction) 11.

#3961 Ἡσαῦ (acc.sing.masc.of Ἡσαῦ, direct object of ἐμίσησα).

King James Version

Esau - Rom.9:13; Heb.11:20; 12:16.

Revised Standard Version

Esau - Rom.9:13; Heb.11:20; 12:16.

Meaning: The Hebrew word means "hairy." The first born son of Isaac and Rebecca; brother of Jacob - Rom.9:13; Heb.11:20; 12:16.

ἐμίσησα (1st.per.sing.aor.act.ind.of μισέω, constative) 542.

Translation - "As it is written, 'Jacob I loved, but Esau I hated.' "

Comment: The quotation is from Malachi 1:2,3, where the immediate reference is to the Edomites, the descendants of Esau. *Cf.* Obadiah 1-21. But Paul uses the passage to reveal the sovereign discrimination of God between two people even before they were born. Discrimination when employed by man is evil, because men are unable to judge properly since we do not have of the facts involved. But divine discrimination is judging between two on a basis that, though inexplicable to men, is not without justification in the divine counsels. Indeed we shall learn in verse 20 that the sovereign God need not give account to anyone for His decisions. This strong statement was certain to arouse opposition from Paul's readers and he anticipates it in

Verse 14 - "What shall we say then? Is there unrighteousness with God? God forbid."

Τί οὖν ἐροῦμεν; μὴ ἀδικία παρὰ τῷ θεῷ; μὴ γένοιτο.

"What shall we say then? Is there injustice on God's part? By no means!" RSV

Τί (acc.sing.neut.of τίς, interrogative pronoun, direct object of ἐροῦμεν) 281.
οὖν (inferential conjunction) 68.
ἐροῦμεν (1st.per.pl.fut.act.ind.of εἶπον, deliberative) 155.
μὴ (negative conjunction in rhetorical question, which expects a negative answer) 87.
ἀδικία (nom.sing.fem.of ἀδικία, subject of ἐστιν understood) 2367.
παρὰ (preposition with the locative, with persons) 154.
τῷ (loc.sing.masc.of the article in agreement with θεῷ) 9.
θεῷ (loc.sing.masc.of θεός, sphere) 124.
μὴ (negative conjunction with the optative) 87.
γένοιτο (3d.per.sing.aor.opt.of γίνομαι, voluntative) 113.

Translation - *"What then shall we conclude? That there is injustice in God's dealings? Of course not!"*

Comment: We have the future indicative in a deliberative question followed by rhetorical question, which expects "No" for an answer and an emotional rejoinder. God chose Isaac instead of Ishmael; God chose Jacob instead of Esau. To what conclusion does the natural man come in contemplation of these facts? The worm's eye view is that God is partial and discriminatory, and therefore unjust. From the human point of view it is an open and shut case. There is no question that God chose one and not the other. The question is whether or not such behavior constitutes unrighteousness? By whose standard of ethics must the question be judged? This is the crucial point. Since when does the creature call the Creator into court to defend Himself? Whatever men may think, God does not regard His decisions as being wrong. And God is the party of the first part.

Before giving his answer, Paul alludes to Scripture and cites the example of Pharaoh.

Verse 15 - *"For he saith to Moses, I will have mercy on whom I will have mercy, and I will have compassion on whom I will have compassion."*

τῷ Μωϋσεῖ γὰρ λέγει, Ἐλεήσω ὅν ἄν ἐλεῶ, καὶ οἰκτιρήσω ὅν ἄν οἰκτίρω.

"For he says to Moses, 'I will have mercy on whom I have mercy, and I will have compassion on whom I have compassion.' " . . . *RSV*

τῷ (dat.sing.masc.of the article in agreement with Μωϋσεῖ) 9.

Μωϋσεῖ (dat.sing.masc.of Μωϋσῆς, indirect object of λέγει) 715.

γὰρ (causal conjunction) 105.

λέγει (3d.per.sing.pres.act.ind.of λέγω, historical) 66.

Ἐλεήσω (1st.per.sing.fut.act.ind.of ἐλεέω, predictive) 430.

ὅν (acc.sing.masc.of ὅς, relative pronoun, direct object of ἐλεήσω) 65.

ἄν (contingent particle with the subjunctive in a third-class condition) 205.

ἐλεῶ (1st.per.sing.pres.act.subj.of ἐλεέω, third-class condition) 430.

καὶ (continuative conjunction) 14.

#3962 οἰκτιρήσω (1st.per.sing.fut.act.ind.of οἰκτείρω, predictive).

   King James Version

have compassion on - Rom.9:15,15.

   Revised Standard Version

have compassion on - Rom.9:15,15.

Meaning: From οἰκτερέω - "to pity" "to have compassion for" Rom.9:15,15.

ὅν (acc.sing.masc.of ὅς, relative pronoun, direct object of οἰκτιρήσω) 65.

ἄν (contingent particle with the subjunctive in a third-class condition) 205.

οἰκτίρω (1st.per.sing.pres.act.subj.of οἰκτείρω, third-class condition) 3962.

Translation - "Because He said to Moses, 'I will have mercy upon whom I have mercy, and I will have compassion for whom I have compassion."

Comment: Note the future indicative in the apodosis which here precedes the protasis in a third-class condition. God is not promising Moses that He will have mercy on anyone, but if He does, without specifying upon whom, when, where, how or why, He will be merciful. This is the force of ἄν and the subjunctive.

The quotation is from Exodus 33:19 in an interesting context. Israel had just broken all of God's laws at the foot of Mount Sinai at the very time that God was giving the law to Moses. Moses then prayed his intercessory prayer in which he expressed the same burden for Israel that Paul expressed in Romans 9:3. Note that in each case the potential imperfect is used. "I could wish . . . κ.τ.λ." in Romans 9:3 and "Yet now, if thou wilt forgive their sin —; and if not blot me I pray thee out . . . κ.τ.λ." (Exodus 32:32). Then Moses begged God not to lead them further unless He went with them and revealed His divine glory (Exodus 33:18). God acquiesced in Moses' request and announced to Moses that the decisions as to who should live and who should die were up to Him alone. It is the divine prerogative, contingent upon nothing outside of God. The statement is as strongly Calvinistic as Greek grammar can make it. If those who are inclined to argue about it had been with Moses in the clift of the rock and had seen God's "afterglow" (Exodus 33:22,23) they might be more inclined to agree that God should be allowed to direct affairs in His kingdom as He sees fit. Who else do they wish to appoint to make the eternal decisions?

Paul also had seen the glory of the sovereign God and what he learned there became the basis for his theology (2 Cor.12:1-4).

Verse 16 - "So then it is not of him that willeth, nor of him that runneth, but of God that sheweth mercy."

ἄρα οὖν οὐ τοῦ θέλοντος οὐδὲ τοῦ τρέχοντος, ἀλλὰ τοῦ ἐλεῶντος θεοῦ.

"So it depends not upon man's will or exertion, but upon God's mercy." . .
RSV

ἄρα (illative particle) 995.
οὖν (conjunction with double illative emphasis) 68.
οὐ (negative conjunction with the indicative) 130.
τοῦ (abl.sing.masc.of the article in agreement with θέλοντος) 9.
θέλοντος (pres.act.part.abl.sing.masc.of θέλω, substantival, source) 88.
οὐδὲ (disjunctive particle) 452.
τοῦ (abl.sing.masc.of the article in agreement with τρέχοντος) 9.
τρέχοντος (pres.act.part.abl.sing.masc.of τρέχω, substantival, source) 1655.
ἀλλὰ (alternative conjunction) 342.
τοῦ (abl.sing.masc.of the article in agreement with θεοῦ) 9.
ἐλεῶντος (pres.act.part.abl.sing.masc.of ἐλεέω, adjectival, ascriptive, in agreement with θεοῦ) 430.
θεοῦ (abl.sing.masc.of θεός, source) 124.

Translation - "Thus neither the one who wills it nor the one who goes for it is the source, but the merciful God."

Comment: Here we have an excellent example of the difference between the participle as a noun and as an adjective. τοῦ θέλοντος and τοῦ τρέχοντος are substantives. τοῦ ἐλεῶντος is an ascriptive adjective in the attributive position (between the article and the noun) defining God. All are in the ablative case, indicating source. Who originates salvation and how is it originated? It is not the one who wills (decides) to be saved. This verse should be enough to lay to rest the nonesense that the unsaved man is a *free* moral agent. Nor is it the one who works for it. Thus prayers for me "That I might hold out faithful and gain a home in heaven" are ill advised. When a church member responds to the question "Are you saved?" by saying "I hope so" he indicates that he is still on the track, running with all possible speed, but that the issue is still in doubt. The Source of our salvation is "the merciful God" and He will "be true" even though every man be a liar (Rom.3:4).

Verse 16 draws the logical conclusion from Exodus 33:19 as cited in Romans 9:15. Neither the human will nor the exertion of human effort are productive of salvation. Only God's mercy is. If Paul had been diplomatic he would have left the matter there. He has already fanned the natural wisdom of the unregenerate mind into smoldering resentment. The unsaved, with eyes aglow with ersatz zeal for fair play, fly to the rescue of Ishmael and Esau. One can see them now carrying signs in Lafayette Park across Pennsylvania Avenue from the White House. It is certain that there will be speeches about human rights, for the depraved are always certain about what is fair and what is unfair. Poor Ishmael! Poor, poor Esau!! But Paul seems deliberately intent upon antagonizing the "fair play" critics further. *Quem Juppiter vult perdere dementat prius* - "Whom God would destroy He first sends mad." (James DuPort, *Homeri gnomologia*).

God deals in what His critics call an arbitrary fashion not only with the descendants of His covenant patriarch Abraham, but also with a pagan Egyptian king.

Verse 17 - "For the scripture saith unto Pharaoh, Even for this same purpose have I raised thee up, that I might show my power in thee, and that my name might be declared throughout all the earth."

λέγει γὰρ ἡ γραφὴ τῷ Φαραὼ ὅτι Εἰς αὐτὸ τοῦτο ἐξήγειρά σε ὅπως ἐνδείξωμαι ἐν σοὶ τὴν δύναμίν μου, καὶ ὅπως διαγγελῇ τὸ ὄνομά μου ἐν πάσῃ τῇ γῇ.

"For the scripture says to Pharaoh, 'I have raised you up for the very purpose of showing my power in you, so that my name may be proclaimed in all the earth."

λέγει (3d.per.sing.pres.act.ind.of λέγω, historical) 66.

γὰρ (causal conjunction) 105.

ἡ (nom.sing.fem.of the article in agreement with γραφή) 9.

γραφὴ (nom.sing.fem.of γραφή, subject of λέγει) 1389.
τῷ (dat.sing.masc.of the article in agreement with Φαραώ) 9.
Φαραώ (dat.sing.masc.of Φαράω, indirect object of λέγει) 3106.
ὅτι (recitative) 211.
Εἰς (preposition with the accusative, purpose) 140.
αὐτὸ (acc.sing.neut.of αὐτός, intensive) 16.
τοῦτο (acc.sing.neut.of οὗτος, purpose) 93.

#3963 ἐξήγειρά (1st.per.sing.1st.aor.act.ind.of ἐξεγείρω, culminative).

King James Version

raise up - Rom.9:17; 1 Cor.6:14.

Revised Standard Version

raise up - Rom.9:17; 1 Cor.6:14.

Meaning: A combination of ἐκ (#19) and ἐγείρω (#125). To raise up in the sense of physical resurrection from the dead in 1 Cor.6:14. To elevate to a position of political power - Rom.9:17.

σε (acc.sing.masc.of σύ, direct object of ἐξήγειρά) 104.
ὅπως (conjunction with the subjunctive in a sub-final clause) 177.
ἐνδείξωμαι (1st.per.sing.aor.mid.subj.of ἐνδείκνυμαι, sub-final) 3842.
ἐν (preposition with the locative of place) 80.
σοὶ (loc.sing.masc.of σύ, place) 104.
τὴν (acc.sing.fem.of the article in agreement with δύναμίν) 9.
δύναμίν (acc.sing.fem.of δύναμις, direct object of ἐνδείξωμαι) 687.
μου (gen.sing.masc.of ἐγώ, possession) 123.
καὶ (adjunctive conjunction joining sub-final clauses) 14.
ὅπως (conjunction with the subjunctive in a sub-final clause) 177.
διαγγελῇ (3d.per.sing.pres.pass.subj.of διαγγέλλω, sub-final) 2361.
τὸ (nom.sing.neut.of the article in agreement with ὄνομά) 9.
ὄνομά (nom.sing.neut.of ὄνομα, subject of διαγγελῇ) 108.
μου (gen.sing.masc.of ἐγώ, possession) 123.
ἐν (preposition with the locative, place) 80.
πάσῃ (loc.sing.fem.of πᾶς, in agreement with γῇ) 67.
τῇ (loc.sing.fem.of the article in agreement with γῇ) 9.
γῇ (loc.sing.fem.of γῇ, place) 157.

Translation - "Because the scripture said to Pharaoh, 'For this very purpose I have elevated you to leadership in order (and with the result) that I might demonstrate in you my power, and that my name might be declared in all the earth."

Comment: εἰς αὐτὸ τοῦτο in a purpose construction, with αὐτὸ in the intensive attributive position - "The same" or "This very." The ὅπως clauses, joined by adjunctive καὶ are sub-final, indicating both purpose and result. God raised up Pharaoh in a political sense. He gave him great prominence and the responsibility of leadership in Egypt at the time when he would be certain to come into conflict with God, Who was pledged to Abraham, Isaac and Jacob. Verse 18 adds that God "hardened" Pharaoh's will. The quotation is from Exodus 9:16, in which the LXX uses διετηρήθης instead of ἐξήγειρα and introduces the first sub-final clause with ἵνα instead of ὅπως. Also, instead of δύναμίν we have ἰσχύν.

Verse 18 - "Therefore hath he mercy on whom he will have mercy, and whom he will he hardeneth."

ἄρα οὖν ὃν θέλει ἐλεεῖ, ὃν δὲ θέλει σκληρύνει.

"So then he has mercy upon whomever he wills, and he hardens the heart of whomever he wills." . . . RSV

ἄρα (illative conjunction in emphasis) 995.
οὖν (illative conjunction in emphasis) 68.
ὃν (acc.sing.masc.of ὅς, relative pronoun, direct object of ἐλεεῖ) 65.
θέλει (3d.per.sing.pres.act.ind.of θέλω, aoristic) 88.
ἐλεεῖ (3d.per.sing.pres.act.ind.of ἐλεέω, aoristic) 430.
ὃν (acc.sing.masc.of ὅς, relative pronoun, direct object of σκληρύνει) 65.
δὲ (adversative conjunction) 11.
θέλει (3d.per.sing.pres.act.ind.of θέλω, aoristic) 88.
σκληρύνει (3d.per.sing.pres.act.ind.of σκληρύνω, aoristic) 3461.

Translation - "So then He shows mercy to whom He wills, and whom He wills He makes obdurate."

Comment: Paul does not hesitate to attribute the cause of Pharaoh's obstinate inflexibility to God. This is what the Greek says. It would serve only a sinister purpose to explain it away.

God's Wrath and Mercy

(Romans 9:19-29)

Verse 19 - "Thou wilt say then unto me, Why doth he yet find fault? For who hath resisted his will?"

Ἐρεῖς μοι οὖν, Τί (οὖν) ἔτι μέμφεται; τῷ γὰρ βουλήματι αὐτοῦ τίς ἀνθέστηκεν;

"You will say to me then, 'Why does he still find fault? For who can resist his will?' " . . . RSV

Ἐρεῖς (2d.per.sing.fut.act.ind.of εἴρω, predictive) 155.
μοι (dat.sing.masc.of ἐγώ, indirect object of Ἐρεῖς) 123.
οὖν (inferential conjunction) 68.

Τί (acc.sing.neut.of τίς, interrogative pronoun, cause) 281.
(οὖν) (inferential conjunction) 68.
ἔτι (adverbial) 448.

#3964 μέμφεται (3d.per.sing.pres.mid.ind.of μέμφομαι, aoristic).

King James Version

find fault - Rom.9:19; Heb.8:8.

Revised Standard Version

find fault - Rom.9:19; Heb.8:8.

Meaning: To blame; to find fault. Absolutely in Romans 9:19, where what explains it is found in verses 17,18. In Heb.8:8, where the object is αὐτούς (Israel).

τῷ (dat.sing.neut.of the article in agreement with βουλήματι) 9.
γὰρ (causal conjunction) 105.
βουλήματι (dat.sing.neut.of βούλημα, personal disadvantage) 3750.
αὐτοῦ (gen.sing.masc.of αὐτός, possession) 16.
τίς (nom.sing.masc.of τίς, interrogative pronoun, subject of ἀνθέστηκεν, direct question) 281.
ἀνθέστηκεν (3d.per.sing.perf.act.ind.of ἀνθίστημι, intensive) 527.

Translation - "You will therefore say to me, 'Why then is He still finding fault? For who has ever successfully resisted His will?'"

Comment: Τί here in the sense of διὰ τί in a causal sense - "Because (or on account of) what?" ἀνθέστηκεν, the intensive perfect, thus asks, "Who has at any time in the past resisted God's will so successfully that, as a result, he is at present still standing in opposition to it?" Many people have resisted God's will once and did not live long enough to continue to resist it. But who has resisted God's will until he has gotten away with it?

This question is often asked by determinists who insist that there can be no assessment of guilt in the absence of freedom of choice. If Ishmael, Esau and Pharaoh were excluded from God's favor before they were born in a way that made it impossible for them to escape their place in life, why should God blame them? It recalls the dialogue between Zeno and his slave, who asked, "If I was predestined to steal your purse why do you beat me for it?" To which Zeno replied, "I was predestined to beat you for it." But Zeno was not God. He himself was an actor upon the stage. God is not predestined by a super-God to find fault with those who, by His own decision, deserve to be blamed. Paul offers no answer to this problem except to cite God's prerogative as Creator, and to say that God in perfect justice could have condemned the entire race. Thus God should be thanked that while He was suffering the insolence of all mankind, He determined to save some, who deserved damnation no less than those He did not save. He further replies by showing the presumption of the creature in criticizing the Creator. Verse 20 recalls Job 38:1 - 40:2 with emphasis upon the last verse.

Verse 20 - "*Nay but, O man, who art thou that repliest against God? Shall the thing formed say to him that formed it, Why hast thou made me thus?*"

ὦ ἄνθρωπε, μενοῦνγε σὺ τίς εἶ ὁ ἀνταποκρινόμενος τῷ θεῷ; μὴ ἐρεῖ τὸ πλάσμα τῷ πλάσαντι, Τί με ἐποίησας οὕτως;

"*But who are you, a man, to answer back to God? Will what is molded say to its molder, 'Why have you made me thus?' *" . . . RSV

ὦ (exclamation) 1177.

ἄνθρωπε (voc.sing.masc.of ἄνθρωπος, address) 341.

#3965 μενοῦνγε (compound emphatic particle).

> King James Version

nay but - Rom.9:20.
yea doubtless - Phil.3:8.
yes verily - Rom.10:18.

> Revised Standard Version

but who are you - Rom.9:20.
Indeed - Phil.3:8; Rom.10:18.

Meaning: A combination of μέν (#300), οὖν (#68) and γε (#2449). Nay rather; nay surely. Used in argumentation where what follows is used to correct the argument of what precedes - Rom.9:20; 10:18; Phil.3:8.

σὺ (nom.sing.masc.of σύ, subject of εἶ) 104.
τίς (nom.sing.masc.of τίς, interrogative pronoun, predicate nominative) 281.
εἶ (2d.per.sing.pres.ind.of εἰμί, aoristic, in direct question) 86.
ὁ (nom.sing.masc.of the article in agreement with ἀνταποκρινόμενος) 9.
ἀνταποκρινόμενος (pres.mid.part.nom.sing.masc.of ἀνταποκρίνομαι, substantival, in apposition with τίς) 2521.
τῷ (dat.sing.masc.of the article in agreement with θεῷ) 9.
θεῷ (dat.sing.masc.of θεός, personal disadvantage) 124.
μὴ (negative conjunction with the indicative in rhetorical question which expects a negative reply) 87.
ἐρεῖ (3d.per.sing.fut.act.ind.of εἴρω, deliberative) 155.
τὸ (nom.sing.neut.of the article in agreement with πλάσμα) 9.

#3966 πλάσμα (nom.sing.neut.of πλάσμα, subject of ἐρεῖ).

> King James Version

thing formed - Rom.9:20.

> Revised Standard Version

what is molded - Rom.9:20.

Meaning: Cf. πλάσσω (#3967) - that which is made, formed, molded, designed. Metaphorically in Rom.9:20.

τῷ (dat.sing.masc.of the article in agreement with πλάσαντι) 9.

#3967 πλάσαντι (1st.aor.act.part.dat.sing.masc.of πλάσσω, substantival, indirect object of ἐρεῖ).

     King James Version

form - Rom.9:20; 1 Tim.2:13.

     Revised Standard Version

molder - Rom.9:20.
formed - 1 Tim.2:13.

Meaning: to form, to mold as clay or wax. With reference to the potter - Rom.9:20; with reference to God, the Creator of the human body - 1 Tim.2:13.

τί (acc.sing.neut.of τίς, interrogative pronoun, cause, direct question) 281.
με (acc.sing.masc.of ἐγώ, direct object of ἐποίησας) 123.
ἐποίησας (2d.per.sing.aor.act.ind.of ποιέω, constative) 127.
οὕτως (demonstrative adverb) 74.

Translation - "*But who indeed are you, O man, who is arguing with God? The thing designed does not say to the designer, 'Why did you make me like this?' does it?*"

Comment: γε (#2449) in μενοῦνγε (#3965) serves to heighten the force of the particles with which it is joined. Here it intensifies the irony which otherwise we would have in μενοῦν. Note the emphatic use of σύ - "O Man, who are you! The one criticizing God!?" The question is asked in incredulity and expects "No" for an answer. Τὸ πλάσμα depends upon τῷ πλάσαντι for its very existence. The question should not be "Why did you make me as you did?" It should be, "Why did you make me at all?" And yet, even that question is useless since the Creator has already made the creature and has made him as he was. A humble creature would ask the Creator to make him over into a new creature - the new birth (2 Cor.5:17). The utter futility of the creature's question in the Creator's court is the point, plus the sinful presumption of blaming the Creator for the creature's condition instead of begging the Creator to change the condition.

     What the creature really means is something like this: I am glad that I was created for if I had not been I would not exist. The fact is that I was created in the condition in which I now find myself. And I cannot help it. That is beyond my control. Therefore I am not to blame for what I think and how I behave. Therefore it is unfair for the Creator to hold me accountable for that for which I accept no moral responsibility. I would rather complain about it than ask the Creator to make me over so that I can, in perfect freedom, be like Him and conform to His standards.

Verse 21 - "Hath not the potter power over the clay, of the same lump, to make one vessel unto honour, and another unto dishonour?"

ἢ οὐκ ἔχει ἐξουσίαν ὁ κεραμεὺς τοῦ πηλοῦ ἐκ τοῦ αὐτοῦ φυράματος ποιῆσαι ὃ μὲν εἰς τιμὴν σκεῦος, ὁ δὲ εἰς ἀτιμίαν;

"Has the potter no right over the clay, to make out of the same lump one vessel for beauty and another for menial use?" . . . RSV

ἢ (disjunctive) 465.
οὐκ (negative conjunction with the indicative, in rhetorical question, which expects a positive reply) 130.
ἔχει (3d.per.sing.pres.act.ind.of ἔχω, static) 82.
ἐξουσίαν (acc.sing.fem.of ἐξουσία, direct object of ἔχει) 707.
ὁ (nom.sing.masc.of the article in agreement with κεραμεὺς) 9.
κεραμεὺς (nom.sing.masc.of κεραμεύς, subject of ἔχει) 1620.
τοῦ (gen.sing.masc.of the article in agreement with πηλοῦ) 9.
πηλοῦ (gen.sing.masc.of πηλός, description) 2393.
ἐκ (preposition with the ablative of source) 19.
τοῦ (abl.sing.neut.of the article in agreement with φυράματος) 9.
αὐτοῦ (abl.sing.neut.of αὐτός, in agreement with φυράματος, intensive) 16.

#3968 φυράματος (abl.sing.neut.of φύραμα, source).

King James Version

lump - Rom.9:21; 11:16; 1 Cor.5:6,7; Gal.5:9.

Revised Standard Version

lump - Rom.9:21; 11:16; 1 Cor.5:6,7; Gal.5:9.

Meaning: Cf. φυράω - "to mix." Hence, any substance mixed with water and kneaded to form a mass of material for molding. Clay - Rom.9:21; 11:16; dough - 1 Cor.5:6,7; Gal.5:9. All passages are using the word metaphorically.

ποιῆσαι (aor.act.inf.of ποιέω, noun use, in apposition with ἐξουσίαν) 127.
ὃ (acc.sing.neut.of ὅς, relative pronoun, direct object of ποιῆσαι) 65.
μὲν (particle of affirmation) 300.
εἰς (preposition with the accusative, purpose) 140.
τιμὴν (acc.sing.fem.of τιμή, purpose) 1619.
σκεῦος (acc.sing.neut.of σκεῦος, direct object of ποιῆσαι) 997.
ὃ (acc.sing.neut.of ὅς, relative pronoun, direct object of ποιῆσαι) 65.
δὲ (adversative conjunction) 11.
εἰς (preposition with the accusative, purpose) 140.
ἀτιμίαν (acc.sing.fem.of ἀτιμία, purpose) 3808.

Translation - "Or does not the potter have authority over the clay to make from the same lump one which is a vase of high value and one a pot of cheap construction?"

Comment: The rhetorical question anticipates a positive reply. τοῦ πηλοῦ can be taken either as a genitive of description, joined with κεραμεύς - "the potter of the clay" or as a genitive of reference, which is essentially the same idea - "the potter has authority with reference to the clay." ἐκ τοῦ αὐτοῦ φυράματος - an ablative of source, with αὐτοῦ in the intensive attributive position - "the same lump." The difference in the finished product is not in the raw material, because both products came from the same lump of clay. The difference is in the design of the artist - in this case the Sovereign God. The clay is still the same clay. One product is a vase of high value. *Cf.*#1619 for the cost-price meaning of τιμή and τιμάω (#1142) and related words. The other product is a menial cook-pot of small value.

God, the Potter in Paul's analogy, must work with the material at hand. It consists of depraved, fallen human nature, all of which deserves only to be abandoned, but for the love of God which rules otherwise. Grace makes one a vase, conformed to Christ's image (Rom.8:29). Justice makes another a menial pot. What is wrong with that? To say that this shows partiality is true. Partiality in human beings is wrong, but such a criticism judges God by human _ standards and is a wicked egotistical presumption.

Verse 22 - "What if God, willing to shew his wrath, and to make his power known, endured with much longsuffering the vessels of wrath fitted to destruction:"

εἰ δὲ θέλων ὁ θεὸς ἐνδείξασθαι τὴν ὀργὴν καὶ γνωρίσαι τὸ δυνατὸν αὐτοῦ ἤνεγκεν ἐν πολλῇ μακροθυμίᾳ σκεύη ὀργῆς κατηρτισμένα εἰς ἀπώλειαν,

"What if God, desiring to show his wrath and to make known his power, has endured with much patience the vessels of wrath made for destruction, . . . " . . .

RSV

εἰ (conditional particle in first-class elliptical condition) 337.

δὲ (adversative conjunction) 11.

θέλων (pres.act.part.nom.sing.masc.of θέλω, adverbial, concessive) 88.

ὁ (nom.sing.masc.of the article in agreement with θεὸς) 9.

θεὸς (nom.sing.masc.of θεός, subject of ἤνεγκεν) 124.

ἐνδείξασθαι (aor.mid.inf.of ἐνδείκνυμαι, epexegetical) 3842.

τὴν (acc.sing.fem.of the article in agreement with ὀργὴν) 9.

ὀργὴν (acc.sing.fem.of ὀργή, direct object of ἐνδείξασθαι) 283.

καὶ (adjunctive conjunction joining infinitives) 14.

γνωρίσαι (aor.act.inf.of γωνρίζω, epexegetical) 1882.

τὸ (acc.sing.neut.of the article in agreement with δυνατὸν) 9.

δυνατὸν (acc.sing.neut.of δυνατός, direct object of γνωρίσαι) 1311.

αὐτοῦ (gen.sing.masc.of αὐτός, possession) 16.

ἤνεγκεν (3d.per.sing.aor.act.ind.of φέρω, culminative) 683.

ἐν (preposition with the locative, time period) 80.

πολλῇ (loc.sing.fem.of πολύς, in agreement with μακροθυμίᾳ) 228.

μακροθυμίᾳ (loc.sing.fem.of μακροθυμία, time period) 3832.

σκεύη (acc.pl.neut.of σκεῦος, direct object of ἤνεγκεν) 997.

ὀργῆς (gen.sing.fem.of ὀργή, description) 283.

κατηρτισμένα (perf.pass.part.acc.pl.neut.of καταρτίζω, adjectival, restrictive, predicate position, in agreement with σκεύη) 401.

εἰς (preposition with the accusative, purpose) 140.

ἀπώλειαν (acc.sing.fem.of ἀπώλεια, purpose) 666.

Translation - "But though God, although intending to display His wrath and make known His power, with great self-restraint postponed punishment upon objects of His wrath which had been made ready for destruction, . . . "

Comment: Paul has begun a first-class condition with εἰ and the indicative in ἤνεγκεν, but his thought trails away and the apodosis is never added. It is another case of Paul's mind running ahead of his pen. The participles are concessive. God's ultimate purpose is to display His wrath against sin and His power to enforce His will. The former is the evidence of His holiness and the latter demonstrates His sovereignty. If He had not wished to display His wrath, He could have been accused of complicity with sin, which would be a denial of His holiness. If He had not wished to display His power in the presence of the awesome power of evil, His sovereignty could be called in question. To question either God's holiness or His sovereign power to enthrone His administration of justice in the universe is to sweep away the eternal hope which is the essence of the Christian faith. Thus God, since He is God, must will ultimately to demonstrate universally both holiness and sovereignty, which in the face of Satan's opposition calls for wrath and power - τὴν ὀργὴν καὶ τὸ δυνατὸν αὐτοῦ.

Despite this fact, however (concessive θέλων) God, in love and mercy withheld punishment against the non-elect, even though it taxed His forebearance (Gen.6:3; Rom.2:4). To prove His love, He endured the insults of sinners, even though they had been in the past and therefore currently (perfect tense in κατηρτισμένα) designed for destruction. To exert power and to exercise wrathful judgment upon sinners on the first occasion of their rebellion would be to indicate a spiteful urge to send them to hell. God knew from the beginning that their ultimate destiny was destruction, but He nevertheless postponed punishment at great personal sacrifice. To postpone it forever, in the face of their continued rebellion, would be complicity in their sin.

Critics can reply that God could have elected to save everyone, even Satan and his demons, and Calvinists, who are stuck with it, can only reply that nevertheless the Scriptures teach that God did not so choose. Arminians have a logical system, as do the Universalists, if by "logical" we mean that which conforms to human thinking, while Calvinists are faced with the revelation of Scripture does not commend itself to human logic. We thus accept what the Bible says, like little children (Mt.11:25,26; 18:3) and reaffirm our faith that, however difficult it is for us to understand it now, we are sure that the Judge of all the earth will always do right (Gen.18:25).

Verse 23 - ". . . and that he might make known the riches of his glory on the vessels of mercy, which he had afore prepared unto glory."

καὶ ἵνα γνωρίσῃ τὸν πλοῦτον τῆς δόξης αὐτοῦ ἐπὶ σκεύη ἐλέους, ἃ προητοίμασεν εἰς δόξαν,

". . . in order to make known the riches of his glory for the vessels of mercy, which he has prepared beforehand for glory, . . . "   RSV

καὶ (continuative conjunction) 14.
ἵνα (conjunction with the subjunctive in a sub-final clause) 114.
γνωρίσῃ (3d.per.sing.aor.act.subj.of γνωρίζω, sub-final) 1882.
τὸν (acc.sing.masc.of the article in agreement with πλοῦτον) 9.
πλοῦτον (acc.sing.masc.of πλοῦτος, direct object of γνωρίσῃ) 1050.
τῆς (gen.sing.fem.of the article in agreement with δόξης) 9.
δόξης (gen.sing.fem.of δόξα, description) 361.
αὐτοῦ (gen.sing.masc.of αὐτός, possession) 16.
ἐπὶ (preposition with the accusative of extent) 47.
σκεύη (acc.pl.neut.of σκεῦος, extent) 997.
ἐλέους (gen.sing.neut.of ἔλεος, description) 795.
ἃ (acc.pl.neut.of ὅς, relative pronoun, direct object of προητοίμασεν) 65.

#3969 προητοίμασεν (3d.per.sing.aor.act.ind.of προετοιμάζω, culminative).

     King James Version

ordain before - Eph.2:10.
prepare before - Rom.9:23.

     Revised Standard Version

prepare beforehand - Rom.9;23; Eph.2:10.

Meaning: A combination of πρό (#442) and ἑτοιμάζω (#257). To prepare before. To make ready someone or something for future destiny. With reference to the good works of the Christian - Eph.2:10; to prepare the elect for salvation, followed by εἰς δόξαν - Rom.9:23.

     εἰς (preposition with the accusative, purpose) 140.
δόξαν (acc.sing.fem.of δόξα, purpose) 361.

Translation - ". . . and that He might display the riches of His glory upon objects of mercy, whom He previously prepared for glory."

Comment: καὶ joins the ἵνα sub-final clause to the concessive participle θέλων in verse 22. God, wishing to display His wrath and power, and also by the contrast, intending thus to make known the riches of His glory . . . κ.τ.λ. By visiting His holy wrath upon sinners, God prominently displays His glory and grace to the elect, since both saints and sinners are molded from the same lump of clay (verse 21). Note the participial phrase κατηρισμένα εἰς ἀπώλειαν in contrast to ἃ προητοίμασεν εἰς δόξαν - "Having been and hence now completely designed for destruction" (a perfect tense present result of a preterite punctiliar action) and "which he prepared before (in a completed timeless action of the aorist) for glory." This arbitrary decision making cuts across ethnic lines, as we learn in

Verse 24 - "Even us whom he hath called, not of the Jews only, but also of the Gentiles."

οὓς καί ἐκάλεσεν ἡμᾶς οὐ μόνον ἐξ Ἰουδαίων ἀλλὰ καὶ ἐξ ἐθνῶν;

". . . even us whom he has called, not from the Jews only but also from the Gentiles?" . . . RSV

οὓς (acc.pl.masc.of ὅς, relative pronoun, direct object of ἐκάλεσεν) 65.
καὶ (ascensive conjunction) 14.
ἐκάλεσεν (3d.per.sing.aor.act.ind.of καλέω, constative) 107.
ἡμᾶς (acc.pl.masc.of ἐγώ, direct object of ἐκάλεσεν) 123.
οὐ (negative conjunction with the indicative) 130.
μόνον (acc.sing.neut.of μόνος, adverbial) 339.
ἐξ (preposition with the partitive genitive) 19.
Ἰουδαίων (gen.pl.masc.of Ἰουδαῖος, partitive) 143.
ἀλλὰ (adversative conjunction) 342.
καὶ (adjunctive conjunction, joining substantives) 14.
ἐξ (preposition with the partitive genitive) 19.
ἐθνῶν (gen.pl.neut.of ἔθνος, partitive) 376.

Translation - "Even us, whom He called, not only from among Jews, but also from among Gentiles."

Comment: ἅ of verse 23 is neuter to agree with σκεύη, as Paul was speaking in a figure of speech. Now (verse 24) οὓς, referring to the same people, is masculine, since Paul is now applying the figure and we have the real gender instead of the grammatical. Also ἡμᾶς, the object of προτοίμασεν.

God's calling is subject only to His sovereign will. It includes some from among both Jews and Gentiles, as the partitive genitives indicate. Paul had made this point before in Rom.4:7-16 and he will make it again (Eph.2:11-22). Now he supports it with a quotation from Hosea.

Verse 25 - "As he saith also is Osee, I will call them my people, which were not my people: and her beloved, which was not beloved."

ὡς καὶ ἐν τῷ Ὡσηὲ λέγει, Καλέσω τὸν οὐ λαόν μου λαόν μου καὶ τὴν οὐκ ἠγαπημένην ἠγαπημένην.

"As indeed he says in Hosea, 'Those who were not my people I will call my people, and her who was not beloved I will call my beloved.' " . . . RSV

ὡς (particle introducing a comparative clause) 128.
καὶ (emphatic conjunction) 14.

ἐν (preposition with the locative of place) 80.
τῷ (loc.sing.masc.of the article in agreement with Ὡσηὲ) 9.

#3970 Ὡσηὲ (loc.sing.masc.of Ὡσηέ, place).

King James Version

Osee - Rom.9:25.

Revised Standard Version

Hosea - Rom.9:25.

Meaning: The Hebrew word for "deliverance." The Son of Beeri, a contemporary of Isaiah; a well known Hebrew prophet - Rom.9:25.

λέγει (3d.per.sing.pres.act.ind.of λέγω, historical) 66.
Καλέσω (1st.per.sing.fut.act.ind.of καλέω, predictive) 107.
τὸν (acc.sing.masc.of the article in agreement with λαόν) 9.
οὐ (negative conjunction with the indicative) 130.
λαόν (acc.sing.masc.of λαός, direct object of καλέσω) 110.
μου (gen.sing.masc.of ἐγώ, relationship) 123.
λαόν (acc.sing.masc.of λαός, predicate accusative) 110.
μου (gen.sing.masc.of ἐγώ, relationship) 123.
καὶ (adjunctive conjunction joining substantives) 14.
τὴν (acc.sing.fem.of the article in agreement with ἠγαπημένην) 9.
οὐκ (negative conjunction with the indicative) 130.
ἠγαπημένην (perf.pass.part.acc.sing.fem.of ἀγαπάω, substantival, direct object of καλέσω) 540.
ἠγαπημένην (perf.pass.part.acc.sing.fem.of ἀγαπάω, substantival, predicate accusative) 540.

Translation - "As indeed He said in Hosea, 'I will call those who are not my people my people, and those not beloved beloved.' "

Comment: Instead of an apodosis to complete εἰ . . . ἤνεγκεν in verse 22, Paul continues with the comparative clause introduced by ὡς. The quotation is from Hosea 2:23, where the LXX has ἀγαπήσω τὴν οὐκ ἠγαπημένην, καὶ ἐγὼ τῷ οὐ λαῷ μου Λαός μου εἶ σύ, καὶ αὐτὸς ἐρεῖ κύριοσ ὁ θεός μου εἶ σύ - "I will love the one not loved, and I will say to those not my people, you are my people and he shall say, You are the Lord my God." *Cf.* Eph.1:6; John 10:16.

Those of verse 25 who were not beloved as the people of God are those of ἐξ ἐθνῶν of verse 24. Not all Gentiles are elect; nor are all Jews non-elect. God's choice is based upon His own will, without regard to race, blessing or lack of blessing. Genetic descent from Abraham is no guarantee of salvation. Nor is the fact that one has been given the Mosaic law or the Levitical order of worship.

In verse 26 Paul cites another passage from Hosea.

Verse 26 - "And it shall come to pass that in the place where it was said unto them, Ye are not my people, there shall they be called the children of the living God."

καὶ ἔσται ἐν τῷ τόπῳ οὗ ἐρρέθη αὐτοῖς, Οὐ λαός μου ὑμεῖς, ἐκεῖ κληθήσονται υἱοὶ θεοῦ ζῶντος.

"And in the very place where it was said to them, 'You are not my people,' they will be called 'sons of the living God.' " . . . *RSV*

καὶ (continuative conjunction) 14.
ἔσται (3d.per.sing.fut.ind.of εἰμί, predictive) 86.
ἐν (preposition with the locative of place) 80.
τῷ (loc.sing.masc.of the article in agreement with τόπῳ) 9.
τόπῳ (loc.sing.masc.of τόπος, place) 1019.
οὗ (gen.sing.masc.of ὅς, relative pronoun, in a relative adjectival clause) 65.
ἐρρέθη (3d.per.sing.aor.pass.ind.of ἐρρήθην, constative) 116.
αὐτοῖς (dat.pl.masc.of αὐτός, indirect object of ἐρρέθη) 16.
Οὐ (negative conjunction with the indicative) 130.
λαός (nom.sing.masc.of λαός, predicate nominative) 110.
μου (gen.sing.masc.of ἐγώ, relationship) 123.
ὑμεῖς (nom.pl.masc.of σύ, subject of verb understood) 104.
ἐκεῖ (adverb of place) 204.
κληθήσονται (3d.per.pl.fut.pass.ind.of καλέω, predictive) 107.
υἱοὶ (nom.pl.masc.of υἱός, predicate nominative) 5.
θεοῦ (gen.sing.masc.of θεός, relationship) 124.
ζῶντος (pres.act.part.gen.sing.masc.of ζάω, adjectival, restrictive, predicate position, in agreement with θεοῦ) 340.

Translation - "And it shall be that in the place where it was said to them, 'You are not my people,' there they shall be called sons of the living God."

Comment: The quotation is from Hosea 1:10. By ἐν τῷ τόπῳ οὗ ἐρρέθη αὐτοῖς is meant the parts of the earth, outside the promised Palestine territory, which was given by covenant to Abraham's seed. Thus, thanks to the world-wide missionary enterprise (Mt.28:18-20; Rev.5:6) throughout the Gentile world, where once God said to Gentiles, "You are not my people" we, the elect from among the Gentiles (Acts 15:14-18; Eph.3:1-11) are now called the sons of God. Not all Gentiles are to be so designated.

This selection principle is also to be applied to the physical sons and daughters of Abraham, as we see in

Verse 27 - "Esaias also crieth concerning Israel, Though the number of the children of Israel be as the sand of the sea, a remnant shall be saved."

Ἡσαΐας δὲ κράζει ὑπὲρ τοῦ Ἰσραήλ, Ἐὰν ᾖ ὁ ἀριθμὸς τῶν υἱῶν Ἰσραὴλ ὡς ἡ ἄμμος τῆς θαλάσσης, τὸ ὑπόλειμμα σωθήσεται.

"And Isaiah cries out concerning Israel: 'Though the number of the sons of Israel be as the sand of the sea, only a remant of them will be saved;' " .. RSV

Ἡσαΐας (nom.sing.masc.of Ἡσαΐας, subject of κράζει) 255.

δὲ (continuative conjunction) 11.

κράζει (3d.per.sing.pres.act.ind.of κράζω, historical) 765.

ὑπὲρ (preposition with the genitive of reference) 545.

τοῦ (gen.sing.masc.of the article in agreement with Ἰσραήλ) 9.

Ἰσραήλ (gen.sing.masc.of Ἰσραήλ, reference) 165.

Ἐὰν (conditional particle in a third-class condition) 363.

ᾖ (3d.per.sing.pres.subj.of εἰμί, third-class condition) 86.

ὁ (nom.sing.masc.of the article in agreement with ἀριθμὸς) 9.

ἀριθμὸς (nom.sing.masc.of ἀριθμός, subject of ᾖ) 2278.

τῶν (gen.pl.masc.of the article in agreement with υἱῶν) 9.

υἱῶν (gen.pl.masc.of υἱός, designation) 5.

Ἰσραὴλ (gen.sing.masc.of Ἰσραήλ, relationship) 165.

ὡς (particle in a comparative clause) 128.

ἡ (nom.sing.fem.of the article in agreement with ἄμμος) 9.

ἄμμος (nom.sing.fem.of ἄμμος, subject of the verb εἰσίν understood) 701.

τῆς (gen.sing.fem.of the article in agreement with θαλάσσης) 9.

θαλάσσης (gen.sing.fem.of θάλασσα, description) 374.

τὸ (nom.sing.neut.of the article in agreement with ὑπόλειμμα) 9.

#3971 ὑπόλειμμα (nom.sing.neut.of ὑπόλειμμα, subject of σωθήσεται).

King James Version

remnant - Rom.9:27.

Revised Standard Version

remnant of them - Rom.9:27.

Meaning: cf. κατάλειμμα (Sinaiticus D F G. rel. *cf.*LXX, Isa.10:22). *Cf.* ὑπολείπω (#3980). A remnant; a part of the whole - Rom.9:27.

σωθήσεται (3d.per.sing.fut.pass.ind.of σώζω, predictive) 109.

Translation - "And Isaiah shouted with reference to Israel, 'Though the number of the sons of Israel be as the sand of the sea, the remnant will be saved.' "

Comment: Ἐὰν and the subjunctive ᾖ here in the protasis and the future indicative in the apodosis of a third-class condition. It has a concessive sense. "Even though (if it is) and despite the fact that the population of Israel (may be) as the sand of the sea, only a remnant will be saved." The quotation is from Isa.10:22. God's promise to Abraham (Gen.13:16) refers to his physical descendants. Out of that great number, some will be saved. Isaiah did not tell us how great a remnant. Keep in mind that all who die in infancy, whether Jews or Gentiles are *safe*. Keep in mind also that many Hebrews have become Hebrew Christians and are members of the Body of Christ. In addition to these 144,000, representing the twelve tribes of Israel, will be saved at the Second Coming of Messiah (Rev.7:1-8) to constitute the nucleus of the Jewish nation in the Kingdom of the Heavens over which Messiah will reign forever.

The prophecy of Genesis 15:5 refers to the spiritual seed of Abraham (Gal.3:7). These are the "remnant" to whom Paul is referring. They are "stars" (Gen.15:5) not "grains of sand" or "bits of dust" (Gen.13:16) and are also not numbered among the 144,00 of Rev.7:1-8.

Just as circumcision was the act by which the physical sons of Israel were marked and thus permanently identified as a Jew, so the birth from above (John 3:3,7; 1 Peter 1:23) permanently seals (Eph.4:30) the elect as members of the Body of Christ. We have already heard from Paul that the circumcision that means salvation for the believer, whether he be Jew or Gentile, is not the surgical operation that marks the Jewish boy for life, but the circumcision "of the heart" by which Paul means regeneration (Rom.2:28-29). A remnant of those physically circumcised have been and will be spiritually circumcised. They are spiritual Israel.

When Paul says that only a remnant of physical Israel will be saved, he does not mean to imply, nor does he say that *all* of the Gentiles will be saved. The election process of God applies to Gentiles as well.

Verse 28 - "For he will finish the work, and cut it short in righteousness: because a short work will the Lord make upon the earth."

λόγον γὰρ συντελῶν καὶ συντέμνων ποιήσει κύριος ἐπὶ τῆς γῆς.

". . . for the Lord will execute his sentence upon the earth with rigor and dispatch." . . . RSV

λόγον (acc.sing.masc.of λόγος, direct object of ποιήσει) 510.
γὰρ (causal conjunction) 105.
συντελῶν (pres.act.part.nom.sing.masc.of συντελέω, adverbial, modal) 1952.
καὶ (adjunctive conjunction joining participles) 14.

#3972 συντέμνων (pres.act.part.nom.sing.masc.of συντέμων, adverbial, modal).

King James Version

cut short - Rom.9:28.

Revised Standard Version

execute - Rom.9:28.

Meaning: A combination of σύν (#1542) and τέμνω - "to cut." Hence to cut to pieces; to cut completely; to cut short; make a quick end of - joined to λόγον - to expedite the fulfillment of a prophecy - Rom.9:28.

ποιήσει (3d.per.sing.fut.act.ind.of ποιέω, predictive) 127.
κύριος (nom.sing.masc.of κύριος, subject of ποιήσει) 97.

ἐπὶ (preposition with the genitive, place description) 47.

τῆς (gen.sing.fem.of the article in agreement with γῆς) 9.

γῆς (gen.sing.fem.of γῆ, place description) 157.

Translation - "For the Lord will implement the fulfillment of His promise upon the earth, with rigor and with no delay."

Comment: The participles are modal, serving as adverbs to modify ποιήσει. The rigorous and swift work of God in closing the age of grace and ushering in the Kingdom age is described in Revelation 1:4-22:5. This short seven years will be the last act on the drama, which began in the Garden of Eden when God saved Adam and Eve and continued throughout the Old Testament age. Infants died and went to heaven. Many adults were given the gift of faith as exercised by Abraham. A category described in Romans 2:12-16 will be included in God's gracious redemptive plan. After Pentecost the church, charged with the great commission, has carried the gospel to the ends of the earth. The work is still going on, and will be brought to completion "in the days of the voice of the seventh angel, when he shall begin to sound . . ." (Rev.10:7). Then the "mystery. . . that the Gentiles should be fellowheirs and of the same body, and partakers of his promise in Christ by the gospel" (Eph.3:3-6) will be finished. And since the seventh trumpet is the "last trump" (1 Cor.15:52), at that time Christ will return. There will be resurrection for the dead in Christ and rapture for the living. There will also be judgment because His coming will also be "in flaming fire, taking vengeance on them that know not God, and that obey not the gospel of our Lord Jesus Christ, who shall be punished with everlasting destuction from the presence of the Lord, and from the glory of his power." (2 Thess.1:7-9). That is the day "When He shall come to be glorified in his saints, and to be admired in all them that believe . . . in that day" (2 Thess.1:10).

The degeneration of world society at the end of the age will be so great that the Lord will be forced to intervene in order to rescue His experiment on this planet. More accurately it is not an experiment as though the outcome is in doubt in the mind of Him Who planned it all before the foundation of the world.

Because we are creatures subject to the categories of time and space, it often seems to us that the time until the end of the age is passing too slowly. Thus we ". . . have need of patience, that, after (we) have done the will of God, (we) might receive the promise. For yet a little while, and he that shall come will come, and will not tarry" (Heb.10:36-37). Our timeless God has already cut the time short "for the elect's sake" for had He not done so "there should no flesh be saved" (Mt.24:22). This is the thought of

Verse 29 - "And as Esaias said before, Except the Lord of Sabaoth had left us a seed, we had been as Sodoma, and been made like unto Gomorrha."

καὶ καθὼς προείρηκεν Ἡσαΐας, Εἰ μὴ κύριος Σαβαὼθ ἐγκατέλιπεν ἡμῖν σπέρμα, ὡς Σόδομα ἂν ἐγενήθημεν καὶ ὡς Γόμορρα ἂν ὡμοιώθημεν.

"And as Isaiah predicted, 'If the Lord of hosts had not left us children, we

would have fared like Sodom and been made like Gomorrah.' " . . . RSV

καὶ (continuative conjunction) 14.

καθὼς (compound particle in a comparative clause) 1348.

προείρηκεν (3d.per.sing.perf.act.ind.of προεῖπον, intensive) 1501.

Ἡσαΐας (nom.sing.masc.of Ἡσαΐας, subject of προείρηκεν) 255.

Εἰ (conditional particle in a second-class condition, contrary to fact) 337.

μὴ (negative conjunction in a second-class condition) 87.

κύριος (nom.sing.masc.of κύριος, subject of ἐγκατέλιπεν) 97.

#3973 Σαβαὼθ gen.sing.masc., description).

King James Version

Sabaoth - Rom.9:29; James 5:4.

Revised Standard Version

hosts - Rom.9:29; James 5:4.

Meaning: Plural for the Hebrew word meaning "an army." Hence, the Commander of the Army. "Lord of hosts." Leader of the army of heaven - *cf.* Rev.19:11-16. Rom.9:29; James 5:4.

ἐγκατέλιπεν (3d.per.sing.aor.act.ind.of ἐγκαταλείπω, culminative, in a second-class, contrary to fact condition) 1654.

ἡμῖν (dat.pl.masc.of ἐγώ, personal advantage) 123.

σπέρμα (acc.sing.neut.of σπέρμα, direct object of ἐγκατέλιπεν) 1056.

ὡς (particle in a comparative clause) 128.

Σόδομα (nom.sing.neut.of Σόδομα, subject of ἔστιν understood) 871.

ἂν (contingent particle in a second-class condition) 205.

ἐγενήθημεν (1st.per.pl.aor.pass.ind.of γίνομαι, second-class condition) 113.

καὶ (adjunctive conjunction joining comparative clauses) 14.

ὡς (particle in a comparative clause) 128.

Γόμορρα (nom.sing.fem.of Γόμορρα,subject of ἔστιν) 872.

ἂν (contingent particle in a second-class condition) 205.

ὡμοιώθημεν (1st.per.pl.1st.aor.pass.ind.of ὁμοιόω, second-class condition) 575.

Translation - "And as Isaiah predicted, 'If the Lord of Hosts had not preserved for us our children, we would have become like Sodom is and we would have been made like Gomorrah.' "

Comment: We have a second-class, contrary to fact condition, with εἰ and secondary tenses in both the protasis and the apodosis. God did leave for Israel succeeding generations and it was for their sake that God did not wipe out the nation and leave them like Sodom and Gomorrah. Peter pointed out to Israel at Pentecost that the promise of salvation ". . . is unto you, and to your children, and to all that are afar off, even as many as the Lord our God shall call." (Acts 2:39).

This does not say that *all* of the physical children of Abraham will be saved, but it does say that some of them will be. There has never been a generation of Jews who have not had children or grandchildren whom God purposed to call and save. Thus even though any given Jew might not repent and be saved, for the sake of his unborn descendants, some of whom were to be saved, God spared his life. To put it the other way, if God had wiped out the Jewish race as He did Sodom and Gomorrah there would have been no Jews since. Divine judgment fell upon Sodom and Gomorrah. Thus no descendants of those who perished are to be found in the Body of Christ, but Lot and his daughters escaped. Even though the Ammonites and Moabites are the descendants of parents conceived in incest, individual Ammonites and Moabites can be saved. Ruth, the grandmother of David was a Moabitess. Indeed Ammonites and Moabites are included in the company described in Revelation 5:9.

Isaiah's prophecy referred specifically to Israel, but it also means that the human family as a whole will be spared total destruction at the hands of an avenging Lord of Hosts, until the last elect soul for whom Christ died has been born, called and regenerated to find his place in the Body of Christ.

God's children, born and saved in whatever age, will live in resurrection glory to see the fulfillment of all that God promised to Abraham, Isaac, Jacob, Judah and David. In Romans 1:18-32, Paul gave us a picture of the social, economic and political chaos that results from apostasy. In the last days of the last days (Heb.1:2) many will turn away from God and the inner tensions of a tightly integrated and increasingly depraved world society will bring the world to antediluvian moral conditions and force God to act in judgment as He did against Sodom and Gomorrah. The one bright hope for the future is that God is under eternal obligations to Abraham to postpone that judgment until His "mystery" (Eph.3:1-11; Rev.10:7) is complete. When that is done, then Christ will return in judgment (2 Thess.1:7-10) to rescue the world from its self-imposed folly and bring eternal order out of chaos. There is utterly no reason for optimism in any analysis of the current world situation that leaves out of account the personal intervention of the Lord of Sabaoth. This is the *weltanschauung* of Christian theology. The eschatologist whose system does not include the theology of election and effectual call is astray. Our Lord will remain at the Father's right hand until His enemies have been made His footstool (Psalm 110:1). In the interim the Holy Spirit is calling out a people for His name. Prophecy buffs (!) should stop looking for the rapture and the mark of the beast, and start praying for the completion of the Body of Christ. When the missionary enterprise is finished (Mt.28:18-20; Acts 1:8) and   the last elect is saved, , Messiah will come back. Not before. If He had intended to leave someone out He would have destroyed the world long ago.

Israel and the Gospel

(Romans 9:30-10:4)

Verse 30 - "What shall we say then? That the Gentiles which followed not after righteousness, have attained to righteousness, even the righteousness which is of faith."

Τί οὖν ἐροῦμεν; ὅτι ἔθνη τὰ μὴ διώκοντα δικαιοσύνην κατέλαβεν δικαιοσύνην, δικαιοσύνη δὲ τὴν ἐκ πίστεως.

"What shall we say, then? That Gentiles who did not pursue righteousness have attained it, that is, righteousness through faith;" . . . RSV

Τί (acc.sing.neut.of τίς, interrogative pronoun, in direct question, object of ἐροῦμεν) 281.

οὖν (inferential conjunction) 68.

ἐροῦμεν (1st.per.pl.fut.act.ind.of εἶπον, deliberative) 155.

ὅτι (conjunction introducing an object clause in indirect discourse) 211.

ἔθνη (nom.pl.neut.of ἔθνος, subject of κατέλαβεν) 376.

τὰ (nom.pl.neut.of the article in agreement with διώκοντα) 9.

μὴ (negative conjunction with the participle) 87.f

διώκοντα (pres.act.part.nom.pl.neut.of διώκω, substantival, in apposition with ἔθνη) 434.

δικαιοσύνην (acc.sing.fem.of δικαιοσύνη, direct object of διώκοντα) 322.

κατέλαβεν (3d.per.sing.aor.act.ind.of καταλαμβάνω, culminative) 1694.

δικαιοσύνην (acc.sing.fem.of δικαιοσύνη, direct object of κατέλαβεν) 322.

δικαιοσύνην (acc.sing.fem.of δικαιοσύνη, in apposition) 322.

δὲ (adversative conjunction) 11.

τὴν (acc.sing.fem.of the article in agreement with δικαιοσύνην) 9.

ἐκ (preposition with the ablative of source) 19.

πίστεως (abl.sing.fem.of πίστις, source) 728.

Translation - "To what conclusion then shall we come? That the Gentiles that did not pursue righteousness have obtained it, but it is the righteousness that comes from faith."

Comment: Paul began this chapter by telling us that his heart was breaking because his Jewish brethren were not saved. Then he introduced the subject of the decrees of God. Isaac was chosen because his birth came about because of the faith of Abraham and Sarah. Isaac was the miracle baby. Ishmael was rejected. His birth was the result of Abraham's trust in his own resources. No miracle was involved when Ishmael was born. Then, again to stress the doctrine of decrees, Paul says that Jacob was chosen rather than Esau, even though the rule as interpreted by human custom favored the first-born. Again God's ways are not necessarily our ways (Isa.55:9).

And then again, as though Paul's readers were not already sufficiently mystified, he introduced Pharaoh and the treatment which he received at the hands of a sovereign God, after which he replied to the critics who advanced the view that God was unfair in His dealings with Pharaoh and therefore at fault. Paul supported his defense of the Almighty by citing passages from Hosea and Isaiah.

We see the logic of Paul's approach in the section which begins in verse 30. The Gentiles were saved by faith *precisely because they were not given the law* and all of the other advantages listed in Romans 9:1-5. Had they been given the advantages given to the Jews, they would have been misled to believe that righteousness was the reward for their obedience to the law. This is the mistake that the Jews made, as Paul points out in verse 31. The Jews misunderstood God's purpose in handing down to them the code of ethics in the Ten Commandments and the rule book for their national life as it spoke in terms of morals, politics, sociology, economics and psychology. Had they understood that the law was given to them so that they might note the contrast between its holy demands and their sinful life style and thus come humbly and in repentance to ask for salvation on the grace and faith basis, they might have done so. In fact, many of them did, as they looked forward in faith, beyond the animal sacrifice at the brazen altar to the true "Lamb of God" (John 1:29; 1 Cor.5:7). Paul discusses the reason why God gave the law to Israel at greater length in Galatians 3:19ff.

There are many barriers on the roadway that otherwise would lead man to God. James E. Duncan, Jr. has suggested slavery to sin, separation, death, the sin nature, sovereignty and identification (*The Reason for Joy*, 12-19 *et passim.*). There is another. Sinful man will never attain to righteousness as long as he entertains his exalted opinion of his own merit, an opinion which is enhanced by his *supposed* adherence to God's rule of ethics. People who think that they are "good" are not like little children (Mt.18:3; 11:25-27). It is ironical. To gain righteousness (δικαιοσύνη) one must refuse to pursue it. He who gains it does so, not by diligent pursuit, and what he gains is the righteousness which has faith as its source. This is why the Jews for the salvation of whom Paul prayed so earnestly, were not yet saved as he says in verses 31,32.

Verse 31 - "But Israel, which followed after the law of righteousness, hath not attained to the law of righteousness."

Ἰσραὴλ δὲ διώκων νόμον δικαιοσύνης εἰς νόμον οὐκ ἔφθασεν.

". . . but that Israel who pursued the righteousness which is based on law did not succeed in fulfilling that law." . . . RSV

Ἰσραὴλ (nom.sing.masc.of Ἰσραήλ, subject of ἔφθασεν) 165.
δὲ (adversative conjunction) 11.
διώκων (pres.act.part.nom.sing.masc.of διώκω, adverbial, concessive) 434.
νόμον (acc.sing.masc.of νόμος, direct object of διώκων) 464.
δικαιοσύνης (gen.sing.fem.of δικαιοσύνη, description) 322.
εἰς (preposition with the accusative of extent) 140.

νόμον (acc.sing.masc.of νόμος, extent) 464.
οὐκ (negative conjunction with the indicative) 130.
ἔφθασεν (3d.per.sing.aor.act.ind.of φθάνω, constative) 996.

Translation - "But Israel, although they tried to obey a righteous law, did not attain its righteousness."

Comment: δὲ is adversative. Unlike the Gentiles, who achieved the goal, not by trying to achieve it but by taking it by faith as a gift, Israel pursued it relentlessly. How relentlessly they pursued it can be appreciated by listening to the prayer of the Pharisee in Luke 18:9-12 and to the testimony of Paul in Philippians 3:4-6. The Jews were motivated by their misunderstanding of the purpose of the law and the real message of the prophets. Deluded by their idea that they could achieve the standard which God held before them (Exodus 19:8) and unaware that God gave them the law only that they might see by the contrast between God's standard and their own that they were sinners, they were unaware that God's special gifts to them represented His attempt to lead them to repentance (Gal.3:19-25; Rom.2:4). Thus they were frustrated (Rom.10:3). But God is sovereign, and though Israel as a nation failed, He in sovereign grace chose some individuals (Rom.9:24). At this point He has not finished choosing from among the Jews, those whom He will call to salvation and incorporate into the Body of Christ. He will also choose a remnant nationally (Rev.7:1-8) so that the promise to Abraham will be honored. The nation could have attained righteousness if they had accepted their Messiah and His authenticating works, but they nailed Him on a cross. *Cf.* ἔφθασεν (#996) in Mt.12:28; Lk.11:20.

Verse 32 - "Wherefore? Because they sought it not by faith, but as it were by the works of the law. For they stumbled at that stumblingstone;"

διὰ τί; ὅτι οὐκ ἐκ πίστεως ἀλλ' ὡς ἐξ ἔργων. προσέκοψαν τῷ λίθῳ τοῦ προσκόμματος,

"Why? Because they did not pursue it through faith, but as if it were based on works. They have stumbled over the stumbling stone, . . . " . . . RSV

διὰ (preposition with the accusative, cause) 118.
τί (acc.sing.neut.of τίς, interrogative pronoun, cause) 281.
ὅτι (conjunction introducing a subordinate causal clause) 211.
οὐκ (negative conjunction with the indicative) 130.
ἐκ (preposition with the ablative of source) 19.
πίστεως (abl.sing.fem.of πίστις, source) 728.
ἀλλ' (alternative conjunction) 342.
ὡς (particle in a comparative clause) 128.
ἐξ (preposition with the ablative of source) 19.
ἔργων (abl.pl.neut.of ἔργον, source) 460.
προσέκοψαν (3d.per.pl.aor.act.ind.of προσκόπτω, constative) 352.
τῷ (instru.sing.masc.of the article in agreement with λίθῳ) 9.
λίθῳ (instru.sing.masc.of λίθος, cause) 290.

τοῦ (gen.sing.neut.of the article in agreement with προσκόμματος) 9.

#3974 προσκόμματος (gen.sing.neut.of πρόσκομμα, description).

King James Version

offence - Rom.14:20.
stumbling - 1 Pet.2:8; Rom.9:32,33.
stumbling block - Rom.14:13; 1 Cor.8:9.

Revised Standard Version

stumbling - Rom.9:32; 14:13.
make men stumble - Rom.9:33; 1 Pet.2:8.
stumbling block - 1 Cor.8:9.

Meaning: Cf. προσκόπτω (#352). A stone or other obstruction against which the foot may strike to cause one to stumble. One Christian's enlightened liberty to eat meat, formerly dedicated to idols, without personal offence, may become a stumbling block to a less enlightened Christian who has doubts about the propriety of such practice - 1 Cor.8:9. In this sense also in Rom.14:13,20. Due to Israel's misconception of Messiah's role, His life, teaching and death became a stumbling block which gave to them what they thought to be a legitimate reason for rejecting Him - Rom.9:32,33; 1 Pet.2:8.

Translation - "Why not? Because they looked to works as the source, not to faith. They stumbled because of the stone of stumbling."

Comment: Note διὰ τί for cause in #'s 118 and 281. ὅτι is causal. Paul omits the verb, but his meaning is clear, since ἐκ πίστεως and ἐξ ἔργων are ablative phrases of source. The Jews failed to attain righteousness because they sought it at the wrong source. They did not seek it through faith, where it can be found. They sought it through their own works which could never be accepted by God as righteousness. And thus they stumbled. Their misconception was that since God had given them the law, He intended that the law should be the source of their salvation. God did not mislead them; they misled themselves.

Verse 33 - "As it is written, Behold I lay in Sion a stumblingstone and rock of offence; and whosoever believeth on him shall not be ashamed."

καθὼς γέγραπται, Ἰδοὺ τίθημι ἐν Σιὼν λίθον προσκόμματος καὶ πέτραν σκανδάλου, καὶ ὁ πιστεύων ἐπ' αὐτῷ οὐ καταισχυνθήσεται.

". . . as it is written, 'Behold, I am laying in Zion a stone that will make men stumble, a rock that will make them fall: and he who believes in him will not be put to shame.' " . . . RSV

καθὼς (compound particle in a comparative clause) 1348.
γέγραπται (3d.per.sing.perf.pass.ind.of γράφω, intensive) 156.
Ἰδοὺ (exclamation) 95.

τίθημι (1st.per.sing.pres.act.ind.of τίθημι, historical) 455.

ἐν (preposition with the locative of place) 80.

Σιών (loc.sing.masc.of Σιών, place) 1345.

λίθον (acc.sing.masc.of λίθος, direct object of τίθημι) 290.

προσκόμματος (gen.sing.masc.of πρόσκομμα, description) 3974.

καὶ (concessive conjunction) 14.

πέτραν (acc.sing.fem.of πέτρα, direct object of τίθημι) 695.

σκανδάλου (gen.sing.neut.of σκάνδαλον, description) 1082.

καὶ (continuative conjunction) 14.

ὁ (nom.sing.masc.of the article in agreement with πιστεύων) 9.

πιστεύων (pres.act.part.nom.sing.masc.of πιστεύω, substantival, subject of καταισχυνθήσεται) 734.

ἐπ' (preposition with the instrumental of cause) 47.

αὐτῷ (instru.sing.masc.of αὐτός, cause) 16.

οὐ (negative conjunction with the indicative) 130.

καταισχυνθήσεται (3d.per.sing.fut.pass.ind.of καταισχύνω, predictive) 2505.

Translation - "Just as it stands written, 'Behold I have placed in Zion a stone of stumbling and a rock of offence. But the one who believes upon Him will not be brought down in disgrace.'"

Comment: The quotation is from Isaiah 8:14; 28:16. A comparison reveals that Paul has given only an approximation of the LXX, but the essence is there. 1 Pet.2:6-8 quotes the prophet more accurately. It was in Zion (Jerusalem, the capital city of David's eternal kingdom) that the Messiah appeared in triumphal presentation (Luke 19:29-40). *Cf.* #695 for πέτρα as opposed to πέτρος (#387). *Cf.* #1082 - the trigger on the trap that ensnared Israel. God set a trap for Israel, just as He hardened Pharaoh's heart (Rom.9:18).

This kind of theology will offend only those unregenerates who imagine themselves possessed with sufficient intellectual and moral sophistication to permit them to sit in judgment upon the sovereign and omniscient God.

καὶ seems to be concessive. For the believer, Christ is not the trigger in the trap, but a great foundation rock (Mt.7:24) upon which we build, never in the long run to be brought down in disgrace, ". . . though now for a season, if need be, (we) are in heaviness through manifold temptations, that the trial of (our) faith, being much more precious than gold that perisheth, though it be tried with fire, might be found unto praise and honour and glory at the appearing of Jesus Christ." (1 Pet.1:6,7). *Cf.* Rom.5:5; 10:11; 1 Pet.2:6.

Romans 10:1 - "Brethren my heart's desire and prayer to God for Israel is, that they might be saved."

Ἀδελφοί, ἡ μὲν εὐδοκία τῆς ἐμῆς καρδίας καὶ ἡ δέησις πρὸς τὸν θεὸν ὑπὲρ αὐτῶν εἰς σωτηρίαν.

"Brethren, my heart's desire and prayer to God for them is that they may be saved." . . . RSV

'Αδελφοί (voc.pl.masc.of ἀδελφός, address) 15.

ἡ (nom.sing.fem.of the article in agreement with εὐδοκία) 9.

μὲν (particle of affirmation) 300.

εὐδοκία (nom.sing.fem.of εὐδοκία, subject of ἐστίν understood) 952.

τῆς (gen.sing.fem.of the article in agreement with καρδίας) 9.

ἐμῆς (gen.sing.fem.of ἐμός, possessive pronoun, in agreement with καρδίας) 1267.

καρδίας (gen.sing.fem.of καρδία, description) 432.

καὶ (adjunctive conjunction joining nouns) 14.

ἡ (nom.sing.fem.of the article in agreement with δέησις) 9.

δέησις (nom.sing.fem.of δέησις, subject of ἐστίν understood) 1796.

πρὸς (preposition with the accusative of extent) 197.

τὸν (acc.sing.masc.of the article in agreement with θεὸν) 9.

θεὸν (acc.sing.masc.of θεός, extent) 124.

ὑπὲρ (preposition with the ablative, "in behalf of") 545.

αὐτῶν (abl.pl.masc.of αὐτός, "in behalf of") 16.

εἰς (preposition with the accusative, purpose) 140.

σωτηρίαν (acc.sing.fem.of σωτηρία, purpose) 1852.

Translation - "Brethren, the desire of my heart and my prayer to God for them is for their salvation."

Comment: μὲν the particle of affirmation adds weight to Paul's statement, added perhaps because he may have felt that his audience would not really believe that he was telling the truth about his burden for the salvation of the Jews. On the contrary Paul is in deep earnest about it. The desire of his heart (genitive of description) is expressed in his petition to God (accusative of extent) in reference to them (the ablative use of ὑπέρ). Both the ablative (in behalf of) and the genitive (in reference to) ideas in αὐτῶν are admissible. εἰς with the accusative here is clearly purpose. The context must decide. *Cf.*Mt.12:41 where εἰς and the accusative is found in a causal construction. Note #1796 and its distinction from προσευχή (#1238). Thus Paul repeats the thought of Rom.9:1-3. Sinaiticus P Ψ 33 88 2495 and Chrysostom have αὐτῶν ἐστιν, while K 81 104 181 326 330 436 451 614 629 630 1241 1877 1984 1985 2492 and some Fathers have τοῦ Ἰσραὴλ ἐστιν. The United Bible Societies' Committee is confident that αὐτῶν is the proper reading. In any case the context indicates clearly that Paul is talking about Israel.

Note that Paul's prayer was directed πρὸς τὸν θεόν. The same phrase describes the place of fellowship with God which Ὁ Λόγος occupied in the eternal past (John 1:1). Note also 1 John 1:2 where we have πρὸς τὸν πατέρα. The Pharisee prayed πρὸς ἑαυτὸν (Luke 18:11) !! Let prayer orators at church take note.

Verse 2 - "For I bear them record that they have a zeal of God, but not according to knowledge."

μαρτυρῶ γὰρ αὐτοῖς ὅτι ζῆλον θεοῦ ἔχουσιν, ἀλλ' οὐ κατ' ἐπίγνωσιν.

μαρτυρῶ (1st.per.sing.pres.act.ind.of μαρτυρέω, aoristic) 1471.
γὰρ (causal conjunction) 105.
αὐτοῖς (dat.pl.masc.of αὐτός, reference) 16.
ὅτι (conjunction introducing indirect discourse) 211.
ζῆλον (acc.sing.masc.of ζῆλος, direct object of ἔχουσιν) 1985.
θεοῦ (gen.sing.masc.of θεός, description) 124.
ἔχουσιν (3d.per.pl.pres.act.ind.of ἔχω, present progressive retroactive) 82.
ἀλλ' (adversative conjunction) 342.
οὐ (negative conjunction with the indicative) 130.
κατ' (preposition with the accusative, standard) 98.
ἐπίγνωσιν (acc.sing.fem.of ἐπίγνωσις, standard) 3817.

Translation - "*Because I will say this for them, that they have a divine zeal, but it is not according to divine knowledge.*"

Comment: Paul's concern for the salvation of the Jews arises from what he knows about them. Thus γὰρ is causal. Paul was directing this epistle to the church at Rome, not to the unsaved Jews directly. Thus αὐτοῖς is a dative of reference, not of indirect object. He was talking about them, not to them. θεοῦ without the article is a genitive of reference or description, not of possession. The Jews were zealots with reference to their relation with God, although their efforts were misguided. Misguided and irrational zeal is tragic. It indicates sincerity, even devotion, but a lack of understanding. Note that Paul uses ἐπίγνωσιν, (#3817), not γνῶσις (#1856). They lacked the superior knowledge that comes only from the revelation of the Holy Spirit. They had the knowledge that comes from human rational analysis.

The Jews were making the same mistake that all the unsaved make when they assume that the way to heaven is the way of the good works that have their source only in the flesh. Their confusion is analyzed in

Verse 3 - "*For they being ignorant of God's righteousness, and going about to establish their own righteousness, have not submitted themselves unto the righteousness of God.*"

ἀγνοοῦντες γὰρ τὴν τοῦ θεοῦ δικαιοσύνην, καὶ τὴν ἰδίαν ζητοῦντες στῆσαι, τῇ δικαιοσύνῃ τοῦ θεοῦ οὐχ ὑπετάγησαν.

"*For, being ignorant of the righteousness that comes from God, and seeking to establish their own, they did not submit to God's righteousness.*" . . . RSV

ἀγνοοῦντες (pres.act.part.nom.pl.masc.of ἀγνοέω, adverbial, causal) 2345.
γὰρ (causal conjunction) 105.
τὴν (acc.sing.fem.of the article in agreement with δικαιοσύνην) 9.
τοῦ (abl.sing.masc.of the article in agreement with θεοῦ) 9.
θεοῦ (abl.sing.masc.of θεός, source) 124.
δικαιοσύνην (acc.sing.fem.of δικαιοσύνη, direct object of ἀγνοοῦντες) 322.
καὶ (adjunctive conjunction joining participles) 14.
τὴν (acc.sing.fem.of the article in agreement with δικαιοσύνην) 9.
ἰδίαν (acc.sing.fem.of ἴδιος, possessive pronoun, in agreement with δικαιοσύνην, understood) 778.

ζητοῦντες (pres.act.part.nom.pl.masc.of ζητέω, adverbial, causal) 207.
στῆσαι (aor.act.inf.of ἵστημι, epexegetical) 180.
τῇ (dat.sing.fem.of the article in agreement with δικαιοσύνη) 9.
δικαιοσύνῃ (dat.sing.fem.of δικαιοσύν, reference) 322.
τοῦ (abl.sing.masc.of the article in agreement with θεοῦ) 9.
θεοῦ (abl.sing.masc.of θεός, source) 124.
οὐχ (negative conjunction with the indicative) 130.
ὑπετάγησαν (3d.per.pl.2d.aor.pass.ind.of ὑποτάσσω, culminative) 1921.

Translation - "It is because they know nothing about the righteousness that comes from God and are trying to establish   their own that they have not been made subject to God's righteousness."

Comment: The participles are causal. Paul is analyzing the reason why the zeal of the Jews (verse 2) is οὐ κατ' ἐπίγνωσιν. He who depends upon his own knowledge is certain to forego all possibility of possessing the superior knowledge that is understood only by those who accept the revelation of the Holy Spirit in the Word of God. The unregenerate have a philosophy and they are prepared to expound it with a zeal that often exceeds that of the child of God, who has superior knowledge (ἐπίγνωσις #3817) at his command. "There is a way that seemeth right unto a man, but the end thereof are the ways of death." (Proverbs 14:12; 16:25).

The attempt to establish self-righteousness, of course, grows out of the ignorance of divine righteousness. All men wish for righteousness, although the unsaved wished to define it. Christians define it in terms of the Holy Spirit's message in the New Testament. Knowing nothing of the true righteousness the unregenerate thus are motivated with great zeal to develop and demonstrate their own. Witness the Pharisee of Luke 18:11,12 and the religious experience of Saul of Tarsus, before he became Paul the Apostle. The harder they work at it the more certain they become that it is the real thing. How could a just God fail to reward my sincere efforts to do right? So it is with all self-righteous people whose great delusion is that salvation is something which they are capable of achieving through their own merit. They ignore the law of God because of their superficial view of it, but they obey their interpretation of it. When the Holy Spirit reveals to the elect what God's righteousness is (John 16:8-10) they hasten to the cross and empty tomb and find Christ.

Verse 4 - "For Christ is the end of the law for righteousness to every one that believeth."

τέλος γὰρ νόμου Χριστὸς εἰς δικαιοσύνην παντὶ τῷ πιστεύοντι.

"For Christ is the end of the law, that every one who has faith may be justified." . . . RSV

τέλος (nom.sing.neut.of τέλος, predicate nominative) 881.
γὰρ (causal conjunction) 105.
νόμου (gen.sing.masc.of νόμος, description) 464.
Χριστὸς (nom.sing.masc.of Χριστός, subject of ἔστιν understood) 4.

εἰς (preposition with the accusative, purpose) 140.

δικαιοσύνην (acc.sing.fem.of δικαιοσύνη, purpose) 322.

παντὶ (dat.sing.masc.of πᾶς, in agreement with πιστεύοντι) 67.

τῷ (dat.sing.masc.of the article in agreement with πιστεύοντι) 9.

πιστεύοντι (pres.act.part.dat.sing.masc.of πιστεύω, substantival, personal advantage) 734.

Translation - *"For Christ is the end of the law for righteousness to every one who believes."*

Comment: One meaning is that the ultimate purpose (τέλος) of the law is to bring us to believe in Christ in order that we may have righteousness. This righteousness in Christ is available to believers, whoever and wherever they may be, without regard to their personal observance of the formal or ethical requirements of the law.

It is also true that Christ is the end of the law in the sense that in His incarnation experience upon the earth He fulfilled it in the sense of Mt.5:17. In all the human family there was only one, Jesus Christ, upon whose record not a single transgression of the law of God was entered before the court. It was this spotless record of righteousness which He exchanged for our sin, as God forsook Him for three hellish hours upon the cross. That is why the believer has Christ's righteousness in the exchange (2 Cor.5:21).

What must man do if he is to merit heaven on the basis of the law of God? This is the subject of verse 5.

Salvation for All

(Romans 10:5-21)

Verse 5 - *"For Moses describeth the righteousness which is of the law, That the man which doeth those things shall live by them."*

Μωϋσῆς γὰρ γράφει τὴν δικαιοσύνην τὴν ἐκ τοῦ νόμου ὅτι ὁ ποιήσας ἄνθρωπος ζήσεται ἐν αὐτῇ.

"Moses writes that the man who practices the righteousness which is based on the law shall live by it." . . . *RSV*

Μωϋσῆς (nom.sing.masc.of Μωϋσῆς, subject of γράφει) 715.

γὰρ (explanatory conjunction) 105.

γράφει (3d.per.sing.pres.act.ind.of γράφω, historical) 156.

τὴν (acc.sing.fem.of the article in agreement with δικαιοσύνην) 9.

δικαιοσύνην (acc.sing.fem.of δικαιοσύνη, reference) 322.

τὴν (acc.sing.fem.of the article in agreement with δικαιοσύνην) 9.

ἐκ (preposition with the ablative, source) 19.

τοῦ (abl.sing.masc.of the article in agreement with νόμου) 9.

νόμου (abl.sing.masc.of νόμος, source) 464.

ὅτι (conjunction introducing indirect discourse) 211.

ὁ (nom.sing.masc.of the article in agreement with ἄνθρωπος) 9.

ποιήσας (aor.act.part.nom.sing.masc.of ποιέω, adjectival, ascriptive, in agreement with ἄνθρωπος) 127.

ἄνθρωπος (nom.sing.masc.of ἄνθρωπος, subject of ζήσεται) 341.

ζήσεται (3d.per.sing.fut.mid.ind.of ζάω, predictive) 340.

ἐν (preposition with the locative, instrumental usage) 80.

αὐτῇ (loc.sing.fem.of αὐτός, means) 16.

Translation - "Now Moses wrote about the righteousness of the law that the man who has done that which is required will live because of it."

Comment: αὐτῇ has as its antecedent δικαιοσύνην. Legalism says that life comes because of the righteousness which is generated by obeying the law. There is a variety of variant readings: ὅτι τὴν δικαιοσύνην τὴν ἐκ νόμου; 1984 omits ὅτι; A has ὅτι τήν δικαιοσύνην τὴν ἐκ πίστεως, in the last clause. Dᵍʳ has ὁ ποιήσας ἄνθρωπος ζήσεται ἐν αὐτοῖς; B 33 (33* ταῦτα) 33c 436 1881 itₓ has ὁ ποιήσας αὐτὰ ἄνθρωπος ζήσεται ἐν αὐτῇ; p46 Sinaiticus K P ψ 88 and other miniscules have ὁ ποιήσας αὐτὰ ἄνθρωπος ζήσεται ἐν αὐτοῖς; others are ὁ ποιήσας αὐτὰ ζήσεται ἐν αὐτοῖς and ὁ ποιήσας αὐτὴν ἄνθρωπος ζήσεται ἐν αὐτῇ. All the variant readings say essentially the same thing.

On the contrary, salvation by faith is described in verse 6-13.

Verse 6 - "But the righteousness which is of faith speaketh on this wise, Say not in thine heart who shall ascend into heaven? (that is, to bring Christ down from above:)"

ἡ δὲ ἐκ πίστεως δικαιοσύνη οὕτως λέγει, Μὴ εἴπῃς ἐν τῇ καρδίᾳ σου, Τίς ἀναβήσεται εἰς τὸν οὐρανόν; τοῦτ' ἔστιν Χριστὸν καταγαγεῖν;

"But the righteousness based on faith says, 'Do not say in your heart, 'Who will ascend into heaven:' (that is, to bring Christ down)' " . . . RSV

ἡ (nom.sing.fem.of the article in agreement with δικαιοσύνη) 9.

δὲ (adversative conjunction) 11.

ἐκ (preposition with the ablative of source) 19.

πίστεως (abl.sing.fem.of πίστις, source) 728.

δικαιοσύνη (nom.sing.fem.of δικαιοσύνη, subject of λέγει) 322.

οὕτως (adverbial) 74.

λέγει (3d.per.sing.pres.act.ind.of λέγω, static) 66.

Μὴ (negative conjunction with the subjunctive in a prohibition) 87.

εἴπῃς (2d.per.sing.aor.act.subj.of εἶπον, prohibition) 155.

ἐν (preposition with the locative of place, metaphorical) 80.

τῇ (loc.sing.fem.of the article in agreement with καρδίᾳ) 9.

καρδίᾳ (loc.sing.fem.of καρδία, place, metaphorical) 432.

σου (gen.sing.masc.of σύ, possession) 104.

Τίς (nom.sing.masc.of τίς, the interrogative pronoun, subject of ἀναβήσεται, direct question) 281.

ἀναβήσεται (3d.per.sing.fut.mid.ind.of ἀναβαίνω, deliberative) 323.
εἰς (preposition with the accusative of extent) 140.
τὸν (acc.sing.masc.of the article in agreement with οὐρανόν) 9.
οὐρανόν (acc.sing.masc.of οὐρανός, extent) 254.
τοῦτ' (nom.sing.neut.of οὗτος, subject of ἔστιν) 93.
ἔστιν (3d.per.sing.pres.ind.of εἰμί, aoristic) 86.
Χριστὸν (acc.sing.masc.of Χριστός, direct object of καταγαγεῖν) 4.
καταγαγεῖν (aor.act.inf.of κατάγω, purpose) 2056.

Translation - "But the righteousness which has faith as its source speaks like this: 'Do not begin to say in your heart, 'Who will ascend into heaven?' - that is to bring Christ down. . . "

Comment: The legalist need not look for a Saviour since he thinks he has the means of salvation in the Mosaic law. To reject that concept is to look elsewhere for a Saviour. What does God's by-faith covenant of righteousness say? First of all it tells us what not to say. We are forbidden to entertain in the heart (μὴ εἴπῃς - "do not say it even once") "Who will go to heaven?" For what purpose? τοῦτ' ἔστιν is epexegetical - "for the purpose of bringing Messiah down." Note the aorist subjunctive in εἴπῃς instead of the imperative in the prohibition. καταγαγεῖν is an infinitive of purpose.

We need look no further in heaven for Messiah, to bring Him down, since He has already come down to earth from heaven. The new covenant therefore forbids us to look for any further incarnation (John 14:6; Acts 4:12). It is a little late for the Reverend Moon or Joseph Smith or any other self-appointed Messiah to assume the role which Jesus so admirably filled two thousand years ago.

We should also not expect Messiah to rise from the dead, since He has already risen. This is the thought of

Verse 7 - "Or, who shall descend into the deep," (that is, to bring up Christ from the dead)."

ἤ, Τίς καταβήσεται εἰς τὴν ἄβυσσον; τοῦτ' ἔστιν Χριστὸν ἐκ νεκρῶν ἀναγαγεῖν.

". . . or 'Who will descend into the abyss?' (that is, to bring Christ up from the dead)." . . . RSV

ἤ (disjunctive) 465
Τίς (nom.sing.masc.of τίς, interrogative pronoun, subject of καταβήσεται, direct question) 281.
καταβήσεται (3d.per.sing.fut.mid.ind.of καταβαίνω, deliberative) 324.
εἰς (preposition with the accusative of extent) 140.
τὴν (acc.sing.fem.of the article in agreement with ἄβυσσον) 9.
ἄβυσσον (acc.sing.fem.of ἄβυσσος, extent) 2231.
τοῦτ' (nom.sing.neut.of οὗτος, subject of ἔστιν) 93.
ἔστιν (3d.per.sing.pres.ind.of εἰμί, aoristic) 86.

Χριστὸν (acc.sing.masc.of Χριστός, direct object of ἀναγαγεῖν) 4.
ἐκ (preposition with the ablative of separation) 19.
νεκρῶν (abl.pl.masc.of νεκρός, separation) 749.
ἀναγαγεῖν (aor.act.inf.of ἀνάγω, purpose) 329.

Translation - "Or, 'Who will descend into the abyss?' - that is to resurrect Christ from the dead."

Comment: Scripture also forbids us to begin to ask Τίς καταβήσεται . . . .κ.τ.λ. Again τοῦτ' ἔστιν is epexegetical, to explain the purpose of a trip into the realms of death. We need not look for a resurrected Saviour. He has already risen. Thus, in verses 6 and 7 Paul is saying that Messiah, to Whom legalism witnesses (Rom.3:21b) has already come down from heaven (John 1:14; Gal.4:4) and He has died, been buried and has risen from the dead (Heb.13:20).

These fundamental facts, so essential to salvation through faith, are already historical events. Redemption's plan which involved Messiah's incarnation, life, death and resurrection is already complete. Those who wish to be saved need not cast about for a plan of salvation. We already have a plan of salvation.

Verse 8 - "But what saith it? The word is nigh thee even in thy mouth, and in thy heart: that is, the word of faith, which we preach."

ἀλλὰ τί λέγει; Ἐγγύς σου τὸ ῥῆμά ἐστιν, ἐν τῷ στόματί σου καὶ ἐν τῇ καρδίᾳ σου, τοῦτ' ἔστιν τὸ ῥῆμα τῆς πίστεως ὃ κηρύσσομεν.

"But what does it say? The word is near you, on your lips and in your heart (that is, the word of faith which we preach);" . . . RSV

ἀλλὰ (alternative conjunction) 342.
τί (acc.sing.neut.of τίς, interrogative pronoun, direct question, direct object of λέγει) 281.
λέγει (3d.per.sing.pres.act.ind.of λέγω, aoristic) 66.
Ἐγγύς (nom.sing.neut.of ἐγγύς, predicate adjective) 1512.
σου (gen.sing.masc.of σύ, place description) 104.
τὸ (nom.sing.neut.of the article in agreement with ῥῆμα) 9.
ῥῆμα (nom.sing.neut.of ῥῆμα, subject of ἔστιν) 343.
ἔστιν (3d.per.sing.pres.ind.of εἰμί, present progressive retroactive) 86.
ἐν (preposition with the locative of place) 80.
τῷ (loc.sing.neut.of the article in agreement with στόματί) 9.
στόματί (loc.sing.neut.of στόμα, place) 344.
σου (gen.sing.masc.of σύ, possession) 104.
καὶ (adjunctive conjunction joining prepositional phrases) 14.
ἐν (preposition with the locative of place, metaphorical) 80.
τῇ (loc.sing.fem.of the article in agreement with καρδίᾳ) 9.
καρδίᾳ (loc.sing.fem.of καρδία, place) 432.
σου (gen.sing.masc.of σύ, possession) 104.
τοῦτ' (nom. sing.neut.of οὗτος, subject of ἔστιν) 93.
ἔστιν (3d.per.sing.pres.ind.of εἰμί, aoristic) 86.
τὸ (nom.sing.neut.of the article in agreement with ῥῆμα) 9.

ῥῆμα (nom.sing.neut.of ῥῆμα, predicate nominative) 343.

τῆς (gen.sing.fem.of the article in agreement with πίστεως) 9.

πίστεως (gen.sing.fem.of πίστις, description) 728.

ὅ (nom.sing.neut.of ὅς, relative pronoun, adjectival, in agreement with ῥῆμα) 65.

κηρύσσομεν (1st.per.pl.pres.act.ind.of κηρύσσω, present progressive retroactive) 249.

Translation - "But what does it say? The word is near you - in your mouth and in your heart - that is, the word of faith which we have been preaching."

Comment: We do not need a new incarnation in order to discover the way of salvation (Deut.30:12); nor that someone should resurrect Messiah from the grave (Deut.30:12-14). What does it say? It is present with us, upon our lips and in our hearts, as near as the breath we breathe, ready to be believed and ready to be spoken. τοῦτ' ἔστιν is another epexegetical clause. It is the message of faith which Paul was preaching as he wrote this and that he had been preaching since his conversion in Damascus. Here we have an excellent example of the retroactive use of the present progressive tense. The context tells us that Paul was not only preaching the "word of faith" when he wrote those lines, but also that he had been preaching it in the past.

Note that it is a "word of faith" (ῥῆμα τῆς πίστεως) which can be taken both as a genitive of description and an ablative of source. If we had no faith the message would mean nothing, as indeed is the case with the unregenerate. Thus the ablative of source. And the message has content which can be accepted and appropriated only by faith. Thus also the genitive of description. It is not a message of experience, although once it is accepted by faith, experience, such as was never known before is ours. Nor is it a message of reason, although once accepted it is found to be infinitely more reasonable than the philosophical explanations of alternative systems that seek to explain reality without it. If untaught evangelists and miscellaneous "soul winners" realized that the gospel is a message of faith, not of experience, nor of reason, they would cease their attempts to argue sinners into the kingdom of God, for "the natural man receiveth not the things of the Spirit of God, for they are foolishness unto him; neither can he know them, because they are spiritually discerned." (1 Cor.2:14). Paul was so intellectual on Mars Hill that he impressed the Athenians but he did not win many to Christ. And he was so "foolish" in Corinth, his next stop, that he had a revival that lasted two and one-half years. The gospel of Christ is not irrational, but it is super-rational, just as God's ways are higher than ours and His thoughts higher than ours (Isa.55:9). The Gnostics are the only ones unfortunate enough to think that they know as much as God!

Salvation is an inner experience of faith in the truth of a set of propositions that no one, employing only human reason, will believe, and a personal commitment, not to an outward observance of laws, signs, portents, rituals, liturgies and/or emotional public outbursts, but to a way of life that yields the convert's physical, emotional and intellectual assets to the Holy Spirit that He is not grieved (Eph.4:30) but free to reproduce His fruits (Gal.5:22,23) and the resurrection life style of our risen Lord (Gal.5:16) in us. He will also enrich us with whatever gifts He, in His sovereign wisdom, knows we need in order to do the work which has been assigned to us, as members of the Body of Christ (1 Cor.12:1-31; Eph.2:10).

The work which was requisite so that the court of heaven can, without a violation of holiness, declare righteous those who are not righteous has already been done. Messiah has already come, lived, died, gone to Sheol, risen up from Sheol and ascended into heaven (Eph.4:8-10). It needs only to be believed in the heart, where it is already implanted and confessed upon the lips where it is already is being formulated. We do not need any oversexed Bedouin shieks or any Korean capitalists with delusions of grandeur, who go about, either in the seventh or the twentieth centuries seducing the sophomores. They are already sufficiently seduced by the nihilists. What we need is what we have - the Holy Spirit, Who has written a Book and Who is now going about in society teaching it to those whom God has selected. But since we do not know whom God has selected, we should be obedient to His commission and preach the gospel to every one. We do so with the knowledge of course that though not all will accept it, some will. That is the way it was when Paul preached it and that is how it has always been and always will be until the days when the seventh angel shall begin to sound his last trumpet call (Rev.10:7). Then the Holy Spirit's work will be finished and the Body of Christ will have received her last member.

Verse 9 - "That if thou shalt confess with thy mouth the Lord Jesus, and shalt believe in thine heart that God hath raised him from the dead, thou shalt be saved."

ὅτι ἐὰν ὁμολογήσῃς ἐν τῷ στόματί σου κύριον Ἰησοῦν, καὶ πιστεύσῃς ἐν τῇ καρδίᾳ σου ὅτι ὁ θεὸς αὐτὸν ἤγειρεν ἐκ νεκρῶν, σωθήσῃ.

". . . because, if you confess with your lips that Jesus is Lord and believe in your heart that God raised him from the dead, you will be saved." . . . RSV

ὅτι (conjunction introducing indirect discourse) 211.

ἐὰν (conditional particle in a third-class condition) 363.

ὁμολογήσῃς (2d.per.sing.aor.act.subj.of ὁμολογέω, third-class condition) 688.

ἐν (preposition with the locative of place) 80.

τῷ (loc.sing.neut.of the article in agreement with στόματί) 9.

στόματί (loc.sing.neut.of στόμα, instrumental use, means) 344.

σου (gen.sing.masc.of σύ, possession) 104.

κύριον (acc.sing.masc.of κύριος, direct object of ὁμολογήσῃς) 97.

Ἰησοῦν (acc.sing.masc.of Ἰησοῦς, apposition) 3.

καὶ (adjunctive conjunction joining verbs) 14.

πιστεύσῃς (2d.per.sing.aor.act.subj.of πιστεύω, third-class condition) 734.

ἐν (preposition with the locative, instrumental use, means) 80.

τῇ (loc.sing.fem.of the article in agreement with καρδίᾳ) 9.

καρδίᾳ (loc.sing.fem.of καρδία, instrumental use, means) 432.

σου (gen.sing.masc.of σύ, possession) 104.

ὅτι (conjunction introducing an object clause in indirect discourse) 211.

ὁ (nom.sing.masc.of the article in agreement with θεὸς) 9.

θεὸς (nom.sing.masc.of θεός, subject of ἤγειρεν) 124.

αὐτὸν (acc.sing.masc.of αὐτός, direct object of ἤγειρεν) 16.

ἤγειρεν (3d.per.sing.aor.act.ind.of ἐγείρω, culminative) 125.

ἐκ (preposition with the ablative of separation) 19.

νεκρῶν (abl.pl.masc.of νεκρός, separation) 749.

σωθήσῃ (2d.per.sing.fut.pass.ind.of σώζω, predictive) 109.

Translation - ". . . that if you confess with your mouth Jesus as Lord and believe in your heart that God has raised Him from the dead, you will be saved."

Comment: It is possible to take the first ὅτι as causal, as the Revised Standard Version does. It is a matter of editing. The United Bible Societies' Committee has placed a period at the end of verse 8. If that is proper (there was no division between letters in the original autographs and, of course, no punctuation marks) then οτι is causal. If the period should not be there, then it is possible to take ὅτι as introducing indirect discourse. The context will support either idea. It seems to me that Paul is adding in verse 9 a definition of τὸ ῥῆμα τῆς πίστεως ὃ κηρύσσομεν - "the word of faith which we preach." What was this "word of faith" which he preached? It is "that . . . κ.τ.λ."

We have a third-class condition in which Paul is saying nothing about whether anyone will confess and believe. But he is saying that *if* anyone does, he will be saved. The dogmatic assertion in the apodosis is contingent upon the two conditions in the protases, which, being subjunctive and introduced by ἐὰν leave the issue in doubt. Paul was sure of course that some would confess and believe, but he is not saying who they are.

The word of faith is on the lips and in the heart (verse 8). Now we have only to employ it. An open confession by word of mouth (or by signs in the case of mutes) to the effect that Jesus, once dead and now alive forever, is one's Lord, coupled with a steadfast heart faith that this Jesus, Whom one has just acknowleged as Lord, has actually been raised from the dead, is the two-fold condition for salvation. The conclusion is indicative mood certitude - "you will be saved." To make the open confession without holding the heart-felt conviction is hypocrisy. It is also nonesense. Who wants to say that a dead Galilean carpenter is his Lord?

To say that Jesus is Lord is not a confession to be taken lightly. If He is Lord in the sense of Ephesians 1:20-23; Philippians 2:9-11; Deuteronomy 4:35,39; 10:17; Psalm 100:3; 1 Kings 8:60; Psalm 92:8; Isaiah 30:18; Daniel 2:47; Acts 10:36; Romans 14:9; 1 Timothy 6:15; Revelation 17:14 and Revelation 19:6, normal prudence and some wisdom would dictate that if we say publicly that He is our Lord we had better mean it. And that means that we will do all within our power to obey Him and and disobey Him at our peril, although the peril involved in the event of disobedience is not the peril of damnation. The "convert" who follows the formula of Romans 10:9 flippantly is already in peril of damnation.

Verse 10 - "For with the heart man believeth unto righteousness, and with the mouth confession is made unto salvation."

καρδίᾳ γὰρ πιστεύεται εἰς δικαιοσύνην, στόματι δὲ ὁμολογεῖται εἰς σωτηρίαν.

"For man believes with his heart and so is justified, and he confesses with his lips and so is saved." . . . RSV

καρδίᾳ (instrumental sing.fem.of καρδία, means) 432.
γὰρ (causal conjunction) 105.
πιστεύεται (3d.per.sing.pres.pass.ind.of πιστεύω, static) 734.
εἰς (preposition with the accusative, purpose) 140.
δικαιοσύνην (acc.sing.fem.of δικαιοσύνη, result) 322.
στόματι (instru.sing.neut.of στόμα, means) 344.
δὲ (continuative conjunction) 11.
ὁμολογεῖται (3d.per.sing.pres.pass.ind.of ὁμολογέω, static) 688.
εἰς (preposition with the predicate accusative) 140.
σωτηρίαν (acc.sing.fem.of σωτηρία, predicate accusative) 1852.

Translation - "For in the heart the gospel is believed and righteousness results, and by the mouth the confession that one is saved is made."

Comment: γὰρ is causal. καρδίᾳ and στόματι are instrumentals of means. The verbs πιστεύεται and ὁμολογεῖται are impersonal passives. εἰς δικαιοσύνη is result and εἰς σωτηρίαν is a predicate accusative. It is when the sinner believes in his heart that he is justified. This is concurrent with the birth from above (John 3:3,7; 1 Pet.1:23) and the baptism of the Holy Spirit into the Body of Christ (1 Cor.12:13). We can be certain that he will tell it. And that is what he does with his mouth. The Scriptures teach elsewhere that belief in the heart that Jesus is Lord, if it is genuine, will not go unconfessed, but it is not the open confession that saves. Goodspeed both makes and misses the point with his "For with their minds men believe and are made upright" (that is good, as he sees result in εἰς δικαιοσύνην) "and with their lips they make the acknowledgement and are saved." He should have said, "they make the acknowledgement *that* they are saved."

The association of the act of believing with righteousness is one of Paul's oft-repeated themes. *Cf.* Rom.4:3; Gen.15:6 *et al.* The use of καρδία as the agent of cognitive acquiesence and commitment is common in the New Testament, as indeed in common modern idiom. Recall Senator Goldwater's appeal in 1964 to the voters, "In your heart you know that I am right." No one uses καρδία in these contexts in an anatomical sense and those who accuse Paul of using it in this sense indicate that they are hard pressed for a sensible argument.

The question, "Can man be saved by believing if he never confesses with his mouth?" can be countered with the rhetorical question, "Can any one who truly believes remain silent about it?"

Verse 11 - "Fot the scripture saith, Whosoever believeth on him shall not be ashamed."

λέγει γὰρ ἡ γραφή, Πᾶς ὁ πιστεύων ἐπ' αὐτῷ οὐ καταισχυνθήσεται.

"The scripture says, 'No one who believes in Him will be put to shame.'" ...
RSV

λέγει (3d.per.sing.pres.act.ind.of λέγω, present progressive retroactive) 66.
γὰρ (causal conjunction) 105.
ἡ (nom.sing.fem.of the article in agreement with γραφή) 9.
γραφή (nom.sing.fem.of γραφή, subject of λέγει) 1389.
Πᾶς (nom.sing.masc.of πᾶς in agreement with πιστεύων) 67.
ὁ (nom.sing.masc.of the article in agreement with πιστεύων) 9.
πιστεύων (pres.act.part.nom.sing.masc.of πιστεύω, substantival, subject of καταισχυνθήσεται) 734.
ἐπ' (preposition with the instrumental, cause) 47.
αὐτῷ (instru.sing.masc.of αὐτός, cause) 16.
οὐ (negative conjunction with the indicative) 130.
καταισχυνθήσεται (3d.per.sing.fut.pass.ind.of καταισχύνω, predictive) 2505.

Translation - "Because the Scripture has been saying, 'He who believes upon Him will not ultimately be ashamed.'"

Comment: The quotation is from Isaiah 28:16 where the LXX uses οὐ μὴ καταισχυνθῇ the emphatic aorist subjunctive passive.

In interpreting this verse the exegete must remember that he is reading Greek and thus he must think like a Greek. Literally, in English, the verse reads, "All the believers in Him shall not be ashamed" which implies in English that some believers will and others will not. We get the same meaning in English if we say, "Not all the believers in Him will be ashamed," which again implies that some will experience embarrassment, but that others will not. The subject of the Greek sentence is ὁ πιστεύων - "the believers" and it is modified by Πᾶς. Thus the subject is "All the believers" and the predicate says of them that they will not be ashamed. Thus every Christian is to escape embarrassment eventually, although many will experience the offence of the cross as they witness for Christ. But every Christian, whether he has been a faithful witness for Christ and thus incurred the wrath and scorn of the unsaved or not, can look forward to the Second Coming when all of the children of God will be vindicated before the eyes of our critics. Not all Christians have studied their Bibles enough to know that ultimately we will be vindicated. Those who have are not ashamed now, even though we face the opposition of the world. Since Christians are not ashamed of Christ, they are certain to confess their faith publicly at least at the time when they experience for the first time the peace and joy of the Holy Spirit as He baptizes them into the Body of Christ.

The English idiom is little understood by Madison Avenue as they write the television commercials. How often we have heard, "All aspirins are not alike." This means that all aspirins are different, which means that each Bayer is different from every other Bayer! I should like for the Bayer people to tell me which of the many Bayers in the bottle is the best of all, since they have already said that they are all different. When one has a headache he should not settle for any but the best.

Verse 12 - "For there is no difference between the Jew and the Greek: for the same Lord over all is rich unto all that call upon him."

οὐ γάρ ἐστιν διαστολὴ Ἰουδαίου τε καὶ Ἕλληνος, ὁ γὰρ αὐτὸς κύριος πάντων, πλουτῶν εἰς πάντας τοὺς ἐπικαλουμένους αὐτόν.

"For there is no distinction between Jew and Greek; the same Lord is Lord of all and bestows his riches upon all who call upon him." . . . RSV

οὐ (negative conjunction with the indicative) 130.
γάρ (inferential conjunction) 105.
ἐστιν (3d.per.sing.pres.ind.of εἰμί, aoristic) 86.
διαστολὴ (nom.sing.fem.of διαστολή, subject of ἐστιν) 3872.
Ἰουδαίου (gen.sing.masc.of Ἰουδαῖος, reference) 143.
τε (correlative particle) 1408.
καὶ (adjunctive conjunction joining nouns) 14.
Ἕλληνος (genitive sing.masc.of Ἕλλην, reference) 2373.
ὁ (nom.sing.masc.of the article in agreement with κύριος) 9.
γάρ (causal conjunction) 105.
αὐτὸς (nom.sing.masc.of αὐτός, in agreement with κύριος, intensive) 16.
κύριος (nom.sing.masc.of κύριος, subject of ἐστιν understood) 97.
πάντων (gen.pl.masc.of πᾶς, relationship) 67.
πλουτῶν (pres.act.part.nom.sing.masc.of πλουτέω, substantival, predicate nominative) 1834.
εἰς (preposition with the accusative of extent) 140.
πάντας (acc.pl.masc.of πᾶς, in agreement with ἐπικαλουμένους) 67.
τοὺς (acc.pl.masc.of the article in agreement with ἐπικαλουμένους) 9.
ἐπικαλουμένους (pres.mid.part.acc.pl.masc.of ἐπικαλέω, substantival, extent) 884.
αὐτόν (acc.sing.masc.of αὐτός, direct object of ἐπικαλουμένους) 16.

Translation - "Therefore with reference to Jew and Greek no difference exists, because the same Lord of all is generous to all who call upon Him."

Comment: Whether we take Ἰουδαίου and Ἕλληνος as ablatives of source or genitives of reference the thought is the same. If ablative, the characteristics which have their source in Jews on the one hand and in Greeks on the other do not provide grounds for saying that there is a difference. It is simpler to say that with reference to (genitive) Jews and Greeks it can be said that there is no difference. Note the intensive attributive position in αὐτός. πλουτῶν, the substantival participle is a predicate nominative, in agreement with κύριος. Or we can say that it is a predicate adjective, since Paul has left out the copula. ἐπικαλουμένους is also a participle used like a noun. The verse is full of interesting Greek grammar and syntax. It is good practice for the beginning

Greek student.

In the discussion beginning with verse 1 Paul has been arguing that the Gentile is more fortunate than the Jew. The Mosaic law and Jesus, Who is a living embodiment of its morals, served as stumbling blocks to trip up the Jew and delude him into the futile quest for righteousness, while the Gentile, free from the seductive influences of legalism, to which the Pharisees fell victim, found righteousness by faith. Does this mean that the individual Jew cannot be saved? Or course not. Nor does it mean that the individual Gentile was totally free from the delusion that he could work out his own salvation on some basis of his own creation. Salvation is an individual matter and it is available to Jew and Gentile alike. But though all who call upon the Lord, whether they be Jew or Gentile, will find that He is rich, generous and gracious to them when they come to Him with humility, no one will call until he has been made to realize that there is only one source of righteousness. That source is Jesus Christ, Who alone lived the life in the flesh that demonstrated the holiness with which righteousness is associated. Only the Holy Spirit can convince the self-righteous sinner, Jew or Gentile, that his "righteousness" smells like what Isaiah said it did (Isaiah 64:6) and that the only righteousness which passes heaven's test is that of Jesus Christ (John 16:7-11). All who are thus convinced will come to Christ and none will be rejected (John 6:37). Race, color, cultural background, social, economic or intellectual status have nothing to do with it.

We will now see that the call upon the Lord is the fifth step in a six-step sequence which begins when God commissions a preacher to preach.

Verse 13 - "For whosoever shall call upon the name of the Lord shall be saved."

Πᾶς γὰρ ὃς ἂν ἐπικαλέσηται τὸ ὄνομα κυρίου σωθήσεται.

"For 'every one who calls upon the name of the Lord will be saved.'"... RSV

Πᾶς (nom.sing.masc.of πᾶς, subject of σωθήσεται) 67.
γὰρ (inferential conjunction) 105.
ὃς (nom.sing.masc.of ὅς, relative pronoun, in agreement with πᾶς, in a more probable condition) 65.
ἂν (contingent particle in the relative clause, more probable condition) 205.
ἐπικαλέσηται (3d.per.sing.1st.aor.mid.subj.of ἐπικαλέω, more probable condition) 884.
τὸ (acc.sing.neut.of the article in agreement with ὄνομα) 9.
ὄνομα (acc.sing.neut.of ὄνομα, direct object of ἐπικαλέσηται) 108.
κυρίου (gen.sing.masc.of κύριος, possession) 97.
σωθήσεται (3d.per.sing.fut.pass.ind.of σώζω, more probable condition) 109.

Translation - "Therefore every one who calls upon the name of the Lord will be saved."

Comment: γὰρ is inferential, as the statement of verse 13, a quotation from Joel 2:32, follows as a result of verse 12. Paul uses the relative pronoun ὃς with ἂν in a protasis of a more probable condition. Th.. construction takes the subjunctive. "When the contingent or indefinite idea is supplied by the context, or the context and the nature of the relative the subjunctive is used. . , Theprotasis of a more probable future condition may be expressed by the use of a relative pronoun with ἄν. . . This construction is sometimes found in the future indicative without ἄν (cf.Mt.10:32). In the New Testament we sometimes find ἐάν instead of ἄν. This was current Koine usage, as is abundantly evidenced by the papyri." (Mantey, *Manual*, 273). *Cf.* Mt.5:19; 10:43; James 2:10. Paul's expectation is that some will call and he is certain that all who do will be saved. But the caller, if and when he calls does not initiate the action as an uncaused result. His call is contingent upon his faith, which is contingent upon his hearing the Word of God, which is contingent upon it being preached, which is contingent upon the preacher being sent, which is contingent upon the will of God to send him. Thus God initiates a chain of events by sending a preacher, who goes and preaches, so that his audience hears. Those in the audience who really *hear* believe and when they believe they call and when they call they are saved. Some in the audience hear in the sense that they receive auditory sensations so that they are able to discern what is said, but they do not hear in the sense Romans 10:14. (Eph.2:8,9).

Dr.Walter Taylor, for many years director of the Pacific Garden Mission, the famous light house of the gospel of Christ on South State Street in Chicago, once said to the author, "These men come into the mission night after night and hear the gospel and hear the gospel and hear the gospel - and then one night they come in and *hear* the gospel." Those who *hear* the gospel are given the gift of faith. Thus they believe and call and are saved. Paul develops all of this in verse 14-21. *Cf.* Joel 2:32 and note that the call results from the outpouring of the Holy Spirit.

A man came forward one night in the Pacific Garden Mission. He was very drunk, hungry, ill clad, cold, sick, lonely and discouraged. He was also under the powerful influence of the Holy Spirit. As we prayed on our knees at the altar I directed his attention to Romans 10:13 - "Whosoever shall call upon the name of the Lord will be saved." He did not know how to pray, but he understood what that verse said. He said, "Lord, Lord, Lord, Lord, Lord!!" He was saved. Unfortunately some people who know how to "pray" do not know what the verse says.

Verse 14 - "How then shall they call on him in whom they have not believed? And how shall they believe in him of whom they have not heard? And how shall they hear without a preacher?"

Πῶς οὖν ἐπικαλέσωνται εἰς ὃν οὐκ ἐπίστευσαν; πῶς δὲ πιστεύσωσιν οὗ οὐκ ἤκουσαν; πῶς δὲ ἀκούσωσιν χωρὶς κηρύσσοντος;

"But how are men to call upon him in whom they have not believed? And how are they to believe in him of whom they have never heard? And how are they to hear without a preacher?" . . . RSV

Πῶς (interrogative conjunction in rhetorical question) 627.
οὖν (inferential conjunction) 68.

ἐπικαλέσωνται (3d.per.pl.1st.aor.mid.subj.of ἐπικαλέω, deliberative) 884.

εἰς (preposition with the accusative of extent) 140.

ὅν (acc.sing.masc.of ὅς, relative pronoun, direct object of ἐπίστευσαν) 65.

οὐκ (negative conjunction with the indicative) 130.

ἐπίστευσαν (3d.per.pl.aor.act.ind.of πιστεύω, culminative) 734.

πῶς (interrogative conjunction in rhetorical question) 627.

δὲ (continuative conjunction) 11.

πιστεύσωσιν (3d.per.pl.1st.aor.act.subj.of πιστεύω, deliberative) 734.

οὗ (gen.sing.masc.of ὅς, objective genitive) 65.

οὐκ (negative conjunction) 130.

ἤκουσαν (3d.per.pl.aor.act.ind.of ἀκούω, culminative) 148.

πῶς (interrogative conjunction in rhetorical question) 627.

δὲ (continuative conjunction) 11.

ἀκούσωσιν (3d.per.pl.aor.act.subj.of ἀκούω, deliberative) 148.

χωρὶς (preposition with the ablative of separation) 1077.

κηρύσσοντος (pres.act.part.abl.sing.neut.of κνρύσσω, substantival, separation) 249.

Translation - "How then can they call upon him whom they do not believe? And how can they believe in him of whom they have not heard? And how can they hear without a preacher?"

Comment: The demonstrative pronouns before the relatives ὅν and οὗ are missing. It is not always necessary to have them, particularly in examples where the case of the demonstrative, if present, would be the same as the relative as εἰς τοῦτον before ὅν; but even when the case would not be the same the demonstrative may not be present. If present, here before οὗ it would be τούτῳ after πιστεύσωσιν.

These questions with the subjunctives ἐπικαλέσωνται, πιστεύσωσιν and ἀκούσωσιν are rhetorical, not interrogative. Paul is forcibly stating the obvious by putting the questions rhetorically, with the deliberative subjunctive. No one calls upon another for help if he does not believe in him. No one believes another if he does not understand him. Note οὗ, the genitive, after ἤκουσαν - "if he does not hear with understanding." *Cf.* Rom.10:18 where, though no object is joined to ἤκουσαν , if it were joined it would be τὸ εὐαγγέλιον, an accusative case object, indicating audible though not perceptive hearing.

If they are to hear about Christ there must be preaching. Thus the preacher is a necessary link in this chain of events.

Verse 15 - "And how shall they preach, except they be sent? As it is written, How beautiful are the feet of them that preach the gospel of peace, and bring glad tidings of good things."

πῶς δὲ κηρύξωσιν ἐὰν μὴ ἀποσταλῶσιν; καθὼς γέγραπται, Ὡς ὡραῖοι οἱ πόδες τῶν εὐαγγελιζομένων ἀγαθά.

"And how can men preach unless they are sent? As it is written, 'How beautiful

are the feet of those who preach good news!' " . . . RSV

πῶς (interrogative conjunction in rhetorical question) 627.

δὲ (continuative conjunction) 11.

κηρύξωσιν (3d.per.pl.aor.act.subj.of κηρύσσω, deliberative) 249.

ἐὰν (conditional particle in a third-class condition) 363.

μὴ (negative conjunction with the subjunctive) 87.

ἀποσταλῶσιν (3d.per.pl.aor.act.subj.of ἀποστέλλω, third-class condition) 215.

καθὼς (compound particle in a comparative clause) 1348.

γέγραπται (3d.per.sing.perf.pass.ind.of γράφω, intensive) 156.

ὡς (exclamation) 128.

ὡραῖοι (nom.pl.masc.of ὡραῖος, predicate adjective) 1465.

οἱ (nom.pl.masc.of the article in agreement with πόδες) 9.

πόδες (nom.pl.masc.of πούς, subject of εἰσίν, understood) 353.

τῶν (gen.pl.masc.of the article in agreement with εὐαγγελιζομένων) 9.

εὐαγγελιζομένων (pres.mid.part.gen.pl.masc.of εὐαγγελίζομαι, substantival, possession) 909.

ἀγαθά (acc.pl.neut.of ἀγαθός, direct object of εὐαγγελιζομένων) 547.

Translation - "And how shall they preach if they are not sent out? In keeping with what is written, 'How beautiful the feet of those who are proclaiming the good news.' "

Comment: Still another rhetorical question, this time in the form of a third-class condition, to complete the cycle. ἐὰν μὴ and the subjunctive in the protasis is regular, but note also the deliberative subjunctive in the apodosis. "If they are not sent out, how can they preach?" The quotation is from Isaiah 52:7 where a fuller version is provided by the LXX. ὡς ὥρα ἐπὶ τῶν ὀρέων ὡς πόδες εὐαγγελιζομένου ἀκοὴν εἰρήνης ὡς εὐαγγελιζόμενος ἀγαθά. *Cf.* also Nahum 1:15. The relative particle ὡς is used here as an exclamation. *Cf.* Eph.6:15. Some MSS add πόδες τῶν εὐαγγελιζομένων εἰρήνην though the United Bible Societies' Committee reject the addition with an A degree of certitude.

Thus the cycle is complete. It starts in the sovereign will of God who sends out preachers who preach. All in the audience hear audibly, while some also hear perceptively. Those who do believe and call. When they call they are saved. But those who do hear and believe do so only by divine grace.

"How beautiful upon the mountains. . . " The mother of a little girl who lived in a cabin at the timber line on the cog road of Pike's Peak, quoted Isaiah's passage to three Baptist preachers who were climbing the mountain. We paused at the cabin for a bowl of soup and a cup of coffee. One of the preachers led the little girl to Christ. She had been listening to Charles E. Fuller on the "Old Fashioned Revival Hour" and needed only the guidance of a verse of scripture. As the preacher's left to resume their climb up the cog road, the mother with tears of joy quoted the passage.

Verse 16 - "But they have not all obeyed the gospel. For Esaias saith, Lord, who hath believed our report?"

Ἀλλ' οὐ πάντες ὑπήκουσαν τῷ εὐαγγελίῳ. Ἠσαΐας γὰρ λέγει, Κύριε, τίς ἐπίστευσεν τῇ ἀκοῇ ἡμῶν;

"But they have not all heeded the gospel; for Isaiah says, 'Lord, who has believed what he has heard from us?' " . . . RSV

Ἀλλ' (adversative conjunction) 342.

οὐ (negative conjunction with the indicative) 130.

πάντες (nom.pl.masc.of πᾶς, subject of ὑπήκουσαν) 67.

ὑπήκουσαν (3d.per.pl.aor.act.ind.of ὑπακούω, ingressive) 760.

τῷ (dat.sing.neut.of the article in agreement with εὐαγγελίῳ) 9.

εὐαγγελίῳ (dat.sing.neut.of εὐαγγέλιον, advantage) 405.

Ἠσαΐας (nom.sing.masc.of Ἠσαΐας, subject of λέγει) 255.

γὰρ (causal conjunction) 105.

λέγει (3d.per.sing.pres.act.ind.of λέγω, historical) 66.

Κύριε (voc.sing.masc.of κύριος, address) 97.

τίς (nom.sing.masc.of τίς, interrogative pronoun, subject of ἐπίστευσεν, direct question) 281.

ἐπίστευσεν (3d.per.sing.aor.act.ind.of πιστεύω, ingressive) 734.

τῇ (dat.sing.fem.of the article in agreement with ἀκοῇ) 9.

ἀκοῇ (dat.sing.fem.of ἀκοή, advantage) 409.

ἡμῶν (gen.pl.masc.of ἐγώ, possession) 123.

Translation - "But not all have begun to obey the gospel. Because Isaiah said, 'Lord, who has begun to believe our message?' "

Comment: For those who miss the distinction between ἀκούω and the genitive (Rom.10:14) and ἀκούω with the accusative, it would appear that everyone who "hears" the gospel preached in the sense of audible sensation, will believe, call and be saved. Such is not the case, as Paul points out in verse 16. Not all who were in the audience when the gospel was preached obeyed it. The Mars Hill sermon in Athens is not a good example because Paul's message there, although scholarly and true in all that he said did not spell out with clarity the plan of salvation.   But even in Corinth where many heard Paul preach, not all believed, though many did. The Corinthian ministry is a good example for Paul, in keeping with his resolve, preached the gospel faithfully, clearly and forcefully (1 Cor.2:1-5).

Note the difference between verse 11 and verse 16, with reference to the position of οὐ. In verse 11 it is joined to the verb. In verse 16 it is joined to the substantive. A literal translation of verse 11 fails to conform to English usage, but in verse 16, it is good English to translate literally - "Not all obeyed the gospel." Some did; others did not.

To support his contention Paul cites Isaiah's complaint of Isaiah 53:1, who adds καὶ ὁ βραχίων κυρίου τίνι ἀπεκαλύφη;. Not all began to obey the gospel, nor did all begin to believe the message. I have taken these aorists as ingressive, because incipient perception of the message of the gospel of Christ and incipient faith in it are the results of the function of the Holy Spirit (John 16:7-11). What the Holy Spirit begins He finishes. The non-elect do not even begin to understand the message of the gospel and that is why they do not begin to accept it. This is true even though from a purely intellectual point of view they may grasp the logic of the doctrines of atonement and justification. This is why the didactic approach to exegesis of the Scriptures should be reserved for those who have already been discipled and immersed in water. This is the order of the Great Commission (Mt.28:18-20). *Cf.* our discussion of the difference between μαθητεύω (#1094) and διδάσκω (#403) in *The Renaissance New Testament*, 3, 621-626. After sinners have been "taught of God" (John 6:45) they are in a position to be taught by Christian educators. To those who do not begin to hear, obey and believe the gospel when they "hear" it, it smells like death. Only to those who are "taught of God" does it smell like life (2 Cor.2:14-17). The only evangelists who are "sufficient for these things" are those who "make clear the savour of his knowledge . . . in every place."

An insurance salesman in Western Missouri knew a great deal about actuarial tables and statistical probability, and could make very clear to a prospect why the premiums were what they were and what the odds were that it was better for the prospect to buy than not to buy. After an hour filled with his didactic eloquence, the prospect knew practically all that is to be known about life insurance. But he did not buy the contract. The sales manager took the brilliant agent aside and employed what is commonly known in the industry as the KISS principle - "Keep it simple, stupid!" The salesman got the message and became a successful representative of the company. Preachers who do not know the difference between preaching the gospel of Christ and teaching the theology of Christianity should employ the KISS principle. Paul was brilliant on Mars Hill, but only the Ph.D's understood him and they were not impressed. In Corinth Paul was simplicity itself and the Holy Spirit used his message to "teach" the elect.

The "strong arm of the Lord" is not revealed to all. But those who truly hear the gospel experience the generation of faith, which enables them to begin to believe. This is the message of

Verse 17 - "So then faith cometh by hearing, and hearing by the word of God."

ἄρα ἡ πίστις ἐξ ἀκοῆς, ἡ δὲ ἀκοὴ διὰ ῥήματος Χριστοῦ.

"So faith comes from what is heard, and what is heard comes by the preaching

ἄρα (illative particle) 995.
ἡ (nom.sing.fem.of the article in agreement with πίστις) 9.
πίστις (nom.sing.fem.of πίστις, subject of verb understood) 728.
ἐξ (preposition with the ablative of source) 19.
ἀκοῆς (abl.sing.fem.of ἀκοή, source) 409.
ἡ (nom.sing.fem.of the article in agreement with ἀκοή) 9.

δὲ (continuative conjunction) 11.

ἀκοή (nom.sing.fem.of ἀκοή, subject of verb understood) 409.

διὰ (preposition with the ablative, intermediate agent) 118.

ῥήματος (abl.sing.neut.of ῥῆμα, intermediate agent) 343.

Χριστοῦ (gen.sing.masc.of Χριστός, description) 4.

Translation - "Obviously then faith results from hearing and hearing is provided by the word of Christ."

Comment: Isaiah preached but he did not conclude that all who heard were saved, though he knew that some heard and were saved while others heard (genitive case) but did not hear (accusative case) and thus they were not saved. So he asked the Lord to sort them out - "Lord who really heard me?" Thus Paul concluded in verse 17 (ἄρα, emphatic inferential) that faith has its source in hearing, while hearing is administered by the agency of the word of Christ. Sinaiticus A D♭,c K P Ψ and many miniscules read θεοῦ instead of Χριστοῦ, but the earlier MSS read Χριστοῦ.

Not only do the non-elect reject what is heard; they also reject Christ's miracles. *Cf.* John 12:37,38. *Cf.* Heb.4:2 which reveals the missing element.

Note the difference between the ablative of source in ἐξ ἀκοῆς and the ablative of intermediate agent in διὰ ῥήματος and the genitive of description in Χριστοῦ. The "word about Christ" is the administration agent by which the true hearing, which is the source of the faith that saves comes to the believer. Paul provides the definition of the "word about Christ" in 1 Cor.15:1-4. When these truths - that Christ died for our sins, was buried and rose again, and that these things were all foretold in the Old Testament Scriptures are faithfully preached, those who hear (accusative case) by virtue of the auspices of the Holy Spirit will experience the incipient obedience to and faith in the gospel. To them what they have just heard (phenomena) and perceived, thanks to the Holy Spirit (noumena), smells to them like life - the life that is eternal.

Verse 18 - "But I say, Have they not heard: Yes, verily their sound went into all the earth, and their words unto the ends of the world."

ἀλλὰ λέγω, μὴ οὐκ ἤκουσαν; μενοῦνγε, Εἰς πᾶσαν τὴν γῆν ἐξῆλθεν ὁ φθόγγος αὐτῶν, καὶ εἰς τὰ πέρατα τῆς οἰκουμένης τὰ ῥήματα αὐτῶν.

"But I ask, have they not heard? Indeed they have; for 'Their voice has gone out to all the earth, and their words to the ends of the world.' " . . . RSV

ἀλλὰ (adversative conjunction) 342.

λέγω (1st.per.sing.pres.act.ind.of λέγω, aoristic) 66.

μὴ (negative conjunction in rhetorical question which expects a negative reply) 87.

οὐκ (negative conjunction with the indicative, to negate ἤκουσαν) 130.

ἤκουσαν (3d.per.pl.aor.act.ind.of ἀκούω, culminative, rhetorical question) 148.

μενοῦνγε (compound emphatic particle) 3965.
εἰς (preposition with the accusative of extent) 140.
πᾶσαν (acc.sing.fem.of πᾶς, in agreement with γῆν) 67.
τὴν (acc.sing.fem.of the article in agreement with γῆν) 9.
γῆν (acc.sing.fem.of γῆ, extent) 157.
ἐξῆλθεν (3d.per.sing.aor.ind.of ἐξέρχομαι, culminative) 161.
ὁ (nom.sing.masc.of the article in agreement with φθόγγος) 9.

#3975 φθόγγος (nom.sing.masc.of φθόγγος, subject of ἐξῆλθεν).

King James Version

sound - Rom.10:18; 1 Cor.14:7.

Revised Standard Version

voice - Rom.10:18.
distinct notes - 1 Cor.14:7.

Meaning: Cf. φθέγγομαι (#3036). Hence, a sound, not necessarily one that conveys a distinct message. The distinction between sounds is derived from the context in 1 Cor.14:7, not from the meaning of φθόγγοις. With reference to the "voices" and the testimony of nature in Psalm 19:4, which Paul quotes in Romans 10:18.

αὐτῶν (gen.pl.masc.of αὐτός, possession) 16.
καὶ (continuative conjunction) 14.
εἰς (preposition with the accusative of extent) 140.
τὰ (acc.pl.neut.of the article in agreement with πέρατα) 9.
πέρατα (acc.pl.neut.of πέρας, extent) 1016.
τῆς (gen.sing.fem.of the article in agreement with οἰκουμένης) 9.
οἰκουμένης (gen.sing.fem.of οἰκουμένη, description) 1491.
τὰ (nom.pl.neut.of the article in agreement with ῥήματα) 9.
ῥήματα (nom.pl.neut.of ῥῆμα, subject of ἐξῆλθεν) 343.
αὐτῶν (gen.pl.masc.of αὐτος, possession) 16.

Translation - "But I ask, 'They failed to hear, did they not?' Indeed they did! Their sound went out unto all the earth and their words unto the furthest extent of civilization.' "

Comment: μή, the interrogative particle expects "yes" as an answer, while οὐκ negatives the verb ἤκουσαν. "They heard, did they not?" μενοῦνγε then adds, "Yes, indeed they did hear." The quotation is from Psalm 19:4 and refers to a message understood by some but not by others. *Cf.* Rom.2:7-10. *Cf.* #3975 - a sound, not a clear and distinct communication, though used by some to bring salvation (Psalm 19:7-9).

Verse 19 - "But I say, Did not Israel know? First, Moses saith, I will provoke you to jealousy by them that are no people, and by a foolish nation, I will anger you."

ἀλλὰ λέγω, μὴ Ἰσραὴλ οὐκ ἔγνω; πρῶτος Μωϋσῆς λέγει, Ἐγὼ παραζηλώσω ὑμᾶς ἐπ᾽ οὐκ ἔθνει, ἐπ᾽ ἔθνει ἀσυνέτῳ παροργιῶ ὑμᾶς.

"Again I ask, did Israel not understand? First Moses says, 'I will make you jealous of those who are not a nation; with a foolish nation I will make you angry.' " . . . RSV

ἀλλὰ (adversative conjunction) 342.
λέγω (1st.per.sing.pres.act.ind.of λέγω, aoristic) 66.
μὴ (negative particle in rhetorical question, expecting a negative reply) 87.
Ἰσραὴλ (nom.sing.masc.of Ἰσραὴλ, subject of ἔγνω) 165.
οὐκ (negative particle with the indicative) 130.
ἔγνω (3d.per.sing.2d.aor.act.ind.of γινώσκω, constative) 131.
πρῶτος (nom.sing.masc.of πρῶτος, adverbial) 487.
Μωϋσῆς (nom.sing.masc.of Μωϋσῆς, subject of λέγει) 715.
λέγει (3d.per.sing.pres.act.ind.of λέγω, historical) 66.
Ἐγὼ (nom.sing.masc.of ἐγώ, subject of   παραζηλώσω) 123.

#3976 παραζηλώσω (1st.per.sing.fut.act.ind.of παραζηλόω, predictive).

   King James Version

provoke to emulation - Rom.11:14.
provoke to jealousy - Rom.10:19; 11:11; 1 Cor.10:22.

   Revised Standard Version

make you jealous - Rom.10:19; 11:11,14.
provoke to jealousy - 1 Cor.10:22.

Meaning: A combination of παρά (#154) and ζηλόω (#3105). To incite or provoke to jealousy. παρά in composition is similar to the German *an*. With reference to Israel as a nation when their Messiah was accepted by the Gentiles - Rom.10:19; 11:11,14. With reference to God's jealous anger as worship offered to demons is also offered to Him - 1 Cor.10:22.

ὑμᾶς (acc.pl.masc.of σύ, direct object of παραζηλώσω) 104.
ἐπ᾽ (preposition with the instrumental of means) 47.
οὐκ (negative particle with the indicative) 130.
ἔθνει (instru.sing.neut.of ἔθνος, means) 376.
ἐπ᾽ (preposition with the instrumental of means) 47.
ἔθνει (instru.sing.neut.of ἔθνος, means) 376.
ἀσυνέτῳ (instru.sing.neut.of ἀσύνετος, in agreement with ἔθνει) 1159.

#3977 παροργιῶ (1st.per.sing.fut.act.ind.of παροργίζω, predictive).

   King James Version

anger - Rom.10:19.
provoke to wrath - Eph.6:4.

Revised Standard Version

make angry - Rom.10:19.
provoke to anger - Eph.6:4.

Meaning: A combination of παρά (#154) and ὀρίζω (#479). To exasperate; provoke to wrath; make angry. Gentile salvation provokes national Israel to wrath - Rom.10:19; unwise fathers provoke their children - Eph.6:4.

ὑμᾶς (acc.pl.masc.of σύ, direct object of παροργιῶ) 104.

Translation - "*But I say, 'Did Israel not know?' Moses first said, 'I will make you jealous with a nation of no standing; by people who do not think I will anger you.' "*

Comment: μὴ Ἰσραὴλ οὐκ ἔγνω is the same idiom that we had in verse 18. "οὐ is the negative of the verb while μή is the interrogative particle expecting the answer "no." The English translation expects the answer "yes" because it ignores μή and translates only οὐ. Cf. 1 Cor.9:4,5; 11:22; Ro.10:18,19.The construction is in the LXX (Judg.6:13,etc.) and in classic Greek." (Robertson, *Grammar*,918). Paul puts the question so as to elicit the positive response, and then, to prove his point, he cites Moses in Deut.32:21, the first half of which has αὐτοὶ παρεζήλωσάν με ἐπ᾽ οὐ θεῷ, παρώξυνάν με ἐν τοῖς εἰδώλοις αὐτῶν - "They provoked me by that which is not God; they angered me with their idols." And then God added, as if in retaliation, "I will make them jealous by that which is not (in Israel's estimation) a nation, and anger them with an ignorant people." This is what Jesus meant in Mt.8:10,11,12 and Mt.21:33-46.

Now Paul adds that as if Moses' statement was not enough to irritate the Jews, Isaiah makes it even stronger.

Verse 20 - "*But Esaias is very bold, and saith, I was found of them that sought me not; I was made manifest unto them that asked not after me.*"

Ἡσαΐας δὲ ἀποτολμᾷ καὶ λέγει, Εὑρέθην (ἐν) τοῖς ἐμὲ μὴ ζητοῦσιν, ἐμφανὴς ἐγενόμην τοῖς ἐμὲ μὴ ἐπερωτῶσιν.

"*Then Isaiah is so bold as to say, 'I have been found by those who did not seek me; I have shown myself to those who did not ask for me.' "* . . . RSV

Ἡσαΐας (nom.sing.masc.of Ἡσαΐας, subject of ἀποτολμᾷ) 255.
δὲ (adversative conjunction) 11.

#3978 ἀποτολμᾷ (3d.per.sing.pres.act.ind.of ἀποτολμάω, historical).

King James Version

be very bold - Rom.10:20.

Revised Standard Version

is so bold - Rom.10:20.

Meaning: A combination of ἀπό (#70) and τολμάω (#1430). Hence, to derive courage to dare to be bold; with λέγει, to be forthright in speech - Rom.10:20.

καὶ (continuative conjunction) 14.
λέγει (3d.per.sing.pres.act.ind.of λέγω, historical) 66.
Εὑρέθην (1st.per.sing.1st.aor.pass.ind.of εὑρίσκω, culminative) 79.
ἐν (preposition with the locative, instrumental use, means) 80.
τοῖς (loc.pl.masc.of the article in agreement with ζητοῦσιν) 9.
ἐμὲ (acc.sing.masc.of ἐμός, direct object of ζητοῦσιν) 1267.
μὴ (negative particle with the participle) 87.
ζητοῦσιν (pres.act.part.loc.pl.masc.of ζητέω, means) 207.
ἐμφανὴς (nom.sing.masc.of ἐμφανής, predicate adjective) 3233.
ἐγενόμην (1st.per.sing.2d.aor.mid.ind.of γίνομαι, culminative) 113.
τοῖς (dat.pl.masc.of the article in agreement with ἐπερωτῶσιν) 9.
ἐμὲ (acc.sing.masc.of ἐμός, direct object of ἐπερωτῶσιν) 1267.
μὴ (negative particle with the participle) 87.
ἐπερωτῶσιν (pres.act.part.dat.pl.masc., substantival, indirect object) 973.

Translation - "But Isaiah was so bold as to say, 'I was discovered by those not seeking me; I made myself manifest to those not asking for me.' "

Comment: ἀποτολμᾷ with λέγει has the effect of being adverbial, with the action of ἀποτολμᾷ defining λέγει. "Isaiah said boldly . . . "   *Cf.* Luke 6:48 - "he went and dug." Hill people say, "He up and did it!" "He has gone and done it!"
   The Jews were working so hard to obey both the Torah and the Talmud and gain righteousness (Rom.10:2,3). The Gentiles were not working at it at all. The Jews, to whom pertained the adoption, the glory, the covenants, the law, the service of God and the promises (Rom.9:4) rejected the Messiah. The Gentiles accepted Him. In search of the Saviour whom they did not find, even though He was in their midst, the Jews were told that the Gentiles, whom they despised, and who were not looking for a Saviour would find Him. Jesus performed His miracles and taught, in keeping with Moses and the Prophets, in order to reveal Himself to Israel as their Messiah, but to no avail. Then He made Himself manifest to the Gentiles who were not asking for enlightenment. The quotation of verses 20,21 is from Isaiah 65:1,2.
   The converts in Jesus' ministry were the Apostles who were Jews. At Pentecost three thousand more Jews accepted Christ. The next day the number grew to five thousand. It was not until some time later that the first Gentiles were reached. Even the Hebrew Christians doubted at first that it was proper to preach the gospel to the Gentiles. And the unregenerate Jews never did accept it. Thus their jealousy and anger.

Verse 21 - "But to Israel he saith, All day long I have stretched forth my hands unto a disobedient and gainsaying people."

πρὸς δὲ τὸν Ἰσραὴλ λέγει, Ὅλην τὴν ἡμέραν ἐξεπέτασα τὰς χεῖράς μου πρὸς λαὸν ἀπειθοῦντα καὶ ἀντιλέγοντα.

"But to Israel he says, 'All day long I have held out my hands to a disobedient and contrary people.' " . . . RSV

πρὸς (preposition with the accusative of extent, with a verb of speaking) 197.
δὲ (adversative conjunction) 11.
τὸν (acc.sing.masc.of the article in agreement with Ἰσραὴλ) 9.
Ἰσραὴλ (acc.sing.masc.of Ἰσραὴλ, extent, with a verb of speaking) 165.
λέγει (3d.per.sing.pres.act.ind.of λέγω,historical) 66.
Ὅλην (acc.sing.fem.of ὅλος, in agreement with ἡμέραν) 112.
τὴν (acc.sing.fem.of the article in agreement with ἡμέραν) 9.
ἡμέραν (acc.sing.fem.of ἡμέρα, time extent) 135.

#3979 ἐξεπέτασα (1st.per.sing.aor.act.ind.of ἐκπετάννθμι, constative).

King James Version

stretch forth - Rom.10:21.

Revised Standard Version

hold out - Rom.10:21.

Meaning: A combination of ἐκ (#19) and πετάννυμι - "to spread" or "to stretch." Hence to spread out or stretch forth. Followed by τὰς χεῖράς μου in Rom.10:21 and Isaiah 65:2, LXX.

τὰς (acc.pl.fem.of the article in agreement with χεῖράς) 9.
χεῖράς (acc.pl.fem.of χείρ, direct object of ἐξεπέτασα) 308.
μου (gen.sing.masc.of ἐγώ, possession) 123.
πρὸς (preposition with the accusative of extent) 197.
λαὸν (acc.sing.masc.of λαός, extent) 110.
ἀπειθοῦντα (pres.act.part.acc.sing.masc.of ἀπειθέω, adjectival, restrictive, predicate position, in agreement with λαὸν) 1996.
καὶ (adjunctive conjunction joining participles) 14.
ἀντιλέγοντα (pres.act.part.acc.sing.masc.of ἀντιλέγω, adjectival, restrictive, predicate position, in agreement with λαὸν) 1903.

Translation - "But to Israel He said, 'All day long I have stretched out my hands to a people always disobedient and argumentative.' "

Comment: In ἐξεπέτασα we have an excellent example of the constative aorist. "This use of the aorist contemplates the action in its entirety. It takes an occurrence and, regardless of its extent of duration, gathers it into a single whole. We have here the basal, unmodified force of the aorist tense." (Mantey, *Manual*, 196).

There had been many pleas for Israel to repent, but the entire offer of salvation to Israel as a nation is here viewed as complete, though the gospel offer is always open to individual Jews. The quotation is from Isaiah 65:2. *Cf.* Acts 13:45; Titus 1:9; Luke 2:34; 20:27 for other uses of ἀντιλέγω. *Cf.*#1996 for Israel's disobedience. Thus Israel heard but they did not hear with spiritual perception, and they knew about the gospel, having often heard its appeal, but their knowledge was never mixed with faith (Heb.4:2).

The argument of Chapter 10, taken alone, might lead some to an amillenial position that God's promise to Abraham, as it relates to a future earthly inheritance, will not be fulfilled. Premillenialists (who are not necessarily associated with pretribulation rapturists) view the coming millenial reign of Messiah with Israel as His chosen nation literally and object by pointing to the fact that the Abrahamic and Davidic covenants are unconditional, and cannot therefore be abrogated, despite Israel's unfaithfulness. They also suggest that the amillenialists take a closer look at the 11th chapter of Romans.

The Remnant of Israel

(Romans 11:1-10)

Romans 11:1 - *"I say then, Hath God cast away his people? God forbid. For I also am an Israelite, of the seed of Abraham, of the tribe of Benjamin."*

Λέγω οὖν, μὴ ἀπώσατο ὁ θεὸς τὸν λαὸν αὐτοῦ; μὴ γένοιτο. καὶ γὰρ ἐγὼ Ἰσραηλίτης εἰμί, ἐκ σπέρματος Ἀβραάμ, φυλῆς Βενιασμείν.

"I ask, then, has God rejected his people? By no means! I myself am an Israelite, a descendant of Abraham, a member of the tribe of Benjamin." . . .

RSV

Λέγω (1st.per.sing.pres.act.ind.of λέγω, aoristic) 66.

οὖν (inferential conjunction) 68.

μὴ (negative particle in rhetorical question expecting a negative response) 87.

ἀπώσατο (3d.per.sing.aor.mid.ind.of ἀπωθέω, culminative) 3126.

ὁ (nom.sing.masc.of the article in agreement with θεὸς) 9.

θεὸς (nom.sing.masc.of θεός, subject of ἀπώσατο) 124.

τὸν (acc.sing.masc.of the article in agreement with λαὸν) 9.

λαὸν (acc.sing.masc.of λαός, direct object of ἀπώσατο) 110.

αὐτοῦ (gen.sing.masc.of αὐτός, relationship) 16.

μὴ (negative particle with the optative, voluntative) 87.

γένοιτο (3d.per.sing.2d.aor.opt.of γίνομαι, voluntative) 113.

καὶ (adjunctive conjunction) 14.

γὰρ (causal conjunction) 105.

ἐγὼ (nom.sing.masc.of ἐγώ, subject of εἰμί) 123.

Ἰσραηλίτης (nom.sing.masc.of Ἰσραηλίτης, predicate nominative) 1967.

εἰμί (1st.per.sing.pres.ind.of εἰμί, aoristic) 86.

ἐκ (preposition with the ablative of source) 19.

σπέρματος (abl.sing.neut.of σπέρμα, source) 1056.

'Αβραάμ (gen.sing.masc.of 'Αβραάμ, description) 7.

φυλῆς (abl.sing.fem.of φυλῇ, source) 1313.

Βενιαμείν (gen.sing.masc.of Βενιαμείν, description) 3295.

Translation - "I say then, 'God has not rejected His people has He?' Certainly not! For I also am an Israelite, a descendant of Abraham of the tribe of Benjamin."

Comment: Paul asks an incredulous rhetorical question that expects a negative reply, and follows it with his favorite emphatic disclaimer, μὴ γένοιτο (*Cf*.#87 for other uses of μή with the optative). Has God pushed His people away from Him? By no means! Then Paul cites himself as exhibit "A" to the contrary. Note that ἐγώ is emphatic.

This however does not involve the point at issue between pre and amillenialists. Paul was a Hebrew Christian, a member of the Body of Christ, one of the spiritual sons of Abraham by faith (Gal.3:7). There are many Hebrew Christians in the Body of Christ and they do not prove that Israel *as a nation* has a future in the economy of God. This point is made, however, as Paul goes on.

A variant reading adds τὴν κληρονομίαν after λαόν - "his chosen people."

Verse 2 - "God hath not cast away his people which he foreknew. Wot ye not what the scripture saith to Elias? How he maketh intercession to God against Israel, saying, . . . "

οὐκ ἀπώσατο ὁ θεὸς τὸν λαὸν αὐτοῦ ὅν προέγνω. ἢ οὐκ οἴδατε ἐν 'Ηλίᾳ τί λέγει ἡ γραφή; ὡς ἐντυγχάνει τῷ θεῷ κατὰ τοῦ 'Ισραήλ, . . .

"God has not rejected his people whom he foreknew. Do you not know what the scripture says to Elijah, how he pleads with God against Israel?" . . . RSV

οὐκ (negative particle with the indicative) 130.

ἀπώσατο (3d.per.sing.aor.mid.ind.of ἀπωθέομαι, culminative) 3126.

ὁ (nom.sing.masc.of the article in agreement with θεὸς) 9.

θεὸς (nom.sing.masc.of θεός, subject of ἀπώσατο) 124.

τὸν (acc.sing.masc.of the article in agreement with λαὸν) 9.

λαὸν (acc.sing.masc.of λαός, direct object of ἀπώσατο) 110.

αὐτοῦ (gen.sing.masc.of αὐτός, relationship) 16.

ὅν (acc.sing.masc.of ὅς, relative pronoun, direct object of προέγνω) 65.

προέγνω (3d.per.sing.2d.aor.act.ind.of προγινώσκω, constative) 3655.

ἢ (disjunctive) 465.

οὐκ (negative particle with the indicative) 130.

οἴδατε (2d.per.pl.perf.act.ind.of οἶδα, intensive) 144b.

ἐν (preposition with the dative of reference) 80.

'Ηλίᾳ (dat.sing.masc.of 'Ηλείας, reference) 921.

τί (acc.sing.neut.of τίς, interrogative pronoun, direct object of λέγει, indirect question) 281.

λέγει (3d.per.sing.pres.act.ind.of λέγω, historical) 66.

ἡ (nom.sing.fem.of the article in agreement with γραφή) 9.

γραφή (nom.sing.fem.of γράφή, subject of λέγει) 1389.

ὡς (conjunction introducing a definite temporal clause, contemporaneous time) 128.

ἐντυγχάνει (3d.per.sing.pres.act.ind.of ἐντυγχάνω, definite, contemporaneous, temporal clause) 3649.

τῷ (dat.sing.masc.of the article in agreement with θεῷ) 9.

θεῷ (dat.sing.masc.of θεός, indirect object of ἐντυγχάνει) 124.

κατά (preposition with the genitive, opposition) 98.

τοῦ (gen.sing.masc.of the article in agreement with Ἰσραήλ) 9.

Ἰσραηλ (gen.sing.masc.of Ἰσραήλ, opposition) 165.

Translation - "God has not rejected His people, whom He foreknew. Now you do remember, do you not what the scripture said with reference to Elijah when he was protesting to God against Israel?"

Comment: The dogmatic statement, quoted from 1 Samuel 12:22 and Psalm 94:14 is the answer to the rhetorical question of verse 1. Samuel added ὅτι ἐπιεικῶς κύριος προσελάβετο ὑμᾶς αὐτῷ εἰς λαόν - "because it has pleased Jehovah to make you a people unto himself." (LXX, 1 Samuel 12:22 RV), and in Psalm 94:14 David added καὶ τὴν κληρονομίαν αὐτοῦ οὐκ ἐγκαταλείφει - "and His inheritance He will not forsake." (LXX, Ps.94:14). Thus the question is decided on the basis of the sovereign will of God (1 Samuel 12:22) and it is also a matter of God's personal honor (Psalm 94:14).

Cf.#3655 for the meaning of προγινώσκω and its other uses. God has foreknown Israel as a nation in the same way that He has foreknown the elect as individuals. ἡ (#465) can here be taken as introductory to an argumentative explanation. The question with οὐκ and the indicative expects "yes" for an answer. See the translation *supra*. οἴδατε - present memory as a result of past learning. ὡς in a temporal sense, translated by the KJV "when" and "as."

Although Paul's question to the Roman Christians expects a positive answer, one wonders how many of them, especially those who were Gentiles, were familiar with the Elijah story in 1 Kings. We may be sure that the Hebrew Christians in his audience knew about it.

What did God say with reference to Elijah's prayer in the mountain cave in Horeb? (1 Kings 19:10,14). First of all, what was his prayer? And this we have in

Verse 3 - "Lord, they have killed thy prophets, and digged down thine altars; and I am left alone, and they seek my life."

Κύριε, τοὺς προφήτας σου ἀπέκτειναν, τὰ θυσιαστήριά σου κατέσκαφαν, κἀγὼ ὑπελείφθην μόνος, καὶ ζητοῦσιν τὴν ψυχήν μου.

"Lord, they have killed thy prophets, they have demolished thy altars, and I alone am left, and they seek my life." . . . RSV

Κύριε (voc.sing.masc.of κύριος, address) 97.

τοὺς (acc.pl.masc.of the article in agreement with προφήτας) 9.

προφήτας (acc.pl.masc.of προφήτης, direct object of ἀπέκτειναν) 119.

σου (gen.sing.masc.of σύ, relationship) 104.

ἀπέκτειναν (3d.per.pl.1st.aor.act.ind.of ἀποκτείνω, culminative) 889.

τὰ (acc.pl.neut.of the article in agreement with θυσιαστήριά) 9.

θυσιαστήριά (acc.pl.neut.of θυσιαστήριον, direct object of κατέσκαφαν) 484.

σου (gen.sing.masc.of σύ, possession) 104.

κατέσκαφαν (3d.per.pl.aor.act.ind.of κατασκάπτω, culminative) 3338.

καἀγὼ (continuative conjunction and first personal pronoun, crasis) 178.

#3980 ὑπελείφθην (1st.per.sing.aor.pass.ind.of ὑπολείπω, culminative).

King James Version

leave - Rom.11:3.

Revised Standard Version

leave - Rom.11:3.

Meaning: A combination of ὑπό (#117) and λείπω (#2636). To leave behind; in the passive, to be left behind. To be left remaining. With reference to Elijah who thought that he was the lone (μόνος) survivor - Rom.11:3.

μόνος (nom.sing.masc.of μόνος, predicate adjective) 339.

καὶ (continuative conjunction) 14.

ζητοῦσιν (3d.per.pl.pres.act.ind.of ζητέω, present progressive retroactive) 207.

τὴν (acc.sing.fem.of the article in agreement with ψυχήν) 9.

ψυχήν (acc.sing.fem.of ψυχή, direct object of ζητοῦσιν) 233.

μου (gen.sing.masc.of ἐγώ, possession) 123.

Translation - "*Lord, they have killed your prophets, demolished your altars and I alone have been left, and they have been seeking my life.*"

Comment: The three aorist verbs are culminative. Elijah was assessing the current situation. The prophets had been killed; the altars had been torn down; only he had been left. Elijah, the overwrought prophet of God, had just come from his notable victory over the prophets of Baal. Read the story in 1 Kings 18 and 19. The priests of Baal, like the modern "charismatics" leaped about the altar, cut themselves with knives and implored their god to speak, while Elijah stood aside, where he would not get stepped on, and indulged in some fine divine sarcasm. When the Baal preachers had exhausted their resources, without avail, Elijah prayed for fifteen seconds and the fire fell from heaven, devoured the sacrifice, the altar and the stones and "licked up the water that was in the trench." The people fell upon their faces and cried out again and again, "The Lord He is the God! The Lord He is the God!" The "front door" revival resulted in a "back door" revival. Elijah slew the priests of Baal - 450 of Jezebel's favorite preachers.

One would think that after that Elijah would be invincible, but when he heard that Jezebel had vowed to kill him as he had killed her priests, he fled post haste and did not stop until he got to Beersheba, a little more than 100 miles to the south. Jezebel was not in pursuit. She only threatened to kill him. But now, seized with a sudden attack of paranoia, Elijah prayed that the Lord would take away his life before the agents of Jezebel had the privilege.

It is a picture of pessimism. If, indeed, Elijah alone was left to be faithful to the God of the covenant and if he wanted to die, then God's promise to redeem Israel as a nation would fail and Baal or some other pagan deity would rise to supplant Him. Elijah was praying like an amillenialist. Apparently he thought that the promises of God to Abraham, Isaac, Jacob and David were conditioned upon the faithfulness of His people, and that Israel had failed. If the party of the second part in a conditional covenant fails to fulfill it the party of the first part is under no further obligation. But not all of Israel had failed as we see in verse 4.

The current counterpart is modern Israel, regathered to Palestine in unbelief, with much of the power of the state in the hands of reformed and/or atheistic Jews who reject the Biblical basis for Zionism. Israel, since 1948 has shown increasing signs of paranoia. Fuelling her pessimism with repeated references to the Holocaust in which six million Jews died, and pointing for justification for her feelings to the enmity of the Arab world, which surrounds her, and to the determination of the Palestine Liberation Organization to gain self-determination, to say nothing of the hatred of Colonel Muammar el-Qaddafi, of Lybia, who has vowed to exterminate them, they have taken the view that the entire Gentile world has forsaken them and that if they survive they must fight for survival with no one to help. Thus in June, 1982 they have invaded Lebanon in an attack which could escalate into World War III in the Middle East. But, although modern Israel has lost sight of God's promises to their forefathers, the God of their forefathers has not forgotten. Not every man in Israel has bowed the knee to Baal.

Verse 4 - "But what saith the answer of God unto him? I have reserved to myself seven thousand men, who have not bowed the knee to the image of Baal."

ἀλλὰ τί λέγει αὐτῷ ὁ χρηματισμός; Κατέλιπον ἐμαυτῷ ἑπτακισχιλίους ἄνδρας, οἵτινες οὐκ ἔκαμψαν γόνυ τῇ Βάαλ.

"But what is God's reply to him? 'I have kept for myself seven thousand men who have not bowed the knee to Baal.' " . . . RSV

ἀλλὰ (adversative conjunction) 342.

τί (nom.sing.neut.of τίς, interrogative pronoun, direct question, predicate nominative) 281.

λέγει (3d.per.sing.pres.act.ind.of λέγω, aoristic) 66.

αὐτῷ (dat.sing.masc.of αὐτός, indirect object of λέγει) 16.

ὁ (nom.sing.masc.of the article in agreement with χρηματισμός) 9.

#3981 χρηματισμός (nom.sing.masc.of χρηματισμός, subject of λέγει).

King James Version

answer of God - Rom.11:4.

Revised Standard Version

God's reply - Rom.11:4.

Meaning: Cf. χρηματίζω (#195). An oracle; a divine response; instruction from a heavenly source - Rom.11:4.

κατέλιπον (1st.per.sing.aor.act.ind.of καταλείπω, constative) 369.
ἐμαυτῷ (dat.sing.masc.of ἐμαυτοῦ, personal interest) 723.

#3982 ἑπτακισχιλίους (acc.pl.masc.of ἑπτακισχίλιος, in agreement with ἄνδρας).

King James Version

seven thousand - Rom.11:4.

Revised Standard Version

seven thousand - Rom.11:4.

Meaning: A combination of ἑπτά (#1024) and χίλιοι (#5278). Hence, seven thousand - Rom.11:4.

ἄνδρας (acc.pl.masc.of ἀνήρ, direct object of κατέλιπον) 63.
οἵτινες (nom.pl.masc.of ὅστις, indefinite relative pronoun, adjectival, subject of ἔκαμψαν) 163.

οὐκ (negative particle with the indicative) 130.

#3983 ἔκαμψαν (3d.per.pl.aor.act.ind.of κάμπω, ingressive).

King James Version

bow - Rom.11:4; 14:11; Eph.3:14; Phil.2:10.

Revised Standard Version

bow - Rom.11:4; 14:11; Eph.3:14; Phil.2:10.

Meaning: To bend or bow. Followed by γόνυ - to bow the knee in worship. Of Baal - Rom.11:4; of God, followed by ἐμοί - Rom.14:11; joined to ἐν τῷ ὀνόματι Ἰησοῦ, of the final judgment when all shall admit that Christ is God - Phil.2:10; Paul's prayer, joined with τὰ γόνατά μου πρὸς τὸν πατέρα - Eph.3:14.

γόνυ (acc.sing.neut.of γόνυ, direct object of ἔκαμψαν) 2052.
τῇ (dat.sing.fem.of the article in agreement with Βάαλ) 9.

#3984 Βάαλ (dat.sing.fem.of Βάαλ, personal advantage).

King James Version

Baal - Rom.11:4.

Revised Standard Version

Baal - Rom.11:4.

Meaning: Chief deity of the Phoenicians, Babylonians, Caananites and Assyrians. Associated with Astarte. Feminine here in Romans 11:4, following the custom of the LXX in the writings of Jeremiah, Hosea and Zephaniah. It was written in the feminine to indicate Jewish contempt for an inferior deity, though in 1 Kings 19:18 it reads τῷ Βάαλ. *Cf.* Jeremiah 2:8,28; 7:9; Hos.2:8; Tobit 1:5B.

Translation - "But what does the divine messenger reply to him? 'I have left for myself seven thousand men who have not once bowed a knee to Baal.' "

Comment: Israel's wholesale apostasy cannot abrogate God's promises to Abraham, Isaac, Jacob, Judah and David (Rom.3:3,4). There will always be a remnant. In Elijah's day there were 7000. In the tribulation period, three and one-half years before Messiah returns there will be 144,000 (Rev.7:1-8). Never since God first made the promise to Abraham has there been a time when every living Jew apostatized to break the covenant of circumcision.

God has not promised to save all of the physical descendants of Abraham.. He did say that in Abraham and in his seed (Christ) all of the nations of the earth would be blessed. But this means more than the coming of the Messiah, though, of course, it does mean that. God has also promised to perpetuate David's throne (2 Samuel 7:10-17), The twelve Apostles will sit on twelve judgment thrones to administer justice to the twelve tribes of Israel (Acts 26:7; Mt.19:28).

Paul next says that in the first century, at the time of his writing of the epistle, God has His remnant.

Verse 5 - "Even so then at this present time also there is a remnant according to the election of grace."

οὕτως οὖν καὶ ἐν τῷ νῦν καιρῷ λεῖμμα κατ' ἐκλογὴν χάριτος γέγονεν.

"So too at the present time there is a remnant, chosen by grace." . . . RSV

οὕτως (demonstrative adverb) 74.
οὖν (inferential conjunction) 68.
καὶ (ascensive conjunction) 14.
ἐν (preposition with the locative, time point) 80.
τῷ (loc.sing.masc.of the article in agreement with καιρῷ) 9.
νῦν (temporal adverb) 1497.
καιρῷ (loc.sing.masc.of καιρός, time point) 767.

#3985 λεῖμμα (nom.sing.neut.of λεῖμμα, subject of γέγονεν).

King James Version

remnant - Rom.11:5.

Revised Standard Version

remnant - Rom. 11:5.

Meaning: Cf. λείπω (#2636). A remnant. A small number salvaged from destruction out of a larger number. Elect Israel - Rom. 11:5.

κατ' (preposition with the accusative, standard) 98.
ἐκλογὴν (acc.sing.fem.of ἐκλογή, standard) 3189.
χάριτος (abl.sing.fem.of χάρις, source) 1700.
γέγονεν (3d.per.sing.perf.ind.of γίνομαι, intensive) 113.

Translation - "Thus then, even at this time, there is a remnant according to the election of grace."

Comment: οὕτως connects the Old Testament fact of God's remnant of 7000 in Elijah's day with God's covenant in Paul's day. καὶ is either adjunctive and/or ascensive.. *Cf.* #767 for other locative phrases ἐν τῷ νῦν καιρῷ. Note that γέγονεν is perfect tense. As a result of God's first choice in electing grace, the present situation prevails. There is now a remnant, and there will always be until the covenant promise is fulfilled. The perfect tense does not perpetuate the status of the elect into the future for the perfect tense, *per se* is never proleptic, but since God once made a choice by grace, His will prevails, since the calling of God is without repentance (Rom. 11:29). The proleptic force of the election is not in the perfect tense, but in the eternal certainty of the realization of God's will.

That Paul was not speaking of the 144,000 of Rev. 7:1-8 is clear from his temporal phrase - ἐν τῷ νῦν καιρῷ. "Even now (at the time that Paul wrote) God has a remnant."

Verse 6 - "And if by grace, then is it no more of works; otherwise grace is no more grace. But if it be of works, then is it no more grace: otherwise work is no more work."

εἰ δὲ χάριτι, οὐκέτι ἐξ ἔργων, ἐπεὶ ἡ χάρις οὐκέτι, γίνεται χάρις.

"But if it is by grace, it is no longer on the basis of works; otherwise grace would no longer be grace." . . . RSV

εἰ (conditional particle in a first-class condition) 337.
δὲ (continuative conjunction) 11.
χάριτι (instru.sing.fem.of χάρις, means) 1700.
οὐκέτι (temporal adverb) 1289.
ἐξ (preposition with the ablative of source) 19.
ἔργων (abl.pl.neut.of ἔργον, source) 460.
ἐπεὶ (subordinating conjunction, introducing a causal clause) 1281.
ἡ (nom.sing.fem.of the article in agreement with χάρις) 9.
χάρις (nom.sing.fem.of χάρις, subject of ἐστίν, understood) 1700.
οὐκέτι (temporal adverb) 1289.
γίνεται (3d.per.sing.pres.ind.of γίνομαι, static) 113.
χάρις (nom.sing.fem.of χάρις, subject of γίνεται) 1700.

Translation - "And since it is by grace, it no longer comes from works; otherwise grace is longer grace."

Comment: This is the same point that Paul made in Romans 4:3-5. χάρις and ἔργον are antithetical. If either is the source of salvation the other is automatically excluded. Salvation cannot be said to be the joint result of a dual source. Verse 5 made it clear that the election flows from grace - κατ' ἐκλογὴν χάριτος. Since it is grace (εἰ and a first-class condition) it is no longer works. The root is grace and the fruit is salvation. But salvation also produces its fruit - the "good works which God hath before ordained that we should walk in them" (Eph.2:10). Thus salvation, the fruit of grace is the root of works. The order must be - grace, salvation, works. Any other sequence makes no sense and destroys the gospel of Christ. These fruit/root and cause/result relationships must not be confused. Thus both legalism and antinomianism are destroyed. We are saved by the faith which is ours because of God's grace, but it is a faith that works. Works do not generate faith, but faith generates works. So the two cannot be separated, but the order must be understood. *Cf.* our comments on James 2:14-18.

The variant readings support the last two sentences of the KJV which only state the reverse proposition. None of the earliest MSS support the expanded text. They were unnecessarily added. Paul had already made the point clearly.

Verse 7 - "What then? Israel hath not obtained that which he seeketh for; but the election hath obtained it, and the rest were blinded."

τί οὖν; ὃ ἐπιζητεῖ Ἰσραήλ, τοῦτο οὐκ ἐπέτυχεν, ἡ δὲ ἐκλογὴ ἐπέτυχεν. οἱ δὲ λοιποὶ ἐπωρώθησαν.

"What then? Israel failed to obtain what it sought. The elect obtained it, but the rest were hardened, . . . " . . . RSV

τί (nom.sing.neut.of τίς, interrogative pronoun, subject of the verb understood) 281.

οὖν (inferential conjunction) 68.

ὃ (acc.sing.neut.of ὅς, relative pronoun, adjectival, in agreement with τοῦτο) 65.

ἐπιζητεῖ (3d.per.sing.pres.act.ind.of ἐπιζητέω, present progressive retroactive) 637.

Ἰσραήλ (nom.sing.masc.of Ἰσραήλ, subject of ἐπιζητεῖ and ἐπέτυχεν) 165.

τοῦτο (acc.sing.neut.of οὗτος, anaphoric, direct object of ἐπέτυχεν) 93.

οὐκ (negative particle with the indicative) 130.

#3986 ἐπέτυχεν (3d.per.sing.2d.aor.act.ind.of ἐπιτυγχάνω, constative).

King James Version

obtain - Rom.11:7,7; Heb.6:15; 11:33; James 4:2.

Revised Standard Version

obtain - Rom.11:7,7; Heb.6:15; James 4:2.

Meaning: A combination of ἐπί (#47) and τυγχάνω (#2699). Thus, to happen to hit upon a thing; to achieve, attain, acquire. Followed by an accusative of reference to salvation - Rom.11:7,7; absolutely in James 4:2; by a genitive - τῆς ἐπαγγελίας in Heb.6:15; 11:33. The word in the New Testament speaks of men and women who, after much frustration in seeking blindly and in the wrong places and ways, finally hit upon God's plan for them. The Jews did not find salvation - Rom.11:7a; the elect did - Rom.11:7b. Abraham finally did, after much straying - Heb.6:15; so also the Fathers - Heb.11:33; with reference to backslidden Christians in James 4:2.

ἡ (nom.sing.fem.of the article in agreement with ἐκλογή) 9.

δὲ (adversative conjunction) 11.

ἐκλογὴ (nom.sing.fem.of ἐκλογή, subject of ἐπέτυχεν) 3189.

ἐπέτυχεν (3d.per.sing.aor.act.ind.of ἐπιτυγχάνω, constative) 3986.

οἱ (nom.pl.masc.of the article in agreement with λοιποὶ) 9.

δὲ (continuative conjunction) 11.

λοιποὶ (nom.pl.masc.of λοιπός, subject of ἐπωρώθησαν) 1402.

ἐπωρώθησαν (3d.per.pl.aor.pass.ind.of πωρόω, constative) 2282.

Translation - "What then? That for which Israel sought so diligently - that she did not acquire. But the elect hit upon it, and the rest were hardened."

Comment: Note the exact shade of meaning of ἐπιτυγχάνω (#3986). The nation of Israel exhausted her imagination in an attempt to please God. The law, the prophets, the priests, the fathers, the traditions - all of these were tried. Then she turned to idols - Baal, Moloch, etc. It was a frantic search that went on endlessly. Note the present progressive retroactive tense in ἐπιζητεῖ, with the intensive prepositional prefix. "They had been intensively (ἐπί) seeking for salvation." But they did not chance to find it. The elect did, however, find salvation and the rest of Israel were made callous. Note the references under #2282. In each case it was Israel who was made callous. Every verb is passive except John 12:40, where Israel is the object of the verb. The context of Paul's argument indicates that the elect referred to are elect Jews who were saved, while οἱ λοιποὶ are the other Jews who were not saved. Paul deals with the elect from among the Gentiles in verses 11-24. The gospel was preached "to the Jew first" (Rom.1:16) and the first believers were Jews.

Verse 8 - (According as it is written, God hath given them the spirit of slumber, eyes that they should not see, and ears that they should not hear;) unto this day."

καθὼς γέγραπται, Ἔδωκεν αὐτοῖς ὁ θεὸς πνεῦμα κατανύξεως, ὀφθαλμοὺς τοῦ μὴ βλέπειν καὶ ὦτα τοῦ μὴ ἀκούειν, ἕως τῆς σήμερον ἡμέρας.

". . . as it is written, 'God gave them a spirit of stupor, eyes that should not see and ears that should not hear, down to this very day.' " . . . RSV

καθὼς (compound particle in a comparative clause) 1348.

γέγραπται (3d.per.sing.perf.pass.ind.of γράφω, intensive) 156.

Ἔδωκεν (3d.per.sing.aor.act.ind.of δίδωμι, constative) 362.
αὐτοῖς (dat.pl.masc.of αὐτός, indirect object of ἔδωκεν) 16.
ὁ (nom.sing.masc.of the article in agreement with θεὸς) 9.
θεὸς (nom.sing.masc.of θεός, subject of ἔδωκεν) 124.
πνεῦμα (acc.sing.neut.of πνεῦμα, direct object of ἔδωκεν) 83.

#3987 κατανύξεως (gen.sing.fem.of κατάνυξις, description).

King James Version

slumber - Rom.11:8.

Revised Standard Version

stupor - Rom.11:8.

Meaning: Cf. κατανύσσω (#2999). A combination of κατά (#98) and νύξις - "pricking" "stabbing" or "stinging." Hence a severe pricking or stabbing. Thus insensibility or torpor of mind caused by trauma. πνεῦμα κατανύξεως - "a spirit of stupor" with the result that they were insenitive to the claims of the gospel - Rom.11:8; Isa.29:9,10.

ὀφθαλμοὺς (acc.pl.masc.of ὀφθαλμός, direct object of ἔδωκεν) 501.
τοῦ (gen.sing.neut.of the article with the infinitive in a purpose construction) 9.
μὴ (negative particle with the infinitive) 87.
βλέπειν (pres.act.inf.of βλέπω, noun use, gen.sing.neut., purpose) 499.
καὶ (adjunctive conjunction, joining nouns) 14.
ὦτα (acc.pl.neut.of οὖς, direct object of ἔδωκεν) 887.
τοῦ (gen.sing.neut.of the article with the infinitive, purpose) 9.
μὴ (negative particle with the infinitive) 87.
ἀκούειν (pres.act.inf.of ἀκούω, noun use, genitive sing.neut., purpose) 148.
ἕως (preposition with the genitive of time description) 71.
τῆς (gen.sing.fem.of the article in agreement with ἡμέρας) 9.
σήμερον (adverbial, intensive) 579.
ἡμέρας (gen.sing.fem.of ἡμέρα, time description) 135.

Translation - "Just as it is written, 'God gave to them a spirit of stupor - eyes that they might not see and ears that they might not hear, unto this very day.' "

Comment: The quotation is from Isaiah 29:10 and Deuteronomy 24:4. πνεῦμα κατανύξεως means a psychological condition, the result of suffering, that renders the patient incapable of listening with perception to what is said. The victim is apathetic, unresponsive, detached. Cf. νωθρός in Heb.5:11; 6:12. Dull.

Israel as a nation has suffered greatly, chiefly because of her own sin against superior light. The suffering resulted in κατάνυξις. The articular infinitives are sub-final. Israel saw and heard the prophets. They listened to Jesus and saw what He did, but except for the elect, who were rescued from their torpor by the Holy Spirit, they did not respond. Note how Paul makes God responsible for this condition, just as he did in the case of Pharaoh. This condition had persisted ἔως τῆς σήμερον ἡμέρας - "unto this very day" *i.e.* the day when Paul wrote these lines. Meanwhile individual Jews, the physical descendants of Abraham, had become Christian members of the Body of Christ. This will continue until the end of the age. Paul has not said that God will deny to national Israel her special place in His economy.

Paul quotes David in Psalm 69:23 to support his point in

Verse 9 - "And David saith, Let their table be made a snare, and a trap, and a stumbling block, and a recompence unto them."

καὶ Δαυὶδ λέγει, Γενηθήτω ἡ τράπεζα αὐτῶν εἰς παγίδα καὶ εἰς θήραν καὶ εἰς σκάνδολον καὶ εἰς ἀνταπόδομα αὐτοῖς,

"And David says, 'Let their feast become a snare and a trap, a pitfall and a retribution for them; . . .' " . . . RSV

καὶ (continuative conjunction) 14.
Δαυὶδ (nom.sing.masc.of Δαυίδ, subject of λέγει) 6.
λέγει (3d.per.sing.pres.act.ind.of λέγω, historical) 66.
Γενηθήτω (3d.per.sing.2d.aor.pass.impv.of γίνομαι, entreaty) 113.
ἡ (nom.sing.fem.of the article in agreement with τράπεζα) 9.
τράπεζα (nom.sing.fem.of τράπεζα, subject of γενηθήτω) 1176.
αὐτῶν (gen.pl.masc.of αὐτός, possession) 16.
εἰς (preposition with the accusative, purpose) 140.
παγίδα (acc.sing.fem.of παγίς, purpose) 2738.
καὶ (adjunctive conjunction joining prepositional phrases) 140.
εἰς (preposition with the accusative, purpose) 140.

#3988 θήραν (acc.sing.fem.of θήρα, purpose).

King James Version

trap - Rom.11:9.

Revised Standard Version

trap - Rom.11:9.

Meaning: From Homer down, a hunting of wild beasts, with a view to their destruction. Hence, figuratively, as applied to men, a trap - Rom.11:9.

καὶ (adjunctive conjunction joining prepositional phrases) 14.
εἰς (preposition with the accusative, purpose) 140.
σκάνδαλον (acc.sing.neut.of σκάνδαλον, purpose) 1082.
καὶ (adjunctive conjunction joining prepositional phrases) 14.
εἰς (preposition with the accusative, purpose) 140.
ἀνταπόδομα (acc.sing.neut.of ἀνταπόδομα, purpose) 2527.
αὐτοῖς (dat.pl.masc.of αὐτός, personal disadvantage) 16.

Translation - *"And David said, 'Let their table be made a snare and a trap and a stumbling block and a punishment for them.'"*

Comment: The εἰς phrases with the accusative are purpose. The quotation is from Psalm 69:23. David had just said, in verse 22 καὶ ἔδωκαν εἰς τὸ βρῶμά μου χολήν,καὶ εἰς τὴν δίψαν μου ἐπότισάν με ὄξος - "they gave me also gall for my meat; and in my thirst they gave me vinegar to drink." The Psalm is Messianic. It describes the crucifixion of Jesus (Mt.27:34; Mk.15:23; Lk.23:36; John 19:29). Thus we understand the figure of ἡ τράπεζα - any banquet feast in contrast to the "food" the Jews served to Jesus on the cross. Another possible interpretation has it that since they crucified the "Bread of Life" (John 6:35-51), ἡ τράπεζα may refer to the Table of Shewbread in the Levitical service (Heb.9:2). In any case the point is the same. The retribution visited upon Israel for the murder of the Son of God is that their own table became a snare, a trap, a stumbling block and a retaliation of punishment against them. As they rejected the true Bread from heaven their own bread poisoned them. The true "Light of the world" (John 8:12) was temporarily extinguished and the false light of Rabbinical Judaism led them down the road to damnation, while it did nothing to banish the darkness of their theology. The "Water of Life" (John 4:14; 7:37,38) was poured out in death (John 2:7,8) and Israel's water became the bitter, poisoned water of Marah (Exod.15:23-25), since they rejected the tree (Calvary) that otherwise would make the water sweet and life-giving.

Thus God gave them a spirit of stupor (verse 8), but it was in just retribution for their crucifixion of their own Messiah. When one has turned his back upon the only Light there is, there is no other light to see. They would not have been any better off if they had not been made dull. When there is no light to behold neither those who are dull nor those who are perceptive can see it. God did not tell Abraham that there would be no divine punishment for individuals among his descendants. He did tell him that after the family of Abraham had produced the incarnate Son of God, a nucleus would survive to see the fulfillment of all that which He promised to Abraham, Isaac, Jacob, Judah and David. God is still committed in an unconditional promise to elevate Israel, as a nation, to a place of world prominence in the administration of Messiah's Kingdom of the Heavens.

When we fail to distinguish between the individual Jew and the Jewish nation, we are forced to one of two false conclusions. If there is no distinction to be considered then we must conclude that every one who has Jacob's blood in his veins will be saved, even those who crucified Christ, or that God will condemn every Jew for what was done by the Jews who crucified Jesus. Jews who were not present in Jerusalem the day Jesus was murdered, cannot be blamed for what happened, although he can be blamed and punished for rejecting Jesus in his heart. By the same reasoning he can be saved, as many Hebrews have been, if he accepts Jesus as his Messiah.

Verse 10 - *"Let their eyes be darkened, that they may not see, and bow down their back alway."*

σκοτισθήτωσαν οἱ ὀφθαλμοὶ αὐτῶν τοῦ μὴ βλέπειν, καὶ τὸν νῶτον αὐτῶν διὰ παντὸς σύγκαμφον.

". . . let their eyes be darkened so that they cannot see, and bend their backs forever." . . . RSV

σκοτισθήτωσαν (3d.per.pl.aor.pass.impv.of σκοτίζω, entreaty) 1504..

οἱ (nom.pl.masc.of the article in agreement with ὀφθαλμοὶ) 9.

ὀφθαλμοὶ (nom.pl.masc.of ὀφθαλμός, subject of σκοτισθήτωσαν) 501.

αὐτῶν (gen.pl.masc.of αὐτός, possession) 16.

τοῦ (gen.sing.neut.of the article, in an articular infinitive of purpose) 9.

μὴ (negative particle with the infinitive) 87.

βλέπειν (pres.act.inf.of βλέπω, gen.sing.neut., purpose) 499.

καὶ (continuative conjunction) 14.

τὸν (acc.sing.masc.of the article in agreement with νῶτον) 9.

#3989 νῶτον (acc.sing.masc.of νῶτος, direct object of σύγκαμφον).

King James Version

back - Rom.11:10.

Revised Standard Version

backs - Rom.11:10.

Meaning: The back - Rom.11:10.

διὰ (preposition with the genitive in a time expression) 118.

παντὸς (gen.sing.neut.of πᾶς, time description) 67.

#3990 σύγκαμφον (2d.per.sing.1st.act.impv.of συγκάμπτω, entreaty)

King James Version

bow down - Rom.11:10.

Revised Standard Version

bend - Rom.11:10.

Meaning: to bend or bow down the back; in a figurative reference to a prisoner bending his back to pass under a yoke of perpetual bondage. David (Psalm 69:24) prays that Israel, who rejected the freedom of God's truth might be perpetually subjected to error, as a slave is perpetually bowed under a yoke of bondage - Rom.11:10.

Translation - "Let their eyes be darkened, that they do not see, and may they bend their back always under a yoke of bondage."

Comment: τοῦ μὴ βλέπειν is another example of purpose as we had it twice in verse 8. The last clause in David's prayer, "bend their backs forever" is a commentary on Mt.6:22,23. Rejected light can only lead to permanent servitude in darkness. *Cf.* also Phil.2:10,11. *Cf.#67* for other uses of διὰ παντός, conveying the idea of time extension. The quotation is from Psalm 69:24. *Cf.* Rom.1:21; Eph.4:17,18 for the reason why intellectual blindness occurs. Intellectual confusion follows the determination of the will to reject God and His truth. Witness the total chaos in the Social Sciences as a result of Herbert Spencer's *Synthetic Philosophy*, in which he tried to coordinate all truth with the dogma of organic evolution.

This passage would lend strong support to amillenialism, with its view that Israel forfeited all future blessing from God when she rejected her Messiah, if it were not for what follows.

The Salvation of the Gentiles

(Romans 11:11-24)

Verse 11 - "I say then, Have they stumbled that they should fall? God forbid: but rather through their fall salvation is come unto the Gentiles, for to provoke them to jealousy."

Λέγω οὖν, μὴ ἔπταισαν ἵνα πέσωσιν; μὴ γένοιτο. ἀλλὰ τῷ αὐτῶν παραπτώματι ἡ σωτηρία τοῖς ἔθνεσιν, εἰς τὸ παραζηλῶσαι αὐτούς.

"So I ask, have they stumbled so as to fall? By no means! But through their trespass salvation has come to the Gentiles, so as to make Israel jealous." ...
RSV

Λέγω (1st.per.sing.pres.act.ind.of λέγω, aoristic) 66.

οὖν (inferential conjunction) 68.

μὴ (negative particle with the indicative in rhetorical question which expects a negative response) 87.

#3991 ἔπταισαν (3d.per.pl.aor.act.ind.of πταίω, in rhetorical question, constative).

King James Version

fall - 2 Pet.1:10.
offend - James 2:10; 3:2,2.
stumble - Rom.11:11.

Revised Standard Version

stumble - Rom.11:11.
fail - James 2:10.
make mistakes - James 3:2,2.
fall - 2 Pet.1:10.

Meaning: Cf. πίπτω (#187). To fall. Always intransitive in the New Testament. With reference to Israel's apostasy at Calvary - Rom.11:11; to transgres any part of the moral law; to sin - James 2:10; to err; to make a mistake - James 3:2a; to make a mistake in speech, either in diction, grammar, syntax or pronunciation - James 3:2b. With reference to the backslidden Christian who fails to live up to his privileges and disgraces himself - 2 Pet.1:10.

ἵνα (conjunction with the subjunctive, purpose) 114.

πέσωσιν (3d.per.pl.aor.act.subj.of πίπτω, purpose) 187.

μή (negative particle with the optative) 87.

γένοιτο (3d.per.sing.aor.opt.of γίνομαι, voluntative) 113.

ἀλλά (alternative conjunction) 342.

τῷ (instru.sing.neut.of the article in agreement with παραπτώματι) 9.

αὐτῶν (gen.pl.masc.of αὐτός, possession) 16.

παραπτώματι (instru.sing.neut.of παράπτωμα, means) 585.

ἡ (nom.sing.fem.of the article in agreement with σωτηρία) 9.

σωτηρία (nom.sing.fem.of σωτηρία, subject of verb understood) 1852.

τοῖς (dat.pl.neut.of the article in agreement with ἔθνεσιν) 9.

ἔθνεσιν (dat.pl.neut.of ἔθνος, personal advantage) 376.

εἰς (preposition with the accusative, purpose) 140.

τό (acc.sing.neut.of the article in agreement with παραζηλῶσαι, articular infinitive of purpose) 9.

παραζηλῶσαι (aor.act.inf.of παραζηλόω, purpose) 3976.

αὐτούς, (acc.pl.masc.of αὐτός, general reference) 16.

Translation - "Now I ask, 'They did not stumble in order that they might fall, did they?' Certainly not! But that, by their lapse, salvation might come to the Gentiles, in order that they might be made jealous."

Comment: The ἵνα clause is final (purpose). It is rhetorical question and Paul expected a negative reply. Keep in mind that God made them stumble (veres 7-9). Now Paul asks incredulously, did God make them step aside from the path of righteousness in order that He might forever deprive Israel, as a nation from His economy of blessing?

The question is preposterous. If Paul had asked it directly (οὐ ἔπταισαν, instead of μή ἔπταισαν), hoping for a positive reply, he would have indicated that his own thinking was astray. God could not abrogate His promise to Abraham and David in any case, even if Israel did fail, since the two covenants involved are unconditional. Let the student study them carefully in search of an "if clause." He will not find it. (Gen.12:1-3; 15:1-7; 2 Samuel 7:10-17). Whether Israel is faithful, unfaithful, obedient or disobedient has nothing to do with it. Thus the intended result is not Israel's ultimate punishment, although individuals in Israel who rejected Messiah must pay the price.

What then is the purpose? What did God have in mind? Let us suppose that Israel had not failed. If she had accepted her Messiah and enthroned Him in Jerusalem on David's throne, there would have been no crucifixion and thus there would have been no redemption for anyone - Jews or Gentiles. The purpose of the incarnation was the vicarious death of Messiah, which was contingent upon Israel's rejection of Jesus. Thus, by means of Israel's lapse two results followed: (1) redemption for the elect, both Jew and Gentile, was accomplished upon the cross, and (2) when salvation, purchased by our Lord at Calvary, was delivered to the Gentiles, the Jews were made jealous. They had always supposed that since God had made them His favored nation and had given them all of the advantages listed in Romans 9:4,5, the uncircumcised Gentile was beyond the Pale.

Our Lord told them that this was not true. He spoke of a sheepfold, over which He, the Good Shepherd, had control and said that the flock would include "other sheep which are not of this (Jewish) fold (whom) also (He) must bring, (who would) hear (His) voice." The result would be that "there shall be one fold and one shepherd." (John 10:16). He healed the servant of a Roman soldier, much to the disgust of the Pharisees, and warned them that "many would come from the east and west and (would) sit down with Abraham, and Isaac, and Jacob, in the kingdom of heaven, but the children of the kingdom (would) be cast out into outer darkness (where there would be) weeping and gnashing of teeth." (Mt.8:1-13). He offered a Samaritan prostitute, who was an outcast on two counts - her genetics and her lifestyle - a drink of the water of everlasting life (John 4:1-26). These incidents and many more in the ministry of our Lord confused the Jews, but only because of their ill conconceived ideas of the divine *weltanschauung*. Nor was their confusion the fault of the Old Testament message. It was the fault of their failure to interpret it, because the Old Testament, while not revealing the "mystery" of Ephesians 3:1-11, as fully as it was later revealed to Paul, pointed clearly to the New Testament message that redemption would be provided for the elect from every "kindred, and tongue, and people and nation" (Rev.5:9). Those Jews with the spiritual insight to read and understand the messages of the Old Testament prophets, knew that the Jew had no corner on salvation.

All of this was so obvious to Paul that he followed his incredulous question with his favorite explosive denial - μὴ γένοιτο. In this passage Paul tolled the death knell for amillenialism, though some of the brethren have not heard it yet.

Verse 12 - "Now if the fall of them be the riches of the world, and the diminishing of them the riches of the Gentiles, how much more their fulness?"

εἰ δὲ τὸ παράπτωμα αὐτῶν πλοῦτος κόσμου καὶ τὸ ἥττημα αὐτῶν πλοῦτος ἐθνῶν, πόσῳ μᾶλλον τὸ πλήρωμα αὐτῶν.

"Now if their trespass means riches for the world, and if their failure means riches for the Gentiles, how much more will their full inclusion mean!" . . . RSV

εἰ (conditional particle in a first-class condition) 337.

δὲ (explanatory conjunction) 11.

τὸ (nom.sing.neut.of the article in agreement with παράπτωμα) 9.

παράπτωμα (nom.sing.neut.of παράπτωμα, subject of ἔστιν understood) 585.

αὐτῶν (gen.pl.masc.of αὐτός, possession) 16.
πλοῦτος (nom.sing.masc.of πλοῦτος, predicate nominative) 1050.
κόσμου (gen.sing.masc.of κόσμος, possession) 360.
καὶ (continuative conjunction) 14.
τὸ (nom.sing.neut.of the article in agreement with ἥττημα) 9.

#3992 ἥττημα (nom.sing.neut.of ἥττημα, subject of ἐστιν, understood).

King James Version

diminishing - Rom.11:12.
fault - 1 Cor.6:7.

Revised Standard Version

failure - Rom.11:12.
defeat - 1 Cor.6:7.

Meaning: Cf. ἡττάομαι (#4400) and ἥττων (#4208). Defeat, failure, loss, diminution of status. With reference to Israel's lapse when she rejected the Messiah - Rom.11:12; loss of spiritual blessing caused by litigation between Christians - 1 Cor.6:7.

αὐτῶν (gen.pl.masc.of αὐτός, possession) 16.
πλοῦτος (nom.sing.masc.of πλοῦτος, predicate nominative) 1050.
ἐθνῶν (gen.pl.neut.of ἔθνος, possession) 376.
πόσῳ (instru.sing.neut.of πόσος, measure) 603.
μᾶλλον (adverbial) 619.
τὸ (nom.sing.neut.of the article in agreement with πλήρωμα) 9.
πλήρωμα (nom.sing.neut.of πλήρωμα, subject of verb understood) 805.
αὐτῶν (gen.pl.masc.of αὐτός, possession) 16.

Translation - "Now, since their lapse resulted in riches for the world and their loss riches for the Gentiles, how much more will result from their fullness?"

Comment: The verbs are missing but the context is clear that εἰ must be supplied with the indicative to provide a first-class condition in which the protasis condition is true. Paul had just said in versee 11 that Israel's lapse resulted in Gentile salvation. Now (explanatory δὲ) since that is true (εἰ in a first-class condition), the moral lapse of Israel, in rejecting Messiah, resulted in the riches of salvation for the entire world (Rom.8:19-23) and a place for Gentiles in the Body of Christ. These riches will consist, in addition to the spiritual salvation of the elect, both Jew and Gentile, of the rescue of the physical world from the curse of sin. The creation, "made subject to vanity" albeit without its consent, need not wait forever to be "delivered from the bondage of disintegration into the glorious liberty of the children of God" (Rom.8:21).

The deliberative question follows: How much greater will be the riches that flow from Israel's fulfillment? What is this πλήρωμα? It cannot mean the salvation of the individual Jew, since Jews were already included in the Body of

Christ, and that result which flowed from Israel's national rejection had already been realized. It can only mean the salvation of the Jewish nation as a whole - something that will take place when Messiah returns and saves the 144,000 Jews of the remnant, who shall then have fulfilled for them, the physical seed of Abraham, all that God promised to Abraham and David. If Israel is to have no prospect of future national glory, as she enjoys the reign of King David's Greater Son (2 Sam.7:12,13; Lk.1:32,33), then there is no future fulfillment (τὸ πλήρωμα) for her beyond the fullness of salvation for individual elect Jews, who, like Gentiles, are incorporated into the Body of Christ. If this were true, Paul's argument in verse 12 would be without meaning.

All the blessings that are now enjoyed and that are to be enjoyed by a sin-cursed world come from God, the only sovereign Who is able to do anything about our misfortunes, and they come from Him solely because Messiah, the Seed-of-the Woman Serpent Bruiser (Gen.3:15; Heb.2:14), paid the sin debt upon the cross. If a holy God has no way to be gracious that does not compromise His justice, then His judgment must remain in force as He pronounced it in the Garden of Eden. But at the cross "Mercy and truth met together; righteousness and peace kissed each other, as truth (sprang) out of the earth and righteousness (looked) down from heaven" (Psalm 85:10,11). There the Judge of all the earth (John 5:22), because He loved us, found a way to absorb the punishment for sin which we deserved, and He paid the debt in full, with the result that now He is free in total justice to lift the curse from us, since He bore it "in His own body on the tree" (1 Pet.2:24). His crucifixion would not have occurred and the redemption that results from it would not be forthcoming if Israel had not failed. Israel failed officially, but when she did God overruled her failure and found the way to justify those who could never have been justified by the law of Moses (Acts 13:38,39) and to lift from the physical universe the curse that now agonizes it.

Verse 13 - "For I speak to you Gentiles, inasmuch as I am the apostle of the Gentiles, I magnify mine office."

Ὑμῖν δὲ λέγω τοῖς ἔθνεσιν. ἐφ' ὅσον μὲν οὖν εἰμί ἐγὼ ἐθνῶν ἀπόστολος, τὴν διακονίαν μου δοξάζω,

"Now I am speaking to you Gentiles. Inasmuch then as I am an apostle to the Gentiles, I magnify my ministry." . . . RSV

Ὑμῖν (dat.pl.masc.of σύ, indirect object of λέγω) 104.

δὲ (explanatory conjunction) 11.

λέγω (1st.per.sing.pres.act.ind.of λέγω, aoristic) 66.

τοῖς (dat.pl.masc.of the article in agreement with ἔθνεσιν) 9.

ἔθνεσιν (dat.pl.masc.of ἔθνος, in apposition with ὑμῖν) 376.

ἐφ' (preposition with the accusative, degree of measure) 47.

ὅσον (acc.sing.neut.of ὅσος, degree of measure) 660.

μὲν (particle of affirmation) 300.

οὖν (inferential conjunction) 68.

εἰμί (1st.per.sing.pres.ind.of εἰμί, static) 86.

ἐθνῶν (gen.pl.neut.of ἔθνος, description) 376.
ἀπόστολος (nom.sing.masc.of ἀπόστολος, predicate nominative) 844.
τὴν (acc.sing.fem.of the article in agreement with διακονίαν) 9.
διακονίαν (acc.sing.fem.of διακονία, direct object of δοξάζω) 2442.
μου (gen.sing.masc.of ἐγώ, possession) 123.
δοξάζω (1st.per.sing.pres.act.ind.of δοξάζω, present progressive retroactive) 461.

Translation - *"Now I am speaking to you,the Gentiles. In view of the fact, therefore, that I am an apostle to the Gentiles, I am exercising my ministry to its greatest advantage."*

Comment: *Cf.* #660 for other instances of ἐφ' ὅσον. Since Paul, a Hebrew Christian, had a special commission to carry the gospel to the Gentiles, he was in a strong position to take full advantage of his ministry, in a way that he explains in

Verse 14 - *"If by any means I may provoke to emulation them which are my flesh, and might save some of them."*

εἰ πως παραζηλώσω μου τὴν σάρκα καὶ σώσω τινὰς ἐξ αὐτῶν.

". . . in order to make my fellow Jews jealous, and thus save some of them." . . .
                                                                                  RSV

εἰ (conditional particle in a third-class condition) 337.
πῶς (interrogative conjunction) 3700.
παραζηλώσω (1st.per.sing.pres.act.subj.of παραζηλόω, third-class condition) 3976.
μου (gen.sing.masc.of ἐγώ, relationship) 123.
τὴν (acc.sing.fem.of the article in agreement with σάρκα) 9.
σάρκα (acc.sing.fem.of σάρξ, direct object of παραζηλώσω) 1202.
καὶ (adjunctive conjunction joining verbs) 14.
σώσω (1st.per.sing.aor.act.subj.of σώζω, third-class condition) 109.
τινὰς (acc.pl.masc.of τίς, indefinite pronoun, direct object of σώσω) 486.
ἐξ (preposition with the partitive genitive) 19.
αὐτῶν (gen.pl.masc.of αὐτός, partitive) 16.

Translation - *". . . if somehow I may make my own flesh and blood jealous, and save some of them."*

Comment: εἰ with the subjunctive in a third-class condition is not a "vulgarism" as Radermacher (*New Testament Greek,* 162, as cited in Robertson, *Grammar,* 1017) charges, since it is classic usage and is also found in the κοινή and later writers. *Cf.*#3700 for εἰ πως,now with the optative,now with the future indicative or subjunctive. The context must measure the degree of doubt, though in no case is there certitude. Here Paul does not know, of course, who, if any of the Jews will respond to his gospel. He only says that his ministry is particularly significant since he is the Apostle, specifically charged with the responsibility of evangelistic work among the Gentiles. Thus he, a Hebrew Christian, who is devoting his life to evangelizing Gentiles, is in a strong position to arouse in unsaved Jews a national jealousy which he can turn to advantage. When they see their Messiah, Jesus Christ, being offered as Saviour to Gentiles, they may wish to know why they cannot enjoy His salvation too.

The Jews can escape this feeling of jealousy if they are assured from their own study of the Old Testament that Jesus' claim to Messiahship is not well founded. But after hearing Paul connect the prophecies and covenants of the Old Testament with the events in the life, death, burial and resurrection of Jesus, they were apt to find it difficult to refute Paul's message that Jesus, the Jewish Messiah, first offered to them, was now being offered to the Gentiles.

Thus, in this way Paul hoped that some would be saved.

I have translated μου τὴν σάρκα as we often hear it in the modern idiom - "my own flesh and blood."

Verse 15 - "For if the casting away of them be the reconciling of the world what shall the receiving of them be, but life from the dead?"

εἰ γὰρ ἡ ἀποβολὴ αὐτῶν καταλλαγὴ κόσμου, τίς ἡ πρόσλημψις εἰ μὴ ζωὴ ἐκ νεκρῶν;

"For if their rejection means the reconciliation of the world, what will their acceptance mean but life from the dead?" . . . RSV

εἰ (conditional particle in a first-class condition) 337.
γὰρ (inferential conjunction) 105.
ἡ (nom.sing.fem.of the article in agreement with ἀποβολὴ) 9.
ἀποβολὴ (nom.sing.fem.of ἀποβολή, subject of verb understood) 3727.
αὐτῶν (gen.pl.masc.of αὐτός, designation) 16.
καταλλαγὴ (nom.sing.fem.of καταλλαγή, predicate nominative) 3900.
κόσμου (gen.sing.masc.of κόσμος, description) 360.
τίς (nom.sing.neut.of τίς, interrogative pronoun, predicate nominative) 281.
ἡ (nom.sing.fem.of the article in agreement with πρόσλημψις) 9.

#3993 πρόσλημψις (nom.sing.fem.of πρόσλημψις, subject of verb understood).

King James Version

receiving - Rom.11:15.

Revised Standard Version

acceptance - Rom.11:15.

Meaning: A combination of πρός (#197) and λῆψις (#4596). The act of receiving; reception; receiving. With reference to the elect Jews into the Body of Christ - Rom.11:15.

εἰ (conditional particle in an elliptical condition) 337.

μή (negative particle in a first-class condition) 87.

ζωή (nom.sing.fem.of ζωή, subject of verb understood) 668.

ἐκ (preposition with the ablative of separation) 19.

νεκρῶν (abl.pl.masc.of νεκρός, separation) 749.

Translation - "So since their repudiation has resulted in a reconciliation of the world of equal value, what is their reception if it is not life from the dead?"

Comment: The copulas are not needed and their omission is in line with classic idiom and should not be regarded as ellipsis. *Cf.* #3900 for the concept of an even trade. If when God cast aside national Israel, temporarily, He gained an equal value in the reconciliation of the world unto Himself through the redemption of the Messiah, rejected by His own people (John 1:11) and lifted up on a cross, then it follows that any future restoration of Israel, individually or nationally, in whole or in part, is a marginal asset, like life out of death.

God's assets were not diminished when Israel crucified Jesus. What He lost in Israel He gained in the Gentile Bride of Christ. Now as Israel returns in repentance and faith, every such case of regeneration is a marginal increment. The verse must be seen in the light of accounting procedures and principles. The future restoration of the nation of Israel in keeping with God's promises to Abraham and David will be still greater profit.

Paul resorts to analogy in

Verse 16 - "For if the firstfruit be holy, the lump is also holy; and if the root be holy, so are the branches."

εἰ δὲ ἡ ἀπαρχὴ ἀγία, καὶ τὸ φύραμα. καὶ εἰ ἡ ῥίζα ἀγία, καὶ οἱ κλάδοι.

"If the dough offered as first fruits is holy, so is the whole lump; and if the root is holy, so are the branches." . . . RSV

εἰ (conditional particle in a first-class condition) 337.

δὲ (explanatory conjunction) 11.

ἡ (nom.sing.fem.of the article in agreement with ἀπαρχὴ) 9.

ἀπαρχὴ (nom.sing.fem.of ἀπαρχή, subject of the verb understood) 3946.

ἀγία (nom.sing.fem.of ἄγιος, predicate adjective) 84.

καὶ (adjunctive conjunction joining nouns) 14.

τὸ (nom.sing.neut.of the article in agreement with φύραμα) 9.

φύραμα (nom.sing.neut.of φύραμα, subject of the verb understood) 3968.

καὶ (continuative conjunction) 14.

εἰ (conditional particle in a first-class condition) 337.

ἡ (nom.sing.fem.of the article in agreement with ῥίζα) 9.

ῥίζα (nom.sing.fem.of ῥίζα, subject of the verb understood) 293.

ἀγία (nom.sing.fem.of ἄγιος, predicate adjective) 84.

καὶ (adjunctive conjunction joining nouns) 14.

οἱ (nom.pl.masc.of the article in agreement with κλάδοι) 9.

κλάδοι (nom.pl.masc.of κλάδος, subject of the verb understood) 1071.

Translation - "Now since the firstfruit is holy so also is the lump; and since the root is holy so also are the branches."

Comment: These are first-class conditions as the context makes clear. As in verse 15 the absence of the copulas does not indicate ellipsis. The lump of dough from which the firstfruit was taken is holy. This is obvious since it produced the firstfruit which, in the protasis is declared holy. An unholy lump of dough could not produce a holy firstfruit. In the second condition the order of proof is reversed. The assumption that   the root is holy is found in the protasis. The conclusion therefore is that the branches, which have the root as their source are also holy. Holy dough produces holy firstfruit and holy roots produce holy branches. It is probable that Paul's reference to dough (τὸ φύραμα) is connected with Numbers 15:20 where we have ἀπαρχὴν φυράματος ὑμῶν ἄρτον, ἀπαρχὴν ἀφόριεῖτε αὐτό (LXX) - "You shall offer up a cake of the first of your dough for an heave offering. . . κ.τ.λ." In the passage φυράματος (dough) is an ablative of source, indicating that the dough is the source of the "cake" (ἀπαρχὴν) which is translated "first fruits" in the KJV. This is in line with Paul's statement that if the first production from the lump is holy the lump also is holy.

Further penetration into our verse centers our attention upon the word ἀπαρχή, translated "first fruits." (#3946). We know the relation between the first fruit and the lump of dough from which it is produced, and the relation between the root and the branches from which it grows. Now what is meant by ἀπαρχή and what are the roots and branches? (#'s 293 and 1071).

ἀπαρχή is used in the New Testament to refer to the new nature of the regenerated believer. Further the source of τὴν ἀπαρχὴν is said to be τοῦ πνεύματος - "those who have the first fruit which has the Spirit as its source" (Rom.8:23). In James 1:18 we learn that the "Father of lights" regenerated us "with the word of truth," His purpose being that "we should be a kind of firstfruits of His creatures." The Jewish remnant of Revelation 14:4 is said to be the first fruits (ἀπαρχή) to God and to the Lamb. Jesus, our resurrected Lord is said to be the "first fruits of those who have been asleep" (ἀπαρχὴ τῶν κεκοιμημένων) in 1 Cor.15:20. *Cf.* also 1 Cor.15:23 where the word is used absolutely and identified with Χριστός. Epaenatus was the first convert in Asia (Rom.16:5) and the family of Stephanas, the first fruits of the gospel in Achaia (1 Cor.16:15). In 2 Thess.2:13 ἀπαρχήν underlies the English "salvation" of the KJV, which is essentially the same thought that we found in Romans 8:23 and James 1:18.

So much for the research. Now let us apply it.

Our Lord Jesus Christ is the first fruit of the lump of dough. He is holy so the lump that produced Him is also holy. What produced Him? Why was He born? The answer must be the Abrahamic covenant. God promised the patriarch that in him *and in his seed* all the nations would be blessed. It took a great many miracles to fulfill this promise. First Isaac, the miracle baby was born. Then throughout the history of the descendants of Abraham, God miraculously delivered them again and again from the extermination which Satan was determined to impose upon them. If the family of Abraham, as it descended through Isaac, could be destroyed, neither the Abrahamic covenant could be implemented, with its promise of universal blessing through Jesus Christ, nor could the Adamic covenant, with its promise that the "seed of the woman" would destroy the kingdom of Satan (Gen.3:15; Heb.2:14). Thus Genesis 3:15 is a part of the holy lump from which our Lord, the first fruit, would come, just as the Abrahamic covenant was (Gen.12:1-3; 15:1-21). Abraham lied to an Egyptian Pharaoh about his wife and risked losing her to a pagan. But God intervened and the Pharaoh lost interest in her, despite her seductive beauty. Then Abraham took matters into his own hands and married Hagar, who produced Ishmael, but God, after waiting thirteen years to teach Abraham a lesson, overruled his secular humanism. The Epyptians enslaved the Israelites for more than two hundred years, but God delivered them, in keeping with His covenant promise to Abraham, Isaac and Jacob. Pharaoh pursued with his war chariots and would have killed them all or taken them back to slavery, as Satan tried to drown them in the Red Sea, but they danced and sang,

> Sing unto the Lord, for He hath triumphed gloriously;
> The horse and his rider hath He thrown into the sea.

They would have died from poisoned water, but God provided the tree that removed the poison and made the waters of Marah potable (Exod .15:22-25). They would have starved, but God sent quails for temporary relief and manna for the next thirty-eight years (Ex.16:1-36).   They would have perished for water, but God told Moses to smite the rock in Horeb and they drank from its life-giving flow (Exodus 17; Numbers 20). After thirty-eight years of wandering in the desert they were brought across Jordan to the land which had been promised in the covenant. Abraham, their father had sojourned there, nearly five hundred years before, living in tents. He was content to see the land which some day he and his children will own, even though he did not own it then, because he looked for a city, which has foundations, the builder and maker of which is God (Heb.11:9,10). But God gave it to his children, as Joshua drove out the pagans. They lived in its cities and built some of their own. But they backslid and turned to Baal, Moloch and Astarte. If God's promise to Abraham had been contingent upon Israel's merits they would have perished at the hands of their enemies, who surrounded them on every side, but it was unconditioned, and God, in self defense delivered them to the Babylonians for seventy years. But He brought back a remnant. Subject to Gentile rule under the Medes, Persians, Greeks and Romans, they finally saw and heard Jesus of Nazareth, the fulfillment of the promises of God to Adam and Eve and to Abraham and Sarah, but they could not grasp His message, nor accept His claim to Messiahship and they were scattered north and east and south and west, where for the next 1878 years (from A.D. 70 to 1948) they were driven into the ghettos, subjected to pogroms and at the command of Adolf Hitler incinerated in the gas furnaces. Six million died in a decade, but the nation survives. The lump from which they came, the covenants which God made with Adam and Abraham, are holy (that is, wholly dedicated to the purposes of the sovereign God) and all the first fruits which derive from those covenants are also holy, and dedicated to the purposes of the sovereign God. The lump produced the Messiah, Who gave full proof of His Messiahship when He arose from the dead (1 Cor.15:20 ,23). The lump has produced the saints of God (Rom.8:23; James 1:18). They too are holy because God has wholly dedicated them to the fulfillment of His sovereign purpose (Eph.2:10; Rom.8:28-39). And the lump will still produce the 144,000 elect Jews, 12,000 from each tribe, who will form the nucleus of the nation Israel (Rev.7:1-8; 14:4). God has not yet made Abraham's seed as numerous as the sands of the sea and the stars of the heavens. Three and one-half million walked through the Red Sea at the Exodus. These all died in the wilderness in the next forty years, except those under twenty at Kadesh Barnea. The nation reached her highest population in the reign of Solomon. They may have numbered twenty million at one time. Scattered to the ends of the earth in the Diaspora in A.D.70, they fled south to Spain and Africa, east to the Orient and north and west to Europe. They divided culturally between the Ashkenazim, who speak Yiddish and lived in northern and western Europe, and the Sephardim, who lived in Spain, Portugal and/or Asia, some of whom came to North America in the 18th and 19th centuries. The Ashkenazim are generally considered culturally superior to their Sephardic brethren. They occupy most of the positions of leadership in Israel at present, although birth rates among the Sephardim are higher and they now outnumber the Ashkenazim. There is some evidence among close observers that the cultural and economic superiority of the Northwest European Jews in Israel, and the numerical superiority of the Sephardim is a source of some discord which may affect the short-run development of the nation.

When Hitler rose to power in the decade following World War I there were about sixteen million Jews in the world. Six million died at the hands of the Nazis. The present world population is in excess of twelve million, between three and four million of whom live in Palestine, with at least that many more in New York City. Thus God has not yet done for Abraham what He has promised to do. It is for demographers with their slide rules to estimate how many sons and daughters of Abraham will result from one thousand years of perfect peace and prosperity as the 144,000, saved on the day of the Second Coming of Messiah, represent Him in the Kingdom of the Heavens.

In Rom.16:5 and 1 Cor.16:15, Paul uses ἀπαρχή in an accommodated sense. Epaenatus and Stephanas and his family may be called "the first fruits of first fruits" in Rome and Corinth respectively, as they were the first whom Paul led to Christ in his ministry in those two cities.

Thus the lump of holy dough has already produced the cakes which are presented to the Lord as a "heave offering." Our Lord, risen from the dead was One. Every time another soul is saved, we have another cake of holy dough, for were it not for the faith of Abraham and God's promise to Him we would not be saved (Gal.3:7). And the nation Israel is yet to be regenerated to become another cake of holy dough.

We have yet to deal with the figure of the root and the branches. This is the subject of verses 17-24.

Verse 17 - "And if some of the branches be broken off, and thou, being a wild olive tree, wert graffed in among them, and with them partakest of the root and fatness of the olive tree, . . . "

Εἰ δέ τινες τῶν κλάδων ἐξεκλάσθησαν, σὺ δὲ ἀγριέλαιος ὢν ἐνεκεντρίσθης ἐν αὐτοῖς καὶ συγκοινωνὸς τῆς ῥίζης τῆς πιότητος τῆς ἐλαίας ἐγένου, . . .

"But if some of the branches were broken off, and you, a wild olive shoot, were grafted in their place to share the richess of the olive tree, . . . " . . . RSV

Εἰ (conditional particle in a second-class contrary to fact condition) 337.
δὲ (adversative conjunction) 11.
τινες (nom.pl.masc.of τις, indefinite pronoun, subject of ἐξεκλάσθησαν) 486.
τῶν (gen.pl.masc.of the article in agreement with κλάδων) 9.
κλάδων (gen.pl.masc.of κλάδος, partitive genitive) 1071.

#3994 ἐξεκλάσθησαν (3d.per.pl.aor.pass.ind.of ἐκκλάω, in a second-class condition).

King James Version

break off - Rom.11:17,19,20.

Revised Standard Version

break off - Rom.11:17,19,20.

Meaning: A combination of ἐκ (#19) and κλάω (#1121); to break off; to break out of. With reference to breaking branches off of a tree or bush - Rom.11:17,19,20.

σὺ (nom.sing.masc.of σύ, subject of ἐνεκεντρίσθης) 104.
δὲ (adjunctive conjunction joining clauses in a second-class condition) 11.

#3995 ἀγριέλαιος (nom.sing.masc.of ἀγριέλαιος, predicate nominative).

King James Version

olive tree which is wild - Rom.11:24.
wild olive tree - Rom.11:17.

Revised Standard Version

wild olive shoot - Rom.11:17.
wild olive tree - Rom.11:24.

Meaning: A combination of ἄγριος (#269) and ἐλαία (#1341). Hence, a wild olive tree. Tristram, *Natural History of the Bible,* 377, as cited in Thayer, p.9, says, "The wild olive must not be confounded with the Oleaster or Oil Tree." Smith, *A Dictionary of Greek and Roman Antiquities,* 317, associates it with κότινος and says, "It is a wild sort of olive tree, differing in some respects from the domesticated olive, as crabs do from apples." Distinguished from καλλιέλαιος (# 4001) in Rom.11:24. In analogy, it is applied to the Gentile Christian - Rom.11:17.

ὤν (pres.part.nom.sing.masc.of εἰμί, adverbial, concessive) 86.

#3996 ἐνεκεντρίσθης (2d.per.sing.1st.aor.pass.ind.of ἐγκεντρίζω, in a second-class condition).

King James Version

graff in - Rom.11:17,19,23,23.
graff into - Rom.11:24,24.

Revised Standard Version

graff in - Rom.11:17,19,23,23.
graff into - Rom.11:24,24.

Meaning: A combination of ἐν (#80) and κεντρίζω - "to stimulate." Hence, to cut into, in order to engraft a scion; to inoculate; graft in. Only in Romans 11:17,19, 23,23,24,24 of the Gentile Christians who are made a part of the program for which Israel's Messianic program was designed. They are likened to a wild scion which is engrafted into a cultivated plant.

ἐν (preposition with the locative, with plural pronouns, association) 80.
αὐτοῖς (loc.pl.masc.of αὐτός, association) 16.
καί (adjunctive conjunction joining nouns) 14.

#3997 συγκοινωνὸς (nom.sing.masc.of συγκοινωνός, predicate nominative).

King James Version

companion - Rev.1:9.
partaker - 1 Cor.9:23.
partake - Rom.11:17; Phil.1:7.

Revised Standard Version

share - Rom.11:17; 1 Cor.9:23; Rev.1:9.
partaker - Phil.1:7.

Meaning: A combination of σύν (#1542) and κοιωνωνός (#1470). Hence, a partaker with; fellow companion; joint partner. Followed by a genitive of description in Rom.11:17; 1 Cor.9:23; Phil.1:7. Followed by ἐν and a locative of sphere - Rev.1:9.

τῆς (gen.sing.fem.of the article in agreement with ῥίζης) 9.
ῥίζης (gen.sing.fem.of ῥίζα, description) 293.
τῆς (gen.sing.fem.of the article in agreement with πιότητος) 9.

#3998 πιότητος (gen.sing.fem.of πιότης, description).

King James Version

fatness - Rom.11:17.

Revised Standard Version

richness - Rom.11:17.

Meaning: Cf. πίων - "fat." Hence, fatness, richness. With reference to the life giving qualities of a tree. Followed by an ablative of source - Rom.11:17.
τῆς (abl.sing.fem.of the article in agreement with ἐλαίας) 9.
ἐλαίας (abl.sing.fem.of ἐλαία, source) 1341.
ἐγένου (2d.per.sing.2d.aor.mid.ind.of γίνομαι, second-class condition) 113.

Translation - "But if some of the branches were broken off and you, although a wild olive branch, were grafted in with them, and you made yourself a fellow participant of the nourishment from the olive tree, . . . "

Comment: We have here a second-class condition with secondary tenses in the protasis (ἐξεκλάσθησαν, ἐνεκεντρίσθης and ἐγένου) and a present imperative in the apodosis (verse 18). The student should keep in mind that although a second-class contrary to fact condition ". . . states a thing as if it were untrue or unreal," it may "in actual fact be true." Note this in Luke 7:39. Jesus was a prophet and He did know what sort of woman she was, but the Pharisee stated his proposition as though both the premise in the protasis and the conclusion in the apodosis were false. So it is here. (Mantey, *Manual*, 289).

Some of the branches had been broken out, although Paul implies with his second-class condition that they had not. The Roman Christians had in fact been grafted in and they were, in fact, partaking of the life-giving nourishment of the Jewish olive tree. Not all of Abraham's descendants were still under the covenant. Witness the Pharisees to whom Jesus spoke the words of John 8:44.

σὺ is emphatic. The concessive participle ὤν also indicates that Paul was being deprecatory. The cultural background of the Roman Christians to whom Paul wrote this epistle could not be favourably compared with that of the Jews. They had come out of paganism and by the grace of God had been called into membership in the Body of Christ. But they were only wild, inferior, boorish branches. Despite this fact they had been engrafted by the Holy Spirit into fellowship with the Hebrew Christians who made up the first members of the Body of Christ. αὐτοῖς refers to these Hebrew Christians.

When a Gentile in the House of Commons made a derogatory remark about Benjamin Disraeli, the Prime Minister, the Jew responded, "My ancestors were writing music, poetry and law when yours were running naked through the moors of northern Europe in quest of the wild boar." The Jews who rejected Jesus had a rich history of cultural refinement (Rom.9:4,5). And not all of them rejected their Messiah.

Paul is making Judaism, with its vested interest in the Abrahamic covenant, the root of the Christian system, as indeed it is. Witness the preaching of Jesus and the Apostles as they tied the message of the Old Testament to the history and philosophy of the New. The Judeo-Christian tradition is in line with this. The gospel was "to the Jew first and also to the Greek" (Rom. 1:16) and the advantage of prior position was enjoyed by the Jews (Rom.3:1). Paul is about to place the Gentile Christian is proper perspective *vis a vis* the Jew.

Verse 18 - *"Boast not thyself against the branches. But if thou boast, thou bearest not the root, but the root thee."*

μὴ κατακαυχῶ τῶν κλάδων. εἰ δὲ κατακαυχᾶσαι, οὐ σὺ τὴν ῥίζαν βαστάζεις ἀλλὰˋ ῥίζα σέ.

_."*. . . do not boast over the branches. If you do boast, remember it is not you that support the root, but the root that supports you."* . . . RSV

μὴ (negative particle with the imperative) 87.

#3999 κατακαυχῶ (2d.per.sing.pres.mid.impv. of κατακαυχάομαι, command).

King James Version

boast against - Rom.11:18,18.
glory - James 3:14.
rejoice against - James 2:13.

Revised Standard Version

boast over - Rom.11:18,18.
triumph over - James 2:13.
boast - James 3:14.

Meaning: A combination of κατά (#98) and καυχάομαι (#3847). Hence, to boast against or exult over another; in the middle voice to declare oneself superior to another. Gentile Christians should not consider themselves superior to Jews - Rom.11:18,18. Mercy is immune to judgment - James 2:13; error should not exult itself above truth - James 3:14.

τῶν (gen.pl.masc.of the article in agreement with κλάδων) 9.
κλάδων (gen.pl.masc.of κλάδος, description) 1071.
εἰ (conditional particle in a first-class condition) 337.
δὲ (causal conjunction) 11.
κατακαυχᾶσαι (2d.per.sing.pres.mid.ind.of κατακαυχάομαι, first-class condition) 3999.
οὐ (negative particle with the indicative) 130.
σὺ (nom.sing.masc.of σύ, subject of βαστάζεις, emphatic) 104.
τὴν (acc.sing.fem.of the article in agreement with ῥίζαν) 9.
ῥίζαν (acc.sing.fem.of ῥίζα, direct object of βαστάζεις) 293.
βαστάζεις (2d.per.sing.pres.act.ind.of βαστάζω, static) 306.

ἀλλά (alternative conjunction) 342.

ἡ (nom.sing.fem.of the article in agreement with ῥίζα) 9.

ῥίζα (nom.sing.fem.of ῥίζα, subject of βαστάζει, understood) 293.

σέ (acc.sing.masc.of σύ, direct object of βαστάζει, understood) 104.

Translation - "Stop boasting about your advantage over the branches, because as you boast remember that you do not bear the root, but the root bears you."

Comment: μή with the present imperative means "do not continue to boast" or "stop boasting." This indicates that the Roman Christians were congratulating themselves that God had chosen to eliminate national Israel from His program in order that the Gentiles might be saved. This is precisely what amillenialism says. The view that God held Israel to account for the murder of His Son to the point that He abrogated His promise to Abraham, as that promise relates to a future for the nation, and that the promises to the patriarchs and to King David are to be interpreted allegorically - this is the essence of amillenialism. The Gentile Christians in Rome apparently were entertaining this error and Paul demands that they abandon it. δέ is causal in one of the few contexts where the causal is demanded. The thought is, "Stop boasting, because, since you are boasting (first-class condition) I must remind you that you did not produce the root. It was the other way around." God did not call out the Gentiles, enter into covenant relations with them and provide that the Jews might also be included. God did call Abraham and vouchsafe to him His promise.

The root in the analogy stands in relation to the branches as the lump of dough did to the first fruit loaf of the heave offering. God's promises to Adam and Eve and to Abraham and Sarah are the Old Testament roots from which the tree with its branches have grown. The Gentiles are branches, originally inferior from a cultural point of view to the natural branches, the Jews, who were prepared for their role in the economy of God by the advantages listed in Romans 9:3,4. What Gentile can point back in history to "the adoption, and the glory, and the covenants, and the giving of the law, and the service of God, and the promises?" What Gentile can point to his "fathers" as the patriarchs of a line that produced the Messiah, the Hope of the World?

The Hebrew Christians are not better, as members of the Body of Christ, than their Gentile brothers and sisters in Christ, for in Him, all who believe are equal in that all have the imputed righteousness of Christ. But Gentile Christians should always remember that when God brought salvation to the world, He chose to do so by calling out a man with whom He entered into covenant relations and from whose line He produced a nation that, for all of its backslidings, produced the Philosopher-King that Plato dreamed about but could not produce. Gentile Christians should remember that in His incarnation, our Lord was a Jew.

Thus Paul keeps the root/branch relationship straight just as he had properly related the holy dough to the holy loaf of bread.

That God could cut out a natural olive branch and engraft an inferior wild olive branch into the stock, with the result that the engrafted branch receives the same rich nourishment from the root that the natural branches enjoy, is a cause of humble rejoicing, not for antiSemitic hubris.

In verse 19 Paul anticipates the argument of the Gentile Christians, states it and lays the ground for his rebuttal.

Verse 19 - "Thou wilt say then, The branches were broken off, that I might be graffed in."

ἐρεῖς οὖν, Ἐξεκλάσθησαν κλάδοι ἵνα ἐγὼ ἐγκεντρισθῶ.

"You will say, 'Branches were broken off so that I might be grafted in." . . .
RSV

ἐρεῖς (2d.per.sing.fut.act.ind.of εἴρω, predictive) 155.
οὖν (inferential conjunction) 68.
ἐξεκλάσθησαν (3d.per.pl.aor.pass.ind.of ἐκκλάω, constative) 3994.
κλάδοι (nom.pl.masc.of κλάδος, subject of ἐξεκλάσθησαν) 1071.
ἵνα (conjunction with the subjunctive in a final clause) 114.
ἐγὼ (nom.sing.masc.of ἐγώ, subject of ἐγκεντρισθῶ) 123.
ἐγκεντρισθῶ (1st.per.sing.aor.pass.subj.of ἐγκεντρίζω, purpose) 3996.

Translation - "So you are going to say, 'Branches were broken out in order that I might be engrafted.' "

Comment: The implication of the Gentile argument is that God prefers Gentiles to Jews, and that He was forced to choose between the two. This is the force of the purpose clause, as though God could not have grafted in the wild olive branches without first of all removing the natural branches. It is true that there would have been no redemption for the race if God had not decreed the plan of redemption as He did. If the Jews had not rejected Jesus, all of Adam's race, Jew and Gentile would have been sent to hell, for in that event our Lord would not have paid our sin debt. Thus a Jewish Messiah, rejected by His own people was nailed on a cross where He died for the sins of Israel and also of the Gentiles. The result is that God can now save both Jews and Gentiles, through the sacrifice of His Son. That Jewish natural branches were set aside temporarily in order that Gentile wild branches might be grafted in does not mean that in election God showed a preference for Gentiles over Jews.

Paul replies that if the Jew, with all of his natural advantages (Rom.9:3,4) did not believe, in how much more danger is the Gentile who has only faith?

Verse 20 - "Well: because of unbelief they were broken off, and thou standest by faith. Be not highminded, but fear."

καλῶς. τῇ ἀπιστίᾳ ἐξεκλάσθησαν, σὺ δὲ τῇ πίστει ἕστηκας. μὴ ὑψηλὰ φρόνει, ἀλλὰ φοβοῦ.

"That is true. They were broken off because of their unbelief, but you stand fast only through faith. So do not become proud, but stand in awe." . . . RSV

καλῶς (adverbial) 977.

τῇ (instru.sing.fem.of the article in agreement with ἀπιστίᾳ) 9.

ἀπιστίᾳ (instru.sing.fem.of ἀπίστια, cause) 1103.

ἐξεκαλάσθησαν (3d.per.pl.aor.pass.ind.of ἐκκλάω, constative) 3994.

σὺ (nom.sing.masc.of σύ, subject of ἕστηκας, emphatic) 104.

δὲ (continuative conjunction) 11.

τῇ (instru.sing.fem.of the article in agreement with πίστει) 9.

πίστει (instru.sing.fem.of πίστις, means) 728.

ἕστηκας (2d.per.sing.perf.act.ind.of ἵστημι, intensive) 180.

μὴ (negative particle with the imperative, in a prohibition) 87.

ὑφηλὰ (acc.pl.neut.of ὑφηλός, direct object of φρόνει) 358.

φρόνει (2d.per.sing.pres.act.impv.of φρονέω, prohibition) 1212.

ἀλλὰ (alternative conjunction) 342.

φοβοῦ (2d.per.sing.pres.mid.impv.of φοβέομαι, command) 101.

Translation - "Indeed! Because of unbelief they were broken off, and you have been standing by faith. Stop regarding yourself so highly, but always be afraid."

Comment: *Cf.* Mk.12:32 for καλῶς in the sense of "I agree." There is a little touch of irony in it here in Romans 11:20. Paul agrees with his imaginery critics in order to pursue the point. The natural branches (the Jews) were cut out of the tree because of lack of faith (Heb.4:2). Israel demanded Messiah's death because they did not believe that Jesus was, in fact, their Messiah, despite His evidence, both in word and deed. Note how He lost His crowd the day after He fed the five thousand because of the theology which He preached in John 6. (John 6:66-68).

σὺ is emphatic. *"You,* you gained your position and as a result, you are now standing (perfect tense in ἕστηκας) by faith." The inference is that the Gentile Christian is not morally superior to the outcast Jew. Christians are not such because of moral excellence or intellectual achievement. Salvation is not character or good works. It is by faith. Now Paul calls upon the Roman Christians to stop being conceited (present imperative with μή in φρόνει). On the contrary they are ordered to continue in humiltiy and fear.

Why should they fear?

Verse 21 - "For if God spared not the natural branches, take heed lest he also spare not thee."

εἰ γὰρ ὁ θεὸς τῶν κατὰ φύσιν κλάδων οὐκ ἐφείσατο, οὐδὲ σοῦ φείσεται.

"For if God did not spare the natural branches, neither will he spare you." . . .
                                                                                    RSV

εἰ (conditional particle in a second-class contrary to fact condition) 337.

γὰρ (causal conjunction) 105.

ὁ (nom.sing.masc.of the article in agreement with θεὸς) 9.

θεὸς (nom.sing.masc.of θεός, subject of ἐφείσατο) 124.

τῶν (gen.pl.masc.of the article in agreement with κλάδων) 9.

κατὰ (preposition with the accusative, standard) 98.

φύσιν (acc.sing.fem.of φύσις, standard) 3811.

κλάδων (gen.pl.masc.of κλάδος, description) 1071.

οὐκ (negative particle with the indicative) 130.

ἐφείσατο (3d.per.sing.aor.mid.ind.of φείδομαι, constative) 3533.

οὐδὲ (disjunctive particle) 452.

σοῦ (gen.sing.masc.of σύ description) 104.

φείσεται (3d.per.sing.fut.mid.ind.of φείδομαι, predictive) 3533.

Translation - *"Because if God did not spare the natural branches, neither will He spare you."*

Comment: γὰρ is causal, as Paul explains why the Gentile Christian should fear. It is because God did not spare the natural branches of the olive tree. The first-class condition assumes as true the premise in the protasis. God did indeed cut out the natural branches because they had no faith (Heb.4:2).

At first glance there appears to be a flaw in Paul's logic. The natural branches (unsaved Jews) were cut out because they had no faith. But Paul had just said in verse 20 that the wild olive branches (Gentile Christians) had taken their place in the economy of God and thus were standing by faith. So the difference is that the Christians had faith while the Jews did not. Can a Christian be repudiated by God if he has faith? If so, this is counter to all that Paul teaches elsewhere. We must, then draw the conclusion that when Paul warns the Gentile Christians that they may be cut out, he is not talking about a loss of their salvation. God will not be indifferent to the sinful pride of Christians, who, though they have faith and thus are saved, are not immune from divine punishment if they misunderstand the basis for their standing.   φείσεται (#3533) simply means to spare from punishment, without designating what kind of punishment. Paul is not threatening the Roman saints with the loss of salvation, but he is saying that God will not be indifferent to an attitude such as he described in verse 19. Note the passages (#3533) where the verb is used of sparing the Corinthians further pain, but in a context that has nothing to do with the loss of salvation.

The persons cut out from the Jewish "root" were unlike the Gentile Christians whom Paul is now addressing. The Jews who crucified Christ were unbelievers, despite the fact that they were the physical seed of Abraham; the Roman Christians who accepted Christ were believers, despite the fact that they were born pagans, described in this context as wild branches of the olive tree and therefore inferior. But a respectable pagan should understand why he is saved and not draw unwarranted inferences from the fact, unless he wishes to invite divine punishment.

There is no warning here that the saints may yet be excluded from the Kingdom of God. The passage does not support Arminianism.

Verse 22 - *"Behold therefore the goodness and severity of God: on them which fell, severity; but toward thee, goodness, if thou continue in his goodness: otherwise thou also shalt be cut off."*

ἴδε οὖν χρηστότητα καὶ ἀποτομίαν θεοῦ. ἐπὶ μὲν τοὺς πεσόντας ἀποτομία,
ἐπὶ δὲ σὲ χρηστότης θεοῦ, ἐὰν ἐπιμένῃς τῇ χρηστότητι, ἐπεὶ καὶ σὺ ἐκκοπήσῃ.

*"Note then the kindness and severity of God: severity toward those who have
fallen, but God's kindness to you, provided you continue in his kindness;
otherwise you too will be cut off." . . . RSV*

ἴδε (2d.per.sing.aor.act.impv.of ὁράω, command) 144a.
οὖν (inferential conjunction) 68.
χρηστότητα (acc.sing.masc.of χρηστότης, direct object of ἴδε) 3830.
καὶ (adjunctive conjunction joining nouns) 14.

#**4000** ἀποτομίαν (acc.sing.fem.of ἀποτομία, direct object of ἴδε).

King James Version

severity - Rom.11:22,22.

Revised Standard Version

severity - Rom.11:22,22.

Meaning: Cf. ἀποτέμνω - "to cut off" "to sever." Cf.ἀποτόμως (#4411).
ἀποτομίαν therefore is the characteristic of one who is strict; willing to punish.
Opposed to χρηστότης (#3830) in Rom.11:22,22.

θεοῦ (gen.sing.masc.of θεός, description) 124.
ἐπὶ (preposition with the accusative of extent) 47.
μὲν (particle of affirmation) 300.
τοὺς (acc.pl.masc.of the article in agreement with πεσόντας) 9.
πεσόντας (aor.act.part.acc.pl.masc.of πίπτω, substantival, extent) 187.
ἀποτομία (nom.sing.fem.of ἀποτομία, *oratio variata*) 4000.
ἐπὶ (preposition with the accusative of extent) 47.
δὲ (adversative conjunction) 11.
σὲ (acc.sing.masc.of σύ, extent) 104.
χρηστότης (nom.sing.masc.of χρηστότης, *oratio variata*) 3830.
θεοῦ (gen.sing.masc.of θεός, description) 124.
ἐὰν (conditional particle in a third-class condition) 363.
ἐπιμένῃς (2d.per.sing.pres.act.subj.of ἐπιμένω, third-class condition) 2379.
τῇ (loc.sing.fem.of the article in agreement with χρηστότητι) 9.
χρηστότητι (loc.sing.fem.of χρηστότης, sphere) 3830.
ἐπεὶ (subordinating conjunction) 1281.
καὶ (adjunctive conjunction) 14.
σὺ (nom.sing.masc.of σύ, subject of ἐκκοπήσῃ) 104.
ἐκκοπήσῃ (2d.per.sing.2d.fut.pass.ind.of ἐκκόπτω, predictive) 297.

*Translation - "Observe then divine goodness and severity: to the fallen severity,
but to you divine goodness, if you continue in goodness. Otherwise you too will
be cut off."*

Comment: ἀποτομία and χρηστότης, nominatives with no verb, are examples of *oratio variata*, which is difficult to distinguish from anacoluthon. The third-class condition reverses the usual order of protasis and apodosis. "If you continue in the sphere of God's goodness, His goodness will continue to be extended to you. Otherwise you will be cut off."

This is punishment, indeed, though not eternal damnation. *Cf.* 1 Cor.9:27 and Heb.6:8, in both of which passages ἀδόκιμος (#3818) occurs. *Cf.*#2379 for other instances where ἐπιμένω is followed by a locative of sphere.

Note the connection between God's goodness and His severity. Israel fell because of unbelief and crucified Messiah; thus God is in a position to provide redemption for and grant faith to the Gentile, thus to be good to him, while being severe with those who fell. Israel's fall resulted in the redemption and regeneration of the Gentiles and the promotion and conclusion of the "mystery" (Eph.3:1-11), which is the establishment of the Gentile church.. Israel's unbelief resulted in Gentile faith. God's severity to Israel comes at the same time as His goodness to the church.

Paul has hinted at the possibility that some Gentiles would not continue in faith (verse 22). In verse 23 he openly suggests the possibility, even probability, that Israel will not continue in her unbelief.

Verse 23 - "And they also, if they abide not still in unbelief, shall be graffed in: for God is able to graff them in again."

κἀκεῖνοι δέ ἐὰν μὴ ἐπιμένωσιν τῇ ἀπιστίᾳ, ἐγκεντρισθήσονται, δυνατὸς γὰρ ἐστιν ὁ θεὸς πάλιν ἐγκεντρίσαι αὐτούς.

"And even the others, if they do not persist in their unbelief, will be grafted in, for God has the power to graft them in again." . . . RSV

κἀκεῖνοι (nom.pl.masc.of κἀκεῖνος, subject of ἐγκεντρισθήσονται, emphatic) 1164.

δὲ (continuative conjunction) 11.

ἐὰν (conditional particle in a third-class condition) 363.

μὴ (negative particle with the subjunctive in a third-class condition) 87.

ἐπιμένωσιν (3d.per.pl.pres.act.subj.of ἐπιμένω, in a third-class condition) 2379.

τῇ (loc.sing.fem.of the article in agreement with ἀπιστίᾳ) 9.

ἀπιστίᾳ (loc.sing.fem.of ἀπιστία, sphere) 1103.

ἐγκεντρισθήσονται (3d.per.pl.fut.pass.ind.of ἐγκεντρίζω, predictive) 3996.

δυνατὸς (nom.sing.masc.of δυνατός, predicate adjective) 1311.

γὰρ (causal conjunction) 105.

ἐστιν (3d.per.sing.pres.ind.of εἰμί, static) 86.

ὁ (nom.sing.masc.of the article in agreement with θεὸς) 9.

θεὸς (nom.sing.masc.of θεός, subject of ἐστιν) 124.

πάλιν (adverbial) 355.

ἐγκεντρίσαι (aor.act.inf.of ἐγκεντρίζω, complementary) 3996.

αὐτούς (acc.pl.masc.of αὐτός, direct object of ἐγκεντρίσαι) 16.

Translation - "And even the others, if they do not continue in their unbelief, will be engrafted, because God is able to graft them in again."

Comment: κἀκεῖνοι is ascensive and emphatic. The third-class condition, with ἐάν and the subjunctive in ἐπιμένωσιν in the protasis expresses some doubt as to whether or not the Jews will persist in their unbelief, but if they do not remain obdurate they are assured of their place in the parental stock. The apodosis is certain if they fulfill the condition in the protasis. Paul adds, almost as an afterthought that which is obvious - God is able to perform such an engrafting operation. Note that he puts δυνατός in emphasis. Indeed if God could engraft the Gentiles into the parental stock He can restore the Jew.

This is the thought of

Verse 24 - "For if thou wert cut out of the olive tree which is wild by nature, and wert graffed contrary to nature into a good olive tree, how much more shall these, which be the natural branches, be graffed into their own olive tree?"

εἰ γὰρ σὺ ἐκ τῆς κατὰ φύσιν ἐξεκόπης ἀγριελαίου καὶ παρὰ φύσιν ἐνεκεντρίσθης εἰς καλλιέλαιον, πόσῳ μᾶλλον οὗτοι οἱ κατὰ φύσιν ἐγκεντρισθήσονται τῇ ἰδίᾳ ἐλαίᾳ.

"For if you have been cut from what is by nature a wild olive tree, and grafted, contrary to nature, into a cultivated olive tree, how much more will these natural branches be grafted back into their own olive tree." . . . RSV

εἰ (conditional particle in a second-class condition) 337.

γὰρ (causal conjunction) 105.

σὺ (nom.sing.masc.of σύ, subject of ἐξεκόπης and ἐνεκεντρίσθης) 104.

ἐκ (preposition with the ablative of source) 19.

τῆς (abl.sing.fem. of the article in agreement with ἀγριελαίου) 9.

κατὰ (preposition with the accusative, standard) 98.

φύσιν (acc.sing.fem.of φύσις, standard) 3811.

ἐξεκόπης (2d.per.sing.2d.aor.pass.ind.of ἐκκόπτω, second-class condition) 297.

ἀγριελαίου (abl.sing.fem.of ἀγριέλαιος, source) 3995.

καὶ (adjunctive conjunction joining verbs) 14.

παρὰ (preposition with the accusative, opposition) 154.

φύσιν (acc.sing.fem.of φύσις, opposition) 3811.

ἐνεκεντρίσθης (2d.per.sing.1st.aor.pass.ind.of ἐγκεντρίζω, second-class condition) 3996.

εἰς (preposition with the accusative of extent) 140.

#4001 καλλιέλαιον (acc.sing.masc.of καλλιέλαιος, extent).

King James Version

good olive tree - Rom.11:24.

Revised Standard Version

cultivated olive tree - Rom.11:24.

Meaning: Cf. κάλλος - the Attic form of καλός (#296) plus ἐλεία (#1341). Hence, a beautiful, cultivated olive tree - one which is the object of horticultural care, as opposed to ἀγριέλαιος (#3995) in Rom.11:24.

πόσῳ (instru.sing.neut.of πόσος, measure) 603.

μᾶλλον (adverbial) 619.

οὗτοι (nom.pl.masc.of οὗτος, subject of ἐγκεντρισθήσονται) 93.

οἱ (nom.pl.masc.of the article in agreement with οὗτοι) 9.

κατὰ (preposition with the accusative, standard) 98.

φύσιν (acc.sing.fem.of φύσις, standard) 3811.

ἐγκεντρισθήσονται (3d.per.pl.fut.pass.ind.of ἐγκεντρίζω, deliberative) 3996.

τῇ (loc.sing.fem.of the article in agreement with ἐλαίᾳ) 9.

ἰδίᾳ (loc.sing.fem.of ἴδιος, possessive pronoun, in agreement with ἐλαίᾳ) 778.

ἐλαίᾳ (loc.sing.fem.of ἐλαία, place) 1341.

Translation - "For if you were cut out of an olive tree, wild by nature, and contrary to nature, were grafted into a cultivated olive tree, how much more will these who are natural branches be engrafted into their own olive tree?"

Comment: εἰ ... ἐξεκόπης ... ἐνεκεντρίσθης is a second-class condition, since the secondary tenses are found in the protasis. Remember that it states the premise as though it is false, whereas in fact it may be true. In this case the premise is true. The Gentile Christians were taken from a culture inferior to that of the Jews and grafted into the Judeo-Christian tradition. As Christians they could look back upon a religion tradition far more refined and sophisticated than that from which they came. The Romans Christians had been selected by divine grace from what Paul, in the olive tree analogy, calls a naturally wild and uncultivated tree, far inferior to καλλιέλαιον (#4001). The pagan culture from which the Gentiles came to Christ had none of the advantages that flowed from the Judaistic tradition, which advantages Paul has listed in Romans 3:1,2; 9:4,5.

Nevertheless we Gentile Christians are the scions of Judaism and we enjoy the fullest fruition which is available from the parental root, which is manifest in the first fruits (ἀπαρχή) - in the miracle of regeneration and in the resurrection of the body of our Lord (Rom.8:23; James 1:18; 1 Cor.15:20,23). To be cut out of ἀγριελαίου (#3995) and grafted into καλλιέλαιον (#4001) is a miracle of divine grace and power. Now, since that is already a fact, although Paul states it as if it were not a fact, how much easier will it be for those branches, now cut out, but which are the natural branches to be grafted back into their own olive tree! It is wholly unwarranted to suppose that God has damned the entire Jewish race because of the crimes of the Pharisees in Jerusalem who crucified their Messiah, particularly in view of the fact that the sole purpose for the incarnation of Messiah was the redemption for the race which He accomplished on the cross.

God is under the most sacred and inviolate treaty obligations to Abraham, Isaac, Jacob, Judah and David and His promises to them cannot be abrogated. Paul now procedes to discuss this in more detail.

The Restoration of Israel

(Romans 11:25-36)

Verse 25 - "For I would not, brethren, that ye should be ignorant of this mystery, lest ye should be wise in your own conceits; that blindness in part is happened to Israel, until the fulness of the Gentiles be come in."

Οὐ γὰρ θέλω ἡμᾶς ἀγνοεῖν, ἀδελφοί, τὸ μυστήριον τοῦτο, ἵνα μὴ ἦτε (ἐν) ἑαυτοῖς φρόνιμοι, ὅτι πώρωσις ἀπὸ μέρους τῷ Ἰσραὴλ γέγονεν ἄχρις οὗ τὸ πλήλωμα τῶν ἐθνῶν εἰσέλθῃ,

"*Lest you be wise in your own conceits, I want you to understand this mystery, brethren: a hardening has come upon part of Israel, until the full number of the Gentiles be come in, . . .*" *. . . RSV*

Οὐ (negative particle with the indicative) 130.

γὰρ (inferential conjunction) 105.

θέλω (1st.per.sing.pres.act.ind.of θέλω, aoristic) 88.

ὑμᾶς (acc.pl.masc.of σύ, general reference) 104.

ἀγνοεῖν (pres.act.inf.of ἀγνοέω, noun use, accusative, direct object of θέλω) 2345.

ἀδελφοί (voc.pl.masc.of ἀδελφός, address) 15.

τὸ (acc.sing.neut.of the article in agreement with μυστήριον) 9.

μυστήριον (acc.sing.neut.of μυστήριον, general reference) 1038.

τοῦτο (acc.sing.neut.of οὗτος, in agreement with μυστήριον) 93.

ἵνα (conjunction with the subjunctive, negative purpose) 114.

μὴ (negative particle with the subjunctive) 87.

ἦτε (2d.per.pl.pres.subj.of εἰμί, negative purpose) 86.

ἐν (preposition with the loc.with plural pronouns, association) 80.

ἑαυτοῖς (loc.pl.masc.of ἑαυτοῦ, association) 288.

φρόνιμοι (nom.pl.masc.of φρόνιμος, predicate adjective) 693.

ὅτι (conjunction introducing an object clause in indirect discourse) 211.

πώρωσις (nom.sing.fem.of πώρωσις, subject of γέγονεν) 2109.

ἀπὸ (preposition with the partitive ablative) 70.

μέρους (abl.sing.neut.of μέρος, partitive) 240.

τῷ (dat.sing.masc.of the article in agreement with Ἰσραήλ) 9.

Ἰσραὴλ (dat.sing.masc.of Ἰσραήλ, personal disadvantage) 165.

γέγονεν (3d.per.sing.2d.perf.ind.of γίνομαι, intensive) 113.

ἄχρις (preposition with the genitive, time description) 1517.

οὗ (gen.sing.neut.of ὅς, time description) 65.

τὸ (nom.sing.neut.of the article in agreement with πλήρωμα) 9.

πλήρωμα (nom.sing.neut.of πλήρωμα, subject of εἰσέλλθῃ) 805.

τῶν (gen.pl.neut.of the article in agreement with ἐθνῶν) 9.

ἐθνῶν (gen.pl.neut.of ἔθνος, description) 376.

εἰσέλθῃ (3d.per.sing.2d.aor.subj.of εἰσέρχομαι, indefinite temporal clause) 234.

Translation - "So I do not want you to be ignorant of this mystery, brethren, lest you be unduly impressed with your own erudition, that partial blindness has been visited upon Israel, until such time as the fullness of the Gentiles is accomplished."

Comment: ὑμᾶς, an accusative of general reference with the infinitive ἀγνοεῖν is the object of θέλω. The infinitive in turn has τὸ μυστήριον as its object. *Cf.* #1038 for the use of μυστήριον, particularly as Paul uses it elsewhere in the same sense in which he uses it here. He defines it in Eph.3:3-9, with particular emphasis upon Eph.3:6. Here the μυστήριον does not refer to the Gentile bride of Christ, but to the fact that until such time as that μυστήριον is complete, Israel as a nation will be partially blind. ἀπὸ μέρους is adverbial, defining the verb γέγονεν, not adjectival defining Israel. It is not that a part of Israel is totally blind, while others can see, but that all of Israel is partially blind.

Judaism has a great deal of truth in it. Indeed, when it was properly interpreted as the Apostles, with the guidance of the Holy Spirit, preached   at Pentecost and on later occasions, Judaism has all of the truth needed to guide the sinner home to salvation. It was the misunderstanding of their own Old Testament scriptures that caused the partial blindness. They were, and many still are, blind to the fact that the Christian Saviour, Jesus Christ, is indeed the Jewish Messiah. For ἀπὸ μέρους in this adverbial sense *cf.* 2 Cor.1:14; 2:5; Rom.15:15,24. Note Mk.3:5 for πώρωσις in connection with the Jews.

This partial blindness, or insensibility to God's truth will not always hinder Israel, although it will continue to confuse them until (ἄχρις οὗ, a genitive relative indefinite temporal clause) such time as the program of God will become complete, as that program concerns the Gentile Bride of Christ. This visit to "the Gentiles, to take out of them a people for His name" (Acts 15:14) will be completed at the end of the seven year tribulation period (Rev.10:7). Then Christ will come (1 Cor.15:51) and the 144,000 Jews (Rev.7:1-8) will have their blindness and hardness of heart removed as a nation is born in a day (Isa.66:8; Zech.13,14).

If Israel as a nation, because of her crucifixion of the Messiah, is to be punished eternally and never allowed a place in the economy of God, then Paul's statement that her blindness is only partial and temporary is wrong. Paul should have said that Israel will be totally, not partially, blind forever, not ἄχρις οὗ ... κ.τ.λ. *Cf.* Luke 21:24.

The "times of the Gentiles" when Gentile powers will exercise hegemony over Palestine and "the fullness of the Gentiles" which speaks of the evangelistic program of the Holy Spirit to call out the Body of Christ, are co-terminous. When the fullness of the Gentiles occurs, the times of the Gentiles will cease. Note the perfect tense in γέγονεν - a past partial blinding with durable present results, although not extending forever into the future. The temporal clause is indefinite, as the subjunctive in εἰσέλθῃ indicates, because Paul did not know, nor do we at the moment (June 10,1982) when the last elect soul for whom Christ died, will be effectually called into His body.

Verse 26 - "And so all Israel shall be saved: as it is written, There shall come out of Sion, the Deliverer, and shall turn away ungodliness from Jacob."

καὶ οὕτως πᾶς 'Ισραὴλ σωθήσεται, καθὼς γέγραπται, Ἥξει ἐκ Σιὼν ὁ ῥυόμενος, ἀποστρέφει ἀσεβείας ἀπὸ 'Ιακώβ.

". . . *and so all Israel will be saved; as it is written, 'The Deliverer will come from Zion, he will banish ungodliness from Jacob' "* . . . RSV

καὶ (continuative conjunction) 14.

οὕτως (demonstrative adverb) 74.

πᾶς (nom.sing.masc.of πᾶς, in agreement with 'Ισραὴλ) 67.

'Ισραὴλ (nom.sing.masc.of 'Ισραὴλ, subject of σωθήσεται) 165.

σωθήσεται (3d.per.sing.fut.pass.ind.of σώζω, predictive) 109.

καθὼς (compound particle in a comparative clause) 1348.

γέγραπται (3d.per.sing.perf.pass.ind.of γράφω, intensive) 156.

Ἥξει (3d.per.sing.fut.act.ind.of ἥκω, predictive) 730.

ἐκ (preposition with the ablative of separation) 19.

Σιὼν (abl.sing.masc.of Σιὼν separation)l 1345.

ὁ (nom.sing.masc.of the article in agreement with ῥυόμενος) 9.

ῥυόμενος (pres.mid.part.nom.sing.masc.of ῥύομαι, substantival, subject of ἥξει) 584.

ἀποστρέφει (3d.per.sing.fut.act.ind.of ἀποστρέφω, predictive) 539.

ἀσεβείας (gen.sing.fem.of ἀσέβεια, description) 3794.

ἀπὸ (preposition with the ablative of separation) 70.

'Ιακώβ (abl.sing.masc.of 'Ιακώβ, separation) 12.

Translation - "*And thus all Israel will be saved, as it is written, 'The Deliverer will come out of Zion: He will turn ungodliness away from Jacob.' "*

Comment: We cannot push πᾶς to mean the quantitative whole of the descendants of Abraham. The word is not ἅπας (#639). πᾶς is used for "all" in a less-than-literal sense, for example in Mt.3:5 where we are not to believe that every person in Judea and in all of the region around Jordan was standing on the banks of the Jordan River listening to John preach. *Cf.* our discussion of the difference between πᾶς and ὅλος (#112). Paul does not mean that 100% of those who have descended from Abraham and Isaac are, by virtue of that fact, to be saved. This would contradict what he said in Romans 2:28,29. Certainly Judas Iscariot (John 6:70; 17:12) and the Pharisees referred to in John 8:44 are not included. Nor is any other Jew who is without faith. We are to understand the phrase πᾶς'Ισραὴλ in a national sense - all the tribes of Israel will be represented in the group made up of the 144,000 Jews who will be saved at the Second Coming of Messiah. Through them Messiah will fulfill all that He promised to Abraham, Isaac, Jacob, Judah and David.. *Cf.* Acts 2:36 where Peter uses πᾶς οἶκος 'Ισραὴλ in the same nationalistic sense. On ἀποστρέφει, *cf.*Acts 3:26. Israel's sin in the late 20th century is the sin of irreverence and disrespect for the God of their fathers. Messiah will cure this. *Cf.* #3794. The quotation is from

Isaiah 59:20,21. *Cf.* also Psalm 14:7. The student should read the entire chapter (Isa.59). Paul has quoted a part of it before (Rom.3:15-17) and he will allude to it again (Eph.6:14-17). Note especially Isa.59:19-21 and apply it to the final battle of Armageddon (Zech.14:1-4; Rev.19:11-16; Psalm 2:1-6). God must rescue Israel on that last day because of His covenant obligations with His people.

Verse 27 - "For this is my covenant with them, when I shall take away their sins."

καὶ αὕτη αὐτοῖς ἡ παρ' ἐμοῦ διαθήκη, ὅταν ἀφέλωμαι τὰς ἁμαρτίας αὐτῶν.

". . . and this will be my covenant with them when I take away their sins." . . .
                                                                          RSV

καὶ (continuative conjunction) 14.
αὕτη (nom.sing.fem.of οὗτος, in agreement with διαθήκη) 93.
αὐτοῖς (instru.pl.masc.of αὐτος, association) 16.
ἡ (nom.sing.fem.of the article in agreement with διαθήκη) 9.
παρ' (preposition with the ablative of source) 154.
ἐμοῦ (abl.sing.masc.of ἐμός, source) 1267.
διαθήκη (nom.sing.fem.of διαθήκη, subject of verb understood) 1575.
ὅταν (temporal conjunction with the subjunctive in an indefinite temporal clause) 436.
ἀφέλωμαι (1st.per.sing.2d.aor.mid.subj.of ἀφαιρέω, indefinite temporal clause) 1594.
τὰς (acc.pl.fem.of the article in agreement with ἁμαρτίας) 9.
ἁμαρτίας (acc.pl.fem.of ἁμαρτία, direct object of ἀφέλωμαι) 111.
αὐτῶν (gen.pl.masc.of αὐτος, possession) 16.

Translation - "And this covenant is from me to them, when I take away their sins."

Comment: Why should God turn irreverence from Jacob? (verse 26). Because He has a covenant with them. The phrase παρ'ἐμοῦ, an ablative of source, is in the attributive position, like an adjective modifying διαθήκη. " This (is) with them the from me covenant." God is the source of the promise. He mixed the holy dough in the first place, from which the holy first fruits have derived.

The quotation is from Isaiah 59:20,21 and Isaiah 27:9. What the blood of bulls and goats (Heb.10:4) cannot do, God can do by the blood of the true Lamb (John 1:29; 1 Cor.5:7).

Note that God's covenant of grace with man, by which He obligates Himself to save the elect in consideration of nothing of merit in the elect, but solely on a basis of grace through faith, is tied to His covenant of redemption with His Son. God will do what He chooses to do for whomever He chooses to do it, but what He does can be done only on a redemptive basis, in which the holy demands of His righteous law are fully met. God cannot bless Abraham's seed and elevate them to a place of world leadership with first taking away their sins.

To say that God can do nothing for man apart from what Jesus Christ did at the cross, is not to deny His omnipotence. God's omnipotence can be denied only when He is overcome by forces outside Himself. He is limited by the limitations of His own nature. Thus His holiness demands His righteousness and He cannot justly overlook sin in the absence of redemption. That is why His plans to save man are tied to His plan to send His Son to redeem us.

Verse 28 - "As concerning the gospel, they are enemies for your sakes: but as touching the election, they are beloved for the fathers' sakes."

κατὰ μὲν τὸ εὐαγγέλιον ἐχϑροὶ δι' ὑμᾶς, κατὰ δὲ τὴν ἐκλογὴν ἀγαπητοὶ διὰ τοὺς πατέρας.

"As regards the gospel they are enemies of God, for your sake; but as regards election they are beloved for the sake of their forefathers." . . . RSV

κατὰ (preposition with the accusative of reference) 98.
μὲν (particle of affirmation) 300.
τὸ (acc.sing.neut.of the article in agreement with εὐαγγέλιον) 9.
εὐαγγέλιον (acc.sing.neut.of εὐαγγέλιον, reference) 405.
ἐχϑροὶ (nom.pl.masc.of ἐχϑρός, predicate nominative) 543.
δι' (preposition with the accusative, cause) 118.
ὑμᾶς (acc.pl.masc.of σύ, cause) 104.
κατὰ (preposition with the accusative of reference) 98.
δὲ (adversative conjunction) 11.
τὴν (acc.sing.fem.of the article in agreement with ἐκλογὴν) 9.
ἐκλογὴν (acc.sing.fem.of ἐκλογή, reference) 3189.
ἀγαπητοὶ (nom.pl.masc.of ἀγαπητός, predicate nominative) 327.
διὰ (preposition with the accusative, cause) 118.
τοὺς (acc.pl.masc.of the article in agreement with πατέρας) 9.
πατέρας (acc.pl.masc.of πατήρ, cause) 238.

Translation - "With reference to the gospel they are in fact enemies because of you, but with reference to the election they are beloved because of the fathers."

Comment: The μὲν . . . δὲ sequence indicates two points of view with opposite results flowing from them. The Jews who rejected Jesus are God's enemies because they see the gospel of the Messiah Whom they rejected and murdered, being preached to Gentiles who are saved and incorporated into the Body of Christ. Thus the Jews are jealous and angry with God. Had they not been enemies of God, they would have accepted His Son as their Messiah and there would have been no redemption on the cross. But for the sake of the Gentiles as well as for the sake of the Jews, Christ had to die. Thus the wrath of the Jews against Messiah, which culminated in His death worked for the benefit of the Gentiles. It is therefore because of the Gentiles (δι' ὑμᾶς) and their need of salvation that God's plan included hardening Israel's attitude against Jesus, to bring about redemption for all at Calvary. What happened to Israel was because of (for the sake of) the Gentiles.

But there is another consideration. With reference to the fact that God chose

Abraham and announced to him that He would make him a great nation, despite what either he (Genesis 16) or his children (John 19:15) might do, the Jews are beloved of God, not because of their own behavior (indeed in spite of it) but because of the fact that they are the physical children of Abraham. It is because of the patriarchs, to whom God is obligated in an unconditional covenant, that God loves Israel and will seal for salvation 12,000 of them out of every tribe (Rev.7:1-8).

This view will correct, if we let it, two extreme positions. Extreme Judaism repudiates Calvary as an unfortunate incident that should not have happened, in which an inconsequential teacher was murdered for no good reason, since Judaism, with its law and its ceremony, can provide salvation for every one. The Jew, by obedience to his own faith, and the Gentile by receiving circumcision and subscribing to the Torah as interpreted by the Talmud are able to save themselves. The uncircumcised Gentile, under this system, is written off as a heathen.

The other extreme says that God's only concern is the salvation of the Gentiles and such elect Jews as He may choose, who will repudiate Judaism totally and become members of the mystical Body of Christ. Thus Israel as a nation has no future, having forfeited all claim to God's further consideration when they crucified Christ. This is the view of amillenialism. Our verse says that God is looking at both sides of the coin. For the sake of the Gentile elect, Israel was made an enemy of God, nailed her Messiah on a cross, where He paid the redemption price for the Body of Christ. But for the sake of the patriarchs, God did not cast off His beloved Israel forever.

The premillenial view, stripped to be sure of its pretribulation rapture doctrine, a cocklebur under the saddle that has bothered us for the last 150 years, alone conforms to verse 28.

Verse 29 - "For the gifts and calling of God are without repentance."

ἀμεταμέλητα γὰρ τὰ χαρίσματα καὶ ἡ κλῆσις τοῦ θεοῦ.

"For the gifts and the call of God are irrevocable." . . . RSV

#4002 ἀμεταμέλητα (nom.pl.neut.of ἀμεταμέλητος, predicate adjective).

King James Version

not to be repented of - 2 Cor.7:10.
without repentance - Rom.11:29.

Revised Standard Version

irrevocable - Rom.11:29.
brings no regret - 2 Cor.7:10.

Meaning: α privative and μεταμέλομαι (#1371). Hence, that which is not to be regretted or changed. With reference to God's decrees - Rom.11:29; in litotes in 2 Cor.7:10, a vast understatement. No change in the emotional reaction to a decision.

γὰρ (causal conjunction) 105.

τὰ (nom.pl.neut.of the article in agreement with χαρίσματα) 9.

χαρίσματα (nom.pl.neut.of χάρισμα, subject of verb understood) 3790.

καὶ (adjunctive conjunction joining nouns) 14.

ἡ (nom.sing.fem.of the article in agreement with κλῆσις) 9.

#4003 κλῆσις (nom.sing.fem.of κλῆσις, subject of verb understood).

King James Version

calling - Rom.11:29; 1 Cor.1:26; 7:20; Eph.1:18; 4:1,4; Phil.3:14; 2 Thess.1:11; 2 Tim.1:9; Heb.3:1; 2 Pet.1:10.

Revised Standard Version

call - Rom.11:29; 1 Cor.1:26; Phil.3:14; 2 Thess.1:11; Heb.3:1; 2 Pet.1:10.
state - 1 Cor.7:20.
to which he has called you - Eph.1:18; 4:1.
that belongs to your call - Eph.4:4.
calling - 2 Tim.1:9.

Meaning: Cf. καλέω (#107). An invitation; a summons. In the New Testament always of God's call to the elect, either of Israel or the Gentiles, for salvation. Followed by a genitive of description, τοῦ θεοῦ in Rom.11:29; Eph.1:18; Phil.3:14 (joined with ἄνω); followed by a genitive of possession, ὑμῶν in 1 Cor.1:26; Eph.4:1,4; 2 Pet.1:10; followed by ἡ ἐκλήθη in 1 Cor.7:20. In 2 Thess.1:11 we have ἀξιώσῃ τῆς καλήσεως; followed by ἀγίᾳ in 2 Tim.1:9; followed by ἐπουρανίῳ in Heb.3:1.

τοῦ (gen.sing.masc.of the article in agreement with θεοῦ) 9.

θεοῦ (gen.sing.masc.of θεός, description) 124.

Translation - "Because the gifts and the call of God are immutable."

Comment: Goodspeed has "for God does not change his mind about those to whom he gives his blessings or sends his call." This makes the point which Paul wants to make but it ignores the meaning of ἀμεταμέλητα, which refers more to the emotions than to the intellect, although, of course the divine intellect is involved in the decision. #4002 refers to a lack of change in the emotional side of God's will to call Israel rather than the rational element. Thus all passages that refer to God's steadfast love for Abraham and his descendants support this verse. God "feels" about His call and the gifts He chooses to bestow as He always has. He wanted Abraham to become a great nation. He still wants it. To say otherwise is to say that God's emotions have undergone a change, and that now He does not want what He wanted before, at a time when He was in error. The irrevocabiltiy and immutability of His counsel is grounded in His will which is influenced by His emotions. God is not going to change His decision. God is not an "Indian giver."

Amillenialists will be the last to say that God has evolved and that His more recent development provides desires and decisions that reverse decisions made when He was in error! It is incumbent upon them therefore to show that God's promises to Abraham and David were conditioned upon human merit, as the Mosaic covenant was. The premillenialist can rest his case upon the facts that (1) God gave unconditional promises to the patriarchs, (2) God cannot change His mind about it, and (3) God is powerful enough to do what He wants to do.

It is not likely that our Lord will read theology textbooks and exegetical commentaries upon what He has written, including this one, before He decides how further to proceed. He already knows precisely what He is going to do, and what He does will be in perfect conformity to what He has written in His Word, whether any of us understand it or not. As a matter of fact, since God is not subject to time and space categories, He does not look forward or back upon anything. All is the eternal present to Him.

Verse 30 - "For as ye in times past have not believed God, yet have now obtained mercy through their unbelief, . . . "

ὥσπερ γὰρ ὑμεῖς ποτε ἠπειθήσατε τῷ θεῷ, νῦν δὲ ἠλεήθητε τῇ τούτων ἀπειθείᾳ, . . .

"Just as you were once disobedient to God but now have received mercy because of their disobedience, . . . " . . . RSV

ὥσπερ (intensive particle introducing a comparative clause) 560.
γὰρ (inferential conjunction) 105.
ὑμεῖς (nom.pl.masc.of σύ, subject of ἠπειθήσατε and ἠλεήθητε, emphatic) 104.
ποτε (temporal particle) 2399.
ἠπειθήσατε (2d.per.pl.aor.act.ind.of ἀπειθέω, constative) 1996.
τῷ (dat.sing.masc.of the article in agreement with θεῷ) 9.
θεῷ (dat.sing.masc.of θεός, person) 124.
νῦν (temporal particle) 1497.
δὲ (concessive conjunction) 11.
ἠλεήθητε (2d.per.pl.1st.aor.pass.ind.of ἐλεέω, constative) 430.
τῇ (instru.sing.fem.of the article in agreement with ἀπειθείᾳ) 9.
τούτων (gen.pl.masc.ofd οὗτος, possession) 93.

#4004 ἀπειθείᾳ (instru.sing.fem.of ἀπείθεια, cause).

King James Version

disobedience - Eph.2:2; 5:6; Col.3:6.
unbelief - Rom.11:30,32; Heb.4:6,11.

Revised Standard Version

disobedience - Rom.11:30,32; Eph.2:2; 5:6; Heb.4:6,11.

Meaning: Cf. ἀπειθής (#1800); ἀπειθέω (#1996). α privative plus πείθω

(#1629). Hence, disobedience, lack of persuasion sufficient to motivate obedience. Lack of belief and hence lack of obedience. With reference to Israel's unbelief *in re* Messiah, at His first advent - Rom.11:30; everyone's unbelief - Rom.11:32; Heb.4:11. In the phrase ἐν τοῖς υἱοῖς τῆς ἀπειθείας - meaning unregenerate sinners - Eph.2:2; 5:6; Col.3:6. Israel at Kadesh Barnea - Heb.4:6.

Translation - "Therefore just as you formerly disobeyed God, though now you have been treated mercifully because of their unbelief. . ."

Comment: ὥσπερ (#560) is the intensive form of ὡς. περ which is added to ὡς is from περί (#173) and means "all the way." It is therefore intensive and extensive. "Precisely" or "exactly" as, are good translations of ὥσπερ. γάρ is inferential. Paul is explaining the inference that can be drawn from his statement in verse 29 that God's decisions are final.

Once, before the Roman Christians were saved, they disbelieved God and were disobedient to the gospel, although (concessive δέ) now (νῦν) they have been treated mercifully. ποτε conflicts with νῦν - "Then and now." οὕτως of verse 31 goes with ὥσπερ and leaves δέ in a concessive sense. The concessive δέ seems smoother than the adversative ("but"), though either will serve.

Why did the Gentiles, formerly disobedient, later receive mercy? Because (τῇ. . . ἀπειθείᾳ) of Israel's disobedience. This is the theme that has run through the 11th chapter. The sentence continues in

Verse 31 - "Even so have these also now not believed, that through your mercy they also may obtain mercy."

οὕτως καὶ οὗτοι νῦν ἠπείθησαν τῷ ὑμετέρῳ ἐλέει ἵνα καὶ αὐτοὶ νῦν ἐλεηθῶσιν.

". . . so they have now been disobedient in order that by the mercy shown to you they also may receive mercy." . . . RSV

οὕτως (demonstrative adverb) 74.
καὶ (adjunctive conjunction joining pronouns) 14.
οὗτοι (nom.pl.masc.of οὗτος, subject of ἠπείθησαν) 93.
νῦν (temporal adverb) 1497.
ἠπείθησαν (3d.per.pl.aor.act.ind.of ἀπειθέω, gnomic) 1996.
τῷ (instru.sing.neut.of the article in agreement with ἐλέει) 9.
ὑμετέρῳ (instru.sing.neut.of ὑμέτερος, in agreement with ἐλέει) 2127.
ἐλέει (instru.sing.neut.of ἔλεος, cause) 795.
ἵνα (conjunction introducing a sub-final clause) 114.
καὶ (adjunctive conjunction joining pronouns) 14.
αὐτοὶ (nom.pl.masc.of αὐτός, subject of ἐλεηθῶσιν) 16.
νῦν (temporal adverb) 1497.
ἐλεηθῶσιν (3d.per.pl.1st.aor.pass.subj.of ἐλεέω, sub-final) 430.

Translation - ". . . in the same way also these now have been disobedient, in order (and with the result) that because of your mercy, they now may be treated mercifully."

Comment: οὕτως is joined with ὥσπερ - "Just as . . . even so also." οὗτοι is deictic as is αὐτοί in the last clause. "These" and "they." Paul wants the Jews emphasized in verse 31 as he emphasized the Gentile Christians in verse 30. The aorist ἠπείθησαν, is gnomic (timeless). joined with νῦν. The Jews had been disobedient and were, at the time of Paul's writing, still unbelieving. The instrumental causal phrase τῇ ὑμέτερῳ ἐλέει is out of order thus to show emphasis.

What is the mercy shown to the Gentile Bride of Christ because of which Israel may obtain mercy? Verse 25 seems to provide the answer to the question. When the "fulness of the Gentiles" (verse 25) occurs, God will then again turn to Israel, to fulfill His promise to them. National Israel had to await her turn, and were set aside temporarily while God showed mercy to the Gentiles. Once that is done, because of the completion of God's redemptive program for the Gentile Bride of Christ (Rev.10:7), Israel will come into her own in terms of verses 26 and 27.

This has nothing to do with the fact that individual Hebrews may become Christians to be incorporated into the Body of Christ during the church age, just as the earliest Christians were Jews. The context however seems to show that Paul is speaking of national salvation in verses 26 and 27. To refer to the Church, composed of elect saints, Jews and Gentiles, as "spiritual Israel" and to point to them as the fulfillment of all of God's promises to the patriarchs. is to ignore Paul's distinction between ὑμεῖς (verse 30) and οὗτοι and αὐτοί (verse 31). "You" on the one hand (verse 30) and "these" and "they" on the other (verse 31) are not the same people. In verse 30 he is speaking of members of the Gentile church. In verse 31 he is speaking of the Jews as a nation. Amillenialists also obscure the distinction between ποτε ("then") and νῦν ("now").

Verse 32 - "For God hath concluded them all in unbelief, that he might have mercy upon all."

συνέκλεισεν γὰρ ὁ θεὸς τοὺς πάντας εἰς ἀπείθειαν ἵνα τοὺς πάντας ἐλεήσῃ.

"For God has consigned all men to disobedience, that he may have mercy upon all." . . . RSV

συνέκλεισεν (3d.per.sing.aor.act.ind.of συγκλείω, constative) 2048.
γὰρ (causal conjunction) 105.
ὁ (nom.sing.masc.of the article in agreement with θεὸς) 9.
θεὸς (nom.sing.masc.of θεός, subject of συνέκλεισεν) 124.
τοὺς (acc.pl.masc.of the article in agreement with πάντας) 9.
πάντας (acc.pl.masc.of πᾶς, direct object of συνέκλεισεν) 67.
εἰς (preposition with the predicate accusative) 140.
ἀπείθειαν (acc.sing.fem.of ἀπείθεια, adverbial) 4004.
ἵνα (conjunction with the subjunctive in a sub-final clause) 114.
τοὺς (acc.pl.masc.of the article in agreement with πάντας) 9.
πάντας (acc.pl.masc.of πᾶς, direct object of ἐλεήσῃ) 67.
ἐλεήσῃ (3d.per.sing.aor.act.subj.of ἐλεέω, sub-final) 430.

Translation - "Because God has included all in the category of unbelief in order (and with the result) that He might be merciful to all."

Comment: It is difficult to find an English verb to use in the metaphorical sense to fit συγκλείω (#2048), used properly in Luke 5:6 of the capture and imprisonment of a number of fish in a net. God has caught us all in His net. He views the entire race, Jews and Gentiles, as unbelieving and disobedient sinners. *Cf.* Gal.3:22,23 where Paul uses the word in the same sense as in Rom.11:32. The sub-final (purpose and result) clause with ἴνα follows - "in order (and with the result) that He may be merciful to all." All men are in the same predicament; all will receive the same treatmenet. τοὺς πάντας here without the substantive. We can supply λάους or ἀνθρώπους, meaning all classes of people. The verse does not teach universalism. God will be merciful to all classes of people (Rev.5:9).

Paul thus brings to a close his doctrinal section of the epistle by repeating the argument with which he opened it. All classes of men are lost - Heathen (Rom.1:18-32), the cultured Gentile (Rom.2:1-16) and the Jew (Rom.2:17-29). But God has provided a way to show mercy to each class of men. Even the unenlightened heathen may find mercy (Rom.2:6-11). Jew and Gentile alike can find his place in the economy of God. Individual Jews who repent and believe become members of the Body of Christ, along with Gentiles who also enter on an individual basis. National Israel will not be forgotten when God has completed His Gentile enterprise (Acts 15:14). All salvation of course depends solely upon the elective choice of a sovereign God Who is answerable only to Himself.

We cannot penetrate into the details of God's own counsel, as Paul observes in verse 33. Indeed, the attempt to do so is a wicked presumption of which only a pseudo-sophisticated Gnostic is capable.

Verse 33 - "O the depths of the riches both of the wisdom and knowledge of God! How unsearchable are his judgments, and his ways past finding out!"

Ὦ βάθος πλούτου καὶ σοφίας καὶ γνώσεως θεοῦ. ὡς ἀνεξεραύνητα τὰ κρίματα αὐτοῦ καὶ ἀνεξιχνίαστοι αἱ ὁδοὶ αὐτοῦ.

"O the depth of the riches and wisdom and knowledge of God! How unsearchable are his judgments and how inscrutable his ways!" . . . RSV

Ὦ (exclamation) 1177.
βάθος (nom.sing.neut.of βάθος, nominative absolute) 1031.
πλούτου (gen.sing.masc.of πλοῦτος, description) 1050.
καὶ (adjunctive conjunction joining nouns) 14.
σοφίας (gen.sing.fem.of σοφία, description) 934.
καὶ (adjunctive conjunction joining nouns) 14.
γνώσεως (gen.sing.fem.of γνῶσις, description) 1856.
θεοῦ (gen.sing.masc.of θεός, possession) 124.
ὡς (exclamation) 128.

#**4005** ἀνεξεραύνητα (nom.pl.neut.of ἀνεξεραύνητα, predicate adjective).

King James Version

unsearchable - Rom.11:33.

Revised Standard Version

unsearchable - Rom.11:33.

Meaning: α privative plus ἐκ (#19) plus ἐρευνάω (#2099). Hence, that which cannot be researched, discovered or ascertained. Unsearchable. With reference to the rationale behind God's judgments - Rom.11:33.

τὰ (nom.pl.neut.of the article in agreement with κρίματα) 9.
κρίματα (nom.pl.neut.of κρίμα, subject of ἐστιν understood) 642.
αὐτοῦ (gen.sing.masc.of αὐτός, possession) 16.
καὶ (adjunctive conjunction joining clauses) 14.

#4006 ἀνεξιχνίαστοι (nom.pl.masc.of ἀνεξιχνίαστος, predicate adjective).

King James Version

past finding out - Rom.11:33.
unsearchable - Eph.3:8.

Revised Standard Version

inscrutable - Rom.11:33.
unsearchable - Eph.3:8.

Meaning: α privative plus ἐξιχνιάζω - "to trace out." Hence unsearchable. Not subject to research. Joined with αἱ ὁδοὶ αὐτοῦ in Rom.11:33; with πλοῦτον τοῦ Χριστοῦ in Eph.3:8.

αἱ (nom.pl.fem.of the article in agreement with ὁδοὶ) 9.
ὁδοὶ (nom.pl.fem.of ὁδός, subject of ἐστιν understood) 199.
αὐτοῦ (gen.sing.masc.of αὐτός, possession) 16.

Translation - "O the depth of riches, both of divine wisdom and knowledge! How unsearchable His decisions and inscrutable His ways!"

Comment: βάθος is an interjectional nominative and ὡς is an exclamation. *Cf.* this also in Rom.10:15. The conclusion is an example of synonymous parallelism. The two predicate adjectives (#'s 4005 and 4006) means essentially the same. Note the genitive without the article in θεοῦ as descriptive.

God's thoughts, His philosophy, the rationale behind His decrees defy human analysis. *Cf.* Isa.45:15; 55:8,9; Rom.9:20; Mt.5:3; 11:25; 18:3. The hiss of the serpent can be discerned unmistakably in the effort to find a theology that man can understand in all of its parts. Unregenerate philosophers and theologians would never write what Paul has written here, and they are contemptuous of what he has written. Their theology is clear to them because it is the product of their own intellectual creation. The divine riches in wisdom and knowledge (philosophy and science) are indeed abysmal as is the ignorance of the antisupernaturalists who strive to explain away what they refuse to accept. God's riches are hid in Christ (Col.2:3). That is where the believer is also hidden (Col.3:3). King Midas, locked inside Fort Knox is not more delighted than the Christian who understands this. In Christ we are in close contact with the wisdom and knowledge of God, but we did not get there by demanding to understand it all with our present intellectual capability. Nor will any other lost sinner.

Paul closes this section with an awe-inspiring statement about the sovereign majesty of God.

Verse 34 - "For who hath known the mind of the Lord? Or who hath been His counsellor?"

Τίς γὰρ ἔγνω νοῦν κυρίου; ἢ τίς σύμβουλος αὐτοῦ ἐγένετο;

"For who has known the mind of the Lord, or who has been his counselor?" ...
                                                                    RSV

Τίς (nom.sing.masc.of τίς, interrogative pronoun, subject of ἔγνω) 281.
γὰρ (inferential conjunction) 105.
ἔγνω (3d.per.sing.2d.aor.act.ind.of γινώσκω, constative) 131.
νοῦν (acc.sing.masc.of νοῦς, direct object of ἔγνω) 2928.
κυρίου (gen.sing.masc.of κύριος, description) 97.
ἢ (disjunctive) 465.
τίς (nom.sing.masc.of τίς, interrogative pronoun, predicate nominative) 281.

#4007 σύμβουλος (nom.sing.masc.of σύμβουλος, subject of ἐγένετο).

King James Version

counsellor - Rom.11:34.

Revised Standard Version

counselor - Rom.11:34.

Meaning: A combination of σύν (#1542) and βουλή (#2163). *Cf.* συμβουλεύω (#1556); συμβούλιον (#980). A counselor; an advisor - Rom.11:34.

αὐτοῦ (gen.sing.masc.of αὐτός, relationship) 16.
ἐγένετο (3d.per.sing.aor.ind.of γίνομαι, constative) 113.

Translation - "So who has ever known the Lordly mind: or who ever became His counselor?"

Comment: Rhetorical questions rising to splendid heights of literary grandeur as Paul challenges the unbelieving rationalist to step forward. No further comment is in order. It is time to worship. The quotation is from Isaiah 40:13,14. Eliphaz, the Temanite hurled a similar challenge at Job (Job 15:8). *Cf.* also Jer.23:18; 1 Cor.2:16.

Verse 35 - "*Or who hath first given to him, and it shall be recompensed unto him again?*"

ἢ τίς προέδωκεν αὐτῷ, καὶ ἀνταποδοθήσεται αὐτῷ;

"*Or who has given a gift to him that he might be repaid?*" . . . RSV

ἢ (disjunctive) 465.
τίς (nom.sing.masc.of τίς, interrogative pronoun, subject of προέδωκεν) 281.

#4008 προέδωκεν (3d.per.sing.aor.act.ind.of προδίδωμι, constative).

King James Version

give first - Rom.11:35.

Revised Standard Version

give a gift - Rom.11:35.

Meaning: A combination of πρό (#442) and δίδωμι (#362). To give first, with a view to expecting something in return - Rom.11:35.

αὐτῷ (dat.sing.masc.of αὐτός, indirect object of προέδωκεν) 16.
καὶ (continuative conjunction) 14.
ἀνταποδοθήσεται (3d.per.sing.fut.pass.ind.of ἀνταποδίδωμι, predictive) 2529.
αὐτῷ (dat.sing.masc.of αὐτός, indirect object of ἀνταποδοθήσεται) 16.

Translation - "*Or who ever gave first to Him so that God is obligated to repay?*"

Comment: *Cf.* Job.41:11. The translation is free. Goodspeed has, "Or who has advanced anything to him, for which he will have to be repaid?"- a translation which correctly translates the passive in ἀνταποδοθήσεται. The idea is that God needs nothing from us, either in the way of advice or material gift and He will be in no man's debt. On the contrary, we learn in

Verse 36 - "*For of him, and through him, and to him, are all things: to whom be glory forever, Amen.*"

ὅτι ἐξ αὐτοῦ καὶ δι' αὐτοῦ καὶ εἰς αὐτὸν τὰ πάντα, αὐτῷ ἡ δόξα εἰς τοὺς αἰῶνας. ἀμήν.

"*For from him and through him and to him are all things. To him be glory for ever. Amen.*" . . . RSV

ὅτι (conjunction introducing a subordinate causal clause) 211.
ἐξ (preposition with the ablative of source) 19.
αὐτοῦ (abl.sing.masc.of αὐτός, source) 16.
καὶ (adjunctive conjunction joining prepositional phrases) 14.
δι' (preposition with the ablative of agent) 118.

αὐτοῦ (abl.sing.masc.of αὐτός, agent) 16.

καὶ (adjunctive conjunction joining prepositional phrases) 14.

εἰς (preposition with the accusative, purpose) 140.

αὐτὸν (acc.sing.masc.of αὐτός, purpose) 16.

τὰ (nom.pl.neut.of the article in agreement with πάντα) 9.

πάντα (nom.pl.neut.of πᾶς subject of ἐστιν understood) 67.

αὐτῷ (dat.sing.masc.of αὐτος, personal advantage) 16.

ἡ (nom.sing.fem.of the article in agreement with δόξα) 9.

δόξα (nom.sing.fem.of δόξα, subject of the verb understood) 361.

εἰς (preposition with the accusative, time extent) 140.

τοὺς (acc.pl.masc.of the article in agreement with αἰῶνας) 9.

αἰῶνας (acc.pl.masc.of αἰών, time extent) 1002.

ἀμήν (explicative) 466.

Translation - "Because from Him and by His agency and unto Him are all things. To Him be glory into the ages! Amen."

Comment: He is Source and Agent of everything, and it is all for Him. This statement of God's role in creation, preservation and consummation expresses His eternity, His omnipotence, omniscience and omnipresence. Thus He is Sovereign. As such He is eternally adequate to keep His own counsel. Who dare to question or gainsay Him?

A division of the Epistle to the Romans, commonly taught has the first eight chapters devoted to the doctrine of soteriology. This they call the Doctrinal Section. Chapters nine, ten and eleven are commonly referred to as Dispensational, while chapters twelve through sixteen are called Practical. This division seems to suggest that there is little if any connection between the doctrine of salvation and the *weltanschauung* set forth in the portion called dispensational. But the theological history of the "last days" (Heb.1:2) with its relations between Israel as a nation and the calling out of the Body of Christ cannot be separated from the work of the Holy Spirit as He directs the worldwide missionary enterprise until the "mystery" of Ephesians 3:1-11 is completed "in the days of the voice of the seventh angel when he shall begin to sound. . . " (Rev.10:7). Our Lord Who sits at the Father's right hand, will remain there until His enemies have been made His footstool (Psalm 110:1). He will not return to take His bride until the last member of her body has been incorporated. Thus the plan of the ages, when viewed scripturally is seen in soteriological rather than in dispensational terms.

As for the designation of the last five chapters, it should never be suggested that doctrinal truth is not practical and that practical truth need not concern itself with doctrine.

The New Life in Christ

(Romans 12:1-8)

Romans 12:1 - "I beseech you therefore, brethren, by the mercies of God, that ye present your bodies a living sacrifice, holy, acceptable unto God, which is your reasonable service."

Παρακαλῶ οὖν ὑμᾶς, ἀδελφοί, διὰ τῶν οἰκτιρμῶν τοῦ θεοῦ, παραστῆσαι τὰ σώματα ὑμῶν θυσίαν ζῶσαν ἁγίαν εὐάρεστον τῷ θεῷ, τὴν λογικὴν λατρείαν ὑμῶν.

"I appeal to you therefore, brethren, by the mercies of God, to present your bodies as a living sacrifice, holy and acceptable to God, which is your sp iritual worship." . . . RSV

Παρακαλῶ (1st.per.sing.pres.ac.ind.of παρακαλέω, aoristic) 230.
οὖν (inferential conjunction) 68.
ὑμᾶς (acc.pl.masc.of σύ, direct object of παρακαλῶ, 104).
ἀδελφοί (voc.pl.masc.of ἀδελφός, address) 15.
διὰ (preposition with the ablative, intermediate agent) 118.
τῶν (abl.pl.masc.of the article in agreement with οἰκτιρμῶν) 9.

#4009 οἰκτιρμῶν (abl.pl.masc.of οἰκτιρμός, intermediate agent).

King James Version

mercy - Rom.12:1; 2 Cor.1:3; Phil.2:1; Col.3:12; Heb.10:28.

Revised Standard Version

mercy - Rom.12:1; 2 Cor.1:3; Heb.10:28.
sympathy - Phil.2:1.
compassion - Col.3:12.

Meaning: Cf. οἰκτείρω (#3962); οἰκτίρμων (#2134). The viscera, which was thought to be the seat of compassion. Hence, mercy, pity, compassion. Followed by τοῦ θεοῦ in Rom.12:1; with ὁ πατὴρ τῶν οἰκτιρμῶν in 2 Cor.1:3; with σπλάγχνα in Phil.2:1; Col.3:12. Absolutely in Heb.10:28.

τοῦ (gen.sing.masc.of the article in agreement with θεοῦ) 9.
θεοῦ (gen.sing.masc.of θεός, description) 124.
παραστῆσαι (aor.act.inf.of παρίστημι, purpose) 1596.
τὰ (acc.pl.neut.of the article in agreement with σώματα) 9.
σώματα (acc.pl.neut.of σῶμα, direct object of παραστῆσαι) 507.
ὑμῶν (gen.pl.masc.of σύ, possession) 104.
θυσίαν (acc.sing.fem.of θυσία, apposition) 796.
ζῶσαν (pres.act.part.acc.sing.fem.of ζάω, adjectival, restrictive, predicate position, in agreement with θυσίαν) 340.
ἁγίαν (acc.sing.fem.of ἅγιος, in agreement with θυσίαν) 84.

#4010 εὐάρεστον (acc.sing.neut.of εὐάρεστος, predicate accusative).

King James Version

acceptable - Rom.12:1,2; 14:18; Eph.5:10; 2 Cor.5:9.
please well - Tit.2:9.
well pleasing - Phil.4:18; Col.3:20.
that which is well pleasing - Heb.13:21.

Revised Standard Version

acceptable - Rom.12:1,2; 14:18.
well pleasing - Eph.5:10.
pleasing - Phil.4:18; Heb.13:21.
pleases - Col.3:20.
aim to please - 2 Cor.5:9.
give satisfaction - Tit.2:9.

Meaning: εὐ plus ἀρεστός (#2384); well pleasing, acceptable, that of which one approves. Followed by τῷ θεῷ in Rom.12:1; 14:18; Phil.4:18; in modification of τὸ θέλημα τοῦ θεοῦ in Rom.12:2; with τῷ κυρίῳ in Eph.5:10; Col.3:20; followed by ἐνώπιον αὐτοῦ, with reference to ὁ θεός in Heb.13:21. Followed by αὐτῷ in 2 Cor.5:9. With reference to earthly masters in Tit.2:9. Elsewhere in reference to God.

τῷ (dat.sing.masc.of the article in agreement with θεῷ) 9.
θεῷ (dat.sing.masc.of θεός, person) 124.
τὴν (acc.sing.fem.of the article in agreement with λατρείαν) 9.

#4011 λογικὴν (acc.sing.fem.of λογικός, in agreement with λατρείαν).

King James Version
of the word - 1 Pet.2:2.
reasonable - Rom.12:1.

Revised Standard Version

spiritual - Rom.12:1; 1 Pet.2:2.

Meaning: Cf.λόγος (#510). Hence, rational, reasonable, logical. With reference to Christian dedication to God - Rom.12:1; in definition of the word of God - 1 Pet.2:2.

λατρείαν (acc.sing.fem.of λατρεία, apposition) 2787.
ὑμῶν (gen.pl.masc.of σύ, possession) 104.

Translation - "*I am asking you, therefore, brethren, by the mercies of God, to offer your bodies as a sacrifice, alive, holy, (an offering) acceptable to God, which offer is your logical service.*"

Comment: Paul began this epistle with a presentation of God as creator, Who was angry with men who knew some truth, but were suppressing it because they wished to sin (Rom.1:18). The human mind, even though unaided by Holy Spirit revelation, was able to grasp the revelation of natural theology, and thus they understood His eternal power and deity (Rom. 1:19,20). Their partial intellectual light, which they rejected and because they rejected it, became darkness (Rom. 1:21; Mt.6:22,23), and their partial wisdom, because they perverted it, became foolishness (Rom. 1:22). Thus the Gentile heathen world was condemned.

The cultivated Gentiles were no better than their uncivilized brothers for the same reason (Rom.2:1-5).

Likewise the Jew, and for the same reason - a propensity to commit sin and a reluctance to live by God's ethical standard, traded the spiritual reality of the Mosaic revelation for a formal and meaningless system of offering dead animal sacrifices, which offerings God hated (Hosea 6:6), and even turned to idolatry as a substitute religion (Jeremiah 44:3,4; Malachi 1:7,8).

Thus God placed all men, Jew and Gentile, pagan and cultured, in the same category of condemnation (Rom.3:9-19).

After his section on justification in Romans 3:21-8:39, which is the most exhaustive and systematic treatment of the doctrine of salvation in the New Testament, Paul deals in chapters 9-11 with the *weltanschauung* by which we are to understand how He is dealing with the Jew as a national people, to whom He is obligated in an unconditional covenant, and how His dealings with Israel coordinates with His calling out the Body of Christ. At the close of this section Paul emphasizes this theme (Rom.11:32) and now he warns his readers, Jew and Gentile alike, who have since had the benefit of His revelation of Christ, the Messiah, and the fulness of the Holy Spirit, not to make the same mistake again.

Man's original mistake was his attempt to compress the idea of God into his own limited intellectual framework and thus to reduce God and His words and works to something that he could understand. Man, because he would rather sin than be holy, must know it all, or reject as false what he cannot understand. Thus he has enthroned his own intellect even though it meant that first he had to pull the sovereign God from His throne. His philosophy says, "I will admit that nothing exists which is beyond the sweep and scope of my experience and/or reason. If I cannot experience it and if it does not appeal to my reason, I will reject it. I refuse to be naive. The role of the humble child is distasteful to me. If that is what God is, and if that kind of ethics is what He demands, I will exchange Him for a deity of my own creation, whose ethical tolerance is more to my liking and whose rationale I can understand." (Rom. 1:22-25).

In opposition to this deification of human wisdom, Paul declares that God's wisdom is infinite and that man, apart from revelation, is incapable of following God's thoughts (Rom. 11:33,34). Moreover God needs nothing that man can provide and is in no sense dependent upon him (Rom. 11:35). *Au contraire* He is the Creator and as such totally adequate in and of Himself (Rom. 11:36). This was Paul's point in Rom. 1:19,20. Thus his argument, beginning in Rom. 1:18 and ending in Rom. 11:36 has swung full circle.

What then is his conclusion as he opens the section of the epistle in which we are to see the practical fruit that grows from this supernatural root? First he reminds us that as regenerated children of God we are surrounded on all sides by the mercies of God. We have called διὰ τῶν οἰκτιρμῶν the ablative of indirect agency, and it can be so construed. But διά, which is related to δύο (#385) always suggests duality. Witness δι' ὕδατος in 1 Peter 3:20, where Noah and his family are said to have been delivered "in between two waters" - those coming down from the open windows of heaven and those coming up from the fountains of the great deep which were broken up (Gen.7:11). Paul now says that the mercies of God are the indirect agents on the basis of which he appeals to us, and he also suggests that they surround us on every side. We are surrounded by the merciful ministrations of God. They provide a basis upon which Paul can appeal to us for our total devotion.

God still asks for sacrifice. But the Christian's body (and all that it entails - physical strength and skills, intelligence and personality quotients) is a living sacrifice (Gal.2:20; 1 Cor.6:19,20; 3:16,17; 6:9-13). God wants no greasy smoke from the burning entrails of a goat, but a living, human body, the temple of the Holy Spirit. The Romans looked in the entrails but we look back at the cross and empty tomb, up to the right hand of God where our Advocate sits and within to the Holy Spirit our Counselor and Guide. Thus our bodies are alive, holy and acceptable to God.

The last clause τὴν λογικὴν λατρείαν ὑμῶν, in apposition with the infinitive παραστῆσαι is now capable of being understood. That we should do this is logical only to one who understands Paul's total soteriolgical system, which he has given us in Romans 3:21-11:36.

Of course it is logical in the light of our baptism by the Holy Spirit (Rom.6:3,4) into the Body of Christ, which results in our complete identification with Him in death, burial and resurrection (Rom.6:1-23).

Jews and Gentiles alike should make the sacrifice since God's dispensationalism has provided that He will certainly honor His sovereign promises to both of them (Rom.11:25-31). The Christian in his living worship of total dedication to God is doing something which to the unregenerate mind is utterly irrational; but it is logical to him, since he is now the recipient of a new life and a superior level of understanding.

These concepts will be honed as the students runs the various references in the analyses of #'s 4009, 1596, 507, 796, 340, 4010, 4011 and 2787. Paul's entire argument for the victorious life (Romans 12-16) is based upon this analysis. Only on this basis is it λογικός (#4011).

In verse 2 Paul says that the Christian will escape conformity to the world and experience transformation into the real and therefore viable sphere of God's kingdom, only by an intellectual revolution. It is a great verse in support of education. And note that we avoided redundancy. We did not call it "Christian" Education, since there is really no other kind.

Verse 2 - "And be not conformed to this world, but be ye transformed by the renewing of your mind, that ye may prove what is that good, and acceptable, and perfect will of God."

καὶ μὴ συσχηματίζεσθε τῷ αἰῶνι τούτῳ, ἀλλὰ μεταμορφοῦσθε τῇ ἀνακαινώσει τοῦ νοός, εἰς τὸ δοκιμάζειν ὑμᾶς τὶ τὸ θέλημα τοῦ θεοῦ, τὸ ἀγαθὸν καὶ εὐάρεστον καὶ τέλειον.

"Do not be conformed to this world but be transformed by the renewal of your mind, that you may prove what is the will of God, what is good and acceptable and perfect." . . . RSV

καὶ (emphatic conjunction) 14.

μὴ (negative particle, with the imperative) 87.

#4012 συσχηματίζεσθε (2d.per.pl.pres.mid.impv.of συσχηματίζω, prohibition).

King James Version

be conformed to - Rom.12:2.
fashion one's self according to - 1 Pet.1:14.

Revised Standard Version

be conformed to - Rom.12:2; 1 Pet.1:14.

Meaning: A combination of σύν (#1542) and σχηματίζω - "to form" "to fashion." *Cf.*σχῆμα (#4163). Hence, to form oneself like something else. To conform; to shape one's policy in conformity with another. Followed by an instrumental of association - Rom.12:2; 1 Pet.1:14.

τῷ (instru.sing.masc.of the article in agreement with αἰῶνι) 9.
αἰῶνι (instru.sing.masc.of αἰών, association) 1002.
τούτῳ (instru.sing.masc.of οὗτος, in agreement with αἰῶνι) 93.
ἀλλὰ (alternative conjunction) 342.
μεταμορφοῦσθε (2d.per.pl.pres.pass.impv.of μεταμορφόω, command) 1222.
τῇ (instrumental sing.fem.of the article in agreement with ἀνακαινώσει) 9.

#4013 ἀνακαινώσει (instru.sing.fem.of ἀνακαίνωσις, means).

King James Version

renewing - Rom.12:2; Tit.3:5.

Revised Standard Version

renewal - Rom.12:2; Tit.3:5.

Meaning: A combination of ἀνά (#1059) and καίνωσις - "renovation" "newness." *Cf.* καινός (#812); καινότης (#3910). Hence, a complete change for the better. *Cf.* ἀνακαινός (#4302). The philosophical regeneration of the Christian - Rom.12:2; the new birth - Titus 3:5.

τοῦ (gen.sing.masc.of the article in agreement with νοός) 9.
νοός (gen.sing.masc.of νοῦς, description) 2928.
εἰς (preposition with the accusative articular infinitive, purpose) 140.
τὸ (acc.sing.neut.of the article, in agreement with δοκιμάζειν) 9.
δοκιμάζειν (pres.act.inf.of δοκιμάζω, noun use, accusative of purpose) 2493.
ὑμᾶς (acc.pl.masc.of σύ, general reference) 104.

τί (acc.sing.neut.of τίς, interrogative pronoun, predicate accusative) 281.

τὸ (acc.sing.neut.of the article in agreement with θέλημα) 9.

θέλημα (acc.sing.neut.of θέλημα, direct object of δοκιμάζειν) 577.

τοῦ (gen.sing.masc.of the article in agreement with θεοῦ) 9.

θεοῦ (gen.sing.masc.of θεός, possession) 124.

τὸ (acc.sing.neut.of the article in agreement with ἀγαθὸν) 9.

ἀγαθὸν (acc.sing.neut.of ἀγαθός, in agreement with θέλημα) 547.

καὶ (adjunctive conjunction joining adjectives) 14.

εὐάρεστον (acc.sing.neut.of εὐάρεστος, in agreement with θέλημα) 4010.

καὶ (adjunctive conjunction joining adjectives) 14.

τέλειον   (acc.sing.neut.of τέλειος, in agreement with θέλημα) 553.

Translation - *"In fact stop allowing yourselves to be conformed to this age, but be always transformed by a regenerating of your way of thinking, in order that you may ascertain what the good and acceptable and perfect will of God is."*

Comment: καὶ is emphatic as well as continuative. The suggestion of verse 1 is positive and is reinforced by its negative counterpart in verse 2. One cannot obey verse 1 without obeying verse 2. A Christian who continues to conform to this age is not an acceptable living sacrifice in worship of God. Thus Paul's demand - "Stop yielding to the pressure to conform in this age which the world constantly imposes." The present tense in the injunction indicates that Paul's audience was guilty.

This age (#1002) is the time period between Calvary, when the Light of the World was crucified (John 8:12) and night settled down (John 9:4) during which no man can make a *permanent* profit, and the Second Coming of Messiah. It is an evil age, under the control of Satan (Eph.2:2). Check all of the references to αἰών (#1002) that relate to this age, for its characteristics. Paul had a low opinion of it as well he might and as every Christian should have. The saints are no match for its machinations (Lk.16:8), but God has turned its wisdom to foolishness (1 Cor.1:20). It is evil (Gal.1:4) and it is dominated by the supernatural powers of evil (Eph.6:12). Demas succombed to its wiles (2 Tim.4: 10). We are to live in it but not in conformity to it (Tit.2:12). These are some of the applications which can be made. See the entire list under #1002.

The urge to conform to the world is a hallmark of personal insecurity. He who feels that he must conform is to the degree that he yields a slave. Christians "know the truth" and are thus made free (John 8:32,36).

The world tells us that there is safety in numbers. Democracy insists that the greatest good for all concerned is served when the general will is enacted into law and enforced by the police power of the state. But democracy assumes that the voters are men and women of good will. No Bible student believes that. Thus, as Winston Churchill once said, democracy is the worst system of government ever devised by man except one - its alternative, by which he meant the dictatorship of one evil man, like Adolf Hitler.

Darwin and those since who have been led astray by his theory assure us that the penalty for failure to conform to the environment is extinction. Thus they explain Tyrannosauros, Brontosaurus and the hairy mammoths found frozen to death within the Arctic Circle, being "willingly ignorant of (the fact) that by the word of God the heavens were of old, and the earth standing out of the water and in the water, whereby the world that then was, being overflowed with water, perished." (2 Pet.3:10. The dinosaurs did not die because they gradually lost the struggle with their environment over millions of years; they died in the flood. But the evolutionists of this age cannot grant the fact of the flood and the story about Noah's ark, because that does not fit their philosophy of uniformitarianism. Of course all facts which do not fit their philosophy are immediately rejected as fiction. Evolution as Darwin taught it is a legitimate inference that can properly be drawn from the empirical evidence of the fossil index, only if it is the only possible explanation. The Biblical account of the deluge, even if it were not true, does at least provide another possible explanation, and thus makes the dogma of Darwinism unacceptable.

So far from teaching that conformity is the way of life, Paul here says that those who conform to this age will never know what is the good, acceptable and total will of God and can never enjoy a viable way of life. This age is universally brainwashed by its diabolical god (2 Cor.4:4) who is said to have been a murderer from the beginning who has never been known to tell the truth. When he lies, as he always does, he is speaking from the depths of his own mendacious resources, for he is a liar and the father of all lies (John 8:44). Thus spake our Lord, Who is "the Way, *THE TRUTH*, and therefore the Life" (John 14:6).

The only safety is in the individuality that finds by empirical research the perfect will of God. Why should anyone wish to be conformed to something with which he does not agree? Because he is insecure. This is not the picture of the victorious Christian, ". . . for God has not given us the spirit of fear, but of power and of love and of a sound mind" (2 Tim.1:7). There is an alternative policy for us. Transformation! See what it did to Jesus (Mt.17:2; Mk.9:2) where the same verb is used (μεταμορφορέω #1222). How can the Christian experience it? By looking at Jesus (2 Cor.3:18) where the same word is used again. Thus the mind of the child of God is regenerated and he is given a new philosophical model (Rom.12:2). This regeneration is the work of the Holy Spirit (Titus 3:5) Who dwells within our physical bodies, after He has baptized us into the Body of Christ (1 Cor.12:13; 6:19,20). Note that νοός refers, not only to the rational faculty, but also to the philosophical model which is holds (#2928).

The only way that a backslidden Christian can cease conforming to the world and begin being transformed is τῇ ἀνακαινώσει τοῦ νοός - "by means of the regeneration of his mind and the philosophical model which he believes." Christians who think conformably to the will of God as it was displayed in Jesus of Nazareth and revealed in the New Testament, do not live outside the will of God. As a man "thinketh in his heart, so is he" (Proverbs 23:7). Show me the Christian who went astray in his conduct and I will show you a Christian who got his eyes and mind off of Jesus Christ and His Word and temporarily adopted the philosophy of this age.

A major cause of spiritual decline among Christians in the late 20th century is the pervasive influence of the mass media which feeds a constant stream of anti-

Christian philosophy to the audience. Few Christians can watch it consistently and escape its evil influence. Once the mind conforms to Satan's philosophy the body is not long in conforming to his ethics. This does not mean that the Christian cannot live victoriously in contact with the world and must flee from it to the desert monastery or to the top of a pole as the ascetics did. If we avoided all contact with the unsaved world and its ideas and influences we could not carry out the great commission to witness the gospel of Christ. The ascetic who flees from Satan lest he backslide thereby admits that he cannot live the victorious life under fire. But the child of God who obeys Paul's admonition in our verse has his mind continuously transformed. Thus he is immune to the devil's blandishments because he knows his Bible well enough and is in close enough contact with the indwelling Holy Spirit that he can appreciate the superficiality of the world's philosophy. Thus he reacts to it with the contempt which only it deserves.

The empirical result of nonconformity to this age and transformation to God is expressed in the articular infinitive in εἰς and the accusative which denotes purpose and result. Such Christians will be certain (τὸ δοκιμάζειν) to know the will of God, at least as it relates to his own life. Something unavailable to the unsaved mind (Rom.11:33,35) is now made available to the transformed mind of the child of God. This is the work of the Holy Spirit (Eph.5:9,10). Such a Christian does not foresee the future, but by daily yielding his mind to Christ he understands the present and sees in it the beauty and wisdom of the good, acceptable and complete will of God. To fellowship with Christ (Col.2:3) in an appreciation of all of the wisdom and knowledge, the philosophy and science of God (Rom.11:33) is the highest level of Christian concentration. It provides a personal security and the mental health which all of the material well being of this godless age cannot provide.

That the Christian is incorporated forever into a relationship with God the Father, Jesus Christ, His Son and the Holy Spirit that will never cease is mind-boggling until we remember that the birth from above is a miracle which only God can perform. We are involved in the miracle, but it is God not the Christian who performed it. Thus by faith we rejoice in that which we cannot explain. What we can understand is that incorporation into the Body of Christ, in Whom "are hid all the treasures of wisdom and knowledge" is matriculation into the university that takes all truth as its curriculum. As students, first at the undergraduate and then at the graduate level, we have the greatest library in the universe at our disposal and we sit in the classes of the greatest teacher, Who is closer to us than hands and feet and the air which we breathe. We shall never graduate, for it will take more than one eternity (!) to learn all that our Lord knows.

Paul renews the warning that the pitfall of the defeated Christian is bad philosophy in

Verse 3 - "For I say, through the grace given unto me, to every man that is among you, not to think of himself more highly than he ought to think; but to think soberly, according as God hath dealt to every man the measure of faith."

Λέγω γὰρ διὰ τῆς χάριτος τῆς δοθείσης μοι παντὶ τῷ ὄντι ἐν ὑμῖν μὴ ὑπερφρονεῖν παρ' ὃ δεῖ φρονεῖν, ἀλλὰ φρονεῖν εἰς τὸ σωφρονεῖν, ἑκάστῳ ὡς ὁ θεὸς ἐμέρισεν μέτρον πίστεως.

"For by the grace given to me I bid every one among you not to think of himself more highly than he ought to think, but to think with sober judgment, each according to the measure of faith which God has assigned him." . . . RSV

Λέγω (1st.per.sing.pres.act.ind.of λέγω, aoristic) 66.

γὰρ (inferential conjunction) 105.

διὰ (preposition with the ablative of means) 118.

τῆς (abl.sing.fem.of the article in agreement with χάριτος) 9.

χάριτος (abl.sing.fem.of χάρις, means) 1700.

τῆς (abl.sing.fem.of the article in agreement with δοθείσης) 9.

δοθείσης (aor.pass.part.abl.sing.fem.of δίδωμι, adjectival, restrictive, in agreement with χάριτος) 362.

μοι (dat.sing.masc.of ἐγώ, indirect object of δοθείσης) 123.

παντὶ (dat.sing.masc.of πᾶς in agreement with ὄντι) 67.

τῷ (dat.sing.masc.of the article in agreement with ὄντι) 9.

ὄντι (pres.part.dat.sing.masc.of εἰμί, substantival, indirect object of λέγω) 86.

ἐν (preposition with the locative with plural pronouns, association) 80.

ὑμῖν (loc.pl.masc.of σύ, association) 104.

μὴ (negative particle with the infinitive) 87.

#4014 ὑπερφρονεῖν (pres.act.inf.of ὑπερφρονέω, indirect discourse).

King James Version

think highly - Rom.12:3.

Revised Standard Version

think highly - Rom.12:3.

Meaning: A combination of ὑπέρ (#545) and φρονέω (#1212). To assume a lofty attitude. The context in Rom.12:3 indicates an unwarranted opinion of oneself.

παρ' (preposition with the accusative of extent) 154.

ὃ (acc.sing.neut.of ὅς, relative pronoun, extent) 65.

δεῖ (3d.per.sing.pres.ind.of δεῖ, impersonal) 1207.

φρονεῖν (pres.act.inf.of φρονέω, complementary) 1212.

ἀλλὰ (alternative conjunction) 342.

φρονεῖν (pres.act.inf.of φρονέω, indirect discourse) 1212.

εἰς (preposition with the accusative, consecutive) 140.

τὸ (acc.sing.neut.of the article in agreement with σωφρονεῖν) 9.

σωφρονεῖν (pres.act.inf.of σωφρονέω, acc.sing.neut. result) 2224.

ἑκάστῳ (dat.sing.masc.of ἕκαστος, ind.object of ἐμέρισεν) 1217.

ὡς (particle introducing a comparative clause) 128.

ὁ (nom.sing.masc.of the article in agreement with θεὸς) 9.

θεὸς (nom.sing.masc.of θεός, subject of ἐμέρισεν) 124.

ἐμέρισεν (3d.per.sing.aor.act.ind.of μερίζω, culminative) 993.

μέτρον (acc.sing.neut.of μέτρον, direct object of ἐμέρισεν) 643.

πίστεως (gen.sing.fem.of πίστις, definition) 728.

Translation - "*So by the grace which has been given to me I say to every one in your fellowship that you must not entertain a higher opinion of yourself than you ought, but that you must think objectively, to the full extent to which God has measured out to each one a measure of faith.*"

Comment: This warning against egotism is a warning to reject the philosophy of the age. The unregenerate are all guilty of overestimation of themselves. This egocentric subjectivity inflates one's conception of his intellelctual powers. Agnostics, who prate about their inability to know anything, regard this as a mark of intellectual superiority and are proud of it. The skepticism, which is indeed the mark of a mature mind, is useful as we listen to the salesman who has the Brooklyn Bridge to sell at a bargain, but the skeptic has gone much too far when he tells us that there is nothing certain for those who wish to be objective. His attitude can be called humility, only when we realize that it is humility on parade and that pride in one's humility is not humility at all. This was the sin of the heathen that turned them away from God (Rom.1:21-22).

Paul has recommended a regeneration of the mind in verse 2. The result of such a transformation is objectivity. The objective view is that view which is in line with the facts. Paul is saying that no mature thinker claims sophistication to a degree greater than that which the facts warrant.

The alternative advice which he gives is that we must think in such a manner as to achieve the result (εἰς τὸ σωφρονεῖν is ecbatic) of knowing exactly what our capabilities are. And to know one's capabilities is to recognize one's limitations. Full recognition, both of capabilities and limitations, is sober thinking. (#2224).

Sobriety, which is objectivity, freedom from false views and hubris, is defined in the epexegetic clause ἑκάστῳ ὡς ὁ θεὸς ἐμέρισεν μέτρον πίστεως - "on the scale by which God has issued to every man some given measure of faith." God, in sovereign wisdom has given to every member of the Body of Christ gifts as it has pleased Him to bestow (1 Cor.12:1-11). One of these gifts is faith. It is the duty of every Christian to find out what gifts he has and to what extent he possesses them. Then he will think of himself exactly as he should. This means that we will live up to our potential, but accept in humility our limitations. This is the road to mental health, personal security and efficiency in Christian service. No Christian with this attitude will attract attention to himself with a false display of humility and the statement that he would help if he could, but he has no talent. That is nonesense. Every Christian has a gift of some sort. Nor will he assure all and sundry that there is no problem that he cannot solve. The eye in the body is for seeing and the ear for hearing. Neither has both optical and auditory capabilities. That is why every member in the Body of Christ needs the ministry of every other member.

There would be fewer divisions within the Body of Christ if this advice given were heeded by the saints. Although no one, saved or unsaved should entertain exaggerated notions about his own abilities, Paul is not addressing the unsaved agnostic in this passage. He is directing it to the members of the Body of Christ. Our potential for reaching the heights in education and thus enjoying fellowship with our Lord in the widest areas of mutual understanding is a function of two variables. We are to achieve transformation by the regeneration of our minds and thus escape conformity with the world according to the "measure of faith" which the Holy Spirit has given to us. Some Christians have been given more faith than others. Humble Christians recognize this fact and pray   for an increase of faith (Luke 17:5). No Christian that I have ever seen had very much for there are few sycamine trees being transplated in the sea (Lk.17:6). But some Christians have more faith than others. The other variable is the degree of intelligence which we possess. Intelligence quotients differ. The range reaches from idiots to genius. Idiots and imbeciles are mental infants and they will go the heaven on the same basis that God saves normal babies who die in infancy. Morons have enough intelligence to make moral judgments and are capable of trusting Christ for salvation. Above the moron range there are Christians with average I.Q's - (the average college I.Q.is 110) and others, so blessed that they discover that E equals MC squared. Indeed tests cannot be devised to measure intelligence for those in the upper ranges of the third standard deviation above the norm. No one really knows the difference between an I.Q. of 180 and another of 200. The parable of the sower (Mt.13) describes some who received the seed of the gospel, experienced its germination, which we take to be the new birth, but "because they had no deepness of earth . . . when the sun was up they were scorched, and because they had no root they withered away" (Mt.13:5,6). But there was life for a moment, as is proved by the germination. Such Christians, through no fault of their own, can never become great students of the Word of God, but they can give to God all of the mental resources which they have, and, when these resources, mixed with varying amounts of faith, are dedicated to the service of God, they produce more fruit than others with more intelligence and less faith.

High intelligence, dedicated wholly to the Lord and a great measure of faith combine for the optimum combination for fruit bearing. Sober thinking takes into account the degree of native intelligence and the measure of faith and, once these factors are evaluated, the sincere Christian lays it all upon the altar before the Lord and trusts Him to do what He will with what we have. This is our logical service (verse 1). The intelligence is a function of genetics and the measure of faith is the function of the sovereign will of the Holy Spirit. The Christian can do nothing about either of these, but he is in complete control of the question as to what he is going to do with what he has. This is why some Christians with less mental power and more faith than others do more for the Lord than their peers. When we add the third element, our willingness to yield what we have to God, we begin to understand the failures of some Christians and the success of others.

Doctrinal disputes have marred the fellowship within some Christian communions, when those with intelligence and faith enough to understand predestination, to give a good example, are intolerant of others who cannot. Or those with less mental power and faith charge with heresy those who see in the Word of God something which they cannot discern. If every Christian, wherever he may stand on the scale between low intelligence and little faith and high intelligence and great faith (at least as great as the mustard seed) would think soberly, he would conclude that the real basis for fellowship between Christians is incorporation into the Body of Christ. The low grade moron who has trusted Christ is a member of that mystic body as is the genius, who, no thanks to his intelligence, has been incorporated into it. God has specific good works for both and each will be held responsible at the judgment seat of Christ (2 Cor.5:10) for what he has done in life with the mental resources with which he was born and the faith which the Holy Spirit has given unto him.

This seems to be Paul's thought when, after he describes his own determination to know Christ in the power of His resurrection, the fellowship of His suffering and conformity unto His death in order to attain the highest level of Christian efficiency, he says, "Let us therefore, as many as be perfect (full grown) be thus minded, and if in any thing ye be otherwise minded, God shall reveal even this unto you. Nevertheless, whereto we have already attained, let us walk by the same rule, let us mind the same thing." (Phil.3:10-16). This seems to say that every Christian must recognize that every other Christian, at any given moment, has developed to the point from which he must view the issues, and cannot view them from any other higher point. Once we understand this we will learn a little Christian temperant toleration, which is one of the fruits of the Holy Spirit (Gal.5:22,23).

An industrial plant operates at its greatest cost efficiency when the total task is divided among many workers, each of whom recognizes his job in the division of labor and performs it faithfully. The worker on the line with little skill may be able to provide the cotter pin without which the final product cannot function. Who is to say that he is not important?

This is the thought of

Verse 4 - "For as we have many members in one body, and all members have not the same office, . . . "

καθάπερ γὰρ ἐν ἑνὶ σώματι πολλὰ μέλη ἔχομεν, τὰ δὲ μέλη πάντα οὐ τὴν αὐτὴν ἔχει πρᾶξιν, . . .

"For as in one body we have many members, and all the members do not have the same function, . . . " . . . RSV

καθάπερ (compound intensive particle in a comparative clause) 3883.

γὰρ (causal conjunction) 105.

ἐν (preposition with the locative of place) 80.

ἑνὶ (loc.sing.neut.of εἷς, in agreement with σώματι) 469.

σώματι (loc.sing.neut.of σῶμα, place) 507.

πολλὰ (acc.pl.neut.of πολύς, in agreement with μέλη) 228.

μέλη (acc.pl.neut.of μέλος, direct object of ἔχομεν) 506.

ἔχομεν (1st.per.pl.pres.act.ind.of ἔχω, aoristic) 82.

τὰ (nom.pl.neut.of the article in agreement with μέλη) 9.

δὲ (adversative conjunction) 11.

μέλη (nom.pl.neut.of μέλος, subject of ἔχει) 506.

πάντα (nom.pl.neut.of πᾶς, in agreement with μέλη) 67.

οὐ (negative particle with the indicative) 130.

τὴν (acc.sing.fem.of the article in agreement with πρᾶξιν) 9.

αὐτὴν (acc.sing.fem.of αὐτός, in agreement with πρᾶξιν, intensive) 16.

ἔχει (3d.per.sing.pres.act.ind.of ἔχω, aoristic) 82.

πρᾶξιν (acc.sing.fem.of πρᾶξις, direct object of ἔχει) 1218.

Translation - *"Because just as in one body we have many organs, but not all the organs have the same function, . . . "*

Comment: Paul develops this analogy in greater detail in 1 Cor. 12:12-26. Here he devotes two verses to it. The point here is not so much the unity of the Body of Christ, but the differing nature of the gifts, thus to pursue the thought presented in the last half of verse 3.

Verse 5 - ". . . so we, being many, are one body in Christ, and every one members one of another."

οὕτως οἱ πολλοὶ ἓν σῶμά ἐσμεν ἐν Χριστῷ, τὸ δὲ καθ᾽ εἷς ἀλλήλων μέλη.

". . . so we, though many, are one body in Christ, and individually members one of another." . . . RSV

οὕτως (demonstrative adverb) 74.

οἱ (nom.pl.masc.of the article in agreement with πολλοὶ) 9.

πολλοὶ (nom.pl.masc.of πολύς, in apposition) 228.

ἓν (nom.sing.neut.of εἷς, in agreement with σῶμά) 469.

σῶμά (nom.sing.neut.of σῶμα, predicate nominative) 507.

ἐσμεν (1st.per.pl.pres.ind.of εἰμί, static) 86.

ἐν (preposition with the locative, association) 80.

Χριστῷ (instru.sing.masc.of Χριστός, association) 4.

τὸ (acc.sing.neut.of the article, with καθ᾽ εἷς) 9.

καθ᾽ (preposition with the accusative, distributive) 98.

εἷς (acc.sing.masc.of εἷς, distributive) 469.

ἀλλήλων (gen.pl.masc.of ἀλλήλων, reciprocal) 1487.

Translation - *" . . . so we, the many, are one body in Christ and every one is a member with the others."*

Comment: οὕτως correlates with καθάπερ in verse 4 - "Precisely as . . . so we . . . κ.τ.λ." οἱ πολλοὶ is in apposition with "we" in ἐσμεν, while ἓν σῶμα is the predicate nominative. The saints individually are many, but collectively we are united to form His body. The division of labor is such that the labor of each individual is coordinated with that of all of the others.

Weymouth translates, "so collectively we form one body in Christ, while individually we serve as organs for one another." Paul is fighting against the tendency of the saints to regard themselves too highly and he stresses that every Christian is a vital member of the Body of Christ without whom the Body would be incomplete. Hence there is equal status and importance for all, though not all have equal endowment for service.

Verse 6 - "Having then gifts differing according to the grace that is given to us, whether prophecy, let us prophesy according to the proportion of faith."

ἔχοντες δὲ χαρίσματα κατὰ τὴν χάριν τὴν δοθεῖσαν ἡμῖν διάφορα, εἴτε προφητείαν κατὰ τῇ ἀναλογίαν τῆς πίστεως,

"Having gifts that differ according to the grace given to us, let us use them: if prophecy, in proportion to our faith;" . . . RSV

ἔχοντες (pres.act.part.nom.pl.masc.of ἔχω, adverbial, conditional) 82.
δὲ (inferential conjunction) 11.
χαρίσματα (acc.pl.neut.of χάρισμα, direct object of ἔχοντες) 3790.
κατὰ (preposition with the accusative, distributive) 98.
τὴν (acc.sing.fem.of the article in agreement with χάριν) 9.
χάριν (acc.sing.fem.of χάρις, distributive) 1700.
τὴν (acc.sing.fem.of the article in agreement with χάριν) 9.
δοθεῖσαν (aor.pass.part.acc.sing.fem.of δοθεῖσαν, adjectival, ascriptive, emphatic attributive position, in agreement with χάριν) 362.
ἡμῖν (dat.pl.masc.of ἐγώ, indirect object of δοθεῖσαν) 123.

#4015 διάφορα (acc.pl.neut.of διάφορος, in agreement with χαρίσματα).

King James Version

differing - Rom.12:6.
diverse - Heb.9:10.
more excellent - Heb.1:4; 8:6.

Revised Standard Version

that differ - Rom.12:6.
more excellent - Heb.1:4; 8:6.
various - Heb.9:10.

Meaning: Cf. διαφέρω (#620). Different; varying in kind. Gifts - Rom.12:6; washings - Heb.9:10; in the comparative degree, with reference to Christ's name - Heb.1:4 and His ministry - Heb.8:6.

#4016 εἴτε (disjunctive conditional particle in indirect question)

King James Version

if - 1 Cor.14:27.
whether - Rom.12:6; 1 Cor.3:22a; 8:5a; 10:31a; 12:13a,c,26a; 13:8,8,8; 14:7; 2

Thess.2:15a; Col.1:16a,20a; 1 Pet.2:13; 1 Cor.15:11a; 2 Cor.1:6; 1 Thess.5:10a; 2 Cor.12:2,2,3; 5:10,13,13; 8;23; Eph.6:8.

or - Rom.12:7,7,8; 1 Cor.3:22b,c,d,e,f,g,h; 8:5b; 10:31b,c; 12:13b,d,26b; 14:7; 2 Cor.5:9b; Phil.1:18b,20b,27b; 2 Thess.2:15b; Col.1:16b,c,d, 20b; 1 Pet.2:14; 1 Cor.15:11b; 12:26b; 2 Cor.1:6b; 1 Thess.5:10b; 2 Cor.5:10; 8;23b; 12:3; Eph.6:8.

   Revised Standard Version

if - Rom.12:6,7a; 1 Cor.12:26a,b; 14:27; 2 Cor.1:6a,b.

not translated -2 Cor.5:10a; Rom.12:7ab,8; 1 Cor.8:5a; 2 Cor.1:6a; 5:8; 8:23; Eph.6:8.

whether - 1 Cor.3:22a; 2 Cor.5:9a; Phil.1:18a,20a,27a; Col.1:16a,20a; 1 Pet.2:13; 1 Cor.15:11a; 1 Thess.5:10a; 2 Cor.12:2a,3; 1 Cor.10:31a; 12:13a,c; 14:7.

either - 2 Thess.2:15a.

or - 1 Cor.3:22b,c,d,e,f,g,h; 8:5b; 2 Cor.5:9b; Phil.1:18b,20b,27b; 2 Thess.2:15b; Col.1:16b,c,d, 20b; 1 Pet.2:14; 1 Cor.15:11b; 1 Thess.5:10b; 2 Cor.12:2b; 5:10; 8;23b; 12:3; Eph.6:8.

as for - 1 Cor.13:8a,b,c.

Meaning: A disjunctive conjunction - "whether - or." With no verb following - Rom.12:6,7,7,8; 1 Cor.3:22; 8:5; 2 Cor.8;23; 12:3; 2 Cor.5:9 with a participle; Phil.1:18,20,27; 2 Thess.2:15; Col.1:16,20; 1 Pet.2:13,14. εἴτε οὖν . . . εἴτε - 1 Cor.12:13; 15:11. Followed by the present indicative - 1 Cor.12:26; 10:31a,b,c; 13:8; 14:27; 2 Cor.1:6. Followed by the present subjunctive - 1 Thess.5:10 (where the subjunctive is used because of ζήσωμεν in the leading clause); "whether. . . or" in indirect question, after οὐκ οἶδα in 2 Cor.12:2,3.

προφητείαν (acc.sing.fem.of προφητεία, direct object of ἔχοντες) 1041.
κατὰ (preposition with the accusative, distributive) 98.
τὴν (acc.sing.fem.of the article in agreement with ἀναλογίαν) 9.

#4017 ἀναλογίαν (acc.sing.fem.of ἀναλογία, distributive).

   King James Version

proportion - Rom.12:6.

   Revised Standard Version

proportion - Rom.12:6.

Meaning: Cf. ἀναλογίζομαι (#5061) ἀνάλογος - "according to a λόγος; hence, proportionate, conformable. Thus ἀναλογία is a proportion - synonymous with μέτρον (#643). κατὰ τὴν ἀναλογίαν πίστεως - equals κατὰ τὸ μέτρον πίστεως which God has given - Rom.12:6.

τῆς (gen.sing.fem.of the article in agreement with πίστεως) 9.
πίστεως (gen.sing.fem.of πίστις, description) 728.

Translation - *"So since we have gifts that differ according to the grace which was given to us, whether it be prophecy, let us exercise it according to the degree of faith. . . "*

Comment: The participle ἔχοντες is an excellent example of the adverbial conditional usage. It functions as the protasis of a conditional sentence. *Cf.* Acts 15:29; Lk.3:11 and Heb.2:3 for other examples. Since there is no other verb in the sentence some grammarians have taken ἔχοντες as an indicative, while others have called the absence of the verb anacoluthon or ellipsis. The papyrii has numerous such uses, and its use does not mark the writer as an uneducated person. Robertson says, ". . . the participle in itself is never imperative nor indicative, though there seem to be examples in the New Testament, as in the papyrii, where, because of ellipsis or anacoluthon, the participle carries on the work either of the indicative or the imperative" (*Grammar*, 1133).It seems simpler to call ἔχοντες an adverb in a first-class condition and supply the verb.

Every Christian has some gift/gifts (1 Cor.12:4-11), but they differ in quantity in keeping with the sovereign will of the Giver. Whatever the gift may be we should exercise it to the full extent of the proportion of faith which has been given to us.

It is important to remember that Paul wrote this to the Romans before the canon of New Testament literature was complete. In the first century, when the churches did not have available the New Testament to guide them, special gifts of specialized knowledge and prophecy and, when needed, miraculous ability to speak in a foreign language, were given to the Apostles and perhaps to others. These gifts were needed for the preaching of the gospel on some occasions, and for the instruction to the churches in matters of doctrine and practice, which instruction was later incorporated into the New Testament literaure. The ability to speak in a language, other than one's own native dialect, ceased (παύσονται) and the gifts of prophecy and knowledge were phased out (καταργηθήσονται) when the complete revelation (τὸ τέλειον) was finished (1 Cor.13:8-10). Thus Paul's instruction to the Romans to exercise the gift of prophecy, although fitting at the time, is no longer fitting, since all of the revelation which the Holy Spirit wishes us to have is in the New Testament. There is no further need for new revelations. Those who claim to have supernatural ability to supplement the message of the New Testament with Spirit inspired "prophecies" are seeking to add to that which is already perfect. There have been no prophets or purveyors of supernatural knowledge, who received their inspiration from outside the New Testament since the first century.

It is important, in this connection to note that 1 Cor.13 does not say that other gifts of the Holy Spirit, such as teaching or ministering (Rom.12:7) have been phased out, for these and other gifts do not seek to supplement the message of the New Testament. *Cf.* our full discussion of this matter *en loc* 1 Cor.11-14.

There is practical guidance here and warning against misuse of the gifts. (1) The Christian should not make grandiose plans to serve the Lord in a way that calls for greater gifts than he possesses, and (2) he should plan to use the gift or gifts which he has to the fullest extent possible. Many Christians underutilize their gifts and thus fail to reach their potential for God's service. Others, with misplaced zeal, seem unwilling to accept the position in the Body of Christ allotted to them. Both of these errors are productive of much mischief. Both paralysis (underutilization) and St.Vitus Dance (hyperactivity) are considered serious neurological disorders.

Verse 7 - "Or ministry, let us wait on our ministering: or he that teacheth, on teaching."

εἴτε διακονίαν ἐν τῇ διακονίᾳ, εἴτε ὁ διδάσκων ἐν τῇ διδασκαλίᾳ,

". . . *if service, in our serving; he who teaches, in his teaching;*" . . . RSV

εἴτε (disjunctive particle in indirect question) 4016.
διακονίαν (acc.sing.fem.of διακονία, direct object of ἔχοντες) 2442.
ἐν (preposition with the locative of sphere) 80.
τῇ (loc.sing.fem.of the article in agreement with διακονίᾳ) 9.
διακονίᾳ (loc.sing.fem.of διακονία, sphere) 2442.
εἴτε (disjunctive conjunction in indirect question) 4016.
ὁ (nom.sing.masc.of the article in agreement with διδάσκων) 9.
διδάσκων (pres.act.part.nom.sing.masc.of διδάσκω, substantival, subject of verb understood) 403.
ἐν (preposition with the locative of sphere) 80.
τῇ (loc.sing.fem.of the article in agreement with διδασκαλίᾳ) 9.
διδασκαλίᾳ (loc.sing.fem.of διδασκαλία, sphere) 1150.

Translation - "or rendering service by serving, or the teacher by teaching, . . . " . . .
RSV

Comment: The hortatory verbs are omitted. Whatever the gift, let him exercise it, with the thought that the gift came from God and the exercise of it fulfills God's will for the recipient. Prophets should prophesy as often as the Holy Spirit gives them something to say. They should also keep in mind that they are only temporary prophets, used by the Holy Spirit to guide the first century churches until He has finished inspiring the New Testament. There were no prophets in the sense in which Paul is using this word in our passage after the New Testament was completed, for the reason that they were no longer needed. Indeed their presence in the church in the 20th century creates a problem that comes close to creating about them an antiChristian cult.

But the office of deacon has not been phased out, and deacons should serve wherever and however they are needed. Deacons should also keep in mind that they are not the dictators in their local churches. Deacons have a difficult time obeying Paul's instructions in the first half of verse 3.

Teachers should teach and be patient when their students seem slow to learn. Theirs is a vital function which is mentioned in the Great Commission (Mt.28:18-20).

There should never be any attempt to rank these functions in some supposed order of dignity or prestige. It is sufficiently prestigious to have been invited into the Body of Christ and there is equal dignity attached to every member of the Body. A gift that has a heavenly origin is never involved in a task that is menial.

The hint that we should be patient runs through this entire passage. Let us remember that our risen Lord is "head over all things to his church, which is his body" (Eph.1:22,23) and that His program is on schedule. God is not in a hurry, and it is incongruous to hope that One Who is not subject to the categories of time and space will accelerate His efforts. The only concern for the yielded child of God is that he discerns his part in the division of labor in the economy of God and that he dedicate himself to it with his full potential.

Verse 8 - "Or he that exhorteth on exhortation: he that giveth let him do it with simplicity; he that ruleth with diligence; he that showeth mercy with cheerfulness."

εἴτε ὁ παρακαλῶν ἐν τῇ παρακλήσει, ὁ μεταδιδοὺς ἐν ἁπλότητι, ὁ προϊστάμενος ἐν σπουδῇ, ὁ ἐλεῶν ἐν ἱλαρότητι.

"he who exhorts, in his exhortation; he who contributes, in liberality; he who gives aid, with zeal; he who does acts of mercy, with cheerfulness." . . . RSV

εἴτε (disjunctive conjunction in indirect question) 4016.

ὁ (nom.sing.masc.of the article in agreement with παρακαλῶν) 9.

παρακαλῶν (pres.act.part.nom.sing.masc.of παρακαλέω, substantival, subject of verb understood) 230.

ἐν (preposition with the locative of sphere) 80.

τῇ (loc.sing.fem.of the article in agreement with παρακλήσει) 9.

παρακλήσει (loc.sing.fem.of παράκλησις, sphere) 1896.

ὁ (nom.sing.masc.of the article in agreement with μεταδιδοὺς) 9.

μεταδιδοὺς (pres.act.part.nom.sing.masc.of μεταδίδωμι, substantival, subject of verb understood) 1942.

ἐν (preposition with the locative, instrumental use, manner) 80.

#4018 ἁπλότητι (instru.sing.masc.of ἁπλότης, manner).

King James Version

bountifulness - 2 Cor.9:11.
liberality - 2 Cor.8:2.
simplicity - Rom.12:8; 2 Cor.1:12; 11:3.
singleness - Eph.6:5; Col.3:22.
liberal - 2 Cor.9;13.

Revised Standard Version

liberality - Rom.12:8; 2 Cor.8:2.
holiness - 2 Cor.1:12.
generosity - 2 Cor.9:11,13.
sincere - 2 Cor.11:3.
singleness - Eph.6:5; Col.3:22.

Meaning: singleness, simplicity, sincerity, mental honesty. Without pretense or dissimulation. Absolutely in Rom.12:8; 2 Cor.1:12; 9:11; 11:13; grammatically absolute, but in a context indicating sincerity in giving money - 2 Cor.8:2; 9:11,13. Followed by τῆς καρδίας in Eph.6:5; followed by καρδίας in Col.3:22.

ὁ (nom.sing.masc.of the article in agreement with προϊστάμενος) 9.

#4019 προϊστάμενος (pres.mid.part.nom.sing.masc.of προΐστημι, substantival, subject of verb understood).

King James Version

be over - 1 Thess.5:12.
maintain - Titus 3:8,14.
rule - Rom.12:8; 1 Tim.3:4,5,12; 5:17.

Revised Standard Version

give aid - Rom.12:8.
be over - 1 Thess.5:12.
manage - 1 Tim.3:4,5,12.
rule - 1 Tim.5:17.
apply oneself - Tit.3:8,14.

Meaning: A combination of πρό (#442) and ἵστημι (#180). Transitively, to set or place over or before; to be over, superintend, rule, manange. In an administrative capacity in a church - Rom.12:8; 1 Thess.5:12; 1 Tim.5:17; in the family - 1 Tim.3:4,5,12. To supervise one's own life to maintain good works - Tit.3:8,14.

ἐν (preposition with the locative, instrumental use, manner) 80.
σπουδῇ (loc.sing.fem.of σπουδή, manner) 1819.
ὁ nom.sing.masc.of the article in agreement with ἐλεῶν) 9.
ἐλεῶν (pres.act.part.nom.sing.masc.of ἐλεέω, substantival, subject of verb understood) 430.
ἐν (preposition with the locative, instrumental use, manner) 80.

#4020 ἱλαρότητι (instru.sing.masc.of ἱλαρότης, manner).

King James Version

cheerfulness - Rom.12:8.

Revised Standard Version

cheerfulness - Rom.12:8.

Meaning: Cf. ἱλαρός (#4350). Joyousness, readiness of mind, cheerfulness, hilarity - Rom.12:8.

Translation - "... or the comforter with sympathy; the one who shares with pure *motive; the administrator with diligence; the one who is being merciful, with cheerfulness."*

Comment: Every Christian should perform his service to Christ by exercising the gift which by divine grace is his. Preachers, deacons, teachers and exhorters are to do that for which they are equipped (verse 7,8), though Paul does not suggest how it should be done except κατὰ τὴν ἀναλογίαν τῆς πίστεως - "to the fullest extent of their ability, as that ability is determined by their faith." However, wealthy Christians should share their financial assets in sincerity, not with an assumed air of superiority of donor over recipient, not with any ulterior motive in mind. God gave them their wealth and therefore it is His money; they are only the stewards of it. Some benefactors who give but not ἐν ἁπλότητι hurt the recipient with their attitude more that they help with their money.

Supervisors should take their administrative duties seriously. Those who go about dispensing mercy should be cheeful, even hilarious about it.

All of these suggestions from Paul are designed to improve human relations in society, both in and out of the local church. The fundamental fact to remember is found in verses 4-6. The unity of the members of the Body of Christ elevates all to the same position of dignity. All are regenerated; all are endowed with some gift/ gifts to the extent of the will of the Holy Spirit. No one is superior to anyone else. Let all function, therefore, in his own way, keeping always in mind that his contribution to the united effort of the body comes only by the grace of God. There would never be a schism in a local church, or in a great denominational body, if this practical policy, based upon this revealed truth were pursued.

Rules of the Christian Life

(Romans 12:9-21)

Verse 9 - "Let love be without dissimulation. Abhor that which is evil; cleave to that which is good."

Ἡ ἀγάπη ἀνυπόκριτος. ἀποστυγοῦντες τὸ πονηρόν, κολλώμενοι τῷ ἀγαθῷ.

"Let love be genuine; hate what is evil, hold fast to what is good;" . . . RSV

Ἡ (nom.sing.fem.of the article in agreement with ἀγάπη) 9.

ἀγάπη (nom.sing.fem.of ἀγάπη, subject of the verb understood) 1490.

#4021 ἀνυπόκριτος (nom.sing.fem.of ἀνυπόκρτος, predicate adjective).

King James Version

unfeigned - 2 Cor.6:6; 1 Tim.1:5; 2 Tim.1:5; 1 Pet.1:22.
without dissimulation - Rom.12:9.
without hypocrisy - James 3:17.

Revised Standard Version

genuine - Rom.12:9; 2 Cor.6:6.
sincere - 1 Tim.1:5; 2 Tim.1:5; 1 Pet.1:22.
without insincerity - James 3:17.

Meaning: α privative plus ὑποκρίνομαι (#2691). Hence, unfeigned, sincere, honest, without pretense. ἡ ἀγάπη ἀνυπόκριτος - "when you say or show to someone that you love him, mean it. Do not be two-faced." Joined with ἀγάπη in Rom.12:9; 2 Cor.6:6; with πίστις in 1 Tim.1:5; 2 Tim.1:5; with σοφία in James 3:17; with φιλαδελφία in 1 Pet.1:22.

#4022 ἀποστυγοῦντες (pres.act.part.nom.pl.masc.of ἀποστυγέω, adverbial, imperatival).

King James Version

abhor - Rom.12:9.

Revised Standard Version

hate - Rom.12:9.

Meaning: A combination of ἀπό (#70) and στυγέω - "to hate" "to abhor." Fritzsche regards ἀπό in composition here as expressing separation - "Turn away in abhorrence." To hate something and be repelled by it. Others regard ἀπό as intensive. These ideas are not mutually exclusive. Followed by τὸ πονηρόν in Rom.12:9.

τὸ (acc.sing.neut.of the article in agreement with πονηρόν) 9.
πονηρόν (acc.sing.neut.of πονηρός, direct object of ἀποστυγοῦντες) 438.
κολλώμενοι (pres.mid.part.nom.pl.masc.of κολλάομαι, adverbial, imperatival) 1288.
τῷ (instru.sing.neut.of the article in agreement with ἀγαθῷ) 9.
ἀγαθῷ (instru.sing.neut.of ἀγαθός, association) 547.

Translation - "Let love be sincere. Turn in disgust from evil. Cling to that which is good."

Comment: The first phrase serves as an independent sentence, despite the fact that there is no verb. We know exactly what Paul means. Our expressions of love, both verbal and pragmatic must be sincere. The participles ἀποστυγοῦντες and κολλώμενοι are imperatival and serve to support independent clauses. Whether a participle in an independent clause without a main verb is indicative or imperative is decided only by the context. Here these are clearly imperative. Note the intensity involved in each - "Turn in disgust and revulsion away from evil" and "glue yourself (middle voice) to the good." *Cf.#*'s 4022 and 1288.

The Christian in the 1980's with a television set in his home has plenty of opportunity to practice the second admonition. These admonitions are nonesense to the existentialist with his ethical relativism, which, according to his boast, elevates him to such a high state of sophistication that he is unable to tell the difference between good and evil. Indeed, without the aid of supernatural guidance, which in 1 Cor.12:10 is called the gift of "discerning of spirits," it is difficult, in a complicated social structure to discern the difference in all cases. But Paul is assuming that his readers are regenerated members of the Body of Christ and that the Holy Spirit lives within (1 Cor.6:19,20). The Christian may not know the difference between right and wrong and good and evil but the indwelling Holy Spirit does and He bears witness with our spirit (Rom.8:16).

The ethical relativist without Christ finds it possible to designate as good anything that he wishes to approbate, however evil it obviously is. Woe unto him! (Isa.5:20). *Cf.* Psalm 97:10.

Aleatoric "music" and da da "art," neither of which is subject to any known principle is lauded by some elements in modern society, despite the fact that canons of good taste are obviously flaunted. Most Christians know the difference but neglect to obey the admonitions of this verse. Thus as they warm themselves at the enemy's fire they get burned (John 18;25; 1 Thess.5:22). Many evil causes are supported by Christian capital while good causes are left without support. In a country guided by first amendment freedoms, the rights of minorities to write, compose, paint, produce and sell whatever they choose is vouchsafed, and Christians err in their misguided zeal to legislate against these minority rights. We cannot in America, in any constitutional way, deprive a citizen of his right to produce trash. The Christian attack upon his efforts consists of education of the public, with the result that enough Christians will "turn in disgust away from evil" that sales will decline to the point that his production will no longer be economically possible. The boycott of that which is evil, in a free society, is the only effective method of control. As long as many professed Christians reward evil, there is little probability that evil can be driven from the market place. Indeed the description of the course of this age in the Scriptures argues against the probability of success for those who wish to keep American decent. A vigorous spiritual revival of revealed New Testament religion, with its ethical reevaluation of the status quo could turn America around. The problem which those who view the current scene from the Christian point of view face is that of not knowing where we are on God's clock. If we are as close to the end of the age as some think, there will be no reversal in the headlong trend to evil until our Lord returns. But this is something that no Christian can know at the moment (June 14, 1982).

Verse 10 - "Be kindly affectioned one to another with brotherly love; in hono preferring one another."

τῇ φιλαδελφίᾳ εἰς ἀλλήλους φιλόστοργοι, τῇ τιμῇ ἀλλήλους προηγούμεν-οι,

"love one another with brotherly affection; outdo one another in showing honor." . . . RSV

τῇ (instru.sing.fem.of the article in agreement with φιλαδελφίᾳ) 9.

#4023 φιλαδελφίᾳ (instru.sing.fem.of φιλαδελφία, manner).

King James Version

brotherly kindness - 2 Pet.1:7,7.
brotherly love - Rom.12:10; 1 Thess.4:9; Heb.13:1.
love of the brethren - 1 Pet.1:22.

Revised Standard Version

brotherly affection - Rom.12:10; 2 Pet.1:7,7.
love of the brethren - 1 Thess.4:9; 1 Pet.1:22.
brotherly love - Heb.13:1.

Meaning: A combination of φιλέω (#566) and ἀδελφός (#15). *Cf.* φίλος (#932), φιλία (#1108), φίλη (#2542), φιλανθρωπία (#3756) and others in φιλ - Love of brothers and sisters. Always in the New Testament of the love of a Christian for another Christian . A stepping stone to ἀγάπη (2 Pet.1:7b) and the fruit of εὐσέβεια (2 Pet.1:7a). Rom.12:10; 1 Thess.4:19; Heb.13:1; 1 Pet.1:22.

εἰς (preposition with the accusative of extent) 140.
ἀλλήλους (acc.pl.masc.of ἀλλήλων, extent) 1487.

#4024 φιλόστοργοι (nom.pl.masc.of φιλόστοργος, predicate adjective).

King James Version

be kindly affectioned - Rom.12:10.

Revised Standard Version

love - Rom.12:10.

Meaning: A combination of φίλος (#932) and στοργή - "love, affection." Hence, mutual affection between parents and children, husbands and wives, close friends - Rom.12:10.

τῇ (loc.sing.fem.of the article in agreement with τιμῇ) 9.
τιμῇ (loc.sing.fem.of τιμή, sphere) 1619.
ἀλλήλους (acc.pl.masc.of ἀλλήλων, direct object of προηγούμενα) 1487.

#4025 προηγούμενα (pres.mid.part.nom.pl.masc.of προηγέομαι, imperatival).

King James Version

prefer - Rom.12:10.

Revised Standard Version

outdo - Rom.12:10.

Meaning: A combination of πρό (#442) and ἡγέομαι (#162). To go ahead as a leader; show the way; outdo another; excell. With a locative of sphere in Rom.12:10. - "Give more honor to your brother than he gives to you."

Translation - "Cultivate fondness for each other by means of brotherly kindness. Let each outdo the other in showing honor."

Comment: Again in the first half of the verse we have no verb. *Cf.* verse 9. φιλόστοργοι is a predicate adjective in the nominative case but the verb is missing. If present, it would be ἔστω (#86). προηγούμενοι is another imperatival participle. It is an interesting concept - "run ahead of each other in your zeal to honor." It is difficult to imagine the unity of a church congregation where each member sought to excel all others in giving (not receiving) honor. Obedience to this imperative calls for complete self-effacement, another indication of the greatest personal security, the basis for mental health.

In view of the fact that τιμή (#1619) is the value of something, which value is often expressed in terms of cost and price, in the monetary sense, Paul may also mean to include a redistribution of the wealth, not in obedience to a mandate from the state but in compliance of a personal wish to help others (Eph.4:28). The idea that each is to seek to outdo the others in this function brings to mind the potlatch of the Kwakiutl Indians of the Pacific Northwest, although their motives are not Christian. The purpose of the potlatch is to demonstrate personal wealth and the contempt which one feels for it as evidenced by giving it away. The Christian is to outdo his brother/sister in honor from selfless motives of love.

Verse 11 - "Not slothful in business; fervent in spirit; serving the Lord."

τῇ σπουδῇ μὴ ὀκνηροί, τῷ πνεύματι ζέοντες, τῷ κυρίῳ δουλεύοντες,

"Never flag in zeal, be aglow with the Spirit, serve the Lord." . . . RSV

τῇ (loc.sing.fem.of the article in agreement with σπουδῇ) 9.
σπουδῇ (loc.sing.fem.of σπουδή, sphere) 1819.
μὴ (negative particle with the imperative) 87.
ὀκνηροί (nom.pl.masc.of ὀκνηρός, predicate adjective) 1539.
τῷ (instru.sing.neut.of the article in agreement with πνεύματι) 9.
πνεύματι (instru.sing.neut.of πνεῦμα, means) 83.
ζέοντες (pres.act.part.nom.pl.masc.of ζέω, adverbial, imperative) 3456.
τῷ (dat.sing.masc.of the article in agreement with κυρίῳ) 9.
κυρίῳ (dat.sing.masc.of κύριος, personal advantage) 97.
δουλεύοντες (pres.act.part.nom.pl.masc.of δουλεύω, adverbial, imperatival) 604.

Translation - "Do not be lazy in the diligent pursuit of your duties; burn with the zeal of the Spirit; always serve the Lord."

Comment: The pattern continues with no main verbs, but with the participles carrying the independent clauses imperatively. That is why we have μὴ with the adjective ὀκνηροί, where normally we would expect οὐκ. τῇ σπουδῇ μὴ ὀκνηροί is really tautological. Literally it says, "in the sphere of your diligence do not be lazy." It is an admonition to avoid procrastination. Whatever there is to do for the Lord, do it (2 Cor.6:2).

Whether we take τῷ πνεύματι to mean the human spirit or the Holy Spirit the result is the same, since the human spirit depends upon the Holy Spirit for guidance and motivation. Thus our translation - "burn with the zeal of the Spirit." We could translate, "Be on fire with the Holy Spirit." There are many passages that teach that Christian zeal is the work of the Holy Spirit.

Note the present participle δουλεύοντες - "always serving the Lord."

The admonition to "burn with the zeal of the Lord" should not be interpreted to approbate the behavior of some super-emotional people who call themselves "charismatics" who respond in public to forces which they assume to be heavenly, but which are in many cases the result of the skills of powerful mob psychologists, former cheer leaders at football games, and now song leaders and preachers in religious services. Nadab and Abihu offered "strange fire" before the Lord and learned that it is impossible to fool God (Lev.10:1; Numbers 3:4; 26:61). Emotional hyper-ventilation is not to be confused with the filling of the Holy Spirit. The zeal of which the Holy Spirit is the Source manifests itself in the fruits which He produces (Gal.5:22,23) and effective use of the gifts which He gives (1 Cor.12:1-11), not in acrobatic feats and inspired vociferations in public worship services for the amusement of wicked little boys on the back seat. One need not be concerned about how high zealous people jump, so long as they walk straight for God when they come down. It is the walk of the straight path that forces the skeptic to make a distinction between the burning zeal of the Holy Spirit that Paul speaks about in our passage and the "strange fire" of the modern Nadab and Abihu.

Verse 12 - "Rejoicing in hope; patient in tribulation; continuing instant in prayer."

τῇ ἐλπίδι χαίροντες, τῇ θλίφει ὑπομένοντες, τῇ προσευχῇ προσκαρτεροῦντες,

"Rejoice in your hope, be patient in tribulation, be constant in prayer." . . .
RSV

τῇ (instrumental sing.fem.of the article in agreement with ἐλπίδι) 9.
ἐλπίδι (instru.sing.fem.of ἐλπίς, cause) 2994.
χαίροντες (pres.act.part.nom.pl.masc.of χαίρω, imperatival) 182.
τῇ (loc.sing.fem.of the article in agreement with θλίφει) 9.
θλίφει (loc.sing.fem.of θλίφις, accompanying circumstance) 1046.
ὑπομένοντες (pres.act.part.nom.pl.masc.of ὑπομένω, imperatival) 880.
τῇ (loc.sing.fem.of the article in agreement with προσευχῇ) 9.

προσευχῇ (loc.sing.fem.of προσευχή, sphere) 1238.

προσκαρτεροῦντες (pres.act.part.nom.pl.masc.of προσκαρτερέω, imperatival) 2113.

Translation - "You have hope! Be glad! Be patient in the face of tribulation. Persist in prayer."

Comment: *Cf.* Rom.5:1-5 for the connection between hope (ἐλπίς) and joy (χαίρω). The locative of accompanying circumstance with the participle as it is often found with verbs. Persistence in the sphere of one's prayer life.

A quick review of the functions of Christian service that results from a correct understanding of our position in the Body of Christ yields: sincere love, disgust for evil, devotion to good (verse 9); fondness, brotherly love and self-effacement with a zeal to honor others (verse 10); diligent application to duty, flaming zeal and consistent service (verse 11) and joy because of hope, patience under trial and constant prayer (verse 12).

The list goes on through verse 21.   Paul is as intensely practical now as he was theoretical in chapters 1-8. We have the connection between the social and the theological gospel in economic terms in

Verse 13 - "Distributing to the necesssity of saints; given to hospitality."

ταῖς χρείαις τῶν ἁγίων κοινωνοῦντες, τὴν φιλοξενίαν διώκοντες.

"Contribute to the needs of the saints, practice hospitality." . . . RSV

ταῖς (instru.pl.fem.of the article in agreement with χρείαις) 9.

χρείαις (instru.pl.fem.of χρεία, cause) 317.

τῶν (gen.pl.masc.of the article in agreement with ἁγίων) 9.

ἁγίων (gen.pl.masc.of ἅγιος, definition) 84.

#4026 κοινωνοῦντες (pres.act.part.nom.pl.masc.of κοινωνέω, imperatival).

King James Version

be made partaker of - Rom.15:27.
be partaker of - 1 Tim.5:22; Heb.2:14; 1 Pet.4:13; 2 John 11.
communicate - Gal.6:6; Phil.4:15.
distribute - Rom.12:13.

Revised Standard Version

contribute - Rom.12:13.
come to share - Rom.15:27.
participate in - 1 Tim.5:22.
share - Heb.2:14; 1 Pet.4:13; 2 John 11; Gal.6:6.
enter into partnership - Phil.4:15.

Meaning: Cf. κοινωνία (#3001), κοινωνός (#1470), κοινόω (#1152), κοινός (#2295) and κοινωνικός (#4795). To share; to divide what one has with others; to be a fellow-partaker; to be made a partner; to commune or have fellowship with. To share physical things with those in need - Rom.12;13; Gal.6:6; Phil.4:15; to participate in the spiritual blessings of the gospel of Christ - Rom.15:27; to be fellow participants in sin and false teaching - 1 Tim.5:22; 2 John 11. With reference to human nature in the incarnation - Heb.2:14. With reference to the Christian's participation with Christ in suffering - 1 Pet.4:13. Thus we have a sermon outline: (1) Fellowship in sin; (2) Fellowship in flesh and blood; (3) Fellowship in the gospel; (4) Fellowship in Christ's sufferings; (5) Fellowship in wealth.

τὴν (acc.sing.fem.of the article in agreement with φιλοξενίαν) 9.

#4027 φιλοξενίαν (acc.sing.fem.of φιλοξενία, direct object of διώκοντες).

King James Version

hospitality - Rom.12:13.
to entertain strangers - Heb.13:2.

Revised Standard Version

hospitality - Rom.12:13; Heb.13:2.

Meaning: A combination of φίλος (#932) and ξένος (#1547). Hence, a love for strangers; kindness to strangers; hospitality. *Cf.* φιλόξενος (#4730). Rom.12:13; Heb.13:2.

διώκοντες (pres.act.part.nom.pl.masc.of διώκω, imperatival) 434.

Translation - "*Share what you have when the saints need it. Follow a policy of hospitality.*"

Comment: Spiritual fellowship with the saints is an empty profession, if, when they need financial help, we do not also share our material blessings. Spiritual, intellectual and material fellowship with those in need is the highest fellowship possible. It extends also to strangers. *Cf.* #434 for other cases of διώκω in this sense.

We have it in the other sense in

Verse 14 - "*Bless them which persecute you: bless, and curse not.*"

εὐλογεῖτε τοὺς διώκοντας, εὐλογεῖτε καὶ μὴ καταρᾶσθε.

"*Bless those who persecute you; bless and do not curse them.*" . . . *RSV*

εὐλογεῖτε (2d.per.pl.pres.act.impv.of εὐλογέω, command) 1120.
τοὺς (acc.pl.masc.of the article in agreement with διώκοντας) 9.
διώκοντας (pres.act.part.acc.pl.masc.of διώκω, substantival, direct object of εὐλογεῖτε) 434.
εὐλογεῖτε (2d.per.pl.pres.act.impv.of εὐλογέω, command) 1120.

καὶ (continuative conjunction) 14.

μὴ (negative particle with the imperative) 87.

καταρᾶσθε (2d.per.pl.pres.mid.impv.of καταράομαι, prohibition) 1550.

Translation - "Always bless your persecutors; always bless and stop cursing."

Comment: In εὐλογεῖτε we finally have a main verb, serving in the imperative for the imperatival participles in verses 9-13. There is not a single main verb in any of the independent clauses after verse 5. We had, either ellipsis or the imperative use of the participle. In verse 15 we will see the infinitive in an imperatival use. *Cf.* Lk.6:28 for Jesus' statement of it.

Paul now enjoins blessing upon all, and also demands that Christians cease retaliating. Note μὴ with the imperative in prohibition in the present tense - "Do not go on cursing." Here is instruction to the Christian in regard to his relationship with the unsaved.

A variant reading has διώκοντας ὑμᾶς. Origin has ἐχθροὺς ὑμῶν. Origin generally thought that he knew more about how it ought to have been written than the Holy Spirit!

Verse 15 - "Rejoice with them that do rejoice, and weep with them that weep."

χαίρειν μετὰ χαιρόντων, κλαίειν μετὰ κλαιόντων.

"Rejoice with those who rejoice, weep with those who weep." . . . RSV

χαίρειν (pres.act.inf.of χαίρω, imperatival) 182.

μετὰ (preposition with the genitive, fellowship) 50.

χαιρόντων (pres.act.part.gen.pl.masc.of χαίρω, substantival, fellowship) 182.

κλαίειν (pres.act.inf.of κλαίω, imperatival) 225.

μετὰ (preposition with the genitive, fellowship) 50.

κλαιόντων (pres.act.part.gen.pl.masc.of κλαίω, substantival, fellowship 225.

Translation - "Rejoice with the joyous and weep with those who weep."

Comment: The infinitives χαίρειν and κλαίειν now, rather than the participles serve the imperatival function, while the participles serve as substantives. The imperative infinitive ". . . is the only independent use of the Greek infinitive, and is not of very frequent occurrence." (Mantey, *Manual*, 216). "It is of ancient origin, being especially frequent in Homer," (Burton, *Moods and Tenses*, 146). "The construction suggests a close kinship between the infinitive and imperative." *(Mantey,* Ibid.) " . . . the probability is that imperative forms like δεῖξαι . . . are infinitive in origin" (Robertson, *Grammar*, 943). "Though this idiom is rare in the New Testament, it is a current Koine usage, for the papyri contain many occurrences of it." (Mantey,*Ibid.*) Its rarity in the New Testament is a "matter of surprise." (Moulton, *Prolegomena to the Grammar of New Testament Greek*, 180, as cited in *Ibid.) Cf.* also Phil.3:16 and Titus 2:2 for other examples. "An example of the imperative infinitive in patristic Greek may be found in the Didache, 14:3: προσφέρειν μοι θυσίαν καθαράν, - *offer to me a pure sacrifice." (Mantey, Ibid., 217).*

Christians are united in unity in the Body of Christ with all other Christians. Thus we are to empathize with each other. *Cf.* 1 Cor.12:25,26. When others are sad we are sympahtetic and sad with them. The good fortune of others is enough to give us joy. How could it ever be any other way? The analogy to the human body is apt. Who has not ached all over because of an infected tooth? A splinter under a finger nail creates excruciating pain, not only to the injured part but to the entire body as well. Older people testify that arthritis delibitates the entire body. How often sullen jealousy is seen on the face and in the speech of one church member because another has been made glad. How often have church members enjoyed a degree of satisfaction from the misfortunes of others.

Verse 16 - "Be of the same mind one toward another. Mind not high things, but condescend to men of low estate. Be not wise in your own conceits."

τὸ αὐτὸ εἰς ἀλλήλους φρονοῦντες, μὴ τὰ ὑφηλὰ φρονοῦντες ἀλλὰ τοῖς ταπεινοῖς συναπαγόμενοι. μὴ γίνεσθε φρόνιμοι παρ᾿ ἑαυτοῖς.

"Live in harmony with one another; do not be haughty, but associate with the lowly; never be conceited." . . . RSV

τὸ (acc.sing.neut.of the article in agreement with αὐτὸ) 9.

αὐτὸ (acc.sing.neut.of αὐτός, direct object of φρονοῦντες) 16.

εἰς (preposition with the accusative of extent) 140.

ἀλλήλους (acc.pl.masc.of ἀλλήλων, extent) 1487.

φρονοῦντες (pres.act.part.nom.pl.masc.of φρονέω, imperatival) 1212.

μὴ (negative particle with the participle) 87.

τὰ (acc.pl.neut.of the article in agreement with ὑφηλὰ) 9.

ὑφηλὰ (acc.pl.neut.of ὑφηλός, direct object of φρονοῦντες) 358.

ἀλλὰ (alternative conjunction) 342.

τοῖς (instru.pl.masc.of the article in agreement with ταπεινοῖς) 9.

ταπεινοῖς (instru.pl.masc.of ταπεινός, association) 957.

#4028 συναπαγόμενοι (pres.mid.part.nom.pl.masc.of συναπάγω, imperatival).

King James Version

carry away with - Gal.2:13.
lead away with - 2 Pet.3:17.
condescend to - Rom.12:16.

Revised Standard Version

associate - Rom.12:16.
carry away with - Gal.2:13; 2 Pet.3:17.

Meaning: A combination of σύν (#1542), ἀπό (#70) and ἄγω (#876). Hence, to lead or bring away in company with. In the passive voice, in a metaphorical sense, to be convinced of a variant theory - Gal.2:13; 2 Pet.3:17. Properly, in the

middle voice to go along with some one in fellowship. It means "condescend" -
"step down to a lower position" only because the context has ταπεινός (#957).
Rom.12:16.

μὴ (negative particle with the imperative) 87.
γίνεσθε (2d.per.pl.pres.impv.of γίνομαι, prohibition) 113.
φρόνιμοι (nom.pl.masc.of φρόνιμος, predicate adjective) 693.
παρ' (preposition with the locative, with persons, sphere) 154.
ἑαυτοῖς (loc.pl.masc.of ἑαυτός, sphere) 288.

*Translation - "Always regard one another in the same way. Stop thinking about
prestige, but always associate with the lowly. Stop being conceited."*

Comment: Again we have participles used like imperatives in independent
clauses, with no main verbs. Thus in the first three clauses. Finally we have a
present imperative in the prohibition of the fourth clause. Note that the
participles and the verb are all in the present tense. There is no reason why a
Christian should ever cease to entertain the attitudes enjoined here. μὴ . . .
φρονοῦντες and μὴ γίνεσθε are prohibitions in the present tense. "Stop thinking
about prestige - Do not continue to think . . . κ.τ.λ." and "Do not continue to
regard yourself as wise . . "

It is the Christian's business to find out what his potential is and humbly thank
God for his gifts, be they few or many. Underestimation of oneself is just as bad
as overestimation, though Paul does not warn us against it in this passage. His
warning against ambition in the second clause, if heeded by all, would prevent a
great many frustrations. One great source of personality disequilibrium is the
frustration that results from the difference between the achievement level (where
we really are) and the ego level (the heights to which we may aspire). All social
gradation, which is such a threat to the unity of the Body of Christ, would
disappear if we obeyed the third and fourth injunctions. Witness the assumed
superiority of the wealthy and socially advantaged Christian in his relation to the
less wealthy members of the congregation, or the disdain of certain sophisticated
theologians for others who hold doctrinal views considered naive. The point is
that the internal unity of the Body of Christ is disrupted and the "lofty" cannot
help the "men of low estate" if they do not condescend. This is the same advice
that Paul gave in verse 3.

*Verse 17 - "Recompense to no man evil for evil. Provide things honest in the sight
of all men."*

μηδενὶ κακὸν ἀντὶ κακοῦ ἀποδιδόντες. προνοούμενοι καλὰ ἐνώπιον πάντων
ἀνθρώπων.

*"Repay no one evil for evil, but take thought for what is noble in the sight of
all." . . . RSV*

μηδενὶ (dat.sing.masc.of μηδείς, personal disadvantage) 713.
κακὸν (acc.sing.neut.of κακός, direct object of ἀποδιδόντες) 1388.

ἀντί (preposition with the genitive, "instead of") 237.
κακοῦ (gen.sing.neut.of κακός, "instead of") 1388.
ἀποδιδόντες (pres.act.part.nom.pl.masc.of ἀποδίδωμι, imperatival) 495.

#4029 προνοούμενοι (pres.mid.part.nom.pl.masc.of προνοέω, imperatival).

King James Version

provide for - 2 Cor.8:21; 1 Tim.5:8.
provide - Rom.12:17.

Revised Standard Version

take thought - Rom.12:17.
aim at - 2 Cor.8:21.
provide for - 1 Tim.5:8.

Meaning: A combination of πρό (#442) and νοέω (#1160). Hence, to think ahead; anticipate; plan for future needs, thus to forestall exigencies. Followed by an object - καλά ("things noble") in Rom.12:17; 2 Cor.8:21. Followed by the genitive - 1 Tim.5:8.

καλά (acc.pl.neut.of καλός, direct object of προνοούμενοι) 296.
ἐνώπιον (preposition with the genitive, with persons) 1798.
πάντων (gen.pl.masc.of πᾶς, in agreement with ἀνθρώπων) 67.
ἀνθρώπων (gen.pl.masc.of ἄνθρωπος, adverbial) 341.

Translation - "Never retaliate against evil with evil. Always make prior arrangements to behave nobly before all men."

Comment: Again we have the present participle ἀποδιδόντες, in an independent clause, in an imperatival usage. Literally it says, "Always (durative action in the present tense) pay back to nobody evil for evil." προνοούμενοι is still another imperatival participle - present tense in the middle voice. The word means "to think ahead" and therefore denies the false interpretation that some put upon Mt.6:34, by which they forbid savings accounts and insurance policies. On the contrary *cf.* 1 Tim.5:8. However, the KJV "honest" has led some to an interpretation that includes only financial matters, so that they make it mean "plan ahead to pay your honest debts." Indeed this is included since financial responsibility is also καλός (#296), but καλός covers a great many more virtues than honesty in business affairs. Thus the translation - "Plan always (aim at) to be noble before all men." κακὸν ἀντὶ κακοῦ reminds us of ὀφθαλμὸν ἀντὶ ὀφθαλμοῦ (Mt.5:38). *Cf.* also 1 Thess.5:15; 1 Pet.3:9.

The two clauses of verse 17 are the negative and positive sides of the same principle. It is really a restatement of Mt.7:12.

Verse 18 - "It it be possible, as much as lieth in you, live peaceably with all men."

εἰ δυνατόν, τὸ ἐξ ὑμῶν μετὰ πάντων ἀνθρώπων εἰρηνεύοντες.

"If possible, so far as it depends upon you, live peaceably with all." . . . *RSV*

εἰ (conditional particle in an elliptical condition) 337.
δυνατόν (acc.sing.neut.of δυνατός, predicate adjective) 1311.
τό (acc.sing.neut.of the article, extent) 9.
ἐξ (preposition with the ablative of source) 19.
ὑμῶν (abl.pl.masc.of σύ, source) 104.
μετά (preposition with the genitive of fellowship) 50.
πάντων (gen.pl.masc.of πᾶς, in agreement with ἀνθρώπων) 67.
ἀνθρώπων (gen.pl.masc.of ἄνθρωπος, fellowship) 341.
εἰρηνεύοντες (pres.act.part.nom.pl.masc.of εἰρηνεύω, imperatival) 2356.

Translation - "If possible, to the extent that it depends upon you, live in peace with all men."

Comment: This conditional clause is elliptical. We have no verb and cannot tell, from a grammatical point of view whether it is a first or second class condition. If the elided verb, had it been present, were in one of the primary tenses, the condition would be first class. If a secondary tense (imperfect, aorist, pluperfect) second-class. If the latter it would be contrary to fact. The context however suggests some doubt about it. To what extent can a Christian live in peace with others? The preposition phrase τὸ ἐξ ὑμῶν is an accusative of extent, and the ablative ἐξ ὑμῶν indicates that the source of one's restraint comes from within the Christian. To what extent do peaceful relationships depend upon the inner resources of the child of God? If we knew that Paul meant to write a second-class condition, we could translate "if it were possible" (with the implication that in some cases it is not) and say that Paul was being realistic. If it is a first-class condition, we should translate "since it is possible" and say that Paul was saying that, since the Holy Spirit indwells the believer, and since one of His fruits is peace, it is possible. In which case the phrase τὸ ἐξ ὑμῶν would mean "to the extent that you yield yourself to the Holy Spirit." There have been occasions when Christians have been goaded into fisticuffs beyond their powers of endurance. *Cf.* Rom.7:15.

The question arises whether a Christian is ever justified in using violence in self-defense or in the defense of others. The pacifistic theologians (Quakers and others) struggle with this question. The view that I have taken in the translation, with some hesitancy, is that we are to make every provision on our part for peaceable relations with others. We should leave no stone unturned to maintain peace. Perhaps both ideas can be drawn from the text. *Cf.* Mk.9:50; 2 Cor.13:11; 1 Thess.5:13.

There seems to be some support for our view in

Verse 19 - "Dearly beloved, avenge not yourselves, but rather give place unto wrath: for it is written, Vengeance is mine; I will repay, saith the Lord."

μὴ ἑαυτοὺς ἐκδικοῦντες, ἀγαπητοί, ἀλλὰ δότε τόπον τῇ ὀργῇ, γέγραπται γάρ, Ἐμοὶ ἐκδίκησις, ἐγὼ ἀνταποδώσω, λέγει κύριος.

"Beloved, never avenge yourselves, but leave it to the wrath of God; for it is written, 'Vengeance is mine, I will repay, says the Lord.' " . . . RSV

μή (negative particle with the participle in a prohibition) 87.

ἑαυτούς (acc.pl.masc.of ἑαυτός, direct object of ἐκδικοῦντες) 288.

ἐκδικοῦντες (pres.act.part.nom.pl.masc.of ἐκδικέω, imperatival) 2523.

ἀγαπητοί (voc.pl.masc.of ἀγαπητός, address) 327.

ἀλλά (alternative conjunction) 342.

δότε (2d.per.pl.aor.act.impv.of δίδωμι, command) 362.

τόπον (ac.sing.masc.of τόπος, direct object of δότε) 1019.

τῇ (loc.sing.fem.of the article in agreement with ὀργῇ) 9.

ὀργῇ (loc.sing.fem.of ὀργή, sphere) 283.

γέγραπται (3d.per.sing.perf.pass.ind.of γράφω, intensive) 156.

γάρ (causal conjunction) 105.

Ἐμοί (dat.sing.masc.of ἐμός, possession) 1267.

ἐκδίκησις (nom.sing.fem.of ἐκδίκησις, subject of verb understood) 2625.

ἐγώ (nom.sing.masc.of ἐγώ, subject of ἀνταποδώσω, emphatic) 123.

ἀνταποδώσω (1st.per.sing.fut.act.ind.of ἀνταποδίδωμι, predictive) 2529.

λέγει (3d.per.sing.pres.act.ind.ofd λέγω; historical) 66.

κύριος (nom.sing.masc.of κύριος, subject of λέγει) 97.

Translation - "Stop avenging yourselves, beloved; rather step aside when confronted with wrath, because it is written, 'Vengeance belongs to me. I will retaliate' said the Lord."

Comment: μή and the imperatival present participle is a present tense prohibition and forbids a continuation of a policy which was already in force - "Do not continue to avenge yourselves." The text is not clear whether τῇ ὀργῇ means God's wrath, that of an assailant or that of the Christian himself. If the former, δότε τόπον means to step aside and leave the resolution of the matter up to God, Who is angry because of injustice. If the second, δοτε τόπον means to run! It is difficult to have a fight when there is only one combatant present. If the latter, it means "because you are angry, do not trust yourself to act, but step aside and God, Who can be trusted to act wisely will act in His own time and in His own way." All three ideas are good advice.

The causal clause with γάρ seems to support the idea that God's wrath is meant. The quotation is from Deut.32:35. *Cf.* Heb.10;30; 2 Thess.1:16; James 1:19; 1 Tim.2:8; Col.3:8; Eph.4:31. When one's own interest is involved, failure to recognize one's own limitations can be a serious mistake. It is a mistake also to think of one's self as a judge (John 5:22,27). God's judgments are superior to our own. If the ancients had understood this they would not have met their fate (Rom.1:18-22). There would be no problem if we all heeded the warnings of Rom.12:3,16.

Paul's advice, if followed, would eliminate all church congregational strife and inter-societal warfare. The vigilantes and other heresy hunters, who feel sufficiently erudite to combine within their sphere of jurisdiction legislative, judicial and executive functions should take heed. Speaking from the bench they say, "You did it." A quick change to the legislative chamber and they say, "It was wrong." Another quick change of hat and they speak with the police power of the executive, "I must punish you." This is the kind of dictatorship that every Christian practices when he "gets even." Carried to its logical extreme it would return society to anarchy in a state of nature where life is "nasty, brutish and short." For if the vigilantes are following the proper course, then everyone should become a vigilante in the event that more control over society is needed. The Social Contract, upon which democracy is built, provides that the individual delegate his personal legislative, judicial and executive powers to the state in return for the state's promise to protect his personal and property rights. If Christian morality prevailed throughout society, the state would not be needed and anarchy would be the proper rule. Where there is no danger there is no need for political control. Christian morality, however, does not prevail in society and, as immorality and amorality increases, the state finds itself less and less able to fulfill its social contract obligations. Thus as violence fills society, Christians must either be willing to pay more taxes for more and better police protection or they must be willing to surrender their rights, since the alternative is to take up arms. This policy our verse forbids.

In view of these things, we can draw an inference which Paul suggests in

Verse 20 - "Therefore, if thine enemy hunger, feed him; if he thirst, give him drink: for in so doing thou shalt heap coals of fire on his head."

ἀλλὰ ἐὰν πεινᾷ ὁ ἐχθρός σου, φώμιζε αὐτόν, ἐὰν διψᾷ, πότιζε αὐτόν. τοῦτο γὰρ ποιῶν ἄνθρακας πυρὸς σωρεύσεις ἐπὶ τὴν κεφαλὴν αὐτοῦ.

"No, 'if your enemy is hungry, feed him; if he is thirsty, give him drink; for by so doing you will heap burning coals upon his head.' " . . . RSV

ἀλλὰ (alternative conjunction) 342.
ἐὰν (conditional particle with the subjunctive in a third-class condition) 363.
πεινᾷ (3d.per.sing.pres.act.subj.of πεινάω, third-class condition) 335.
ὁ (nom.sing.masc.of the article in agreement with ἐσθρός) 9.
ἐχθρός (nom.sing.masc.of ἐχθρός, subject of πεινᾷ) 543.
σου (gen.sing.masc.of σύ, relationship) 104.

#4030 φώμιζε (2d.per.sing.pres.act.impv.of φωμίζω, command).

King James Version

bestow to feed - 1 Cor.13:3.
feed - Rom.12:20.

Revised Standard Version

feed - Rom.12:20.
give away - 1 Cor.13:3.

Meaning: Cf. φωμίον (#2766), φωμός - "morsel," "bit." Hence, to put a bit of food into the mouth; to feed - Rom.12:20; followed by πάντα τὰ ὑπαρχοντά μου - "to give away a little at a time all my property (all that I control) - 1 Cor.13:3.

αὐτόν (acc.sing.masc.of αὐτός, direct object of φώμιζε) 16.
ἐὰν (conditional particle in a third-class condition) 363.
διφᾷ (3d.per.sing.pres.act.subj.of διφάω, third-class condition) 427.
πότιζε (2d.per.sing.pres.act.impv.of ποτίζω, command) 900.
αὐτόν (acc.sing.masc.of αὐτός, direct object of πότιζε) 16.
τοῦτο (acc.sing.neut.of οὗτος, direct object of ποιῶν) 93.
γὰρ (causal conjunction) 105.
ποιῶν (pres.act.part.nom.sing.masc.of ποιέω, adverbial, instrumental) 127.

#4031 ἄνθρακας (acc.pl.masc.of ἄνθραξ, direct object of σωρεύσεις).

King James Version

coal - Rom.12:20.

Revised Standard Version

coal - Rom.12:20.

Meaning: live coals of fire. Thayer says, ". . . a proverbial expression, fr. Prs.25:22, signifying to call up, by the favors you confer on your enemy, the memory in him of the wrong he has done you (which shall pain him as if live coals were heaped on his head), that he may the more readily repent. The Arabians call things that cause very acute mental pain, *burning coals of the heart and fire in the liver.*" *Cf.* Genesius, *Thesaurus*, I, 280. - Rom.12:20.

πυρὸς (gen.sing.neut.of πῦρ, description) 298.

#4032 σωρεύσεις (2d.per.sing.fut.act.ind.of σωρεύω, predictive).

King James Version

heap - Rom.12:20.
lade - 2 Tim.3:6.

Revised Standard Version

heap - Rom.12:20.
burdened - 2 Tim.3:6.

Meaning: Cf.σωρός - "a heap" or "a pile" especially of corn. Hence to pile up or pile upon. Figuratively in Rom.12:20, to increase one's moral obligation to do right; to be addicted to sin - 2 Tim.3:6.

ἐπὶ (preposition with the accusative of extent) 47.
τὴν (acc.sing.fem.of the article in agreement with κεφαλὴν) 9.
κεφαλὴν (acc.sing.fem.of κεφαλή, extent) 521.
αὐτοῦ (gen.sing.masc.of αὐτός, possession) 16.

Translation - "On the contrary, if your enemy is hungry, feed him; if he is thirsty, give him drink, because by doing this you will heap burning coals upon his head."

Comment: ἀλλά is the alternative conjunction. There is a better way to solve the problem of violence. The positive mandamus of verse 20 is as strong as the negative injunction of verse 19. "Stop avenging yourselves" (verse 19) means no more than a policy of neutrality toward your enemies. This is insufficient. We must take positive steps of treating our enemies as though they were our loved ones, or even ourselves. You have an enemy? Has he wronged you? You are in the process of getting even? Paul's order is, "Stop retaliating against him." Apply the rule of Mt.7:12. If he is hungry or thirsty give him food and drink. Whatever his need, do all you can to meet it. In verse 13 we were ordered to divide our wealth with needy Christians. Now we are told to divide it also with our enemies, whether they be Christian or not.

Why should we do this? The γὰρ clause is causal. The participle ποιῶν is adverbial and instrumental. The distinction between the instrumental and modal participle is sometimes hard to discern. The instrumental indicates the *means* by which the action of the main verb is accomplished, while the modal indicates the *manner* in which it is accomplished. It is by means of your action of feeding and giving drink to your hungry and thirsty enemy, that you are placing him under great moral obligation to regret the injury he has perpetrated upon you. Your example of the Golden Rule (Mt.7:12) may provoke him to repentance. Note carefully #4031. The antecedent of τοῦτο is the set of imperatives in the two third-class conditional clauses.

The entire teaching of verses 17-20 is summed up in

Verse 21 - "Be not overcome of evil, but overcome evil with good."

μὴ νικῶ ὑπὸ τοῦ κακοῦ, ἀλλὰ νίκα ἐν τῷ ἀγαθῷ τὸ κακόν.

"Do not be overcome by evil, but overcome evil with good." . . . *RSV*

μὴ (negative particle with the imperative) 87.
νικῶ (2d.per.sing.pres.pass.impv.of νικάω, prohibition) 2454.
ὑπὸ (preposition with the ablative of agent) 117.
τοῦ (abl.sing.neut.of the article in agreement with κακοῦ) 9.
κακοῦ (abl.sing.neut.of κακός, agent) 1388.
ἀλλὰ (alternative conjunction) 342.
νίκα (2d.per.sing.pres.act.impv.of νικάω, command) 2454.
ἐν (preposition with the locative, instrumental use, means) 80.
τῷ (loc.sing.masc.of the article in agreement with ἀγαθῷ) 9.
ἀγαθῷ (loc.sing.masc.of ἀγαθός, instrumental use, means) 547.
τὸ (acc.sing.neut.of the article in agreement with κακόν) 9.
κακόν (acc.sing.neut.of κακός, direct object of νίκα) 1388.

Translation - "Stop being conquered by evil; on the contrary always be victorious over evil by means of the good."

Comment: The present tenses here, in both imperatives νικῶ and νίκα are used like perfects. "The root has the sense of completion" (Robertson, *Grammar,* 881). The Roman Christians were being defeated. Paul says, "Put a stop to it, and reverse the situation." As Robertson points out, the root νικ speaks of victory in the past, the results of which are still available. Thus the admonition is that just as we have been victorious over evil in the past, so we are to continue. Note the articles with the adjectives. They need not be translated, but they point definitely to the substantives.

Paul writes as though he believed that there is a distinct difference between ὁ ἀγαθός and ὁ κακός. Further that they are antithetical and thus mutally exclusive in the final analysis. *Cf.* our comment on Rom.12:9. The good is stronger than the evil as the last clause implies (John 1:5; Gal.5:16; 1 John 4:4). It should be remembered that Paul is addressing Christians (Rom.1:7) and that they have the indwelling Holy Spirit witnessing with their own spirits (Rom.8:16). The unsaved man cannot obey verse 21. He has no good with which to overcome his evil (Rom.7:18). Indeed verse 21 was not addressed to the unsaved.

Obedience to Rulers

(Romans 13:1-7)

Romans 13:1 - *"Let every soul be subject unto the higher powers. For there is no power but of God: the powers that be are ordained of God."*

Πᾶσα ψυχὴ ἐξουσίαις ὑπερεχούσαις ὑποτασσέσθω. οὐ γὰρ ἔστιν ἐξουσία εἰ μὴ ὑπὸ θεοῦ, αἱ δὲ οὖσαι ὑπὸ θεοῦ τεταγμέναι εἰσίν.

"Let every person be subject to the governing authorities. For there is no authority except from God, and those that exist have been instituted by God."...
. *RSV*

Πᾶσα (nom.sing.fem.of πᾶς in agreement with ψυχή) 67.
ψυχή (nom.sing.fem.of ψυχή, subject of ὑποτασσέσθω) 233.
ἐξουσίαις (dat.pl.fem.of ἐξουσία, personal advantage) 707.

#4033 ὑπερεχούσαις (pres.act.part.dat.pl.fem.of ὑπερέχω, adjectival, restrictive, in agreement with ἐξουσίαις).

King James Version

pass - Phil.4:7.
better - Phil.2:3.
excellency - Phil.3:8.
higher - Rom.13:1.
supreme - 1 Pet.2:13.

Revised Standard Version

pass - Phil.4:7.

better - Phil.2:3.
surpassing worth - Phil.3:8.
supreme - 1 Pet.2:13.
governing - Rom.13:1.

Meaning: In the New Testament always intransitively. As a participial adjective or a substantive. A combination of ὑπέρ (#545) and ἔχω (#82), thus to be possessed of a higher τίνα. The context determines what. Joined with ἐξουσίαις to denote higher political authority in Rom.13:1; with βασιλεῖ in the same sense in 1 Pet.2:13. As a predicate adjective with an ablative of comparison in Phil.2:3; as a participial substantive, followed by a genitive of description in Phil.3:8. As a participial adjective in the emphatic attributive position in Phil.4:7.

ὑποτασσέσθω (3d.per.sing.pres.mid.impv.of ὑποτάσσω, command) 1921.
οὐ (negative particle with the indicative) 130.
γὰρ (causal conjunction) 105.
ἔστιν (3d.per.sing.pres.ind.of εἰμί, static) 86.
ἐξουσία (nom.sing.fem.of ἐξουσία, subject of ἔστιν) 707.
εἰ (conditional particle in an elliptical first-class condition) 337.
μὴ (negative particle in an elliptical first-class condition) 87.
ὑπὸ (preposition with the ablative of source) 117.
θεοῦ (abl.sing.masc.of θεός, source) 124.
αἱ (nom.pl.fem.of the article in agreement with ἐξουσίαι, understood) 9.
δὲ (continuative conjunction) 11.
οὖσαι (pres.part.nom.pl.fem.of εἰμί, adjectival, in agreement with ἐξουσίαι) 86.
ὑπὸ (preposition with the ablative of agent) 117.
θεοῦ (abl.sing.masc.of θεός, agent) 124.
τεταγμέναι (perf.pass.part.nom.pl.fem.of τάσσω, perfect periphrastic, adjectival, in agreement with ἐξουσίαι understood) 722.
εἰσίν (3d.per.pl.pres.ind.of εἰμί, static, perfect periphrastic) 86/.

Translation - *"Let every soul place himself under subjection to those having superior authority, because no authority exists except that which has God as its source; and those who are authorities are in power because they have been so appointed by God."*

Comment: This verse is not friendly to democracy as it is currently understood in political science. Paul begins by ordering all Christians to make themselves subject to those having higher authority. ὑποτασσέσθω is middle voice - "Submit yourselves to ἐξουσίαις ὑπερεχούσαις - those having superior authority. A variant reading has πάσαις ἐξουσίαις ὑπερεχούσαις ὑποτάσσεσθε - "You (plural) subject yourselves to all having higher authority." Thus the right of revolution, the heart of Rousseau's philosophy and the essence of Thomas Jefferson's statement in the Declaration of Independence, is swept away. There is no way to reconcile Paul's statement here with Jefferson's statement "That whenever any form of government becomes destructive to these ends, it is the right of the people to alter or abolish it, and to institute new government, laying its foundation on such principles and organizaing its powers in such forms, as to them shall seem most likely to affect their safety and happiness."

The difficulty is resolved in the fact that Paul was not writing to the unsaved, and Jefferson was not writing to Christians. Democracy, with its right of revolution, is perhaps the best way for the unsaved to establish the authority to maintain whatever order can be achieved in a world of unsaved people, who are destined for God's judgment. Since the day that man murdered the Son of God, it has been "man's day" not God's (1 Cor.4:3). It is night and has been since the Light of the World (John 8:12) was plunged into darkness on a cross. The world did not see Him rise from the dead and would not have believed it if they had. Unregenerates since who have refused to follow Jesus Christ have walked in darkness (John 8:12). The activities of the unsaved, however sincere they imagine them to be, cannot show a societal profit (John 9:4). Man rejected the rule of God on earth and God has chosen to allow man to rule the world, under the superior domination of Satan (Eph.2:2; 2 Cor.4:4; 1 John 5:19) until man has, by his ungodly, though highly sophisticated stupidity, driven world society into utter chaos. When the world, operated by the unsaved in man's day has lost it viability, God will send His Son to rescue His experiment upon earth and at that time what form of government exists, be it anarchy, democracy, oligarchy or monarchy (a euphemism for dictatorship), will give place to the benevolent and wise rule of Plato's Heavenly Philosopher-King, the Lord Jesus Christ.

This is not to say that God does not know nor care what is happening on the earth in the church age, but His concern is related only to how world events and earthly conditions affect His one purpose in this age, which is to call out the Body of Christ, His Church (Acts 15:14). When that task is finished (Rev.10:7) God will intervene and put an end to "man's day" with its unChristian worship of man, which is the essence of democracy.

Though Christ, once crucified, is at the Father's right hand until His enemies are made His footstool (Psalm 110:1) God has not surrendered one iota of His authority. He has not abdicated His throne. Thus Paul's statement, following his mandamus to the Christian to submit tamely to whatever political authority exists, that no king, dictator, president or other world ruler, however chosen, whether by heredity as a king, by vote as a democratic leader or by force as a dictator, is exercising his authority in and of himself. "If the authority is not from God (ablative of source in ὑπὸ θεοῦ) is does not exist." Or to put it otherwise, whatever authority is exercised by puny man is his, only by divine permission. Further that the existing politicians and what few statesmen may chance to be among them hold their positions as such, with all police, judicial and legislative powers as a result of their having been appointed to such positions by God (ablative of agent in ὑπὸ θεοῦ). This is what τεταγμέναι εἰσίν, the perfect periphrastic says. God at various times in the past has granted to miscellaneous clowns - Nero, Adolph Hitler or Richard Nixon, the privilege of being the political leader and these leaders remained in power only so long as God was willing to suffer them. Then they were dismissed, some with dignity and others not, and their places were taken by other clowns.

Presumably, if God's plan to save the elect is hindered under a given ruler's administration, he will be removed, for God is able to remove any politician from the earthly scene, or strip him of his political power, whenever He chooses to do so. Otherwise the Lord seems to be remarkably indifferent to what happens down here, so long as His business of calling to salvation those for whom Christ died is not hindered. If society chooses at the polls to substitute fools for knaves that is society's affair. God probably had little if anything to do with it. He permits the dog and pony show, which frequently changes the act to a battle of the frogs and mice (witness the Falkland Islands crisis of 1982) to go on, so long as His own program of evangelism is not hindered. History demonstrates that the Holy Spirit is able to save the elect under any form of human government so long as the Word of God, either surreptitiously or openly, is proclaimed.

Meanwhile what is the Christian's obligation to human government? He is to submit to the existing power on the throne in the knowledge that the ruler is there only with delegated power and is subject totally to God's permissive will. Violent overthrow of governments is forbidden to the child of God. There seems to be no need to push this injunction against violent revolution to include a ban on the Christian's freedom to speak, advise and vote for or against his government. Paul did not discuss this since democracy was not practised within the Roman Empire in the first century, though there was a brief democratic experiment in Greece four centuries before. Paul was telling the Roman saints to subject themselves to Caligula or Claudius or Nero, however depraved they might be. Nero was not sovereign, for all of his tyranny, but God is sovereign and He attended to Nero in His own time and way. Romans 12:17 forbids revolt, even against the Emperor. "Pay back to no man (not even Nero) evil for evil."

Paul gave this same advice to Christian slaves with regard to their relationship with their masters, not because Paul favored human slavery, but because it is better for a Christian slave to submit to a cruel unsaved master than it is to kill him (Col.3:22).

The truth lying behind all of this injunction against social and political revolution is that the course of this age is set in God's plan and it can progress only down to total frustration and judgment. Social and political justice can come to stay only when Christ returns. Meanwhile the Christian's role is to witness to the unsaved about the good news of the gospel of Christ and humbly endure whatever injustice the world decides to impose upon him.

The difficulty that the Christian faces when considering his proper role in promoting justice here and now, is that he does not know how long this age will run before the Second Coming. Will Christ come back in his life time? Or is the end of the age one hundred, one thousand or perhaps ten thousand years in the future? There is no answer to this question at this time (June 15, 1982), though end-time Christians will know the date, seven years before the end. The fact remains that no one knows the date now.

By living the Golden Rule every day (Mt.7:12) and by witnessing, not only to the saving grace of God in the gospel, but also to the beauty of social, economic and political justice inherent in the teaching of the New Testament, the Christian can function as the "salt of the earth" (Mt.5:13) and the "light of the world" (Mt.5:14). And by his vote, if he lives in a democracy, he may be able to mitigate a bad situation temporarily. Paul does not forbid his participation in politics in this way. But if he is powerless to change the policy of his country except by physical force, Romans 13:1 forbids him to use it.

This philosophy of submission to authority can also be applied in a church congregation where agitation to dismiss a pastor is present, or on a college campus, where student radicals are demanding the professional, if not the physical life of the administration. But nothing that Paul says in his epistles to Christians applies to the behavior of the unsaved. So long as the sinner is outside of Christ his attitude and actions are a matter of infinite divine indifference. Of course this does not apply to the elect who are as yet uncalled by the Holy Spirit. In God's own time, place and manner, the Holy Spirit will visit each of God's elect in irresistible grace and incorporate him into the Body of Christ. At that moment everything he does is the concern of the indwelling Holy Spirit. And since our passage says that political rulers, even though unsaved, are in power only at the sufferance of God, He is concerned about what they do only if their policies should seek to interfere with His divine purpose in calling out the church. Russia has been under the dictatorship of atheists for more than sixty years, and prior to that, under the dictatorship of the Czars, who may or may not have been regenerated but atheism in Russia, enforced by the secret police, effected in Siberian prison camps and influenced by state-controlled media has not been able to prevent the Holy Spirit from calling to the cross millions of God's elect. There are "thirty million Russian Orthodox and three million evangelicals" there today "an influential part of Russian society." (Richard Shumaker, "Three Significant Happenings in Moscow Raise Hope for Church in USSR," *Eternity*, June, 1982, 8).

In recent years a movement has been growing in the United States, supported with great determination, chiefly by the political and economic right and by fundamentalist preachers, to capture the national government, not in a violent *coup d' etat*, to be sure, but at the polls, amend the constitution and legislate the country into conformity with the ethics of the New Testament. This attempt to make America   Christian is linked with the economics of the Classical and Neo-Classical schools, which advocate the survival of the fittest, as the Social Darwinists preached it, in keeping with the theory of evolution as taught by Charles Darwin. It is ironical that from the same platform and out of the same mouth comes an attack upon Darwinism, and a demand that Biblical creationsim be taught in the public schools at the expense of unsaved tax payers, and at the same time a demand that the economy of the country be turned over to the Social Darwinists, as represented by the giant multinational corporations. Perhaps this anomaly results from the fact that most Bible expositors are not at home in the Social Sciences, particularly economics and they are unable to discern the inconsistency of their position. They seem to believe that since 1933 the United States has been particularly unChristian and unscriptural in the administration of the "welfare state." Left-wing Social Scientists look upon the welfare state, not only as a means of making Capitalism viable, and thus qualifying as the best friend that Capitalism has, but also the head-on collision with Communism. Furthermore it is a practical application of Paul's admonitions in Romans 12:9-21, with special attention to verses 13 and 20.

To use the police power of the state to enforce Biblical ethics upon unsaved citizens and/or to enjoin them against acts or words which the Bible condemns is to bridge the gap between church and state which the founding fathers so wisely wrote into the constitution. If it be argued, as the so-called Moral Majority does, that if it is wrong to legislate against what the Bible calls sin, then it is wrong to legislate against murder, rape, theft and perjury, since these are forbidden in the Ten Commandments, the reply is that murder, rape, theft and perjury are acts which deny to their victims the personal and property rights to which citizens of the state are entitled, and which the social contract is sworn to maintain. It is not illegal to murder a man because murder is sin, but because murder deprives the victim of his right to life, liberty and pursuit of happiness. It is not illegal to rape, because it is sin but because it is an invasion of the right to privacy of the victim. Theft is not illegal because it is sin. Thieves, burglars and robbers are taking away property without due process of law. The witness who bears false witness under oath is, to be sure, a sinner, for the Bible says, "Thou shalt not bear false witness," but he is also a felon because his false testimony may deprive a citizen of equal protection under the law. Thus the state is justified in legislating against crimes, but to say that the state is justified in legislating against sins, if the sins so forbidden do not deny personal or property rights, is to make the state an enforcement agency for Biblical Christianity. And in America there are tax payers who do not believe in the Bible.

If one believes as I do that human life is a gift of God and that it begins at conception, then he must conclude that the state, under the constitution, must forbid abortion of an unborn fetus, on the grounds that the baby, although as yet unborn is a human being, although he is not yet a citizen. Citizenship is defined in the 14th amendment as the status enjoyed by "All persons *born* or naturalized in the United States, and subject to the jurisdiction thereof."Until the baby is born it is not a citizen and is not subject to the jurisdiction of the state. The courts cannot indict and condemn the unborn fetus.But though not a citizen,the baby is a human being, and as such has a moral right to live, even if he has no constituional right to live. But this is a view that depends upon the Biblical truth that God is the author of life.

The inconsistency of the proponent of abortion is his unwillingness to sanction murder after the child is born. If it is right to kill the fetus, why is it wrong to indulge in infanticide? The only difference between the fetus and the three-year-old, or the teen-ager or the superannuate is one of development. If a fetus should be destroyed because his presence takes away the mother's right over her own body, then all human beings should be killed for the same reason. For in our crowded society everyone except the hermit in a cave is infringing upon the personal rights of those around him. If the high school student were not here to use the car, his father would have a chance to use it once in a while. So we had better be careful how we speak of what ought or ought not be done in order to protect our "rights." I own an automobile. It was paid for with my money. I buy the gasoline it burns and pay taxes to build and maintain the highway on which I drive it. But the state tells me that I have no "right" to drive it faster than fifty-five miles per hour. I do not contest the rule on the grounds that my "rights" have been impaired, because I realize that the state is seeking to prevent an accident that will deprive others of their lives and liberties. Of course it is possible to argue about whether or not fifty-five miles per hour is a safe limit. Safety on the highways is, in part, a function of the skills of the driver. Some drivers are dangerous before they put the car in gear!

Thus for one who wishes to think these problems down to their roots, it is impossible to be consistent and stay atop the earth.

Those who wish to use their influence through the democratic process, however, to make America a Christian nation, despite the fact that the first amendment declares that "Congress shall make no law respecting an establishment of religion, or prohibiting the free exercise thereof," are overlooking a clear body of truth, clearly taught in the New Testament. "Christians are the church, the Body of Christ. Christians are also members of the state. Can we separate the same individual?" (Robert McBurney, "The Subterfuge of Church and State Separation," *Southern Baptist Advocate,* III, 2, p.5). The article goes on to argue that Christians have the same obligation to interact with the other members of the corporate state as they have to interact with the other corporate members of the Body of Christ. All of which is perfectly logical, and we must agree, but only if the premise is sound. The truth is the Christians are not corporate members of the state in the same sense in which we are corporate members of the Body of Christ. The Body of Christ,into which we were incorporated by the baptism of the Holy Spirit (1 Cor.12:13; Gal.3:27), and in which we enjoy the same intimate association with each other as that enjoyed by our Lord with His Father (John 17:21), is a theocracy. The corporate state is a democracy. Only one will should prevail within the Body of Christ. That is the will of the Holy Spirit who indwells each member of the body. Indeed were it not for Him there would be no Body of Christ. There is also only one will in the democratic corporate body of the state, and that is the "general will" that Jean Jacques Rousseau talked about. And that general will is the composite result of the views, expressed by the exercise of free speech and a free press, and registered in free elections on periodic occasions. Not all of the citizens of the corporate state are indwelt by the Holy Spirit. Some are. Some are not. Those who are not may not even believe that there is a Holy Spirit, or if they did, that He had any authority over them in the exercise of what they call their freedom and their rights.

Each member of the corporate state agrees to obey the general will in exchange for the state's protection of his right to life, liberty and property. Thus if he breaks the social contract and transgresses the general will, he has forfeited his right to the state's protection of his property. The state is under no obligation to protect even the right to life of a murderer if he murders his victim within the jurisdiction in which murder is a capital crime. Lesser crimes are to be punished with the alienation of lesser amounts of liberty or property. Thus armed robbery justifies the state is depriving the robber of his liberty for twenty years, and driving forty-five in a twenty mile speed zone justifies the state is depriving the transgressor of fifty-six dollars.

So, the superficial thinker will conclude that what ought and what ought not be done in a democratic state is decided by the majority of its citizens. To which we object that this assumes that the majority is always right and therefore that the general will of the majority must be the best guide to public policy. A moment of reflection about this premise will reveal how shabby it is. Indeed, from the unsaved man's point of view, however shabby it may be, it is the best that can be done, to which Winston Churchill agreed with his famous statement that although democracy was the worst possible system of government ever devised by man, it was better than its alternative. That the majority is always right is a premise based upon the idea that the voters who make up the majority are good people. It is not inconsistent for the unsaved to preach this, because they do not believe what the Bible says about the depravity and stupidity of man, but it is a little strange for a fundamentalist preacher, who is supposed to believe what the Bible says about man's basic goodness to preach that democracy is a good system, because it is based upon the votes of good people.

Most elections are decided upon a margin of very few votes. A majority of 51% is not unusual. A popular expression has it that the election is "too close to call." But democracy depends upon the view that what is decided in a democratic state is good because all of the misguided people expressed their opinion on the same day during the time between the opening and the closing of the polls. Some were misguided on one issue; the others on another. Some were too much influenced by the politicians; others too little. We are also asked to believe that after the politicians are elected and installed in their respective positions, be they legislators, judges or executives, they listen to the wishes of their constituents.

It is not strange that even the best democracies in the world are in decline. Social Scientists find it easy to point out the flaws in society and easy also to recommend scenarios which, if followed will set all things right, but they also find it impossible to implement their plans. Ours is a petty generation. That is what the Bible says

The Bible clearly teaches that the Christian is a citizen, not of an earthly government, but of heaven. *Cf.* our discussion or Phil.3:20 - "ye are a colony of Heaven." Paul wrote to the Corinthians that "we are ambassadors for Christ." (2 Cor.5:20). An ambassador is a citizen of a nation which he represents and the interests of which he seeks to promote in a country where he is an alien. He is often out of sympathy with the policies of the country where he is a diplomatic guest and in which he enjoys diplomatic immunity, but he is not subject to the jurisdiction of his host country and if he is a good diplomat who understands the rules of the game, he does not interfere in its internal affairs. Paul was a citizen of Rome in an earthly and temporal sense, a status of which he was justifiably proud, but, after he was "born from above" he was in a heavenly and eternal sense a member of "the colony of heaven" (Phil.3:20). And that is why he admonished other ambassadors for Christ to obey the laws and to be subject to the political rulers of the earthly regimes where they were stationed temporarily to represent the moral and spiritual values of the Kingdom of the Heavens.

But it is significant that the Apostles sought neither to gain control of the Roman government nor to legislate Christian morality into the Roman code. They did not because they knew that they were not there for that purpose. They were there to be "witnesses unto (Christ) both in Jerusalem, and in all Judea, and in Samaria, and unto the uttermost part of the earth" (Acts 1:8). They did not seek to change the behavior of their unsaved neighbors; they did seek to change their philosophy. They understood that when a sinner's philosophy is changed his life style will take care of itself. Admonitions to holy living in the New Testament are directed exclusively to Christians, never to the unsaved. For if a man rejects Christ his moral standards, be they Victorian or vicious, beatific or bestial, Puritanical or pig-sty, are not going to make any difference in his destiny. They might impact one way or the other upon society, but the Apostles were not called to reform Roman society. They were called to witness the good news of the gospel of Christ, so that the Holy Spirit could "take out . . . a people for His name" (Acts 15:14).

It is true that the early Christians were mistaken when they expected Christ to return to earth within their lifetime, but they were not mistaken when they understood that He would return when the world-wide missionary enterprise is finished. Contemporary Christians do not know that our Lord will return before this generation passes away, because we do not know that "this generation" is the one to witness "the Abomination of Desolation spoken of by Daniel the prophet" (Mt.24:15), but we are not mistaken about what our role is in the economy of God. It is the same as the role assigned to the first century Christians at Pentecost. We are "witnesses unto (Him)" and "ambassadors for (Him)." We are to represent His interests and secure His designs upon the world. Whatever else happens in the moral world of unbelieving sinners, is really none of the Ambassador's business. Paul did not believe in human slavery, nor in Roman brutality, nor in gladiatorial slaughter in the Coliseum, nor in the pornographic orgies of Nero's court, but Paul did not use his television ministry to gain support at the polls for legislators in the Roman Senate who would vote to outlaw what Nero wanted to do. What Paul did was to win to Christ in Nero's prison a young runaway slave named Onesimus. It was God who took care of Nero and it was the barbarians three hundred years later who visited the wrath of God upon the Roman Empire.

But some may still wish to ask, "Why should a Christian submit to injustice?" The answer lies in the fact that he is already dead to sin and this world and alive in Jesus Christ. "We know that we are of God, but the entire world lies asleep in the evil one" (1 John 5:19). The believer is in Christ, but the world has only a short time to "enjoy" life. Then it faces eternity in complete frustration in hell. The Christian has only a short time to endure the same contradictions of sinners that Jesus faced (Heb.13:1-3). The world could not understand Him, so it hated Him "without a cause" and it will hate the Christian for the same reason (John 15:18-25), but the Christian faces eternity with the sure promise of total fulfillment in glory, not to be compared with present trials (Rom.8:18; 2 Cor.4:17,18). Since the child of God is "marching to a different drum" and in the opposite direction, motivated and guided by a different spirit and anticipating a different destiny, he can afford to suffer in gracious silence. Indeed, if he seeks vindication before the world's bar of justice he demonstrates an incredible naivete and a woeful lack of knowledge of the Scriptures.

Communists will regard the New Testament teaching to the Christian on this point as a reactionary "pie in the sky" fallacy. So be it. It is clearly what the New Testament teaches. But it teaches it only to the Christian, not to the unsaved. The Bible has nothing whatever to say to the unbeliever upon this or any other subject, except "repent and believe the gospel." If a sinner is not going to obey the gospel then his only hope for a little happiness upon this earth, before he goes to the place where there will be no happiness, lies in the amelioration of society's ills that flows from democracy with its right to revolution, and he should revolt in his own behalf every time his rights are denied to him. He should think only of himself. His rights alone are important, for this is a jungle where only the fittest survive. The unfit will leave their tracks in the mud for some misguided Darwinist to contemplate a billion years hence. The revolt will help society temporarily but democracy cannot reverse the foreordained course of this age, that Paul described on Mars Hill. It will end in chaos and divine judgment and be followed by Messiah's kingdom (Rev.11:15). Romans 13:1-2 is talking about relationships between the Christian and the unregenerate political, social and economic power structure. The relationship of one Christian to another Christian is a different matter. The Christian employer will pay his Christian employee a fair wage (Col.4:1). There is no such thing as a Christian master who exploits a Christian slave. Fellow members of the same Body of Christ are united in mystic union with the Godhead and with each other. We have not belonged to this world since we became Christians.

Verse 2 - "Whosoever therefore resisteth the power resisteth the ordinance of God: and they that resist shall receive to themselves damnation."

ὥστε ὁ ἀντιτασσόμενος τῇ ἐξουσίᾳ τῇ τοῦ θεοῦ διαταγῇ ἀνθέστηκεν, οἱ δὲ ἀνθεστηκότες ἑαυτοῖς κρίμα λήμφονται.

"Therefore he who resists the authorities resists what God has appointed, and those who resist will incur judgment." . . . RSV

ὥστε (conjunction with the indicative, actual result) 752.
ὁ (nom.sing.masc.of the article in agreement with ἀντιτασσόμενος) 9.
ἀντιτασσόμενος (pres.mid.part.nom.sing.masc.of ἀντιτάσσομαι, substantival subject of ἀνθέστηκεν) 3437.
τῇ (loc.sing.fem.of the article in agreement with ἐξουσίᾳ) 9.
ἐξουσίᾳ (loc.sing.fem.of ἐξουσία, opposition, after ἀντί in composition) 707.
τῇ (loc.sing.fem.of the article in agreement with διαταγῇ) 9.
τοῦ (gen.sing.masc.of the article in agreement with θεοῦ)9.
θεοῦ (gen.sing.masc.of θεός, possession) 124.
διαταγῇ (loc.sing.fem.of διαταγή, oppisition after ἀντί in composition) 3152.
ἀνθέστηκεν (3d.per.sing.perf.act.ind.of ἀνθίστημι, consummative) 527.
οἱ (nom.pl.masc.of the article in agreement with ἀνθεστηκότες) 9.
δὲ (continuative conjunction) 11.
ἀνθεστηκότες (perf.act.part.nom.pl.masc.of ἀνθίστημι, substantival, subject of λήμφονται) 527.

ἑαυτοῖς (dat.pl.masc.of ἑαυτός, personal disadvantage) 288.
κρίμα (acc.sing.neut.of κρίμα, direct object of λήμφονται) 642.
λήμφονται (3d.per.pl.fut.mid.ind.of λαμβάνω, predictive) 533.

Translation - ". . . with the result that the one who arrays himself against the authority has taken a stand against the ordinance of God and those who resist will be convicted."

Comment: With the infinitive ὥστε "expresses conceived or intended result, but with the indicative (only two occurrences in the New Testament) it expresses actual result." (Mantey, *Manusal*, 286). The two places are John 3:16 and Rom.13:2. "But actual result may also be expressed by the infinitive with ὥστε (Mt.8;24; 12:22; Lk.5:7)." (*Ibid.*). However wicked the head of state may be, his position is by God's appointment and therefore he has jurisdiction over the people by God's appointment. The Christian who indulges in civil disobedience may expect to be indicted, convicted and punished.

Paul does not however tell the Christian to obey the civil ruler when to do so involves disobedience to God. We recall the statement of Peter and John, "We ought to obey God rather than man" (Acts 5:29) and "Whether it be right in the sight of God to hearken unto you more than unto God, judge ye. For we cannot but speak the things which we have seen and heard" (Acts 4:19,20).

This is the question of the Naturalism of Sir William Blackstone versus the Positivism of Jeremy Bentham that has been debated by students of jurisprudence. Does law originate in the moral law of God as set forth in the Bible, as the Naturalists contend, or in the general will of the people in a democracy as the Positivists say? For Blackstone, it is impossible for a legislative assembly to enact into law an immoral practice. Andrew Jackson, on the bench of the Federal District Court in Nashville, stated the Blackstone view when he instructed a jury, charged with the responsibility of deciding a case involving the line fence between two farmers, by saying, "Do what is *right* between these parties. That is what the law always means." Bentham insisted, not that an immoral law was good, but that it was the law, if it was the will of the majority, while Blackstone would say that if the will of the majority resulted in placing an immoral statute on the books, it was null and void, and could with impunity be transgressed. This is not to say that Bentham favored immorality. His advice to those who objected to a law on moral grounds was "Obey punctually and censure freely." Thus, for Bentham, the protest against an immoral law might be strong enough to induce the legislature to change it.

Paul's instruction is that the Christian is to obey the will of the state, except in cases where obedience to the state involves disobedience to God. Thus he was not a Positivist. Was Martin Luther King a Positivist? He boldly disobeyed segregation laws because he thought them immoral. This sounds like Naturalism, but, although he freely censured them, he paid the penalty by going to jail. He did not use violence to overthrow the state.

Verse 3 - "*For rulers are not a terror to good works but to the evil. Wilt thou then not be afraid of the power? Do that which is good, and thou shalt have praise of the same.*"

οἱ γὰρ ἄρχοντες οὐκ εἰσὶν φόβος τῷ ἀγαθῷ ἔργῳ ἀλλὰ τῷ κακῷ. θέλεις δὲ μὴ φοβεῖσθαι τὴν ἐξουσίαν; τὸ ἀγαθὸν ποίει, καὶ ἕξεις ἔπαινον ἐξ αὐτῆς.

"For rulers are not a terror to good conduct, but to bad. Would you have no fear of him who is authority? Then do what is good, and you will receive his approval." . . . RSV

οἱ (nom.pl.masc.of the article in agreement with ἄρχοντες) 9.

γὰρ (explanatory conjunction) 105.

ἄρχοντες (pres.act.part.nom.pl.masc.of ἄρχω, substantival, subject of εἰσίν) 816.

οὐκ (negative particle with the indicative) 130.

εἰσὶν (3d.per.pl.pres.ind.of εἰμί, aoristic) 86.

φόβος (nom.sing.masc.of φόβος, predicate nominative) 1131.

τῷ (dat.sing.neut.of the article in agreement with ἔργῳ) 9.

ἀγαθῷ (dat.sing.neut.of ἀγαθός, in agreement with ἔργῳ) 547.

ἔργῳ (dat.sing.neut.of ἔργον, reference) 460.

ἀλλὰ (adversative conjunction) 342.

τῷ (dat.sing.neut.of the article in agreement with ἔργῳ, understood) 9.

κακῷ (dat.sing.neut.of κακός, in agreement with ἔργῳ understood) 1388.

θέλεις (2d.per.sing.pres.act.ind.of θέλω, direct question) 88.

δὲ (adversative conjunction) 11.

μὴ (negative particle in direct question which expects a negative response) 87.

φοβεῖσθαι (pres.mid.inf.of φοβέομαι, complementary) 101.

τὴν (acc.sing.fem.of the article in agreement with ἐξουσίαν) 9.

ἐξουσίαν (acc.sing.fem.of ἐξουσία, direct object of φοβεῖσθαι) 707.

τὸ (acc.sing.neut.of the article in agreement with ἀγαθὸν) 9.

ἀγαθὸν (acc.sing.neut.of ἀγαθός, direct object of ποίει) 547.

ποίει (2d.per.sing.pres.act.impv.of ποιέω, command) 127.

καὶ (continuative conjunction) 14.

ἕξεις (2d.per.sing.fut.act.ind.of ἔχω, predictive) 82.

ἔπαινον (acc.sing.masc.of ἔπαινος, direct object of ἕξεις) 3853.

ἐξ (preposition with the ablative of source) 19.

αὐτῆς (abl.sing.fem.of αὐτός, source) 16.

Translation - "*Now the rulers are not a threat to the good work but to the evil. But you do not wish to be afraid of the authority do you? Always do the good and you will have approval from him.*"

Comment: γὰρ seems explanatory. In verse 2 Paul has warned that the government official has enforcement power over the wrong doer. However there is another side to the story. *Cf.*#1131 with particular notice of 1 Pet.3:14 for φόβος in this sense - "wrath, the source of fear." Note that τῷ ἀγαθῷ and τῷ κακῷ both have the article, distinguishing one class of persons and deeds from another class. If some in Paul's audience say, "But I do not wish to live in fear of the authority. I want to live peaceably with my government." The formula is simple: "Always do the good and the result will be that you will always have his approval." The antecedent of αὐτῆς is τὴν ἐξουσίαν, with which it agrees in gender and number, though of course αὐτῆς derives its case from its use in its own clause. If we supply ἐξουσίας after αὐτῆς we have αὐτῆς in the attributive position with the translation "the same." The same authority whom you should fear if you break the law will praise you if you do the right thing.

God's purpose in ordaining public officials to administer society is that some order may be maintained, even though the people are unregenerate. Some order is necessary if the Holy Spirit is to work through individual Christians, fellowshipping with each other in local church congregations to carry out God's primary purpose in this age - the calling to salvation of the elect. This is the thought in

Verse 4 - "For he is the minister of God to thee for good. But if thou do that which is evil, be afraid; for he beareth not the sword in vain: for he is the minister of God, a revenger to execute wrath upon him that doeth evil."

θεοῦ γὰρ διάκονός ἐστιν σοὶ εἰς τὸ ἀγαθόν. ἐὰν δὲ τὸ κακὸν ποιῇς, φοβοῦ, οὐ γὰρ εἰκῇ τὴν μάχαιραν φορεῖ. θεοῦ γὰρ διάκονός ἐστιν, ἔκδικος εἰς ὀργὴν τῷ τὸ κακὸν πράσσοντι.

". . . for he is God's servant for your good. But if you do wrong, be afraid, for he does not bear the sword in vain; he is the servant of God to execute his wrath on the wrongdoer." . . . RSV

θεοῦ (gen.sing.masc.of θεός, possession) 124.

γὰρ (causal conjunction) 105.

διάκονός (nom.sing.masc.of διάκονος, predicate nominative) 1334.

ἐστιν (3d.per.sing.pres.ind.of εἰμί, aoristic) 86.

σοὶ (dat.sing.masc.of σύ, reference) 104.

εἰς (preposition with the accusative, purpose) 140.

τὸ (acc.sing.neut.of the article in agreement with ἀγαθόν) 9.

ἀγαθόν (acc.sing.neut.of ἀγαθός, purpose) 547.

ἐὰν (conditional particle with the subjunctive in a third-class condition) 363.

δὲ (adversative conjunction) 11.

τὸ (acc.sing.neut.of the article in agreement with κακὸν) 9.

κακὸν (acc.sing.neut.of κακός, direct object of ποιῇς) 1388.

ποιῇς (2d.per.sing.pres.act.subj.of ποιέω, third-class condition) 127.

φοβοῦ (2d.per.sing.pres.mid.impv.of φοβέομαι, command) 101.

οὐ (negative particle with the indicative) 130.

γὰρ (causal conjunction) 105.

#4034 εἰκῇ (adverbial).

King James Version

in vain - Rom.13:4; 1 Cor.15:2; Gal.3:4,4; 4:11; Col.2:18.

Revised Standard Version

in vain - Rom.13:4; 1 Cor.15:2; Gal.3:4,4,; 4:11.
without reason - Col.2:18.

Meaning: Without purpose; for no real reason - Rom.13:4, *i.e.,* the officer does does not carry a sword in a scabbard for vain display. He will draw it and use it if it is necessary. Col.2:18 - no reason for the false teachers' pretense of sophistication; without success - Gal.3:4,4; 4:11. Vainly, without the proper reason; from improper motives - 1 Cor.15:2.

τὴν (acc.sing.fem.of the article in agreement with μάχαιραν) 9.
μάχαιραν (acc.sing.fem.of μάχαιρα, direct object of φορεῖ) 896.
φορεῖ (3d.per.sing.pres.act.ind.of φορέω, aoristic) 913.
θεοῦ (gen.sing.masc.of θεός, possession) 124.
γὰρ (causal conjunction) 105.
διάκονός (nom.sing.masc.of διάκονος, predicate nominative) 1334.
ἐστιν (3d.per.sing.pres.ind.of εἰμί, aoristic) 86.

#4035 ἔκδικος (nom.sing.masc.of ἔκδικος, predicate nominative).

King James Version

avenger - 1 Thess.4:6.
revenger - Rom.13:4.

Revised Standard Version

to execute - Rom.13:4.
avenger - 1 Thess.4:6.

Meaning: A combination of ἐκ (#19) and δίκη (#3761). Therefore, one who exacts a penalty from (ἐκ) a wrong-doer. An avenger. Executor - Rom.13:4, followed by a dative of reference - in 1 Thess.4:6.
εἰς (preposition with the accusative, purpose) 140.
ὀργὴν (acc.sing.fem.of ὀργή, purpose) 283.
τῷ (dat.sing.masc.of the article in agreement with πράσσοντι) 9.
τὸ (acc.sing.neut.of the article in agreement with κακὸν) 9.
κακὸν (acc.sing.neut.of κακός, direct object of πράσσοντι) 1388.
πράσσοντι (pres.act.part.dat.sing.masc.of πράσσω, substantival, reference) 1943.

Translation - "*Because he is a divine administrator for your good. But if you are doing evil, be afraid. Because he is not carrying the sword for display, because he is a divine administrator, an avenger to punish the one who does evil.*"

Comment: Note θεοῦ γὰρ διάκονός - in emphasis in both clauses. Paul's wants the point understood that civil authority is by God's appointment. His purpose is the good of society, but we should not presume upon this fact, as though he would never use his police power, for if that were true he could not protect society. There is the other side. The evil doer, if, in fact, he persists in evil, should fear. Because the ruler has a sword and it is not worn for display but for use. Laws, enacted by the legislature and adjudicated by the courts are of no force until enforced by the executive with his police power.

Three reasons for law and its enforcement have been cited in justification for the existence of the state, as an alternative to anarchy. (1) The state exists for the protection of society. (2) The state also exists to uphold the dignity of its courts, and (3) the state exists for the rehabilitation of the criminal. Authorities differ as to the order of importance of these. Paul in his last clause mentions a fourth. The ruler is an agent of God to visit divine wrath upon those who transgress His law. Thus Paul takes his place on the side of Naturalism. God, Who is the Source of morality has defined morals in terms of His code and human legislative acts should conform to what God calls morals.

It has been almost 2000 years since man excluded Messiah from His own world (John 1:11), yet world society, ultimately destined to lose its fight to maintain decency and justice and fail, has remained viable despite man's sin. The reason is that God has always had His servants, some of whom have not been Christians, who enforced law in keeping with God's moral code. Some of these have been Christians; others not, but for public administration purposes they are servants of God.

There are two reasons why the Christian should comply with the laws of the state. They are set forth in

Verse 5 - "Wherefore ye must needs be subject, not only for wrath, but also for conscience sake."

διὸ ἀνάγκη ὑποτάσσεσθαι, οὐ μόνον διὰ τὴν ὀργὴν ἀλλὰ καὶ διὰ τὴν συνείδησαν.

"Therefore one must be subject, not only to avoid God's wrath but also for the sake of conscience." . . . RSV

διὸ (consecutive conjunction) 1622.
ἀνάγκη (nom.sing.fem.of ἀνάγκη, subject of the verb understood) 1254.
ὑποτάσσεσθαι (pres.mid.inf.of ὑποτάσσω, in apposition with ἀνάγκη) 1921.
οὐ (negative particle with the indicative) 130.
μόνον (acc.sing.neut.of μόνος, adverbial) 339.
διὰ (preposition with the accusative, cause) 118.
τὴν (acc.sing.fem.of the article in agreement with ὀργὴν) 9.
ὀργὴν (acc.sing.fem.of ὀργή, cause) 283.
ἀλλὰ (adversative conjunction) 342.
καὶ (adjunctive conjunction joining prepositional phrases) 14.
διὰ (preposition with the accusative, cause) 118.
τὴν (acc.sing.fem.of the article in agreement with συνείδησιν) 9.
συνείδησιν (acc.sing.fem.of συνείδησις, cause) 3590.

Translation - "The result is that it is imperative for you to submit, not only because of fear of punishment but also for the sake of your conscience."

Comment: *Cf.*#1622 for all of the uses of διό, the consecutive conjunction. Its force in this context depends upon verse 4. Since the ruler is God's duly appointed representative for purposes of approbation of the good and opprobrium for evil "It is imperative for you to submit." Since the verb is missing it is possible to take the infinitive as the subject of the elided verb and consider ἀνάγκη as a predicate nominative, in which case the translation would be "To submit is a necessity." I have taken ἀνάγκη as the subject of the clause and placed the infinitive in apposition. Both approaches are good Greek grammar and the result is the same. Note the οὐ μόνον . . . ἀλλὰ καὶ sequence - "not only. . . but also" καὶ can also be taken here as ascensive - "not only . . . but even. . ." The διὰ phrases are causal. The wrath of God and fear of punishment is reason enough to obey the law of the state, but for the Christian citizen there is a greater reason - τὴν συνείδησιν - Christians are law-abiding citizens on principle. The Golden Rule, which Kant called the Categorical Imperative (Mt.7;12) is sufficient Scriptural and moral warrant for the child of God to obey the law of the land. He wishes others to do so because if they did not his own personal and property rights would be in jeopardy. What he wishes others to do for him is what he must do for others.

Here Paul is approving of Rousseau's teaching that submission to the "general will" if it demands good behavior is the surest safeguard to personal freedom. "Ye shall know the truth and the truth shall make you free" (John 8:32,36).

Paul is also in support of Blackstone, a point which we discussed in more detail in our comment on verse 2. Blackstone and other Naturalists in jurisprudence, opposed Positivists such as Jeremy Bentham, the Utilitarian philosopher and John Austin, the English jurist, by saying that a law that is not a "good' law in the moral sense is not in fact a law and need not be obeyed. The Utilitarians agreed that laws *should* be moral, but they insisted that immoral law, if it is the "general will" is indeed law nonetheless and must be obeyed promptly while being censured freely. To this view Paul would object since he says that the magistrate and executive officer rule for the public good.

Verse 6 - "For, for this cause pay ye tribute also: for they are God's ministers attending continually upon this very thing."

διὰ τοῦτο γὰρ καὶ φόρους τελεῖτε, λειτουργοὶ γὰρ θεοῦ εἰσιν εἰς αὐτὸ τοῦτο προσκαρτεροῦντες.

"For the same reason you also pay taxes, for the authorities are ministers of God, attending to this very thing." . . . RSV

διὰ (preposition with the accusative, cause) 118.
τοῦτο (acc.sing.neut.of οὗτος, cause) 93.
γὰρ (causal conjunction) 105.
καὶ (adjunctive conjunction joining prepositional phrases) 14.
φόρους (acc.pl.masc.of φόρος, direct object of τελεῖτε) 2692.
τελεῖτε (2d.per.pl.pres.act.ind.of τελέω, present progressive retroactive) 704.

#4036 λειτουργοὶ (nom.pl.masc.of λειτουργός, predicate nominative)

King James Version

he that ministereth - Phil.2:25.
minister - Rom.13:6; 15:16; Heb.1:7; 8:2.

Revised Standard Version

minister - Phil.2:25; Rom.13:6; 15:16; Heb.8:2.
servants - Heb.1:7.

Meaning: A combination of ἐργάζομαι (#691) and λῖτος, an unused word from λήϊτος - "public" *i.e.* belonging to the state. Hence, a public worker; public servant; public administrator; politician. With reference to civil officials - Rom.13:6; of Paul in his ministry to the Gentiles - Rom.15:16; with reference to heavenly creatures, other than angels, such as cherubim, seraphim, heavenly elders - Heb.1:7; of Christ,the administrator of the heavenly tabernacle - Heb.8:2. Epaphroditus, Paul's helper - Phil.2:25.

γὰρ (causal conjunction) 105.
θεοῦ (gen.sing.masc.of θεός, description) 124.
εἰσιν (3d.per.pl.pres.ind.of εἰμί, aoristic) 86.
εἰς (preposition with the accusative, purpose) 140.
αὐτὸ (acc.sing.neut.of αὐτός, in agreement with τοῦτο, intensive) 16.
τοῦτο (acc.sing.neut.of οὗτος, purpose) 93.
προσκαρτεροῦντες (pres.act.part.nom.pl.masc.of προσκαρτερέω, substantival, subject of εἰσιν) 2113.

Translation - *"Because this is why you also pay taxes, because those who are attending to this same thing are divine public administrators."*

Comment: The context alone can decide whether τέλειτε is indicative or imperative, since the spelling is the same of both forms. It seems here only to be indicative. The Roman Christians had already been paying taxes, before they were saved and before they saw Paul or received his letter. Paul is commenting on the fact that the tax collector is designated as such on divine authority. It is God's arrangement that this should be so. They spend all of their time at their task and are therefore entitled to a living from it. So also with the law enforcement agents. Thus Paul has added a second obligation. The Christian must obey the law and he must pay taxes to maintain the government.

He sums up the Christian's obligation to the state in

Verse 7 - *"Render therefore to all their dues: tribute to whom tribute is due; custom to whom custom; fear to whom fear; honour to whom honour."*

ἀπόδοτε πᾶσιν τὰς ὀφειλάς, τῷ τὸν φόρον τὸν φόρον, τῷ τὸ τέλος τὸ τέλος; τῷ τὸν φόβον, τῷ τὴν τιμὴν τὴν τιμήν.

"Pay all of them their dues, taxes to whom taxes are due, revenue to whom revenue is due, respect to whom respect is due, honor to whom honor is due." ...
RSV

ἀπόδοτε (2d.per.pl.aor.act.impv.of ἀποδίδωμι, command) 495.

πᾶσιν (dat.pl.masc.of πᾶς, indirect object of ἀπόδοτε) 67.

τὰς (acc.pl.fem.of the article in agreement with ὀφειλάς) 9.

ὀφειλάς (acc.pl.fem.of ὀφειλή, direct object of ἀπόδοτε) 1280.

τῷ (dat.sing.masc.of the article in agreement with κελεύοντι, understood) 9.

τὸν (acc.sing.masc.of the article in agreement with φόρον) 9.

φόρον (acc.sing.masc.of φόρος, direct object of κελεύοντι understood) 2692.

τὸν (acc.sing.masc.of the article in agreement with φόρον) 9.

φόρον (acc.sing.masc.of φόρος, direct object of ἐπόδοτε) 2692.

τῷ (dat.sing.masc.of the article in agreement with κελεύοντι understood) 9.

τὸ (acc.sing.neut.of the article in agreement with τέλος) 9.

τέλος (acc.sing.neut.of τέλος, direct object of κελεύοντι) 881.

τῳ (dat.sing.masc.of the article in agreement with κελεύοντι understood) 9.

τὸν (acc.sing.masc.of the article in agreement with φόβον) 9.

φόβον (acc.sing.masc.of φόβος, direct object of κελεύοντι) 1131.

τὸν (acc.sing.masc.of the article in agreement with φόβον) 9.

φόβον (acc.sing.masc.of φόβος, direct object of ἀπόδοτε) 1131.

τῷ (dat.sing.masc.of the article in agreement with κελεύοντι) 9.

τὴν (acc.sing.fem.of the article in agreement with τιμήν) 9.

τιμὴν (acc.sing.fem.of τιμή, direct object of κελεύοντι) 1619.

τὴν (acc.sing.fem.of the article in agreement with τιμήν) 9.

τιμήν (acc.sing.fem.of τιμή, direct object of ἀπόδοτε) 1619.

Translation - "Pay to all what you owe -to him who demands property tax, property tax; to the revenue agent excise tax; to him who demands respect, respect; to him who demands honor, honor."

Comment: *Cf.* #'s 2692, 881 and 1243 (which does not occur here but is mentioned in connection with #881 in Mt.17:25) for three kinds of taxes: (1) property tax, (2) excise tax levied at the end of the production process and hence τέλος, and (3) poll tax (#1243). The Christian has three types of obligation to his government: (1) financial (φόρος καὶ τέλος), (2) respect for the man in power, not because of his qualities or character, necessarily, but because of the office which he holds by God's appointment, and (3) honor to anyone, in or out of public office, whose character and achievement warrant it. Winer suggests that κελεύοντι be supplied as the missing verb.

In the next section Paul turns to the Christian's obligation, not to the state, but to private individuals.

Brotherly Love

(Romans 13:8-10)

Verse 8 - "Owe no man anything, but to love one another: for he that loveth another hath fulfilled the law."

Μηδενὶ μηδὲν ὀφείλετε, εἰ μὴ τὸ ἀλλήλους ἀγαπᾶν, ὁ γὰρ ἀγαπῶν τὸν ἕτερον νόμον πεπλήρωκεν.

"Owe no one anything, except to love one another; for he who loves his neighbor has fulfilled the law." . . . RSV

Μηδενὶ (dat.sing.masc.of μηδείς, personal advantage) 713.

μηδὲν (acc.sing.neut.of μηδείς, direct object of ὀφείλετε) 713.

ὀφείλετε (2d.per.pl.pres.act.impv.of ὀφείλω, command) 1277.

εἰ (conditional particle in a first-class elliptical condition) 337.

μὴ (negative particle in a first-class elliptical condition) 87.

τὸ (acc.sing.neut.of the article in agreement with ἀγαπᾶν) 9.

ἀλλήλους (acc.pl.masc.of ἀλλήλων, general reference) 1487.

ἀγαπᾶν (pres.act.inf.of ἀγαπάω, direct object of ὀφείλετε) 540.

ὁ (nom.sing.masc.of the article in agreement with ἀγαπῶν) 9.

γὰρ (causal conjunction) 105.

ἀγαπῶν (pres.act.part.nom.sing.masc.of ἀγαπάω, substantival, subject of πεπλήρωκεν) 540.

τὸν (acc.sing.masc.of the article in agreement with ἕτερον) 9.

ἕτερον (acc.sing.masc.of ἕτερος, direct object of ἀγαπῶν) 605.

νόμον (acc.sing.masc.of νόμος, direct object ofd πεπλήρωκεν) 464.

πεπλήρωκεν (3d.per.sing.perf.act.ind.of πληρόω, consummative) 115.

Translation - "Owe nothing to anyone, except to love one another; because he loves another is fulfilling the law."

Comment: εἰ μὴ is disjunctive. "Owe nothing to anyone except to love. . . " The articular infinitive τὸ ἀγαπᾶν is the object of ὀφείλετε. This passage is taken too frequently as applying only to financial obligations. They are included certainly, but so are all other moral and social obligations. μηδενὶ μηδὲν - "not one thing to not one person" is all inclusive. The participle ὁ ἀγαπῶν is the substantive. "The lover has fulfilled, is fulfilling and will continue to fulfill the law." This is the force of the present tense in ἀγαπῶν and the consummative perfect in πεπλήρωκεν. The present perfect is gnomic (timeless) and has a proleptic extension into the future, but only because of the durative action in the present participle. The perfect tense is never proleptic in itself. The one who is always loving his neighbor is always fulfilling the law. Here the context permits us to add that love also fulfills human statutes that are enacted on naturalistic principles. If laws are moral (and this is Paul's assumption in this passage - *cf.* verse 4) there is no reason why the Christian citizen should not obey them. And he does this automatically when he loves others. ἕτερος (#605) is the only dual pronominal in the New Testament - "the second of a pair." Thus Christian love is a distinctly personal thing. The Christian and one other - the one nearest him.

Verse 9 - "For this, Thou shalt not commit adultery, Thou shalt not kill, Thou shalt not steal, Thou shalt not bear false witness, Thou shalt not covet; and if

there be any other commandment, it is briefly comprehended in this saying,
namely, Thou shalt love thy neighbour as thyself."

τὸ γὰρ Οὐ μοιχεύσεις, Οὐ φονεύσεις, Οὐ κλέφεις, Οὐκ ἐπιθυμήσεις, καὶ εἴ τις
ἑτέρα ἐντολή, ἐν τῷ λόγῳ τούτῳ ἀνακεφαλαιοῦται, (ἐν τῷ) Ἀγαπήσεις τὸν
πλησίον σου ὡς σεαυτόν.

"The commandments, 'You shall not commit adultery, You shall not kill, You
shall not steal, You shall not covet,' and any other commandment, are summed
up in this sentence, 'You shall love your neighbor as yourself.' " . . . RSV

τὸ (nom.sing.neut.of the article, nominative absolute) 9.
γὰρ (causal conjunction) 105.
Οὐ (negative particle with the indicative) 130.
μοιχεύσεις (2d.per.sing.fut.act.ind.of μοιχεύω, imperatival) 498.
Οὐ (negative particle with the indicative) 130.
φονεύσεις (2d.per.sing.fut.act.ind.of φονεύω, imperatival) 476.
Οὐ (negative particle with the indicative) 130.
κλέφεις (2d.per.sing.fut.act.ind.of κλέπτω, imperatival) 597.
Οὐκ (negative particle with the indicative) 130.
ἐπιθυμήσεις (2d.per.sing.fut.act.ind.of ἐπιθυμέω, imperatival) 500.
καὶ (continuative conjunction) 14.
εἰ (conditional particle in a first-class condition) 337.
τις (nom.sing.fem.of τις, indefinite pronoun, in agreement with ἐντολή) 486.
ἑτέρα (nom.sing.fem.of ἕτερος, in agreement with ἐντολή) 605.
ἐντολή (nom.sing.fem.of ἐντολή, subject of ἐστιν understood) 472.
ἐν (preposition with the locative of place) 80.
τῷ (loc.sing.masc.of the article in agreement with λόγῳ) 9.
λόγῳ (loc.sing.masc.of λόγος, place) 510.
τούτῳ (loc.sing.masc.of οὗτος, in agreement with λόγῳ) 93.

#4037 ἀνακεφαλαιοῦται (3d.per.sing.pres.pass.ind.of ἀνακεφαλαιόομαι,
present progressive retroactive).

King James Version

be briefly comprehended - Rom.13:9.
gathered together in one - Eph.1:10.

Revised Standard Version

summed up - Rom.13:9.
unite - Eph.1:10.

Meaning: A combination of ἀνά (#1059) and κεφαλή (#521). *Cf.* κεφάλαιον
(#3588), κεφαλαιόω (#2683). To sum up; to bring together in summary; to
summarize. The particular elements of the moral code can be summed up in a
word - Rom.13:9. God will bring together under one Head, Christ, all of His
works in all dispensations, and with all groups - Eph.1:10.

(*ἐν*) (preposition with the locative of place) 80.

(*τῷ*) (loc.sing.neut.of the article, place) 9.

Ἀγαπήσεις (2d.per.sing.fut.act.ind.of ἀγαπάω, imperatival) 540.

τὸν (acc.sing.masc.of the article in agreement with πλησίον) 9.

πλησίον (acc.sing.masc.of πλησίον, direct object of ἀγαπήσεις) 541.

σου (gen.sing.masc.of σύ, relationship) 104.

ὡς (particle in a comparative clause) 128.

σεαυτόν (acc.sing.masc.of σεαυτός, direct object of ἀγαπήσεις) 347.

Translation - "Because the commandments - 'Do not commit adultery, Do not commit murder, Do not steal, Do not covet' — and if there is any other commandment, it is summarized in this, to wit, 'You shall love your neighbor as yourself.' "

Comment: The definite article τὸ, a nominative absolute, joins the list of commandments which follow. We supply ἐστίν with εἰ in a first-class condition. Paul means that the representative list of commandments which he gives seems to represent all of God's commands. We need not list them all. We can say it all with Leviticus 19:18.

All of the commandments except one ("Honor thy father and thy mother") are injunctions against evil. Since love never generates evil, the positive approach to holiness is love. This is Paul's point in

Verse 10 - "Love worketh no ill to his neighbour: therefore love is the fulfilling of the law."

ἡ ἀγάπη τῷ πλησίον κακὸν οὐκ ἐργάζεται. πλήρωμα οὖν νόμου ἡ ἀγάπη.

"Love does no wrong to a neighbor; therefore love is the fulfilling of the law." .

. . RSV

ἡ (nom.sing.fem.of the article in agreement with ἀγάπη) 9.

ἀγάπη (nom.sing.fem.of ἀγάπη, subject of ἐργάζεται) 1490.

τῷ (dat.sing.neut.of the article, personal interest) 9.

πλησίον (acc.sing.neut.of πλήσιος, extent) 541.

κακὸν (acc.sing.masc.of κακός, direct object of ἐργάζεται) 1388.

οὐκ (negative particle with the indicative) 130.

ἐργάζεται (3d.per.sing.pres.mid.ind.of ἐργάζομαι, static) 691.

πλήρωμα (nom.sing.neut.of πλήρωμα, predicate nominative) 805.

οὖν (inferential conjunction) 68.

νόμου (gen.sing.masc.of νόμος, description) 464.

ἡ (nom.sing.fem.of the article in agreement with ἀπάπη) 9.

ἀγάπη (nom.sing.fem.of ἀγάπη, subject of ἐστίν understood) 1490.

Translation - "Love does not generate evil for a neighbor, so love is a fulfilling of law."

Comment: Paul sums up this section on practical Christian ethics by saying that

Christ in the heart is not a system of rigid adherence to a long list of moral injunctions, which insist that the Christian must not do this and that. Rather Christ is a positive resurrection personality Who generates love in the heart and hence could never harm anyone. The Christian whose heart overflows with the fruits of the Holy Spirit, one of which is love, automatically keeps the law of the universe, whether promulgated by God or man.

The Approach of the Day of Christ

(Romans 13:11-14)

Verse 11 - "And that, knowing the time, that now it is high time to awake out of sleep: for now is our salvation nearer than when we believed."

Καὶ τοῦτο εἰδότες τὸν καιρόν, ὅτι ὥρα ἤδη ὑμᾶς ἐξ ὕπνου ἐγερθῆναι, νῦν γὰρ ἐγγύτερον ἡμῶν ἡ σωτηρία ἢ ὅτε ἐπιστεύσαμεν.

"Besides this you know what hour it is, how it is full time now for you to wake from sleep. For salvation is nearer to us now than when we first believed;" . . .
RSV

καὶ (continuative conjunction) 14.
τοῦτο (acc.sing.neut.of οὗτος, adverbial) 93.
εἰδότες (perf.act.part.nom.pl.masc.of ὁράω, adverbial, causal) 144b.
τὸν (acc.sing.masc.of the article in agreement with καιρόν) 9.
καιρόν (acc.sing.masc.of καιρός, direct object of εἰδότες) 767.
ὅτι (conjunction introducing an object clause in indirect discourse) 211.
ὥρα (nom.sing.fem.of ὥρα, subject of ἔστιν, understood) 735.
ἤδη (temporal adverb) 291.
ὑμᾶς (acc.pl.masc.of ἐγώ, general reference) 104.
ἐξ (preposition with the ablative of separation) 19.
ὕπνου (abl.sing.masc.of ὕπνος, separation) 126.
ἐγερθῆναι (aor.pass.inf.of ἐγείρω, noun use, in apposition with ὥρα) 125.
νῦν (temporal adverb) 1497.
γὰρ (causal conjunction) 105.
ἐγγύτερον (acc.sing.neut.of ἐγγύς, comparative predicate adjective) 1512.
ἡμῶν (gen.pl.masc.of ἐγώ, possession) 123.
ἡ (nom.sing.fem.of the article in agreement with σωτηρία) 9.
σωτηρία (nom.sing.fem.of σωτηρία, subject of ἔστιν understood) 1852.
ἢ (disjunctive) 465.
ὅτε (conjunction with the indicative in a definite temporal clause) 703.
ἐπιστεύσαμεν (1st.per.pl.aor.act.ind.of πιστεύω, ingressive) 734.

Translation - "Further, because we know the situation - that the hour is already upon us that we should wake up, for now is our salvation nearer than when we first believed."

Comment: The word is καιρόν, not χρόνος. Paul is not talking about the hour of the day or night, but about the period of time in which he then wrote, in relation to the day when Christ will return. He is preparing his audience for the hortatory subjunctives ἀποθώμεθα and ἐνδυσώμεθα in verse 12, περιπατήσωμεν in verse 13 and the imperative ἐνδύσασθε in verse 14. Christians must cast off the works of darkness, put on the armor of light, walk honestly and put on the Lord Jesus. Why? εἰδότες, the perfect participle is causal. Because we know what time it is. In modern parlance we sometimes say, "It is later than you think." The ὅτι object clause is indirect discourse, with the infinitive ἐγερθῆναι in apposition with ὥρα. What hour? The time to wake up. Why should we? Our salvation, by which Paul means their deliverance from this present evil world, not their justification, is nearer than when we first believed (ingressive aorist in ἐπιστεύσαμεν). They were saved in the justification sense when they believed, but their salvation in the glorification sense is still in the future. The statement is really redundant. Obviously, whatever "salvation" Paul had in mind was at some time in his future and thus with every passing moment it was nearer than it was at the time when they first accepted Christ.

It is possible that Paul was not speaking of the Second Coming of Messiah, although it was widely believed by the first century Christians that He would return within their lifetime, but of their deaths at the hands of the Roman Emperor. In any case the point is that they had no time to waste. Each moment we live reduces the amount of time available to us to serve the Lord. The folly of wasted time for the Christian is the point. Abraham Lincoln's observation that one should not waste time, since time is the "stuff from which life is made" is to the point. Every moment of spiritual apathy (ὕπνος) is an opportunity cost that no Christian should be willing to pay.

After two more observations about the lateness of the time, Paul closes the chapter with admonitions for victorious Christian living. *Cf.* Eph.5:14.

Verse 12 - "The night is far spent, the day is at hand; let us therefore cast off the works of darkness, and let us put on the armour of light."

ἡ νὺξ προέκοφεν, ἡ δὲ ἡμέρα ἤγγικεν. ἀποθώμεθα οὖν τὰ ἔργα τοῦ σκότους, ἐνδυσώμεθα δὲ τὰ ὅπλα τοῦ φωτός.

"the night is far gone, the day is at hand. Let us then cast off the works of darkness and put on the armor of light;" . . . RSV

ἡ (nom.sing.fem.of the article in agreement with νὺξ) 9.
νὺξ (nom.sing.fem.of νύξ, subject of προέκοφεν) 209.
προέκοφεν (3d.per.sing.aor.act.ind.of προκόπτω, culminative) 1923.
ἡ (nom.sing.fem.of the article in agreement with ἡμέρα) 9.
δὲ (continuative conjunction) 11.
ἡμέρα (nom.sing.fem.of ἡμέρα, subject of ἔγγικεν) 135.
ἤγγικεν (3d.per.sing.perf.act.ind.of ἐγγίζω, aoristic present perfect) 252.
ἀποθώμεθα (1st.per.pl.2d.aor.mid.subj.of ἀποτίθημι, hortatory) 1106.
οὖν (inferential conjunction) 68.
τὰ (acc.pl.neut.of the article in agreement with ἔργα) 9.

ἔργα (acc.pl.neut.of ἔργον, direct object of ἀποθώμεθα) 460.
τοῦ (gen.sing.masc.of the article in agreement with σκότους) 9.
σκότους (gen.sing.masc.of σκότος, description) 602.
ἐνδυσώμεθα (1st.per.pl.1st.aor.mid.subj.of ἐνδύω,hortatory) 613.
δὲ (continuative conjunction) 11.
τὰ (acc.pl.neut.of the article, in agreement with ὅπλα) 9.
ὅπλα (acc.pl.neut.of ὅπλον, direct object of ἐνδυσώμεθα) 2804.
τοῦ (gen.sing.neut.of the article in agreeement with φωτός) 9.
φωτός (gen.sing.neut.of φῶς, description) 379.

Translation - "The night is almost gone, and the day is near. So let us lay aside the activities of the darkness and let us equip ourselves with the weapons of light."

Comment: Note the culminative aorist in προέκοφεν and the aoristic present perfect in ἤγγικεν. The night was almost gone and the day was approaching. We have a similar juxtaposition in Phil.3:12 with ἔλαβον ἤ ἤδη τετελείωμαι.

In John 9:4 Jesus defined the night as the time following His death, and characterized by the fact that man's efforts in the night would be ineffectual. It has been "night" since man murdered the "Light of the world" (John 8:12). The night of man's sin and rebellion against God has been lengthened, spread thin by hammering (#1923). Satan and his sin program is prolonged. Man's empty philosophy lengthens into more ungodliness (2 Tim.2:16). Evil men and seducers string out their folly (2 Tim.3:13). But there is a limit beyond which God will not allow it to go (2 Tim.3:9).

Here is evidence that Paul looked upon the end of the age and the second advent of Messiah as very close at hand. Apparently he hoped that Jesus would return to earth during his lifetime. At any rate the time was short and he advocates the rigid training of a soldier of Christ. On ἀποθώμεθα cf. Jam.1:21; Heb.12:1; 1 Pet.2:1; Eph.4:22,25; Col.3:8. This shedding of what Paul calls the activities of darkness includes psychological and philosophical as well as physical sins. *Cf.* Eph.5:11; Col.1:21; 2 Tim.4:18. The weapons of light are both defensive (armor) and offensive (attack equipment). *cf.* 2 Cor.10:4.

Verse 13 - "Let us walk honestly, as in the day; not in rioting and drunkenness, not in chambering and wantonness,not in strife and envying."

ὡς ἐν ἡμέρᾳ εὐσχημόνως περιπατήσωμεν, μὴ κώμοις καὶ μέθαις, μὴ κοίταις καὶ ἀσελγείαις, μὴ ἔριδι καὶ ζήλῳ.

"let us conduct ourselves becomingly as in the day, not in reveling and drunkenness, not in debauchery and licentiousness, not in quarreling and jealousy." . . . RSV

ὡς (particle in a comparative clause) 128.
ἐν (preposition with the locative, time point) 80.
ἡμέρᾳ (loc.sing.fem.of ἡμέρα, time point) 135.

#4038 εὐσχημόνως (adverbial).

King James Version

decently - 1 Cor.14:40.
honestly - Rom.13:13; 1 Thess.4:12.

Revised Standard Version

decently - 1 Cor.14:40.
command the respect - 1 Thess.4:12.
becomingly - Rom.13:13.

Meaning: Cf. εὐσχήμων (#2872); hence, in a proper seemly manner; decently. With reference to the Christian walk - Rom.13:13; 1 Thess.4:12. Of the administration of the program of the local church - 1 Cor.14:40.

περιπατήσωμεν (1st.per.pl.1st.aor.act.subj. of περιπατέω, hortatory) 384.
μή (negative particle with the subjunctive) 87.

#4039 κώμοις (instru.pl.masc.of κῶμος, means).

King James Version

revelling - Gal.5:21; 1 Pet.4:3.
rioting - Rom.13:13.

Revised Standard Version

reveling - Rom.13:13.
carousing - Gal.5:21.
reveals - 1 Pet.4:3.

Meaning: cf. κεῖμαι (#295) - "a revel, carousal, *i.e.* in the Greek writings prop. a nocturnal and riotous procession of half-drunken and frolicsome fellows who after supper parade through the streets with torches and music in honor of Bacchus or some other deity, and sing and play before the houses of their male and female friends; hence used generally of feasts and drinking parties that are protracted till late at night and indulge in revelry - Rom.13:13; Gal.5:21; 1 Pet.4:3" (Thayer, 367).

καί (adjunctive conjunction joining nouns) 14.
μέθαις (instru.pl.fem.of μέθη, means) 2735.
μή (negative particle with the subjunctive) 87.
κοίταις (instru.pl.fem.of κοίτη, means) 2448.
καί (adjunctive conjunction joining nouns) 14.
ἀσελγείαις (instru.pl.fem.of ἀσέλγεια, means) 2303.
μή (negative particle with the subjunctive) 87.
ἔριδι (instru.sing.fem.of ἔρις, means) 3819.
καί (adjunctive conjunction joining nouns) 14.

ζήλῳ (instru.sing.masc.of ζῆλος, means) 1985.

Translation - "Let us walk properly as in the day, not with reveling and drunkenness; not with immorality and seduction; not with brawling and jealousy."

Comment: *Cf.* comment on verse 11. περιπατήσωμεν is another hortatory subjunctive explaining καὶ ποιεῖτε τοῦτο of verse 11. "Lay aside . . . darkness; be clothed . . . light" (verse 12) and "Let us walk properly. . . " Paul defines the Christian walk negatively. It is not reveling, drunkenness, seduction, adultery, strife or jealousy. The positive side is presented in

Verse 14 - "But put ye on the Lord Jesus Christ, and make not provision for the flesh, to fulfil the lusts thereof."

ἀλλὰ ἐνδύσασθε τὸν κύριον Ἰησοῦν Χριστόν, καὶ τῆς σαρκὸς πρόνοιαν μὴ ποιεῖσθε εἰς ἐπιθυμίας.

"But put on the Lord Jesus Christ, and make no provision for the flesh, to gratify its desires." . . . RSV

ἀλλὰ (alternative conjunction) 342.

ἐνδύσασθε (2d.per.pl.1st.aor.mid.impv.of ἐνδύω, command) 613.

τὸν (acc.sing.masc.of the article in agreement with κύριον) 9.

κύριον (acc.sing.masc.of κύριος, direct object of ἐνδύσασθε) 97.

Ἰησοῦν (acc.sing.masc.of Ἰησοῦς, apposition) 3.

Χριστόν (acc.sing.masc.of Χριστός, apposition) 4.

καὶ (continuative conjunction) 14.

τῆς (gen.sing.fem.of the article in agreement with σαρκὸς) 9.

σαρκὸς (gen.sing.fem.of σάρξ, description) 1202.

πρόνοιαν (acc.sing.fem.of πρόνοια, direct object of ποιεῖσθε) 3614.

μὴ (negative particle with the imperative) 87.

ποιεῖσθε (2d.per.pl.pres.mid.impv.of ποιέω, prohibition) 127.

εἰς (preposition with the accusative, purpose) 140.

ἐπιθυμίας (acc.pl.fem.of ἐπιθυμία, purpose) 2186.

Translation - "But wrap the Lord Jesus Christ around you, and do not plan ahead for the gratifications of the flesh."

Comment: This is the same thought as the last clause of verse 12. Christ is the weapon of light that confronts and defeats the machinations of darkness. Note that the overt sin of the flesh is preceded by the covert sin of the lecherous thought. The diabolical order is adultery and murder in a thought, then in a look, then in an act (Mt.5:2-7, 21-22, 28). Paul does not promise the believer that his flesh will not present a problem. The sanctification that removes, not only the desire, but even the ability to sin is the glorification experience of the believer at the Second Coming (Phil.3:20,21; 1 John 3:1-2). Until then the Christian is chained to a "body of death" (Rom.7:24) and has the struggle that Paul describes in Rom.7:9-25. Indeed the passage warns us that the flesh is always with us and that the only way to escape is to surround ourselves ("wrap yourself in" or "put on") with the Greater Personality of the resurrected Christ (1 John 4:4). No Christian who is totally dominated by the Holy Spirit, and who thus is using all of the resurrection power of our Lord, will surrender to temptation regardless of his surroundings and the power of Satan's seduction. But since most Christians do not avail ourselves of all of this spiritual power, even though it is always available, it is well to utilize our own common sense and control our behavior in such a fashion as never to be presented with the easy opportunity to sin. This is what Paul means by the last clause of our verse. "Do not plan ahead in order to sin." Rather let us "plan ahead" to avoid the social situation that makes it easy to sin. This planning will depend upon the nature of the temptation. Not all Christians are beset with the same temptations. Some are amenable to illicit sex; others to theft; others to violence; others to the psychological sins, such as jealousy and argumentation. The victorious Christian will indulge in self-analysis and know where his weaknesses lie. He will then plan ahead to avoid the situations in which his particular weakness can be best exploited. The Christian who is attracted to an improper sex partner, should avoid that person, and in no case be maneuvered into a meeting where no others are present. The same Christian, with a weakness for sex, might safely walk through the aisles of a department store all day with never the thought of shop lifting, since he is not a kleptomaniac. The Casper Milquetoast type need not worry about the sin of violence, at least not as long as there is an opportunity to flee. The Christian whose tendency is toward too high an opinion of the soundness of his theological or political views, should remember that if he gets into an argument he may lose control and commit the sins connected with oral strife. In some cases oral strife escalates into fisticuffs or worse.

Thus Paul tells us not only to yield to the superior power of the indwelling Holy Spirit, Who will clothe us with the holiness of Jesus Christ, but also to use our own intelligence and common sense and stay away from the social situations in which we are most severely tempted to yield to the flesh. The alcoholic should stay out of the bars. So also should Carrie Nation have, but for a different reason. It is not probable that she was tempted to violence except in saloons. The President of the Women's Christian Temperance Union, who probably does not like the taste of liquor anyway should have no difficulty in such an environment.

In Chapter 14 Paul suggests the Christian attitude toward other Christians with scruples which we do not share.

Do Not Judge Your Brother

(Romans 14:1-12)

Romans 14:1 - "Him that is weak in the faith receive you, but not to doubtful disputations."

Τὸν δὲ ἀσθενοῦντα τῇ πίστει προσλαμβάνεσθε, μὴ εἰς διακρίσεις διαλογισμῶν.

"As for the man who is weak in faith, welcome him, but not for disputes over opinions." . . . RSV

Τὸν (acc.sing.masc.of the article in agreement with ἀσθενοῦντα) 9.

δὲ (explanatory conjunction) 11.

ἀσθενοῦντα (pres.part.acc.sing.masc.of ἀσθενέω, substantival, direct object of προσλαμβάνεσθε) 857.

τῇ (loc.sing.fem.of the article in agreement with πίστει) 9.

πίστει (loc.sing.fem.of πίστις, sphere) 728.

προσλαμβάνεσθε (2d.per.pl.pres.mid.impv.of προσλαμβάνω, command) 1210.

μὴ (negative particle with the imperative) 87.

εἰς (preposition with the accusative, purpose) 140.

#4040 διακρίσεις (acc.pl.fem.of διάκρισις, purpose).

King James Version

discerning - 1 Cor.12:10.
to discern - Heb.5:14.
doubtful - Rom.14:1.

Revised Standard Version

disputes - Rom.14:1.
to distinguish - 1 Cor.12:10; Heb.5:14.

Meaning: A combination of διά (#118) and κρίνω (#531). *Cf.* also διακρίνω (#1195). The act of distinguishing differences between things; discerning; judgment. Followed by a genitive of description, διαλογισμῶν in Rom.14:1; πνευμάτων in 1 Cor.12:10; with καλοῦ τε καὶ κακοῦ in Heb.5:14.

διαλογισμῶν (gen.pl.masc.of διαλογισμός, description) 1165.

Translation - *"Now do not receive the one who is weak in faith for the purpose of debate."*

Comment: The prohibition is not against receiving the weak brother. It is rather against the motive which might impel us to receive him. Indeed the prohibition implies that we are to receive him, but we are not to do so for the purpose of debating with him about his views.

Such a debate could only result in his frustration since the weakness of his faith is in the premise. His views are indefensible, but only to those who are more mature in their experience and understanding of the Word of God. To him, at his stage of growth in grace, they are vital. There is therefore a great danger that if we debate with him about his views, and he, unable to support them, is routed in the discussion, he will become disillusioned and his growth in grace will be stunted.

The context which follows indicates doubts about ethical practices, rather than theological points,although of course to the intellectually advanced mind,it is impossible to separate ethics from theology. Those who reject the Christian theology have no logical right to entertain moral scruples about anything, although most unregenerates have not thought that deeply into the problem, or, if they have, they have not the courage to live the lives which their nihilism dictates.

But the child of God, recently "born from above" and without the opportunity to study the Word in depth may very likely espouse views which his later more mature knowledge and wisdom will lead him to abandon. But we are not talking about his views as they may develop later. We are concerned with what he believes now and the life style which his current views dictate. He is saved; he is delighted to be saved; he is zealous to become a better Christian and he is mistaken about something about which he is very certain he is right.

What is the proper policy for the church with reference to him?

He should be received in a way that tells him that the church is delighted to have him in the fellowship. The analogy to physical birth applies. When the baby is born, the parents, siblings and friends are delighted and take him home from the hospital with great pomp and circumstance. They lavish their love on him, give loving attention to his needs and proudly display him even to those who are not particularly interested in the display. But they do not immediately argue with him about the Pythagorean theorem, supply-side economics or E equals MC squared.

But misguided and overzealous Christians do this all the time to the new babes in Christ. Immediately it becomes important that the newcomer understand that he may eat anything he likes, work or play golf on Saturday (or is it Sunday?) or do anything else which Christian liberty allows. He must also quickly grasp the intricate theology of the Calvinistic TULIP and he must understand that the church either is or is not going through the Great Tribulation.

It is scant wonder that many babes in Christ do not reveal the growth in grace that normally we have a right to expect.

The requirements for membership in a New Testament church do not include the doctorate in theology. They do include repentance and faith, open confession of the candidate's acceptance of Jesus Christ as Lord and Saviour and immersion in water. The church should then extend the hand and heart of fellowship and full membership, despite the fact that the candidate may at this early date be confused about what the Christian life style really is. The Great Commission places education ($\delta\iota\delta\acute{a}\sigma\kappa o\nu\tau\epsilon\varsigma$) after discipleship and immersion (Mt.28:18-20). The purpose of Christian fellowship is not to turn the worship into a debate over philosophical, theological or ethical questions.

This is not to say that the church should never seek to elevate Christians to a mature understanding of the New Testament. Far from it! But it is to say that a wise pastor and his people do not take the new convert to the foot of a wall, ten thousand feet in height, and say, "Climb it." But they do begin very carefully to teach him how to climb the first ten feet.

Christians should be more concerned about tolerance than about exactitude in debateable questions of orthodoxy. This advice, if it is followed, will prevent schism in the local church over questions, with reference to which honest minds may differ.

This plea for tolerance in theological and ethical matters which Paul has made neither justifies nor demands tenure in the church membership for outright heretics. An honest lack of understanding of what the Bible teaches is one thing, and it is to be both expected and excused, particularly among the babes in Christ. But an outright and deliberate rejection of what one admits that the Bible teaches is heresy and must be dealt with. The local New Testament church "is the house of God, which is the church of the living God, the pillar and ground of the truth" (1 Tim.3:15). When it continues to approbate and reward views which openly repudiate the New Testament, which is the foundation of the Christian system, it loses its status as a New Testament church. What is the role of the Bible believer in such a situation? He should do what he can, under the guidance of the Holy Spirit to change the situation, and if he fails, he has no other course open to him than to find his fellowship in a church that has no doubts about the authority of the New Testament.

Paul is not speaking here about theological questions as such. In such contexts his advice is not in terms of tolerance for error. *Cf.*Titus 3:10; 2 Cor.6:14-18). He is speaking, for example about what Christians may or may not eat, in

Verse 2 - "For one believeth that he may eat all things: another, who is weak eateth herbs."

ὃς μὲν πιστεύει φαγεῖν πάντα, ὁ δὲ ἀσθενῶν λάχανα ἐσθίει.

"One believes he may eat anything, while the weak man eats only vegetables."
. . *RSV*

ὃς (nom.sing.masc.of ὅς, demonstrative pronoun, subject of πιστεύει) 65.
μὲν (particle of affirmation) 300.
πιστεύει (3d.per.sing.pres.act.ind.of πιστεύω, aoristic) 724.
φαγεῖν (aor.act.inf.of ἐσθίω, indirect declaration) 610.
πάντα (acc.pl.neut.of πᾶς, direct object of φαγεῖν) 67.
ὁ (nom.sing.masc.of the article in agreement with ἀσθενῶν) 9.
δὲ (adversative conjunction) 11.
ἀσθενῶν (pres.act.part.nom.sing.masc.of ἀσθενέω, substantival, subject of ἐσθίει) 857.
λάχανα (acc.pl.neut.of λάχανον, direct object of ἐσθίει) 1069.
ἐσθίει (3d.per.sing.pres.act.ind.of ἐσθίω, customary) 610.

Translation - "In fact one believes that he may eat everything, but the weak customarily eat only vegetables."

Comment: ὃς cannot have ἀσθενοῦντα in verse 1 as its antecedent, though they agree in number and gender, because ἀνθενοῦντα is represented in verse 2 as the vegetarian, while ὃς is strong in faith and eats everything. ὃς here is not relative but demonstrative.

Some Christians in the first century had scruples against eating meat which had first been offered in sacrifice to idols and then sold in the markets, on the ground that to do so was to lend financial support to a pagan institution, and thus be charged with complicity in idolatry. Others, more mature, saw no connection between the facts that (1) the meat was offered first to a dumb idol, and (2) subsequently offered for sale as a food. Thus they bought and ate the meat with a clear conscience. Paul returns to the question about eating such meat in verse 6 and offers a full discussion of the question in 1 Cor.8:4-13.

Christians often make dietary choices on grounds other than theological, and should not be criticized. What one eats or does not eat is a matter of personal liberty, and has nothing directly to do with Christianity.

A missionary friend who spent many years in the Chad region of what was then French Equatorial Africa told of her delight when several dozen fresh eggs were flown into the compound. She and her family had not seen an egg for months. They bought several dozen and took them home with instructions to the native house boy to cook and fry them, as they anticipated an orgy of eating eggs. The house boy turned green and said, "Are you going to eat those eggs? Anyone who would eat eggs would eat anything!" It is all a matter of acculturation. Another missionary came home after ten years of uninterrupted service in Africa. His little son, who was born in Africa, came down with some illness. The doctor noted that he had no appetite and asked him if there was anything that he wanted especially to eat. The lad said, "Grasshoppers." Who in America is to say that eggs are fit to eat and that grasshoppers are not? Maybe the house boy in Africa and the little boy knew something that we do not know.

One must be possessed of a special measure of bigotry to insist that others conform in all matters to what one believes to be proper. Supreme confidence in one's opinions, with no dilution of humility is the stuff of which bigots are made. In view of the fact that only in Christ are all of the treasures of wisdom and knowledge hid, and that no one else knows as much as He, bigotry in the Christian is especially obnoxious and revolting.

Verse 3 - "Let not him that eateth despise him that eateth not: and let not him which eateth not judge him that eateth: for God hath received him."

ὁ ἐσθίων τὸν μὴ ἐσθίοντα μὴ ἐξουθενείτω, ὁ δὲ μὴ ἐσθίων τὸν ἐσθίοντα μὴ κρινέτω, ὁ θεὸς γὰρ αὐτὸν προσελάβετο.

"Let not him who eats despise him who abstains, and let not him who abstains pass judgment on him who eats; for God has welcomed him." . . . RSV

ὁ (nom.sing.masc.of the article in agreement with ἐσθίων) 9.

ἐσθίων (pres.act.part.nom.sing.masc.of ἐσθίω, substantival, subject of ἐξουθενείτω) 610.

τὸν (acc.sing.masc.of the article in agreement with ἐσθίοντα) 9.

μὴ (negative particle with the participle) 87.

ἐσθίοντα (pres.act.part.acc.sing.masc.of ἐσκθίω, substantival, direct object of ἐξουθενείτω) 610.

μὴ (negative particle with the imperative) 87.

ἐξουθενείτω (3d.per.sing.pres.act.impv.of ἐξωθενέω, prohibition) 2628.

ὁ (nom.sing.masc.of the article in agreement with ἐσθίων) 9.

δὲ (continuative conjunction) 11.

μὴ (negative particle with the participle) 87.

ἐσθίων (pres.act.part.nom.sing.masc.of ἐσθίω, substantival, subject of κρινέτω) 610.

τὸν (acc.sing.masc.of the article in agreement with ἐσθίοντα) 9.

ἐσθίοντα (pres.act.part.acc.sing.masc.of ἐσθίω, substantival, direct object of κρινέτω) 610.

μὴ (negative particle with the imperative) 87.

κρινέτω (3d.per.sing.pres.act.impv.of κρίνω, prohibition) 531.

ὁ (nom.sing.masc.of the article in agreement with θεὸς) 9.

θεὸς (nom.sing.masc.of θεός, subject of προσελάβετο) 124.

γὰρ (causal conjunction) 105.

αὐτὸν (acc.sing.masc.of αὐτός, direct object of προσελάβετο) 16.

προσελάβετο (3d.per.sing.aor.mid.ind.of προσλαμβάνω, culminative) 1210.

Translation - *"The one who eats should never entertain contempt for the one who does not, and the one who does not should never condemn the one who does, beause God has taken him in."*

Comment: The participles are substantives, subject and object - the eaters and the non-eaters. Neither should judge the other. The mature Christian may be tempted to be contemptuous of the overscrupulous babe in Christ. The babe in Christ may have a tendency to be self-righteous about his taboo and tend to judge older Christians. Neither should yield to these tendencies. Let us at least give the non-eater credit for the sincerity of his conviction and the zeal with which he obeys it. Kindly disposition is often a camouflage for amused contempt.

Most pastors have seen both of these errors in the church and the trouble in human relations which they cause. The overzealous, with pride in their humble obedience to a rule, commit the sin of judging others for behavior which they consider off limits. A dear Christian woman had not studied this passage despite the fact that she was a faithful witness for Christ in her community, a warrior in prayer and a daily Bible reader. She went to her pastor and told him that she was praying about his golf. The pastor thanked her, asked her to continue in prayer in the hope that his game would improve, especially on the greens. The woman burst out laughing, went home and came back the next day to apologize to her pastor and say that now she realized that his golf was none of her business. The pastor then asked her to pray that his preaching might be more effective. She did and it was. His golf game did not improve.

Why should there be no condemnation? The causal clause with γὰρ tells us why. God has received both the Christian who eats meat offered to idols and him who does not. If eating meat is such a sin as to dishonor God, then it should be condemned by all. Apparently God does not take this view of it. But God has also accepted the Christian who abstains.

The issue comes down to this: whether a child of God, whom God has accepted, eats meat or only vegetables is of concern only to him and to God, and the sophisticated Christian will not intrude into something that is none of his affair. Paul deals with the problem with a bit of asperity in

Verse 4 - "Who art thou that judgest another man's servant? To his own master he standeth or falleth. Yea, he shall be holden up: for God is able to make him stand."

σὺ τίς εἶ ὁ κρίνων ἀλλότριον οἰκέτην; τῷ ἰδίῳ κυρίῳ στήκει ἢ πίπτει. σταθήσεται δέ, δυνατεῖ γὰρ ὁ κύριος στῆσαι αὐτόν.

"Who are you to pass judgment on the servant of another? It is before his own master that he stands or falls. And he will be upheld, for the Master is able to make him stand." . . . RSV

σὺ (nom.sing.masc.of σύ, subject of εἶ) 104.

τίς (nom.sing.masc.of τίς, interrogative pronoun, predicate nominative, in direct question) 281.

εἶ (2d.per.sing.pres.ind.of εἰμί, aoristic) 86.

ὁ (nom.sing.masc.of the article in agreement with κρίνων) 9.

κρίνων (pres.act.part.nom.sing.masc.of κρίνω, substantival, in apposition with σύ) 104.

ἀλλότριον (acc.sing.masc.of ἀλλότριος, in agreement with οἰκέτην) 1244.

οἰκέτην (acc.sing.masc.of οἰκέτης, direct object of κρίνων) 2572.

τῷ (dat.sing.masc.of the article in agreement with κυρίῳ) 9.

ἰδίῳ (dat.sing.masc.of ἴδιος, in agreement with κυρίῳ) 778.

κυρίῳ (dat.sing.masc.of κύριος, personal interest) 97.

στήκει (3d.per.sing.pres.act.ind.of στήκω, static) 1957.

ἢ (disjunctive) 465.

πίπτει (3d.per.sing.pres.act.ind.of πίπτω, static) 187.

σταθήσεται (3d.per.sing.fut.pass.ind.of ἵστημι, predictive) 180.

δὲ (intensive conjunction) 11.

#4041 δυνατεῖ (3d.per.sing.pres.act.ind.of δυνατέω, static).

King James Version

able - Rom.14:4; 2 Cor.9:8.
be mighty - 2 Cor.13:3.

Revised Standard Version

able - Rom.14:4; 2 Cor.9:8.
powerful - 2 Cor.13:3.

Meaning: Cf. δυνατός (#1311). To be powerful, mighty. Followed by an infinitive in Rom.14:4; 2 Cor.9:8. Opposed to ἀσθενέω (#857) in 2 Cor.13:3.

γὰρ (causal conjunction) 105.

ὁ (nom.sing.masc.of the article in agreement with κύριος) 9.
κύριος (nom.sing.masc.of κύριος, subject of δυνατεῖ) 97.
στῆσαι (aor.act.inf.of ἵστημι, complementary) 180.
αὐτόν (acc.sing.masc.of αὐτός, direct object of στῆσαι) 16.

Translation - "*You?! Who are you who is judging another man's servant? To his own lord he stands or falls. In fact he will be made to stand, because the Lord is able to make him stand.*"

Comment: σύ is emphatic. "You" as Paul points a finger. In modern parlance we say, "Who do you think you are?" δέ is intensive. After Paul had suggested that a Christian may either stand or fall, but that whatever happens, it is the Lord's problem, not ours, he hastens to add that the Christian will stand, because God is able to see to it that He does.

The anxious critic need not be concerned that his brother who has it wrong is going to be lost, or even that he is going to ruin his Christian testimony. If eating meat or refusing to eat meat is bad, God, Whose responsibility it is, will do the job of correcting His mistaken servant. God needs no help with His discipline problems.

Another issue among the saints is the question of whether or not one day is holier than the others. The Sabbath question has divided the church for centuries. Paul speaks to the issue in

Verse 5 - "*One man esteemeth one day above another; another esteemeth every day alike. Let every man be fully persuaded in his own mind.*"

ὃς μὲν (γὰρ) κρίνει ἡμέραν παρ' ἡμέραν, ὃς δὲ κρίνει πᾶσαν ἡμέραν. ἕκαστος ἐν τῷ ἰδίῳ νοῒ πληροφορείσθω.

"*One man esteems one day as better than another, while another man esteems all days alike. Let every one be fully convinced in his own mind.*" . . . RSV

ὃς (nom.sing.masc.of ὅς, demonstrative, subject of κρίνει) 65.
μὲν (affirmative particle) 300.
(γὰρ) (explanatory conjunction) 105.
κρίνει (3d.per.sing.pres.act.ind.of κρίνω, aoristic) 531.
ἡμέραν (acc.sing.fem.of ἡμέρα, direct object of κρίνει) 135.
παρ' (preposition with the accusative of extent, comparison - "better") 154.
ἡμέραν (acc.sing.fem.of ἡμέρα, extent, comparison) 135.
ὃς (nom.sing.masc.of ὅς, demonstrative pronoun, subject of κρίνει) 65.
δὲ (adversative conjunction) 11.
κρίνει (3d.per.sing.pres.act.ind.of κρίνω, aoristic) 531.
πᾶσαν (acc.sing.fem.of πᾶς, in agreement with ἡμέραν) 67.
ἡμέραν (acc.sing.fem.of ἡμέρα, direct object of κρίνει) 135.
ἕκαστος (nom.sing.masc.of ἕκαστος, subject of πληροφορείσθω) 1217.
ἐν (preposition with the locative of place) 80.
τῷ (loc.sing.masc.of the article in agreement with νοῒ) 9.
ἰδίῳ (loc.sing.masc.of ἴδιος, in agreement with νοῒ) 778.

νοΐ (loc.sing.masc.of *νούς*, place) 2928.

πληροφορείσθω (3d.per.sing.pres.pass.impv.of *πληροφορέω*, command) 1708.

Translation - *"Now the fact is that one reveres one day more than another, but another man judges every day alike; let each man be fully convinced in his own mind."*

Comment: We have two more uses of *ὅς* as a demonstrative pronoun, as we found it in verse 2. *γὰρ* is explanatory, as Paul prepares to apply the principle established in verses 1-4 to another issue where a difference of opinion exists. *μὲν* is emphatically affirmative and followed by *δὲ* which can be either adversative or concessive. *Cf.*#154 for *παρά* and the accusative of extent in comparison. Some Christians believe that one day of seven is holier than the other six. Is it Saturday, the Jewish Sabbath day, or Sunday, the Christian "first day of the week" on which we celebrate the resurrection of our Lord?

Some Christians, this writer among them, believe that Saturday is a day of physical and economic rest and that Sunday is a day of celebration and worship. Unfortunately controversy over these issues has produced more heat than light. The way to gain light on the question is to ban the heat. Why must Christians feel insulted when other Christians disagree with them on some point? Humble Christians, who recognize that they do not know it all, and are ashamed that they know so little, possess the humility which is prerequisite to knowledge (2 Pet.1:5), and rejoice in the opportunity to discuss disputed points of Scripture interpretation (as indeed of secular theory) with others whom they love and respect as colleagues in the Body of Christ. Paul and Peter disagreed briefly about Peter's social discrimination against Gentile Christians, an action wholly inconsistent with Peter's theology as he had learned it in the home of Cornelius, but there is no record that they became enemies. On the contrary Peter was grateful to Paul for the correction and Paul did not react to the controversy with a feeling that he was better than Peter because he understood the point better.

It is the Christian's duty to search the Scriptures (John 6:39; 2 Tim.2:15; 3:16,17) in reference to controversial points in order to ascertain what the true views are. In this way each man constructs a rationale that honestly satisfies him. It is in this way that each Christian does his own thinking and stands upon his own intellectual discernment, and thus escapes the intellectual slavery that results when one accepts institutional dogma. A Baptist who believes in baptism by immersion in water "because I am a Baptist and that is what Baptists believe" is a slave to the Baptist denomination. A Presbyterian who believes in sprinkling babies because "I have carefully studied the Scriptures and I am convinced that the Greek verb *βαπτίζω* means "to sprinkle" may or may not be correct, but at least he is doing his own thinking and standing on his own convictions, not following church tradition blindly. Baptists who are also Bible students are amused to find immersed Presbyterians.

Paul did not say that no discussion should be had between parties who honestly disagree on a point. Elsewhere he suggests that it should (Gal.6:1). Let the discussions be had, just as Paul pointed out to Peter the inconsistency of his action (Gal.2:11-14), but after all is said, no one should adopt a position which he does not truly believe on the basis of deference to superior authority. This is slovenly - unworthy of the child of God. The "winner" in a debate that ends on those terms is not a good teacher, for no teacher uses his authority over the student to gain his point. If the point which the "teacher" is trying to establish cannot be made on solid grounds of New Testament Greek exegesis, it is untrue and the teacher and the student should exchange places.

Paul tells each of us to find out what the Bible teaches. We are to convince ourselves that our intellectual model is soundly based on good exegesis and possesses the solidity of inner consistency and coherence. This is the only truth that also corresponds to reality. Who wants to believe in that which is unreal? Once the study has been conducted, with no desire on the part of any student to "prove his point" but rather to discover only what the truth is, each Christian should procede on the basis of his own judgment. Only thus can we offer to God in worship whatever we do. This is the thought in verse 6.

This discussion should not close without pointing to the distinction which must be made between focal and peripheral truths. Some teachings of the Christian revelation are so important that without them, there is no Christianity. Others, while important in the sense that everything God says is important, can be ignored, neglected or misinterpreted without doing structural damage to the Christian faith. The Calvinistic Presbyterian with a firm faith in the TULIP is closer to the truth of God, despite the fact that he sprinkles babies, than the Last-Point Calvinists among the Baptists who hold firmly to immersion in water for believers only. An amillenialist who believes in the virgin birth is a better Bible student than a Premillenialist who does not, although a Premillenialist who rejects the incarnation is rare, if not non-existent. Correctitude on the focal points does not give us the right to be careless about the periphery, for everything that God has said is to be obeyed. On the other hand orthodoxy on the periphery has too often been the source of so much spiritual pride that the hair-splitting fanatics have ignored, neglected and misinterpreted the central truths of the faith. Thus institutional dogma destroys the gospel and dishonors God.

Verse 6 - "He that regardeth the day regardeth it unto the Lord; and he that regardeth not the day, to the Lord he doth not regard it. He that eateth eateth to the Lord, for he giveth God thanks; and he that eateth not, to the Lord he eateth not, and giveth God thanks."

ὁ φρονῶν τὴν ἡμέραν κυρίῳ φρονεῖ. καὶ ὁ ἐστίων κυρίῳ ἐσθίει, εὐχαριστεῖ γὰρ τῷ θεῷ. καὶ ὁ μὴ ἐσθίων κυρίῳ οὐκ ἐσθίει, καὶ εὐχαριστεῖ τῷ θεῷ.

"He who observes the day, observes it in honor of the Lord. He also who eats, eats in honor of the Lord, since he gives thanks to God, while he who abstains, abstains in honor of the Lord and gives thanks to God." . . . RSV

ὁ (nom.sing.masc.of the article in agreement with φρονῶν) 9.

φρονῶν (pres.act.part.nom.sing.masc.of φρονέω, substantival, subject of φρονεῖ) 1212.

τὴν (acc.sing.fem.of the article in agreement with ἡμέραν) 9.

ἡμέραν (acc.sing.fem.of ἡμέρα, direct object of φρονῶν) 135.

κυρίῳ (dat.sing.masc.of κύριος, personal advantage) 97.

φρονεῖ (3d.per.sing.pres.act.ind.of φρονέω, aoristic) 1212.

καὶ (continuative conjunction) 14.

ὁ (nom.sing.masc.of the article in agreement with ἐσθίων) 9.

ἐσθίων (pres.act.part.nom.sing.masc.of ἐσθίω, substantival, subject of ἐσθίει) 610.

κυρίῳ (dat.sing.masc.of κύριος, personal advantage) 97.

ἐσθίει (3d.per.sing.pres.act.ind.of ἐσθίω, aoristic) 610.

εὐχαριστεῖ (3d.per.sing.pres.act.ind.of εὐχαριστέω, aoristic) 1185.

γὰρ (causal conjunction) 105.

τῷ (dat.sing.masc.of the article in agreement with θεῷ) 9.

θεῷ (dat.sing.masc.of θεός, indirect object of εὐχαριστεῖ) 124.

καὶ (continuative conjunction) 14.

ὁ (nom.sing.masc.of the article in agreement with ἐσθίων) 9.

μὴ (negative particle with the participle) 87.

ἐσθίων (pres.act.part.nom.sing.masc.of ἐσθίω, substantival, subject of ἐσθίει) 610

κυρίῳ (dat.sing.masc.of κύριος, personal advantage) 97.

οὐκ (negative particle with the indicative) 130.

ἐσθίει (3d.per.sing.pres.act.ind.of ἐσθίω, aoristic) 610.

καὶ (continuative conjunction) 14.

εὐχαριστεῖ (3d.per.sing.pres.act.ind.of εὐχαριστέω, aoristic) 1185.

τῷ (dat.sing.masc.of the article in agreement with θεῷ) 9.

θεῷ (dat.sing.masc.of θεός, indirect object of εὐχαριστεῖ) 124.

Translation - *"The one who observes a day does so to honor the Lord, and the eater eats for the Lord's glory; therefore he gives thanks to God; and the one who never eats is abstaining for the Lord and he is thanking God."*

Comment: The grammar and syntax is all perfectly regular. Every Christian is assumed to do or to refrain from doing whatever is his choice for the personal honor of God. This is demonstrated by the fact that he accompanies his act or his abstinence with a prayer of gratitude to the Lord. Why would he do so if he did not think that his action (or the lack of it) would please God?

Since then whatever is done or not done is designed to honor God, which is the highest ethical act that a Christian can perform, there is no room for criticism. The critic criticizes on the assumption that (1) he is a personal bodyguard of God's honor who knows perfectly what God likes and dislikes, and (2) that his "erring" brother is doing that which displeases God. In order for these assumptions to be true, the critic would have to be God!

Of course this teaching applies only to the areas of behavior where no definite rule, such as the Ten Commandments, has been handed down. One who says that adultery is evil is not a bigot for having said it, since the injunction is a part of revelation. But the critic of the vegetarian or the vegetarian who criticizes the meat-eater is playing God. And that is a role which any thespian should know is hard to play.

Verse 7 - "For none of us liveth to himself, and no man dieth to himself."

οὐδεὶς γὰρ ἡμῶν ἑαυτῷ ζῇ, καὶ οὐδεὶς ἑαυτῷ ἀποθνῄσκει.

"None of us lives to himself, and none of us dies to himself." . . . *RSV*

οὐδεὶ (nom.sing.masc.of οὐδείς, subject of ζῇ) 446.
γὰρ (causal conjunction) 105.
ἡμῶν (gen.pl.masc.of ἐγώ, partitive) 123.
ἑαυτῷ (dat.sing.masc.of ἑαυτοῦ, personal interest) 288.
ζῇ (3d.per.sing.pres.act.ind.of ζάω, static) 340.
καὶ (continuative conjunction) 14.
οὐδεὶς (nom.sing.masc.of οὐδείς, subject of ζῇ) 446.
ἑαυτῷ (dat.sing.masc.of ἑαυτοῦ, personal interest) 288.
ἀποθνῄσκει (3d.per.sing.pres.act.ind.of ἀποθνῄσκω, static) 774.

Translation - "Because no one of us lives for himself and not one dies for himself."

Comment: Every Christian lives and dies for the ultimate glory of God and not for his own selfish interest and advantage (Eph.2:7). When he repents and believes on Christ, he is sealed by the Holy Spirit (Eph.1:13,14), Who takes up His residence in his body (1 Cor.6:19,20) and guarantees his bodily resurrection (Eph.4:30; Rom.8:11). God, Who initiated the program of redemption for and in the Christian will perfect it until His death (Rom.8:29,30). Thus God has a Creator's and Redeemer's interest in each Christian, and God has already assigned to him certain good works which he is to perform for God's glory (Eph.2:10; 2 Tim.4:6,7; Rev.3:2). All that he does as long as he lives and on the day he dies, is God's personal concern. Whether he eats meat or only vegetables and whether he worships alike on all days or singles out one day above the others, is his own personal business between him and God alone. The only requirement is that he must be satisfied in his own mind that he is doing the proper thing and is sincere in his attempt to glorify God.

These things being so, it follows that God will hold each of His children responsible for his stewardship at the judgment seat of Christ (1 Cor.3:11-15; 2 Cor.5:10; Rev.11:18)

Verse 8 - "For whether we live we live unto the Lord, and whether we die we die unto the Lord: whether we live therefore, or die, we are the Lord's."

ἐάν τε γὰρ ζῶμεν, τῷ κυρίῳ ζῶμεν, ἐάν τε ἀποθνῄσκωμεν, τῷ κυρίῳ ἀποθνῄσκωμεν. ἐάν τε οὖν ζῶμεν ἐάν τε ἀποθνῄσκωμεν, τοῦ κυρίου ἐσμέν.

"If we live, we live to the Lord, and if we die, we die to the Lord; so then, whether we live or whether we die, we are the Lord's." . . . *RSV*

ἐάν (conditional particle with the indicative in a first-class condition) 363.

τε (correlative particle) 1408.

γὰρ (inferential conjunction) 105.

ζῶμεν (1st.per.pl.pres.act.ind.of ζάω, first-class condition) 340.

τῷ (dat.sing.masc.of the article in agreement with κυρίῳ) 9.

κυρίῳ (dat.sing.masc.of κύριος, personal advantage) 97.

ζῶμεν (1st.per.pl.pres.act.ind.of ζάω, progressive present) 340.

ἐάν (conditional particle in a first-class condition) 363.

τε (correlative particle) 1408.

ἀποθνῄσκωμεν (1st.per.pl.pres.act.subj.of ἀποθνῄσκω, third-class condition) 774.

τῳ (dat.sing.masc.of the article in agreement with κυρίῳ) 9.

κυρίῳ (dat.sing.masc.of κύριος, personal advantage) 97.

ἀποθνῄσκομεν (1st.per.pl.pres.act.ind.of ἀποθνῄσκω, third-class condition) 774.

ἐάν (conditional particle in a third-class condition) 363.

τε (correlative particle) 1408.

οὖν (inferential conjunction) 68.

ζῶμεν (1st.per.pl.pres.act.ind.of ζάω, first-class condition) 340.

ἐάν (conditional particle in a third-class condition) 363.

τε (correlative particle) 1408.

ἀποθνῄσωμεν (1st.per.pl.pres.act.subj.of ἀποθνῄσκω, third-class condition) 774.

τοῦ (gen.sing.masc.of the article in agreement with κυρίου) 9.

κυρίου (gen.sing.masc.of κύριος, possession) 97.

ἐσμέν (1st.per.pl.pres.ind.of εἰμί, static) 86.

Translation - "And therefore, since we live we live for the Lord's benefit and if we die, we die for the Lord. Therefore since we live and if we die we belong to the Lord."

Comment: ἐάν is sometimes used with the indicative mode in first-class conditions, in which the assumption is that the statement in the protasis is true. *Cf.* #363. "In general the difference between εἰ and ἐάν is considerably lessened in the κοινή, though it must be remembered that ἐάν was never confined to the subjunctive, nor εἰ to the indicative and optative." (Robertson, *Grammar,* 1009, 1010). Since in form ζῶμεν is either indicative of subjunctive, only the context can help us. There is no doubt that Paul and the Roman Christians were alive, though Paul had some doubt that they would die, since he hoped for Messiah's return in their lifetime. Hence we have ἐάν τε ἀποθνῄσκωμεν in both protases, which is clearly subjunctive. Robertson reminds us that there is "considerable support . . . for ἐάν τε ἀποθνῄσκομεν in Rom.14:8" (*Ibid.*), though he does not cite the variant MSS. The United Bible Societies' Committee cite no variant readings for the passage. To read ἐάν τε ἀποθνῄσκομεν (indicative) is to deny that Paul expected to be raptured without death. We have no choice but to follow the text, which indicates that Paul accepted the physical life as an obvious fact and conjectured (in a third-class condition) about whether or not they would die. Hence our translation *supra*. They certainly were alive at the time of the writing and they might die. The verbs in the three apodoses are, of course, indicative. Since Christians live and if they die, in any and all cases, we live and/or die for the Lord's glory and we belong to the Lord. Thus each Christian is responsible to the Lord in life and death (Phil.1:20,21).

The preservtion of the saints (the P in the TULIP) is clearly taught in this passage, since Paul fails to qualify the last condition. Hence the conclusion follows. The saints belong to the Lord - by right of redemption and creation. This verse strengthens what he said in verse 7.

Verse 9 - "For to this end Christ both died and rose, and revived, that he might be Lord both of the dead and the living.'

εἰς τοῦτο γὰρ Χριστὸς ἀπέθανεν καὶ ἔζησεν ἵνα καὶ νεκρῶν καὶ ζώντων κυριεύσῃ.

"For to this end Christ died and lived again, that he might be Lord both of the dead and of the living." . . . RSV

εἰς (preposition with the accusative, purpose) 140.
τοῦτο (acc.sing.neut.of οὗτος, purpose) 93.
γὰρ (causal conjunction) 105.
Χριστὸς (nom.sing.masc.of Χριστός, subject of ἀπέθανεν and ἔζησεν) 4.
ἀπέθανεν (3d.per.sing.aor.act.ind.of ἀποθνήσκω, constative) 774.
καὶ (adjunctive conjunction joining verbs) 14.
ἔζησεν (3d.per.sing.aor.act.ind.of ζάω, ingressive) 340.
ἵνα (conjunction with the subjunctive in a sub-final clause) 114.
καὶ (correlative conjunction) 14.
νεκρῶν (gen.pl.masc.of νεκρός, description) 749.
καὶ (adjunctive conjunction joining nouns) 14.
ζώντων (pres.act.part.gen.pl.masc.of ζάω, substantival, description) 340.
κυριεύσῃ (3d.per.sing.aor.act.subj.of κυριεύω, purpose/result) 2776.

Translation - "Because it was for this purpose that Christ died and took up His life again, in order (and with the result) that of both dead and living He might be Sovereign."

Comment: The ἵνα clause with κυριεύσῃ is in apposition to the purpose accusative phrase εἰς τοῦτο. Note that ἔζησεν is inchoative (*i.e.* the emphasis is upon the beginning of the action). The precise reason for Christ's death and resurrection was that, just as He was Sovereign over His own physical body (John 10:17,18), so also He became Sovereign over His mystical Body, composed of all the elect for whom He died, who would be incorporated into it by the Holy Spirit (1 Cor.12:13; Gal.3:27), whether they be alive or dead.

Note the similarity of the type of argument in Rom.4:9-12 in another connection. Is Christ the Lord of the Christian in death? In life? Yes, to both, since He also died and rose again. Variant readings insert ἀνέστη - "he stood up" along with ἀπέθανεν and ἔζησεν, which explains the strange KJV reading.

The variant reading adds nothing to the thought. *Cf.* 1 Tim.6:15 for #2776.

Verse 10 - "But why dost thou judge thy brother? Or why dost thou set at nought thy brother? for we shall all stand before the judgment seat of Christ."

συ δὲ τί κρίνεις τὸν ἀδελφόν σου; ἢ καὶ σὺ τί ἐξουθενεῖς τὸν ἀδελφόν σου; πάντες γὰρ παραστησόμεθα τῷ βήματι τοῦ θεοῦ.

"Why do you pass judgment on your brother? Or you, why do you despise your brother? For we shall all stand before the judgment seat of God;" . . . RSV

σὺ (nom.sing.masc.of σύ, subject of κρίνεις, emphatic) 104.
δὲ (adversative conjunction) 11.
τί (acc.sing.neut.of τίς, interrogative pronoun, cause) 281.
κρίνεις (2d.per.sing.pres.act.ind.of κρίνω, present progressive) 531.
τὸν (acc.sing.masc.of the article in agreement with ἀδελφόν) 9.
ἀδελφόν (acc.sing.masc.of ἀδελφός, direct object of κρίνεις) 15.
σου (gen.sing.masc.of σύ, relationship) 104.
ἢ (disunctive) 465.
σὺ (nom.sing.masc.of σύ, subject of ἐξουθενεῖς, emphatic) 104.
τί (acc.sing.neut.of τίς, interrogative pronoun, cause) 281.
ἐξουθενεῖς (2d.per.sing.pres.act.ind.of ἐξουθενέω, present progressive) 2628.
τὸν (acc.sing.masc.of the article in agreement with ἀδελφόν) 9.
ἀδελφόν (acc.sing.masc.of ἀδελφός, direct object of ἐξουθενεῖς) 15.
σου (gen.sing.masc.of σύ, relationship) 104.
πάντες (nom.pl.masc.of πᾶς, subject of παραστησόμεθα) 67.
γὰρ (causal conjunction) 105.
παραστησόμεθα (1st.per.pl.fut.mid.ind.of παρίστημι, predictive) 1596.
τῷ (loc.sing.neut.of the article in agreement with βήματι) 9.
βήματι (loc.sing.neut.of βῆμα, place, after παρά in composition) 1628.
τοῦ (gen.sing.masc.of the article in agreement with θεοῦ) 9.
θεοῦ (gen.sing.masc.of θεός, possession) 124.

Translation - "But you — Why are you sitting in judgment upon your brother? Or you — why do you even treat your brother with contempt? Because all of us shall stand before the judgment seat of God."

Comment: There is nothing in the text to indicate that one of these questions is directed to the vegetarian and the other to the meat eater. σύ is emphatic in both questions. This Christian not only judges his brother but views him contemptuously. Verse 3 uses ἐξουθενέω with the meat eater and κρίνω with the vegetarian, which may explain Montgomery's translation - "But you (the abstainer), why do you pass judgment on your brother? Or you again (the non-abstainer), why do you despise yours?. . . "

Τί without διά - "on account of what?" or "Why?" *Cf.*2 Cor.5:10 where Paul says the same thing to the Corinthians. The fact is sobering, for what Christian can contemplate the judgment of his own life,. Though the issue there will be rewards, not salvation,the prospect of 1 Cor.3:15 is enough to give us pause when we feel inclined to sit in judgment upon the failures of our Christian brother. *Cf.* Mt.7;1-5.

Verse 11 - "For it is written, As I live, saith the Lord, every knee shall bow to me, and every tongue shall confess to God."

γέγραπται γάρ, Ζῶ ἐγώ, λέγει κύριος, ὅτι ἐμοὶ κάμφει πᾶν γόνυ, καὶ πᾶσα γλῶσσα ἐξομολογήσεται τῷ θεῷ.

"for it is written, 'As I live, says the Lord, every knee shall bow to me, and every tongue shall give praise to God.' " . . . RSV

γέγραπται (3d.per.sing.perf.pass.ind.of γράφω, intensive) 156.
γάρ (causal conjunction) 105.
Ζῶ (1st.per.sing.pres.act.ind.of ζάω, exclamation) 340.
ἐγώ (nom.sing.masc.of ἐγώ, subject of Ζῶ) 123.
λέγει (3d.per.sing.pres.act.ind.of λέγω, historical) 66.
κύριος (nom.sing.masc.of κύριος, subject of λέγει) 97.
ὅτι (conjunction introducing an object clause in indirect discourse) 211.
ἐμοὶ (dat.sing.masc.of ἐμός, dative of person) 1267.
κάμφει (3d.per.sing.fut.act.ind.of κάμπτω, predictive) 3983.
πᾶν (nom.sing.neut.of πᾶς, in agreement with γόνυ) 67.
γόνυ (nom.sing.neut.of γόνυ, subject of κάμφει) 2052.
καὶ (continuative conjunction) 14.
πᾶσα (nom.sing.fem.of πᾶς, in agreement with γλῶσσα) 67.
γλῶσσα (nom.sing.fem.of γλῶσσα, subject of ἐξομολογήσεται) 1846.
ἐξομολογήσεται (3d.per.sing.fut.mid.ind.of ἐξομολογέω, predictive) 275.
τῷ (dat.sing.masc.of the article in agreement with θεῷ) 9.
θεῷ (dat.sing.masc.of θεός, indirect object of ἐξομολογήσεται) 124.

Translation - "Because it is written, 'As I live, says the Lord, to me every knee will bow and every tongue will confess to God.' "

Comment:Ζῶ here in emphasis as God swears by His own sovereign existence. The quotation is from Isaiah 45:23, where the LXX introduces the ὅτι clause with οἱ λόγοι μοι - "my word shall not return,namely (ὅτι) that every knee shall bow . . . κ.τ.λ." Thus Paul supports the last clause of verse 10. *Cf.* Phil.2:10,11 where Paul extends this to every universal tongue, saved and unsaved, men, demons and angels. Here the context indicates that he means the tongue of every Christian, while the confession will be in regard to his peccadillos, as well as more serious violations of the moral code. "I ate meat offered to idols." "I ate no meat." "I regarded one day above another." "I regarded all days alike." The list can be extended indefinitely. "I smoked." "I had a cocktail." The point is that God will attend to each of us, and therefore that we should refrain from judging each other in those twilight areas where the ethics is debateable. Paul is not talking about those areas which are expressly forbidden. However, though the weak in faith are not to judge the liberty in Christ of the strong, the strong are not to exercise their liberty in a way that causes the weak Christian to stumble. This is the thought of verses 13-23.

Verse 12 - "So then everyone of us shall give account of himself to God."

ἄρα (οὖν) ἕκαστος ἡμῶν περὶ ἑαυτοῦ λόγον δώσει τῷ θεῷ.

"So each of us shall give account of himself to God." . . . RSV

ἄρα (illative particle) 995.
οὖν (continuative conjunction) 68.
ἕκαστος (nom.sing.masc.of ἕκαστος, subject of δώσει) 1217.
ἡμῶν (gen.pl.masc.of ἐγώ, partitive genitive) 123.
περὶ (preposition with the genitive of reference) 173.
ἑαυτοῦ (gen.sing.masc.of ἑαυτοῦ, reference) 288.
λόγον (acc.sing.masc.of λόγος, direct object of δώσει) 510.
δώσει (3d.per.sing.fut.act.ind.of δίδωμι, predictive) 362.
τῷ (dat.sing.masc.of the article in agreement with θεῷ) 9.
θεῷ (dat.sing.masc.of θεός, indirect object of δώσει) 124.

Translation - "Thus, then each of us shall submit himself to God for an audit."

Comment: Literally it says "each one of us shall give an explanation about himself to God." Some MSS omit τῷ θεῷ. It is the same thought as that expressed in the last clause of verse 10. *Cf.* 2 Cor.5:10; 1 Cor.3:13-15; Rev.11:18; Lk.14:4. That Paul is speaking of Christians is clear from the context. Note also that he says ἕκαστος ἡμῶν - "each of us" not "each of them" with reference to the unsaved. Thus Paul includes himself and the Roman Christians to whom he is writing.

There is danger that the so-called "mature" Christian will presume upon Paul's argument of Romans 14:1-12 and conclude that he may exercise his freedom in Christ to the point where he loses his influence with others and even inadvertantly causes the spiritual downfall of some. To forestall this danger, Paul adds the material of verses 13-23.

Do Not Make Your Brother Stumble

(Romans 14:13-23)

Verse 13 - "Let us not therefore judge one another any more: but judge this rather that no man put a stumblingblock or an occasion to fall in his brother's way."

Μηκέτι οὖν ἀλλήλους κρίνωμεν, ἀλλὰ τοῦτο κρίνατε μᾶλλον, τὸ μὴ τιθέναι πρόσκομμα τῷ ἀδελφῷ ἢ σκάνδαλον.

"Then let us no more pass judgment on one another, but rather decide never to put a stumbling block or hindrance in the way of a brother." . . . RSV

μηκέτι (negative temporal adverb) 1368.

οὖν (inferential conjunction) 68.

ἀλλήλους (acc.pl.masc.of ἀλλήλων, direct object of κρίνωμεν) 1487.

κρίνωμεν (1st.per.pl.pres.act.subj.of κρίνω, hortatory) 531.

ἀλλά (alternative conjunction) 342.

τοῦτο (acc.sing.neut.of οὗτος, direct object of κρίνωμεν) 93.

κρίνατε (2d.per.pl.1st.aor.act.impv.of κρίνω, command) 531.

μᾶλλον (adverbial) 619.

τό (acc.sing.neut.of the article in agreement with τιθέναι) 9.

μή (negative particle with the infinitive) 87.

τιθέναι (pres.act.inf.of τίθημι, noun use, in apposition with τοῦτο) 455.

πρόσκομμα (acc.sing.neut.of πρόσκομμα, direct object of τιθέναι) 3974.

τῷ (loc.sing.masc.of the article in agreement with ἀδελφῷ) 9.

ἀδελφῷ (loc.sing.masc.of ἀδελφός, place) 15.

ἤ (disjunctive) 465.

σκάνδαλον (acc.sing.neut.of σκάνδαλον, direct object of τιθέναι) 1082.

Translation - "Let us not be judging one another any longer, but consider this rather that you stop putting a stumbling block or an obstacle in your brother's path."

Comment: The first clause repeats the ban on censor among christians. *Cf.* verses 3,10. Thus, three times in thirteen verses, Paul told the Roman church to stop assuming the role of judge. μηκέτι - "never again." οὖν gets it support from verses 11,12.

Now Paul changes the emphasis. "Consider this. . . " The articular infinitive τό μή τιθέναι is appositional to τοῦτο, *i.e.* it explains what Paul meant by τοῦτο. The Christian should not behave in a way that will result in the spiritual downfall of another, even if this means that he gives up some of his liberty in Christ. *Cf.#*'s 3974 and 1082 for "stumbling blocks." The remainder of the chapter is devoted to this injunction.

In 1 Corinthians 8 Paul discusses this problem again with the church in Corinth and again he says that the Christian who has certain scruples which he regards unnecessary is "weak" in the faith. And yet he tells us to be careful not to offend such Christians, lest we disillusion them and cause their downfall. Does this mean that we are not to lead them into a deeper understanding of their position in Christ and enable them to take a more mature look? Obviously it does not. Otherwise we would be remiss in our obligations in the field of Christian education.

A farmer in Northern Indiana, one of the godliest men in the community had convictions about working on Sunday. Three years after his pastor came to the community he said that when the pastor came three years before, his conscience hurt him on Sunday when he threw a forkful of hay into the manger for his horses. He added that, thanks to the gentle teaching of his pastor on the question of the Sabbath law, he had come to understand that Sunday was a day of worship and that feeding the horses did not violate the law of the Sabbath. He had not understood that the Sabbath came on Saturday. If that pastor had been unduly critical, censorious and contemptuous of the man's honest, if misguided convictions, he could have created the psychological block that would have proved his downfall. Fortunately the pastor had spoken "the truth in love" (Eph.4:15) and patience and the weak faith and faulty understanding of the brother was corrected.

Verse 14 - "I know, and am persuaded by the Lord Jesus, that there is nothing unclean of itself: but to him that esteemeth any thing to be unclean, to him it is unclean."

οἶδα καὶ πέπεισμαι ἐν κυρίῳ Ἰησοῦ ὅτι οὐδὲν κοινὸν δι' ἑαυτοῦ. εἰ μὴ τῷ λογιζομένῳ τι κοινὸν εἶναι ἐκείνῳ κοινόν.

"I know and am persuaded in the Lord Jesus that nothing is unclean in itself; but it is unclean for any one who thinks it unclean." . . . RSV

οἶδα (1st.per.sing.perf.ind.of ὁράω, intensive) 144b.

καὶ (adjunctive conjunction joining verbs) 14.

πέπεισμαι (1st.per.sing.perf.pass.ind.of πείθω, intensive) 1629.

ἐν (preposition with the locative, instrumental use, association) 80.

κυρίῳ (loc.sing.masc.of κύριος, association) 97.

Ἰησοῦ (loc.sing.masc.of Ἰησοῦ, apposition) 3.

ὅτι (conjunction introducing an object clause in indirect discourse) 211.

οὐδὲν (nom.sing.neut.of οὐδείς, subject of ἔστιν understood) 446.

κοινὸν (nom.sing.neut.of κοινός, predicate adjective) 2295.

δι' (preposition with the ablative, with an abstract idea) 118.

ἑαυτοῦ (abl.sing.neut.of ἑαυτοῦ, abstract idea) 288.

εἰ (conditional particle in an elliptical condition) 337.

μὴ (negative particle with the infinitive) 87.

τῷ (dat.sing.masc.of the article in agreement with λογιζομένῳ) 9.

λογιζομένῳ (pres.mid.part.dat.sing.masc.of λογίζομαι, substantival, person) 2611.

τι (acc.sing.neut.of τις, indefinite pronoun, general reference) 486.

κοινὸν (acc.sing.neut.of κοινός, predicate adjective) 2295.

εἶναι (pres.inf.of εἰμί, object of λογιζομένῳ indirect discourse) 86.

ἐκείνῳ (dat.sing.masc.of ἐκεῖνος, person) 246.

κοινόν (acc.sing.neut.of κοινός, predicate adjective) 2295.

Translation - "I have learned and I am now convinced that in the Lord Jesus nothing is unclean of itself, except to the one who thinks that it is unclean. To that man it is unclean."

Comment: Both οἶδα and πέπεισμαι are perfect tenses. They indicate that Paul's present conviction is the result of a past learning experience. ὅτι introduces indirect discourse. "Nothing is unclean of itself, in its relation to the Lord Jesus." Since He is Creator of all things (Col.1:16; John 1:3) it is obvious that everything He created glorifies Him (Rev.4:11). Nothing therefore is inherently κοινόν. The sin comes when we indulge in something which we have evaluated as unclean.

The participle τῷ λογιζομένῳ has as its object the infinitive εἶναι in the accusative case, with τι an accusative of general reference. Because of the fact that one judges something (τι) to be unclean (εἶναι κοινόν), the result is that it is unclean to that person. Paul's grasp of this concept which he had not always understood, is the mark of a mature Christian. Babes in Christ have not yet thought deeply into the matter. To say that something (meat, drink, a given policy of worship on a given day, etc.) is evil in and of itself, is to say that there is an area of life outside of Christ. On the contrary He has brought everything He created into His redemptive and regenerative purview. Thus ἐν αὐτῷ nothing is κοινόν δι' ἑαυτοῦ - "of itself" *i.e.* by virtue of its own inherent nature. This is a great truth for the mature Christian, but he does not live in isolation and he has an influence on less developed Christians, to whom he owes a spiritual obligation. This fact reduces the area of his free behavior.

Verse 15 - "But if thy brother be grieved with thy meat, now walkest thou not charitably. Destroy not him with thy meat, for whom Christ died."

εἰ γὰρ διὰ βρῶμα ὁ ἀδελφός σου λυπεῖται, οὐκέτι κατὰ ἀγάπην περιπατεῖς. μὴ τῷ βρώματί σου ἐκεῖνον ἀπόλλυε ὑπὲρ οὗ Χριστὸς ἀπέθανεν.

"If your brother is being injured by what you eat, you are no longer walking in love. Do not let what you eat cause the ruin of one for whom Christ died." . . .

RSV

εἰ (conditional particle in a first-class condition) 337.

γὰρ (inferential conjunction) 105.

διὰ (preposition with the accusative, cause) 118.

βρῶμα (acc.sing.neut.of βρῶμα, cause) 1118.

ὁ (nom.sing.masc.of the article in agreement with ἀδελφός) 9.

ἀδελφός (nom.sing.masc.of ἀδελφός, subject of λυπεῖται) 15.

σου (gen.sing.masc.of σύ, relationship) 104.

λυπεῖται (3d.per.sing.pres.pass.ind.of λυπέω, first-class condition) 1113.

οὐκέτι (negative temporal adverb) 1289.

κατὰ (preposition with the accusative, standard) 98.

ἀγάπην (acc.sing.fem.of ἀγάπη, standard) 1490.

περιπατεῖς (2d.per.sing.pres.act.ind.of περιπατέω, present progressive retroactive) 384.

μὴ (negative conjunction with the imperative, prohibition) 87.

τῷ (instru.sing.neut.of the article in agreement with βρώματί) 9.

βρώματί (instru.sing.neut.of βρῶμα, cause) 1118.

σου (gen.sing.masc.of σύ, possession) 104.

ἐκεῖνον (acc.sing.masc.of ἐκεῖνος, direct object of ἀπόλλυε) 246.

ἀπόλλυε (2d.per.sing.pres.act.impv.of ἀπόλλυμι, prohibition) 208.

ὑπὲρ (preposition with the ablative, "instead of") 545.

οὗ (abl.sing.masc.of ὅς, relative pronoun, "instead of") 65.

Χριστὸς (nom.sing.masc.of Χριστός, subject of ἀπέθανεν) 4.

ἀπέθανεν (3d.per.sing.aor.act.ind.of ἀποθνήσκω, culminative) 774.

Translation - "So if your brother is offended because you eat meat you are not walking in love. Stop destroying with your food that one for whom Christ died."

Comment: γὰρ is inferential. Paul has just intimated in the last clause of verse 14 that the overscrupulous attitude of the babe in Christ toward meat makes it a sin for him to eat it. Now, since that is so, he will be offended if the mature Christian eats meat. Since therefore he is offended (εἰ and a first-class condition) because of what you eat (διὰ βρῶμα) the conclusion is that you are not conducting yourself in keeping with the standards that love requires (κατὰ ἀγάπην). A Christian motivated by the love of Christ will not continue deliberately to exercise his freedom in Christ, when he knows that his behavior is a source of confusion and perhaps disillusionment for a younger and weaker saint. Since he is offended and what you eat is the reason for his offense you are not walking charitably unless you give up your meat.

Then Paul adds the injunction, "Stop destroying (μή with the present imperative) him (ἐκεῖνον) for whom Christ died." ἐκεῖνον is the antecedent for the relative pronoun οὗ. Thus the moral obligation to sacrifice one's lifestyle, in order not to hinder the spiritual growth of others is clear.

There is some relief from this hard rule. He can eat meat when he is alone if he is certain that God, Who is always watching, is not offended (verse 22). The spiritual health of the members of the Body of Christ is more important than the gratification of an appetite of the flesh, however legitimate it may be.

Verse 16 - "Let not then your good be evil spoken of."

μὴ βλασφημείσθω οὖν ὑμῶν τὸ ἀγαθόν.

"So do not let what is good to you be spoken of as evil." . . . RSV

μή (negative particle with the imperative) 87.

βλασφημείσθω (3d.per.sing.pres.pass.impv.of βλασφημέω, prohibition) 781.

οὖν (inferential conjunction) 68.

ὑμῶν (gen.pl.masc.of σύ, possession) 104.

τὸ (nom.sing.neut.of the article in agreement with ἀγαθόν) 9.

ἀγαθόν (nom.sing.neut.of ἀγαθός, subject of βλασφημείσθω) 547.

Translation - "So do not allow your good behavior to be criticized."

Comment: What you and other Christians who are equally mature and hence uncondemned by your life style do must not be allowed to become a bone of contention, because other weaker Christians consider your behavior improper.

A note of caution must be added. What Paul has said applies only to cases where the objections to one's life style are sincere. Insincere Christians and even unsaved people, who are aware of this principle could feign offense at anything the Christian does and thus dominate his life entirely. To illustrate the point with an extreme example, suppose that someone objects to the use of the automobile? And comes back the next week and says that he does not believe that you should wear a necktie?

Why should the mature child of God yield his freedom in Christ to the pressures of less enlightened believers? We have already seen that we should in order to avoid stunting the spiritual growth of others. There is another reason in

Verse 17 - "For the kingdom of God is not meat and drink; but righteousness, and peace, and joy in the Holy Ghost."

οὐ γάρ ἐστιν ἡ βασιλεία τοῦ θεοῦ βρῶσις καὶ πόσις, ἀλλὰ δικαιοσύνη καὶ εἰρήνη καὶ χαρὰ ἐν πνεύματι ἁγίῳ.

"For the kingdom of God does not mean food and drink but righteousness and peace and joy in the Holy Spirit;" . . . *RSV*

οὐ (negative particle with the indicative) 130.
γάρ (causal conjunction) 105.
ἐστιν (3d.per.sing.pres.ind.of εἰμί, static) 86.
ἡ (nom.sing.fem.of the article in agreement with βασιλεία) 9.
βασιλεία (nom.sing.fem.of βασιλεία, subject of ἐστιν) 253.
τοῦ (gen.sing.masc.of the article in agreement with θεοῦ) 9.
θεοῦ (gen.sing.masc.of θεός, description) 124.
βρῶσις (nom.sing.fem.of βρῶσις, predicate nominative) 594.
καὶ (adjunctive conjunction joining nouns) 14.
πόσις (nom.sing.fem.of πόσις, predicate nominative) 2292.
ἀλλὰ (alternative conjunction) 342.
δικαιοσύνη (nom.sing.fem.of δικαιοσύνη, predicate nominative) 322.
καὶ (adjunctive conjunction joining nouns) 14.
εἰρήνη (nom.sing.fem.of εἰρήνη, predicate nominative) 865.
καὶ (adjunctive conjunction joining nouns) 14.
χαρὰ (nom.sing.fem.of χαρά, predicate nominative) 183.
ἐν (preposition with the locative, instrumental use, association) 80.
πνεύματι (instru.sing.neut.of πνεῦμα, association) 83.
ἁγίῳ (instru.sing.neut.of ἅγιος, in agreement with πνεύματι) 84.

Translation - "Because the kingdom of God is not meat and drink, but righteousness and peace and joy in association with the Holy Spirit."

Comment: Paul has just asked the mature Christian to surrender those pleasures which do not offend his conscience but constitute stumbling blocks for weaker Christian brethren. This is not too much to ask since the gifts of salvation, administered by the Holy Spirit, are of a much higher quality than the physical pleasures of food and drink.

The standing of the believer in Christ is one of sonship with God and joint heirship with Jesus Christ (Rom.8:17). The Holy Spirit produces His fruits in our lives (Gal.5:22,23). To run roughshod over the tender feelings of less enlightened saints for the sake of fleshly gratification of a steak or a glass of wine, or a golf game, fishing trip or an evening at the opera, even though we can enjoy these things with a clear conscience, when we know that our participation is being monitored by others whose own spiritual development is being hindered by our freedom, is to manifest an attitude of loveless unconcern for them.

Verse 18 - "For he that in these things serveth Christ is acceptable to God, and approved of men."

ὁ γὰρ ἐν τούτῳ δουλεύων τῷ Χριστῷ εὐάρεστος τῷ θεῷ καὶ δόκιμος τοῖς ἀνθρώποις.

"He who thus serves Christ is acceptable to God and approved by men." . . .
RSV

ὁ (nom.sing.masc.of the article in agreement with δουλεύων) 9.
γὰρ (inferential conjunction) 105.
ἐν (preposition with the locative of sphere) 80.
τούτῳ (loc.sing.neut.of οὗτος, sphere) 93.
δουλεύων (pres.act.part.nom.sing.masc.of δουλεύω, substantival, subject of ἐστιν understood) 604.
τῷ (dat.sing.masc.of the article in agreement with Χριστῷ) 9.
Χριστῷ (dat.sing.masc.of Χριστός, personal advantage) 4.
εὐάρεστος (nom.sing.masc.of εὐάρεστος, predicate adjective) 4010.
τῷ (dat.sing.masc.of the article in agreement with θεῷ) 9.
θεῷ (dat.sing.masc.of θεός, personal interest) 124.
καὶ (adjunctive conjunction joining adjectives) 14.

#4042 δόκιμος (nom.sing.masc.of δόκιμος, predicate adjective).

King James Version

approved - Rom.14:18; 16:10; 2 Cor.10:18; 13:7; 2 Tim.2:15.
tried - James 1:12.
which is approved - 1 Cor.11:19.

Revised Standard Version

approved - Rom.14:18; 16:10; 2 Tim.2:15.
genuine - 1 Cor.11:19.
accepted - 2 Cor.10:18.
meet the test - 2 Cor.13:7.
stand the test - James 1:12.

Meaning: Cf. δέχομαι (#867). Tried, tested and found acceptable. In Gen.23:16 and 2 Chron.9:17 (LXX) of money or precious metals thus demonstrated under trial to be genuine. With reference to Christians who have demonstrated by their high ethical behavior that they are δόκιμος before God and man - Rom.14:18; 16:10; 2 Tim.2:15; 1 Cor.11:19; 2 Cor.10:18; 13:7; James 1:12.

τοῖς (dat.pl.masc.of the article in agreement with ἀνθρώποις) 9.
ἀνθρώποις (dat.pl.masc.of ἄνθρωπος, personal interest) 341.

Translation - "Therefore he that is serving Christ in this manner is acceptable to

God and approved by men."

Comment: γάρ is inferential because (1) though it is good for a Christian to enjoy his freedom in Christ, (2) he is commanded not to allow his good to become the occasion for evil talk about him by those Christians who, being less enlightened, are more scrupulous (verse 16). Besides (3) the kingdom of God does not consist of physical comforts, but psychological and spiritual blessings which are the gifts of the Holy Spirit (verse 17). "Therefore" (inferential γάρ) the one who serves Christ by giving up his privileged freedoms out of concern lest he cause his weak brother to stumble, is acceptable to God and approved by men, even perhaps the unsaved world. ἐν τούτῳ refers to the Christian's obedience to verses 15 and 16.

Paul here tells us how to be δόκιμος (#4042). *Cf.* 1 Cor.9:27; Heb.6:8 where he fears that the Christian may become ἀδόκιμος (#3818).

Verse 19 - "Let us therefore follow after the things which make for peace, and things wherewith one may edify another."

ἄρα (illative particle) 995.

οὖν (continuative conjunction) 68.

τά (acc.pl.neut.of the article, direct object of διώκωμεν) 9.

τῆς (gen.sing.fem.of the article in agreement with εἰρήνης) 9.

εἰρήνης (gen.sing.fem.of εἰρήνη, description) 865.

διώκωμεν (1st.per.pl.pres.act.subj.of διώκω, hortatory) 434.

καί (adjunctive conjunction joining substantives) 14.

τά (acc.pl.neut.of the article, direct object of διώκωμεν) 9.

τῆς (gen.sing.fem.of the article in agreement with οἰκοδομῆς) 9.

οἰκοδομῆς (gen.sing.fem.of οἰκοδομή, description) 1481.

τής (gen.sing.fem.of the article in agreement with οἰκοδομῆς) 9.

εἰς (preposition with the accusative, extent) 140.

ἀλλήλους (acc.pl.masc.of ἀλλήλων, extent) 1487.

Translation - "Let us then pursue a policy of peace and edification of one another."

Comment: Sinaiticus A B G^gr P 048 0209 and some miniscules and Chrysostom have the indicative διώκομεν instead of the hortatory subjunctive of the text. "The question whether in this verse Paul describes the Christian ideal (the indicative διώκομεν continuing the statements made in verses 17 and 18), or whether he now begins his exhortation (the subjunctive διώκωμεν) leading to κατάλθε in ver.20a), is extremely difficult to answer. Despite the slightly superior uncial support for διώκομεν, . . . and despite the circumstance that elsewhere in Romans the phrase ἄρα οὖν is always followed by the indicative (5.18; 7.3,25; 8.12; 9.16,18; cf.14.12), the Committee felt that, on the whole, the context here calls for the hortatory subjunctive (cf.the imperatives in ver.13 and ver.20)." (Metzger, *A Textual Commentary on the Greek New Testament*, 532).

The subjunctive exhortation fits the context better than the indicative statement of fact. Apparently the Romans were not trying to pursue peace and edify each other. Note that peaceful relations with other members of the Body of Christ that result in the mutual edifying of all of the saints is more important than the personal freedom of the mature Christian to engage in practices, thought by some to be evil. The right to eat meat is challenged by the higher right to meet the obligation to others in the interest of the good of all. This is a high service which we can render to Christ (verse 18).

Verse 20 - "For meat destroy not the work of God. All things indeed are pure; but it is evil for that man who eateth with offence."

μὴ ἕνεκεν βρώματος κατάλυε τὸ ἔργον τοῦ θεοῦ. πάντα μὲν καθαρά, ἀλλὰ κακὸν τῷ ἀνθρώπῳ τῷ διὰ προσκόμματος ἐσθίοντι.

"Do not, for the sake of food, destroy the work of God. Everything is indeed clean, but it is wrong for any one to make others fall by what he eats;" . . . RSV

μὴ (negative particle with the imperative) 87.

ἕνεκεν (improper preposition with the genitive, "for the sake of") 435.

βρώματος (gen.sing.neut.of βρῶμα, reference) 1118.

κατάλυε (2d.per.sing.pres.act.impv.of καλαλύω, prohibition) 463.

τὸ (acc.sing.neut.of the article in agreement with ἔργον) 9.

ἔργον (acc.sing.neut.of ἔργον, direct object of κατάλυε) 460.

τοῦ (gen.sing.masc.of the article in agreement with θεοῦ) 9.

θεοῦ (gen.sing.masc.of θεός, description) 124.

πάντα (nom.pl.neut.of πᾶς, subject of ἐστιν understood) 67.

μὲν (particle of affirmation) 300.

καθαρά (nom.pl.neut.of καθαρός, predicate adjective) 431.

ἀλλὰ (alternative conjunction) 342.

κακὸν (acc.sing.neut.of κακός, predicate adjective) 1388.

τῷ (dat.sing.masc.of the article in agreement with ἀνθρώπῳ) 9.

ἀνθρώπῳ (dat.sing.masc.of ἄνθρωπος, reference) 341.

τῷ (dat.sing.masc.of the article in agreement with ἐσθίοντι) 9.

διὰ (preposition with the ablative with an abstract idea) 118.

προσκόμματος (abl.sing.neut.of πρόσκομμα, with an abstract idea) 3974.

ἐσθίοντι (pres.act.part.dat.sing.masc.of ἐσθίω, in apposition with ἀνθρώπῳ) 610.

Translation - "For the sake of food do not destroy the handiwork of God. All things are clean, to be sure, but for the man who eats and causes offense it is evil."

Comment: God's program of evangelism and edification of the members of Christ's body is torn down when mature Christians, in the name of personal freedom, ride roughshod over the tender consciences of less mature Christians. Paul orders that this practice cease. Then he reaffirms the view that the sin is not in the thing itself, but in the feeling that indulgence is sin. If one has doubts about it, don't.

Verse 21 - "It is good neither to eat flesh, nor to drink wine, nor anything whereby thy brother stumbleth, or is offended, or is made weak."

καλὸν τὸ μὴ φαγεῖν κρέα μηδὲ πιεῖν οἶνον μηδὲ ἐν ᾧ ὁ ἀδελφός σου πρισκόπτει.

"it is right not to eat meat or drink wine or do anything that makes your brother stumble." . . . RSV

καλὸν (nom.sing.neut.of καλός, predicate adjective) 296.
τὸ (nom.sing.neut.of the article in agreement with φαγεῖν and πιεῖν) 9.
μὴ (negative particle with the infinitive) 87.
φαγεῖν (aor.act.inf.of ἐσθίω, noun use, subject of ἐστιν understood) 610.

#4043 κρέα (acc.sing.neut.of κρέας, direct object of φαγεῖν).

King James Version

flesh - Rom.14:21; 1 Cor.8:13.

Revised Standard Version

meat - Rom.14:21; 1 Cor.8:13.

Meaning: The meat of a sacrificed animal, later offered for sale. The center of a controversy in the church in Rome - Rom.14:21; in Corinth - 1 Cor.8:13.

μηδὲ (negative disjunctive) 612.
πιεῖν (2d.aor.act.inf.of πίνω, noun use, subject of ἐστιν understood) 611.
οἶνον (acc.sing.masc.of οἶνον, direct object of πιεῖν) 808.
μηδὲ (negative disjunctive) 612.
ἐν (preposition with the locative of sphere) 80.
ᾧ (loc.sing.neut.of ὅς, sphere) 65.
ὁ (nom.sing.masc.of the article in agreement with ἀδελφός) 9.
ἀδελφός (nom.sing.masc.of ἀδελφός, subject of προσκόπτει) 15.
σου (gen.sing.masc.of σύ, relationship) 104.
προσκόπτει (3d.per.sing.pres.act.ind.of προσκόπτω, customary) 352.

Translation - "It is noble neither to eat meat nor to drink wine nor to do anything whereby your brother stumbles."

Comment: Paul's emphasis is upon the predicate adjective καλόν, as he puts it first in the sentence. Note that the infinitive πιεῖν is anarthrous. The entire infinitival substantive, the subject of ἐστιν understood is τὸ μὴ φαγεῖν κρέα μηδὲ πιεῖν οἶνον μηδὲ. The noble thing to do is to forego any and all practices, however legitimate, if such practices cause others to stumble. The nobility in such a course lies in the fact that it reveals one's priorities. The edification of the saints of God is more important than the gratification of physical desires for food or drink or any other physical thing, particularly in view of the fact that the kingdom of God is not meat and drink in any case (verse 17). One who would insist upon his meat and drink when he knew that his behavior was stultifying to the development of a weaker Christian is tearing down the word of God (verse 20). There is certainly nothing good about that! Variant readings add λυπεῖται ἢ σκανδαλίζεται ἢ ἀνθενεῖ. They add nothing to the point.

Verse 22 - "Hast thou faith? Have it to thyself before God. Happy is he that condemneth not himself in that thing which he alloweth."

σὺ πίστιν (ἣν) ἔχεις κατὰ σεαυτὸν ἔχε ἐνώπιον τοῦ θεοῦ. μακάριος ὁ μὴ κρίνων ἑαυτὸν ἐν ᾧ δοκιμάζει.

"The faith which you have, keep between yourself and God; happy is he who has no reason to judge himself for what he approves." . . . RSV

σὺ (nom.sing.masc.of σύ, subject of ἔχεις) 104.
πίστιν (acc.sing.fem.of πίστις, direct object of ἔχεις) 728.
(ἣν) (acc.sing.fem.of ὅς, direct object of ἔχε) 65.
ἔχεις (2d.per.sing.pres.act.ind.of ἔχω, aoristic) 82.
κατὰ (preposition with the accusative, general reference) 98.
σεαυτὸν (acc.sing.masc.of σεαυτός, general reference) 347.
ἔχε (2d.per.sing.pres.act.impv.of ἔχω, command) 82.
ἐνώπιον (improper preposition with the genitive of place description) 1798.
τοῦ (gen.sing.masc.of the article in agreement with θεοῦ) 9.
θεοῦ (gen.sing.masc.of θεός, place description) 124.
μακάριος (nom.sing.masc.of μακάριος, predicate adjective) 422.
ὁ (nom.sing.masc.of the article in agreement with κρίνων) 9.
μὴ (negative particle with the participle) 87.
κρίνων (pres.act.part.nom.sing.masc.of κρίνω, substantival, subject of ἐστιν understood) 531.
ἑαυτὸν (acc.sing.masc.of ἑαυτοῦ, direct object of κρίνων) 288.
ἐν (preposition with the locative of sphere) 80.
ᾧ (loc.sing.neut.of ὅς, demonstrative pronoun, sphere) 65.
δοκιμάζει (3d.per.sing.pres.act.ind.of δοκιμάζω, aoristic) 2493.

Translation - "Keep the faith which you have to yourself before God. Happy is the man who does not condemn himself in those things which he approves."

Comment: There is no way to tell whether the first clause is interrogative or declarative. If interrogative Paul expects a positive reply. Paul is calling attention to the spiritual maturity which the Christian addressed thinks he possesses. He has the kind of faith to believe that in Christ all things are pure. Very well. He is fortunate. But since he is associating with weaker Christians who do not share his lofty view, he is ordered to keep his opinions to himself and exercise his liberty in God's presence, but no where else. The beatitude follows. Blessed indeed is the man or woman who does all that he wants to do without the knowledge that what he does is sin. The other side of the question is stated in verse 23. It is possible that some have a higher opinion of their grasp of the ethics of the gospel than the truth of God warrants. The Christian who yields most completely to the Holy Spirit may discover that although he sees nothing wrong in certain things, he is so busy serving the Lord and so delighted in the enjoyment of the fruits of the Spirit (Gal.5:22,23) and in the exercise of His gifts (1 Cor.12:1-11) that he forgets about all his other secular pursuits.

Verse 23 - "And he that doubteth is damned if he eat, because he eateth not of faith: for whatsoever is not of faith is sin."

ὁ δὲ διακρινόμενος ἐὰν φάγῃ κατακέκριται, ὅτι οὐκ ἐκ πίστεως. πᾶν δὲ ὁ οὐκ ἐκ πίστεως ἁμαρτία ἐστίν.

"But he who has doubts is condemned, if he eats, because he does not act from faith; for whatever does not proceed from faith is sin." . . . RSV

ὁ (nom.sing.masc.of the article in agreement with διακρινόμενος) 9.

δὲ (adversative conjunction) 11.

διακρινόμενος (pres.mid.part.nom.sing.masc.of διακρίνομαι, substantival, subject of κατακέκριται) 1195.

ἐὰν (conditional particle in a third-class condition) 363.

φάγῃ (3d.per.sing.aor.act.subj.of ἐσθίω, third-class condition) 610.

κατακέκριται (3d.per.sing.perf.mid.ind.of κατακρίνω, third-class condition) 1012.

ὅτι (conjunction introducing a subordinate causal clause) 211.

οὐκ (negative particle with the indicative) 130.

ἐκ (preposition with the ablative of source) 19.

πίστεως (abl.sing.fem.of πίστις, source) 728.

πᾶν (nom.sing.neut.of πᾶς, in agreement with ὁ) 67.

δὲ (causal conjunction) 11.

ὁ (nom.sing.neut.of ὅς, relative pronoun, subject of ἐστίν) 65.

οὐκ (negative particle) 130.

ἐκ (preposition with the ablative of source) 19.

πίστεως (abl.sing.fem.of πίστις, source) 728.

ἁμαρτία (nom.sing.fem.of ἁμαρτία, predicate nominative) 111.

ἐστίν (3d.per.sing.pres.ind.of εἰμί, static) 86.

Translation - "But if the one who has doubts eats he has already been condemned, because he did not act from faith; because all that is not done by faith is sin."

Comment: In contrast to the happy Christian of verse 22, we see here the one who is overscrupulous. He debates with himself, and perhaps with others the propriety of eating meat. *Cf.#1195.* He is caught between two views. As long as he is not totally convinced that the action is right, he is not therefore motivated by faith (ἐκ πίστεως). And everything not motivated by faith comes from the flesh and is sin.

This discussion must have created great interest in the first century, due to the rising influence of Gnosticism which developed into full flower by A.D.150-200, although in its incipience it plagued the Apostles and the first century Christians. Ascetics would soon argue that all food, whether having been offered to idols or

not was evil, since it perpetuates the flesh which is evil. For the ascetic, with his
Gnostic doctrine that matter is evil and eternal, the only way to escape sin is to
become immaterial. But that is difficult! All that the Gnostic can do is to
apologize, as Plotinus did when he told his students in Rome that he was sorry
that he had a body.

Please Your Fellow Men, Not Yourself

(Romans 15:1-6)

*Romans 15:1 - "We then that are strong ought to bear the infirmity of the weak,
and not to please ourselves."*

Ὀφείλομεν δὲ ἡμεῖς οἱ δυνατοὶ τὰ ἀσθενήματα τῶν ἀδυνάτων βαστάζειν,
καὶ μὴ ἑαυτοῖς ἀρέσκειν.

*"We who are strong ought to bear with the failings of the weak, and not to
please ourselves;" . . . RSV*

Ὀφείλομεν (1st.per.pl.pres.act.ind.of ὀφείλω, static) 1277.
δὲ (explanatory conjunction) 11.
ἡμεῖς (nom.pl.masc.of ἐγώ, subject of ὀφείλομεν) 123
οἱ (nom.pl.masc.of the article in agreement with δυνατοὶ) 9.
δυνατοὶ (nom.pl.masc.of δυνατός, in apposition with ἡμεῖς) 1311.
τὰ (acc.pl.neut.of the article in agreement with ἀσθενήματα) 9.

#4044 ἀσθενήματα (acc.pl.neut.of ἀσθένημα, direct object of βαστάζειν).

King James Version

infirmity - Rom.15:1.

Revised Standard Version

failings - Rom.15:1.

Meaning: Cf. ἀσθενέω (#857); ἀσθένεια (#740). In Romans 15:1, of the error in
judgment with reference to Christian ethics.

τῶν (gen.pl.masc.of the article in agreement with ἀδυνάτων) 9.
ἀδυνάτων (gen.pl.masc.of ἀδύνατος, description) 1310.
βαστάζειν (pres.act.inf.of βαστάζω, complementary) 306.
καὶ (adjunctive conjunction joining infinitives) 14.
μὴ (negative particle with the infinitive) 87.
ἑαυτοῖς (dat.pl.masc.of ἑαυτοῦ, personal advantage) 288.
ἀρέσκειν (pres.act.inf.of ἀρέσκω, complementary) 1110.

*Translation - "Now we who can ought to bear with the failings of those who
cannot and we ought not to please ourselves."*

Comment: Goodspeed has "It is the duty of us who are strong to put up with the weaknesses of those who are immature, and not just to suit ourselves." *"put up with"* is no less plebeian than *"bear with.'* The last clause is the alternative of the first, not final. Paul is presenting both the positive and negative sides of our obligation. "We ought to bear. . . " and "we ought not to please ourselves." The passage is often misinterpreted to mean that the reason the mature Christian "puts up with" his weaker brethren is "in order that he may please himself" *i.e.* with the result that he now congratulates himself that he is kindly disposed toward those who entertain unnecessary scruples about meat, days, etc.

When we give up our own pleasures for the sake of others, we fulfill the law of Christ (Gal.6:2).

Verse 2 - "Let every one of us please his neighbour for his good to edification."

ἔκαστος ἡμῶν τῷ πλησίον ἀρεσκέτω εἰς τὸ ἀγαθὸν πρὸς οἰκοδομήν.

"let each of us please his neighbor for his good, to edify him." . . . RSV

ἔκαστος (nom.sing.masc.of ἔκαστος, subject of ἀρεσκέτω) 1217.
ἡμῶν (gen.pl.masc.of ἐγώ, partitive) 123.
τῷ (dat.sing.masc.of the article, personal advantage) 9.
πλησίον (adverbial) 541.
ἀρεσκέτω (3d.per.sing.pres.act.impv.of ἀρέσκω, command) 1110.
εἰς (preposition with the accusative, purpose) 140.
τὸ (acc.sing.neut.of the article in agreement with ἀγαθὸν) 9.
ἀγαθὸν (acc.sing.neut.of ἀγαθός, purpose) 547.
πρὸς (preposition with the accusative, purpose) 197.
οἰκοδομήν (acc.sing.fem.of οἰκοδομή, purpose) 1481.

Translation - "Let every one of us please his neighbor to make him better in order to edify him."

Comment: *Cf.*#541 for the other instances of πλησίον with τῷ. The two prepositional phrases, each with the accusative, one with εἰς and the other with πρός are purpose. We do not please our neighbor in order that he may be bad, but good. If we did everything for our neighbor that he wanted we might on occasion make him bad. But we are to do all we can for him if the result is good and thus edifying.

This is a good public relations verse. How peaceful society would be if every one obeyed this verse. Modern society is fragmented and pluralistic, as we not only do not try to please and edify our neighbors; we do not even know them well enough to speak to them!

Our example in this matter is our Lord.

Verse 3 - "For even Christ pleased not himself: but as it is written, The reproaches of them that reproached thee fell on me."

καὶ γὰρ ὁ Χριστὸς οὐχ ἑαυτῷ ἤρεσεν. ἀλλὰ καθὼς γέγραπται, Οἱ ὀνειδισμοὶ τῶν ὀνειδιζόντων σε ἐπέπεσαν ἐπ' ἐμέ.

"For Christ did not please himself; but, as it is written, 'The reproaches of those who reproached thee fell on me.' " . . . RSV

καὶ (ascensive conjunction) 14.
γὰρ (causal conjunction) 105.
ὁ (nom.sing.masc.of the article in agreement with Χριστὸς) 9.
Χριστὸς (nom.sing.masc.of Χριστός, subject of ἤρεσεν) 4.
οὐχ (negative conjunction with the indicative) 130.
ἑαυτῷ (dat.sing.masc.of ἑαυτοῦ, personal interest) 288.
ἤρεσεν (3d.per.sing.aor.act.ind.of ἀρέσκω, constative) 1110.
ἀλλὰ (alternative conjunction) 342.
καθὼς (compound particle in a comparative clause) 1348.
γέγραπται (3d.per.sing.perf.pass.ind.of γράφω, intensive) 156.
Οἱ (nom.pl.masc.of the article in agreement with ὀνειδισμοὶ) 9.

#4045 ὀνειδισμοὶ (nom.pl.masc.of ὀνειδισμός, subject of ἐπέπεσεν).

King James Version

reproach - Rom.15:3; 1 Tim.3:7; Heb.10:33; 11:26; 13:13.

Revised Standard Version

reproach - Rom.15:3; 1 Tim.3:7.
abuse - Heb.10:33; 11:26; 13:13.

Meaning: Cf. ὀνειδίζω (#437); ὄνειδος (#1811). A verbal affront; insult; taunt; slur. The insults hurled at our Lord, both during His public ministry and at His crucifixion - Rom.15:3; directed against a bishop - 1 Tim.3:7; against the saints, associated with θλίψις in Heb.10:33. Note that an insult to Moses in Egypt is called the reproach of Christ - Heb.11:26; 13:13.

τῶν (gen.pl.masc.of the article in agreement with ὀνειδιζόντων) 9.
ὀνειδιζόντων (pres.act.part.gen.pl.masc.of ὀνειδίζω, substantival description) 437.
σε (acc.sing.masc.of σύ, direct object of ὀνειδιζόντων) 104.
ἐπέπεσαν (3d.per.pl.aor.act.ind.of ἐπιπίπτω, constative) 1794.
ἐπ' (preposition with the accusative of extent) 47.
ἐμέ (acc.sing.masc.of ἐμός, extent) 1267.

Translation - "*Because even Christ did not please Himself. On the contrary, as it is written, 'The insults of those taunting you fell upon me.' "*

Comment: γὰρ is causal as Paul strengthens his admonition of verse 2 by showing that Christ's behavior is exemplary. καὶ then is ascensive. "If even Christ did not seek to please Himself, but rather suffered unjustly for others, how much more should we?" The mature Christian has a moral right to eat meat, drink wine and do anything not specifically forbidden in Scripture, just as Christ had a right to escape the cross, which He had ample power to do. (John 18:6; Mt.26:52-54). But Christ suffered unjustified reproach (Mt.27:44; Mk.15:32), and it is a small thing if we must forego legitimate pleasures, if by doing so, we edify the weaker saints. The quotation is from Psalm 69:9, which is also cited in John 2:17. The Psalm is Messianic. In it Christ is speaking to the Father. In its local application it is David speaking to God. The world's hatred against the members of the Body of Christ is really directed at Christ, the Head of the Body.

Verse 4 - " For whatsoever things were written aforetime were written for our learning, that we through patience and comfort of the scriptures might have hope."

ὅσα γὰρ προεγράφη, εἰς τὴν ἡμετέραν διδασκαλίαν ἐγράφη, ἵνα διὰ τῆς ὑπομονῆς καὶ διὰ τῆς παρακλήσεως τῶν γραφῶν τὴν ἐλπίδα ἔχωμεν.

"For whatever was written in former days was written for our instruction, that by steadfastness and by the encouragement of the scriptures we might have hope." . . . RSV

ὅσα (nom.pl.neut.of ὅσος, subject of προεγράφη) 660.
γὰρ (causal conjunction) 105.

#4046 προεγράφη (3d.per.sing.2d.aor.pass.ind.of προγράφω, culminative).

     King James Version

ordain before - Jude 4.
set forth evidently - Gal.3:1.
write aforetime - Rom.15:4.
write before - Eph.3:3.

     Revised Standard Version

designated - Jude 4.
publicly portrayed - Gal.3:1.
write - Eph.3:3.
written in former days - Rom.15:4.

Meaning: A combination of πρό (#442) and γράφω (#156). Hence, to write at a previous time. To record before the time in question. With reference to the Old Testament Scriptures, as a guide and comfort to Christians - Rom.15:4; as a revelation of Jesus, the Messiah - Gal.3:1. With reference to a previously written testimony by Paul, prior to his epistle to the Ephesians - Eph.3:3; of the prophecies in relation to apostates - Jude 4. *In re* Gal.3:1 γράφω is sometimes used to mean "to paint" or "to depict" as an artist does. Thus προγράφω in Gal.3:1 can mean "to set before the eyes of the Galatians, the word picture of the sufferings of Christ." *cf.* comment on Gal.3:1.

εἰς (preposition with the accusative, purpose) 140.

τὴν (acc.sing.fem.of the article in agreement with διδασκαλίαν) 9.

ἡμετέραν (acc.sing.fem.of ἡμέτερος, in agreement with διδασκαλίαν) 2571.

διδασκαλίαν (acc.sing.fem.of διδασκαλία, purpose) 1150.

ἐγράφη (3d.per.sing.2d.aor.pass.ind.of γράφω, culminative) 156.

ἵνα (conjunction with the subjunctive, sub-final) 114.

διὰ (preposition with the ablative, means) 118.

τῆς (abl.sing.fem.of ὑπομονή, means) 2204.

ὑπομονῆς (abl.sing.fem.of ὑπομονή, means) 2204.

καὶ (adjunctive conjunction joining prepositional phrases) 14.

διὰ (preposition with the ablative, means) 118.

τῆς (abl.sing.fem.of the article in agreement with παρακλήσεως) 9.

παρακλήσεως (abl.sing.fem.of παράκλησις, means) 1896.

τῶν (abl.pl.fem.of the article in agreement with γραφῶν) 9.

γραφῶν (abl.pl.fem.of γράφη, source) 1389.

τὴν (acc.sing.fem.of the article in agreement with ἐλπίδα) 9.

ἐλπίδα (acc.sing.fem.of ἐλπίς, direct object ofd ἔχωμεν) 2994.

ἔχωμεν (1st.per.pl.pres.act.subj.of ἔχω, purpose/result) 82.

Translation - *"Because whatever was written previously was written for our instruction, in order (and with the result) that through patience and encouragement from the Scriptures, we might continue to have hope."*

Comment: γὰρ is causal. The so-called "New Hermeneutics" with its existential historicism, which denies that any writer can communicate his thought to a reader of a later generation, will ask Paul why he should support his command of verse 2 by quoting Psalm 69:9 in verse 3. After all, Psalm 69:9 was written centuries before Paul quoted it to the Romans, and Paul cannot distinguish between exegesis and eisegesis anyway. How does Paul know what David meant in Psalm 69:9?

Paul obviously was not a historicist in this extreme sense. No one denies that exegetes must establish *zeitgeist* (the ability to put oneself back chronologically into the time period when something was written, thus to experience "the spirit of the times.").

The study of any ancient writing must be carried on in the light of historical research of that idiom. But many of us, though we admit the difficulty, strongly deny the impossibility of such study, and we still believe that exegesis is one thing and that eisegesis is the opposite, and that we can tell the difference. Paul says here that Old Testament writings were written for a purpose - εἰς τὴν ἡμετέραν διδασκαλίαν ἐγράφη - "they were written in order to instruct us." Then a sub-final ἵνα clause with the subjunctive ἔχωμεν adds that the purpose and result of our instruction is that, by means of patience and comfort we may continue (present subjunctive in ἔχωμεν) to have hope." If nobody knows what the Scriptures mean then this verse about the utility of the Old Testament in enabling New Testament Christians to live victorious lives, is nonesense. Of course, if the historicists are correct, then no one knows what Paul meant in

Romans 14:5 (!) since we are further removed chronologically from Paul now than Paul was from David then! And yet, ironically enough, the existentially inclined "New Hermeneutics" addicts (!) are most zealous to communicate to all of us that no one can communicate anything to anyone else, and therefore that no one knows what Paul or David or even the scholar (!) who is reading the paper means by what he says.

The assumption of the Christian theologian is that it is possible through the historical approach of grammar, lexicology and syntax to discover the concepts set forth in the Greek New Testament. And what Paul says to the Roman saints here is that whatever Old Testament Scripture has been written will instruct us now, with a view to providing from them (ablative of source in γραφῶν) patience and comfort which will be the means (διὰ with the ablative) of giving us continued hope. An ancient Greek idiom often omitted the prepositional prefix on the second use of a verb, with the same meaning as it had in its first usage. Thus here we have προεγράφη followed by ἐγράφη, where ἐγράφη obviously has the same force. Moulton suggests John 1:11,12; 1 Pet.1:10,11; 2 Cor.5:3; Eph.6:13 and Rev.10:10 as other examples (Moulton, *Prol.*, 115 as cited in Robertson, *Grammar*, 563), though Robertson doubts 2 Cor.5:3 and Eph.6:13 especially. The context must decide in each case.

I have been as much interested in the content of Romans 15:4 for its high velocity ammunition against the "New Hermeneutics" as in the message to the Romans saints who knew nothing about this insidious and diabolically clever latest 20th century attack upon Christianity. But let us not lose sight of Paul's point. We are to help the weaker saints. We must make them happy and help them to grow. If this means giving up our own pleasures, however legitimate, so be it. Because Christ did just this, even as Psalm 69:9 prophesied that He would. He is our example in the solution of this ethical problem. Indeed everything in the Old Testament will teach and help us. Note the article τῆς both with ὑπομονῆς and παρακλήσεως as they are used here to separate one quality from another.

Verse 5 - "Now the God of patience and consolation grant you to be likeminded one toward another according to Christ Jesus."

ὁ δὲ θεὸς τῆς ὑπομονῆς καὶ τῆς παρακλήσεως δῴη ὑμῖν τὸ αὐτὸ φρονεῖν ἐν ἀλλήλοις κατὰ Χριστὸν Ἰησοῦν,

"May the God of steadfastness and encouragement grant you to live in such harmony with one another, in accord with Christ Jesus," . . . RSV

ὁ (nom.sing.masc.of the article in agreement with θεὸς) 9.
δὲ (continuative conjunction) 11.
θεὸς (nom.sing.masc.of θεός, subject of δῴη) 124.
τῆς (gen.sing.fem.of the article in agreement with ὑπομονῆς) 9.
ὑπομονῆς (gen.sing.fem.of ὑπομονή, description) 2204.
καὶ (adjunctive conjunction joining nouns) 14.
τῆς (gen.sing.fem.of the article in agreement with παρακλήσεως) 9.

παρακλήσεως (gen.sing.fem.of παράκλησις, description) 1896.
δώη (3d.per.sing.2d.aor.act.opt.of δίδωμι, voluntative) 362.
ὑμῖν (dat.pl.masc.of σύ, indirect object of δώῃ) 104.
τὸ (acc.sing.neut.of the article in agreement with φρονεῖν) 9.
αὐτὸ (acc.sing.neut.of αὐτός, intensive) 16.
φρονεῖν (pres.act.inf.of φρονέω, object of δώῃ) 1212.
ἐν (preposition with the locative, with plural pronouns) 80.
ἀλλήλοις (loc.pl.masc.of ἀλλήλων, place) 1487.
κατὰ (preposition with the accusative, standard) 98.
Χριστὸν (acc.sing.masc.of Χριστός, standard) 4.
Ἰησοῦν (acc.sing.masc.of Ἰησοῦς, apposition) 3.

Translation - *"O that the God of patience and of consolation would give to you the grace to regard one another with equal favor, according to the example of Christ Jesus."*

Comment: Paul puts his prayer in the optative (δώῃ) as if he had scant faith that it would be answered! God is described as the God who is the source of ὑπομονῆς and παρακλήσεως. (James 1:17). Since He is the source, He is described by the genitive of description. The object of δώῃ is the articular infinitive τὸ φρονεῖν. "To regard one another in the *same* way" (intensive αὐτὸ), in keeping with the standard set by our Lord. This recalls Romans 12:3. Such an attitude of total impartiality is a gift that only God can bestow and Paul is not sure that He will do it. Men, even after they have been born again, are so addicted to the function of making judgments that it is very difficult to avoid making discriminatory evaluations. We forget that even the Father does not make judgments, but has committed all judgment unto the Son (John 5:22,27; Mt.7:1-5).

Note the reflexive pronoun used reciprocally - ἐν ἀλλήλοις.

The sentence, which is Paul's prayer, goes on in

Verse 6 - *". . . that ye may with one mind and one mouth glorify God, even the Father of our Lord Jesus Christ."*

ἵνα ὁμοθυμαδὸν ἐν ἑνὶ στόματι δοξάζητε τὸν θεὸν καὶ πατέρα τοῦ κυρίου ἡμῶν Ἰησοῦ Χριστοῦ.

". . . that together you may with one voice glorify the God and Father of our Lord Jesus Christ." . . . RSV

ἵνα (conjunction with the subjunctive in a final clause) 114.
ὁμοθυμαδὸν (adverbial) 2942.
ἐν (preposition with the locative, means) 80.
ἑνὶ (loc.sing.neut.of εἷς, in agreement with στόματι) 469.
στόματι (loc.sing.neut.of στόμα, means) 344.
δοξάζητε (2d.per.pl.pres.act.subj.of δοξάζω, purpose) 461.
τὸν (acc.sing.masc.of the article in agreement with θεὸν) 9.
θεὸν (acc.sing.masc.of θεός, direct object of δοξάζητε) 124.

καὶ (adjunctive conjunction joining nouns) 14.
πατέρα (acc.sing.masc.of πατήρ, direct object of δοξάζητε) 238.
τοῦ (gen.sing.masc.of the article in agreement with κυρίου) 9.
κυρίου (gen.sing.masc.of κύριος, relationship) 97.
ἡμῶν (gen.pl.masc.of ἐγώ, relationship) 123.
Ἰησοῦ (gen.sing.masc.of Ἰησοῦς, apposition) 3.
Χριστοῦ (gen.sing.masc.of Χριστός, apposition) 4.

Translation - ". . . in order that together with one voice you may glorify the God and Father of our Lord Jesus Christ."

Comment: The ἵνα . . . δοξάζητε clause gives the purpose that the answer to Paul's prayer of verse 5 would achieve. The result is complete unity in the church. The intellectual and emotional unity is in ὁμοθυμαδὸν. The vocal unity is in ἐν ἑνὶ στόματι. When a church thinks, emotes and talks in unity, God is certainly glorified. Note that the basis for this unity is psychological. It is when Christians think the same way about each other - τὸ αὐτὸ φρονεῖν ἐν ἀλλήλοις - according to Christ's example - κατὰ Χριστὸν Ἰησοῦν that God is glorified because then Christians think like God. This is a miracle that calls for ἡ ἀνακαίνωσις τοῦ νοός (Rom.12:2).

The Gospel for Jews and Gentiles Alike

(Romans 15:7-13)

Verse 7 - "Wherefore receive ye one another, as Christ also received us to the glory of God."

Διὸ προσλαμβάνεσθε ἀλλήλους, καθὼς καὶ ὁ Χριστὸς προσελάβετο ὑμᾶς, εἰς δόξαν τοῦ θεοῦ.

"Welcome one another, therefore, as Christ has welcomed you, for the glory of God". . . RSV

Διὸ (inferential particle) 1622.
προσλαμβάνεσθε (2d.per.pl.pres.mid.impv.of προσλαμβάνω, entreaty) 1210.
ἀλλήλους (acc.pl.masc.of ἀλλήλων, direct object of προσλαμβάνεσθε) 1487.
καθὼς (compound particle in a comparative clause) 1348.
καὶ (adjunctive conjunction joining substantives) 14.
ὁ (nom.sing.masc.of the article in agreement with Χριστὸς) 9.
Χριστὸς (nom.sing.masc.of Χριστός, subject of προσελάβετο) 4.
προσελάβετο (3d.per.sing.aor.mid.ind.of προσλαμβάνω, culminative) 1210.
ὑμᾶς (acc.pl.masc.of σύ, direct object ofd προσελάβετο) 104.
εἰς (preposition with the accusative, purpose) 140.
δόξαν (acc.sing.fem.of δόξα, purpose) 361.

τοῦ (gen.sing.masc.of the article in agreement with θεοῦ) 9.

θεοῦ (gen.sing.masc.of θεός, description) 124.

Translation - "Therefore always receive one another unto yourselves, just as Christ also took you unto Himself for God's glory."

Comment: The indirect middles here προσλαμβάνεσθε and προσελάβετο are common in the New Testament - "Received unto yourself. *Cf.* #1348 for καθὼς καὶ. B D and some miniscules have ἡμᾶς (us) instead of ὑμᾶς (you), but the Committee follows Sinaiticus A C Db,c G Ψ and many other miniscules with a B degree of confidence.

When any Christian discriminates against another socially, he is apparently forgetting that Christ did not discriminate against him. Otherwise he would never have been called to salvation. This fact needs only to be stated to be believed, which must lead to the conclusion that the bigoted Christian surely has not been asked to think about it. Gentile Christian's particularly are the recipients of God's grace and mercy and should never therefore refuse to receive into their fellowship any other one, however distasteful that person might be. This principle applies not only to Hebrew Christians but to those of other skin color and/or cultural backgrounds. The intimacy of the union of the believer with Jesus Christ and God in the Body of Christ (John 17:21) should be reflected in the intimacy of the fellowship within the local church.

This is Paul's point in verses 8 and 9 and he then supports it with four quotations from the Old Testament in verses 9-12.

Verse 8 - "Now I say that Jesus Christ was a minister of the circumcision for the truth of God, to confirm the promises made unto the fathers."

λέγω γὰρ Χριστὸν διάκονον γεγενῆσθαι περιτομῆς ὑπὲρ ἀληθείας θεοῦ, εἰς τὸ βεβαιῶσαι τὰς ἐπαγγελίας τῶν πατέρων,

"For I tell you that Christ became a servant to the circumcised to show God's truthfulness, in order to confirm the promises given to the patriarchs, ..." ...

RSV

λέγω (1st.per.sing.pres.act.ind.of λέγω, aoristic) 66.

γὰρ (explanatory conjunction) 105.

Χριστὸν (acc.sing.masc.of Χριστός, general reference) 4.

διάκονον (acc.sing.masc.of διάκονος, predicate accusative) 1334.

γεγενῆσθαι (perf.pass.inf.of γίνομαι, accusative, object of λέγω) 113.

περιτομῆς (gen.sing.fem.of περιτομή, description) 2368.

ὑπὲρ (preposition with the ablative "in behalf of") 545.

ἀληθείας (abl.sing.fem.of ἀλήθεια, "in behalf of") 1416.

θεοῦ (gen.sing.masc.of θεός, description) 124.

εἰς (preposition with the infinitive, purpose) 140.

τὸ (acc.sing.neut.of the article, with the infinitive, purpose) 9.

βεβαιῶσαι (aor.act.inf.of βεβαιόω, purpose) 2932.

τὰς (acc.pl.fem.of the article in agreement with ἐπαγγελίας) 9.
ἐπαγγελίας (acc.pl.fem.of ἐπαγγελία, direct object of βεβαιῶσαι) 2929.
τῶν (gen.pl.masc.of the article in agreement with πατέρων) 9.
πατέρων (gen.pl.masc.of πατήρ, possession) 238.

Translation - "Now I am telling you that Christ has been made a servant of the circumcised for the sake of divine truth, in order to fulfill the promises to the fathers."

Comment: The first infinitive γεγενῆσθαι is the object of λέγω with Χριστὸν in general reference. The second purpose infinitive depends upon the first. Messiah was made God's servant with a special ministry to the Jews for the sake of God's truth. This truth, contained in God's promises to Abraham, Isaac, Jacob, Judah and David was to the effect that their family line would produce the Messiah. God delivered what He promised. This was Christ's primary reason for coming to earth. But there was a second purpose that God had in the incarnation, set forth in

Verse 9 - "And that the Gentiles might glorify God for his mercy; as it is written, For this cause I will confess to thee among the Gentiles, and sing unto thy name."

τὰ δὲ ἔθνη ὑπὲρ ἐλέους δοξάσαι τὸν θεόν. καθὼς γέγραπται, Διὰ τοῦτο ἐξομολογήσομαί σοι ἐν ἔθνεσιν, καὶ τῷ ὀνόματί σου ψαλῶ.

". . . and in order that the Gentiles might glorify God for his mercy. As it is written, 'Therefore I will praise thee among the Gentiles, and sing to thy name;' "

τὰ (acc.pl.neut.of the article in agreement with ἔθνη) 9.
δὲ (continuative conjunction) 11.
ἔθνη (acc.pl.neut.of ἔθνος, general refrence) 376.
ὑπὲρ (preposition with the ablative, cause) 545.
ἐλέους (abl.sing.neut.of ἔλεος, cause) 795.
δοξάσαι (aor.act.inf.of δοξάζω, purpose) 461.
τὸν (acc.sing.masc.of the article in agreement with θεόν) 9
θεόν (acc.sing.masc.of θεός, direct object of δοξάσαι) 124.
καθὼς (compound particle in a comparative clause) 1348.
γέγραπται (3d.per.sing.perf.pass.ind.of γράφω, intensive) 156.
Διὰ (preposition with the accusative, cause) 118.
τοῦτο (acc.sing.neut.of οὗτος, cause) 93.
ἐξομολογήσομαι (1st.per.sing.fut.mid.ind.of ἐξομολογέω, predictive) 275.
σοι (dat.sing.masc.of σύ, reference) 104.
ἐν (preposition with the locative, place) 80.
ἔθνεσιν (loc.pl.neut.of ἔθνος, place) 376.
καὶ (continuative conjunction) 14.
τῷ (dat.sing.neut.of the article in agreement with ὀνόμματι) 9.
ὀνόματί (dat.sing.neut.of ὄνομα, advantage) 108.
σοῦ (gen.sing.masc.of σύ, possession) 104.

#4047 ψαλῶ (1st.per.sing.fut.act.ind.of ψάλλω, predictive).

King James Version

make melody - Eph.5:19.
sing - Rom.15:9; 1 Cor.14:15,15.
sing psalms - James 5:13.

Revised Standard Version

sing - Rom.15:9; 1 Cor.14:15,15.
sing praise - James 5:13.

Meaning: I quote *en tout* Julius R. Mantey, *Word Studies in Philo*, (Louisville, Kentucky, 1931), 83-86, an unpublished dissertation, submitted to Southern Baptist Theological Seminary, in partial requirement for the Ph.D. degree.

Inasmuch as some people dogmatically and enthusiastically claim that there is nothing in the New Testament that can be reasonably interpreted in favor of the use of musical instruments, and since they claim that, although the word φάλλω may have denoted playing upon an instrument prior to 100 B.C., it had lost such significance soon after that time and that it meant only to sing or hum during the first century A.D., it may be of interest to note Philo's use of the word, as well as that of Lucian, who lived in the second century A.D.

Dreams, I, S.7, ὁ τοίνυν οὐρανὸς τὸ μουσικῆς ἀρχέτυπον ὄργανον ἄκρως ἡρμόθαι δοκεῖ δι' οὐδὲν ἕτερον, ἢ ἵνα ἐπὶ φάλλενται. - - "Furthermore heaven, the archtype organ seems to be perfectly arranged for nothing else except that hymns, being sung to the honor of the father of all, may be *played* musically (on a stringed instrument)." Note that a participle is used to denote the idea of singing, whereas another word is used to denote playing. If only singing were meant the last word would be superfluous.

But Lucian's use of the word leaves no room at all for doubt as to the fact that it still meant playing upon a stringed instrument in the second century. He shuts out all other meanings by declaring that it is impossible to φάλλω without a lyre. *The Parasite*, S. 17: καὶ αἱ μὲν ἄλλαι τέχναι χωρὶς ὀργάνων οὐδαμῶς τῷ κεκτημένῳ ὑπηρετεῖν δύναται. οὔτε γὰρ αὐλεῖν ἐνι χωρὶς αὐλῶν οὔτε φάλλειν ἄνευ λύρας οὔτε ἱππεύειν ἄνεθ ἵππου. . . "The other arts, moreover, cannot be of use to their possessors without tools, for it is impossible to flute without flutes, or to *strum* without a lyre or to ride on horseback without a horse."

In view of these quotations from the first and second centuries the assertion in Liddell-Scott's lexicon "later to sing to a harp, N.T." may be far from reliable. Where is evidence that it ever meant to sing?

In Ps.33:3 we find ἄσατε αὐτῷ ᾆσμα καινόν, καλῶς φάλατε ἐν ἀλαλαγμῷ - - "sing unto Him a new song; *play* well upon a stringed instrument with shouting." The word which we translate shouting after Liddell and Scott, together with φάλατε, can hardly mean "sing well with shouting." Although some people's singing may well be classified as shouting.

In 1 Sam.16:16 we find φάλλειν ἐν κινύρα . . . φαλῇ ἐν τῇ κινύρᾳ αὐτοῦ. In the 23rd verse of the same chapter is found ἐλάμβανε Δαυὶδ τὴν κινύραν καὶ ἔφαλλεν ἐν χειρὶ αὐτοῦ. This instrument is claimed to have had ten strings. If we try to translate φάλλω here as sing we get into difficulty at once. For it is asserted twice that he "psaloed" on an instrument, and then that he took an instrument and "psaloed" with his hand - not his mouth.

There is some likelihood that φάλλω in Jam.5:13; Rom.15:9 and 1 Cor.14:15,15 may mean to render a psalm. But what is a psalm? According to Abbott-Smith it is "a sacred song sung to musical accompaniment," and according to Liddell and Scott, "a song sung to a stringed instrument." Thus to "psallo" would include the playing upon an instrument even if we should admit that it might be translated to sing at times. Since the New Testament instructs us to "psallv," the benefit of the doubt seems to be decidedly in favor of those who worship God with musical instruments as well as with singing hymns. And since this word regularly connotes the idea of instrumental music thoughout all Greek literature before the New Testament times, during and after, is it not reasonable to assume that God would not assuredly hold guiltless any deviant worshipper who believes in using such music in church, in case it should later be proved that "psallo" means only to sing? The New Testament writers, if they disbelieved in using instrumental music in services of worship were most careless and culpable in using "psallo" in view of its connotation to all Greeks.

But in Eph.5:19 "psallo" evidently has its usual meaning of *strumming* or *playing* upon an instrument. - λαλοῦντες ἑαυτοῖς φαλμοῖς καὶ ὕμνοις καὶ ᾠδαῖς πνευματικαῖς, ἄδοντες καὶ φάλλοντες τῇ καρδίᾳ ὑμῶν τῷ κυρίῳ, εὐχαριστοῦντες πάντοτε. Four ways of being filled with the Spirit are here specified, quoting psalms and hymns and songs, singing, 'playing with your heart to God' and thanksgiving. If 'psallo' means to sing, why did Paul repeat himself by twice mentioning that in the same sentence? He was not given to such redundancy. Ah, but what he does say is that we should both "sing and *play* from the heart to God." Church music then is not only to include playing upon instruments but also - and this is vital to public worship - that the music is not to be just for art's sake, but rather it is to come out of the heart, be genuine, be full of emotion, and it is to be rendered, not to the glory of the participants, but to the glory of God.

Why then should we let the movie and amusement houses monopolize instrumental music when the Bible enjoins us by that means to grow in grace as well as to worship God."

*Cf.*φάω - "to rub, wipe, handle, touch" - hence, to pluck a string.

Translation - " . . . *and that the Gentiles might glorify God because of His mercy, just as it is written, 'On account of this, I will openly speak of you among the Gentiles and I will play an instrument in honor of your name."*

Comment: Two reasons are given why Christ became God's servant: (1) to confirm God's promises to the Jewish patriarchs (verse 8) and, (2) to offer salvation to the Gentiles (verse 9). The infinitives βεβαιῶσαι and δοξάσαι after εἰς indicate purpose. Because He came the Gentiles will glory God ὑπὲρ ἐλέους ("because of mercy"). *Cf.* #545 for ὑπέρ with the ablative in a causal sense.

Paul then cites Psalm 18:49. *Cf.*#4047 - "to sing a psalm, with accompaniment on a musical instrument." *Cf.* comment on verse 7. διὰ τοῦτο - cause. *Cf.*#'s 118 and 93. Because God's purpose in sending Messiah included salvation also for Gentiles, Christ prophesied in Psalm 18:49 that He would openly talk about God among the Gentiles (dative of reference in σοι) and would sing a psalm in honor of God's name. Since God included the Gentiles, the Roman Christians, many of whom were Gentiles could not reasonably exclude anyone from their fellowship. This is Paul's point in the entire 15th chapter.

Verse 10 - *"And again he saith, Rejoice, ye Gentiles, with his people."*

καὶ πάλιν λέγει, Εὐφράνθητε, ἔθνη, μετὰ τοῦ λαοῦ αὐτοῦ.

". . . and again it is said, 'Rejoice, O Gentiles, with his people.' " . . . RSV

καὶ (continuative conjunction) 14.
πάλιν (adverbial) 355.
λέγει (3d.per.sing.pres.act.ind.of λέγω, historical) 66.
Εὐφράνθητε (2d.per.pl.1st.aor.pass.impv. of εὐφραίνω, command) 2479.
ἔθνη (voc.pl.neut.of ἔθνος, address) 376.
μετὰ (preposition with the genitive, fellowship) 50.
τοῦ (gen.sing.masc.of the article in agreement with λαοῦ) 9.
λαοῦ (gen.sing.masc.of λαός, fellowship) 110.
αὐτοῦ (gen.sing.masc.of αὐτός, relationship) 16.

Translation - *"And again He said, 'Be overcome with joy, you Gentiles, in fellowship with His people.' "*

Comment: The quotation is from Deut.32:43. It is a part of the song of Moses, which will be sung again (Rev.15:3). God invites the Gentiles to rejoice with Jews because of salvation. Therefore why should Gentile Christians discriminate against each other? Thus Paul again supports his point.

Verse 11 - *"And again, Praise the Lord, all ye Gentiles: and laud him, all ye people."*

καὶ πάλιν, Αἰνεῖτε, πάντα τὰ ἔθνη, τὸν κύριον, καὶ ἐπαινεσάτωσαν αὐτὸν πάντες οἱ λαοί.

". . . and again, 'Praise the Lord, all Gentiles, and let all the peoples praise him' " . . . RSV

καὶ (continuative conjunction) 14.
πάλιν (adverbial) 355.
Αἰνεῖτε (2d.per.pl.pres.act.impv.of αἰνέω, command) 1881.
πάντα (voc.pl.neut.of πᾶς, in agreement with ἔθνη) 67.
τὰ (voc.pl.neut.of the article in agreement with ἔθνη) 9.
ἔθνη (voc.pl.neut.of ἔθνος, address) 376.
τὸν (acc.sing.masc.of the article in agreement with κύριον) 9.
κύριον (acc.sing.masc.of κύριος, direct object of αἰνεῖτε) 97.
καὶ (continuative conjunction) 14.
ἐπαινεσάτωσαν (3d.per.pl.1st.aor.act.impv.of ἐπαινέω, command) 2568.
αὐτὸν (acc.sing.masc.of αὐτός, direct object of ἐπαινεσάτωσαν) 16.

πάντες (voc.pl.masc.of πᾶς, in agreement with λαοί) 67.
οἱ (voc.pl.masc.of the article in agreement with λαοί) 9.
λαοί (voc.pl.masc.of λαός, address) 110.

Translation - "And again, 'Praise the Lord, all you Gentiles, and heap praises upon Him, you people.' "

Comment: The quotation is from Psalm 117:1. Paul has added ἐπί to the verb as used in Psalm 117:1, LXX. Universal adulation for the Lord is called for, thus indicating that both Gentiles and Jews are included. There is no place for exclusion in Christ. (Rev.5:13).

Verse 12 - "And again Esaias saith, There shall be a root out of Jesse, and he that shall rise to reign over the Gentiles; in him shall the Gentiles trust."

καὶ πάλιν Ἡσαΐας λέγει, Ἔσται ἡ ῥίζα τοῦ Ἰεσσαί, καὶ ὁ ἀνιστάμενος ἄρχειν ἐθνῶν, ἐπ' αὐτῷ ἔθνη ἐλπιοῦσιν.

"... and further Isaiah says, 'The root of Jesse shall come, he who rises to rule the Gentiles; in him shall the Gentiles hope.' " ... RSV

καὶ (continuative conjunction) 14.
πάλιν (adverbial) 355.
Ἡσαΐας (nom.sing.masc.of Ἡσαΐας, subject of λέγει) 255.
λέγει (3d.per.sing.pres.act.ind.of λέγω, historical) 66.
Ἔσται (3d.per.sing.fut.ind.of εἰμί, predictive) 86.
ἡ (nom.sing.fem.of the article in agreement with ῥίζα) 9.
ῥίζα (nom.sing.fem.of ῥίζα, subject of Ἔσται) 293.
τοῦ (gen.sing.masc.of the article in agreement with Ἰεσσαί) 9.
Ἰεσσαί (gen.sing.masc.of Ἰεσσαί, relationship) 30.
καὶ (adjunctive conjunction joining substantives) 14.
ὁ (nom.sing.masc.of the article in agreement with ἀνιστάμενος) 9.
ἀνιστάμενος (pres.mid.part.nom.sing.masc.of ἀνίστημι, substantival, subject of Ἔσται) 789.
ἄρχειν (pres.act.inf.of ἄρχω, purpose) 383.
ἐθνῶν (gen.pl.neut.of ἔθνος, description) 376.
ἐπ' (preposition with the locative with a verb of emotion) 47.
αὐτῷ (loc.sing.masc.of αὐτός, with a verb of emotion) 16.
ἔθνη (nom.pl.neut.of ἔθνος, subject of ἐλπιοῦσιν) 376.
ἐλπιοῦσιν (3d.per.pl.fut.act.ind.(Att.) of ἐλπίζω, predictive) 991.

Translation - "And again Isaiah said, 'The Root out Jesse will appear, even the One standing up in order to rule the Gentiles. They will have their hopes on Him.' "

Comment: The quotation is from Isa.11:1,10. Jesse was the father of David, to whom God gave the kingdom covenant of 2 Samuel 7. The "Root out of Jesse" is therefore David, and King David's Greater Son, the Messiah. But Isaiah went beyond the nationalism of Israel to say that Israel's Messiah would rule the Gentiles as well, that they would pin their hopes on Him and receive Him. *Cf.* Rev.5:5; 22:16. Jesus, the Root of David, once crucified and risen now sits at the Father's right hand while the Holy Spirit directs a worldwide missionary enterprise to preach His blood sacrifice (Rev.5:6) to Gentiles as well as to Jews. He will open the seven year tribulation period by ripping the seals off Daniel's book (Daniel 12:9,10; Rev.5:1-5), thus to signal the beginning of heaven's warfare against the earth dwellers who will have rejected Him. He appears in the denoument (Rev.22:16). Many Gentiles will trust Him as Saviour and thus become members of His Body. In the millenium He will rule all Gentile nations (Mk.10:42).

The true Gentile Ruler came as a servant. Thus again Paul appeals to the Old Testament to support his teaching that God's plan of salvation included the Gentiles to whom he is writing. And thus it is totally illogical that they who are safe in Christ should discriminate in any way against others.

Verse 13 - "Now the God of hope fill you with all joy and peace in believing, that ye may abound in hope, through the power of the Holy Ghost."

ὁ δὲ θεὸς τῆς ἐλπίδος πληρῶσαι ὑμᾶς πάσης χαρᾶς καὶ εἰρήνης ἐν τῷ πιστεύειν, εἰς τὸ περισσεύειν ὑμᾶς ἐν τῇ ἐλπίδι ἐν δυνάμει πνεύματος ἁγίου.

"May the God of hope fill you with all joy and peace in believing, so that by the power of the Holy Spirit you may abound in hope." . . . RSV

ὁ (nom.sing.masc.of the article in agreement with θεὸς) 9.

δὲ (continuative conjunction) 11.

θεὸς (nom.sing.masc.of θεός, subject of πληρῶσαι) 124.

τῆς (gen.sing.fem.of the article in agreement with ἐλπίδος) 9.

ἐλπίδος (gen.sing.fem.of ἐλπίς, description) 2994.

πληρῶσαι (3d.per.sing.1st.aor.act.opt.of πληρόω, voluntative) 115.

ὑμᾶς (acc.pl.masc.of σύ, direct object of πληρῶσαι) 104.

πάσης (abl.sing.fem.of πᾶς, in agreement with χαρᾶς and εἰρήνης) 67.

χαρᾶς (abl.sing.fem.of χαρά, means) 183.

καὶ (adjunctive conjunction joining nouns) 14.

εἰρήνης (abl.sing.fem.of εἰρήνη, means) 865.

ἐν (preposition with the locative, means) 80.

τῷ (loc.sing.neut.of the article in agreement with πιστεύειν) 9.

πιστεύειν (pres.act.inf.of πιστεύω, noun use, loc.sing.neut., means) 734.

εἰς (preposition with the accusative, purpose) 140.

τὸ (acc.sing.neut.of the article in agreement with περισσεύειν) 9.

περισσεύειν (pres.act.inf.of περισσεύω, purpose) 473.

ὑμᾶς (acc.pl.masc.of σύ, general reference) 104.

ἐν (preposition with the locative of sphere) 80.

τῇ (loc.sing.fem.of the article in agreement with ἐλπίδι) 9.

ἐλπίδι (loc.sing.fem.of ἐλπίς, sphere) 2994.

ἐν (preposition with the locative, means) 80.

δυνάμει (loc.sing.fem.of δύναμις, means) 687.
πνεύματος (abl.sing.neut.of πνεῦμα, source) 83.
ἁγίου (abl.sing.neut.of ἅγιος, in agreement with πνεύματος) 84.

Translation - "O that the God of hope would fill you with joy and peace in believing, with the result that you abound by means of the hope that comes from the Holy Spirit."

Comment: In verse 5 Paul directed a prayer to God with scant faith that it would be answered. We have it again here as Paul uses the optative in πληρώσαι. Then he prayed to God the source of patience and comfort. Now he addresses Him as the God of hope. *Cf.* Heb.3:6; 6:11; 7:19; 10:23 for ἐλπίς (#2994) in a genitive of description construction. ἐν τῷ πιστεύειν, the articular infinitive, in a means construction. If Christians would only believe they would be overflowed with joy and peace. There is no greater way to honor the Holy Spirit than to believe. His fruits include joy and peace (Gal.5:22,23). The result would be (εἰς τὸ περισσεύειν ὑμᾶς) that they would abound in hope by means of the Holy Spirit's power. Note the article with ἐλπίδι, though not with δυνάμει. The means is τῇ ἐλπίδι. The means to attain it is δυνάμει that flows from the Holy Spirit.

Paul's Missionary Commission

(Romans 15:14-21)

Verse 14 - "And I myself also am persuaded of you, my brethren, that ye also are full of goodness, filled with all knowledge, able also to admonish one another."

Πέπεισμαι δέ, ἀδελφοί μου, καὶ αὐτὸς ἐγὼ περὶ ὑμῶν, ὅτι καὶ αὐτοὶ μεστοί ἐστε ἀγαθωσύνης, πεπληρωμένοι πάσης (τῆς) γνώσεως, δυνάμενοι καὶ ἀλλήλους νουθετεῖν.

"I myself am satisfied about you, my brethren, that you yourselves are full of goodness, filled with all knowledge, and able to instruct one another." . . . RSV

Πέπεισμαι (1st.per.sing.perf.pass.ind.of πείθω, intensive) 1629.
δὲ (adversative conjunction) 11.
ἀδελφοί (voc.pl.masc.of ἀδελφός, address) 15.
μου (gen.sing.masc.of ἐγώ, relationship) 123.
καὶ (adjunctive conjunction) 14.
αὐτὸς (nom.sing.masc.of αὐτός, intensive, predicate position) 16.
ἐγὼ (nom.sing.masc.of ἐγώ, subject of πέπεισμαι) 123.
περὶ (preposition with the genitive of reference) 173.
ὑμῶν (gen.pl.masc.of σύ, reference) 104.
ὅτι (conjunction introducing an object clause in indirect discourse) 211.
καὶ (adjunctive conjunction joining pronouns) 14.
αὐτοὶ (nom.pl.masc.of αὐτός, intensive) 16.
μεστοί (nom.pl.masc.of μεστός, predicate adjective) 1468.

ἐστε (2d.per.pl.pres.ind.of εἰμί, aoristic) 86.

#4048 ἀγαθωσύνης (abl.sing.fem.of ἀγαθωσύνη, source).

King James Version

goodness - Rom.15:14; Gal.5:22; Eph.5:9; 2 Thess.1:11.

Revised Standard Version

goodness - Rom.15:14; Gal.5:22.
that is good - Eph.5:9.
good resolve - 2 Thess.1:11.

Meaning: Cf. ἀγαθός (#547); ἀγαθοποιέω (#2105), etc. Uprightness in heart and life. The characteristic of doing good. God's gift to the believer - Rom.15:14; Gal.5:22; Eph.5:9; 2 Thess.1:11.

πεπληρωμένοι (perf.pass.part.nom.pl.masc.of πληρόω, adverbial, causal) 115.
πάσης (abl.sing.fem.of πᾶς, in agreement with γνώσεως) 67.
τῆς (abl.sing.fem.of the article in agreement with γνώσεως) 9.
γνώσεως (abl.sing.fem.of γνῶσις, source) 1856.
δυνάμενοι (pres.part.nom.pl.masc.of δύναμαι, adverbial, causal) 289.
καί (adjunctive conjunction joining participles) 14.
ἀλλήλους (acc.pl.masc.of ἀλλήλων, direct object of νουθετεῖν) 1487.
νουθετεῖν (pres.act.inf.of νουθετέω, complementary) 3535.

Translation - "But I myself also am persuaded about you, my brethren, that you yourselves also are full of goodness, having been filled up with all knowledge, able also to set one another on right paths of thought."

Comment: Note πέπεισμαι and πεπληρωμένοι, the perfect tenses indicating present conditions as results of past action. Paul is now convinced, having been persuaded that the Romans are now filled, having received the filling in the past. . . κ.τ.λ.

The intensives, αὐτός and αὐτοί are interesting because rare. *Cf.* #16. δυνάμενοι is a present participle. The basis of Paul's confidence is the fact that they are able to set one another straight in their thinking, since they have been filled with all knowledge.

This optimistic statement is out of harmony with his doubts expressed in verse 5 and 13, but it is good psychology to tell the saints that you have confidence in them. Note that Paul is saying that Christians are supposed to "set one another straight." *Cf.* Gal.6:1,2; Mt.18:15-17.

Paul was aware that what he has said in verse 14 is not altogether in keeping with his previous pessimism about them, and he follows in verse 15 with a partial explanation of his psychology. It is well to remember that at the time of this writing Paul had not yet visited Rome and did not know the Roman Christians personally, except in the cases of those whom he knew from previous associations outside the confines of Italy.

Verse 15 - "Nevertheless, brethren, I have written the more boldly unto you in some sort, as putting you in mind, because of the grace that is given to me of God."

τολμηρότερον δὲ ἔγραφα ὑμῖν ἀπὸ μέρους, ὡς ἐπαναμιμνῄσκων ὑμᾶς διὰ τὴν χάριν τὴν δοθεῖσάν μοι ὑπὸ τοῦ θεοῦ

"But on some points I have written to you very boldly by way of reminder, because of the grace given me by God" . . . RSV

#4049 τολμηρότερον (adverbial).

King James Version

the more boldly - Rom.15:15.

Revised Standard Version

very boldly - Rom.15:15.

Meaning: The neuter comparative of τολμηρός - "bold." *Cf.* τολμάω (#1430). More boldly; with greater boldness - Rom.15:15.

δὲ (adversative conjunction) 11.
ἔγραφα (1st.per.sing.aor.act.ind.of γράφω, epistolary) 156.
ὑμῖν (dat.pl.masc.of σύ, indirect object of ἔγραφα) 104.
ἀπὸ (preposition with the genitive, reference) 70
μέρους (gen.sing.neut.of μέρος, reference) 240.
ὡς (particle with the telic participle) 128.

#4050 ἐπαναμιμνῄσκων (pres.act.part.nom.sing.masc.of ἐπαναμιμνῄσκω, adverbial, telic).

King James Version

put in mind - Rom.15:15.

Revised Standard Version

by way of reminder - Rom.15:15.

Meaning: A combination of ἐπί (#47), ἀνά (#1059) and μιμνῄσκομαι (#485). To call to mind again; to remind again - Rom.15:15.

ὑμᾶς (acc.pl.masc.of σύ, direct object of ἐπαναμιμνῄσκων) 104.
διὰ (preposition with the accusative, cause) 118.
τὴν (acc.sing.fem.of the article in agreement with χάριν) 9.
χάριν (acc.sing.fem.of χάρις, cause) 1700.
τὴν (acc.sing.fem.of the article in agreement with δοθεῖσάν) 9
δοθεῖσάν (aor.pass.part.acc.sing.fem.of δίδωμι, adjectival, ascriptive, in agreement with χάριν) 362.
μοι (dat.sing.masc.of ἐγώ, indirect object of δοθεῖσάν) 123.

ὑπό (preposition with the ablative of agent) 117.
τοῦ (abl.sing.masc.of the article in agreement with θεοῦ) 9.
θεοῦ (abl.sing.masc.of θεός, agent) 124.

Translation - "However I have written more boldy to you in part, so as to remind you again because of the gift which was given to me by God."

Comment: ἔγραφα is an epistolary aorist. "This idiom is merely a matter of standpoint. The writer looks at his letter as the recipient will." (Robertson, *Grammar*, 845). It is a case where the writer "puts himself in the place of his reader and describes as past that which is to himself present, but which will be past to his reader" (Burton, *New Testament Moods and Tenses*, 21). The epistolary aorist occurs in Latin, and is of very frequent occurrence in the papyri. "There is therefore no adequate reason for denying its presence in the New Testament" (Robertson, *Ibid.*,846).

Note διὰ τῆς χάριτος τῆς δοθείσης μοι in Romans 12:3 and διὰ τὴν χάριν τὴν δοθεῖσάν μοι in Romans 15:15.

Cf. #'s 70 and 240 ἀπὸ μέρους meaning "in part." Paul is referring to the parts of the epistle in which he has dealt rather more strongly with the Romans than normally he would have done.He is not apologizing, but explaining that his position as Christ's appointed Apostle to the Gentiles gives him the right, and indeed puts him under a heavy obligation to remind the Christians in Rome of their sin of intolerance. He used the same argument in Romans 12:6 to make the same point.

The sentence goes on in

Verse 16 - "That I should be the minister of Jesus Christ to the Gentiles, ministering the gospel of God, that the offering up of the Gentiles might be acceptable, being sanctified by the Holy Ghost."

εἰς τὸ εἶναί με λειτουργὸν Χριστοῦ Ἰησοῦ εἰς τὰ ἔθνη, ἱερουργοῦντα τὸ εὐαγγέλιον τοῦ θεοῦ, ἵνα γένηται ἡ προσφορὰ τῶν ἐθνῶν εὐπρόσδεκτος, ἡγιασμένη ἐν πνεύματι ἁγίῳ.

". . . to be a minister of Christ Jesus to the Gentiles in the priestly service of the gospel of God, so that the offering of the Gentiles may be acceptable, sanctified by the Holy Spirit." . . . RSV

εἰς (preposition with the accusative of purpose) 140.
τὸ (acc.sing.neut.of the article, with the infinitive, purpose) 9.
εἶναί (pres.inf.of εἰμί, acc.sing.neut., purpose) 86.
με (acc.sing.masc.of ἐγώ, general reference) 123.
λειτουργὸν (acc.sing.masc.of λειτουργός, predicate accusative) 4036.
Χριστοῦ (gen.sing.masc.of Χριστός, description) 4.
Ἰησοῦ (gen.sing.masc.of Ἰησοῦς, apposition) 3.
εἰς (preposition with the accusative of extent) 140.
τὰ (acc.pl.neut.of the article in agreement with ἔθνη) 9.
ἔθνη (acc.pl.neut.of ἔθνος, extent) 376.

#4051 ἱερουργοῦντα (pres.act.part.acc.sing.masc.of ἱερουργέω, adverbial, modal).

King James Version

minister - Rom.15:16.

Revised Standard Version

in priestly service - Rom.15:16.

Meaning: A combination of ἱερόν (#346) and ἔργω - "to work." *Cf.* ἱερουργός - "a sacrificing priest." Hence, to perform a priestly service in the temple. In Rom.15:16 followed by τὸ εὐαγγέλιον τοῦ θεοῦ - *i.e.* to preach and teach the gospel.

τὸ (acc.sing.neut.of the article in agreement with εὐαγγέλιον) 9.
εὐαγγέλιον (acc.sing.neut.of εὐαγγέλιον, direct object of ἱερουργοῦντα) 405.
τοῦ (gen.sing.masc.of the article in agreement with θεοῦ) 9.
θεοῦ (gen.sing.masc.of θεός, description) 124.
ἵνα (conjunction with the subjunctive in a final clause) 114.
γένηται (3d.per.sing.aor.subj.of γίνομαι, final clause) 113.
ἡ (nom.sing.fem.of the article in agreement with προσφορὰ) 9.
προσφορὰ (nom.sing.fem.of προσφορά, subject of γένηται) 3560.
τῶν (gen.pl.neut.of the article in agreement with ἐθνῶν) 9.
ἐθνῶν (gen.pl.neut.ofd ἔθνος, description) 376.

#4052 ευπρόσδεκτος (nom.sing.fem.of εὐπρόσδεκτος, predicate adjective).

King James Version

acceptable - Rom.15:16.
accepted - 1 Pet.2:5; Rom.15:31; 2 Cor.6:2; 8:12.

Revised Standard Version

acceptable - Rom.15:16; 1 Pet.2:5; Rom.15:31; 2 Cor.6:2; 8:12.

Meaning: A combination of εὐ plus πρός (#197) plus δέχομαι (#867). *Cf.* προσδέχομαι (#1895). Well received; accepted with favor. With reference to the Gentile saints accepted by God - Rom.15:16; with reference to Hebrew Christians - 1 Pet.2:5; with reference to money - 2 Cor.8:12; gifts of money from Asia accepted by the Jerusalem saints - Rom.15:31. The proper time to be saved - 2 Cor.6:2.

ἡγιασμένη (perf.pass.part.nom.sing.fem.of ἁγιάζω, in agreement with προσφορὰ) 576.
ἐν (preposition with the locative, means) 80.

πνεύματι (loc.sing.neut.of πνεῦμα, means) 83.

ἁγίῳ (loc.sing.neut.of ἅγιος, in agreement with πνεύματι) 84.

Translation - ". . . *to the end that I might be a public administrator of Christ Jesus for the benefit of the Gentiles, doing the priestly work of the gospel of God, in order that the offering of the Gentiles might be accepted, having been directed by the Holy Spirit.*"

Comment: Verses 15 and 16 explain why Paul wrote so boldly, even with a touch of sarcasm (verses 5,13) to the Roman saints about their bigoted intolerance with each other. It was because of the gift that God gave him and the purpose of the gift. God called Paul "to make him an officially recognized public minister (λειτουργόν) of Christ Jesus specifically for the benefit of the Gentiles (εἰς τὰ ἔθνη, accusative of extent). In carrying out this ministry he occupied himself in the work of ministering the gospel of God. Why? The ἵνα γένηται purpose clause tells us. In order that the offering of Christian service (προσφορά) which the Gentile saints, including the Romans could offer, might be so completely in line with the divine will, as to be acceptable. That ἡ προσφορά can indeed be εὐ'-πρόσδεκτος to God is due to the fact that it is specifically ordained and constantly directed by the Holy Spirit. Note the perfect participle in ἡγιασμένη which is joined to ἡ προσφορά, not to Gentiles. Eph.2:10; 1 Cor.6:19,20.

The rewards for a constant yielding to the indwelling Holy Spirit are incalculable. He has marked out the path of Christian activity for every member of Christ's Body. All that we do after salvation that is contrary to His will, exacts an opportunity cost to us as we forego doing what He wanted us to do at the same time and with those same resources. The resources of all are limited - time, talent, physical strength, money, etc. Since I cannot do everything I must choose what to do. I can either obey the Holy Spirit and walk in His προσφορά or go my own way.

Paul was concerned that he fulfill his own ministry since it was God's gift to him and it carried heavy responsibility and the authority that always goes with responsibility (λειτουργός, #4036). Therefore Paul felt justified in using his authority boldly since his goal was the good of the Roman Christians. All God-called and Holy Spirit-directed preachers have this authority and responsibility. We should not hesitate to speak sternly to the saints if the occasion demands it.

Verse 17 - "*I have therefore whereof I may glory through Jesus Christ in those things which pertain to God.*"

ἔχω οὖν (τὴν) καύχησιν ἐν Χριστῷ Ἰησοῦ τὰ πρὸς τὸν θεόν.

"*In Christ Jesus, then, I have reason to be proud of my work for God.*" . . .
RSV

ἔχω (1st.per.sing.pres.act.ind.of ἔχω, aoristic) 82.

οὖν (inferential conjunction) 68.

(τὴν) (acc.sing.fem.of the article in agreement with καύχησιν) 9.

καύχησιν (acc.sing.fem.of καύχησις, direct object of ἔχω) 3877.

ἐν (preposition with the locative, sphere) 80.
Χριστῷ (loc.sing.masc.of Χριστός, sphere) 4.
Ἰησοῦ (loc.sing.masc.of Ἰησοῦς, apposition) 3.
τά (acc.pl.neut.of the article, adverbial accusative) 9.
πρός (preposition with the accusative of extent) 197.
τόν (acc.sing.masc.of the article in agreement with θεόν) 9.
θεόν (acc.sing.masc.of θεός, extent) 124.

Translation - "*So I have occasion to be proud in Christ Jesus of those things which relate closely to God.*"

Comment: *Cf.* 2 Cor.1:12 where Paul expresses a similar sentiment. He is not boasting of his own accomplishments. This feeling of pride, confidence - even boldness, grows out of his relation to Christ Jesus and it extends only to the things that relate to God - τά πρός τόν θεόν. As an especially called and commissioned Apostle to the Gentiles he was under special obligations and was given special authority to speak to the church.

Verse 18 - "*For I will not dare to speak of any of those things which Christ hath not wrought by me, to make the Gentiles obedient, by word and deed.*"

οὐ γάρ τολμήσω τι λαλεῖν ὧν οὐ κατειργάσατο Χριστὸς δι᾽ ἐμοῦ εἰς ὑπακοὴν ἐθνῶν, λόγῳ καὶ ἔργῳ.

"*For I will not venture to speak of anything except what Christ has wrought through me to win obedience from the Gentiles, by word and deed.*" . . . *RSV*

οὐ (negative particle with the indicative) 130.
γάρ (inferential conjunction) 105.
τολμήσω (1st.per.sing.fut.act.ind.of τολμάω, predictive) 1430.
τι (acc.sing.neut.of τις, the indefinite pronoun, direct object of λαλεῖν) 486.
λαλεῖν (pres.act.inf.of λαλέω, complementary) 815.
ὧν (gen.pl.neut.of ὅς, relative pronoun, reference) 65.
οὐ (negative particle with the indicative) 130.
κατειργάσατο (3d.per.sing.aor.mid.ind.of κατεργάζομαι, culminative) 3815.
Χριστὸς (nom.sing.masc.of Χριστός, subject of κατειράσατο) 4.
δι᾽ (preposition with the ablative of agent) 118.
ἐμοῦ (abl.sing.masc.of ἐμός, agent) 1267.
εἰς (preposition with the accusative, purpose) 140.
ὑπακοὴν (acc.sing.fem.of ὑπακοή, purpose) 3785.
ἐθνῶν (gen.pl.neut.of ἔθνος, description) 376.
λόγῳ (loc.sing.masc.of λόγος, sphere) 510.
καὶ (adjunctive conjunction joining nouns) 14.
ἔργῳ (loc.sing.neut.of ἔργον, sphere) 460.

Translation - "*So I will not venture to say anything about those things which Christ did not accomplish through me, in order to win Gentile obedience, in word and deed.*"

Comment: The two negatives in the literal translation *supra* can be translated more smoothly thus: "So I will venture to speak only of that which Christ accomplished through me. . . κ.τ.λ." or "So I will not venture to speak of anything except that which Christ accomplished through me. . . κ.τ.λ."

Since Paul has been boasting of his authority, given to him by Christ, to rebuke the Roman Christians, he now says that he is not taking credit for what Christ did through others, in bringing the Gentiles to salvation - for example the preacher(s) who first carried the gospel to Rome, led the Romans to Christ, immersed them and set the Roman church in order. Christ did much through others beside Paul and he will not mention any of that, but in verse 19 he mentions the work which the Holy Spirit had done through him elsewhere.

Verse 19 - ". . . through mighty signs and wonders, by the power of the Spirit of God: so that from Jerusalem, and round about unto Illyricum, I have fully preached the gospel of Christ."

ἐν δυνάμει σημείων καὶ τεράτων, ἐν δυνάμει πνεύματος. ὥστε με ἀπὸ Ἰερουσαλὴμ καὶ κύκλῳ μέχρι τοῦ Ἰλλυρικοῦ πεπληρωκέναι τὸ εὐαγγέλιον τοῦ Χριστοῦ,

". . . by the power of signs and wonders, by the power of the Holy Spirit, so that from Jerusalem and as far round as Illyricum I have fully preached the gospel of Christ." . . . RSV

ἐν (preposition with the locative, means) 80.
δυνάμει (loc.sing.fem.of δύναμις, means) 687.
σημείων (gen.pl.neut.of σημεῖον, description) 1005.
καὶ (adjunctive conjunction joining nouns) 14.
τεράτων (gen.pl.neut.of τέρας, description) 1500.
ἐν (preposition with the locative, means) 80.
δυνάμει (loc.sing.fem.of δύναμις, means) 687.
πνεύματος (gen.sing.neut.of πνεῦμα, description) 83.
ὥστε (conjunction with the infinitive in a result clause) 752.
με (acc.sing.masc.of ἐγώ, general reference) 123.
ἀπὸ (preposition with the ablative, separation) 70.
Ἰερουσαλὴμ (abl.sing.masc.of Ἰερουσαλήμ, separation) 141.
καὶ (adjunctive conjunction joining prepositional phrases) 14.
κύκλῳ (loc.sing.masc.of κύκλος, place) 2183.
μέχρι (preposition with the genitive of place description) 948.

#4053 Ἰλλυρικοῦ (gen.sing.neut.of Ἰλλυρικόν, place description).

King James Version

Illyricum - Rom.15:19.

Revised Standard Version

Illyricum - Rom.15:19.

Meaning: An area lying between Italy, Germany, Macedonia and Thrace, between the Adriatic Sea and the Danube River. Modern Yugoslavia - Rom.15:19

πεπληρωκέναι (perf.act.inf.of πληρόω, result) 115.
τό (acc.sing.neut.of the article in agreement with εὐαγγέλιον) 9.
εὐαγγέλιον (acc.sing.neut.of εὐαγγέλιον, direct object of πεπληρωκέναι) 405.
τοῦ (gen.sing.masc.of the article in agreement with Χριστοῦ) 9.
Χριστοῦ (gen.sing.masc.of Χριστός, description) 4.

Translation - ". . . by means of the power of the Spirit as manifested in signs and wonders, with the result that, travelling in a circle from Jerusalem unto Yugoslavia, I have told the good news of Christ to all."

Comment: Paul does not mean that the power of the gospel comes from the signs and wonders; rather that the signs and wonders themselves are the works of the Holy Spirit Who is the source of the power. This passage holds no comfort or support for those mob psychologists, who operate in their self-appointed roles as evangelists and mystify to the point of "conversion" the customers who cannot but be impressed with the "signs and wonders" which they see. In Paul's meetings where the signs and wonders which the Holy Spirit produced were in evidence, it seems that Paul always forgot to pass the collection plates, an oversight of which the modern charlatans are never guilty.

Since Paul wished to preach the gospel in territory where it had never been heard (verse20) he had begun at Jerusalem and his travels described a circle, the northwestern periphery of which reached ᵴthe southern regions of Yugoslavia. Paul does not say that he entered Illyricum (Yugoslavia) but that he came "unto" (μέχρι) it.

The infinitive πεπληρωκέναι is a subject infinitive, indicating result after ὥστε. The perfect tense accents the complete fulfillment of his task. He had preached the full gospel to all of the people in all of the regions with results that would endure.

He tells us in verse 20 why he had chosen the unevangelized fields for his ministry.

Verse 20 - "Yea, so have I strived to preach the gospel,not where Christ was named, lest I should build upon another man's foundation."

οὕτως δὲ φιλοτιμούμενον εὐαγγελίζεσθαι οὐχ ὅπου ὠνομάσθη Χριστός, ἵνα μὴ ἐπ' ἀλλότριον θεμέλιον οἰκοδομῶ,

". . . thus making it my ambition to preach the gospel, not where Christ has already been named, lest I build on another man's foundation,. . ." . . . *RSV*

οὕτως (demonstrative adverb) 74.
δὲ (emphatic conjunction) 11.

#4054 φιλοτιμούμενον (pres.mid.part.acc.sing.masc.of φιλοτιμέομαι, adverbial, causal).

King James Version

labour - 2 Cor.5:9.
strive - Rom.15:20.
study - 1 Thess.4:11.

Revised Standard Version

make my ambition - Rom.15:20.
make my aim - 2 Cor.5:9.
aspire - 1 Thess.4:11.

Meaning: Cf. φιλότιμος - "fond of honor" from φίλος (#932) and τιμή (#1619). The person possessed with this characteristic is ambitious to do something. What the aspiration is the context will reveal. Followed by an infinitive - "to preach" in Rom.15:20; with an infinitive and a predicate adjective in 2 Cor.5:9; followed by three infinitives in 1 Thess.4:11.

εὐαγγελίζεσθαι (pres.mid.inf.of εὐαγγελίζω, complementary) 909.
οὐχ (negative particle with the indicative understood) 130.
ὅπου (relative adverb of place) 592.
ὠνομάσθη (3d.per.sing.aor.pass.ind.of ὀνομάζω, culminative) 2115.
Χριστός (nom.sing.masc.of Χριστός, subject of ὠνομάσθη) 4.
ἵνα (conjunction with the subjunctive, negative purpose) 114.
μή (negative particle with the subjunctive, negative purpose) 87.
ἐπ' (preposition with the accusative of extent) 47.
ἀλλότριον (acc.sing.masc.of ἀλλότριος, in agreement with θεμέλιον) 1244.
θελέλιον (acc.sing.masc.of θεμέλιος, extent) 2143.
οἰκοδομῶ (1st.per.sing.pres.act.subj.of οἰκοδομέω, negative purpose) 694.

Translation - "..... *I did this, in fact, because I was ambitious to preach, not where Christ has already been named, lest I build upon another man's foundation.*"

Comment: This long sentence began in verse 18. It has two main parts: Paul does not wish to speak of the ministry of others. God had worked through them to secure Gentile obedience to the gospel. They had come to Rome in the power of the Holy Spirit, Who had honored their ministry with powerful signs and wonders. Under their ministry the Romans had come to Christ and the Roman church had been established. Rather Paul speaks of his own ministry from Jerusalem to Yugoslavia, in which he fulfilled the gospel in many Gentile cities. This he did, because it was his desire to be known as the pioneer gospel missionary who preached where Christ's name had never yet been heard. Only thus could he avoid building upon another's foundation. *Cf.* 2 Tim.2:19; Eph.1:29; 3:15 for ὀνομάζω (#2115).

We are not told who the Apostles and/or other Christian workers were, who preached first in Rome. Paul here approbates their work.

Verse 21 - "But as it is written, To whom he was not spoken of, they shall see: and they that have not heard shall understand."

ἀλλὰ καθὼς γέγραπται, Οἷς οὐκ ἀνηγγέλη περὶ αὐτοῦ ὄψονται, καὶ οἳ οὐκ ἀκηκόασιν συνήσουσιν.

". . . but as it is written, 'They shall see who have never been told of him, and they shall understand who have never heard of him.' " . . . RSV

ἀλλὰ (adversative conjunction) 342.
καθὼς (compound particle in a comparative clause) 1348.
γέγραπται (3d.per.sing.perf.pass.ind.of γράφω, intensive) 156.
Οἷς (dat.pl.masc.of ὅς, demonstrative pronoun, personal advantage) 65.
οὐκ (negative particle with the indicative) 130.
ἀνηγγέλη (3d.per.sing.2d.aor.pass.ind.of ἀναγγέλλω, constative) 2012.
περὶ (preposition with the genitive of reference) 173.
αὐτοῦ (gen.sing.masc.of αὐτός, reference) 16.
ὄψονται (3d.per.pl.fut.act.ind.of ὁράω, predictive) 144a.
καὶ (continuative conjunction) 14.
οἱ (nom.pl.masc.of the article in agreement with ἀκηκόασιν) 9.
οὐκ (negative particle with the indicative) 130.
ἀκηκόασιν (3d.per.pl.2d.perf.Attic of ἀκούω) 148.
συνήσουσιν (3d.per.pl.fut.act.ind.of συνίημι, predictive) 1039.

Translation - "On the contrary, just as it is written, 'Those to whom no announcement about Him was made shall see, and those having never heard shall understand.' "

Comment: The quotation is from Isaiah 52:15. Note οὐκ here with a relative clause. Other instances are found in Mt.12:2; Mk.2:24; John 6:64; Lk.14:27; John 4:22; Gal.3:10; Rev.9:4. Paul's ministry fulfilled Isaiah's prophecy.

Paul's Plan to Visit Rome

(Romans 15:22-33)

Verse 22 - "For which cause also I have been much hindered from coming to you."

Διὸ καὶ ἐνεκοπτόμην τὰ πολλὰ τοῦ ἐλθεῖν πρὸς ὑμᾶς.

"This is the reason why I have so often been hindered from coming to you." . . .
RSV

Διὸ (conjunction introducing a result clause) 1622.
καὶ (continuative conjunction) 14.
ἐνεκοπτόμην (1st.per.sing.imp.pass.ind.of ἐγκόπτω, iterative) 3617.

τὰ (acc.pl.neut.of the article in agreement with πολλὰ) 9.
πολλὰ (acc.pl.neut.of πολύς, time extent) 228.
τοῦ (abl.sing.neut.of the article in agreement with ἐλθεῖν) 9.
ἐλθεῖν (aor.inf.of ἔρχομαι, object infinitive, abl.sing.neut., after a verb of hindering) 146.
πρὸς (preposition with the accusative of extent) 197.
ὑμᾶς (acc.pl.masc.of σύ, extent) 104.

Translation - *"It is because of this that I have been prevented on many occasions from coming to you."*

Comment: The ablative object infinitive after a verb of hindering is used in its substantival aspect. "My coming to you was prevented (ablative) many times." τὰ πολλὰ is adverbial, an accusative of time extent. Paul's reason for not coming to Rome sooner was his feeling that it was better for him to visit unevangelized fields rather than a field where the gospel had already been preached. However, now he adds that the situation has changed.

Verse 23 - *"But now having no more place in these parts, and having a great desire these many years to come unto you, . ."*

νυνὶ δὲ μηκέτι τόπον ἔχων ἐν τοῖς κλίμασι τούτοις, ἐπιποθίαν δὲ ἔχων τοῦ ἐλθεῖν πρὸς ὑμᾶς ἀπὸ πολλῶν ἐτῶν,

"But now since I no longer have any room for work in these regions, and since I have longed for many years to come to you,. . ." . . . RSV

νυνὶ (temporal adverb) 1497.
δὲ (adversative conjunction) 11.
μηκέτι (negative compound temporal adverb) 1368.
τόπον (acc.sing.masc.of τόπος, direct object of ἔχων) 1019.
ἔχων (pres.act.part.nom.sing.masc.of ἔχω, adverbial, causal) 82.
ἐν (preposition with the locative of place) 80.
τοῖς (loc.pl.neut.of the article in agreement with κλίμασι) 9.

#4055 κλίμασι (loc.pl.neut.of κλίμα, place).

King James Version

part - Rom.15:23.
region - 2 Cor.11:10; Gal.1:21.

Revised Standard Version

region - Rom.15:23; 2 Cor.11:10; Gal.1:21.

Meaning: Cf. κλίνω (#746). Hence, a slope; an area of the earth's surface between the equator and the pole. In the New Testament, a tract of land; a region. Asia Minor - Rom.15:23; Achaia -2 Cor.11:10; Syria and Cilicia - Gal.1:21.

τούτοις (loc.pl.neut.of οὗτος, in agreement with κλίμασι) 93.

#4056 ἐπιποθίαν (acc.sing.fem.of ἐπιποθία, direct object of ἔχων).

King James Version

great desire - Rom.15:23.

Revised Standard Version

have longed - Rom.15:23.

Meaning: Cf. ἐπιποθέω (#3789); ἐπιπόθησις (#4328); ἐπιπόθητος (#4579). Intense longing; strong desire. Followed by an infinitive in the genitive - Rom.15:23.

δέ (adjunctive conjunction joining participles) 11.

ἔχων (pres.act.part.nom.sing.masc.of ἔχω, adverbial, causal) 82.

τοῦ (gen.sing.neut.of the article in agreement with ἐλθεῖν) 9.

ἐλθεῖν (aor.inf.of ἔρχομαι, adnominal) 146.

πρός (preposition with the accusative of extent) 197.

ὑμᾶς (acc.pl.masc.of σύ, extent) 104.

ἀπό (preposition with the ablative of time separation) 70.

πολλῶν (abl.pl.neut.of πολύς, in agreement with ἐτῶν) 228.

ἐτῶν (abl.pl.neut.of ἔτος, time separation) 821.

Translation - "But now, since I have no other place in these areas and also having had a great desire to come to you for many years. . . "

Comment: Paul's great desire to go to Rome had been thwarted many times in the past by his greater desire to evangelize pioneer fields. But now (adversative δέ) two reasons are advanced why he can come to Rome: (1) He had no other open doors in the area in Macedonia, Achaia or other parts of Asia Minor, and (2) the intense urge to visit Rome, which he had felt for many years was still with him. τοῦ ἐλθεῖν is adnominal, in the genitive case as it names the nature of ἐπιποθίαν. A variant reading has ἰκαρῶν instead of πολλῶν.

Verse 24 - "Whensoever I take my journey into Spain I will come to you: for I trust to see you in my journey, and to be brought on my way thitherward by you, if first I be somewhat filled with your company."

ὡς ἄν πορεύωμαι εἰς τὴν Σπανίαν, ἐλπίζω γὰρ διαπορευόμενος θεάσασθαι ὑμᾶς καὶ ὑφ' ὑμῶν προπεμφθῆναι ἐκεῖ ἐὰν ὑμῶν πρῶτον ἀπὸ μέρους ἐμπλησθῶ —

"I hope to see you in passing as I go to Spain, and to be sped on my journey there by you, once I have enjoyed your company for a little." . . . RSV

ὡς (particle with the subjunctive in an indefinite temporal clause) 128.

ἄν (contingent particle with the subjunctive in an indefinite temporal clause) 205.

πορεύωμαι (1st.per.sing.pres.mid.subj.of πορεύομαι, indefinite temporal clause) 170.

εἰς (preposition with the accusative of extent) 140.

τὴν (acc.sing.fem.of the article in agreement with Σπανίαν) 9.

#4057 Σπανίαν (acc.sing.fem.of Σπανία, extent).

King James Version

Spain - Rom.15:24,28.

Revised Standard Version

Spain - Rom.15:24,28.

Meaning: In Paul's day the name applied to all of the land territory south of the Pyrenees Mountains , including all of present day Portugal as well. The classic Greek spelling is ἰσπανία, which was Phonecian or Latin for Ἰβηρία. Paul hoped to visit Spain - Rom.15:24,28. Whether he did or not is not certainly known. The assumption is that he did not.

ἐλπίζω (1st.per.sing.pres.act.ind.of ἐλπίζω, aoristic) 991.

γὰρ (inferential conjunction) 105.

διαπορευόμενος (pres.mid.part.nom.sing.masc.of διαπορεύομαι, adverbial, temporal) 2101.

θεάσασθαι (1st.aor.inf.of θεάομαι, complementary) 556.

ὑμᾶς (acc.pl.masc.of σύ, direct object of θεάσασθαι) 104.

καὶ (adjunctive conjunction joining infinitives) 14.

ὑφ' (preposition with the ablative of agent) 117.

ὑμῶν (abl.pl.masc.of σύ, agent) 104.

προπεμφθῆναι (aor.pass.inf.of προπέμπω, complementary) 3335.

ἐκεῖ (local adverb) 204.

ἐὰν (conditional particle in a third-class condition) 363.

ὑμῶν (abl.pl.masc.of σύ, source) 104.

πρῶτον (acc.sing.neut.of πρῶτος, adverbial) 487.

ἀπὸ (preposition with the ablative, partitive) 70

μέρους (abl.sing.neut.of μέρος, partitive) 240.

ἐμπλησθῶ (1st.per.sing.aor.pass.subj.of ἐμπίπλημι, third-class condition) 1833.

Translation - "If and when I come into Spain, then, as I pass through I hope to see you and with your help be sent on, if first, for a little while I may be blessed with your fellowship."

Comment:ὡς is the temporal particle, most frequently with the indicative in a definite temporal clause, but here and in 1 Cor.11:34; Phil.2:23 with ἄν and the subjunctive. Paul's plans to go to Spain were too definite for the optative and too uncertain for the indicative. The translation, "whenever" or "when if ever" carries too much doubt. "When" implies too much certainty. "If and when" is about right. διαπορευόμενος is temporal. "As I am passings through Rome, enroute to Spain, if and when I go to Spain, I hope to see you . . . " He also hoped that after he had spent a little time with them (ἀπὸ μέρους) they might provide some financial assistance for his further travels in Spain, along with the spiritual blessings which their fellowship would provide. As later history reveals when Paul got to Rome he was Nero's prisoner and had no freedom of choice to leave. The infinitives are complementary, the objects of ἐλπίζω.

Verse 25 - *"But now I go unto Jerusalem to minister unto the saints."*

νυνὶ δὲ πορεύομαι εἰς Ἱερουσαλὴμ διακονῶν τοῖς ἁγίοις.

"At present, however, I am going to Jerusalem with aid for the saints." . . .
RSV

νυνὶ (temporal conjunction) 1497.
δὲ (adversative conjunction) 11.
πορεύομαι (1st.per.sing.pres.mid.ind.of πορεύομαι, futuristic) 170.
εἰς (preposition with the accusative of extent) 140.
Ἱερουσαλήμ (acc.sing.masc.of Ἱερουσαλήμ, extent) 141.
διακονῶν (pres.act.part.nom.sing.masc.of διακονέω, adverbial, telic) 367.
τοῖς (dat.pl.masc.of the article in agreement with ἁγίοις) 9.
ἁγίοις (dat.pl.masc.of ἅγιος, personal advantage) 84.

Translation - *"But now I will soon go to Jerusalem to take help to the saints."*

Comment: δὲ is adversative as Paul turns from a discussion of plans for the more distant future that involve Rome and Spain to speak of his more immediate plans. He was about to leave Corinth to go to Jerusalem for the purpose of taking money given by the Gentile Christians in Macedonia and Greece to the saints in Jerusalem who were suffering from a food shortage. Note the futuristic present in the telic participle διακονῶν. *Cf.* Acts 24:17.

In verse 26 Paul tells us where he got the money which he will soon take to Jerusalem.

Verse 26 - *"For it hath pleased them of Macedonia and Achaia to make a certain contribution for the poor saints which are at Jerusalem."*

ηὐδόκησαν γὰρ Μακεδονία καὶ Ἀχαΐα κοινωνίαν τινὰ ποιήσασθαι εἰς τοὺς πτωχοὺς τῶν ἁγίων τῶν ἐν Ἱερουσαλήμ.

"For Macedonia and Achaia have been pleased to make some contribution for the poor among the saints at Jerusalem." . . . *RSV*

ηὐδόκησαν (3d.per.pl.aor.act.ind.of εὐδοκέω, culminative) 328.
γὰρ (causal conjunction) 105.
Μακεδονία (nom.pl.fem.of Μακεδονία, subject of ηὐδόκησαν) 3360.
καὶ (adjunctive conjunction joining nouns) 14.
Ἀχαΐα (nom.pl.fem.of Ἀχαΐα, subject of ηὐδόκησαν) 3443.
κοινωνίαν (acc.sing.fem.of κοινωνία, general reference) 3001.
τινὰ (acc.sing.fem.of τις, indefinite pronoun, in agreement with κοινωνίαν) 486.

ποιήσασθαι (aor.pass.inf.of ποιέω, object of ηὐδόκησαν) 123.
εἰς (preposition with the accusative, extent) 140.
τοὺς (acc.pl.masc.of the article in agreement with πρωχοὺς) 9.
πτωχοὺς (acc.pl.masc.of πτωχός, extent) 423.
τῶν (gen.pl.masc.of the article in agreement with ἁγίων) 9.
ἁγίων (gen.pl.masc.of ἅγιος, partitive) 84.
τῶν (gen.pl.masc.of the article in agreement with ἁγίων) 9.
ἐν (preposition with the locative, place) 80.
Ἰερουσαλήμ (loc.sing.neut.of Ἰερουσαλήμ, place) 141.

Translation - "Because the Macedonians and Achaians have thought it proper that a certain contribution be made for the poor among the saints in Jerusalem."

Comment: Verse 26 explains the causal participle διακονῶν in verse 25. What sort of ministry? The Gentile Christians in Macedonia (Philippi, Thessalonica, Berea) and Greece (Corinth) thought well of the idea (εὐδοκέω #328) that a "certain token of commonality be made." What better way to promote fellowship than to give to a needy Christian money which could well be used by oneself? The κοινωνία idea is that "we are all in this thing together" - an idea that John Donne expressed very well when he wrote

> *Any man's death diminishes me, because I am involved in Mankind;*
> *And therefore never send to know for whom the bell tolls;*
> *It tolls for thee.*
>
> John Donne, *Devotions*

Donne's concept can be applied to the entire human race, both those who are saved and those who are not, for we share this limited planet as our temporary home and are equally dependent upon it for life, but it applies in a special way to the children of God. (Eph.4:28).

εἰς τοὺς πτωχούς is either an accusative of extent in a predicate usage or purpose. Both ideas are found with εἰς and the accusative. If we take it as purpose we supply "for the relief of." Note how carefully Paul's Greek tells us for whom the money had been given. Not all of the Christians in Jerusalem were poor, as the partitive genitive τῶν ἁγίων indicates. He also limits the charity for those in Jerusalem. This money had been collected locally and entrusted to Paul who was now about to deliver it to Jerusalem.

Verse 27 - "It hath pleased them verily; and their debtors they are   for if the Gentiles have been made partakers of their spiritual things their duty is also to minister unto them in carnal things."

ηὐδόκησαν γάρ, καὶ ὀφειλέται εἰσὶν αὐτῶν. εἰ γὰρ τοῖς πνευματικοῖς αὐτῶν ἐκοινώνησαν τὰ ἔθνη, ὀφείλουσιν καὶ ἐν τοῖς σαρκικοῖς λειτουργῆσαι αὐτοῖς.

"they were pleased to do it , and indeed they are in debt to them, for if the Gentiles have come to share in their spiritual blessings, they ought also to be of service to them in material blessings." . . . RSV

ηὐδόκησαν (3d.per.pl.aor.act.ind.of εὐδοκέω, culminative) 328.

γάρ (causal conjunction) 105.

καὶ (emphatic conjunction) 14.

ὀφειλέται (nom.pl.masc.of ὀφειλέτης, predicate nominative) 581.

εἰσὶν (3d.per.pl.pres.ind.of εἰμί, static) 86.

αὐτῶν (gen.pl.masc.of αὐτός, relationship) 16.

εἰ (conditional particle in a first-class condition) 337.

γάρ (causal condition) 105.

τοῖς (dat.pl.neut.of the article in agreement with πνευματικοῖς) 9.

πνευματικοῖς (dat.pl.neut.of πνευματικός, reference) 3791.

αὐτῶν (gen.pl.masc.of αὐτός, possession) 16.

ἐκοινώνησαν (3d.per.pl.aor.act.ind.of κοινωνέω, culminative) 4026.

τὰ (nom.pl.neut.of the article in agreement with ἔθνη) 9.

ἔθνη (nom.pl.neut.of ἔθνος, subject of ἐκοινώνησαν) 376.

ὀφείλουσιν (3d.per.pl.pres.act.ind.of ὀφείλω, static) 1277.

ἐν (preposition with the locative of sphere) 80.

τοῖς (loc.pl.neut.of the article in agreement with σαρκικοῖς) 9.

#4058 σαρκικοῖς (loc.pl.neut.of σαρκικός, sphere).

King James Version

carnal - 1 Cor.3:3,3,4; 2 Cor.10:4.
fleshly - 2 Cor.1:12; 1 Pet.2:11.
carnal things - Rom.15:27; 1 Cor.9:11.

Revised Standard Version

material blessings - Rom.15:27.
material benefits - 1 Cor.9:11.
men of the flesh - 1 Cor.3:1.
of the flesh - 1 Cor.3:3a,b; 1 Pet.2:11.
worldly - 2 Cor.10:4.
earthly - 2 Cor.1:12.

Meaning: Cf. σάρξ (#1202), σάρκινος (#3924). That which pertains to the flesh; of human origin; having only human power and wisdom. Opposed to πνευματικός (#3791). In an ethical sense, dominated by sinful, fleshly desire. πνευματικός does not mean "immaterial" (Gal.6:1), but "dominated by the Spirit." Thus σαρκικός means "dominated by the flesh." With reference to ethical attitudes - 1 Cor.3:3,3; to ethical actions - 1 Pet.2:11; of human weaponry as inferior to divine - 2 Cor.10:4; of human wisdom as inferior to divine - 2 Cor.1:12; of material values, such as money, as opposed to spiritual benefits flowing from the gospel - Rom.15:27; 1 Cor.9:11.

λειτουργῆσαι (aor.act.inf.of λειτουργέω, complementary) 3272.

αὐτοῖς (dat.pl.masc.of αὐτός, indirect object of λειτουργῆσαι) 16.

Translation - *"Indeed, they were happy to do it, because they are their debtors; for since the Gentiles shared their spiritual blessings they ought also to serve them with material blessings."*

Comment: γὰρ καὶ in a causal and emphatic sense fits the context beautifully here. Paul wished to emphasize that the givers were not importuned with undue pressure. When the Christians in Macedonia and Greece were told of the financial plight of the Hebrew Christians in Palestine, due to the famine (Acts 11:28) they were happy to share their money with those brethren who had shared with them the far greater spiritual blessings of the gospel of Christ.

Here is Christian fellowship across the miles, a fact that means that membership in the Body of Christ is not subject to time or space. The financial blessings served a good purpose. The spiritual blessings created the constructive associations within the Body of Christ that made the share-the-wealth program possible.

Verse 28 - *"When therefore I have performed this, and have sealed to them this fruit, I will come by you into Spain."*

τοῦτο οὖν ἐπιτελέσας, καὶ σφραγισάμενος αὐτοῖς τὸν καρπὸν τοῦτον, ἀπελεύσομαι δι' ὑμῶν εἰς Σπανίαν.

"When therefore I have completed this, and have delivered to them what has been raised, I shall go on by way of you to Spain;" . . . RSV

τοῦτο (acc.sing.neut.of οὗτος, direct object of ἐπιτελέσας) 93.

οὖν (inferential conjunction) 68.

#4059 ἐπιτελέσας (aor.act.part.nom.sing.masc.of ἐπιτελέω, adverbial, temporal).

King James Version

accomplish - Heb.9:6; 1 Pet.5:9.
finish - 2 Cor.8:6.
make - Heb.8:5.
make perfect - Gal.3:3.
perfect - 2 Cor.7:1.
perform - Rom.15:28; 2 Cor.8:11; Phil.1:6.
performance - 2 Cor.8:11.

Revised Standard Version

performing - Heb.9:6.
required - 1 Pet.5:9.
complete - 2 Cor.8:6; Rom.15:28; 2 Cor.8:11.
completing - 2 Cor.8:11.
erect - Heb.8:5.
end - Gal.3:3.
perfect - 2 Cor.7:1.
bring to completion - Phil.1:6.

Meaning: A combination of ἐπί (#47) and τελέω (#704). To bring to an end; complete; execute; accomplish; finish. Followed by τοῦτο in Rom.15:28, of the task of delivering money to Jerusalem; with τὰς λατρείας in Hebrews 9:6; to endure affliction to the end - 1 Pet.5:9; to build the Mosaic tabernacle - Heb.8:5; to finish collecting money - 2 Cor.8:6,11,11; to perfect holiness - 2 Cor.7:1; to complete the salvation experience - Gal.3:3; with reference to the work of evangelism in Philippi - Phil.1:6.

καί (adjunctive conjunction joining participles) 14.
σφραγισάμενος (aor.mid.part.nom.sing.masc.of σφραγίζω, adverbial, temporal) 1686.
αὐτοῖς (dat.pl.masc.of αὐτός, ind.object of σφραγισάμενος) 16.
τόν (acc.sing.masc.of the article in agreement with καρπόν) 9.
καρπόν (acc.sing.masc.of καρπός, direct object of σφραγισάμενος) 284.
τοῦτο (acc.sing.masc.of οὗτος, in agreement with καρπόν) 93.
ἀπελεύσομαι (1st.per.sing.fut.ind.of ἀπέρχομαι, predictive) 239.
δι (preposition with the genitive of place description) 118.
ὑμῶν (gen.pl.masc.of σύ, place description) 104.
εἰς (preposition with the accusative of extent) 140.
Σπανίαν (acc.sing.fem.of Σπανία, extent) 4057.

Translation - "So when I have completed this mission and have delivered the money to them I will come through Rome on my way to Spain."

Comment: The two aorist participles are temporal, indicating action prior to that of the main verb ἀπελεύσομαι. Before he visits Rome on his way to Spain, he must return to Jerusalem and deliver the money safely into the hands of those for whom it has been designated. The participle σφραγισάμενος may carry the idea of receiving from the proper persons in Jerusalem a certified receipt that the money was in fact delivered. Thus Paul takes care to follow his own advice (Rom.12:17b). Then he would be free to go to Spain. δι' ὑμῶν is an excellent example of διά in its basic meaning of "in between two."

Verse 29 - "And I am sure that when I come unto you, I shall come in the fulness of the blessing of the gospel of Christ."

οἶδα δὲ ὅτι ἐρχόμενος πρὸς ὑμᾶς ἐν πληαρώματι εὐλογίας Χριστοῦ ἐλεύσομαι.

"And I know that when I come to you I shall come in the fulness of the blessing of Christ." . . . RSV

οἶδα (1st.per.sing.perf.act.ind.of ὁράω, intensive) 144b.
δέ (continuative conjunction) 11.
ὅτι (conjunction introducing an object clause in indirect discourse) 211.
ἐρχόμενος (pres.part.nom.sing.masc.of ἔρχομαι, adverbial, temporal) 146.
πρός (preposition with the accusative of extent) 197.
ὑμᾶς (acc.pl.masc.of σύ, extent) 104.

ἐν (preposition with the locative, accompanying circumstance) 80.

πληρώματι (loc.sing.neut.of πλήρωμα, accompanying circumstance) 805.

#4060 εὐλογίας (gen.sing.fem.of εὐλογία, description).

King James Version

blessing - Rom.15:29; 1 Cor.10:16; Gal.3:14; Eph.1:3; Heb.6:7; 12:17;
Jam.3:10; 1 Pet.3:9; Rev.5:12,12; 7:12.
bounty - 2 Cor.9:5.
fair speeches - Rom.16:18.
matter of bounty - 2 Cor.9:5.
bountifully - 2 Cor.9:6,6.

Revised Standard Version

blessing - Rom.15:2 9; 1 Cor.10:16; Gal.3:14; Eph.1:3; Heb.6:7; 12:17;
Jam.3:10; 1 Pet.3:9; Rev.5:12,13; 7:12
gift - 2 Cor.9:5a.
willing gift - 2 Cor.9:5b.
fair and flattering words - Rom.16:18.
bountifully - 2 Cor.9:6,6.

Meaning: A combination of εὐ and λόγος (#510). *Cf.* εὐλογέω (#1120);
εὐλογητός (#1849). A song of praise or adulation sung to God - Rev.5:12,13;
7:12; in an evil sense, a beautifully polished but insincere speech - Rom.16:18; the
invocation of blessing upon someone - Heb.12:17; Jam.3:10. A material or
spiritual benefit - some concrete object or act of utility to the recipient - 1 Pet.3:9.
With reference to Paul's blessing in coming to Rome - Rom.15:29; of salvation
and kindred blessings - Eph.1:3; the salvation promised to Abraham is given to
the Gentiles - Gal.3:14; in the analogy of the fruitful field - Heb.6:7; financial
blessing - 2 Cor.9:5,6,6,. The communion cup of blessing - 1 Cor.10:16.

Χριστοῦ (gen.sing.masc.of Χριστός, description) 4.
ἐλεύσομαι (1st.per.sing.fut.mid.ind.of ἔρχομαι, predictive) 146.

*Translation - "And I know that when I come to you I will come with the fulness
of Christ's blessing."*

Comment: Variant readings after εὐλογίας have τοῦ εὐαγγελίου τοῦ Χριστοῦ
and τῆς διδαχῆς τοῦ Χριστοῦ. ἐρχόμενος is temporal. "When I come" (or "as I
come") "I will be coming to you with Christ's fullest blessing."

How could Paul be so certain? Because he believed that his policy of having no
plans except Christ's plans for him always resulted in the Holy Spirit's guidance
for him into Christ's perfect will. If the Christian goes only where, says and does
only what and agrees only to that which the Holy Spirit has in mind for him, he
can be certain that he will always have the fulness of Christ's blessing. Paul came
to Rome, (though, as far as we know, not to Spain) and enjoyed Christ's
blessings to the full (Acts 28:30,21; 2 Tim.4:6-8).

Now he asks the Roman saints to join him in a prayer with four specific requests.

Verse 30 - "Now I beseech you, brethren, for the Lord Jesus Christ's sake, and for the love of the Spirit, that ye strive together with me in your prayers to God for me."

Παρακαλῶ δὲ ὑμᾶς (,ἀδελφοί,) διὰ τοῦ κυρίου Ἰησοῦ Χριστοῦ καὶ διὰ τῆς ἀγάπης τοῦ πνεύματος, συναγωνίσασθαί μοι ἐν ταῖς προσευχαῖς ὑπὲρ ἐμοῦ πρὸς τὸν θεόν.

"I appeal to you, brethren, by our Lord Jesus Christ and by the love of the Spirit to strive together with me in your prayers to God on my behalf," . . . RSV

Παρακαλῶ (1st.per.sing.pres.act.ind.of παρακαλέω, aoristic) 230.
δὲ (explanatory conjunction) 11.
ὑμᾶς (acc.pl.masc.of σύ, direct object of Παρακαλῶ) 104.
(ἀδελφοί) (voc.pl.masc.of ἀδελφός, address) 15.
διὰ (preposition with the ablative of agent) 118.
τοῦ (abl.sing.masc.of the article in agreement with κυρίου) 9.
κυρίου (abl.sing.masc.of κύριος, agent) 97.
ἡμῶν (gen.pl.masc.of ἐγώ, relationship) 123.
Ἰησοῦ (abl.sing.masc.of Ἰησοῦς, apposition) 3.
Χριστοῦ (abl.sing.masc.of Χριστός, apposition) 4.
καὶ (adjunctive conjunction joining prepositional phrases) 14.
διὰ (preposition with the ablative of means) 118.
τῆς (abl.sing.fem.of the article in agreement with ἀγάπης) 9.
ἀγάπης (abl.sing.fem.of ἀγάπη, means) 1490.
τοῦ (gen.sing.neut.of the article in agreement with πνεύματος) 9.
πνεύματος (gen.sing.neut.of πνεῦμα, description) 83.

#4061 συναγωνίσασθαί (1st.aor.inf.of συναγωνίζομαι, object of παρακαλῶ).

King James Version

strive together with - Rom.15:30.

Revised Standard Version

strive together with - Rom.15:30.

Meaning: A combination of σύν (#1542) and ἀγωνίζομαι - "to meet in a contest; to witness a struggle." Hence, in late Greek "to struggle." With σύν it means "to struggle together as partners. *Cf.* ἀγών (#4549). With the personal pronoun in a direct reflexive use and ἐν ταῖς προσευχαῖς - Rom.15:30.

μοι (instru.sing.masc.of ἐγώ, association after σύν in composition) 123.
ἐν (preposition with the locative of sphere) 80.
ταῖς (loc.pl.fem.of the article in agreement with προσευχαῖς) 9.

προσευχαῖς (loc.pl.fem.of προσευχή, sphere) 1238.
ὑπὲρ (preposition with the ablative, "in behalf of") 545.
ἐμοῦ (abl.sing.masc.of ἐμός, "in behalf of") 1267.
πρὸς (preposition with the accusative of extent) 197.
τὸν (acc.sing.masc.of the article in agreement with θεόν) 9.
θεόν (acc.sing.masc.of θεός, extent) 124.

Translation - *"Now I ask for your help, brethren, through our Lord Jesus Christ and by the love of the Spirit that you struggle together with me in your prayers to God in my behalf."*

Comment: δὲ is explanatory. διὰ with the ablative is agency when persons are involved; means when things are involved. It is essentially the same idea. The infinitive is the object of παρακαλῶ. This was Paul's request - that they join him in prayer. The four specific requests are found in the two ἵνα clauses of verse 31,32.

For Paul prayer was a struggle. (*Cf.*#4061). For many Christians, unfortunately it is a perfunctory ceremony.

Verse 31 - *"That I may be delivered from them that do not believe in Judaea; and that my service which I have from Jerusalem may be accepted of the saints."*

ἵνα ῥυσθῶ ἀπὸ τῶν ἀπειθούντων ἐν τῇ Ἰουδαίᾳ καὶ ἡ διακονία μου ἡ εἰς Ἱερουσαλὴμ εὐπρόσδεκτος τοῖς ἁγίοις γένηται,

"... that I may be delivered from the unbelievers in Judea, and that my service for Jerusalem may be acceptable to the saints, ..." ... *RSV*

ἵνα (conjunction with the subjunctive in a final clause) 114.
ῥυσθῶ (1st.per.sing.1st.aor.pass.subj.of ῥύομαι, purpose) 584.
ἀπὸ (preposition with the ablative of separation) 70.
τῶν (abl.pl.masc.of the article in agreement with ἀπειθούντων) 9.
ἀπειθούντων (pres.act.part.abl.pl.masc.of ἀπειθέω, substantival, separation) 1996.
ἐν (preposition with the locative of place) 80.
τῇ (loc.sing.fem.of the article in agreement with Ἰουδαίᾳ) 9.
Ἰουδαίᾳ (loc.sing.fem.of Ἰουδαίας, place) 134.
καὶ (adjunctive conjunction joining verbs) 14.
ἡ (nom.sing.fem.of the article in agreement with διακονία) 9.
διακονία (nom.sing.fem.of διακονία, subject of γένηται) 2442.
μου (gen.sing.masc.of ἐγώ, possession) 123.
ἡ (nom.sing.fem.of the article in agreement with διακονία) 9.
εἰς (preposition with the accusative, static use, like a locative) 140.
Ἱερουσαλὴμ (acc.sing.neut.of Ἱερουσαλήμ place) 141.
εὐπρόσδεκτος (nom.sing.masc.of εὐπρόσδεκτος, predicate adjective) 4052.
τοῖς (dat.pl.masc.of the article in agreement with ἁγίοις) 9.
ἁγίοις (dat.pl.masc.of ἅγιος, personal advantage) 84.
γένηται (3d.per.sing.aor.subj.of γίνομαι, purpose) 113.

Translation - "That I may be delivered from the unbelievers in Judea and that my offering in Jerusalem may be acceptable to the saints."

Comment: The first two prayer requests (verse 30) are found in the double ἵνα clause of purpose. Note the adjunctive καὶ joining the two subjunctives, each of which depends upon ἵνα.

Paul feared the persecution from the Jews in Jerusalem (Acts 20:23: 21:4) - a fear that proved to be justified. But though he was arrested, indicted and tried, he was not convicted, but only because he appealed to Nero. Thus his prayer for deliverance from the Jews in Jerusalem was answered. Otherwise they would have killed him, with or without the approval of the Roman court. The other request, that the saints in Jerusalem would receive him and the gifts which he brought was answered abundantly (Acts 21:17-19).

If we take διακονία (#2442) to mean a mission or journey, then the prepositional phrase εἰς Ἱερουσαλήμ is translated, "my mission to Jerusalem" in reference to the trip. If we take it to mean the money the phrase is used in the locative sense, which was the original static use of εἰς and the accusative of place where. The ideas are not in conflict. What Paul wanted was a safe journey to Jerusalem, a favorable reception from the Christians there, the safe delivery of the money to the proper authorities who would then dispense it where needed, and protection from the Jews who were lying in wait to kill him.

The other two requests are found in

Verse 32 - "That I may come unto you with joy by the will of God and may with you be refreshed."

ἵνα ἐν χαρᾷ ἐλθὼν πρὸς ὑμᾶς διὰ θελήματος θεοῦ συναναπαύσωμαι ὑμῖν.

". . . so that by God's will I may come to you with joy and be refreshed in your company." . . . RSV

ἵνα (conjunction with the subjunctive in a final clause) 114.
ἐν (preposition with the locative, accompanying circumstance) 80.
χαρᾷ (loc.sing.fem.of χαρά, accompanying circumstance) 183.
ἐλθὼν (aor.part.nom.sing.masc.of ἔρχομαι, adverbial, temporal) 146.
πρὸς (preposition with the accusative of extent) 197.
ὑμᾶς (acc.pl.masc.of σύ, extent) 104.
διὰ (preposition with the ablative of means) 118.
θελήματος (abl.sing.neut.of θέλημα, means) 577.
θεοῦ (gen.sing.masc.of θεός, description) 124.

#4062 συναναπαύσωμαι (1st.per.sing.aor.mid.subj.of συναναπαύω, purpose).

King James Version

be refreshed - Rom.15:32.

Revised Standard Version

be refreshed - Rom.15:32.

Meaning: A combination of σύν (#1542), ἀνά (#1059) and παύω (#2044). Hence, literally, "to rest" (παύω) "up" (ἀνά) "together" (σύν). To be refreshed, physically, mentally and spiritually, as Paul visits the Roman Christians - Rom.15:32.

ὑμῖν (instru.pl.masc.of σύ, association) 104.

Translation - "That when I have come to you by the will of God I might have a joyous vacation with you."

Comment: The last two prayer requests are included in the ἵνα clause. Paul was praying that God would permit him to visit Rome and that he might find the time while there to have a joyous vacation in his association with his new friends. We are to take the verb συναναπαύσωμαι in its fullest sense - a time of physical, mental and spiritual rest, recreation and rehabilitation.

The answer to Paul's prayers for rescue from the Jews in Jerusalem and for his return to Rome are connected. God provided for his trip to Rome by the circumstances that rescued him from the Jews. He came to Rome, to be sure, as Nero's prisoner. Only thus did God save him from death in Jerusalem. The trip from Caesarea to Rome was hazardous enough (Acts 27-28). He needed time to recuperate, when he arrived and God provided for him two full years of fellowship with the Roman Christians and fruitful preaching.

Verse 33 - "Now the God of peace be with you all. Amen."

ὁ δὲ θεὸς τῆς εἰρήνης μετὰ πάντων ὑμῶν. ἀμήν.

"The God of peace be with you all. Amen." . . . RSV

ὁ (nom.sing.masc.of the article in agreement with θεὸς) 9.
δὲ (explanatory conjunction) 11.
θεὸς (nom.sing.masc.of θεός, subject of εἴη, understood) 124.
τῆς (gen.sing.fem.of the article in agreement with εἰρήνης) 9.
εἰρήνης (gen.sing.fem.of εἰρήνη, description) 865.
μετὰ (preposition with the genitive of association) 50.
πάντων (gen.pl.masc.of πᾶς, in agreement with ὑμῶν) 67.
ὑμῶν (gen.pl.masc.of σύ, association) 104.
ἀμήν (explicative) 466.

Translation - "Now the God of peace be with all of you. Amen."

Comment: We supply the optative εἴη with the voluntative construction. A variant reading, p46 omits ἀμήν and appends Romans 16:25-27 at this point.

"The doxology ("Now to him who is able to strengthen you . . . be glory for evermore through Jesus Christ!") varies in location; traditionally it has been printed at the close of chap.16 (as verses 25-27), but in some witnesses it occurs at the chose of chap.14, and in another witness (p46) at the close of chap.15.

Moreover, several witnesses have it at the close of both chap.14 and chap.16, and in others it does not occur at all." (Metzger, *A Textual Commentary on the Greek New Testament*, 533).

Personal Greetings

(Romans 16:1-23)

Romans 16:1 - *"I commend unto you Phebe our sister, which is a servant of the church which is at Cenchrea."*

Συνίστημι δὲ ὑμῖν Φοίβην τὴν ἀδελφὴν ἡμῶν, οὖσαν (καὶ) διάκονον τῆς ἐκκλησίας τῆς ἐν Κεγχρεαῖς,

"I commend to you our sister Phoebe, a deaconess of the church at Cenchreae," . . . RSV

Συνίστημι (1st.per.sing.pres.act.ind.of συνίστημι, aoristic) 2328.
δὲ (explanatory conjunction) 11.
ὑμῖν (dat.pl.masc.of σύ, indirect object of συνίστημι) 104.

#4063 Φοίβην (acc.sing.fem.of Φοίβη, direct object of συνίστημι).

    King James Version

Phebe - Rom.16:1.

    Revised Standard Version

Phoebe - Rom.16:1.

Meaning: "bright" or "radiant." Phoebe or Phebe, a deaconess of the church at Cenchrea, a port on the Adriatic coast, a short distance southeast of Corinth - Rom.16:1.

τὴν (acc.sing.fem.of the article in agreement with ἀδελφὴν) 9.
ἀδελφὴν (acc.sing.fem.of ἀδελφή, apposition) 1025.
ἡμῶν (gen.pl.masc.of ἐγώ, relationship) 123.
οὖσαν (pres.part.acc.sing.fem.of εἰμί, adverbial, circumstantial) 86.
καὶ (adjunctive conjunction joining nouns) 14.
διάκονον (acc.sing.fem.of διάκονος, predicate accusative) 1334.
τῆς (gen.sing.fem.of the article in agreement with ἐκκλησίας) 9.
ἐκκλησίας (gen.sing.fem.of ἐκκλησία, description) 1204.
τῆς (gen.sing.fem.of the article in agreement with ἐκκλησίας) 9.
ἐν (preposition with the locative of place) 80.
Κεγχρεαῖς (loc.sing.fem.of Κεγχρεαί, place) 3450.

Translation - *"Now I commend to you Phoebe, our sister, who is also a deaconess of the church in Cenchreae."*

Comment: It is probable that Phoebe carried the letter to Rome from Corinth. *Cf.*#2328 for the basic etymology of σννίστημι. Here we have scriptural warrant for women in the role of deaconess   in the first century church, with Paul's manifest approval. There is no hint as to why she was going to Rome, if for any other reason than to carry Paul's letter. Verse 2 suggests that she would need some kind of help, perhaps to secure lodging and food or to make business contacts.

Verse 2 - "That ye receive her in the Lord, as becometh saints, and that ye assist her in whatever business she hath need of you: for she hath been a succourer of many, and of myself also."

ἵνα προσδέξησθε αὐτὴν ἐν κυρίῳ ἀξίως τῶν ἁγίων, καὶ παραστῆτε αὐτῇ ἐν ᾧ ἂν ὑμῶν χρῄζῃ πράγματι, καὶ γὰρ αὐτὴ προστάτις πολλῶν ἐγενήθη καὶ ἐμοῦ αὐτοῦ.

"that you may receive her in the Lord as befits the saints, and help her in whatever she may require from you, for she has been a helper of many and of myself as well." . . . RSV

ἵνα (conjunction with the subjunctive in a final clause) 114.
προσδέξησθε (2d.per.pl.aor.mid.subj.of προσδέχομαι, purpose) 1895.
αὐτὴν (acc.sing.fem.of αὐτός, direct object of προσδέξησθε) 16.
ἐν (preposition with the locative, association) 80.
κυρίῳ (loc.sing.masc.of κύριος, association) 97.

#4064 ἀξίως (adverbial).

    King James Version

as becometh - Rom.16:2; Phil.1:27.
worthy - Eph.4:1; Col.1:10; 1 Thess.2:12.
after a godly sort - 3 John 6.

    Revised Standard Version

befits - Rom.16:2; 3 John 6.
worthy - Phil.1:27; Eph.4:1; Col.1:10; 1 Thess.2:12.

Meaning: Cf. ἄξιος (#285); ἀξιόω (#2151). An adverb, worthy of, equal to, consistent with the standard suggested by the context. With the genitive of description which follows it in Rom.16:2; Phil.1:27; Eph.4:1; Col.1:10; 1 Thess.2:12; 3 John 6. A study of these genitives of description indicate that Christians are to measure up to saints (Rom.16:2), the gospel of Christ (Phil.1:27), the vocation to which they are called (Eph.4:1 —,) the Lord (Col.1:10) and God (1 Thess.2:12; 3 John 6).

τῶν (gen.pl.masc.of the article in agreement with ἁγίων) 9.
ἁγίων (gen.pl.masc.of ἅγιος, description) 84.

καὶ (adjunctive conjunction joining verbs) 14.

παραστῆτε (2d.per.pl.aor.act.subj.of παρίστημι, purpose) 1596.

αὐτῇ (dat.sing.fem.of αὐτός, personal advantage) 16.

ἐν (preposition with the locative of sphere) 80.

ᾧ (loc.sing.neut.of ὅς, relative pronoun with the subjunctive in a third-class condition) 65.

ἂν (contingent particle with the subjunctive in a third-class condition) 205.

ὑμῶν (abl.pl.masc.of σύ, source) 104.

χρῄζῃ (3d.per.sing.pres.act.subj.of χρῄζω, third-class condition) 638.

πράγματι (loc.sing.neut.of πρᾶγμα, sphere) 1266.

καὶ (emphatic conjunction) 14.

γὰρ (causal conjunction) 105.

αὐτὴ (nom.sing.fem.of αὐτός, subject of ἐγενήθη) 16.

#4065 προστάτις (nom.sing.fem.of προστάτις, predicate nominative).

King James Version

succourer - Rom.16:2.

Revised Standard Version

helper - Rom.16:2.

Meaning: The feminine form of προστάτης, from προΐστημι (#4019), One who stands before in an administrative sense. A helper. A woman who works in a guardian capacity over others. Phoebe was a woman of influence in her church who used her influence for the good of many and gained a position of trust - Rom.16:2.

πολλῶν (gen.pl.masc.of πολύς, description) 228.

ἐγενήθη (3d.per.sing.aor.ind.of γίνομαι, constative) 113.

καὶ (adjunctive conjunction joining substantives) 14.

ἐμοῦ (gen.sing.masc.of ἐμός, description) 1267.

αὐτοῦ (gen.sing.masc.of αὐτός, demonstrative) 16.

Translation - ". . . in order that you may receive her in the Lord in a way consistent with the behavior of saints and that you may stand beside her in whatever practical way she needs you, because she in fact has been a helper of many and of me myself."

Comment: The ἵνα clause has two subjunctives of purpose. "Receive her" and "stand by her." Then Paul adds an indicative clause to the effect that Phoebe had a record of standing by others when they needed her and helping them. He says that he himself was among those whom she had helped. "Receive her ἐν κυρίῳ" - "as a Christian in association with the Lord," *i.e.* as they were associated with the Lord they were to receive her as one who enjoyed the same association (John 17:21). This is a lesson that many Christians, who are guilty of discrimination against other Christians on grounds of race, color, social, economic or ideological differences, have not learned. We are to receive all whom Christ has received. It is well to remember that when Christ received us He was not too favourably impressed with our merits! If our Lord did not reject them on what grounds can we do so?

Paul implies that Phoebe had some other things to do in Rome besides delivering his epistle, if indeed she carried it. One wonders what? Note the relative pronoun in the locative of sphere, with ἄν and the subjunctive in χρήζη - a relative clause functioning as a third-class condition - "If (some doubt about it) she needs your help in any way . . . I am asking you to stand by her."

Verse 3 - "Greet Priscilla and Aquilla, my helpers in Christ Jesus."

Ἀσπάσασθε Πρίσκαν καὶ Ἀκύλαν τοὺς συνεργούς μου ἐν Χριστῷ Ἰησοῦ.

"Greet Γ.isca and Aquila, my fellow workers in Christ Jesus." . . . RSV

Ἀσπάσασθε (2d.per.pl.aor.mid.impv.of ἀσπάζω, command) 551.
Πρίσκαν (acc.sing.fem.of Πρίσκα (dimin.) , direct object of ἀσπάσασθε) 3433.
καὶ (adjunctive conjunction joining nouns) 14.
Ἀκύλαν (acc.sing.masc.of Ἀκύλας, direct object of ἀσπάσασθε) 3429.
τοὺς (acc.pl.masc.of the article in agreement with συνεργούς) 9.

#4066 συνεργούς (acc.pl.masc.of συνεργός, apposition).

King James Version
companion in labor - Phil.2:25.
fellow-helper - 2 Cor.8:23; 3 John 8.
fellow-labourer - Phil.4:3; 1 Thess.3:2; Phm.1,24.
fellow-worker - Col.4:11.
helper - Rom.16:3,9; 2 Cor.1:24.
laborer together with - 1 Cor.3:9.
work fellow - Rom.16:21.

Revised Standard Version
fellow worker - Phil.2:25; 2 Cor.8:23; 3 John 8; Phil.4:3; Phm.1,24; Col.4:11; Rom.16:3,9,21; 1 Cor.3:9.
servant - 1 Thess.3:2.
work with you - 2 Cor.1:24.

Meaning: A combination of σύν (#1542) and ἔργον (#460). *Cf.* ἐργάζομαι (#691). One who works with another; fellow worker. In the gospel ministry. All Christians with God - 1 Cor.3:9; in all other passages various first century Christians with Paul - Paul and Ephaphroditus, Phil.2:25; Titus, 2 Cor.8:23; all Christians and John - 3 John 8; Clement *et al* with Paul, Phil.4:3; Paul and Timothy - 1 Thess.3:2; Paul and Mark, Aristarchus, Demas and Luke - Phm.1,24; Onesimus, Aristarchus, Mark, Jesus Justis and Paul - Col.4:11; Aquilla and Priscilla and Paul - Rom.16:3; Urbane and Stachys - Rom.16:9;

Timothy, Lucius, Jason and Sosipater - Rom. 16:21; Paul and the Corinthians - 2 Cor. 1:24.

μου (gen.sing.masc.of ἐγώ, relationship) 123.
ἐν (preposition with the locative, association) 80.
Χριστῷ (loc.sing.masc.of Χριστός, association) 4.
Ἰησοῦ (loc.sing.masc.of Ἰησοῦς, apposition) 3.

Translation - *"Say hello to Prisca and Aquila, my fellow workers in Christ Jesus."*

Comment: Note that Paul uses the diminutive form of Πρίσκιλλα (#3433), indicating that he knew her and her husband quite well. *Cf.* #'s 3429 and 3433. Paul had many fellow workers (#4066). Except for 3 John 8 the word in the New Testament is Paul's.

We have the explanation for Paul's special regard for Aquila and Prisca in

Verse 4 - *"Who have for my life laid down their own necks: unto whom not only I give thanks, but also all the churches of the Gentiles."*

οἵτινες ὑπὲρ τῆς ψυχῆς μου τὸν ἑαυτῶν τράχηλον ὑπέθηκαν, οἷς οὐκ ἐγὼ μόνος εὐχαριστῶ ἀλλὰ καὶ πᾶσαι αἱ ἐκκλησίαι τῶν ἐθνῶν,

"who risked their necks for my life, to whom not only I but also all the churches of the Gentiles give thanks;" . . . *RSV*

οἵτινες (nom.pl.masc.of ὅστις, relative pronoun, definite use, subject of ὑπέθηκαν, descriptive) 163.
ὑπὲρ (preposition with the ablative, "instead of") 545.
τῆς (abl.sing.fem.of the article in agreement with ψυχῆς) 9.
ψυχῆς (abl.sing.fem.of ψυχή, "instead of") 233.
μου (gen.sing.masc.of ἐγώ, possession) 123.
τὸν (acc.sing.masc.of the article in agreement with τράχηλον) 9.
ἑαυτῶν (gen.pl.masc.of ἑαυτοῦ, possession) 288.
τράχηλον (acc.sing.masc.of τράχηλος, direct object of ὑπέθηκαν) 1252.

#4067 ὑπέθηκαν (3d.per.pl.1st.aor.act.ind.of ὑποτίθημι, constative).

　　　　King James Version

lay down - Rom. 16:4.
put in remembrance - 1 Tim. 4:6.

　　　　Revised Standard Version

risk - Rom. 16:4.
put before - 1 Tim. 4:6.

Meaning: A combination of ὑπό (#117) and τίθημι (#455). To place down or under; to lay down. With τράχηλον - thus to act so as to place one's life in jeopardy - Rom. 16:4; to remind - 1 Tim. 4:6 - or suggest with reference to certain matters set forth in 1 Tim.4:3-5.

οἷς (dat.pl.masc.of ὅς, relative pronoun, indirect object of εὐχαριστῶ) 65.
οὐκ (negative particle with the indicative) 130.
ἐγώ (nom.sing.masc.of ἐγώ, subject of εὐχαριστῶ) 123.
μόνος (nom.sing.masc.of μόνος, adverbial) 339.
εὐχαριστῶ (1st.per.sing.pres.act.ind.of εὐχαριστέω, aoristic) 1185.
ἀλλά (adversative conjunction) 342.
καί (adjunctive conjunction joining substantives) 14.
πᾶσαι (nom.pl.fem.of πᾶς, in agreement with ἐκκλησίαι) 67.
αἱ (nom.pl.fem.of the article in agreement with ἐκκλησίαι) 9.
ἐκκλησίαι (nom.pl.fem.of ἐκκλησία, subject of verb understood) 1204.
τῶν (gen.pl.neut.of the article in agreement with ἐθνῶν) 9.
ἐθνῶν (gen.pl.neut.of ἔθνος, description) 376.

Translation - "*Who laid down their necks to save my life, to whom not only I, but also all of the Gentile churches, give thanks.*"

Comment: οἵτινες here is definite. *Cf.* the *Meaning* article - #163. ὑπέρ with the ablative meaning "instead of." *Cf.*#545,(3). It is probable that the event to which Paul alludes is described in Acts 19:23-41, although Luke does not mention Aquila and Priscilla by name in his account. It is interesting that Paul has οἵτινες (#163), the relative which is most frequently indefinite, although here the context demands οἵ, and then follows it with οἷς (#65) instead of οἷστισι or ὅτοις. Robertson says, "I confess that I fail to see a great deal of difference between οἵτινες and οἷς in Ro.16:4." (*Grammar*, 728). The problem comes up again in Rom.16:7, where we have οἵτινες and οἵ. Normally the adverbial μόνος is written in the neuter gender, though here in the masculine. #339.

Paul and the Gentile churches who knew of the ministry of Aquila and Priscilla were of course, grateful to them.

Verse 5 - "*Likewise greet the church that is in their house. Salute my wellbeloved Epaenetus, who is the firstfruits of Achaia unto Christ.*"

καὶ τὴν κατ' οἶκον αὐτῶν ἐκκλησίαν. ἀσπάσασθε Ἐπαίνετον τὸν ἀγαπητόν μου, ὅς ἐστιν ἀπαρχὴ τῆς Ἀσίας εἰς Χριστόν.

"*greet also the church in their house. Greet my beloved Epaenetus, who was the first convert in Asia for Christ.*" . . . *RSV*

καί (adjunctive conjunction joining nouns) 14.
τήν (acc.sing.fem.of the article in agreement with ἐκκλησίαν) 9.
κατ' (preposition with the accusative, distributive) 98.
οἶκον (acc.sing.masc.of οἶκος, distributive) 784.
αὐτῶν (gen.pl.masc.of αὐτός, possession) 16.
ἐκκλησίαν (acc.sing.fem.of ἐκκλησία, direct object of ἀσπάσασθε) 1204.
ἀσπάσασθε (2d.per.pl.aor.mid.impv.of ἀσπάζομαι, command) 551.

#4068 Ἐπαίνετον (acc.sing.masc.of Ἐπαίνετος, direct object of ἀσπάσασθε).

King James Version

Epaenetus - Rom.16:5.

Revised Standard Version

Epaenetus - Rom.16:5.

Meaning: Cf. ἐπαινέω (#2568). Paul's first convert in Asia - Rom.16:5. The word means "High Praise."

τὸν (acc.sing.masc.of the article in agreement with ἀγαπητόν) 9.
ἀγαπητόν (acc.sing.masc.of ἀγαπητός, in agreement with Ἐπαίνετον) 327.
μου (gen.sing.masc.of ἐγώ, relationship) 123.
ὅς (nom.sing.masc.of ὅς, relative pronoun, subject of ἐστιν, adjectival) 65.
ἐστιν (3d.per.sing.pres.ind.of εἰμί, aoristic) 86.
ἀπαρχή (nom.sing.fem.of ἀπαρχή, predicate nominative) 3946.
τῆς (abl.sing.fem.of the article in agreement with Ἀσίας) 9.
Ἀσίας (abl.sing.fem.of Ἀσίας, source) 2968.
εἰς (preposition with the accusative, extent) 140.
Χριστόν (acc.sing.masc.of Χριστός, extent) 4.

Translation - "*And (greet) the church in their home. Give my regards to Epaenetus, my beloved friend, who is the first convert to Christ from Asia Minor.*"

Comment: Ἀσπάσασθε is the verb in the long sentence which begins in verse 3. This verse is helpful is making the distinction, which is so often confused, between the church (ἡ ἐκκλησία) and the building in which it meets (ὁ οἶκον). The word ἐκκλησία (#1204) is never used in the New Testament to refer to a building. With reference to Epaenetus, the relative pronoun is ὅς, in the next clause, which defines him as being the first convert in Asia Minor. Note that in verse 6, with reference to Μαριάμ, Paul reverts to ἥτις.

Verse 6 - "*Greet Mary, who bestowed much labour on us.*"

ἀσπάσασθε Μαριάμ, ἥτις πολλὰ ἐκοπίασεν εἰς ὑμᾶς.

"*Greet Mary, who has worked hard among you.*" . . . RSV

ἀσπάσασθε (2d.per.pl.aor.mid.impv.of ἀσπάζομαι, command) 551.

#4069 Μαριάμ (acc.sing.fem.of Μαριάμ, direct object of ἀσπάσασθε).

King James Version

Mary - Rom.16:6.

Revised Standard Version

Mary - Rom.16:6.

Meaning: a Christian woman in Rome, mentioned only in Romans 16:6.

ἥτις (nom.sing.fem.of ὅστις, subject of ἐκοπίασεν, definite relative pronoun) 163.

πολλὰ (acc.pl.neut.of πολύς, adverbial accusative) 228.

ἐκοπίασεν (3d.per.sing.aor.act.ind.of κοπιάω, constative) 629.

εἰς (preposition with the accusative, extent) 140.

ὑμᾶς (acc.pl.masc.of σύ, extent) 104.

Translation - "Greet Mary, who has worked so hard for you."

Comment: Mary had done so much work for the church in Rome that Paul had heard about her and her faithful service. Had he met her somewhere before? Or was his knowledge of her work the result of communication with other mutual friends?

Verse 7 - "Salute Andronicus and Junia, my kinsmen, and my fellowprisoners, who are of note among the apostles, who also were in Christ before me."

ἀσπάσασθε Ἀνδρόνικον καὶ Ἰουνιᾶν τοὺς συγγενεῖς μου καὶ συναιχμαλώτους μου, οἵτινές εἰσιν ἐπίσημοι ἐν τοῖς ἀποστόλοις, οἳ καὶ πρὸ ἐμοῦ γέγοναν ἐν Χριστῷ.

"Greet Adronicus and Junias, my kinsmen and my fellow prisoners; they are men of note among the apostles, and they were in Christ before me." . . . RSV

ἀσπάσασθε (2d.per.pl.aor.mid.impv.of ἀσπάζομαι, command) 551.

#4070 Ἀνδρόνικον (acc.sing.masc.of Ἀνδρόνικος, direct object of ἀσπάσασθε).

King James Version

Andronicus - Rom.16:7.

Revised Standard Version

Andronicus - Rom.16:7.

Meaning: A Hebrew Christian in Rome; a relative of Paul who had suffered persecution with him. Well known by the other Apostles - Rom.16:7.

καὶ (adjunctive conjunction joining nouns) 14.

#4071 Ἰουνιᾶν (acc.sing.masc.of Ἰουνίας, direct object of ἀσπάσασθε).

King James Version

Junia - Rom.16:7.

Revised Standard Version

Junias - Rom.16:7.

Meaning: Not to be confused with Ἰουννιανός, although Robertson (*Grammar*, 172) thinks it may be an abbreviation. The KJV translates Junia (a woman's name) The RSV has Junias. *Cf.* Rom.16:15 where the United Bible Societies' Committee has Ἰουλίαν (masculine) with A certitude against a variant reading Ἰουνίαν. ᵖ⁴⁶ on Rom.16:7 has Ἰουλίαν, against which reading the Committee has ruled.   The fact that συγγενεῖς and συναιχμαλώτους, in apposition are masculine, does not help us. The Committee thinks that the feminine form is Ἰουνίαν while Ἰουνιᾶν is in the text challenged, not by Ἰουνίαν but by Ἰουλίαν for which there is scant support. It would appear that Ἰουνιᾶν was a man. He was a relative of Paul and Andronicus (#4070) and a Roman citizen - Rom.16:7.

τοὺς (acc.pl.masc.of the article in agreement with συγγενεῖς) 9.
συγγενεῖς (acc.pl.masc.of συγγενής, apposition) 1815.
μου (gen.sing.masc.of ἐγώ, relationship) 123.

καὶ (adjunctive conjunction joining nouns) 14.

#4072 συναιχμαλώτους (acc.pl.masc.of συναιχμάλωτος, apposition).

King James Version

fellow prisoner - Rom.16:7; Col.4:10; Phm.23.

Revised Standard Version

fellow prisoner - Rom.16:7; Col.4:10; Phm.23.

Meaning: A combination of σύν (#1542), αἰχμάλωτος (#2022). *Cf.* also αἰχμαλωσία (#4492), αἰχμαλωτεύω (#4491) and αἰχμαλωτίζω (#2726). Fellow prisoner. One who joined another in incarceration. Andronicus and Junias with Paul - Rom.16:7; Aristarchus with Paul - Col.4:10; Epaphras with Paul - Phm.23.

μου (gen.sing.masc.of ἐγώ, relationship) 123.
οἵτινες (nom.pl.masc.of ὅστις, definite relative pronoun, subject of εἰσιν) 163.
εἰσιν (3d.per.pl.pres.ind.of εἰμί, static) 86.
ἐπίσημοι (nom.pl.masc.of ἐπίσημος, predicate adjective) 1625.
ἐν (preposition with the locative with plural nouns) 80.
τοῖς (loc.pl.masc.of the article in agreement with ἀποστόλοις) 9.
ἀποστόλοις (loc.pl.masc.of ἀπόστολος, association) 844.
οἱ (nom.pl.masc.of ὅς, definite relative pronoun, subject of γέγοναν) 65.
καὶ (emphatic conjunction) 14.
πρὸ (preposition with the ablative of time separation) 442.
ἐμοῦ (abl.sing.masc.of ἐμός, time separation) 1267.
γέγοναν (3d.per.pl.contr.of 2d.perf.ind.of γίνομαι) 113.
ἐν (preposition with the locative, association) 80.
Χριστῷ (loc.sing.masc.of Χριστός, association) 4.

Translation - "*Give my regards to Andronicus and Junias, my relatives and my*

fellow prisoners, who are well known among the Apostles, who have in fact been
Christians longer than I."

Comment: Paul's relatives, who probably lived in Jerusalem, or in Antioch, since they were well known among the Apostles, and who had become Christians before he did, had gone to jail with him for the cause of Christ. How they came to Rome is not known. ἐπίσμοι - "notable" in the case of Adronicus and Junias; "notorious" in the case of Barabbas (#1625). Outstanding service for good or evil will gain attention from all and admiration and approbation from some, but opprobrium from others. Note again (as in verse 4) that Paul uses οἵτινες and οἱ in the same sense. A variant reading has ὃς καὶ πρὸ ἐμοῦ γέγονεν, which is singular instead of plural and would apply to only one of the men involved. However the United Bible Societies' Committee has opted for the plural reading.

Verse 8 - "Greet Amplias my beloved in the Lord."

ἀσπάσασθε Ἀμπλιᾶτον τὸν ἀγαπητόν μου ἐν κυρίῳ.

"Greet Ampliatus, my beloved in the Lord." . . . RSV

ἀσπάσασθε (2d.per.pl.aor.mid.impv.of ἀσπάζομαι, command) 551.

#4073 Ἀμπλιᾶτον (acc.sing.masc.of Ἀμπλιᾶτος, direct object of ἀσπάσασθε).

King James Version

Amplias - Rom.16:8.

Revised Standard Version

Ampliatus - Rom.16:8.

Meaning: A contraction from the Latin, Ampliatus. A Christian in Rome - Rom.16:8.

τὸν (acc.sing.masc.of the article in agreement with ἀγαπητόν) 9.
ἀγαπητόν (acc.sing.masc.of ἀγαπητός, in agreement with Ἀμπλιᾶτον) 327.
μου (gen.sing.masc.of ἐγώ, relationship) 123.
ἐν (preposition with the locative, association) 80.
κυρίῳ (loc.sing.masc.of κύριος, association) 97.

Translation - "Say hello to Ampliatus, my beloved friend in the Lord."

Comment: The phrases ἐν κυρίῳ and ἐν Χριστῷ can be regarded as cause, means or association, since all three ideas are valid. It is both because and by means of His work that we are in association with Him. And because we are in association with Him, we enjoy fellowship with others who also are in Him. A locative of sphere is also a possible interpretation. Much more research is needed to explain fully how ἐν Χριστῷ speaks of the mystic union of the believer with Christ.

Verse 9 - "Salute Urbane, our helper in Christ, and Stachys my beloved."

ἀσπάσασθε Οὐρβανὸν τὸν συνεργὸν ἡμῶν ἐν Χριστῷ καὶ Στάχυν τὸν ἀγαπητόν μου.

"Greet Urbanus, our fellow worker in Christ, and my beloved Stachys." . . .

RSV

ἀσπάσασθε (2d.per.pl.aor.mid.impv.of ἀσπάζομαι, command) 551.

#4074 Οὐρβανὸν (acc.sing.masc.of Οὐρβανός, direct object of ἀσπάσασθε).

King James Version

Urbane - Rom.16:9.

Revised Standard Version

Urbanus - Rom.16:9.

Meaning: Urbanus, a certain Christian mentioned in Rom.16:9 as a fellow worker with Paul.

τὸν (acc.sing.masc.of the article in agreement with συνεργόν) 9.
συνεργόν (acc.sing.masc.of συνεργός, in apposition) 4066.
ἡμῶν (gen.pl.masc.of ἐγώ, relationship) 123.
ἐν (preposition with the locative, association) 80.
Χριστῷ (loc.sing.masc.of Χριστός, association) 4.
καὶ (adjunctive conjunction joining nouns) 14.

#4075 Στάχυν (acc.sing.masc.of Στάχυς, direct object of ἀσπάσασθε).

King James Version

Stachys - Rom.16:9.

Revised Standard Version

Stachys - Rom.16:9.

Meaning: Cf. with #965. One of Paul's Christian friends in Rome - Rom.16:9.

τὸν (acc.sing.masc.of the article in agreement with ἀγαπητόν) 9.
ἀγαπητόν (acc.sing.masc.of ἀγαπητός, in agreement with Στάχυν) 327.
μου (gen.sing.masc.of ἐγώ, relationship) 123.

Translation - "Remember me to Urbanus, our fellow worker in Christ and to my good friend Stachys.

Comment: Paul's long experience as a gospel missionary throughout Asia Minor resulted in his having led to Christ and worked with a great many people who had since migrated to Rome. It is not clear which of these people whom Paul greets came to Christ directly under his ministry.

Verse 10 - "Salute Apelles approved in Christ. Salute them which are of

Aristobulus' household."

ἀσπάσασθε Ἀπελλῆν τὸν δόκιμον ἐν Χριστῷ. ἀσπάσασθε τοὺς ἐκ τῶν Ἀριστοβούλου.

"Greet Apelles, who is approved in Christ. Greet those who belong to the family of Aristobulus." . . . RSV

ἀσπάσασθε (2d.per.pl.aor.mid.impv.of ἀσπάζομαι, command) 551.

#4076 Ἀπελλῆν (acc.sing.masc.of Ἀπελλης, direct object of ἀσπάσασθε).

King James Version

Apelles - Rom.16:10.

Revised Standard Version

Apelles - Rom.16:10.

Meaning: A Christian in Rome - Rom.16:10.
τὸν (acc.sing.masc.of the article in agreement with δόκιμον) 9.
δόκιμον (acc.sing.masc.of δόκιμος, in agreement with Ἀπελλῆν) 4042.
ἐν (preposition with the locative, association) 80.
Χριστῷ (loc.sing.masc.of Χριστός, association) 4.
ἀσπάσασθε (2d.per.pl.aor.mid.impv.of ἀσπάζομαι, command) 551.
τοὺς (acc.pl. masc.of the article direct object of ἀσπάσασθε) 9.
ἐκ (preposition with the partitive genitive) 19.
τῶν (gen.pl.masc.of the article, partitive genitive) 9.

#4077 Ἀριστοβούλου (gen.sing.masc.of Ἀριστόβουλος, relationship).

King James Version

Aristobulus - Rom.16:10.

Revised Standard Version

Aristobulus - Rom.16:10.

Meaning: A combination of ἄριστος - "best" and βουλή (#2163). Hence, literally "the best counsel." A resident in Rome, some of whose household, either family or servants, were acquaintances of Paul - Rom.16:10.

Translation - "Greet Apelles, approved in Christ. Say hello to those in the household of Aristobulus."

Comment: Note that τῶν is plural. If Paul had meant to greet everyone (τοὺς) in the family of Aristobulus, it would read ἐκ τοῦ Ἀριστοβούλου. But τοὺς is a plural group out of a larger number (τῶν) of Aristobulus' family. The text does not say that Aristobulus was a Christian. Nor that *all* of his family were. In fact the text does not say that any of them were. It does say that Paul wished to be remembered to them.

Verse 11 - "Salute Herodion my kinsman. Greet them that be of the household of Narcissus, which are in the Lord."

ἀσπάσασθε Ἡρῳδίωνα τὸν συγγενῆ μου. ἀσπάσασθε τοὺς ἐκ τῶν Ναρκίσσου τοὺς ὄντας ἐν κυρίῳ.

"Greet my kinsman Herodion. Greet those in the Lord who belong to the family of Narcissus." . . . RSV

ἀσπάσασθε (2d.per.pl.aor.mid.impv.of ἀσπάζομαι, command) 551.

#4078 Ἡρῳδίωνα (acc.sing.masc.of Ἡρῳδίων, direct object of ἀσπάσασθε).

King James Version

Herodion - Rom.16:11.

Revised Standard Version

Herodion - Rom.16:11.

Meaning: A relative of Paul who lived in Rome - Rom.16:11.

τὸν (acc.sing.masc.of the article in agreement with συγγενῆ) 9.
συγγενῆ (acc.sing.masc.of συγγενής, apposition) 1815.
μου (gen.sing.masc.of ἐγώ, relationship) 123.
ἀσπάσασθε (2d.per.pl.aor.mid.impv.of ἀσπάζομαι, command) 551.
τοὺς (acc.pl.masc.of the article, direct object of ἀσπάσασθε) 9.
ἐκ (preposition with the partitive genitive) 19.
τῶν (gen.pl.masc.of the article, partitive genitive) 9.

#4079 Ναρκίσσου (gen.sing.masc.of Νάρκισσος, relationship).

King James Version

Narcissus - Rom.16:11.

Revised Standard Version

Narcissus - Rom.16:11.

Meaning: Narcissus - a resident of Rome in whose household there lived some Christians - Rom.16:11.

τοὺς (acc.pl.masc.of the article in agreement with ὄντας) 9.
ὄντας (pres.part.acc.pl.masc.of εἰμί, substantival, in apposition with τοὺς) 86.
ἐν (preposition with the locative, association) 80.
κυρίῳ (loc.sing.masc.of κύριος, association) 97.

Translation - "Greet Herodion, my relative. Remember me to those who are in the Lord who live with Narcissus."

Comment: The partitive genitive ἐκ τῶν of verse 11 has the same force as in verse 10. Narcissus and Aristobulus may or may not have been Christians, but they each had members of their household who were. τοὺ ὄντας ἐν κυρίῳ is in apposition to the first τοὺς. If we consider the participle restrictive, the implication is that there were those living with Narcissus who were not Christians.

Verse 12 - "Salute Tryphena and Tryphosa, who labour in the Lord. Salute the beloved Persis, which laboured much in the Lord."

ἀσπάσασθε Τρύφαιναν καὶ Τρυφῶσαν τὰς κοπιώσας ἐν κυρίῳ. ἀσπάσασθε Περσίδα τὴν ἀγαπητήν, ἥτις πολλὰ ἐκοπίασεν ἐν κυρίῳ.

"Greet those workers in the Lord, Tryphaena and Tryphosa. Greet the beloved Persis, who has worked hard in the Lord." . . . RSV

ἀσπάσασθε (2d.per.pl.aor.mid.impv.of ἀσπάζομαι, command) 551.

#4080 Τρύφαιναν (acc.sing.fem.of Τρύφαινα, direct object of ἀσπάσασθε).

King James Version

Tryphena - Rom.16:12.

Revised Standard Version

Tryphaena - Rom.16:12.

Meaning: A Christian woman in Rome - Rom.16:12.

καὶ (adjunctive conjunction joining nouns) 14.

#4081 Τρυφῶσαν (acc.sing.fem.of Τρυφῶσα, direct object of ἀσπάσασθε).

King James Version

Tryphosa - Rom.16:12.

Revised Standard Version

Tryphosa -Rom.16:12.

Meaning: A Christian woman in Rome. An associate of Tryphena (#4080) - Rom.16:12.

τὰ (acc.pl.fem.of the article in agreement with κοπιώσας) 9.
κοπιώσας (pres.act.part.acc.pl.fem.of κοπιάω, substantival, in apposition) 629
ἐν (preposition with the locative, association) 80.

κυρίῳ (loc.sing.masc.of κύριος, association) 97.
ἀσπάσασθε (2d.per.pl.aor.mid.impv.of ἀσπάζομαι, command) 551.

#4082 Περσίδα (acc.sing.fem.of Περσίς, direct object of ἀσπάσασθε).

King James Version

Persis - Rom.16:12.

Revised Standard Version

Persis - Rom.16:12.

Meaning: literally — "a Persian woman." A Christian woman in Rome - Rom.16:12.

τὴν (acc.sing.fem.of the article in agreement with ἀγαπητήν) 9.
ἀγαπατήν (acc.sing.fem.of ἀγαπατός, in agreement with Περσίδα) 327.
ἥτις (nom.sing.fem.of ὅστις, definite relative pronoun, subject of ἐκοπίασεν) 163.
πολλά (acc.pl.neut.of πολύς, direct object of ἐκοπίασεν) 228.
ἐν (preposition with the locative, association) 80.
κυρίῳ (loc.sing.masc.of κύριος, association) 97.

Translation - *"Greet Tryphaena and Tryphosa, the workers for the Lord. Say hello to the beloved Persis, who has labored much in the Lord's cause."*

Comment: Paul's memory of people and their accomplishments for the Lord is serving him well.

Verse 13 - *"Salute Rufus, chosen in the Lord, and his mother and mine."*

ἀσπάσασθε Ῥοῦφον τὸν ἐκλεκτὸν ἐν κυρίῳ καὶ τὴν μητέρα αὐτοῦ καὶ ἐμοῦ.

"Greet Rufus, eminent in the Lord, also his mother and mine." . . . RSV

ἀσπάσασθε (2d.per.pl.aor.mid.impv.of ἀσπάζομαι, command) 551.
Ῥοῦφον (acc.sing.masc.of Ῥοῦφον, direct object of ἀσπάσασθε) 2849.
τὸν (acc.sing.masc.of the article in agreement with ἐκλεκτὸν) 9.
ἐκλεκτὸν (acc.sing.masc.of ἐκλεκτός, in agreement with Ῥοῦφον) 1412.
ἐν (preposition with the locative, association) 80.
κυρίῳ (loc.sing.masc.of κύριος, association) 97.
καὶ (adjunctive conjunction joining nouns) 14.
τὴν (acc.sing.fem.of the article in agreement with μητέρα) 9.
μητέρα (acc.sing.fem.of μήτηρ, direct object of ἀσπάσασθε) 76.
αὐτοῦ (gen.sing.masc.of αὐτός, relationship) 16.
καὶ (adjunctive conjunction joining pronouns) 14.
ἐμοῦ (gen.sing.masc.of ἐμός, relationship) 1267.

Translation - *"Greet Rufus, the man chosen in the Lord, and his mother and mine."*

Comment: Paul does not mean that he is Rufus' brother genetically, but that Rufus' mother had treated Paul like her own son. Whether or not Rufus is the son of Simon the Cyreanian (Mk.15:21) is not known. *Cf.* 1 Cor.16:18; Phm.11 for similar constructions.

Verse 14 - "Salute Asyncritus, Phlegon, Hermas, Patrobas, Hermes, and the brethren which are with them."

ἀσπάσασθε Ἀσύγκριτον, Φλέγοντα, Ἑρμῆν, Πατροβᾶν, Ἑρμᾶν, καὶ τοὺς σὺν αὐτοῖς ἀδελφούς.

"Greet Asyncritus, Phlegon, Hermes, Patrobas, Hermas, and the brethren who are with them." . . . RSV

ἀσπάσασθε (2d.per.pl.aor.mid.impv.of ἀσπάζομαι, command) 551.

#4083 Ἀσύγκριτον (acc.sing.masc.of Ἀσύγκριτος, direct object of ἀσπάσασθε).

King James Version

Asyncritus - Rom.16:14.

Revised Standard Version

Asyncritus - Rom.16:14.

Meaning: α privative plus συγκρίνω (#4111). Hence, incomparable. A Christian in Rome - Rom.16:14.

#4084 Φλέγοντα (acc.sing.masc.of φλέγων, direct object of ἀσπάσασθε).

King James Version

Phlegon - Rom.16:14.

Revised Standard Version

Phlegon - Rom.16:14.

Meaning: Cf. φλογίζω (#5127). Hence "burning" ' a Christian in Rome - Rom.16:14.

Ἑρμῆν (acc.sing.masc.of Ἑρμῆς, direct object of ἀσπάσασθε) 3317.

#4085 Πατροβᾶν (acc.sing.masc.of Πατρόβας, direct object of ἀσπάσασθε).

King James Version

Patrobas - Rom.16:14.

Revised Standard Version

Patrobas - Rom.16:14.

Meaning: Contracted from πατρόβιος. "Lightfoot recalls that this proper name, an abbreviated form of Patrobius, was borne by a well-known freedman of Nero (Tacitus, *Hist. i, 49, ii, 95)* and cites two other exx. of it from the inscript." (Moulton & Milligan, *The Vocabulary of the Greek New Testament,* 499). Whether this Christian in Rome was the same man is not known - Rom.16:14.

#4086 Ἑρμᾶν (acc.sing.masc.of Ἑρμᾶς, direct object of ἀσπάσασθε).

King James Version

Hermes - Rom.16:14.

Revised Standard Version

Hermas - Rom.16:14.

Meaning: A Christian in Rome, thought by Origen and others to be the author of "The Shepherd." - Rom.16:14.

καὶ (adjunctive conjunction joining nouns) 14.
τοὺς (acc.pl.masc.of the article in agreement with ἀδελφούς) 9.
σὺν (preposition with the instrumental of association) 1542.
αὐτοῖς (instru.pl.masc.of αὐτός, association) 16.
ἀδελφούς (acc.pl.masc.of ἀδελφός, direct object of ἀσπάσασθε) 15.

Translation - "Remember me to Asynkriton, Phlegon, Hermes, Patrobas, Hermas and the brethren with them."

Comment: Note the absence of the article in the list of proper names.

Verse 15 - "Salute Philologus, and Julia, Nereus, and his sister, and Olympas, and all the saints which are with them."

ἀσπάσασθε Φιλόλογον καὶ Ἰουλίαν, Νηρέα καὶ τὴν ἀδελφὴν αὐτοῦ, καὶ Ὀλυμπᾶν, καὶ τοὺς σὺν αὐτοῖς πάντας ἁγίους.

"Greet Philologus, Julia, Nereus and his sister, and Olympas, and all the saints who are with them." . . . RSV

ἀσπάσασθε (2d.per.pl.aor.mid.impv.of ἀσπάζομαι, command) 551.

#4087 Φιλόλογον (acc.sing.masc.of Φιλόλογος, direct object of ἀσπάσασθε).

King James Version

Philologus - Rom.16:15.

Revised Standard Version

Philologus - Rom.16:15.

Meaning: A combination of φίλος (#932) or φιλέω (#566) and λόγος (#510).

Hence, "fond of talk." A Roman Christian - Rom.16:15.

καὶ (adjunctive conjunction) 14.

#4088 Ἰουλίαν (acc.sing.masc.of Ἰουλία, direct object of ἀσπάσασθε).

King James Version

Julia - Rom.16:15.

Revised Standard Version

Julia - Rom.16:15.

Meaning: A Christian woman in Rome - Rom.16:15.

#4089 Νηρέα (acc.sing.masc.of Νηρεύς, direct object of ἀσπάσασθε).

King James Version

Nereus - Rom.16:15.

Revised Standard Version

Nereus - Rom.16;15.

Meaning: A Christian who lived in Rome - Rom.16:15.

καὶ (adjunctive conjunction joining nouns) 14.
τὴν (acc.sing.fem.of the article in agreement with ἀδελφὴν) 9.
ἀδελφὴν (acc.sing.fem.of ἀδελφή, direct object of ἀσπάσασθε) 1025.
αὐτοῦ (gen.sing.masc.of αὐτός, relationship) 16.
καὶ (adjunctive conjunction joining nouns) 14.

#4090   Ὀλυμπᾶν (acc.sing.masc.of Ὀλυμπᾶς, direct object of ἀσπάσασθε).

King James Version

Olympas - Rom.16:15.

Revised Standard Version

Olympas - Rom.16:15.

Meaning: A Christian in Rome - Rom.16:15.

καὶ (adjunctive conjunction joining nouns) 14.
τοὺς (acc.pl.masc.of the article in agreement with ἁγίους) 9.
σὺν (preposition with the instrumental of association) 1542.
αὐτοῖς (instru.pl.masc.of αὐτός, association) 16.
ἁγίους (acc.pl.masc.of ἅγιος, direct object of ἀσπάσασθε) 84.

Translation - "Say hello to Philologus and Julia, Nereus and his sister, and

Olympas and all the saints with them."

Comment: σὺν αὐτοῖς, an instrumental of association. One wonders about the fortunes of these people whom Paul has greeted in this closing chapter. How many of them died in the Coliseum? Paul has mentioned 25 names, plus a mother, a sister, and other members of the households of Aristobulus and Narcissus, plus other Christians who met in the home of Aquila and Priscilla, plus other saints.

Verse 16 - "Salute one another with an holy kiss. The churches of Christ salute you."

Ἀσπάσασθε ἀλλήλους ἐν φιλήματι ἁγίῳ. Ἀσπάζονται ὑμᾶς αἱ ἐκκλησίαι πᾶσαι τοῦ Χριστοῦ.

"Greet one another with a holy kiss. All the churches of Christ greet you." . . . RSV

Ἀσπάσασθε (2d.per.pl.aor.mid.impv.of ἀσπάζομαι, command) 551.
ἀλλήλους (acc.pl.masc.of ἀλλήλων;, direct object of ἀσπάσασαθε) 1487.
ἐν (preposition with the locative, means) 80.
φιλήματι (loc.sing.neut.of φίλημα, means) 2175.
ἁγίῳ (loc.sing.neut.of ἅγιος, in agreement with φιλήματι) 84.
Ἀσπάζονται (3d.per.pl.pres.mid.ind.of ἀσπάζομαι, aoristic) 551.
ὑμᾶς (acc.pl.masc.of σύ, direct object of ἀσπάζονται) 104.
αἱ (nom.pl.fem.of the article in agreement with ἐκκλησίαι) 9.
ἐκκλησίαι (nom.pl.fem.of ἐκκλησία, subject of ἀσπάζονται) 1204.
πᾶσαι (nom.pl.fem.of πᾶς, in agreement with ἐκκλησίαι) 67.
τοῦ (gen.sing.masc.of the article in agreement with Χριστοῦ) 9.
Χριστοῦ (gen.sing.masc.of Χριστός, possession) 4.

Translation - "Greet one another with a holy kiss. All the churches of Christ send greeting."

Comment: *Cf.*#2175 for similar greetings. "The ancient custom, especially in the East, and particularly among the Jews, of uniting a greeting with a kiss, gave birth to the Christian practice of the ἅγιον φίλημα (1 Pet.5:14), termed ἅγιον because it was no profane thing, but had Christian consecration, expressing the holy Christian fellowship of love." (Meyer, *Romans*, 570).

This concludes Paul's list of greetings to the Romans. In the verses that remain in the epistle, he warns them against trouble makers in the church, includes greetings to the Romans from Corinth and closes with the doxology.

Verse 17 - "Now I beseech you, brethren, mark them which cause divisions and offences contrary to the doctrine which ye have learned, and avoid them."

Παρακαλῶ δὲ ὑμᾶς, ἀδελφοί, σκοπεῖν τοὺς τὰς διχοστασίας καὶ τὰ σκάνδαλα παρὰ τὴν διδαχὴν ἣν ὑμεῖς ἐμάθετε ποιοῦντας, καὶ ἐκκλίνετε ἀπ' αὐτῶν.

"I appeal to you, brethren, to take note of those who create dissensions and difficulties, in opposition to the doctrine which you have been taught; avoid them." . . . RSV

Παρακαλῶ (1st.per.sing.pres.act.ind.ofds παρακαλέω, aoristic) 230.
δὲ (explanatory conjunction) 11.
ὑμᾶς (acc.pl.masc.of σύ, direct object of παρακαλῶ) 104.
ἀδελφοί (voc.pl.masc.of ἀδελφός, address) 15.
σκοπεῖν (pres.act.inf.of σκοπέω, complementary) 2460.
τοὺς (acc.pl.masc.of the article in agreement with ποιοῦντας) 9.
τὰ (acc.pl.fem.of the article in agreement with διχοστασίας) 9.

#4091 διχοστασίας (acc.pl.fem.of διχοστασία, direct object of ποιοῦντας).

King James Version

division - Rom.16:17.
sedition - Gal.5:20.

Revised Standard Version

dissension - Rom.16:17; Gal.5:20.

Meaning: Cf. διχοστατέω - "to stand apart from." Hence, divisions, dissensions, differences of opinion. In Rom.16:17 of the theological views not identical to (παρά) received doctrine. One of the works of the flesh - Gal.5:20.

καὶ (adjunctive conjunction joining nouns) 14.
τὰ (acc.pl.neut.of the article in agreement with σκάνδαλα) 9.
σκάνδαλα (acc.pl.neut.of σκάνδαλον, direct object of ποιοῦντας) 1082.
παρὰ (preposition with the accusative, opposition) 154.
τὴν (acc.sing.fem.of the article in agreement with διδαχὴν) 9.
διδαχὴν (acc.sing.fem.of διδαχή, opposition) 706.
ἣν (acc.sing.fem.of ὅς, relative pronoun, direct object of ἐμάθετε) 65.
ὑμεῖς (nom.pl.masc.of σύ, subject of ἐμάθετε) 104.
ἐμάθετε (2d.per.pl.2d.aor.act.ind.of μανθάνω, constative) 794.
ποιοῦντας (pres.act.part.acc.pl.masc.of ποιέω, substantival, direct object of σκοπεῖν) 127.
καὶ (continuative conjunction) 14.
ἐκκλίνετε (2d.per.pl.pres.act.impv.of ἐκκλίνω, command) 3860.
ἀπ' (preposition with the ablative of separation) 70.
αὐτῶν (abl.pl.masc.of αὐτός, separation) 16.

Translation - "Now I beg you, brethren, to watch out for those who create the dissensions and difficulties, in opposition to the teaching you have learned, and avoid them."

Comment: δὲ is explanatory as Paul begins a new paragraph. σκοπεῖν, the object infinitive in complementary to παρακαλῶ. The object of the infinitive is the trouble makers - τοὺς ... ποιοῦντας. Note that the article τοὺς and its participial substantive are widely separated by the direct objects of ποιοῦντας, the prepositional phrase with παρὰ and the relative pronoun ἥν clause. All three uses of the article are beautifully illustrated in this verse.

τοὺς refers to the individuals who are causing trouble.

τὰς and τὰ separating classes of trouble - theoretical and social, and

τὴν which distinguishes the quality of Christian teaching from the quality of the heresies and stumbling blocks.

παρὰ τὴν διδαχήν - "beside" or "parallel to" and therefore "contrary to" the teaching. *Cf.* #154 for παρά in this sense.

Note the direct attraction of the relative pronoun ἥν to its antecedent διδαχήν.

The last verb is imperative. "Avoid them." There were theological heresies and stumbling blocks (σκάνδαλον #1082) in the Roman church. Their thrust was contrary to orthodox Christian teaching, both in matters of faith and practice. Paul ordered that the church avoid a confrontation with the heretics.

Does this Scripture support the modern movement among conservative theologians who have formally withdrawn in legal and administrative ways, from church bodies that fellowship false teaching? Though the early churches were formally set in order, in the sense that pastors, bishops (overseers) and deacons were named and installed, there was no organizational structure that tied each local church to the others separated by geography. For example, churches in Rome, Ephesus, Corinth, Philippi, Berea, Thessalonica, Galatian country, Antich, Jerusalem etc. had no super church organizational machinery. There was no hierarchy among the clergy after the death of the Apostles, and even the Apostles functioned in advisory capacity only. The problem of church discipline and heresy was a local church matter.

Paul certainly taught that Christians should separate from heretics. This is inherent in the verb ἐκκλίνετε (#3860) and the ablative of separation expressed by ἀπ' αὐτῶν. The action of separation is enjoined upon the Christians, not upon the heretics. The order to the Romans was "Avoid them." This could be done either by dismissing the trouble makers from the fellowship or by withdrawing from the heretics. Titus 3:10 and Mt.18:15-17 seem clearly to say that the heretic is to be dismissed from the church, not the other way around.

This much is certain. Paul regarded a failure to dissociate Christian truth and practice from false teaching and unethical behavior as a danger to the spiritual life of the members of a local church fellowship. He who teaches that which is contrary to the Holy Spirit's revelation in the New Testament, grieves Him (Eph.4:30). In such cases, those in the fellowship who are dominated by the Holy Spirit (πνευματικός) are charged with the responsibility of restoring the heretic to the faith, taking due care not to be carried away themselves by the heresy (Gal.6:1). If their efforts are successful the problem is solved. If not it must be dealt with in another way.

Paul was totally tolerant of any and all teachings and practices outside the church. He was no societal reformer for those who were not saved. He spent no time trying to tell the Romans Emperors how to run the Roman Empire. But he was intolerant of false teaching and practice within the church. The 18th verse fails to make clear whether the trouble makers in Rome were saved or unsaved; inside the fellowship or without.

Verse 18 - "For they that are such serve not our Lord Jesus Christ, but their own belly; and by good words and fair speeches deceive the hearts of the simple."

οἱ γὰρ τοιοῦτοι τῷ κυρίῳ ἡμῶν Χριστῷ οὐ δουλεύουσιν ἀλλὰ τῇ ἑαυτῶν κοιλίᾳ, καὶ διὰ τῆς χρηστολογίας καὶ εὐλογίας ἐξαπατῶσιν τὰς καρδίας τῶν ἀκάκων.

"For such persons do not serve our Lord Christ, but their own appetites, and by fair and flattering words they deceive the hearts of the simple-minded."

οἱ (nom.pl.masc.of the article in agreement with τοιοῦτοι) 9.
γὰρ (causal conjunction) 105.
τοιοῦτοι (nom.pl.masc.of τοιοῦτος, subject of δουλεύουσιν) 785.
τῷ (dat.sing.masc.of the article in agreement with κυρίῳ) 9.
κυρίῳ (dat.sing.masc.of κύριος, personal advantage) 97.
ἡμῶν (gen.pl.masc.of ἐγώ, relationship) 123.
Χριστῷ (dat.sing.masc.of Χριστός, apposition) 4.
οὐ (negative particle with the indicative) 130.
δουλεύουσιν (3d.per.pl.pres.act.ind.of δουλεύω, customary) 604.
ἀλλὰ (alternative conjunction) 342.
τῇ (dat.sing.fem.of the article in agreement with κοιλίᾳ) 9.
ἑαυτῶν (gen.pl.masc.of ἑαυτός, possession) 288.
κοιλίᾳ (dat.sing.fem.of κοιλία, personal advantage) 1008.
καὶ (adjunctive conjunction joining verbs) 14.
διὰ (preposition with the ablative of means) 118.
τῆς (abl.sing.fem.of the article in agreement with χρηστολογίας) 9.

#4092 χρηστολογίας (abl.sing.fem.of χρηστολογία, means).

King James Version

good words - Rom.16:18.

Revised Standard Version

fair words - Rom.16:18.

Meaning: A combination of χρηστός (#959) and λόγος (#510). *Cf.* also others in λόγ - #'s 4011, 3135, 3455, 3845, 2611, 4820, 4778. Fair, pleasant, gracious, easy flowing speech that exudes goodness and tends to convince. In an evil sense - seductive and conducive to false views and immoral behavior - Rom.16:18.

καὶ (adjunctive conjunction joining nouns) 14.
εὐλογίας (abl.sing.fem.of εὐλογία, means) 4060.
ἐξαπατῶσιν (3d.per.pl.pres.act.ind.ofd ἐξαπατάω, customary) 3922.
τὰς (acc.pl.fem.of the article in agreement with καρδίας) 9.

καρδίας (acc.pl.fem.of καρδία, direct object of ἐξαπατῶσιν) 432.
τῶν (gen.pl.masc.of the article in agreement with ἀκάκων) 9.

#4093 ἀκάκων (gen.pl.masc.of ἄκακος, description).

King James Version

harmless - Heb.7:26.
simple - Rom.16:18.

Revised Standard Version

simple minded - Rom.16:18.
blameless - Heb.7:26.

Meaning: α privative plus κακός (#1388). Hence, without guilt; harmless; without guile. So personally free from guile as to be considered naive; characterized by unaffected simplicity - Rom.16:18. In a good sense in Heb.7:26 where it applies to our Lord.

Translation - "Because such men are not serving our Lord Christ, but their own carnal desires, and by means of pleasant words and flattering speeches, they seduce the hearts of the unsophisticated."

Comment: Paul's incisive analysis of the heretics uncovers their base motivation. The concern of these knaves is not to serve the Lord, but to satisfy their own animal passions, whether for moeny, food, sex, prestige or what. He also analyzes their *modus operandi.* They are plausible, eloquent, easy to listen to. Their speeches are laced with insincere flattery. They play the role of the villain in the melodrama that was so popular a century ago. Their performance elicits hisses, boos, catcalls and Bronx cheers from the intellectuals in the audience, to whom they make no positive appeal. They are good salesmen, but they succeed only with the simple minded in the audience.

Paul also analyzes the victim of such demagogy. He is sincere, guileless, so free from impure motives that he is unaware that others are less pure. He is naive, like a child in his thinking, simple minded, immature, in many cases congenitally short of intellectual potential. Such people fall victim to the demagogues. It was the rats that followed the Pied Piper into the river, and later the little children in the city, although the religious Pied Pipers whom Paul attacks, unlike the Hamelin musician of Browning's poem, are well paid for their services. If Christians would ignore the offering plate when it is passed by these soapbox artists they would go away, but there are those in the audience without the power to discriminate between elegance of speech and perspicuity. They are not mature enough to look for content in speech rather than for form.

A great theologian, speaking of a prominent Deist, said, "He uses the language of heaven to teach the doctrines of hell." A simple minded Christian woman once said to her pastor, "I know that he does not believe the Bible but his sermons are so beautiful."

The question often arises whether Christian young people, who have been reared in a Christian home and who have been subject to Biblical disciplines should attend colleges or universities where professors inveigh against Christianty. Are not such people in danger of losing their faith? Not unless they are of the type described here. The mature mind is as skeptical of error as it is of new truth. One who is soldily grounded in Christian Apologetics will find that his faith in the Word of God grows stronger as he listens with growing contempt to the attempts of deists, agnostics, atheists and/or nihilists to destroy it. The Bible is the anvil that wears out the hammers. But one must know the Bible and enough about philosophy and religion to recognize the hammer when he sees one. All Christians who attended secular institutions of higher learning will testify that in the course of their advanced studies they found many new insights that cast a new glow of light upon the Scriptures. Witness the support that the economics of John Maynard Keynes provides for Ephesians 4:28 and the approval of the Freudians of the psychology of 1 Peter 2:1,2. There are many others.

Conversely the Christian whose education has been under the care only of Bible believers may have been hothoused for Fundamentalism and never challenged to think for himself. Such are ill prepared to face the rough and tumble world which they will encounter after graduation. There was no harm to Daniel in the lions' den, nor will there be to Christian young people in an atheistic university, but they must be like Daniel and they must know a lion when they see one. The question in modern Christian education is not, "Where is the Lord God of Elijah?" (2 Kings 2:14). It may well be, "Where is Elijah?"

Verse 19 - "For your obedience is come abroad unto all men. I am glad therefore on your behalf: but yet I would have you wise unto that which is good, and simple concerning evil."

ἡ γὰρ ὑμῶν ὑπακοὴ εἰς πάντας ἀφίκετο. ἐφ᾽ ὑμῖν οὖν χαίρω, θέλω δὲ ὑμᾶς σοφοὺς εἶναι εἰς τὸ ἀγαθόν, ἀκεραίους δὲ εἰς τὸ κακόν.

"For while your obedience is known to all, so that I rejoice over you, I would have you wise as to what is good and guileless as to what is evil;" . . . RSV

ἡ (nom.sing.fem.of the article in agreement with ὑπακοή) 9.
γὰρ (concessive conjunction) 105.
ὑμῶν (gen.pl.masc.of σύ, possession) 104.
ὑπακοὴ (nom.sing.fem.of ὑπακοή, subject of ἀφίκετο) 3785.
εἰς (preposition with the accusative of extent) 140.
πάντας (acc.pl.masc.of πᾶς, extent) 67.

#4094 ἀφίκετο (3d.per.sing.2d.aor.mid.ind.of ἀφικνέομαι, constative).

King James Version

come abroad - Rom.16:18.

Revised Standard Version

known - Rom.16:19.

Meaning: A combination of ἀπό (#70) and ἱκνέομαι - "to come." Hence, to come from a place. With reference to the story of the Roman Christians and their obedience to the gospel - Rom.16:19. *Cf.* Rom.1:8.

ἐφ' (preposition with the instrumental, cause) 47.
ὑμῖν (instru.pl.masc.of σύ, cause) 104.
οὖν (inferential conjunction) 68.
χαίρω (1st.per.sing.pres.act.ind.of χαίρω, aoristic) 182.
θέλω (1st.per.sing.pres.act.ind.of θέλω, aoristic) 88.
δὲ (adversative conjunction) 11.
ὑμᾶς (acc.pl.masc.of σύ, general reference) 104.
σοφοὺς (acc.pl.masc.of σοφός, predicate accusative) 949.
εἶναι (pres.inf.of εἰμί, direct object of θέλω) 86.
εἰς (preposition with the accusative of reference) 140.
τὸ (acc.sing.neut.of the article in agreement with ἀγαθόν) 9.
ἀκεραίου (acc.pl.masc.of ἀκέραιος, predicate accustive) 874.
δὲ (adversative conjunction) 11.
εἰς (preposition with the accusative of reference) 140.
τὸ (acc.sing.neut.of the article in agreement with κακόν) 9.
κακόν (acc.sing.neut.of κακός, accusative of reference) 1388.

Translation - *"Although your obedience has become known to all (and) therefore I rejoice because of you, I want you to be wise with reference to that which is good but unadulterated with reference to that which is evil."*

Comment: The story of the obedience of the Roman Christians was widespread. *Cf.* Rom.1:8 and comment *en loc.* Because of their obedience Paul was glad, yet (adversative δὲ) he was not wholly satisfied with their performance. He had been wishing (present progressive retroactive in θέλω) them to be very sophisticated about what was good, but he also wanted them unadulterated (simple, pure, gullible, unmixed, homogeneous, plain, bare, mere, uniform, elementary, elemental and of a piece) with reference to evil. All of these adjectives are listed in Roget for the concept involved in ἀκεραίους (#874).

The false teachers of verse 18 were attempting to introduce alloys of philosophical error into their minds. When it comes to evil Paul wished them to be unalloyed. Sin is sin and evil is evil, regardless of the fair speeches in which it is presented. This point is particularly apropos since the revival of situation ethics and relative morality. If one becomes philosophical enough he can justify any human behavior on moral grounds. A group of psychiatrists have only recently convinced twelve people that a young man was mentally incompetent to the point that he was unaware that it was wrong to shoot the President of the United States. If one must be totally sane in order to be immoral and felonious then there is no such thing as sin or illegality, for no psychiatrist can *prove* that anyone is totally free from mental aberration. Sin is insanity in a moral universe that is run on natural law which God in creation ordained. It follows then that what is sin, if it is also in violation of the law must be excused. No one should be incarcerated in a prison cell. Everyone who breaks the law should be treated to a stay in a psychopathic ward.

Paul's teaching here is authoritarian to be sure. When God says, "No" He means "No" and we are not to question it or submit His decision to the ramifications of philosophical haul and pull. It is better to be an obedient child, even if our obedience involves simple mindedness than to be the sophisticate who has seduced himself into universal disobedience.

The sophisticated truth is that if we will think the problem of what is the good, the beautiful and the true down to its roots, we will find that the Ten Commandments and the New Testament law of love which fulfills them is the only system that is consistent, coherent and correspondant to reality. Those who are able to think that deeply will rejoice. Those who cannot can at least be obedient.

Must the philosophical struggle about what is good and evil go on forever, is often the question of the Christian who is tired of it. The answer is that it will not, as Paul says in

Verse 20 - "And the God of peace shall bruise Satan under your feet shortly. The grace of our Lord Jesus Christ be with you. Amen."

ὁ δὲ θεὸς τῆς εἰρήνης συντρίψει τὸν Σατανᾶν ὑπὸ τοὺς πόδας ὑμῶν ἐν τάχει. ἡ χάρις τοῦ κυρίου ἡμῶν Ἰησοῦ μεθ' ὑμῶν.

"then the God of peace will soon crush Satan under your feet. The grace of our Lord Jesus be with you." . . . RSV

ὁ (nom.sing.masc.of the article in agreement with θεὸς) 9.
δὲ (continuative conjunction) 11.
θεὸς (nom.sing.masc.of θεός, subject of συντρίψει) 124.
τῆς (gen.sing.fem.of the article in agreement with εἰρήνης) 9.
εἰρήνης (gen.sing.fem.of εἰρήνη, description) 865.
συντρίψει (3d.per.sing.fut.act.ind.of συντρίβω, predictive) 985.
τὸν (acc.sing.masc.of the article in agreement with Σατανᾶν) 9.
Σατανᾶν (acc.sing.masc.of Σατανᾶ, direct object of συντρίψει) 365.
ὑπὸ (preposition with the accusative of extent) 117.
τοὺς (acc.pl.masc.of the article in agreement with πόδας) 9.
πόδας (acc.pl.masc.of πούς, extent) 353.
ὑμῶν (gen.pl.masc.of σύ, possession) 104.
ἐν (preposition with the locative in a time expression) 80.
τάχει (loc.sing.neut.ofd τάχος, time point) 2626.
ἡ (nom.sing.fem.of the article in agreement with χάρις) 9.
χάρις (nom.sing.fem.of χάρις, subject of εἴη understood) 1700.
τοῦ (gen.sing.masc.of the article in agreement with κυρίου) 9.
κυρίου (gen.sing.masc.of κύριος, description) 97.
ἡμῶν (gen.pl.masc.of ἐγώ, relationship) 123.
Ἰησοῦ (gen.sing.masc.of Ἰησοῦς, apposition) 3.
μεθ' (preposition with the genitive of accompaniment) 50.

ὑμῶν (gen.pl.masc.of σύ, accompaniment) 104.

Translation - "And the God of peace will utterly destroy Satan under your feet soon. The grace of our Lord Jesus be with you."

Comment: It is a call for patience. The Roman Christians were attacked from all sides and in various ways. When would God act in their behalf? Not immediately, but soon. *Cf. ἐν τάχει* in other contexts (#2626). Note that in the Revelation it refers not to immediacy but to a time which is contingent upon other events.

Perhaps a local application is being made to Nero, who, though not Satan was Satanically inspired. Paul anticipated the Second Coming of Messiah in the first century. He is saying to the saints that their God is aware of the struggle between light and darkness, good and evil, truth and error and that ultimately the victory will belong to God and the saints will see Satan, now prominent and domineering, utterly crushed beneath their feet. The victory promised to our Lord in Psalm 2:1-12; 110:1 will be their victory.

Meanwhile God's grace will be sufficient. (2 Cor.12:9; Heb.10:36,37).

Verse 21 - "Timotheus my workfellow, and Lucius, and Jason, and Sosipater, my kinsman, salute you."

Ἀσπάζεται ὑμᾶς Τιμόθεος ὁ συνεργός μου, καὶ Λούκιος καὶ Ἰάσων καὶ Σωσίπατρος οἱ συγγενεῖς μου.

"Timothy, my fellow worker, greets you; so do Lucius and Jason and Sosipater, my kinsmen." . . . RSV

Ἀσπάζεται (3d.per.sing.pres.mid.ind.of ἀσπάζομαι, aoristic) 551.
ὑμᾶς (acc.pl.masc.of σύ, direct object of ἀσπάζεται) 104.
Τιμόθεος (nom.sing.masc.of Τιμόθεος, subject of ἀσπάζομαι) 3354.
ὁ (nom.sing.masc.of the article in agreement with συνεργός) 9.
συνεργός (nom.sing.masc.of συνεργός, apposition) 4066.
μου (gen.sing.masc.of ἐγώ, relationship) 123.
καὶ (adjunctive conjunction joining nouns) 14.
Λούκιος (nom.sing.masc.of Λούκιος, subject of ἀσπάζεται) 3269.
καὶ (adjunctive conjunction joining nouns) 14.
Ἰάσων (nom.sing.masc.of Ἰάσων, subject of ἀσπάζεται) 3390.
καὶ (adjunctive conjunction joining nouns) 14.

#**4095** Σωσίπατρος (nom.sing.masc.of Σωσίπατρος, subject of ἀσπάζεται).

      King James Version

      Sosipater - Rom.16:21.

        Revised Standard Version

      Sosipater - Rom.16:21.

Meaning: A relative of Paul. Possibly confused with Σώπατρος (#3501) of Acts

20:4, who was from Berea, while Sosipater was with Paul in Corinth, when Paul wrote the Roman letter. It is however possible that Σώπατρος of Berea (#3501) and Σωσίπατρος, who was with Paul in Corinth when the Roman letter was written (#4095) is the same man. A careful reading of Acts 20-21 does not make the matter clear. Romans 16:21.

οἱ (nom.pl.masc.of the article in agreement with συγγενεῖς) 9.
συγγενεῖς (nom.pl.masc.of συγγενής, apposition) 1815.
μου (gen.sing.masc.of ἐγώ, relationship) 123.

Translation - "Timothy my fellow worker and Lucius and Jason and Sosipater, my relatives send you greeting."

Comment: The Acts account of Paul's ministry in Corinth neither affirms nor denies that those mentioned here were with him in Corinth.

Verse 22 - "I Tertius, who wrote this epistle, salute you in the Lord."

ἀσπάζομαι ὑμᾶς ἐγὼ Τέρτιος ὁ γράψας τὴν ἐπιστολὴν ἐν κυρίῳ.

"I Tertius, the writer of this letter, greet you in the Lord." . . . RSV

ἀσπάζομαι (1st.per.sing.pres.mid.ind.of ἀσπάζομαι, aoristic) 551.
ὑμᾶς (acc.pl.masc.of σύ, direct object of ἀσπάζομαι) 104.
ἐγώ (nom.sing.masc.of ἐγώ, subject of ἀσπάζομαι) 123.

#4096 Τέρτιος (nom.sing.masc.of Τέρτιος, apposition).

King James Version

Tertius - Rom.16:22.

Revised Standard Version

Tertius - Rom.16:22.

Meaning: An amenuensis for Paul, who wrote the Roman epistle - Rom.16:22.

ὁ (nom.sing.masc.of the article in agreement with γράψας) 9.
γράψας (aor.act.part.nom.sing.masc.of γράφω, substantival, apposition) 156.
τὴν (acc.sing.fem.of the article in agreement with ἐπιστολὴν) 9.
ἐπιστολὴν (acc.sing.fem.of ἐπιστολή, direct object of γράψας) 3180.
ἐν (preposition with the locative, association) 80.
κυρίῳ (loc.sing.masc.of κύριος, association) 97.

Translation - "I, Tertius, who has written this letter send you greeting in the Lord."

Comment: This verse is parenthetical as Tertius took the liberty to send his own personal greeting to the Roman Christians.

Verse 23 - "Gaius mine host, and of the whole church, saluteth you. Erastus the chamberlain of the city saluteth you, and Quartus a brother."

ἀσπάζεται ὑμᾶς Γάϊος ὁ ξένος μου καὶ ὅλης τῆς ἐκκλησίας. ἀσπάζεται ὑμᾶς Ἔραστος ὁ οἰκονόμος τῆς πόλεως καὶ Κούαρτος ὁ ἀδελφός.

"Gaius, who is host to me and to the whole church, greets you. Erastus, the city treasurer, and our brother Quartus, greet you." . . . RSV

ἀσπάζεται (3d.per.sing.pres.mid.ind.of ἀσπάζομαι, aoristic) 551.
ὑμᾶς (acc.pl.masc.of σύ, direct object of ἀσπάζεται) 104.
Γάϊος (nom.sing.masc.of Γάϊος, subject of ἀσπάζεται) 3484.
ὁ (nom.sing.masc.of the article in agreement with ξένος) 9.
ξένος (nom.sing.masc.of ξένος, apposition) 1547.
μου (gen.sing.masc.of ἐγώ, relationship) 123.
καὶ (adjunctive conjunction joining substantives) 14.
ὅλης (gen.sing.fem.of ὅλος, in agreement with ἐκκλησίας) 112.
τῆς (gen.sing.fem.of the article in agreement with ἐκκλησίας) 9.
ἐκκλησίας (gen.sing.fem.of ἐκκλησία, relationship) 1204.
ἀσπάζεται (3d.per.sing.pres.mid.ind.of ἀσπάζομαι, aoristic) 551.
Ἔραστος (nom.sing.masc.of Ἔραστος, subject of ἀσπάζεται) 3472.
ὁ (nom.sing.masc.of the article in agreement with οἰκονόμος) 9.
οἰκονόμος (nom.sing.masc.of οἰκονόμος, apposition) 2488.
τῆς (gen.sing.fem.of the article in agreement with πόλεως) 9.
πόλεως (gen.sing.fem.of πόλις, relationship) 243.
καὶ (adjunctive conjunction joining nouns) 14.

#4097 Κούαρτος (nom.sing.masc.of Κούαρτος, subject of verb understood).

King James Version

Quartus - Rom.16:23.

Revised Standard Version

Quartus - Rom.16:23.

Meaning: An unknown Christian in Corinth, an associate of Paul - Rom.16:23.

ὁ (nom.sing.masc.of the article in agreement with ἀδελφός) 9.
ἀδελφός (nom.sing.masc.of ἀδελφός, apposition) 15.

Translation - *"Gaius, my host and host of the entire church sends greeting. Erastus, the city treasurer and Quartus, a brother, also wish to be remembered."*

Comment: Here is further evidence (verses 4,5) that the early churches had no public buildings devoted to worship but met in private homes. The Roman church met with Aquila and Priscilla (Rom.16:5); the church in Corinth met in the home of Gaius. Erastus' greeting to the Roman saints indicates that Christianity in Corinth had reached into the political establishment of the city.

Verse 24 - "The grace of our Lord Jesus Christ be with you all. Amen."

(The United Bible Societies' Committee text, with a B degree of certainty has followed p46,61 vid, Sinaiticus, A B C and some miniscules in omitting verse 24. D Ψ and several miniscules include it while G includes it, but omits Ἰησοῦ Χριστοῦ. P 33 104 256 436 1319 1837, etc.include verse 24 following verse 27. Note that the benediction belongs in verse 20.)

Doxology

(Romans 16:25-27)

Verse 25 - "Now to him that is of power to stablish you according to my gospel, and the preaching of Jesus Christ according to the revelation of the mystery, which was kept secret since the world began,"

Τῷ δὲ δυναμένῳ ὑμᾶς στηρίξαι κατὰ τὸ εὐαγγέλιόν μου καὶ τὸ κήρυγμα Ἰησοῦ Χριστοῦ, κατὰ ἀποκάλυφιν μυστηρίου χρόνοις αἰωνίοις σεσιγημένου.

"Now to him who is able to strengthen you according to my gospel and the preaching of Jesus Christ, according to the revelation of the mystery which was kept secret for long ages. . . . " RSV

Τῷ (dat.sing.masc.of the article in agreement with δυναμένῳ) 9.

δὲ (explanatory conjunction) 11.

δυναμένῳ (pres.mid.part.dat.sing.masc.of δύναμαι, substantival, personal interest) 289.

ὑμᾶς (acc.pl.masc.of σύ, direct object of στηρίξαι) 104.

στηρίξαι (aor.act.inf.of στηρίζω, complementary) 2359.

κατὰ (preposition with the accusative, standard) 98.

τὸ (acc.sing.neut.of the article in agreement with εὐαγγέλιόν) 9.

εὐαγγέλιόν (acc.sing.neut.of εὐαγγέλιον, standard) 405.

μου (gen.sing.masc.of ἐγώ, possession) 123.

καὶ (adjunctive conjunction joining nouns) 14.

τὸ (acc.sing.neut.of the article in agreement with κήρυγμα) 9.

κήρυγμα (acc.sing.neut.of κήρυγμα, standard) 1013.

Ἰησοῦ (gen.sing.masc.of Ἰησοῦς, description) 3.

Χριστοῦ (gen.sing.masc.of Χριστός, apposition) 4.

κατὰ (preposition with the accusative, standard) 98.

ἀποκάλυφιν (acc.sing.fem.of ἀποκάλυφις, standard) 1902.

μυστηρίου (gen.sing.neut.of μυστήριον, description) 1038.

χρόνοις (instrumental pl.masc.of χρόνος, time measure) 168.

αἰωνίοις (instru.pl.masc.of αἰώνιος, in agreement with χρόνοις) 1255.

σεσιγημένου (perf.pass.part.gen.sing.neut.of σιγάω, adjectival, restrictive, in agreement with μυστηρίου) 2330.

Translation - "Now to Him Who is able to solidify your faith in accordance with my gospel and the preaching about Jesus Christ, in keeping with the revelation of the mystery, kept secret since the eternal ages , . . . "

Comment: The doxology begins here and ends with verse 27. ἡ δόζα (verse 27) is the gift of praise offered to τῷ δυναμένῳ in verse 25. "Glory to the Able One. . . κ.τ.λ." στηρίξαι, the complementary infinitive, completes δυναμένῳ and tell us what God is able to do. He can establish, make secure and solidify the Christian (#2359). This solid building of the Christian faith and experience is done along specific lines. It is in keeping with what Paul calls "my gospel" and further defines it as the "preaching about Jesus Christ." This is how God will establish the saints. It will be according to the gospel which he preached which is the proclamation of story of the person and work of Jesus Christ. (1 Cor.15:1-4). The faithful preaching of the gospel of Jesus Christ makes for solid citizenry in the Kingdom of God. The social gospel, with its emphasis upon good works, is essential, but only if it is presented in connection with the theological gospel of the incarntion, life, teaching, miracles, death, burial, resurrection, ascension, high priestly ministry and second coming of our Lord. The theological gospel is foundational; the social gospel is superstructural. Each is essential to the other. Neither would be complete in itself. Christians who are not thoroughly grounded in the theological gospel are not effective social gospel workers, despite their zealous efforts.

Paul's preaching about Jesus Christ was shaped by the revelation of a great mystery which God revealed to him. This mystery had been hidden from before the foundation of the world. There are hints with reference to it in the Old Testament, but it "was not made known unto the sons of men (in previous ages) *as it is now revealed* unto his holy apostles and prophets by the Spirit." (Eph.3:5). The new revelation was to the effect that "the Gentiles should be fellowheirs and of the same body, and partakers of his promise in Christ by the gospel." (Eph.3:6). It was in connection with the unveiling of this new truth that Paul received his call to Apostleship. That is why he refers to it as "my gospel."

Note the instrumental-associative use of χρόνοις αἰωνίοις, to express time. How long had the mystery been kept a secret? From the time in between the beginning (αἰωνίοις) to the present time, set forth by φανερωθέντος δὲ νῦν of verse 26. The perfect passive participle σεσιγημένου points backward interminably to the "time" (!) when God decreed it, since which time it has been kept secret, but now (and for all the future) revealed. But the revealing, with its proleptic (future) results are not to be derived from σεσιγνμένου, but from what follows in verse 26. The perfect tense in never proleptic in itself. Extension of results into the future must be found elsewhere in the context.

The emphasis in Paul's preaching, as he exploited the mystery which God had revealed to him, was upon the fact that salvation was for the Gentiles as well as for the Jews and that this had been the divine plan from the beginning. There is nothing in the gospel of Christ to denigrate a Gentile because he is a Gentile or to give special favor to the Jew because he is a Jew. Once a Gentile Christian understands that he is motivated to be obedient.

Verse 26 - ". . . but now is made manifest, and by the scriptures of the prophets,

*according to the commandment of the everlasting God, made known to all
nations for the obedience of faith."*

φανερωθέντος δὲ νῦν διά τε γραφῶν προφητικῶν κατ᾽ ἐπιταγὴν τοῦ
αἰωνίου θεοῦ εἰς ὑπακοὴν πίστεως εἰς πάντα τὰ ἔθνη γνωρισθέντος,

*". . . but is now disclosed and through the prophetic writings is made known to
all nations, according to the command of the eternal God, to bring about the
obedience of faith —" . . . RSV*

φανερωθέντος (1st.aor.pass.part.gen.sing.neut.of φανερόω, adjectival,
restrictive, in agreement with μυστηρίου) 1960.
δὲ (adversative conjunction) 11.
νῦν (temporal adverb) 1497.
διὰ (preposition with the genitive, means) 118.
τε (correlative particle) 1408.
γραφῶν (gen.pl.fem.of γραφή, means) 1389.

#4098 προφητικῶν (gen.pl.fem.of προφητικός, in agreement with γραφῶν).

King James Version

of prophecy - 2 Pet.1:19.
of the prophets - Rom.16:26.

Revised Standard Version

prophetic writings - Rom.16:26.
prophetic word - 2 Pet.1:19.

Meaning: Cf. προφήτης (#119); προφητεύω (#685); προφητεία (#1041) and
προφῆτις (#1906). Proceding from a prophet. Hence, prophetic. In definition of
γραφῶν in Rom.16:26; defining λόγον in 2 Pet.1:19.

κατ᾽ (preposition with the accusative, standard) 98.

#4099 ἐπιταγὴν (acc.sing.fem.of ἐπιταγή, standard).

King James Version

authority - Tit.2:15.
commandment - Rom.16:26; 1 Cor.7:6,25; 2 Cor.8:8; 1 Tim.1:1; Tit.1:3.

Revised Standard Version

command - Rom.16:26; 1 Cor.7:6,25; 2 Cor.8:8; 1 Tim.1:1; Tit.1:3.
authority - Tit.2:15.

Meaning: A combination of ἐπί (#47) and πάσσω (#732). Cf. also τάγμα
(#4242); ἐπιτάσσω (#2061). Hence, a mandamus or (negatively) an injunction.
An order served upon one by a superior authority. A mandate. With κατά and

the accusative of standard and followed by an ablative of source - Rom. 16:26; where the divine command is implied - 1 Cor. 7:6; as a direct object with κυρίου - 1 Cor. 7:25; with κατά and the divine source implied in 2 Cor. 8:8; expressed - 1 Tim. 1:1; Tit. 1:3. With μετὰ πάσης ἐπιταγῆς, where the source of the authority is divine by implication - Tit. 2:15.

τοῦ (abl.sing.masc.of the article in agreement with θεοῦ) 9.

αἰωνίου (abl.sing.masc.of αἰώνιος, in agreement with θεοῦ) 1255.

θεοῦ (abl.sing.masc.of θεός, source) 124.

εἰς (preposition with the accusative, purpose) 140.

ὑπακοήν (acc.sing.fem.of ὑπακοή, purpose) 3785.

πίστεως (abl.sing.fem.of πίστις, source) 728.

εἰς (preposition with the accusative of extent) 140.

πάντα (acc.pl.neut.of πᾶς, in agreement with ἔθνη) 67.

ἔθνη (acc.pl.neut.of ἔθνος, extent) 376.

γνωρισθέντος (aor.pass.part.gen.sing.neut.adjectival, restrictive, in agreement with μυστηρίου) 1882.

Translation - "... but now brought to light and by the command of the eternal God made known to all the nations by the prophetic Scriptures in order to elicit obedience that comes from faith..."

Comment: Three participles, all adjectival are used to define μυστηρίου in verse 25. The mystery had been "kept secret" (σεσιγημένου) throughout the eternal ages of the past, but it was "brought to light" (φανερωθέντος) and "made known" (γνωρισθέντος). Now in the New Testament age, thanks to Paul's gospel, which he calls τὸ κήρυγμα Ἰησοῦ Χριστοῦ - "the proclaimed message of Jesus Christ" it is known. Paul used the perfect participle to explain that the mystery had been hidden in the past, and it was still hidden until Paul had revealed to him what the mystery was (Eph. 3:1-11). Then he used the aorist participle to say that, due to its unveiling, the fact was no longer a mystery. The aorist results in a present condition of knowing, while the perfect participle results in a past condition of not knowing, until the time of unveiling. The two eras (1) in the past hidden and (2) currently revealed, are set forth by σεσιγημένου ... φανερωθέντος δὲ νῦν. The third participle that defines μυστηρίου is γνωρισθέντος - "make known."

God revealed, first to Paul and then to others, that the Old Testament Scriptures had always taught that Gentiles as well as Jews could be saved. Having revealed this truth to Paul, God ordered it preached to all the Gentile nations (Mt. 28:18-20). For what purpose? εἰς ὑπακοὴν πίστεως, the purpose construction tells us. God wants the gospel of Jesus Christ obeyed. This obedience has its source in the faith with which the sinner believes. This faith is the result of hearing the Word of God preached. Thus the order is (1) revelation of the mystery to Paul, which, after God had pointed it out, Paul saw clearly in the Old Testament Scriptures, (2) the order to preach, (3) the preaching of Paul and others, (4) hearing, (5) faith, (6) obedience. *Cf.* Rom. 10:13-15.

Thus the prophetic writings, once considered relevant to Israel and her sole property, are the source of a truth, previously hidden but now understood, and which, when preached to the Gentiles and the Jews results in their faith which in turn produces their obedience. Obedience to God's will can come only from a divine source, which is faith, which comes only from a divine source, preaching (κήρυγμα) which is nothing unless based upon a divine revelation, the mystery of Christ's body, which revelation comes from a set of divine writings, the prophetic Scriptures. They are the written source. God supervised their writings and directed their authorship. Julius Wellhausen, Otis Eissfeldt and others who gave the world their documentary hypothesis with its JEPD theory of authorship of the Pentateuch, have taught that the prophetic Scriptures are only of human authorship.   Thus they cast doubt upon the reliability of the Scriptures which are the source of Paul's theology and of the evangelistic mission of the New Testament church. Thanks to Samuel Kulling of Basel and others the higher criticism is not universally accepted. We who are "fools for Christ" join Paul, who coined the phrase, in believing that the prophetic writings (γραφῶν προφητικῶν) are authoritative and supernatural, not only in their origin (2 Pet.1:20,21) but also in their results (Rom.16:26,27).

Verse 27 - "To God only wise, be glory through Jesus Christ for ever. Amen."

μόνῳ σοφῷ θεῷ διὰ 'Ιησοῦ Χριστοῦ (ᾧ) ἡ δόξα εἰς τοὺς αἰῶνας. ἀμήν.

"To the only wise God be glory for evermore through Jesus Christ. Amen." . . .
                                                                            RSV

μόνῳ (dat.sing.masc.of μόνος in agreement with θεῷ) 339.

σοφῷ (dat.sing.masc.of σοφός, in agreement with θεῷ) 949.

θεῷ (dat.sing.masc.of θεός, personal advantage) 124.

διὰ (preposition with the ablative of agent) 118.

'Ιησοῦ (abl.sing.masc.of 'Ιησοῦς, agent) 3.

Χριστοῦ (abl.sing.masc.of Χριστός, apposition) 4.

(ᾧ) (dat.sing.masc.of ὅς, relative pronoun, attracted to θεῷ) 65.

ἡ (nom.sing.fem.of the article in agreement with δόξα) 9.

δόξα (nom.sing.fem.of δόξα, subject of ἦ understood) 361.

εἰς (preposition with the accusative of time extent) 140.

τοὺς (acc.pl.masc.of the article in agreement with αἰῶνας) 9.

αἰῶνας (acc.pl.masc.of αἰών, time extent) 1002.

ἀμήν (explicative) 466.

Translation - "To God Who alone is wise, even to Him be glory through Jesus Christ into the ages. Amen."

Comment: The resumptive use of ᾧ helps us with this involved sentence. Paul, emotionally overcome by the grandeur of the wisdom of God's eternal plan, had one of those experiences in which his heart raced ahead of the pen and his grammatical analysis. Hence the anacoluthon. But the meaning of this thrilling doxology is clear.

Thus ends the most scientific statement of the Christian doctrine of salvation in the New Testament.

Paul's First Letter to the Church in Corinth

Greeting and Thanksgiving

(1 Corinthians 1:1-9)

1 Corinthians 1:1 - "Paul, called to be an apostle of Jesus Christ, through the will of God, and Sosthenes, our brother."

Παῦλος κλητὸς ἀπόστολος Χριστοῦ Ἰησοῦ διὰ θελήματος θεοῦ, καὶ Σωσθένης ὁ ἀδελφός,

"PAUL, CALLED BY THE WILL of God to be an apostle of Christ Jesus, and our brother Sosthenes," . . . *RSV*

Παῦλος (nom.sing.masc.of Παῦλος, nominative absolute) 3284.
κλητὸς (nom.sing.masc.of κλητός, in agreement with Παῦλος) 1411.
ἀπόστολος (nom.sing.masc.of ἀπόστολος, predicate nominative) 844.
Χριστοῦ (gen.sing.masc.of Χριστός, possession) 4.
Ἰησοῦ (gen.sing.masc.of Ἰησοῦς, apposition) 3.
διὰ (preposition with the ablative of agency) 118.
θελήματος (abl.sing.neut.of θέλημα, agency) 577.
θεοῦ (gen.sing.masc.of θεός, definition) 124.
καὶ (adjunctive conjunction joining nouns) 14.
Σωσθένης (nom.sing.masc.of Σωσθένης, nominative absolute) 3449.
ὁ (nom.sing.masc.of the article in agreement with ἀδελφός) 9.
ἀδελφός (nom.sing.masc.of ἀδελφός, apposition) 15.

Translation - "Paul, called by the divine will an Apostle of Christ Jesus, and

brother Sosthenes."

Comment: It was Paul who carried the gospel to Corinth and established the church in this important city of the Roman province of Achaia. He was in Ephesus (1 Cor.16:8) where he stayed until Pentecost (Acts 19:1-40). Ephesus is east of Corinth across the Aegean Sea. The letter was written two or three years before he wrote the Roman letter. At that time (*cf.* comment on Romans 1:1) the offering for poor relief in Jerusalem was complete, while as he writes to the Corinthians it is not yet taken (1 Cor.16:1; 2 Cor.9:1-2). We may thus date the first Corinthian letter at c.55-56.

The Corinthian church, situated in a busy commercial center, was sociologically subject to many unchristian environmental influences. Thus the church had a great many problems, theologically, philosophically and ethically. However, it was, among all of the churches which Paul founded, one of the most richly endowed with spiritual gifts (1 Cor.1:4-7). This epistle is a rich gold mine of teaching which came from the pen of Paul as he struggled with the many spiritual problems of the Christians.

Cf.#'s 1411, 1412. As a member of the Body of Christ, Paul's calling was no different from that of all of the elect. It is the result of the Holy Spirit's ministry (John 16:7-11). As an Apostle Paul's calling was special, reserved only for the original twelve, minus Judas Iscariot, not including Matthias, but including Paul who was named to take the place of Judas Iscariot. (*Cf.* Acts 1:15-26; Mt.19:28; Lk.22:30).

Paul spoke of his calling to the Apostleship and defended it stoutly because he was specially chosen to carry the gospel to the Gentiles (Eph.3:1-11). He was frequently challenged by legalistic Hebrew Christians before it became clear to them that Gentiles also were to be included in the Body of Christ.

Verse 2 - "Unto the church of God which is at Corinth, to them that are sanctified in Christ Jesus, called to be saints, with all that in every place call upon the name of Jesus Christ our Lord, both theirs and ours."

τῇ ἐκκλησίᾳ τοῦ θεοῦ τῇ οὔσῃ ἐν Κορίνθῳ, ἡγιασμένοις ἐν Χριστῷ Ἰησοῦ, κλητοῖς ἁγίοις, σὺν πᾶσιν τοῖς ἐπικαλουμένοις τὸ ὄνομα τοῦ κυρίου ἡμῶν Ἰησοῦ Χριστοῦ ἐν παντὶ τόπῳ, αὐτῶν καὶ ἡμῶν.

"To the church of God which is at Corinth, to those sanctified in Christ Jesus, called to be saints together with all those who in every place call on the name of our Lord Jesus Christ, both their Lord and ours:" ... RSV

τῇ (dat.sing.fem.of the article in agreement with ἐκκλησίᾳ) 9.
ἐκκλησίᾳ (dat.sing.fem.of ἐκκλησία, indirect object) 1204.
τοῦ (gen.sing.masc.of the article in agreement with θεοῦ) 9.
θεοῦ (gen.sing.masc.of θεός, possession) 124.
τῇ (dat.sing.fem.of the article in agreement with οὔσῃ) 9.
οὔσῃ (pres.part.dat.sing.fem.of εἰμί, adjectival, ascriptive, emphatic attributive position, in agreement with ἐκκλησίᾳ) 86.
ἐν (preposition with the locative of place) 80.

Κορίνθῳ (loc.sing.masc.of Κόρινθος, place) 3428.

ἡγιασμένοις (perf.pass.part.dat.pl.masc.of ἀγιάζω, indirect object) 576.

ἐν (preposition with the instrumental, association) 80.

Χριστῷ (instru.sing.masc.of Χριστός, association) 4.

Ἰησοῦ (instru.sing.masc.of Ἰησοῦς, apposition) 3.

κλητοῖς (dat.pl.masc.of κλητός, in agreement with ἁγίοις) 1411.

ἁγίοις (dat.pl.masc.of ἅγιος, apposition) 84.

σὺν (preposition with the instrumental of association) 1542.

πᾶσιν (instru.pl.masc.of πᾶς, in agreement with ἐπικαλουμένοις) 67.

τοῖς (instru.pl.masc.of the article in agreement with ἐπικαλουμένοις) 9.

ἐπικαλουμένοις (pres.mid.part.instru.pl.masc.of ἐπικαλέω, substantival, indirect object) 884.

τὸ (acc.sing.neut.of the article in agreement with ὄνομα) 9.

ὄνομα (acc.sing.neut.of ὄνομα, direct object of ἐπικαλουμένοις) 108.

τοῦ (gen.sing.masc.of the article in agreement with κυρίου) 9.

κυρίου (gen.sing.masc.of κύριος, possession) 97.

ἡμῶν (gen.pl.masc.of ἐγώ, relationship) 123.

Ἰησοῦ (gen.sing.masc.of Ἰησοῦς, apposition) 3.

Χριστοῦ (gen.sing.masc.of Χριστός, apposition) 4.

ἐν (preposition with the locative of place) 80.

παντὶ (loc.sing.masc.of πᾶς, in agreement with τόπῳ) 67.

τόπῳ (loc.sing.masc.of τόπος, place) 1019.

αὐτῶν (gen.pl.masc.of αὐτός, possession) 16.

καὶ (adjunctive conjunction joining pronouns) 14.

ἡμῶν (gen.pl.masc.of ἐγώ, possession) 123.

Translation - "To the church of God in Corinth, set apart in Christ Jesus, called saints, with all those who are calling upon the name of our Lord Jesus Christ in every place, their Lord and ours."

Comment: Note the participial adjective τῇ οὔσῃ in the emphatic attributive position. There were other churches but only one in Corinth. They were set apart (ἡγιασμένοις) as God's property to be used exclusively in His service. This is essentially what sanctification means.

Paul also directs the epistle to all the Christians everywhere - a hint that he expected that the letter would be passed from hand to hand, until ultimately it would be read by all Christians of all ages. The geography makes no difference, nor does the age in which the child of God is born. Twentieth century Christians in Peoria may consider this epistle as having been directed to them also. Christ Jesus is the universal Lord (Phil.2:9-11) and to call upon Him (Rom.10:13) is to be incorporated into His body. This is ecumenicity on proper scriptural grounds.

Paul is magnifying his office as an Apostle by pointing out in the last clause that the Lord of the Gentile saints is also the Lord of the Jewish saints. A Hebrew Christian greets Gentiles who have become Christians. In the first century this was a startling idea.

Verse 3 - "Grace be unto you and peace from God our Father, and from the Lord Jesus Christ."

χάρις ὑμῖν καὶ εἰρήνη ἀπὸ θεοῦ πατρὸς ἡμῶν καὶ κυρίου Ἰησοῦ Χριστοῦ.

"Grace to you and peace from God our Father and the Lord Jesus Christ." . . .
                                                                          RSV

χάρις (nom.sing.fem.of χάρις, nominative absolute) 1700.
ὑμῖν (dat.pl.masc.of σύ, indirect object) 104.
καὶ (adjunctive conjunction joining nouns) 14.
εἰρήνη (nom.sing.fem.of εἰρήνη, nominative absolute) 865.
ἀπὸ (preposition with the ablative of source) 70.
θεοῦ (abl.sing.masc.of θεός, source) 124.
πατρὸς (abl.sing.masc.of πατήρ, apposition) 238.
ἡμῶν (gen.pl.masc.of ἐγώ, relationship) 123.
καὶ (adjunctive conjunction joining nouns) 14.
κυρίου (abl.sing.masc.of κύριος, source) 97.
Ἰησοῦ (abl.sing.masc.of Ἰησοῦς, apposition) 3.
Χριστοῦ (abl.sing.masc.of Χριστός, apposition) 4.

Translation - *"Grace unto you and peace from God our Father and Lord Jesus Christ."*

Comment: The triune God is the source of grace and peace. Only favor in spite of demerit can account for our justification. Peace can be defined both as absence of war (Rom.5:1) and absence of worry (Gal.5:22,23).

Verse 4 - *"I thank my God always on your behalf, for the grace of God which is given you by Jesus Christ."*

Εὐχαριστῶ τῷ θεῷ μου πάντοτε περὶ ὑμῶν ἐπὶ τῇ χάριτι τοῦ θεοῦ τῇ δοθείσῃ ὑμῖν ἐν Χριστῷ Ἰησοῦ,

"I give thanks to God always for you because of the grace of God which was given you in Christ Jesus." . . . RSV

Εὐχαριστῶ (1st.per.sing.pres.act.ind.of εὐχαριστέω, present progressive, retroactive) 1185.
    τῷ (dat.sing.masc.of the article in agreement with θεῷ) 9.
    θεῷ (dat.sing.masc.of θεός, indirect object) 124.
    μου (gen.sing.masc.of ἐγώ, relationship) 123.
    πάντοτε (adverbial) 1567.
    περὶ (preposition with the genitive of reference) 173.
    ὑμῶν (gen.pl.masc.of σύ, reference) 104.
    ἐπὶ (preposition with the instrumental of cause) 47.
    τῇ (instru.sing.fem.of the article in agreement with χάριτι) 9.
    χάριτι (instru.sing.fem.of χάρις, cause) 1700.
    τοῦ (abl.sing.masc.of the article in agreement with θεοῦ) 9.
    θεοῦ (abl.sing.masc.of θεός, source) 124.
    τῇ (instru.sing.fem.of the article in agreement with δοθείσῃ) 9.
    δοθείσῃ (aor.pass.part.instru.sing. fem.of δίδωμι, adjectival, emphatic

attributive position, ascriptive, in agreement with χάριτι) 362.
  ὑμῖν (dat.pl.masc.of σύ, indirect object of δοθείση) 104.
  ἐν (preposition with the instrumental of association) 80.
  Χριστῷ (instru.sing.masc.of Χριστός, association) 4.
  Ἰησοῦ (instru.sing.masc.of Ἰησοῦς, apposition) 3.

Translation - "I am always thanking God for you because of the grace from God, the gift given to you in Christ Jesus."

Comment: πάντοτε reinforces the present retroactive duration of the present tense in εὐχαριστῶ. Paul had always given God thanks with reference to the Corinthians since the day he first preached to them and saw them come to Christ. Why? The ἐπὶ instrumental phrase speaks of cause. God had given a great gift to them. Ablative of source in τοῦ θεοῦ (James 1:17). Note how Paul emphasizes the gift - τῇ χάριτι . . . τῆς δοθείση - emphatic attributive position in the participial modifier. What God gives to Christians He gives in association with Jesus Christ.
  The Corinthians seemed to be more enriched with God's gifts than other churches. This is the thought of verses 5-7.

Verse 5 - "That in everything ye are enriched by Him, in all utterance, and in all knowledge."

  ὅτι ἐν παντὶ ἐπλουτίσθητε ἐν αὐτῷ, ἐν παντὶ λόγῳ καὶ πάσῃ γνώσει,

"that in every way you were enriched in him with all speech and all knowledge —" . . . RSV

  ὅτι (conjunction introducing a subordinate causal clause) 211.
  ἐν (preposition with the locative of sphere) 80.
  παντὶ (loc.sing.neut.of πᾶς, sphere) 67.

#4100 ἐπλουτίσθητε (2d.per.pl.1st.aor.pass.ind.of πλουτίζω, culminative).

  King James Version

  enrich - 1 Cor.1:5; 2 Cor.9:11.
  make rich - 2 Cor.6:10.

  Revised Standard Version

  enrich - 1 Cor.1:5; 2 Cor.9:11.
  make rich - 2 Cor.6:10.

Meaning: Cf. πλούσιος (#1306); πλουσίως (#4636); πλουτέω (#1834); πλοῦτος (#1050). To enrich; make rich; endow with wealth. Spiritual gifts to the Corinthian saints - 1 Cor.1:5; 2 Cor.6:10; 9:11.

  ἐν (preposition with the instrumental of association) 80.
  αὐτῷ (instru.sing.masc.of αὐτός, association) 16.
  ἐν (preposition with the locative of sphere) 80.

παντὶ (loc. sing.masc.of πᾶς, in agreement with λόγῳ) 67.
λόγῳ (loc.sing.masc.of λόγος, sphere) 510.
καὶ (adjunctive conjunction joining nouns) 14.
πάσῃ (loc.sing.fem.of πᾶς, in agreement with γνώσει) 67.
γνώσει (loc.sing.fem.of γνῶσις, sphere) 1856.

Translation - *"Because you were made rich in Him in every way - in articulate speech and comprehensive knowledge."*

Comment: ὅτι introduces the causal clause. It can also be taken as an object clause in indirect discourse. The Corinthians were greatly endowed in a variety of spheres. The locatives of sphere ἐν παντὶ λόγῳ ... γνώσει explain the areas of their capabilities. A broad education which takes in πᾶσαν τὴν γνῶσιν (1 Cor.13:2) and an exhaustive vocabulary with which to expound it, is a great gift from God, but there is a greater gift without which all others are useless (1 Cor.13). Note that here γνῶσιν is without the article, while in 1 Cor.13:2 the article in present. Abstract substantives may be used without the article. Perhaps one of the pitfalls that the Corinthians had to overcome was their great endowment of intellectual gifts.

Verse 6 - *"Even as the testimony of Christ was confirmed in you."*

καθὼς τὸ μαρτύριον τοῦ Χριστοῦ ἐβεβαιώθη ἐν ὑμῖν,

"even as the testimony of Christ was confirmed among you — " . . . *RSV*

καθὼς (compound particle in a comparative clause) 1348.
τὸ (nom.sing.neut.of the article in agreement with μαρτύριον) 9.
μαρτύριον (nom.sing.neut.of μαρτύριον, subject of ἐβεβαιώθη) 716.
τοῦ (gen.sing.masc.of the article in agreement with Χριστοῦ) 9.
Χριστοῦ (gen.sing.masc.of Χριστός, reference) 4.
ἐβεβαιώθη (3d.per.sing.1st.aor.pass.ind.of βεβαιόω, culminative) 2932.
ἐν (preposition with the locative, place) 80.
ὑμῖν (loc.pl.masc.of σύ, place) 104.

Translation - *"Even as the testimony with reference to Christ was confirmed among you."*

Comment: Good education and eloquent expression are aids to strong Christian faith if Christ's testimony is received with due humility and faith. The Corinthians grew in grace (2 Pet.3:18) rapidly after they first accepted Christ and were willing to accept Paul's correction and instruction in righteousness, although they were guilty at first of some attitudes that were not Christ-like. Paul deals with these in verse 10-16.

The advantages which they possessed (verse 5) could become hindrances to their growth if they were not sanctified to the glory of God. Satan is able to turn the knowledge and eloquence which the Christian may possess to his own designs if the guidance of the Holy Spirit is not recognized by the child of God.

Verse 7 - "So that ye come behind in no gift; waiting for the coming of our Lord Jesus Christ."

ὥστε ὑμᾶς μὴ ὑστερεῖσθαι ἐν μηδενὶ χαρίσματι, ἀπεκδεχομένους τὴν ἀποκάλυψιν τοῦ κυρίου ὑμῶν Ἰησοῦ Χριστοῦ.

"so that you are not lacking in any spiritual gift, as you wait for the revealing of our Lord Jesus Christ." . . . RSV

ὥστε (conjunction with the infinitive in a result clause) 752.

ὑμᾶς (acc.pl.masc.of σύ, general reference) 104.

μὴ (negative particle with the infinitive) 87.

ὑστερεῖσθαι (pres.mid.inf.of ὑστερέω, in a result clause) 1302.

ἐν (preposition with the locative of sphere) 80.

μηδενὶ (loc.sing.neut.of μηδείς, in agreement with χαρίσματι) 713.

χαρίσματι (loc.sing.neut.of χάρισμα, sphere) 3790.

ἀπεκδεχομένους (pres.mid.part.acc.pl.masc.of ἀπεκδέχομαι, adverbial, temporal) 3939.

τὴν (acc.sing.fem.of the article in agreement with ἀποκάλυψιν) 9.

ἀποκάλυψιν (acc.sing.fem.of ἀποκάλυψις, direct object of ἀπεκδεχομένους) 1902.

τοῦ (gen.sing.masc.of the article in agreement with κυρίου) 9.

κυρίου (gen.sing.masc.of κύριος, description) 97.

ἡμῶν (gen.pl.masc.of ἐγώ, relationship) 123.

Ἰησοῦ (gen.sing.masc.of Ἰησοῦς, apposition) 3.

Χριστοῦ (gen.sing.masc.of Χριστός, apposition) 4.

Translation - "With the result that you are not deficient in a single gift, as you await the appearance of our Lord Jesus Christ."

Comment: ὥστε the consecutive conjunction introduces the infinitive in the consecutive (result) clause. The causes of the result which follows are contained in verse 5 (enriched with gifts) and verse 6 (confirmation of the testimony of Jesus Christ). Thus the Corinthians are second to none among the first century churches in the sphere (locative of sphere) of gifts. They enjoy these gifts and use them for the glory of Christ as they await and anticipate the Second Coming of our Lord (temporal participial adverb in ἀπεκδεχομένους). *Cf.* 1 Pet.1:7,13; 4:13; 2 Thess.1:7 for ἀποκάλυψις (#1902). Note especially 1 Pet.1:13 where Peter advocates total dedication of our intellectual powers in connection with the Second Coming. Paul had just congratulated the Corinthians on their intellect (verse 5).

The dedicated Christian in the late 20th century whose education includes the Social Sciences as well as Bible Theology sees the futility of man-made scenarios to establish a viable world society outside of Christ. Witness the work of Herbert Spencer, Huxley's *Brave New World* and Alvin Toffler, *The Third Wave."*

Christians who believe in the coming of our Lord, but only in a halfhearted manner, because they are deluded by the hope that Christian Liberalism in the late 20th century may yet succeed in turning the world around to save it from collapse, had better put their God-given "Corinthian" gifts (1 Cor.1:5) to work (1 Pet.1:13) as they await Messiah's final Triumphal Entry. The premillenial view that the unregenerate world may yet "make it" on its own resources of wisdom and knowledge is an ambivalence that grows out of poor scholarship in both the Social Sciences (geography, economics, political science, philosophy, demography, sociology, psychology and history) and Bible exegesis. Superficiality, both in the Social Sciences and in what the New Testament clearly teaches results in the Polly Anna view that somehow or other we will figure something out. The non-Christian social scientist of depth is either a pessimist who peddles his gloom or a Stoic. Scholarly premillenialists are optimistic about the future, not despite man's failure on this planet but because of it. The failure of the unregenerate world to bring in the kingdom by repudiating the King is apparent on every side. The modernistic reformers will continue their quest. When they have painted themselves into the last available corner, our Lord, at the Father's right hand, will return. His cue to return will be the effectual call of the last elect soul for whom He died (Rev.10:7). Until the mystery which was revealed in all of its fulness to Paul the Apostle to the Gentiles is complete (Eph.3:1-11; Rev.10:7), God will preserve some order on earth, despite the efforts of the unsaved, either to poison the race, starve it or blow it up with nuclear fission. God will not allow His divine experiment on earth to fail.

The problem which we face is that of not knowing precisely where human history is on God's clock. It is well to remember that it is us, not God, who are creatures subject to the categories of time and space. While we wait with what patience may be given to us (Heb.10:36,37; 2 Pet.1:6) for His return it is well that we exercise our gifts, whatever they may be, to do what we can to alleviate human misery in the name of Christ. Christians should remember that "This world is not our home" and also that "This home is not our world." It is interesting, challenging and not a little sobering to reflect upon how our life style would change if we knew that our Lord would return within the next seven years.

The Corinthians were mistaken in expecting the Second Coming in their lifetime, but they were not mistaken in exercising their spiritual gifts as they waited for Christ to return. Nor are we.

Verse 8 - "Who shall also confirm you unto the end, that ye may be blameless in the day of our Lord Jesus Christ."

ὃς καὶ βεβαιώσει ὑμᾶς ἕως τέλους ἀνεγκλήτους ἐν τῇ ἡμέρᾳ τοῦ κυρίου ἡμῶν Ἰησοῦ (Χριστοῦ).

"who will sustain you to the end, guiltless in the day of our Lord Jesus Christ."
         ... RSV

ὃς (nom.sing.masc.of ὅς, relative pronoun, subject of βεβαιώσει) 65.
καὶ (adjunctive conjunction joining verbs) 14.
βεβαιώσει (3d.per.sing.fut.act.ind.of βεβαιόω, predictive) 2932.
ὑμᾶς (acc.pl.masc.of σύ, direct object of βεβαιώσει) 104.
ἕως (preposition with the genitive in a time expression) 71.

τέλους (gen.sing.neut.of τέλος, time expression) 881.

#4101 ἀνεγκλήτους (acc.pl.masc.of ἀνέγκλητος, in agreement with ὑμᾶς).

King James Version

blameless - 1 Cor.1:8; 1 Tim.3:10; Tit.1:6,7.
unreproveable - Col.1:22.

Revised Standard Version

guiltless - 1 Cor.1:8.
irreproachable - Col.1:22.
blameless - 1 Tim.3:10; Tit.1:6,7.

Meaning: ἀν plus ἐγκαλέω (#3495), which is α privative (with euphonic ν) plus ἐγκαλέω. Hence, one who cannot be called to account. Not subject to indictment. One against whom no charge of malfeasance or nonfeasance can be brought. The promise that Christ's justification of the believer guarantees his preservation unto the end without the threat of a legal indictment for transgression in heaven's court - 1 Cor.1:8; Col.1:22. With reference to deacons whose record in society and in the church is irreproachable - 1 Tim.3:10; of elders (Tit.1:6) and bishops (Tit.1:7) in the same sense.

ἐν (preposition with the locative of time point) 80.
τῇ (loc.sing.fem.of the article in agreement with ἡμέρᾳ) 9.
ἡμέρᾳ (loc.sing.fem.of ἡμέρα, time point) 135.
τοῦ (gen.sing.masc.of the article in agreement with κυρίου) 9.
κυρίου (gen.sing.masc.of κύριος, description) 97.
ἡμῶν (gen.pl.masc.of ἐγώ, relationship) 123.
Ἰησοῦ (gen.sing.masc.ofd Ἰησοῦς, apposition) 3.
(Χριστοῦ) (gen.sing.masc.of Χριστός, apposition) 4.

Translation - "... *who also will vindicate you until the end and (present) you free from indictment on the day of our Lord Jesus Christ.*"

Comment: ὅς, the relative pronoun relates the action of verse 8 to the antecedent in verse 7 - τοῦ κυρίου ἡμῶν Ἰησοῦ Χριστοῦ. While we are waiting for Him to return, we exercise the gifts which the Holy Spirit has given us. The world will scoff at our testimony that He is coming back. Nevertheless we will continue to witness until either (1) we die, or (2) He returns. At the judgment seat of Christ on the day when He returns (Rev.11:15-19) He will vindicate us. The world will then be forced to admit that our witness was true. And we will be blameless if we have exercised our gifts in the way, at the times and in the places where He, Who is Head over all things to His church (Eph.1:22) has directed.

ἕως τέλους means the end of the age, and τῇ ἡμέρᾳ ... Χριστοῦ means the day of the Second Coming. *Cf.* #135. Paul did not tell them how long it would be until the end, though it is probable that both he and they thought that it was near, though not imminent (*i.e.* unannounced by correlating events). But this age of the church has an end (Mt.28:20; Mt.24:30; 1 Cor.15:24) which will come on a definite day. Note the article - ἐν τῇ ἡμέρᾳ - a day clearly defined as that of our Lord Jesus Christ. (Rev.11:15-19; 19:11-21; 6:12-17; 1 Cor.15:51-58; 1 Thess.4:13-18; Phil.3:20,21; 1 John 3:1-3, and many more).

The main point in 1 Cor.1:8 is not the end, nor the day, but that He will keep us blameless until that day. Hallelujah! **p** 46 and B omit Χριστοῦ after Ἰησοῦ.

Verse 9 - "God is faithful, by whom ye were called unto the fellowship of his son Jesus Christ our Lord."

πιστὸς ὁ θεὸς δι' οὗ ἐκλήθητε εἰς κοινωνίαν τοῦ υἱοῦ αὐτοῦ Ἰησοῦ Χριστοῦ τοῦ κυρίου ὑμῶν.

"God is faithful, by whom you were called into the fellowship of his Son, Jesus Christ our Lord." . . . RSV.

πιστὸς (nom.sing.masc.of πιστός, predicate adjective) 1522.
ὁ (nom.sing.masc.of the article in agreement with θεὸς) 9.
θεὸς (nom.sing.masc.of θεός, subject of ἐστιν, understood) 124.
δι' (preposition with the ablative of agent) 118.
οὗ (abl.sing.masc.of ὅς, relative pronoun, agency) 65.
ἐκλήθητε (2d.per.pl.aor.pass.ind.of καλέω, culminative) 107.
εἰς (preposition with the accusative of extent) 140.
κοινωνίαν (acc.sing.fem.of κοινωνία, extent) 3001.
τοῦ (gen.sing.masc.of the article in agreement with υἱοῦ) 9.
υἱοῦ (gen.sing.masc.of υἱός, definition) 5.
αὐτοῦ (gen.sing.masc.of αὐτός, relationship) 16.
Ἰησοῦ (gen.sing.masc.of Ἰησοῦς, apposition) 3.
Χριστοῦ (gen.sing.masc.of Χριστός, apposition) 4.
τοῦ (gen.sing.masc.of the article in agreement with κυρίου) 9.
κυρίου (gen.sing.masc.of κύριος, apposition) 97.
ἡμῶν (gen.pl.masc.of ἐγώ, relationship) 123.

Translation - "God is faithful by Whom you have been called into the fellowship of His Son, Jesus Christ, our Lord."

Comment: This statement justifies our classification of the prepositional phrases ἐν Χριστῷ, ἐν κυρίῳ and ἐν θεῷ as instrumentals of association. The result of God's call to the elect is that they are introduced permanently into the fellowship (communion, association, oneness) of the commonality known as "the Body of Christ."

Note the emphatic position of πιστὸς. God is faithful, with His steadfastness emphasized. This means that He never changes His mind and He keeps His promises. He called us in eternity past and He will always feel the same way about it (Heb.13:8). What He initiates in His foreknowledge and follows with his predestination is implemented in history by His call, justification and glorification. The object of this grace is the believer (Rom.8:29-30). If God were not πιστός then we could have reasonable ground for doubting that His call would eventuate in our permanent salvation. But He *is faithful.* On εἰς κοινωνίαν cf. John 17:21 where total commonality is described.

Divisions in the Church

(1 Corinthians 1:10-17)

Verse 10 - "Now I beseech you, brethren, by the name of our Lord Jesus Christ, that ye all speak the same thing, and that there be no divisions among you; but that ye be perfectly joined together in the same mind and in the same judgment."

Παρακαλῶ δὲ ὑμᾶς, ἀδελφοί, διὰ τοῦ ὀνόματος τοῦ κυρίου ἡμῶν Ἰησοῦ Χριστοῦ, ἵνα τὸ αὐτὸ λέγητε πάντες, καὶ μὴ ᾖ ἐν ὑμῖν σχίσματα, ἦτε δὲ κατηρτισμένοι ἐν τῷ αὐτῷ νοῒ καὶ ἐν τῇ αὐτῇ γνώμῃ.

"I appeal to you, brethren, by the name of our Lord Jesus Christ, that all of you agree and that there be no dissensions among you, but that you be united in the same mind and the same judgment." . . . RSV

Παρακαλῶ (1st.per.sing.pres.act.ind.of παρακαλέω, aoristic) 230.

δὲ (inferential conjunction) 11.

ὑμᾶς (acc.pl.masc.of σύ, direct object of παρακαλῶ) 104.

ἀδελφοί (voc.pl.masc.of ἀδελφός, address) 15.

διὰ (preposition with the ablative of agent) 118.

τοῦ (abl.sing.neut.of the article in agreement with ὀνόματος) 9.

ὀνόματος (abl.sing.neut.of ὄνομα, agency) 108.

τοῦ (gen.sing.masc.of the article in agreement with κυρίου) 9.

κυρίου (gen.sing.masc.of κύριος, possession) 97.

ἡμῶν (gen.pl.masc.of ἐγώ, relationship) 123.

Ἰησοῦ (gen.sing.masc.of Ἰησοῦς, apposition) 3.

Χριστοῦ (gen.sing.masc.of Χριστός, apposition) 4.

ἵνα (conjunction with the subjunctives in a triple purpose clause) 114.

τὸ (acc.sing.neut.of the article in agreement with αὐτὸ) 9.

αὐτὸ (acc.sing.neut.of αὐτός, direct object of λέγητε) 16.

λέγητε (2d.per.pl.pres.act.subj.of λέγω, purpose) 66.

πάντες (nom.pl.masc.of πᾶς, subject of λέγητε) 67.

καὶ (adjunctive conjunction joining purpose clauses) 14.

μὴ (negative particle with the subjunctive) 87.

ᾖ (3d.per.sing. pres.subj.of εἰμί, purpose) 86.

ἐν (preposition with the locative, with plural pronouns) 80.

ὑμῖν (loc.pl.masc.of σύ, place where) 104.

σχίσματα (nom.pl.neut.of σχίσμα, subject of ᾖ) 807.

ἦτε (2d.per.pl.pres.subj.of εἰμί, purpose) 86.

δὲ (adversative conjunction) 11.

κατηρτισμένοι (perf.pass.part.nom.pl.masc.of καταρτίζω, perfect periphrastic, purpose) 401.

ἐν (preposition with the instrumental of means) 80.

τῷ (instru.sing.masc.of the article in agreement with νοΐ) 9.

αὐτῷ (instru.sing.masc.of αὐτός, in agreement with νοΐ) 16.

νοΐ (instru.sing.masc.of νοῦς, means) 2928.

καὶ (adjunctive conjunction joining prepositional phrases) 14.

ἐν (preposition with the instrumental of means) 80.

τῇ (instru.sing.fem.of the article in agreement with γνωμῃ) 9.

αὐτῇ (instru.sing.fem.of αὐτός, in agreement with γνώμῃ) 16.

γνώμῃ (instru.sing.fem.of γνώμη means) 3499.

Translation - "So I am begging you, brethren, on the authority of the name of our Lord Jesus Christ, that all teach the same doctrine and that there be no differences of opinion among you, but that you be restored to the truth by the same rationale and the same conclusion."

Comment: δὲ is inferential. Paul had just told them about the faithful God who had called them into a homogeneity of perfect fellowship with His Son (verse 9). Since that is the divine ideal for them he therefore (inferential δὲ) begs them to implement in fact what God has willed for them. Why should common members of the Body of Christ disagree? The analogy to the physical body is apt. When the nervous system, which under normal conditions allows the head to control the members of the body in harmonious function, malfunctions the result is that the members of the body tend to work at cross purposes. We call those so afflicted awkward or, in more severe cases spastic. When one member of the Body of Christ disagrees, in thought, word or action with another, it is apparent that Christ, the Head of the Body (Eph.1:22) is not in complete control. Someone involved in the dispute is wrong, and there is a possibility that all are wrong to some degree. The cure for this condition is that all parties to the dispute pay more attention to the leadership of the Holy Spirit.

This plea for Corinthian unity is made on the authority of the name of Him unto Whose commonality they had already been called.

The final clauses, introduced by ἵνα have λέγητε, μὴ ᾖ and ἦτε. Paul wanted them all "to voice the same opinion," and that "divisions among you may not exist" while the third is the positive counterpart of the negative of the second clause. Note that it is a perfect periphrastic in the subjunctive, a rare construction in the New Testament. The pefect passive participle κατηρτισμένοι is joined periphrastically with the subjunctive ᾖτε. Cf. #401 for the basic meaning of καραρτίζω. Paul is pleading that they might be permanently restored (the periphrastic durative force with the basic meaning of καταρτίζω) to God's divine ideal set forth in verse 9.

How can this be done? The same rationale must be followed (#2928). If this is done the same conclusion will be reached (#3499).

This verse provides three examples of αὐτός in the intensive attributive position, meaning "same." In the first clause τὸ αὐτὸ means "the same thing." We cannot supply λόγον, since αὐτό is neuter and λόγον is masculine. When a church has dissension, because individual members of the same Body of Christ, have differing views, it is evident that someone is out of fellowship with the Head in glory and with the indwelling Holy Spirit (1 Cor.6:19,20). When the Holy Spirit dictates, the will of God is done, God's views are held by men and peace in society results (Col.3:15).

There is on record the case of a church that will take no definitive action except upon the unanimous vote of its members. The pastor believes that a divided church is evidence that the church is out of fellowship with the Holy Spirit and that in such a case, the only safe thing for the church to do is to pray for a revival! In those cases in which a vast majority of the congregation concur the minority voters ask for special prayer for themselves that they may more perfectly ascertain the will of God or that they be confirmed in their views, in which case the majority is brought to agreement with them. This method of applying Col.3:15 literally may preclude most church actions. Some churches cannot buy a broom without having a fight! Some have split over a piano, only to splinter the split over a tuning fork.

Paul has accused the Corinthians of dissension in their ranks. In verse 11 he tells them where he got his information.

Verse 11 - "For it hath been declared unto me of you, my brethren, by them which are of the house of Chloe, that there are contentions among you."

ἐδηλώθη γάρ μοι περὶ ὑμῶν, ἀδελφοί μου, ὑπὸ τῶν Χλόης ὅτι ἔριδες ἐν ὑμῖν εἰσιν.

"For it has been reported to me by Chloe's people that there is quarreling among you, my brethren." . . . RSV

#4102 ἐδηλώθη (3d.per.sing.aor.pass.ind.of δηλόω, culminative).

King James Version

declare - 1 Cor.1:11; 3:13; Col.1:8.
show - 2 Pet.1:14.
signify - Heb.9:8; 12:27; 1 Pet.1:11.

Revised Standard Version

report - 1 Cor.1:11.
disclose - 1 Cor.3:13.
make known - Col.1:8.
indicate - Heb.9:8; 12:27; 1 Pet.1:11.
show - 2 Pet.1:14.

Meaning: To make manifest to the mind (while ἐμφανίζω - #1666 - means to reveal to the sight); to disclose; relate; inform. With reference to the rumor of contention at Corinth - 1 Cor.1:11; the value of the Christian life at the judgment seat of Christ - 1 Cor.3:13; of the love of the Colossian Christians - Col.1:8; followed by the infinitive in indirect discourse - Heb.9:8 of the significance of the temple worship; of the significance of a verse of Scripture - Heb.12:27; of the meaning of the revelation of the Holy Spirit - 1 Pet.1:11; with reference to information from Jesus to Peter about his death - 2 Pet.1:14.

γάρ (causal conjunction) 105.
μοι (dat.sing.masc.of ἐγώ, indirect object of ἐδηλώϑη) 123.
περὶ (preposition with the genitive of reference) 173.
ὑμῶν (gen.pl.masc.of σύ, reference) 104.
ἀδελφοί (voc.pl.masc.of ἀδελφός, address) 15.
μου (gen.sing.masc.of ἀεγώ, relationship) 123.
ὑπὸ (preposition with the ablative of agent) 117.
τῶν (abl.pl.masc.of the article, agent) 9.

#4103 Χλόης (gen.sing.fem.of Χλόη, relationship).

King James Version

Chloe - 1 Cor.1:11.

Revised Standard Version

Chloe - 1 Cor.1:11.

Meaning: - "tender verdure" - an appelation of Demeter, "The Verdant." Chloe, a Christian woman in Corinth - 1 Cor.1:11.

ὅτι (conjunction introducing an object clause in indirect discourse) 211.
ἔριδες (nom.pl.fem.of ἔρις, subject of εἰσιν) 3819.
ἐν (preposition with the locative, with plural pronouns) 80.
ὑμῖν (loc.pl.masc.of σύ, place) 104.
εἰσιν (3d.per.pl.pres.ind.of εἰμί, aoristic) 86.

Translation - "Because it has been reported to me about you, my brothers, by the family of Chloe that there are contentions among you."

Comment: γάρ is causal. The common practice in most churches is for a pastor not to divulge the source of his information when he brings accusations against the people. Not Paul. He identified his informers and made the charge specific. Chloe's relatives or family, perhaps those who lived in her home, had reported to Paul that the Corinthian church was being troubled by dissension.

There was probably more reason for the first century church to entertain dissenting opinions than for the modern church. The New Testament canon Scripture was not yet complete. In the meantime the Holy Spirit had given the gifts of wisdom, knowledge and prophecy (1 Cor.12:8-11; Rom.12:6-8) to the Apostles who founded the churches and established them in the faith. But until the literature of the New Testament was complete and had been distributed among the churches, the study of Christian theology could not have advanced as it has two thousand years later. There is less reason for the 20th century church to quarrel about doctrine than for them, because we have inherited a vast library of exegetical and homiletical studies. At the first even the Apostles did not agree on some points of doctrine and practice. *Cf.* Galatians 2:11-21.

It was quite natural therefore that the Corinthians should evaluate various preachers who had come to Corinth differently and that each preacher should have developed a following, the members of which would feel a special affinity for one more than for another.

Verse 12 - "Now this I say, that every one of you saith, I am of Paul; and I of Apollos; and I of Cephas; and I of Christ."

λέγω δὲ τοῦτο, ὅτι ἕκαστος ὑμῶν λέγει, Ἐγὼ μὲν εἰμι Παύλου, ' Ἐγὼ δὲ Ἀπολλῶ, Ἐγὼ δὲ Κηφᾶ, Ἐγὼ δὲ Χριστοῦ.

"What I mean is that each one of you says, 'I belong to Paul,' or 'I belong to Apollos,' or 'I belong to Cephas,' or 'I belong to Christ.' " . . . RSV

λέγω (1st.per.sing.pres.act.ind.of λέγω, aoristic) 66.
δὲ (explanatory conjunction) 11.
τοῦτο (acc.sing.neut.of οὗτος, direct object of λέγω) 93.
ὅτι (conjunction introducing an object clause in indirect discourse) 211.
ἕκαστος (nom.sing.masc.of ἕκαστος, subject of λέγει) 1217.
ὑμῶν (gen.pl.masc.of σύ, partitive genitive) 104.
λέγει (3d.per.sing.pres.act.ind.of λέγω, customary) 66.
Ἐγὼ (nom.sing.masc.of ἐγώ, subject of εἰμι) 123.
μέν (correlative particle of affirmation) 300.
εἰμι (1st.per.sing.pres.ind.of εἰμί, aoristic) 86.
Παύλου (abl.sing.masc.of Παῦλος, agent) 3284.
Ἐγὼ (nom.sing.masc.of ἐγώ, subject of εἰμι, understood) 123.
δὲ (adversative conjunction) 11.
Ἀπολλῶ (abl.sing.masc.of Ἀπολλῶς, agent) 3454.
Ἐγὼ (nom.sing.masc.of ἐγώ, subject of εἰμι understood) 123.
δὲ (adversative conjunction) 11.
Κηφᾶ (abl.sing.masc.of Κηφᾶς, agent) 1964.
Ἐγὼ (nom.sing.masc.of ἐγώ, subject of εἰμι, understood) 123.
δὲ (adversative conjunction) 11.
Χριστοῦ (abl.sing.masc.of Χριστός, agent) 4.

Translation - "Let me explain. Each one of you is saying, 'I am of Paul's ministry; but I of Apollos'; but I of Cephas'; but I of Christ.' "

Comment: τοῦτο has the ὅτι clause in apposition to explain Paul's point in verse 11. The dissension in the Corinthian church took the form of hero worship for the particular preacher under the ministry of whom each one was saved. Note the partitive genitive in ὑμῶν. "Each one individually" (ἕκαστος) of the collective group (ὑμῶν) was guilty. Note the μέν . . . δὲ . . . δὲ . . . δὲ contrast. δὲ in the first clause in explanatory. Those following μέν are adversative. We can supply "a follower" as most translations do, and consider Παύλου, Ἀπολλῶ, Κηφᾶ and Χριστοῦ as specifying genitives or, as I have done consider the proper names ablatives of agency.

The error here is a common one among babes in Christ, who are either temporary babes because of a short Christian experience or permanent babes because of low intelligence. It is natural for a recently saved person to be unduly enthusiastic about the person who led him to Christ. It is sad that such persons do not soon learn that Christ alone deserves to be worshipped. It is a poor recommendation of a man's ministry when, after he has left the community, his converts continue to sing his praises instead of worshipping Christ and cooperating with the new pastor. Note that those who said, Ἐγὼ δὲ Χριστοῦ were implying that the others were not Christians at all!

Verse 13 - "Is Christ divided? Was Paul crucified for you? Or were you baptized in the name of Paul?"

μεμέρισται ὁ Χριστός; μὴ Παῦλος ἐσταυρώθη ὑπὲρ ὑμῶν, ἢ εἰς τὸ ὄνομα Παύλου ἐβαπτίσθητε;

"Is Christ divided? Was Paul crucified for you? Or were you baptized in the name of Paul?" . . . RSV

μεμέρισται (3d.per.sing.perf.pass.ind.of μερίζω, intensive) 993.

ὁ (nom.sing.masc.of the article in agreement with Χριστός) 9.

Χριστός (nom.sing.masc.of Χριστός, subject of μεμέρισται) 4.

μὴ (negative particle with the indicative in rhetorical question which expects a negative reply) 87.

Παῦλος (nom.sing.masc.of Παῦλος, subject of ἐσταυρώθη) 3284.

ἐσταυρώθη (3d.per.sing.aor.pass.ind.of σταυρόω, rhetorical question) 1328.

ὑπὲρ (preposition with the ablative, "in behalf of") 545.

ὑμῶν (abl.pl.masc.of σύ, "in behalf of") 104.

ἢ (disjunctive) 465.

εἰς (preposition with the accusative, like a dative, disposition or state of mind) 140.

τὸ (acc.sing.neut.of the article in agreement with ὄνομα) 9.

ὄνομα (acc.sing.neut.of ὄνομα, disposition) 108.

Παύλου (gen.sing.masc.of Παῦλος, possession) 3284.

ἐβαπτίσθητε (2d.per.pl.aor.pass.ind.of βαπτίζω, constative) 273.

Translation - "Has Christ been divided? Paul was not crucified for you was he? Or were you immersed in the name of Paul?"

Comment: p₄₆ 326 1962 and a few other MSS read μή before μεμέρισται, which the United Bible Societies' Committee rejects to follow Sinaiticus A B C D G P Ψ and many miniscules. Without μή it is impossible to tell whether the first clause is declarative or interrogative. It is either "Is Christ now divided?" - expecting "Yes" for an answer or it is an exclamation of dismay - "Christ is divided!" Indeed, since these Corinthian saints (1 Cor.1:2) were all members of Christ's body, though engaging in controversy, the Body of Christ was divided. Paul is appalled! His second question is rhetorical, expecting a negative reply to an obviously sarcastic question. "Paul was not crucified for you was he?" Mature Christians follow only Him Who died for them. The last question is also rhetorical though it expects whatever answer fits the facts. Had the Christians been immersed in Paul's name? Doubtless,they had not!

This question opens the door for a discussion immersion in water in

Verse 14 - *"I thank God that I baptized none of you, but Crispus and Gaius."*

εὐχαριστῶ ὅτι οὐδένα ὑμῶν ἐβάπτισα εἰ μὴ Κρίσπον καὶ Γάϊπν,

"I am thankful that I baptized none of you except Crispus and Gaius;" ...
                                                                    RSV

εὐχαριστῶ (1st.per.sing.pres.act.ind.of εὐχαριστέω, aoristic) 1185.
ὅτι (conjunction introducing an object clause in indirect discourse) 211.
οὐδένα (acc.sing.masc.of οὐδείς, direct object of ἐβάπτισα) 446.
ὑμῶν (gen.pl.masc.of σύ, partitive genitive) 104.
ἐβάπτισα (1st.per.sing.aor.act.ind.of βαπτίζω, constative) 273.
εἰ (conditional particle in an elliptical condition) 337.
μὴ (negative particle in an elliptical condition) 87.
Κρίσπον (acc.sing.masc.of Κρίσπος, direct object of ἐβάπτισα) 3440.
καὶ (adjunctive conjunction joining nouns) 14.
Γάϊον (acc.sing.masc.of Γάϊος, direct object of ἐβάπτισα) 3484.

Translation - *"I am grateful that I immersed not one of you except Crispus and Gaius.*

Comment: A variant reading follows A to add τῷ θεῷ μου, but the best authorities reject it with good support from Sinaiticus B and others. Sinaiticusc C D G P Ψ and several miniscules have εὐχαριστῶ τῷ θεῷ. The ὅτι clause is the object of εὐχαριστῶ. Note the partitive genitive in ὑμῶν. The exceptions were Crispus, Gaius and the family of Stephanas (verse 16). *Cf.*Acts 18:8 for the conversion of Crispus, the Corinthian Jewish synagogue official and Rom.16:23 for Γάϊος, who was Paul's host in Corinth. These he baptized and perhaps a few others whom Paul has forgotten. Others administered the ordinance of immersion in water for the other converts in Corinth.

Paul is not denigrating immersion in water as an ordinance of the church, but he is pointing to the fact that he had not personally baptized the Corinthians, lest the Pauline party in the church be more numerous, a development which he is deploring in this context. He tells us in verse 15 why he wrote verse 14.

There is no comfort here for those who consider immersion unnecessary as an ordinance of the church, nor can the baptismal regenerationists find support for their view that immersion in water is essential to salvation. Verse 17 makes no sense at all if it is true that all those who are not immersed in water are lost, despite whatever else they may believe and do.

Verse 15 - *"Lest any should say that I had baptized in my own name."*

ἵνα μὴ τις εἴπῃ ὅτι εἰς τὸ ἐμὸν ὄνομα ἐβαπτίσθητε.

"lest any one should say that you were baptized in my name." . . . *RSV*

ἵνα (conjunction with the subjunctive in a negative purpose clause) 114.
μή (negative particle with the subjunctive in a negative purpose clause) 87.
τις (nom.sing.masc.of τις, indefinite pronoun, subject of εἴπῃ) 486.

εἴπῃ (3d.per.sing.aor.act.subj.of εἶπον, negative purpose) 155.

ὅτι (conjunction introducing an object clause in indirect discourse) 211.

εἰς (preposition with the accusative, like a dative, disposition) 140.

τὸ (acc.sing.neut.of the article in agreement with ὄνομα) 9.

ἐμὸν (acc.sing.neut.of ἐμός, in agreement with ὄνομα) 1267.

ὄνομα (acc.sing.neut.of ὄνομα, disposition of mind) 108.

ἐβαπτίσθητε (2d.per.pl.aor.pass.ind.of βαπτίζω, constative) 273.

Translation - "*Lest anyone should say that you were immersed in my name.*"

Comment: The negative final clause with ἵνα μή and the subjunctive depends upon the ὅτι clause of verse 14, which is the object of εὐχαριστῶ. Paul's reason for being glad that he had immersed so few is here explained. He was not sorry that they had been baptized. He was not opposed to immersion as such. He was glad he had not personally immersed them. We often hear preachers relate with some pride the stories of how they personally baptized their converts. This is not wrong if those so baptized do not transfer their worship from the Lord to the preacher. Paul might not have written these things if there had been no division based upon personality cults in the Corinthian church.

On the other hand this language is devastating to the baptismal regeneration theology.

Verse 16 - "*And I baptized also the household of Stephanas: besides I know not whether I baptized any other.*"

ἐβάπτισα δὲ καὶ τὸν Στεφανᾶ οἶκον. λοιπὸν οὐκ οἶδα εἴ τινα ἄλλον ἐβάπτισα.

"*(I did baptize also the household of Stephanas. Beyond that, I do not know whether I baptized any one else.)*" . . . *RSV*

ἐβάπτισα (1st.per.sing.aor.act.ind.of βαπτίζω, constative) 273.

δὲ (continuative conjunction) 11.

καὶ (adjunctive conjunction joining nouns) 14.

τὸν (acc.sing.masc.of the article in agreement with οἶκον) 9.

#4104 Στεφανᾶ (gen.sing.masc.of Στεφανᾶς, relationship).

     King James Version

Stephanas - 1 Cor.1:16; 16:15,17.

     Revised Standard Version

Stephanas - 1 Cor.1:16; 16:15,17.

Meaning: A Christian in Corinth whom Paul immersed - 1 Cor.1:16. He was Paul's first convert in Corinth - 1 Cor.16:15,17. Not to be confused with #3081.

οἶκον (acc.sing.masc.of οἶκος, direct object of ἐβάπτισα) 784.

λοιπὸν (acc.sing.neut.of λοιπός, adverbial) 1402.
οὐκ (negative particle with the indicative) 130.
οἶδα (1st.per.sing.perf.act.ind.of ὁράω, intensive) 144b.
εἰ (conditional particle in a mixed condition) 337.
τινα (acc.sing.masc.of τις, indefinite pronoun, in agreement with ἄλλον) 486.
ἄλλον (acc.sing.masc.of ἄλλος, direct object of ἐβάπτισα) 198.
ἐβάπτισα (1st.per.sing.aor.act.ind.of βαπτίζω, constative) 273.

Translation - *"And I also immersed the household of Stephanas; I do not know whether I immersed any other besides."*

Comment: λοιπὸν, the adverbial accusative is really not needed here. The baptism of Stephanas and those of his household is mentioned almost as an afterthought, though he was Paul's first convert in Corinth (1 Cor.16:15,17). There may have been no other Christian in the city to administer the ordinance. After that Paul had established the church, apparently he taught them that the act of immersing a believer in water upon his confession of faith in Christ as Saviour and Lord could be performed by any other Christian upon the authority of the church. Contrary to current popular belief baptism need not be carried out only by an ordained minister, so long as it is done on the authority of the local church. Christian laymen baptized the first converts in Corinth, except for those whom Paul baptized.

Paul puts the subject of water baptism in perspective in

Verse 17 - *"For Christ sent me not to baptize, but to preach the gospel: not with wisdom of words, lest the cross of Christ should be made of none effect."*

οὐ γὰρ ἀπέστειλέν με Χριστὸς βαπτίζειν ἀλλὰ εὐαγγελίζεσθαι, οὐκ ἐν σοφίᾳ λόγου, ἵνα μὴ κενωθῇ ὁ σταυρὸς τοῦ Χριστοῦ.

"For Christ did not send me to baptize but to preach the gospel, and not with eloquent wisdom, lest the cross of Christ be emptied of its power." . . . RSV

οὐ (negative particle with the indicative) 130.
γὰρ (causal conjunction) 105.
ἀπέστειλέν (3d.per.sing.aor.act.ind.of ἀποστέλλω, constative) 215.
με (acc.sing.masc.of ἐγώ, direct object of ἀπέστειλέν) 123.
Χριστὸς (nom.sing.masc.of Χριστός, subject of ἀπέστειλέν) 4.
βαπτίζειν (pres.act.inf.of βαπτίζω, purpose) 273.
ἀλλὰ (alternative conjunction) 342.
εὐαγγελίζεσθαι (pres.mid.inf.of εὐαγγελίζομαι, purpose) 909.
οὐκ (negative particle with the infinitive) 130.
ἐν (preposition with the instrumental of means) 80.
σοφίᾳ (instru.sing.fem. of σοφία, means) 934.
λόγου (abl.sing.masc.of λόγος, source) 510.
ἵνα (conjunction with the subjunctive, negative purpose) 114.
μὴ (negative particle with the subjunctive) 87.
κενωθῇ (3d.per.sing.aor.pass.subj.of κενόω, negative purpose) 3888.

ὁ (nom.sing.masc.of the article in agreement with σταυρὸς) 9.
σταυρὸς (nom.sing.masc.of σταυρός, subject of κενωθῇ) 899.
τοῦ (gen.sing.masc.of the article in agreement with Χριστοῦ) 9.
Χριστοῦ (gen.sing.masc.of Χριστός, description) 4.

Translation - *"Because Christ did not send me to immerse but to tell the good news, not with eloquent wisdom lest the cross of Christ be made ineffective."*

Comment: *Cf.* ἵνα μή here with ὅπως μή in verse 29. οὐ is emphasized. Paul's commission was not to administer the ordinance of water baptism, though Mt.28:18-20 includes immersion in water. Paul means here that his primary function is to proclaim the good news of the gospel. He is not denying that regenerated believers should be immersed in water, for water baptism is a picture of the baptism of the Holy Spirit which introduces the believer into the Body of Christ (1 Cor.12:13; Rom.6:1-4).

God wants His gospel presented in plain unadorned language. *Cf.* our comment on 1 Cor.2:1-2. When Paul first came to Corinth from Athens (Acts 18:1) he was suffering the trauma of having failed in his sermon on Mars Hill (Acts 17:22-31). Only a few were saved (Acts 17:33-34). It was Paul's most scholarly sermon in all of the Book of Acts — and the least fruitful. Paul had yielded to the temptation to demonstrate his own erudition in Athens, the city of scholars. It was magnificent — a magnificent failure as far as results were concerned. But it is to Paul's eternal credit that he analyzed the difficulty and corrected his error forthwith. In Corinth it was not ἐν σοφίᾳ λόγου, because he knew from experience that in a sermon like that the power of the cross is short-circuited. Modern preachers who are too concerned about their I.Q. and too interested in literary achievement should take heed. Many evangelicals, whose basic theology is correct, are as guilty as the modernists.

Christ the Power and Wisdom of God

(1 Corinthians 1:18-31)

Verse 18 - *"For the preaching of the cross is to them that perish foolishness; but unto us which are saved it is the power of God."*

Ὁ λόγος γὰρ ὁ τοῦ σταυροῦ τοῖς μὲν ἀπολλυμένοις μωρία ἐστίν, τοῖς δὲ σῳζομένοις ἡμῖν δύναμις θεοῦ ἐστιν.

"For the word of the cross is folly to those who are perishing, but to us who are being saved it is the power of God." . . . RSV

Ὁ (nom.sing.masc.of the article in agreement with λόγος) 9.
λόγος (nom.sing.masc.of λόγος, subject of ἐστίν) 510.
γὰρ (causal conjunction) 105.
ὁ (nom.sing.masc.of the article in agreement with λόγος) 9.
τοῦ (gen.sing.masc.of the article in agreement with σταυροῦ) 9.

σταυροῦ (gen.sing.masc.of σταυρός, description) 899.

τοῖς (dat.pl.masc.of the article in agreement with ἀπολλυμένοις) 9.

ἀπολλυμένοις (pres.mid.part.dat.pl.masc.of ἀπόλλυμι, substantival, personal interest) 208.

#4105 μωρία (nom.sing.fem.of μωρία, predicate nominative).

King James Version

foolishness - 1 Cor.1:18,21,23; 2:14; 3:19.

Revised Standard Version

folly - 1 Cor.1:18,21,23; 2:14; 3:19.

Meaning: Cf. μωρός (#482); μωραίνω (#444); μωρολογία (#4508). Foolishness, folly, nonesense, vapid and vacuous philosophical discourse, stupid and inane speech. The gospel of Christ is foolishness to the unsaved - 1 Cor.1:18,21,23; 2:14. Conversely, the world's highest wisdom is nonesense to God - 1 Cor.3:19.

ἐστίν (3d.per.sing.pres.ind.of εἰμί, static) 86.

τοῖς (dat.pl.masc.of the article in agreement with ἡμῖν) 9.

σωζομένοις (pres.pass.part.dat.pl.masc.of σώζω, adverbial, causal) 109.

ἡμῖν (dat.pl.masc.of ἐγώ, personal interest) 123.

δύναμις (nom.sing.fem.of δύναμις, predicate nominative) 687.

θεοῦ (gen.sing.masc.of θεός, description) 124.

ἐστιν (3d.per.sing.pres.ind.of εἰμί, static) 86.

Translation - "Because the philosophy of the cross to those who are perishing is nonesense, but to us, because we are saved, it is divine power."

Comment: Paul is explaining why he determined that never again would he attempt to dress up the story of Calvary with worldly erudition as he had done at Mars Hill. Thus γάρ is causal. The philosophy that has as its rationale the death of Jesus Christ upon the cross is such that it can never be acceptable to the lost? Why? Because Satan has blinded the minds of those who are perishing (2 Cor.4:4). Christ's death on the cross is the basis of Paul's gospel. When he preached it it was life unto life for the saved, but death unto death for the lost (2 Cor.2:15), a statement that supports 1 Cor.1:18. What brings life to those elect souls is the power of God, while the same message considered foolishness by the perishing, brings death to them. Only the truth makes us free (John 8:32,36). Since the lost will not have the truth they are seduced into believing the Devil's lie (2 Thess.2:10).

Calvary is nonesense to the lost for at least two reasons: (1) it teaches that man is lost because he is depraved by sin. This view is anathema to the unregenerate mind. Education professors and misguided parents, brainwashed by a college textbook instead of guided by the Book have been telling us for centuries that children are not "bad." They are only uneducated. The first point in the TULIP is Total Depravity and the unsaved will have none of it. Modern heretics come from a long line - The Judaizers in Galatian country, whom Paul opposed in his

Galatian epistle, Pelagius, Arminius, Erasmus, Pestalozzi, Rousseau, Thomas Jefferson, Robert Owen, John Dewey, William Heard Kilpatrick *et al*) - all of these and many more teach that "the fall of man," "original sin," "depravity" and other theological terms are to be regarded with amused contempt and dismissed as unfounded formulations of a bygone age. The idea that man is incapable of earning his own way in God's moral universe is repugnant to the human spirit, and the fact that it happens to be true only adds fuel to the flames of resentment.

The story of the cross also does not lend itself to empirical investigation as that phrase is understood by scientists. It must be accepted "by faith." There is no way to substantiate it by the scientific method. It is argued that Christians defend it because they have a vested interest in it. They are accused of not being tough minded enough to face life without the "good news" that Christ died and rose again. It was Immanuel Kant who proved in his *Critique of Pure Reason* that, although we can deduce noumena from phenomena, as we use the categories of time and space to convert sensations to perceptions which produce concepts, which become science and a rationale for life, we cannot accept the Bible with its stories of a Saviour and predictions of salvation because we did not live in the first century and therefore could not know for certain that the things written are true. It did not seem to bother Kant that by the same reasoning we must disbelieve all written history. Just why we can believe the stories in Gibbon, *The Decline and Fall of the Roman Empire*, but cannot believe the historic record of Matthew, Mark, Luke and John was not explained.

Christians who try to prove the Christian theology by quoting the Scriptures are begging the question. The point in litigation is that the New Testament is a divine revelation and as such that it is true. We cannot assume as true the point being debated and then use it to build our case. Proper Christian Apologetics does not try to argue the world into Christ. We did not get into the Body of Christ by our own thought processes, but by faith. Nor should we try that method in Christian witnessing. We should only preach the gospel, knowing full well, before we open our mouth, that what we are about to say is certain to be regarded as nonesense by the unsaved. When we preach in a scholarly fashion, as Paul did on Mars Hill (Acts 17:22-31) the Holy Spirit is unable to do His supernatural work, but when we preach "foolishness" as Paul did in Corinth, the Holy Spirit effectually calls those for whom Christ died. Compare the results in Athens (Acts 17) and those in Corinth (Acts 18-19).

Note the μὲν . . . δὲ bifurcation between the two definite classes, distinguished by the definite articles - τοῖς μὲν ἀπολλυμένοις and τοῖς δὲ σῳζομένοις. Those in the process of perishing think the gospel is nonesense; those in the process of being saved experience it as the power of God.

Satan wants to unite the world on his own terms (Rev.13:8, 11-17), and he will succeed temporarily. But the cross of Christ has divided mankind (Mt.10:34-36; Dan.12:10; 1 Thess.5:1-5). Christ will unite the elect members of His body (John 17:21). The others will be left to the inevitable consequences of unlimited particularity (the goal of science) without unity (the gift of divine revelation). In gestalt terms there will be no "closure" in hell. Only in heaven. If faith in New Testament revelation is required to put the "many" into logical relations with the "one" the world opts to forego the unity. Christ alone unites particularity into unity. Plato was sure that the ideal oak leaf was in heaven. Aristotle was equally sure that although he could tell the difference between an oak leaf and a rhinoceros, he could also see the difference between one oak leaf and the others on the tree. Because they had no knowledge of the Christ who could confirm both their views,they went their separate ways. Aristotle said, "I love Plato dearly, but I love philosophy more dearly." Christians see no need to cling to one and repudiate the other. For we have our Lord, the Creator of the many who unites them into the one. Man murdered Him and rejects the story that He rose from the dead. So, for the unsaved there is no "unity" except that which he dishonestly borrows from the rationale of his Christian neighbour, which is hardly playing the game of epistemology in keeping with the rules! Man's attempt to unite his world without Christ will always fail. Witness the United Nations (1 Pet.5:3). There can be no union of nations until there is a union of notions. Hell is ultimate disconnectedness (2 Thess.1:9).

My unsaved neighbour thinks that life in a random universe is exciting because unpredictable, but he turns the ignition key on his car with the same assurance that it will start that I do when I crank mine. According to his philosophy, the next time he tries to start it, it may bake a cake or compose a symphony or turn into a monster with a green head. If such should happen no one would be more surprized than my neighbour.

These problems in epistemology are not difficult for the Christian, but he often forgets that he did not understand them either until he was born from above.

Verse 19 - "For it is written, I will destroy the wisdom of the wise, and will bring to nothing the understanding of the prudent."

γέγραπται γάρ,Ἀπολῶ τὴν σοφίαν τῶν σοφῶν, καὶ τὴν σύνεσιν τῶν συνετῶν ἀθετήσω.

"For it is written, 'I will destroy the wisdom of the wise, and the cleverness of the clever I will thwart.'" . . . RSV

γέγραπται (3d.per.sing.perf.pass.ind.of γράφω, intensive) 156.

γάρ (causal conjunction) 105.

Ἀπολῶ (1st.per.sing.fut.act.ind.of ἀπόλλυμι, predictive) 208.

τὴν (acc.sing.fem.of the article in agreement with σοφίαν) 9.

σοφίαν (acc.sing.fem.of σοφία, direct object of ἀπολῶ) 934.

τῶν (gen.pl.masc.of the article in agreement with σοφῶν) 9.

σοφῶν (gen.pl.masc.of σοφός, possession) 949.

καὶ (continuative conjunction) 14.

τὴν (acc.sing.fem.of the article in agreement with σύνεσιν) 9.

σύνεσιν (acc.sing.fem.of σύνεσις, direct object of ἀθετήσω) 1918.

τῶν (gen.pl.masc.of the article in agreement with συνετῶν) 9.

συνετῶν (gen.pl.masc.of συνετός, possession) 950.

ἀθετήσω (1st.per.sing.fut.act.ind.of ἀθετέω, predictive) 2164.

Translation - *"Because it is written, 'I will demolish the wisdom of the wise and the quest for concrescence of the philosophers I will frustrate.' "*

Comment: The verbs ἀπολῶ and ἀθετήσω explain why. Paul used δύναμις (power) in verse 18. Thus γάρ is causal. It is *because* of what is written that the saved see the preaching of the cross in terms of power.

What specifically is the treatment that God promises to mete out to unregenerate philosophy? Disintegration (ἀπολῶ - #208) and ultimate frustration (ἀθετήσω - #2164). The modern unregenerate wisdom (σοφία - #934) that considers the gospel of Christ as nonesense is, of course, the radical empiricism and existentialism which it spawns, which rejects all attempts to achieve concrescence. When all experience is brought into concrete relations we have the merge of the "many" particularities into the "one" unifying principle. This is what Einstein had in mind as he sought until the end of his life for the "unified field" that would explain what to him seemed in conflict. At least the great man had the faith to believe that the unified field existed, even though he did not know where it was. Existentialists are not interested in unifying the universe. They are afraid that if they succeeded they would find it in Christ, Whose moral standards would demand their repentance.

Our Lord is the Great Unifier. The unified field is in Him (Col.2:3). He is the fulfillment of Plato's cry for a Philosopher-King. But empiricists refuse to accept any connection of anything with anything else which cannot be empirically demonstrated. Hence, all history is suspect (Historicism) including the gospel accounts of the historic Jesus. So indeed is prophecy both in the sense of forthtelling and foretelling. Preaching what one knows to be true and foretelling what must surely come to pass is a pastime for fools and/or knaves. Since the gospel of Christ points backward in history to the first century and forward in prophecy to the return of Him who died and rose again, it must be rejected by empiricists. Yet, despite their philosophy they ask us to accept some concrescence, although they say that they do not believe in it.

Isaiah 29:14, quoted here in 1 Cor.1:19, says that God is going to "take their philosophy apart" since, by their own view it is not supposed to put things together anyway. They ask for disconnectedness and noncontiguity and God is going to see that they get it. This is basicly what ἀπόλλυμι (#208) means, and it is the ultimate fate of the empiricism which, in fanatical extremity, rejects all deduction based upon faith - faith in the proposition that the Creator of the jigsaw puzzle intended for us to have the fun of putting it together.

Note that we have not said that empiricism has no place in Christian philosophy. Induction indeed, when joined with deduction, provides certitude. Even John Dewey said this. (John Dewey, *How We Think,* rev.ed., D.C.Heath & Co., 1933, chaps. 6,7,11). Dewey's incurable prejudices against Christianity never allowed him (assuming no deathbed repentance) to carry the epistemological method of this piece to its logical conclusion.

God will also thwart and ultimately embarrass "the understanding of the prudent" which we have translated "the concrescent thinking of the philosophical." Note that σύνεσις (#1918) and συνετός (#950) basicly mean concrescence.

Even unregenerate philosophers who have the proper method will be brought to frustration, not because their method is wrong, for it is not, but because they refused to allow it to bring them to Christ. They have travelled the proper path, methodologically, but have stopped short of the destination to which inevitably it would have led them, for the road which they follow leads to childlike humility and faith at the foot of the cross. Thus their ultimate repudiation. It takes an all powerful Christ to rip the ivy off the hallowed halls of the world's institutions of sophistication (Mt.28:18; 11:25).

Verse 20 - "Where is the wise? Where is the scribe? Where is the disputer of this world? Hath not God made foolish the wisdom of this world?"

ποῦ σοφός; ποῦ γραμματεύς; ποῦ συζητητὴς τοῦ αἰῶνος τούτου; οὐχὶ ἐμώρανεν ὁ θεὸς τὴν σοφίαν τοῦ κόσμου;

"Where is the wise man? Where is the scribe? Where is the debater of this age? Has not God made foolish the wisdom of the world?" . . . RSV

ποῦ (interrogative adverb of place) 142.
σοφός (nom.sing.masc.of σοφός, nominative absolute) 949.
ποῦ (interrogative adverb of place) 142.
γραμματεύς (nom.sing.masc.of γραμματεύς, nominative absolute) 152.
ποῦ (interrogative adverb of place) 142.

#4106 συζητητὴς (nom.sing.masc.of συζητητής, nominative absolute).

King James Version

disputer - 1 Cor.1:20.

Revised Standard Version

debater - 1 Cor.1:20.

Meaning: Cf. συζητέω (#2060); ζήτησις (#1994). A combination of σύν (#1542) and ζητέω (#207). Hence, one who seeks with others to discover truth by debate; a disputer; a debater; a follower of Hegel's method of distilling truth from conflicting views. With reference to the philosophers of the first century who rejected Christian faith in order to continue their "search" for truth. Used in contempt by Paul in 1 Cor.1:20.

τοῦ (gen.sing.neut.of the article in agreement with αἰῶνος) 9.
αἰῶνος (gen.sing.neut.of αἰών, description) 1002.
τούτου (gen.sing.neut.of οὗτος, in agreement with αἰῶνος) 93.
οὐχὶ (negative particle with the indicative) 130.
ἐμώρανεν (3d.per.sing.1st.aor.act.ind.of μωραίνω, constative, rhetorical question, expecting a positive reply) 444.
ὁ (nom.sing.masc.of the article in agreement with θεὸς) 9.
θεὸς (nom.sing.masc.of θεός, subject of ἐμώρανεν) 124.

τὴν (acc.sing.fem.of the article in agreement with σοφίαν) 9.
σοφίαν (acc.sing.fem.of σοφία, direct object of ἐμώρανεν) 934.
τοῦ (gen.sing.masc.of the article in agreement with κόσμου) 9.
κόσμου (gen.sing.masc.of κόσμος, description) 360.

Translation - "Where is the wise? Where is the scribe? Where is the debater of this age? God has demonstrated the folly of the philosophy of this world has He not?"

Comment: Note that the classes referred to here - "wise men. . . scribes. . . debaters" are sufficiently definite, even if, in the case of σοφός, adjectival, without the article. These are nominative absolutes in rhetorical question. Paul is strongly repudiating philosophy, pedantic scholarship and debate where it is prejudicial against Christ. There is a great deal of contempt in Paul's feeling. The οὐχὶ question expects a positive reply. God has indeed embarrassed the radical empiricism of this world. Note that the word here is τὴν σοφίαν, not τὴν σύνεσιν. Even God cannot make σύνεσις foolish, for it is the proper philosophical method. He can thwart it, but only because it stops short of its goal. *Cf.* verse 19. But God can and has rendered σοφίαν utterly vapid and vacuous. How? By determining to save the believer who, by faith, accepts the facts of the gospel of Christ, which facts are matters of history long past. Historicists may preach that no one can understand the writings of previous generations; hence, that history and the conclusions of historians are altogether unreliable, but God makes the reliability and objectivity of history fundamental to salvation. Thus while ἡ σοφία τοῦ κόσμου - "the radical empiricism of the world" - teaches that no one can be sure about the past, and thus condemns itself, by its own method to damnation, the very history which it repudiates is used by God to save those whose approach to certitude includes faith.

What we have just said is what Paul adds in

Verse 21 - "For after that in the wisdom of God the world by wisdom knew not God, it pleased God by the foolishness of preaching to save them that believe."

ἐπειδὴ γὰρ ἐν τῇ σοφίᾳ τοῦ θεοῦ οὐκ ἔγνω ὁ κόσμος διὰ τῆς σοφίας τὸν θεόν, εὐδόκησεν ὁ θεὸς διὰ τῆς μωρίας τοῦ κηρύγματος σῶσαι τοὺς πιστεύοντας.

"For since, in the wisdom of God, the world did not know God through wisdom, it pleased God through the folly of what we preach to save those who believe." . . . RSV

ἐπειδὴ (compound conjunction) 2148.
γὰρ (explanatory conjunction) 105.
ἐν (preposition with the locative, accompanying circumstance) 80.
τῇ (loc.sing.fem.of the article in agreement with σοφίᾳ) 9.
σοφίᾳ (loc.sing.fem.of σοφία, accompanying circumstance) 934.
τοῦ (gen.sing.masc.of the article in agreement with θεοῦ) 9.
θεοῦ (gen.sing.masc.of θεός, description) 124.
οὐκ (negative particle with the indicative) 130.

ἔγνω (3d.per.sing.2d.aor.act.ind.of γινώσκω, constative) 131.

ὁ (nom.sing.masc.of the article in agreement with κόσμος) 9.

κόσμος (nom.sing.masc.of κόσμος, subject of ἔγνω) 360.

διὰ (preposition with the ablative, means) 118.

τῆς (abl.sing.fem.of the article in agreement with σοφίας) 9.

σοφίας (abl.sing.fem.of σοφία, means) 934.

τὸν (acc.sing.masc.of the article in agreement with θεόν) 9.

θεόν (acc.sing.masc.of θεός, direct object of ἔγνω) 124.

εὐδόκησεν (3d.per.sing.aor.act.ind.of εὐδοκέω, constative) 328.

ὁ (nom.sing.masc.of the article in agreement with θεὸς) 9.

θεὸς (nom.sing.masc.of θεός, subject of εὐδόκησεν) 124.

διὰ (preposition with the ablative of means) 118.

τῆς (abl.sing.fem.of the article in agreement with μωρίας) 9.

μωρίας (abl.sing.fem.of μωρία, means) 4105.

τοῦ (gen.sing.neut.of the article in agreement with κηρύγματος) 9.

κηρύγματος (gen.sing.neut.of κήρυγμα, description) 1013.

σῶσαι (aor.act.inf.of σώζω, epexegetical) 109.

τοὺς (acc.pl.masc.of the article in agreement with πιστεύοντας) 9.

πιστεύοντας (pres.act.part.acc.pl.masc.of πιστεύω, substantival, direct object of σῶσαι) 734.

Translation - *"So, because that in the wisdom of God the world by means of philosophy did not know God, God was pleased by means of the nonesense of what is preached to save the believers."*

Comment:ἐπειδὴ here in its causal sense, which makes γὰρ explanatory, as Paul explains his thought in the rhetorical question of verse 20. God ordained that unregenerate philosophy would never lead man to Christ. This is the accompanying circumstance in the locative phrase ἐν τῇ σοφίᾳ τοῦ θεοῦ. We need only to look at what man's thought processes did for him in the beginning (Rom.1:18-32). The sensations of phenomena lead to the concepts of noumena. Thus sense perception and thought direct the unsaved man to recognize divine power and intelligence in an orderly universe, but there is nothing in nature to tell man that God loves Him and that Jesus Christ came to earth to die for him. *Cf.* our discussion of this in comment on Romans 1:18-23.

Jesus was happy about the Father's decree (Mt.11:25; 18:3; 1 Cor.2:9). The world obviously cannot know God by the empirical approach, since empiricism can do nothing but record sensations which are "brute" — *i.e.* isolated from all other sensations. The universal law of causation with its conclusion that all effects have previous causes is not the product of science. It is the product of reason. If man is irrational he can only conclude that he lives in a random universe in which anything can happen and probably will.

So the empiricist cannot know God. He has never tasted, smelt, touched, heard or seen God nor subjected Him to experimentation in a test-tube. He concludes therefore that since test-tube epistemology is the only tough minded way for a mature intellect (!) to be sure of anything, God does not exist, or, if He does He cannot be known. Philosophy and science at best, therefore, can lead only to deism, never to theism. The only book that teaches theism is the Bible and no one takes the Bible seriously until he has accepted its authority on an *a priori* basis. This the philosopher refuses to do.

Since this is the case, God was pleased to save those whom He is determined to save, by means of the content of that which is preached. The gospel of Christ speaks of incarnation (virgin birth!), sinless life, miracles, vicarious death, burial, bodily resurrection, bodily ascenscion, high priestly intercession and second coming. Such nonesense! To be sure, unless it is true, in which case it is the best news that has ever been announced on this wretched planet. One must come to the place where he is like a little child to accept it (Mt.18:3). This kind of gospel is not revealed to PH.D's, but to babes (Mt.11:25). Christians believe the gospel and therefore they "know" (1 John 5:13). But when the Christian uses the word "know" he uses it in a different sense than is found in the mouth of the scientist and/or philosopher. For the Christian "know" is synonymous with "believe" when he is speaking within the context of Christian epistemology. In secular contexts he uses the two words as the empiricist does. Example: Before Henry Aaron did it, I *believed* that he would surpass Babe Ruth's home run record. After he did it I *knew* that he had done it. If the Bible had prophesied that he would, then I would have *known* it in advance. But there is nothing in the Bible about home runs. The empiricist uses the two words synonymously in all contexts since he rejects revelation and refuses to believe anything that he does not know. Witness Tennyson in *In Memoriam* - "We have but faith; we cannot know. For knowledge is of things we see." To which Strong retorted, "This would make sensuous phenomena the only objects of knowledge. Faith in supersensible realities, on the contrary, is the highest exercise of reason." (A. H. Strong, *Systematic Theology*, I, 3).

There is divine irony in God's decree that by simple and tender minded faith the "poor in the sphere of intellect" (Mt.5:3) who could scarcely read a philosophy book, much less understand it can be given eternal life by believing, while an exalted PH.D. with a Phi Beta Kappa key misses eternal life because he considers himself too sophisticated to doubt his epistemological system. He too can be saved, if he is willing to become like a little child (Mt.18:3). Thousands have.

The two approaches to truth employed by the unsaved are set forth in

Verse 22 - *"For the Jews require a sign, and the Greeks seek after wisdom."*

ἐπειδὴ καὶ Ἰουδαῖοι σημεῖα αἰτοῦσιν καὶ Ἕλληνεσ σοφίαν ζητοῦσιν,

"For Jews demand signs and Greeks seek wisdom, . . . RSV

ἐπειδὴ (compound causal conjunction) 2148.
καὶ (ascensive conjunction) 14.
Ἰουδαῖοι (nom.pl.masc.of Ἰουδαῖος, subject of αἰτοῦσιν) 143.
σημεῖα (acc.sing.neut.of σημεῖον, direct object of αἰτοῦσιν) 1005.
αἰτοῦσιν (3d.per.pl.pres.act.ind.of αἰτέω, customary) 537.

καὶ (continuative conjunction) 14.

Ἕλληνες (nom.pl.masc.of Ἕλλήν, subject of ζητοῦσιν) 2373.

σοφίαν (acc.sing.fem.of σοφία, direct object of ζητοῦσιν) 934.

ζητοῦσιν (3d.per.pl.pres.act.ind.of ζητέω, customary) 207.

Translation - "Because Jews are even asking for a sign and Greeks always seek philosophy."

Comment: As γὰρ after ἐπειδή in verse 21 was explanatory, so καὶ after ἐπειδή must be ascensive. Note the causal force of ὅτι in verse 25 and γὰρ in verse 26. The Jews, "an evil and adulterous generation" even went to the lengths of demanding a sign (Mt.12:38-42), and they got none except Christ, our Heavenly Jonah. The men of Nineveh will fare better in the judgment than the Jews who crucified Christ, because they believed Jonah's story (and what a story it was!) while the Jews rejected Jesus' prophecy that He would rise from the dead and they also rejected the witness of the Christians after His resurrection that He had indeed risen.

The Jewish error was philosophical. "Come down from the cross and we will take a look at this empirical evidence. If we think it is conclusive we will believe." They would not have believed if He had come down from the cross as they demanded. They would have found some other way to rationalize their unbelief. The real test was their unwillingness to do God's will (John 7:17). If one is willing to obey God's will he will enjoy the certitude of Christian faith, with or without having seen such miracles as the Jews demanded. But no one is willing to do God's will until he has been made willing by the sovereign Holy Spirit (John 16:7-11).

The Jews were the scientists. The Greeks were the philosophers. The Jews wanted to base faith on experience. The Greeks wanted to base it upon reason. Their demand is this: "Show me that the terms of the gospel of Christ upon which you ask me to believe are reasonable. How does it make sense to say that a Galilean carpenter can save me from the penalty of sin by dying on a cross? And this story about His bodily resurrection? It is well known to Greek philosophers, that resurrection is of the spirit, not of the body."

If the Jews had been given the sign that they demanded, and if the Greeks had become convinced by the philosophical arguments which they invited, then their faith would have been the product of their own experience and thought processes. Paul deals with this problem in 1 Cor.2:1-5. He who believes in and trusts only that which he understands has created a religion for himself no greater than his own perceptive capability. He has in effect become his own saviour. But those who understand the gravity of the sin problem in a moral universe realize that the solution requires more than the resources of fallen man.

Note that there will be empirical evidence ultimately for believers - 1 Cor.15:5-8; Rev.1:7; 19:11-21; Mt.24:30, etc. But the Christian's certitude will not be enhanced by forthcoming empirical evidence. We are sure *now* that Christ is alive. It will be exciting to see Him but we do not need the confirmatory evidence. The fallacy of Jewish and Greek thinking is that they want the empirical evidence, in the case of the Jews, and the logic, in the case of the Greeks, as causes of faith, whereas God has decreed that sensation and logic are the results of faith. The gospel of Jesus Christ makes great sense, but only to the Christian, and Christians are the ones who will see the sign that the Jews demanded. The Jews will see it too, but it will then be too late. It will be scant consolation to go to hell with the knowledge that at last one has been forced to admit that he was wrong (Phil.2:9,10).

Although Greek philosophy cannot bring the sinner to Christ, the Greeks are to be credited with having developed philosophy to its highest point, and as a result, Plato at least reached the point in his thinking where he recognized that he had no real answer to the problem of soul sorrow. That is why he cried out for the Philosopher-King. (*Republic,* 5, 473, D). Philosophy seemed to lead him to the point where he was willing to believe that there was an answer somewhere and to admit that he could not find it by taking thought. He seemed also to express a great desire that the Philosopher-King would some day come. Preachers should be careful about preaching Plato into hell, because he was not baptized by immersion somewhere south of the Mason-Dixon line. Perhaps it is for him that Paul wrote Romans 2:12-16 . The same analysis may apply to thinkers like Albert Einstein, who spent his declining years in eager search for the "unified field" - the formula which had escaped him but which he believed existed, which would explain the universe on a rational basis. He was sure that God was not playing dice with the universe.

Whatever the Jews demand in the way of a sign and the Greeks in the way of a syllogism, all Paul had to offer was the only message that could save them - the story of a Galilean carpenter on a cross between two thieves.

Verse 23 - "But we preach Christ crucified, unto the Jews a stumbling block, and unto the Greeks foolishness."

ἡμεῖς δὲ κηρύσσομεν Χριστὸν ἐσταυρωμένον, Ἰουδαίοις μὲν σκάνδαλον ἔθνεσιν δὲ μωρίαν,

"but we preach Christ crucified, a stumbling block to Jews and folly to Gentiles,. . . " RSV

ἡμεῖς (nom.pl.masc.of ἐγώ, subject of κηρύσσομεν) 123.

δὲ (adversative conjunction) 11.

κηρύσσομεν (1st.per.pl.pres.act.ind.of κηρύσσω, customary) 249.

Χριστὸν (acc.sing.masc.of Χριστός, direct object of κηρύσσομεν) 4.

ἐσταυρωμένον (perf.pass.part.acc.sing.masc.of σταυρόω, adjectival, restrictive, in agreement with Χριστὸν) 1328.

Ἰουδαίοις (dat.pl.masc.of Ἰουδαῖος, personal interest) 143.

μὲν (correlative particle of affirmation) 300.

σκάνδαλον (acc.sing.neut.of σκάνδαλον, apposition) 1082.

ἔθνεσιν (dat.pl.neut.of ἔθνος, personal interest) 376.

δὲ (adversative conjunction) 11.

μωρίαν (acc.sing.fem.of μωρία, apposition) 4105.

Translation - "But we always preach Christ crucified - to the Jews indeed a stumbling block but to the Gentiles nonesense."

Comment: δὲ is definitely adversative. Jews go about demanding a sign; Gentiles seek philosophical certitude on their terms. Does Paul oblige? By no means! His custom was to preach that Messiah was nailed to a cross by the Romans. No better way to trip up a Jew (#1082) whose rationale was in terms of a triumphant King, not a crucified carpenter. Messiah was expected to crucify the Romans, not the other way around. And no better way to repel a philosopher who was looking for the good, the beautiful and the true, not the victim of a mob, dying among thieves. That a Nazarene carpenter, with Jesus' apparent credentials and record should be a Saviour was the height of foolishness to a philosopher.

If both Jews and Greeks reacted to Paul's message, which dealt only with Jesus (Rom.16:25) how then could anyone, either Jew or Gentile be saved? The answer is in

Verse 24 - "But unto them which are called, both Jews and Greeks, Christ, the power of God and the wisdom of God."

αὐτοῖς δὲ τοῖς κλητοῖς, Ἰουδαίοις τε καὶ Ἕλλησιν, Χριστὸν θεοῦ δύναμιν καὶ θεοῦ σοφίαν.

"but to those who are called, both Jews and Greeks, Christ the power of God and the wisdom of God." . . . RSV

αὐτοῖς (dat.pl.masc.of αὐτός, personal interest) 16.
δὲ (adversative conjunction) 11.
τοῖς (dat.pl.masc.of the article in agreement with κλητοῖς) 9.
κλητοῖς (dat.pl.masc.of κλητός, apposition) 1411.
Ἰουδαίοις (dat.pl.masc.of Ἰουδαῖος, apposition) 143.
τε (correlative particle) 1408.
καὶ (adjunctive particle joining nouns) 14.
Ἕλλησιν (dat.pl.masc.of Ἕλλην, apposition) 2373.
Χριστὸν (acc.sing.masc.of Χριστός, direct object of κηρύσσομεν) 4.
θεοῦ (abl.sing.masc.of θεός, source) 124.
δύναμιν (acc.sing.fem.of δύναμις, apposition) 687.
καὶ (adjunctive conjunction joining nouns) 14.
θεοῦ (abl.sing.masc.of θεός, source) 124.
σοφίαν (acc.sing.fem.of σοφία, apposition) 934.

Translation - "But to those (who are) the called ones, both Jews and Greeks, Christ, the power from God and the wisdom from God."

Comment: δὲ, the adversative accentuates the difference in the reaction to the gospel of Christ of those who are the called and those who are not called. This difference is not to be explained by ethnic background and acculturation, because both Jews and Greeks who are called regard Christ differently from Jews and Greeks who, not having been called, judge Jesus on their own misguided terms. An uncalled Jew regarded Jesus as an imposter because when He was challenged for a sign He gave none except the one that for them became a trap stick (Mt.12:40). An uncalled Greek regarded Jesus as a fool. But whether he be Jew or Greek, when he is called by the Holy Spirit, the elect came to see Jesus as both power and wisdom coming from the divine source (ablative of source in θεοῦ). We can think of θεοῦ also as genitive in which case it is descriptive - "divine power and divine wisdom." Thus the difference is in the calling, not in any inherent superiority of one set of sinners over another. (Rom.8:29-30).

In Romans 1:18-20 we learned that when men view the wonders of creation in the natural world they are able to deduce from the observations of the senses an appreciation of the power and intelligence of God the Creator, although they were unable to learn from the same sources that He was also a loving Saviour willing to come to earth in incarnation to die for His elect. All powerful and all wise, as the heavens declared Him to be, He is now seen in the person of Jesus Christ as the embodiment of that power and wisdom. But this is understood only by those who are the objects of the Holy Spirit's effectual call.

The Hero in the story of the incarnation and the cross is the One in Whom are hid all of the treasures of wisdom and knowledge (Col.2:3) and all power is given unto Him in heaven and in earth (Mt.28:18). That God should reveal this in a gospel story that men call foolish and that His power should be revealed in One Whom men viewed as too weak to resist the Roman soldiers who killed Him is the thought in

Verse 25 - "Because the foolishness of God is wiser than men; and the weakness of God is stronger than men."

ὅτι τὸ μωρὸν τοῦ θεοῦ σοφώτερον τῶν ἀνθρώπων ἐστίν, καὶ τὸ ἀσθενὲς τοῦ θεοῦ ἰσχυρότερον τῶν ἀνθρώπων.

"For the foolishness of God is wiser than men, and the weakness of God is stronger than men." . . . RSV

ὅτι (causal conjunction) 211.
τὸ (nom.sing.neut.of the article in agreement with μωρὸν) 9.
μωρὸν (nom.sing.neut.of μωρός, subject of ἐστίν) 482.
τοῦ (gen.sing.masc.of the article in agreement with θεοῦ) 9.
θεοῦ (gen.sing.masc.of θεός, description) 124.
σοφώτερον (nom.sing.neut.comp.of σοφός, predicate adjective, in agreement with μωρὸν) 949.
τῶν (abl.pl.masc.of the article in agreement with ἀνθρώπων) 9.
ἀνθρώπων (abl.pl.masc.of ἄνθρωπος, comparison) 341.
ἐστίν (3d.per.sing.pres.ind.of εἰμί, static) 86.
καὶ (continuative conjunction) 14.
τὸ (nom.sing.neut.of the article in agreement with ἀσθενὲς) 9.
ἀσθενὲς (nom.sing.neut.of ἀσθενής, subject of ἐστίν understood) 1551.
τοῦ (gen.sing.masc.of the article in agreement with θεοῦ) 9.
θεοῦ (gen.sing.masc.of θεός, description) 124.

ἰσχυρότερον (nom.sing.neut.comp.of ἰσχυρός, predicate adjective in agreement with ἀσθενὲς) 303.

τῶν (abl.pl.masc.of the article in agreement with ἀνθρώπων) 9.

ἀνθρώπων (abl.pl.masc.of ἄνθρωπος, comparison) 341.

Translation - "Because the foolishness of God is wiser than men and the weakness of God is stronger then men."

Comment: This is obviously language in accommodation of a point that Paul is making. God is never foolish or weak, but if He were endowed with wisdom and strength only in varying degrees then on His weakest day He would be stronger than man on his strongest day and God's height of folly would still contain more wisdom than man's greatest achievement in wisdom.

The proof of this is seen in God's achievement as an Educator, in

Verse 26 - "For ye see your calling, brethren, how that not many wise men after the flesh, not many mighty, not many noble, are called."

Βλέπετε γὰρ τὴν κλῆσιν ὑμῶν, ἀδελφοί, ὅτι οὐ πολλοὶ σοφοὶ κατὰ σάρκα, ὀυ πολλοὶ δυνατοί, οὐ πολλοὶ εὐγενεῖς.

"For consider your call, brethren; not many of you were wise according to worldly standards, not many were powerful, not many were of noble birth; . . ." RSV

Βλέπετε (2d.per.pl.pres.act.impv.of βλέπω, command) 499.

γὰρ (inferential conjunction) 105.

τὴν (acc.sing.fem.of the article in agreement with κλῆσιν) 9.

κλῆσιν (acc.sing.fem.of κλῆσις, direct object of βλέπετε) 4003.

ὑμῶν (gen.pl.masc.of σύ, possession) 104.

ἀδελφοί (voc.pl.masc.of ἀδελφός, address) 15.

ὅτι (conjunction introducing an object clause in indirect declaration) 211.

οὐ (negative particle with the indicative) 130.

πολλοὶ (nom.pl.masc.of πολύς, in agreement with σοφοὶ) 228.

σοφοὶ (nom.pl.masc.of σοφός, subject of verb understood) 949.

κατὰ (preposition with the accusative, standard) 98.

σάρκα (acc.sing.fem.of σάρξ, standard) 1202.

οὐ (negative particle with the indicative) 130.

πολλοὶ (nom.pl.masc.of πολύς, in agreement with δυνατοί) 228.

δυνατοί (nom.pl.masc.of δυνατός, subject of verb understood) 1311.

οὐ (negative particle with the indicative) 130.

πολλοὶ (nom.pl.masc.of πολύς, in agreement with εὐγενεῖς) 228.

εὐγενεῖς (nom.pl.masc.of εὐγενής, subject of verb understood) 2656.

Translation - "Therefore, consider your calling, brethren, that not many well educated by human standards, not many influential, not many well-bred are called."

Comment: Paul is using the experience of the Corinthian church to prove the argument of verses 18-25. He invites the Corinthians to look around the congregation. By local Corinthian standards the sophisticated, influential and aristocratic citizens of Corinth were not represented in great numbers. A few were there by the same grace of God by which all were called. Paul did not say, "Not any." He said, "Not many." Statisticians will be quick to point out that the aristocrats, highly educated and influential people were a small proportionate part of the total population anyway. Did the aristocratic Christians represent a proportion of the church membership less than, equal to, or greater than their proportion in society? The text does not say, but the inference that it seems we can draw from the entire passage is that they were fewer as a percentage of Christians than as Corinthians. The Corinthian church members had little influence in the city before they were saved, and apart from the unction of the Holy Spirit, they had even less influence after they were saved. For now they were "fools for Christ" who suffered the offense of the cross.

But though their academic, social and political standing in the community was not impressive, they had been enrolled in God's "Jesus Christ University" with the Holy Spirit as the teacher, the New Testament as the text book and a grasp of truth unattainable to those outside of Christ. They were now in a position to be "taught of God" (John 6:45).

Verse 27 - "But God hath chosen the foolish things of the world to confound the wise; and God has chosen the weak things of the world to confound the things which are mighty;"

ἀλλὰ τὰ μωρὰ τοῦ κόσμου ἐξελέξατο ὁ θεὸς ἵνα καταισχύνῃ τοὺς σοφούς, καὶ τὰ ἀσθενῆ τοῦ κόσμου ἐξελέξατο ὁ θεὸς καταισχύνῃ τὰ ἰσχυρά,

". . . but God chose what is foolish in the world to shame the wise, God chose what is weak in the world to shame the strong, . . . " . . . RSV

ἀλλὰ (adversative conjunction) 342.
τὰ (acc.pl.neut.of the article in agreement with μωρὰ) 9.
μωρὰ (acc.pl.neut.of μωρός, direct object of ἐξελέξατο) 482.
τοῦ (gen.sing.masc.of the article in agreement with κόσμου) 9.
κόσμου (gen.sing.masc.of κόσμος, description) 360.
ἐξελέξατο (3d.per.sing.aor.mid.ind.of ἐκλέγω, constative) 2119.
ὁ (nom.sing.masc.of the article in agreement with θεὸς) 9.
θεὸς (nom.sing.masc.of θεός, subject of ἐξελέξατο) 124.
ἵνα (conjunction with the subjunctive in a purpose clause) 114.
καταισχύνῃ (3d.per.sing.aor.act.subj.of καταισχύνω, purpose) 2505.
τοὺς (acc.pl.masc.of the article in agreement with σοφούς) 9.
σοφούς (acc.pl.masc.of σοφός, direct object of καταισχύνῃ) 949.
καὶ (continuative conjunction) 14.
τὰ (acc.pl.neut.of the article in agreement with ἀσθενῆ) 9.
ἀσθενῆ (acc.pl.neut.of ἀσθενής, direct object of ἐξελέξατο) 1551.
τοῦ (gen.sing.masc.of the article in agreement with κόσμου) 9.
κόσμου (gen.sing.masc.of κόσμος, description) 360.

ἐξελέξατο (3d.per.sing.aor.mid.ind.of ἐκλέγω, constative) 2119.
ὁ (nom.sing.masc.of the article in agreement with θεὸς) 9.
θεὸς (nom.sing.masc.of θεός, subject of ἐξελέξατο) 124.
ἵνα (conjunction with the subjunctive, purpose) 114.
καταισχύνῃ (3d.per.sing.aor.act.subj.of καταισχύνω, purpose) 2505.
τὰ (acc.pl.neut.of the article in agreement with ἰσχυρά) 9.
ἰσχυρά (acc.pl.neut.of ἰσχυρός, direct object of καταισχύνῃ) 303.

Translation - "*But God has chosen the stupid things of the world in order to dicomfit the wise men, and the weak things of the world God has chosen to put to rout the strong.*"

Comment: Since God's fools are smarter than the unsaved intellectuals and God's weaklings are stronger than the mightiest forces of Satan (verse 25) He has chosen to use them to embarrass the enemy. Thus "the meek shall inherit the earth" (Mt.5:5) and "the last shall be first" (Mt.19:30). God likes to do things like that (Rom.4:17b). In the contest between God and Satan, good and evil, light and darkness, truth and error, our Lord pits the second team against Satan's varsity. What the enemy regards as stupid and weak is more than enough to defeat him on his best day. Because unregenerate man is walking in the dark (Mt.6:23; John 11:9,10) all of his values are confused. That Christians in this age should expect to be praised by unsaved sinners for anything they do indicates that they do not understand their Bibles very well.

Verse 28 - "*And base things of the world, and things which are despised, hath God chosen, yea, and things which are not to bring to naught things that are.*"

καὶ τὰ ἀγενῆ τοῦ κόσμου καὶ τὰ ἐξουθενημένα ἐξελέξατο ὁ θεός, τὰ μὴ ὄντα, ἵνα τὰ ὄντα καταργήσῃ,

"*God chose what is low and despised in the world, even things that are not, to bring to nothing things that are, . . .*" . . . *RSV*

καὶ (continuative conjunction) 14.
τὰ (acc.pl.neut.of the article in agreement with ἀγενῆ) 9.

#4107 ἀγενῆ (acc.pl.neut.of ἀγενής, direct object of ἐξελέξατο).

King James Version

base things - 1 Cor.1:28.

Revised Standard Version

low things - 1 Cor.1:28.

Meaning: α privative plus γένος (#1090). Opposed to εὐγενής (#2656). Hence, low born; a man of no family; of base antecedents; ignoble; mean; cowardly - 1 Cor.1:28.

τοῦ (gen.sing.masc.of the article in agreement with κόσμου) 9.
κόσμου (gen.sing.masc.of κόσμος, definition) 360.
καὶ (continuative conjunction) 14.
τὰ (acc.pl.neut.of the article in agreement with ἐξουθενημένα) 9.
ἐξουθενημένα (perf.pass.part.acc.pl.neut.of ἐξουθενέω, substantival, direct object of ἐξελέξατο) 2628.
ἐξελέξατο (3d.per.sing.aor.mid.ind.of ἐκλέγω, constative) 2119.
ὁ (nom.sing.masc.of the article in agreement with θεός) 9.
θεός (nom.sing.masc.of θεός, subject of ἐξελέξατο) 124.
τὰ (acc.pl.neut.of the article in agreement with ὄντα) 9.
μὴ (negative particle with the participle) 87.
ὄντα (pres.part.acc.pl.neut.of εἰμί, substantival, direct object of ἐξελέξατο) 86.
ἵνα (conjunction with the subjunctive, purpose) 114.
τὰ (acc.pl.neut.of the article in agreement with ὄντα) 9.
ὄντα (pres.part.acc.pl.neut.of εἰμί, substantival, direct object of καταργήσῃ) 86.
καταργήσῃ (3d.per.sing.aor.act.subj.of καταργέω, purpose) 2500.

Translation - "And the ignoble things of lowly origin of the world and the things which are regarded with contempt God has chosen - the things which do not exist in order to replace the things that now exist."

Comment: This is in further explanation of the thought of verse 27. There is much profit for the student who runs the references for ἐξουθενέω (#2628) and καταργέω (#2500). Note especially Heb.7:14. What is any less prestigious than death on a cross? Yet, by it Christ put Satan, the god of this world, who had death as his chief weapon, out of business. If God can use death on a Roman cross as the supreme means of bringing the world under His sway, so that He can exercise His power over His enemies, then He can use anything - "folly, weakness, low social and political status, contemptible things, even nothing to confound His enemies.

A man who was 100 years old and his wife, who was 90 fathered a great nation. A jawbone of an ass in the hands of a backslider slew the Philistines. A donkey taught a preacher a lesson. The testimony of a little slave girl was used to heal a leper. Jesus paid His taxes with a fish. A little lad's lunch fed a multitude. A handful of Christians spread Christianity throughout the Roman Empire in 300 years. A whale taught a disobedient prophet to obey.

What is the purpose of God's policy of exalting that which the world despises above that which it admires? Could He not have saved the elect with a philosophy that is the object of the admiration of the unsaved? Could He not have appealed to the high and mighty, the rich, the jet set, the intellectual, the socially prominent, the politically powerful? Of course He could have done so, except that, had He done so, the recipients of His grace would never have understood and they would have taken the credit to themselves for what God did. Their salvation would have been viewed by them as something that they had always expected on the ground that they deserved it. This is the point in

Verse 29 - "That no flesh should glory in his presence."

ὅπως μὴ καυχήσηται πᾶσα σὰρξ ἐνώπιον τοῦ θεοῦ.

". . . so that no human being might boast in the presence of God." . . . RSV

ὅπως (conjunction with the subjunctive in a result clause) 177.

μὴ (negative particle with the subjunctive) 87.

καυχήσηται (3d.per.sing.aor.mid.subj.of καυχάομαι, result) 3847.

πᾶσα (nom.sing.fem.of πᾶς, in agreement with σὰρξ) 67.

σὰρξ (nom.sing.fem.of σάρξ, subject of καυχήσηται) 1202.

ἐνώπιον (preposition with the genitive of place description) 1798.

τοῦ (gen.sing.masc.of the article in agreement with θεοῦ) 9.

θεοῦ (gen.sing.masc.of θεός, place description) 124.

Translation - "In order (and with the result) that no human being may boast in the presence of God."

Comment: ὅπως with the subjunctive is usually final, not consecutive, but in a context in which the decrees of God are involved it is sub-final, since what God purposes also results. Actually the line between purpose and result is difficult to draw since purpose is intended result. When man purposes he does not always see the result, fortunately, but when God purposes, the result is certain.

What God has done, He has done in such a way as to make it impossible for man to take the credit. The primary purpose for all that God does is His own glory. This is His privilege and His prerogative as the Party of the First Part. Were it not for Him there would have been no creation and the universe and man would not exist.

The unregenerate mind in wicked presumption rebels at this concept and, without the slightest embarrassment at his colossal pretense, accepts the alternative, which is that God, if He exists at all, should seek man's glory. Thus man makes himself God and ends up doing the same thing for himself that he accuses God of doing for Himself! Witness the philosophical confusion of the lost soul, who is also the "poor soul" so skillfully portrayed by Jackie Gleason. *Cf.* Eph.2:7, which precludes all glory for man.

μὴ . . . πᾶσα σὰρξ does not mean "not all flesh shall glory" which implies that some flesh shall glory, but "all flesh shall not glory" or "no flesh shall glory." The negative μὴ joins the verb, not the noun, while πᾶσα joins the noun σάρξ. All human beings shall refrain from boasting before God. That is why God placed the glorious truths of revelation beyond the scope of experience and reason. Unsaved man can receive sensations, and, although "there is nothing in the intellect without first being in the senses," there is the intellect itself, as Leibnitz pointed out and with his mind the unsaved man can deduce from sensations some truth. But he cannot know that God loves him and that Christ died for Him without revelation and without the Holy Spirit, he does not have the faith to accept revelation. To our Lord goes all of the praise because

Verse 30 - "But of him are ye in Christ Jesus, who of God is made unto us

wisdom, and righteousness, and sanctification, and redemption."

ἐξ αὐτοῦ δὲ ὑμεῖς ἐστε ἐν Χριστῷ Ἰησοῦ ὃς ἐγενήθη σοφία ἡμῖν ἀπὸ θεοῦ,
δικαιοσύνη τε καὶ ἁγιασμὸς καὶ ἀπολύτρωσις,

*"He is the source of your life in Christ Jesus, whom God made our wisdom,
our righteousness and sanctification and redemption;" . . . RSV*

ἐξ (preposition with the ablative of source) 19.

αὐτοῦ (abl.sing.masc.of αὐτός, source) 16.

δὲ (adversative conjunction) 11.

ὑμεῖς (nom.pl.masc.of σύ, subject of ἐστε) 104.

ἐστε (2d.per.pl.pres.ind.of εἰμί, aoristic) 86.

ἐν (preposition with the instrumental of association) 80.

Χριστῷ (instru.sing.masc.of Χριστός, association) 4.

Ἰησοῦ (instru.sing.masc.of Ἰησοῦς, apposition) 3.

ὃς (nom.sing.masc.of ὅς, relative pronoun, subject of ἐγενήθη) 65.

ἐγενήθη (3d.per.sing.aor.pass.ind.of γίνομαι, culminative) 113,

σοφία (nom.sing.fem.of σοφία, predicate nominative) 934.

ἡμῖν (dat.pl.masc.of ἐγώ, personal advantage) 123.

ἀπὸ (preposition with the ablative of source) 70.

θεοῦ (abl.sing.masc.of θεός, source) 124.

δικαιοσύνη (nom.sing.fem.of δικαιοσύνη, predicate nominative) 322.

τε (correlative particle) 1408.

καὶ (adjunctive conjunction joining nouns) 14.

ἁγιασμὸς (nom.sing.masc.of ἁγιασμός, predicate nominative) 3917.

καὶ (adjunctive conjunction joining nouns) 14.

ἀπολύτρωσις (nom.sing.fem.of ἀπολύτρωσις, predicate nominative) 2732.

*Translation - "But He is the Source of your relationship with Christ Jesus, Who
has been made for you wisdom from God, both righteousness and sanctification
and redemption."*

Comment: δὲ is adversative to emphasize the contrast between verses 29 and 30.
No human being should boast before God (verse 29). On the contrary
(adversative δὲ) God is the source of the believer's association with Christ Jesus.
We can also take ἐξ αὐτοῦ as an ablative of agency. God is both the source and
the agent of our salvation. The antecedent of ὅς is Χριστῷ Ἰησοῦ. The relative
clause is causal. The only reason that the believer is in Christ is that Christ gave
us our philosophy from God (ablative of source in τοῦ θεοῦ). The Christian has
taken his course in epistemology (science of knowledge) from God. God is the
source and Christ is the direct agent. He has been rescued from the pitfalls of the
radical empiricism of the existentialist and he has been carried further than John
Dewey was able to lead him, although Dewey's method was correct as far as it
goes.

Note that Paul puts σοφία first. If the Christian does not have access to
holistic epistemology he is ill equipped to witness for the Lord. In Christ "are hid

all of the treasures of philosophy and science" (Col.2:3). With boundless intelligence and pre-planning and possessed of all the power there is, He created a universal jigsaw puzzle, composed of innumerable facts, which, like the pieces in a puzzle make sense only when they relate to other pieces which make up the whole. If they did not fit into the puzzle they would be "brute" *i.e.* meaningless. But they do fit. Thus the universe is not random and life has meaning. To some infinitesimal extent we understand the puzzle. In the case of a small number, a number that closely approximates zero, we have been able to put the pieces together. That is why we can blast off an airplane in Florida, send it around the earth for a week and bring it back safely in California. That is why we can blow up the world in a nuclear exchange. But we do not have the intelligence to drive our cars through an intersection without the guidance of an electric gadget which tells us when to go and when to refrain from going.

Cause and result relationships do exist in the universe which our Lord created. Every one of the multiplied billions of particularities, which philosophers call the "many" fit harmoniously in the "one." Thus the Christian can predicate. He can use adjectives. He can make value judgments. He can order his life in a manner that glorifies God. And when he fails to do so, He has the perceptivity to realize that he has failed and the grace to repent and ask forgiveness.

Since our Lord is our holistic wisdom He is also able to be our justification, sanctification and redemption. Note that τε καὶ . . . καὶ serve to tie these three together. Only the holistic philosopher Who sits at the right hand of God can give us these. Unregenerate philosophy, which deprecates the preaching of the cross as nonesense, can never provide lost man with righteousness, sanctification and redemption. These greatest of all benefits, the goals of philosophers for ages, are available only in Christ.

The devil has his bargain-basement substitutes - self righteousness, physchological autointoxication at an altar which is then declared to be sanctification, and salvation by works. These are available in the world's flea markets at every booth. The statement "I do no sin" really means "Nothing that I do is sin." Only the Christian says, "I am the chief of sinners but Christ's righteousness, holiness and redemption are mine by God's grace."

The world asks, "Who is Christ?"

We reply, "The historic Jesus of Nazareth."

The historicist demands, "How can you be so sure?"

We reply, "Faith."

The world sneers, "Nonesense."

We reply, "Very well. Have it your own way."

But the last word from the world will be "Alas!" and the Christian will enter the new age shouting, "Glory."

The student should run all of the references on #'s 322, 3917 and 2732, in order to appreciate how rich we are in Christ Jesus. Study each use of each word in context and learn to appreciate how this book which the Holy Spirit has written fits together.

Note that sanctification refers to the act of God by which He sets certain people and things apart for His own exclusive use. Note that our Lord "sanctified" Himself - *i.e.* He determined to do nothing but to go to the cross. *Cf.*Eph.2:10.

Verse 31 - "That according as it is written, He that glorieth, let him glory in the Lord."

ἵνα καθὼς γέγραπται, Ὁ καυχώμενος ἐν κυρίῳ καυχάσθω.

". . . therefore, as it is written, 'Let him who boasts, boast of the Lord." . . . RSV

ἵνα (conjunction with γένηται understood, in a purpose clause, ellipsis) 114.
καθὼς (compound adverbial in a comparative clause) 1348.
γέγραπται (3d.per.sing.perf.pass.ind.of γράφω, intensive) 156.
Ὁ (nom.sing.masc.of the article in agreement with καυχώμενος) 9.
καυχώμενος (pres.mid.part.nom.sing.masc.of καυχάομαι, substantival, subject of καυχάσθω) 3487.
ἐν (preposition with the instrumental, association) 80.
κυρίῳ (instru.sing.masc.of κύριος, association) 97.
καυχάσθω (3d.per.sing.pres.impv.of καυχάομαι, command) 3847.

Translation - "In order that it may happen as it is written, 'Let the boaster boast in the Lord.' "

Comment: The quotation is from Jer.9:24. We must supply γένηται in the ellipsis after ἵνα in order to complete the purpose clause. The imperative after ἵνα, of course is due to the quotation. *Cf.* Rom.4:1-3. If there is any boasting to be done, the Lord Who is the source of all that man has that is good, will get the glory (James 1:17).

Proclaiming Christ Crucified

(1 Corinthians 2:1-5)

1 Cor.2:1 - "And I, brethren, when I came to you, came not with excellency of speech or of wisdom, declaring unto you the testimony of God."

Κἀγὼ ἐλθὼν πρὸς ὑμᾶς, ἀδελφοί, ἦλθον οὐ καθ' ὑπεροχὴν λόγου ἢ σοφίας καταγγέλλων ὑμῖν τὸ μυστήριον τοῦ θεοῦ.

"When I came to you, brethren, I did not come proclaiming to you the testimony of God in lofty words or wisdom." . . . RSV

Κἀγὼ (continuative conjunction and ἐγώ, crasis) 178.
ἐλθὼν (aor.mid.part.nom.sing.masc.of ἔρχομαι, adverbial, gnomic) 146.
πρὸς (preposition with the accusative of extent) 197.
ὑμᾶς (acc.pl.masc.of σύ, extent) 104.
ἀδελφοί (voc.pl.masc.of ἀδελφός, address) 15.
ἦλθον (1st.per.sing.aor.mid.ind.of ἔρχομαι, constative) 146.
οὐ (negative particle, with the indicative) 130.
καθ' (preposition with the accusative, standard) 98.

#4108 ὑπεροχὴν (acc.sing.fem.of ὑπεροχή, standard).

King James Version

authority - 1 Tim.2:2.
excellency - 1 Cor.2:1.

Revised Standard Version

high position - 1 Tim.2:2.
lofty - 1 Cor.2:1.

Meaning: A combination of ὑπέρ (#545) and ἔχω (#82). *Cf.* ὑπερέχω (#4033). Prop.elevation, superiority, predominance, high position. In a metaphorical sense, excellence, lofty character. Followed by a genitive of description, λόγου hence, sophisticated speech - ἢ σοφίας - speech of lofty philosophical content - 1 Cor.2:1. With the participle ὄντων and a locative of accompanying circumstances "in a high political position" - 1 Tim.2:2.

λόγου (gen.sing.masc.of λόγος, description) 510.
ἢ (disjunctive) 465.
σοφίας (gen.sing.fem.of σοφία, description) 934.
καταγγέλλων (pres.act.part.nom.sing.masc.of καταγγέλλω, adverbial, temporal) 3023.
ὑμῖν (dat.pl.masc.of σύ, indirect object of καταγγέλλων) 104.
τὸ (acc.sing.neut.of the article in agreement with μυστήριον) 9.
μυστήριον (acc.sing.neut.of μυστήριον, direct object of καταγγέλλων) 1038.
τοῦ (gen.sing.masc.of the article in agreement with θεοῦ) 9.
θεοῦ (gen.sing.masc.of θεός, description) 124.

Translation - "And when I came to you, brethren, I did not come with eloquent speech or lofty philosophy as I declared unto you the mystery of God."

Comment: *Cf.* verse 3. We are not to consider the time of ἐλθών as prior to that of ἦλθον. ἐλθών is a gnomic (timeless) aorist. ἦλθον means "I came before you to preach" when I came to Corinth. καθ' ὑπεροχὴν λόγου ἢ σοφίας - an accusative of standard or rule. Paul was not trying to deliver his sermons in Corinth in keeping with the highest standards of oratory. Indeed, he was determined to achieve the opposite. It was his mistake on Mars Hill in the last sermon that he preached in Athens before he left for Corinth that he delivered his message with the high sounding phraseology and lofty and sophisticated philosophical argumentation with which he hoped to impress the Athenians. Now he was determined to preach simply. His message was "the mystery of God" - τὸ μυστήριον τοῦ θεοῦ. *Cf.*#1038 for the mystery. The Corinthians were told that the fact that they were Gentiles constituted no barrier between them and the God of Abraham, Isaac and Jacob. This was the special message which Paul was commissioned to preach (Eph.3:1-11). Variant readings have μαρτύριον - "witness", εὐαγγέλιον - "gospel" or σωτήριον - "salvation." If anything is capable of inspiring a long and learned exposition it is the "mystery of God." To discuss it in depth would require competence in cosmology, teleology, anthropology, sociology, psychology, even economics and political science. Indeed it takes the entire field of human knowledge as its province. Yet Paul did not argue the mystery of God with the Corinthians. He merely declared it. God was in Christ reconciling the world unto Himself (2 Cor.5:19) and His plan envisaged a homogeneous body of Christ, in fellowship with the Godhead, composed of Jews and every tribe, kingdom, tongue, people and nation of non-Jews, solely on a basis of grace and effectual call, and made possible by the atonement of the Son of God. Paul did not analyze it, or dissect it, or explain it or defend it. He preached it - in simple language. God was determined to save the Gentiles too.

Some may wish to conclude that if this is successful evangelism, an educated ministry is unnecessary, nay, even a hindrance. To which we reply that if evangelism were the only element in the Great Commission we might agree, although it can be argued that it takes an educated man to realize that in evangelism sophistication is out of place. God has ordained to call the elect to repentance and faith when the simple facts of the gospel are preached and this can be and is being done by the most illiterate lay people and even by little children. But the Commission also asks us to teach the saints "all things." It is in our ministry to the Christian, after he has been made a disciple and immersed that dedicated scholarship becomes indispensable. Evangelists and pastor-teachers are given to the church to edify the saints so that they can do the evangelistic work of the ministry (Eph.4:11-16, upon which *cf.* comment). There is nothing that the teacher of Christian theology does not need to know. The evangelist needs only to know that Christ died for sinners to reveal the love of God.

Verse 2 - "For I determined not to know anything among you, save Jesus Christ, and him crucified."

οὐ γὰρ ἔκρινά τι εἰδέναι ἐν ὑμῖν εἰ μὴ Ἰησοῦν Χριστὸν καὶ τοῦτον ἐσταυρωμένον.

"For I decided to know nothing among you except Jesus Christ and him crucified." . . . RSV

οὐ (negative particle with the infinitive) 130.
γὰρ (inferential conjunction) 105.
ἔκρινά (1st.per.sing.aor.act.ind.of κρίνω, constative) 531.
τι (acc.sing.neut.of τις, indefinite pronoun, direct object of εἰδέναι) 486.
εἰδέναι (perf.inf.of οἶδα, direct object of ἔκρινά) 144b.
ἐν (preposition with the locative, with plural pronouns) 80.
ὑμῖν (loc.pl.masc.of σύ, place) 104.
εἰ (conditional particle in an elliptical condition) 337.
μὴ (negative particle in an elliptical condition) 87.
Ἰησοῦν (acc.sing.masc.of Ἰησοῦς, direct object of verb understood) 3.

Χριστὸν (acc.sing.masc.of Χριστός, apposition) 4.

καὶ (adjunctive conjunction joining substantives) 14.

τοῦτον (acc.sing.masc.of οὗτος, direct object of εἰδέναι) 93.

ἐσταυρωμένον (perf.pass.part.acc.sing.masc.of σταυρόω, adverbial, circumstantial) 1328.

Translation - "Because I determined not to know anything while with you except Jesus Christ and Him crucified."

Comment: Paul tells us why he came to Corinth preaching as he did only in the most elemental terms. It was because (γὰρ) he had made a decision (aorist tense in ἔκρινά). When? In past time relative to the time of his first message in Corinth - possibly as he walked along the road from Athens (Acts 18:1), pondering the reason for his relative failure in Athens. The object infinitive after ἔκρινά is εἰδέναι, a perfect infinitive of οἶδα. What he determined to preach to the Corinthians would exclude everything which he knew and could have preached, except Jesus Christ. And when he spoke of Jesus, it would not be Jesus the Creator, Teacher, Sustainer, Author of History, Manipulator of Nations, God of Geography, Unifier of all Knowledge or any other Jesus. It would be only Jesus Christ, the Nazarene carpenter dying on a Roman cross.

He had preached the other Jesus in Athens on Mars Hill (Acts 17:22-31, *cf.* comment *en loc.*) It was a great sermon - Paul's greatest intellectual production in the New Testament. And it was all true. But he left out the Cross! And that is why he failed. He challenged the intellects of the Athenians and the Holy Spirit had little opporunity to work. If Paul had convinced the Athenians, they would have believed and then attributed their salvation to their own intellectual powers to understand a philosophy of which they approved. God would have got no glory out of it at all (1 Cor.1:29-31). No man is saved until he is humble enough to trust in a truth which his intellect tells him is stuff and nonesense. Thus God has decreed. And that is how it is. Paul's sermon on Mars Hill was a masterpiece, but he delivered it to the wrong audience. That is a sermon for the saints, after they have been discipled and immersed in water in the name of the Lord (Mt.28:18-20). On Mars Hill Paul was a Christian educator, but one cannot educate a dead man. At that point the Athenians were being educated by the "god of this world" (2 Cor.4:4). One who is being victimized by the brainwashing of Satan will not believe anything a Christian educator has to say, until the Holy Spirit has first of all convinced him of "sin, and of righteousness and of judgment" (John 16:7-11).

Thus we see the fundamental difference between the approach of the evangelist and that of the pastor-teacher.

Verse 3 - "And I was with you in weakness, and in fear, and in much trembling."

κἀγὼ ἐν ἀσθενείᾳ καὶ ἐν φόβῳ καὶ ἐν τρόμῳ πολλῷ ἐγενόμην πρὸς ὑμᾶς,

"And I was with you in weakness and in much fear and trembling;" ... RSV

κἀγὼ (continuative conjunction and ἐγώ, crasis) 178.

ἐν (preposition with the locative of accompanying circumstance) 80.

ἀσθενείᾳ (loc.sing.fem.of ἀσθένεια, accompanying circumstance) 740.
καὶ (adjunctive conjunction joining prepositional phrases) 14.
ἐν (preposition with the locative of accompanying circumstance) 80.
φόβῳ (loc.sing.masc.of φόβος, accompanying circumstance) 1131.
καὶ (adjunctive conjunction joining prepositional phrases) 14.
ἐν (preposition with the locative, accompanying circumstance) 80.
τρόμῳ (loc.sing.masc.of τρόμος, accompanying circumstance) 2889.
πολλῷ (loc.sing.masc.of πολύς, in agreement with τρόμῳ) 228.
ἐγενόμην (1st.per.sing.aor.ind.of γίνομαι, constative) 113.
πρὸς (preposition with the accusative of extent) 197.
ὑμᾶς (acc.pl.masc.of σύ, extent) 104.

Translation - "And I was with you in weakness and in fear and with much trembling."

Comment: Apparently Paul had no such feelings of inadequacy at Mars Hill. There his was a sense of intellectual superiority as he viewed with disdain the superstitions of the Athenians (Acts 17:22). With great confidence in his own ability to cope with the situation he was delighted with the chance to educate the Greeks. Paul was "showing off" in Athens. An intellectual speaking before intellectuals fears nothing. Rather he accepts the challenge.

In Corinth he felt and demonstrated a weakness because of which God's strength was made perfect (2 Cor.12:9).

Paul's reaction in these two situations seems contrary to what most people would expect. Most would tremble in the presence of the Athenians who were reputed to be great philosophers and feel confident in speaking to the lower middleclass congregation which Paul found in Corinth. Of what, then was Paul afraid in Corinth? It was certainly not the audience. He was confident that he knew more about his subject than they. But he was afraid that he would grieve the Holy Spirit as he had done in Athens. The preacher who has learned to fear God as he preaches is the preacher whose message of salvation the Holy Spirit can use.

Paul pursues the point in

Verse 4 - "And my speech and my preaching was not with enticing words of man's wisdom, but in demonstration of the Spirit and of power."

καὶ ὁ λόγος μου καὶ τὸ κήρυγμά μου οὐκ ἐν πειθοῖ(ς) σοφίας (λόγοις) ἀλλ' ἐν ἀποδείξει πνεύματος καὶ δυνάμεως,

"and my speech and my message were not in plausible words of wisdom, but in demonstration of the Spirit and power," . . . RSV

καὶ (continuative conjunction) 14.
ὁ (nom.sing.masc.of the article in agreement with λόγος) 9.
λόγος (nom.sing.masc.of λόγος, subject of ἦν understood) 510.
μου (gen.sing.masc.of ἐγώ, possession) 123.
καὶ (adjunctive conjunction joining nouns) 14.
τὸ (nom.sing.neut.of the article in agreement with κήρυγμα) 9.

κήρυγμά (nom.sing.neut.of κήρυγμα, subject of ἦν understood) 1013.
μου (gen.sing.masc.of ἐγώ, possession) 123.
οὐκ (negative particle with the indicative) 130.
ἐν (preposition with the instrumental, means) 80.

#4109 πειθοῖς (instru.pl.masc.of πειθός, in agreement with λόγοις).

King James Version

enticing - 1 Cor.2:4.

Revised Standard Version

plausible - 1 Cor.2:4.

Meaning: Cf. πείθω (#1629). Persuasive, convincing, with great intellectual appeal - 1 Cor.2:4.

σοφίας (gen.sing.fem.of σοφία, description) 934.
λόγοις (instru.pl.masc.of λόγός, means) 510.
ἀλλ' (alternative conjunction) 342.
ἐν (preposition with the instrumental of means) 80.

#4110 ἀποδείξει (instru.sing.fem.of ἀπόδειξις, means).

King James Version - 1 Cor.2:4.

demonstration - 1 Cor.2:4.

Revised Standard Version

demonstration - 1 Cor.2:4.

Meaning: Cf. ἀποδείκνυμι (#2989), from ἀπό (#70) and δείκνυμι (#359). A process of showing, demonstrating, of making manifest. A proof by empirical test - Followed by genitives of description - 1 Cor.2:4.

πνεύματος (gen.sing.neut.of πνεῦμα, description) 83.
καὶ (adjunctive conjunction joining nouns) 14.
δυνάμεως (gen.sing.fem.of δύναμις, description) 687.

Translation - "And my speech and my preaching was not by means of persuasive philosophical phraseology, but by means of the demonstration of the Spirit and power."

Comment: Not only what he said (τὸ κήρυγμά μου) but how he said it (ὁ λόγος μου) was of concern to Paul. Thus an important homiletical lesson concerns both content and style. Paul's content in Corinth was nothing more than Christ crucified. His style was utter simplicity. He spurned the language of the philosophers. His appeal was definitely not to the Corinthian mind. In fact the gospel insulted their intelligence as it does the intelligence of all who are perishing (1 Cor.1:18). The content and style of Paul's epistles, since they are directed to the saints, is probably far more sophisticated than his preaching to them before they were saved. We shall never know exactly how Paul preached at first to the Corinthians, but they were not impressed with him (2 Cor.10:10). But, though his personal appearance and the literary style of his discourse was not impressive, if not repulsive, and though the content of his message sounded to them like nonesense, Paul's ministry demonstrated the Holy Spirit's exercise of supernatural power. Look at the results (Acts 18:10).

Verse 5 - "That your faith should not stand in the wisdom of men, but in the power of God."

ἵνα ἡ πίστις ὑμῶν μὴ ᾖ ἐν σοφίᾳ ἀνθρώπων ἀλλ' ἐν δυνάμει θεοῦ.

". . . that your faith might not rest in the wisdom of men but in the power of God." . . . RSV

ἵνα (conjunction with the subjunctive in a sub-final clause) 114.
ἡ (nom.sing.fem.of the article in agreement with πίστις) 9.
πίστις (nom.sing.fem.of πίστις, subject of ᾖ) 728.
ὑμῶν (gen.pl.masc.of σύ, possession) 104.
μὴ (negative particle with the subjunctive) 87.
ᾖ (3d.per.sing.pres.subj.of εἰμί, sub-final) 86.
ἐν (preposition with the locative of sphere) 80.
σοφίᾳ (loc.sing.fem.of σοφία, sphere) 934.
ἀνθρώπων (gen.pl.masc.of ἄνθρωπος, definition) 341.
ἀλλ' (alternative conjunction) 342.
ἐν (preposition with the locative of sphere) 80.
δυνάμει (loc.sing.fem.of δύναμις, sphere) 687.
θεοῦ (gen.sing.masc.of θεός, description) 124.

Translation - "In order (and with the result) that your faith may rest not in the sphere of human reason but in divine power."

Comment: This is the thought of 1 Cor.1:29-31. The purpose of Paul's evangelistic approach (verse 4) was that Christian faith should have a divine rather than a human base. The result was precisely what the purpose hoped for. Thus the ἵνα clause is sub-final (both final and consecutive; purpose and result).
    πίστις is a much overworked, misunderstood and prostituted word in the late 20th century. A sociologist speaks of his *faith* by which he means that man in his sovereign dignity will find a solution to the problem of soul sorrow, through sociology, totally apart from God. A television announcer who listens to many preachers who preach a variety of theological opinions speaks to us of his *faith* but it does not embrace a Trinitarian and Redemptive view of Jesus. Thus *faith* stands in the area of human philosophy and is supported by a rationale from an unregenerate mind which rejects revelation. This is precisely what Paul wished to avoid. Faith, as the word is used by the Christian (which means far more than intellectual assent to a demonstrated truth) exists only ἐν δυνάμει θεοῦ. *Cf.* Heb.12:2 and see comment. The difference is not only one of degree, but also

one of kind. A traveller has faith in the weather report; a coach has faith in the ability of a quarterback. A banker has faith in the man who borrows his money. These are not examples of faith as the New Testament uses the word. Confidence that the future will unfold the predictable is based upon statistical probability, not certitude. A Christian's faith is the result of a supernatural experience, called "birth from above" (John 3:3,7). He *knows* whom he has believed and he knows that God is true even if every man is a liar (2 Tim.1:12; Rom.3:4). This faith is supernatural, not only in its origin (Heb.12:2) but also in the results that flow from it.

The Revelation by God's Spirit

(1 Corinthians 2:6-16)

Verse 6 - "Howbeit we speak wisdom among them that are perfect; yet not the wisdom of this world, nor of the princes of this world, that come to nought."

Σοφίαν δὲ λαλοῦμεν ἐν τοῖς τελείοις, σοφίαν δὲ οὐ τοῦ αἰῶνος τούτου οὐδὲ τῶν ἀρχόντων τοῦ αἰῶνος τούτου τῶν καταργουμένων.

"Yet among the mature we do impart wisdom, although it is not a wisdom of this age or of the rulers of this age, who are doomed to pass away." . . . RSV

Σοφίαν (acc.sing.fem.of σοφία, direct object of λαλοῦμεν) 934.
δὲ (adversative conjunction) 11.
λαλοῦμεν (1st.per.pl.pres.act.ind.of λαλέω, customary) 815.
ἐν (preposition with the locative with plural nouns and pronouns) 80.
τοῖς (loc.pl.masc.of the article in agreement with τελείοις) 9.
τελείοις (loc.pl.masc.of τέλειος, place) 553.
σοφίαν (acc.sing.fem.of σοφία, direct object of λαλοῦμεν) 934.
δὲ (adversative conjunction) 11.
οὐ (negative particle with the indicative) 130.
τοῦ (gen.sing.masc.of the article in agreement with αἰῶνος) 9.
αἰῶνος (gen.sing.masc.of αἰών, description) 1002.
τούτου (gen.sing.masc.of οὗτος, in agreement with αἰῶνος) 93.
οὐδὲ (disjunctive compound particle) 452.
τῶν (gen.pl.masc.of the article in agreement with ἀρχόντων) 9.
ἀρχόντων (gen.pl.masc.of ἄρχων, description) 816.
τοῦ (gen.sing.masc.of the article in agreement with αἰῶνος) 9.
αἰῶνος (gen.sing.masc.of αἰών, description) 1002.
τούτου (gen.sing.masc.of οὗτος, in agreement with αἰῶνος) 93.
τῶν (gen.pl.masc.of the article in agreement with καταργουμένων) 9.
καταργουμένων (pres.pass.part.gen.pl.masc.of καταργέω, substantival, apposition) 2500.

Translation - "But we are teaching philosophy among the fully matured saints, though it is not the philosophy of this age nor of the rulers of this age, who are being superceded."

Comment: Paul's outpouring of contempt upon philosophy was likely to denigrate *all* philosophy in the minds of the Corinthians as indeed it has done among certain ill-advised Christians today. Yet this hasty conclusion cannot be drawn with validity from the passage. Paul is speaking only of ἡ σοφία τοῦ αἰῶνος τούτου - *i.e.* the philosophy of the unregenerate. In modern terms (there is nothing modern about it) it is the radical empiricism and extreme existentialism which blinds the eyes of the unbelieving to the claims of the gospel of Christ. This is enemy territory and Paul's contempt for it knows virtually no bounds. But Paul is a true philosopher, in search of concrescence, the goal of all true philosophy. He sought holism, closure, an epistemic correlation that embraces totality - the universal one which correlates the infinitely multitudinous instances of the many. This holism we find only in Christ (Col.2:3) as we are incorporated by the baptism of the Holy Spirit into His body (1 Cor.12:13). Only those whose quest is that of the "poor in spirit" (Mt.5:3; 18:3; 11:25) will find it.

Worldly philosophy, which is essential egotism, prevents man from becoming a true philosopher. Since empiricists refuse to accept what they cannot understand, on the grounds that to do so marks them as tender minded and intellectually inferior - naive children, who in their insecurity need Linus' blanket (!) - they preclude themselves from fellowship with Christ, in association with Whom the Christian finds all of the science and all of the philosophy there is. They are naive because they spend their time attacking Christians as naive. Indeed some Christians *are* naive, but only because they are "babes in Christ." Unfortunately some Christians never outgrow their spiritual infancy, but that is another problem. The Christian who has only recently been saved and brought into the fellowship of a church by baptism is as yet untaught and thus is not yet academically ready for Paul's Christian philosophy (Heb.5:11-14). But that is only because he has not yet had the time and opportunity to "grow in grace and in the knowledge of our Lord and Saviour, Jesus Christ" (2 Pet.3:18). *Cf.*#553 for all of the uses of τέλειος. It is possible that some Christians who did not grow in grace were denied the growth that they could have had because they did not have access to a pastor-teacher who was equipped to obey the last third of the Great Commission. Many preachers can disciple the lost and immerse them in water and receive them into the fellowship of the church, but are not academically equipped to "teach them to observe all things" that the Great Commission demands. But the Christian whose maturity stands in a position relatively favourable to that of his unsaved peers need never accept second place in intellectual discussion. He must indeed admit that he is a "fool for Christ" but he should quickly ask his unsaved friend. "Whose fool are you?"

Paul is saying that when he found himself in a group of intellectually developed Christians he was delighted to talk philosophy, but he hastens to qualify it by saying that it is not the philosophy of this age nor of the authorities of this age. It will be empirical but not the radical empiricism that says that all knowledge is grounded in sensation. It will include the existential, because the New Testament does teach that the issues of the moment are important. It will have a place for environmentalism, but the behaviorism of John Broadus Watson, the slobbering of Pavlov's dog, the dire predictions of Karl Marx about the future of capitalism and B.F.Skinner's box will be held up to the light of more thorough examination. Situation ethics and secular humanism will be given whatever approval can be found for them. Paul's system has a place for all of that which is valid. The Holy Spirit who wrote the New Testament is not ignorant of anything. Our Lord, Who created it all is aware of it all. Christian philosophy is not fragmentary. It ignores nothing that is real. It is holistic and concrescent. It embraces all that is true because it has no fear of that which is true. Thus it takes the universe of reality as its province. Like a computer programmed for multiple regression it accepts everything that it can use and rejects everything that does not fit into the gestalt.

The mature Christian philosopher owns a "spread" bigger even than any in Texas and he rides the range and presides over all manner of delightful fauna and flora, but this is only because once he was given grace enough and the gift of grace to place his faith in a crucified carpenter. When he did so the "mature" world leaders called him a naive baby, a religious fanatic, the brainwashed slave of some evil guru, but whether he or they knew it or not, he had taken the inchoate step that leads to true philosophical maturity, while his critics, who opted only for the reality available in sense perception, or for sensory data plus the danda of Immanuel Kant, have sealed their fate.

They are in the process of being superseded. *Cf.#2500* for the basic idea in καταργέω.

Having told the Corinthians what the philosophy which he would teach when they were mature enough to follow him, was not, in verse 6 Paul tells them what it is in

Verse 7 - "But we speak the wisdom of God in a mystery, even the hidden wisdom, which God ordained before the world unto our glory."

ἀλλὰ λαλοῦμεν θεοῦ σοφίαν ἐν μυστηρίῳ, τὴν ἀποκεκρυμμένην, ἣν προώρισεν ὁ θεὸς πρὸ τῶν αἰώνων εἰς δόξαν ἡμῶν.

"But we impart a secret and hidden wisdom of God, which God decreed before the ages for our glorification." . . . RSV

ἀλλὰ (alternative conjunction) 342.
λαλοῦμεν (1st.per.pl.pres.act.ind.of λαλέω, customary) 815.
θεοῦ (gen.sing.masc.of θεός, description) 124.
σοφίαν (acc.sing.fem.of σοφία, direct object of λαλοῦμεν) 934.
ἐν (preposition with the locative of sphere) 80.
μυστηρίῳ (loc.sing.neut.of μυστήριον, sphere) 1038.
τὴν (acc.sing.fem.of the article in agreement with σοφίαν) 9.
ἀποκεκρυμμένην (perf.pass.part.acc.sing.fem.of ἀποκρύπτω, adjectival, ascriptive, in agreement with σοφίαν) 2418.

ἥν (acc.sing.fem.of ὅς, relative pronoun, direct object of προώρισεν) 65.

προώρισεν (3d.per.sing.aor.act.ind.of προορίζω, constative) 3042.

ὁ (nom.sing.masc.of the article in agreement with θεὸς) 9.

θεὸς (nom.sing.masc.of θεός, subject of προώρισεν) 124.

πρὸ (preposition with the ablative of time separation) 442.

τῶν (abl.pl.masc.of the article in agreement with αἰώνων) 9.

αἰώνων (abl.pl.masc.of αἰών, time separation) 1002.

εἰς (preposition with the accusative, purpose) 140.

δόξαν (acc.sing.fem.of δόξα, purpose) 361.

ἡμῶν (gen.pl.masc.of ἐγώ, possession) 123.

Translation - "But we speak a divine philosophy in a sphere of hidden mystery kept secret until now which God ordained before the ages for our glory."

Comment: Note the emphasis of θεοῦ, the genitive of description. In verse 6 Paul stressed the fact that his philosophy was not that of the world. Now, in contrast, he points to God as its source. The perfect participle τὴν κεκρυμμ. is feminine gender and cannot therefore refer to μυστηρίῳ, which is neuter. It does refer to σοφίαν. This is true also of the relative clause with ἥν, and for the same reason. The relative pronoun must find an antecedent with which it agrees in gender and number. This is σοφίαν. It was God's philosophy which had been hidden previously and which was forordained before the ages for our glory. *Cf.* Rom.8:29,30; Eph.1:3; 3:4-6.

God's philosophy which is the philosophy of the gospel of Christ as revealed in the Greek New Testament is holistic. There is no reality in the universe which does not comport with its gestalt (pattern). But note that Paul says that when he preached it, the presentation was in the sphere of the mysterious. The gospel preacher is not going to answer all of the questions which his thoughtful critic may wish to ask.

The heart of the gospel is the incarnation. God became a man. A single personality lived on earth and still lives in heaven with two natures - the one divine and the other human. Always God, Jesus became and will forever remain a man. He has two wills, two intellects, two emotional natures. His body was material. He inherited his body from a sinful woman. He was Adam's son but not Adam's seed. Son of God eternally He became the Son of Man. This is a mystery (1 Tim.3:16). The Gnostics cannot accept our Lord as God incarnate because He has a material body and Gnosticism teaches that since God could not have created evil, in view of the fact that there is no doubt that evil exists, therefore evil is also eternal. If so of what does evil consist? And the Gnostic answer is that matter is evil. *Voila!* God is Spirit and good; matter is evil; both are eternal. It follows therefore that Jesus in incarnation in material human form could not be God. Or if He is God His body could not be material. The Arians accepted His humanity and denied His deity. The Docetics accepted His deity and denied His humanity. The Monophysite and Monothelite controversies raged for years. Arians opposed Athanasians. Was Jesus God or not? Did He have two wills or one? Did He have two natures or one? Dogmatists overlooked the truth in their zeal to win an argument. Dogmatists often make mistakes like that. The truth which they ignored is Paul's statement that the preaching of the divine wisdom requires that we accept some things which are to us in our present state of intellectual development, mysterious. The Gnostic will have none of it. He will explain all mysteries, if not to the satisfaction of others, at least to his own satisfaction. He is unwilling for God to know something which he does not know. Thus he rationalizes the gospel down to his human level. *Cf.* our discussion of the pitfals of Gnosticism in the Introduction to Volume 9 of *The Renaissance New Testament.*

No theologian who knows his place before the throne of God will try to explain that which the New Testament declares is a mystery. God's philosophy is not mysterious to Him, but it was to Paul and he knew that when he explained it to the Corinthians it would be mysterious to them also. That is why he warned them that when they grew in grace to the point where they were ready for the more advanced solid food (Heb.5:14) there would still be some things which they would have to take on faith. Christians who understand this do not try to explain the incarnation and the virgin birth. They believe it. The extent to which they consider it nonesense is the extent to which they are asked to be willing to become "fools for Christ." And if they accept it their acceptance is the measure of their humility. Somehow we get the idea that being humble before God is not a bad thing.

This mysterious truth of the incarnation, the redemption which it made possible and the bodily resurrection which followed is something that would have made a difference if the princes of this world had understood it. Had they done so they would not have crucified the Lord of Glory. Jesus said to the Father, when they drove the nails through His hands, "Father . . . they do not know what they are doing." This is the thought in

Verse 8 - "Which none of the princes of this world knew: for had they known it, they would not have crucified the Lord of glory."

ἢν οὐδεὶς τῶν ἀρχόντων τοῦ αἰῶνος τούτου ἔγνωκεν, εἰ γὰρ ἔγνωσαν, οὐκ ἂν τὸν κύριον τῆς δόξης ἐσταύρωσαν.

"None of the rulers of this age understood this; for if they had, they would not have crucified the Lord of glory." . . . RSV

ἢν (acc.sing.fem.of ὅς, relative pronoun, direct object of ἔγνωκεν) 65.
οὐδεὶς (nom.sing.masc.of οὐδείς, subject of ἔγνωκεν) 446.
τῶν (gen.pl.masc.of the article in agreement with ἀρχόντων) 9.
ἀρχόντων (gen.pl.masc.of ἄρχων, partitive genitive) 816.
τοῦ (gen.sing.masc.of the article in agreement with αἰῶνος) 9.
αἰῶνος (gen.sing.masc.of αἰών, description) 1002.
τούτου (gen.sing.masc.of οὗτος, in agreement with αἰῶνος) 93.
ἔγνωκεν (3d.per.sing.perf.act.ind.of γινώσκω, intensive) 131.
εἰ (conditional particle in a second-class condition, contrary to fact) 337.
γὰρ (causal conjunction) 105.

ἔγνωσαν (3d.per.pl.aor.act.ind.of γινώσκω, constative) 131.

οὐκ (negative particle with the indicative) 130.

ἄν (contingent particle in a second-class condition, contrary to fact) 205.

τὸν (acc.sing.masc.of the article in agreement with κύριον) 9.

κύριον (acc.sing.masc.of κύριος, direct object of ἐσταύρωσαν) 97.

τῆς (gen.sing.fem.of the article in agreement with δόξης) 9.

δόξης (gen.sing.fem.of δόξα, description) 361.

ἐσταύρωσαν (3d.per.pl.aor.act.ind.of σταυρόω, constative, second-class condition, contrary to fact) 1328.

Translation - "Which not one of the rulers of this age has ever understood, nor understands now, because if they had known it they would not have crucified the Lord of glory."

Comment: The antecedent of ἥν is σοφίαν just as in verse 7. It was God's philosophy which Paul preached, if he could find an audience mature enough to take it (verse 6). It is not of this world (verse 6), but of God. It is the hidden philosophy which God has always had (verse 7) and decreed that mature Christians should have it too (verse 7) so that they might be glorified (purpose in εἰς δόξαν ἡμῶν). Please note again that it was not the mystery that God ordained and hid. It is the divine philosophy.

Now, in verse 8, still in reference to σοφίαν, Paul adds that not one of this world's leaders has ever understood it. ἔγνωκεν is a perfect tense, indicating a present and continuing condition of ignorance as a result of having never in the past learned it. Their past ignorance is not all that the perfect ἔγνωκεν reveals. It also speaks of their present ignorance. Thus our translation. Having never learned they do not now know. The second-class condition follows, with εἰ and the aorist indicative with ἄν in the protasis and also the aorist in the result clause. This assumes that the premise is false, as indeed it is. If they had understood and appreciated the philosophy of God, which they did not, they would not have crucified our Lord, which they did.

Note τὸν κύριον τῆς δόξης. The article with the δόξης makes it definite, thus forbidding the translation, "the glorious Lord." He is, of course, our "glorious Lord" but this passage says, "the Lord of glory," with "glory" as definite as "Lord." It is not therefore adjectival.

Who are these ἄρχοντες? *Cf.*#816. The word is applied to Satan and his subordinate rulers in the demon world, to the Pharisees, elders, scribes and high priests and to political leaders in general. Once it applies to Christ (Rev.1:5). Which of these were responsible for the act of crucifying Christ? Certainly the Pharisees, Scribes, High Priests and Elders and the demonic hosts. None of them has ever understood God's wisdom, which is centered in the fact that the death of Jesus Christ on the cross is the indispensable basis of all that God does in redemption. Had Christ not been crucified, God would have been powerless to deal with the devastating and totally destructive fact of sin in His universe. It is "through death" that Christ "destroyed him who hath the power of death, that is the devil" (Heb.2:14; Gen.3:15). If they had understood this they would have done everything possible to prevent His death. By crucifying Christ they played directly into the hands of God and brought about their own destruction. The Pharisees were children of hell (John 8:44). If they had understood they would have done all in their power to keep Him alive until He died some insignificant death that in no way fulfilled the Old Testament prophecies about Him.

Paul is not being patronizing with the Pharisees in this passage. It is not that he is saying that the Pharisees were good people who would not have tortured and murdered Jesus if they had known better. He is saying that they were very evil people whose stupidity seduced them into carrying out the crucifixion of Jesus and thus they implemented God's redemptive plan and brought about their own damnation. They were scheduled to be superseded (verse 6).

Preachers who point to Calvary as a tragedy that ought never to have occurred and say that Jesus would be treated with the respect He deserves if He came to earth today, now that man has evolved unto a higher understanding and a more ethical conduct, also do not understand God's philosophy. If they did they would point to Calvary as a great victory. They would also know that the world's philosophy is as AntiChrist now as it was at Calvary, and that if Jesus came to earth today in the same humble manner as He came before, they would run Him out of town.

When He comes again He is going to be the Party of the First Part (2 Thess.1:7-10). That also they do not understand because they think that He is dead.

Verse 9 - "But as it is written, Eye hath not seen, nor ear heard, neither have entered into the heart of man, the things which God hath prepared for them that love him."

ἀλλὰ καθὼς γέγραπται,῍Α ὀφθαλμὸς οὐκ εἶδεν καὶ οὖς οὐκ ἤκουσεν καὶ ἐπὶ καρδίαν ἀνθρώπου οὐκ ἀνέβυ, ἃ ἡτοίμασεν ὁ θεὸς τοῖς ἀγαπῶσιν αὐτόν.

"But, as it is written, 'What no eye has seen, nor ear heard, nor the heart of man conceived, what God has prepared for those who love Him.' " . . . RSV

ἀλλὰ (adversative conjunction) 342.

καθώς (compound particle in a comparative clause) 1348.

γέγραπται (3d.per.sing.perf.pass.ind.of γράφω, intensive) 156.

῍Α (acc.pl.neut.of ὅς, demonstrative pronoun, direct object of εἶδεν and ἤκουσεν) 65.

ὀφθαλμὸς (nom.sing.masc.of ὀφθαλμός, subject of εἶδεν) 501.

οὐκ (negative particle with the indicative) 130.

εἶδεν (3d.per.sing.2d.aor.act.ind.of ὁράω, constative) 144a.

καὶ (continuative conjunction) 14.

οὖς (nom.sing.neut.of οὖς, subject of ἤκουσεν) 887.

οὐκ (negative particle with the indicative) 130.

ἤκουσεν (3d.per.sing.aor.act.ind.of ἀκούω, constative) 148.

καὶ (continuative conjunction) 14.

ἐπὶ (preposition with the accusative of extent) 47.

καρδίαν (acc.sing.fem.of καρδία, extent) 432.

ἀνθρώπου (gen.sing.masc.of ἄνθρωπος, description) 341.

οὐκ (negative particle with the indicative) 130.

ἀνέβη (3d.per.sing.aor.act.ind.of ἀναβαίνω, constative) 323.

ἃ (acc.pl.neut.of ὅς, relative pronoun, direct object of ἡτοίμασεν) 65.

ἡτοίμασεν (3d.per.sing.aor.act.ind.of ἑτοιμάζω, constative) 257.

ὁ (nom.sing.masc.of the article in agreement with θεὸς) 9.

θεὸς (nom.sing.masc.of θεός, subject of ἡτοίμασεν) 124.

τοῖς (dat.pl.masc.of the article in agreement with ἀγαπῶσιν) 9.

ἀγαπῶσιν (pres.act.part.dat.pl.masc.of ἀγαπάω, substantival, personal advantage) 540.

αὐτόν (acc.sing.masc.of αὐτός, direct object of ἀγαπῶσιν) 16.

Translation - "*But just as the Scripture says, 'Those things which the eye has not seen and the ear has not heard and which has not entered into the human heart are the things which God has prepared for those who love Him.*"

Comment: The world leadership cannot think God's thoughts after Him, but Paul is preaching from Isaiah 64:4 and 52:15. Note that Isa.64:4 prepares the quotation with the temporal phrase ἀπὸ τοῦ αἰῶνος - "since the eternal age" which fits Paul's statement in verse 7 - πρὸ τῶν αἰώνων. The clause ἃ ἡτοίμασεν ... αὐτόν is really in apposition to the first three clauses. The things which are seen and heard are objects of science and the things which enter into the heart (thinking realm) of men are objects of human philosophy. Thus neither the scientific method nor the philosophical method can reveal to man what God has in store for those who love Him. *Cf.* Rom.8;28 for τοῖς ἀγαπῶσιν. All that God has prepared (1 Cor.2:9) works together for good (Rom.8:28) to those who love Him.

Paul does not deny that sense perception (eyes and ears) and mental perception (mind and heart) are valuable in their appropriate spheres. Science and reason have taken us to the moon, given us the Pythagorean theorem, demonstrated that it is impossible to square the circle and that the universe through entropy is slowing down to an equilibrium halt. Science has also provided us with nuclear fission, napalm and philosophy of a sort that gave Germany an Adolf Hitler. Existential philosophy has also told us that there is no difference between subject and object and thus that no one can communicate meaningfully with anyone else. It has also said that no mature thinker knows the difference between right and wrong. Science has conceived and spawned discordant noise, which some call music, and chaotic confusion on a canvas that some call art - all of this in an attempt to say that there is no meaning in life and that the universe is insane. Thus man has put on exhibit the handiwork of eye, ear and brain.

But never once since eternity past has he understood what God has in store for those who love Him. How then do we know what these things are?

Cf. Lk.24:38 and Acts 7;23 for the metaphorical use of ἀναβαίνω (#323) in the same sense, once with ἐπί and once with ἐν. Science cannot save us. Reason cannot. But revelation can as we learn in

Verse 10 - "But God hath revealed them unto us by his spirit: for the spirit searcheth all things, yea, the deep things of God."

ἡμῖν δὲ ἀπεκάλυφεν ὁ θεὸς διὰ τοῦ πνεύματος. τὸ γὰρ πνεῦμα πάντα ἐραυνᾷ, καὶ τὰ βάθη τοῦ θεοῦ.

"God has revealed to us through the Spirit. For the Spirit searches everything, even the depths of God." . . . RSV

ἡμῖν (dat.pl.masc.of ἐγώ, indirect object of ἀπεκάλυφεν) 123.

δὲ (adversative conjunction) 11.

ἀπεκάλυφεν (3d.per.sing.aor.act.ind.of ἀποκαλύπτω, culminative) 886.

ὁ (nom.sing.masc.of the article in agreement with θεὸς) 9.

θεὸς (nom.sing.masc.of θεός, subject of ἀπεκάλυφεν) 124.

διὰ (preposition with the ablative of agent) 118.

τοῦ (abl.sing.neut.of the article in agreement with πνεύματος) 9.

πνεύματος (abl.sing.neut.of πνεῦμα, agent) 83.

τὸ (nom.sing.neut.of the article in agreement with πνεῦμα) 9.

γὰρ (causal conjunction) 105.

πνεῦμα (nom.sing.neut.of πνεῦμα, subject of ἐραυνᾷ) 83.

πάντα (acc.pl.neut.of πᾶς, direct object of ἐραυνᾷ) 67.

ἐραυνᾷ (3d.per.sing.pres.act.ind.of ἐρευνάω, customary) 2099.

καὶ (ascensive conjunction) 14.

τὰ (acc.pl.neut.of the article in agreement with βάθη) 9.

βάθη (acc.pl.neut.of βάθος, direct object of ἐραυνᾷ) 1031.

τοῦ (gen.sing.masc.of the article in agreement with θεοῦ) 9.

θεοῦ (gen.sing.masc.of θεός, possession) 124.

Translation - "But God has revealed them unto us by the Spirit; because the Spirit is plumbing the depths of everything, even the deep things of God."

Comment: What neither science nor philosophy can discover, God reveals to the believer by the agency of the Holy Spirit. *Cf.* John 14:16-18; 16:7, 12-15. This is how Peter knew that Jesus was the Messiah (Mt.16:17), which is remarkably parallel to 1 Cor.2:9,10.

The Divine Teacher, the Holy Spirit Himself is a great Scientist and Philosopher. Indeed He is the greatest Research Scientist ever, since He has looked into everything, even (ascensive καὶ) the depths of divine wisdom and knowledge (Col.2:3). Being God, He is coequal, coeval and coeternal with God. Thus the Holy Spirit knows all that God knows.

The omniscient Godhead reveals to the believer, not everything that they know, for they know it all, but everything that God wants us to know now. These are the things that He has prepared for the elect. The recipients of all of this revelation are those who, by the grace of God, have faith in propositional revelation that does not, in its inchoate stage, lend itself either to scientific or philosophical verification. Thus they are looked upon as "fools for Christ" by others who insist that only by sense perception or human deduction can certitude be enjoyed.

The medium which the Holy Spirit uses to reveal God's truth is the Old and New Testaments in their original languages. For those of us who live two thousand years after they were written, there is a problem of *zeitgeist*. Just what did the writers mean to convey when they used a language and an idiom well known to them and to their contemporaries, but strange to us? To what extent are the historicists correct when they say that no writer can communicate to any other reader than those who are his contemporaries? They are wrong, but only because they overstate their case. Communication between Paul in the first century and us in the twentieth century is not impossible - only difficult. That is why we must study the Hebrew Old Testament and the Greek New Testament in the light of historical research. It should be noted that historicists are not as pessimistic about our ability to understand Homer or Thucydides as they are about Paul or Luke. One wonders why?! They seem quite willing to honor the Homeric scholar, but they doubt the ability of any contemporary to interpret Paul. Strange! Could their prejudice against Christianity have anything to do with it? Let us not forget that the unsaved have a bad case of theophobia, as did all of us before the Holy Spirit visited us with His effectual call.

Just as pigs cannot be expected to research the affairs of men, so men cannot be expected to research the things of God. If it takes a man to study men, it takes God to research the counsels of God and to reveal them to man. This is the thought in

Verse 11 - *"For what man knoweth the things of a man save the spirit of man which is in him? Even so the things of God knoweth no man, but the Spirit of God."*

τίς γὰρ οἶδεν ἀνθρώπων τὰ τοῦ ἀνθρώπου εἰ μὴ τὸ πνεῦμα τοῦ ἀνθρώπου τὸ ἐν αὐτῷ; οὕτως καὶ τὰ τοῦ θεοῦ οὐδεὶς ἔγνωκεν εἰ μὴ τὸ πνεῦμα τοῦ θεοῦ.

"For what person knows a man's thoughts except the spirit of the man which is in him? So also no one comprehends the thoughts of God except the Spirit of God." . . . RSV

τίς (nom.sing.masc.of τίς, interrogative pronoun, subject of οἶδεν) 281.
γὰρ (causal conjunction) 105.
οἶδεν (3d.per.sing.perf.act.ind.of ὁράω) 144b.
ἀνθρώπων (gen.pl.masc.of ἄνθρωπος, partitive genitive) 341.
τὰ (acc.pl.neut.of the article, direct object of οἶδεν) 9.
τοῦ (gen.sing.masc.of the article in agreement with ἀνθρώπου) 9.
ἀνθρώπου (gen.sing.masc.of ἄνθρωπος, description) 341.
εἰ (conditional particle in an elliptical condition) 337.
μὴ (negative particle in an elliptical condition) 87.
τὸ (nom.sing.neut.of the article in agreement with πνεῦμα) 9.
πνεῦμα (nom.sing.neut.of πνεῦμα, subject of οἶδεν understood) 83.
τοῦ (gen.sing.masc.of the article in agreement with ἀνθρώπου) 9.
ἀνθρώπου (gen.sing.masc.of ἄνθρωπος, definition) 341.

τὸ (nom.sing.neut.of the article in agreement with πνεῦμα) 9.

ἐν (preposition with the locative of place) 80.

αὐτῷ (loc.sing.masc.of αὐτός, place) 16.

οὕτως (compound particle in a comparative clause) 74.

καὶ (continuative conjunction) 14.

τὰ (acc.pl.neut.of the article, direct object of ἔγνωκεν) 9.

τοῦ (gen.sing.masc.of the article in agreement with θεοῦ) 9.

θεοῦ (gen.sing.masc.of θεός, possession) 124.

οὐδεὶς (nom.sing.masc.of οὐδείς, subject of ἔγνωκεν) 446.

ἔγνωκεν (3d.per.sing.perf.act.ind.of γινώσκω, intensive) 131.

εἰ (conditional particle in an elliptical condition) 337.

μὴ (negative particle in an elliptical condition) 87.

τὸ (nom.sing.neut.of the article in agreement with πνεῦμα) 9.

πνεῦμα (nom.sing.neut.of πνεῦμα, subject of verb understood) 83.

τοῦ (gen.sing.masc.of the article in agreement with θεοῦ) 9.

θεοῦ (gen.sing.masc.of θεός, possession) 124.

Translation - "*For what man except with the human spirit which is in him has understood things in the human spirit? And in the same way no man has ever known things in the divine sphere except the Spirit of God.*"

Comment: Paul is resorting to analogy. All objects of knowledge are divided into two spheres - the human and the divine. The human spirit which God placed in man in creation (*homo sapiens*) is adequate to the task of understanding all those things which fall within the human sphere. What one man with his natural ability to reason can understand, all men with equal intelligence can understand. The inference is that lower forms of life cannot think on the human level. And (continuative καὶ) in the same way (οὕτως) those areas of knowledge which fall within the purview of the divine mind are as far beyond man as human knowledge is beyond the animals. It is no more possible for the human mind, unregenerate and unenlightened by revelation, to know the depths of God's thoughts than it is for pigs to understand algebra or for chickens to know why an airplane flies. Only the Spirit of God can think God's thoughts. Verse 11 therefore restates the argument of verses 9 and 10. Isaiah said the same thing in Isa.55:8,9.

These things being true, how can the Christian claim to understand God? Is he not human? Does he not think on the human level? Yes, he is human and he does think on the human level, but he is a very special kind of human, no thanks to him. He has been "born from above" (John 3:3,7) and in his regeneration he has been made the recipient of a marvelous gift.

Verse 12 - "*Now we have received not the spirit of the world, but the spirit which is of God; that we might know the things that are freely given to us of God.*"

ἡμεῖς δὲ οὐ τὸ πνεῦμα τοῦ κόσμου ἐλάβομεν ἀλλὰ τὸ πνεῦμα τὸ ἐκ τοῦ θεοῦ, ἵνα εἰδῶμεν τὰ ὑπὸ τοῦ θεοῦ χαρισθέντα ἡμῖν.

"Now we have received not the spirit of the world, but the Spirit which is from God, that we might understand the gifts bestowed on us by God.". . . RSV

ἡμεῖς (nom.pl.masc.of ἐγώ, subject of ἐλάβομεν) 123.
δὲ (adversative conjunction) 11.
οὐ (negative particle with the indicative) 130.
τὸ (acc.sing.neut.of the article in agreement with πνεῦμα) 9.
πνεῦμα (acc.sing.neut.of πνεῦμα, direct object of ἐλάβομεν) 83.
τοῦ (gen.sing.masc.of the article in agreement with κόσμου) 9.
κόσμου (gen.sing.masc.of κόσμος, description) 360.
ἐλάβομεν (1st.per.pl.aor.act.ind.of λαμβάνω, culminative) 533.
ἀλλὰ (alternative conjunction) 342.
τὸ (acc.sing.neut.of the article in agreement with πνεῦμα) 9.
πνεῦμα (acc.sing.neut.of πνεῦμα, direct object of ἐλάβομεν) 83.
τὸ (acc.sing.neut.of the article in agreement with πνεῦμα) 9.
ἐκ (preposition with the ablative of source) 19.
τοῦ (abl.sing.masc.of the article in agreement with θεοῦ) 9.
θεοῦ (abl.sing.masc.of θεός, source) 124.
ἵνα (conjunction with the subjunctive in a sub-final clause) 114.
εἰδῶμεν (1st.per.pl.2d.perf.act.subj.of οἶδα, intensive) 144b.
τὰ (acc.pl.neut.of the article in agreement with χαρισθέντα) 9.
ὑπὸ (preposition with the ablative of agent) 117.
τοῦ (abl.sing.masc.of the article in agreement with θεοῦ) 9.
θεοῦ (abl.sing.masc.of θεός, agent) 124.
χαρισθέντα (1st.aor.pass.part.acc.pl.neut.of χαρίζομαι, substantival, direct object of εἰδῶμεν) 2158.
ἡμῖν (dat.pl.masc.of ἐγώ, indirect object of χαρισθέντα) 123.

Translation - "But we have not received the spirit of the world; rather (we have received) the Spirit Who comes from God, in order (and with the result) that we may know the things which have been given to us by God."

Comment: δὲ is adversative as Paul moves to answer the objection which we raised at the close of comment on verse 11. Though Christians are merely human, they have nevertheless received the Spirit of God, not the spirit of the world. (Eph.1:13;John 20:22; 14:16,17; 16:7). They already had the spirit of the world before they were saved. It was sufficient for them to master all the philosophy and science of the earthly sphere, if we assume that they possessed sufficient intelligence. The I.Q.of the unsaved man will limit the degree of his understanding of knowledge in the human sphere, but no unsaved person, however high his I.Q. is able to think God's thoughts after Him. All men have some intelligence, in varying degrees, by virtue of their first human birth and the laws of genetics. But in addition, the child of God has received the Spirit of God. Why? The sub-final clause gives us both the purpose which God had in mind when He saved us and the result which surely follows. It is that we may understand what God has given to us - that to which Paul refers in the last clause of verse 9. Thus, by virtue of the new birth, the Christian, normally equipped by the spirit of the world to discuss matters with the unsaved on the earthly level, can also speak of things on the heavenly level. This is by virtue of the fact that he has been supernaturally equipped. All other things being equal the Christian can be educated to as high a level of philosophical and scientific sophistication as his unsaved peers. He need not defer to any of them. But, thanks to His baptism by the Holy Spirit into the Body of Christ (1 Cor.12:13; Gal.3:27) he can talk sensibly about matters which his unsaved peers can only regard as sheer nonesense. This is why a regenerate child can talk over the heads of a group of unregenerate Ph.D.'s. It may also explain why there are more Mortimer Snerds at prayer meeting than college professors.

Note the emphatic attributive position of the phrase ἐκ τοῦ θεοῦ with τὸ for special emphasis. Also the attributive position of τὰ ὑπὸ τοῦ θεοῦ χαρισθέντα - "the by God having been given unto us things." *Cf.* Rom.8:32, if you want to know how many things!

When the Christian comes to realize how richly endowed he has become by God's grace, it is impossible for him to remain silent. This is the thought of

Verse 13 - "Which things also we speak not in the words which man's wisdom teacheth, but which the Holy Ghost teacheth; comparing spiritual things with spiritual."

ἃ καὶ λαλοῦμεν οὐκ ἐν διδακτοῖς ἀνθρωπίνης σοφίας λόγοις ἀλλ' ἐν διδακτοῖς πνεύματος, πνευματικοῖς πνευματικὰ συγκρίνοντες.

"And we impart this in words not taught by human wisdom but taught by the Spirit, interpreting spiritual truths to those who possess the Spirit." . . . RSV

ἃ (acc.pl.neut.of ὅς, relative pronoun, direct object of λαλοῦμεν) 65.
καὶ (continuative conjunction) 14.
λαλοῦμεν (1st.per.pl.pres.act.ind.of λαλέω, customary) 815.
οὐκ (negative particle with the indicative) 130.
ἐν (preposition with the instrumental of means) 80.
διδακτοῖς (instru.pl.masc.of διδακτός, in agreement with λόγοις) 2290.
ἀνθρωπίνης (gen.sing.fem.of ἀνθρώπινος, description) 3415.
σοφίας (abl.sing.fem.of σοφία, source) 934.
λόγοις (instru.pl.masc.of λόγος, means) 510.
ἀλλ' (alternative conjunction) 342.
ἐν (preposition with the instrumental of means) 80.
διδακτοῖς (instru.sing.masc.of διδακτός, means) 2290.
πνεύματος (abl.sing.neut.of πνεῦμα, source) 83.
πνευματικοῖς (instru.pl.masc.of πνευματικός, association) 3791.
πνευματικὰ (acc.pl.neut.of πνευματικός, direct object of συγκρίνοντες) 3791.

#4111 συγκρίνοντες (pres.act.part.nom.pl.masc.of συγκρίνω, adverbial, circumstantial).

King James Version

compare among - 2 Cor.10:12.
compare with - 1 Cor.2:13; 2 Cor.10:12.

Revised Standard Version

interpreting - 1 Cor.2:13.
compare - 2 Cor.10:12,12.

Meaning: A combination of σύν (#1542) and κρίνω (#531). To judge with or together; to combine, connect. In 1 Cor.2:13 - "to place a discussion of spiritual matters (πνευματικά) among spiritual persons (πνευματικοῖς)." Or to talk about spiritual things in the sphere in which it is proper to discuss them. To do otherwise is referred to as "casting pearls before swine" and "giving holy things to dogs" (Mt.7:6). *Cf.* comment *infra.* In a sense unknown to the earlier Greek - to compare - 2 Cor.10:12,12.

Translation - "Which things we talk about, not with the techinal terms derived from human philosophy, but with teaching skills from the Spirit, as we discuss spiritual matters with spiritual people."

Comment: The antecedent of ἅ is τὰ of verse 12. When we received the Holy Spirit from God (verse 12), He enabled us to understand the things that had been given to us by God (verse 12), and now we are talking about these things (verse 13). How and how not? And with whom? Christians should not use phraseology which denotes concepts which normally we would use in lecturing to an unsaved audience. Our message is dictated by the audience and thus dictates the phraseology which ought to be employed. διδακτοῖς modifies λόγοις, which means, of course, both the words we use and the concepts which the words denote. We should exercise care to avoid connotations, which serve to lead the audience astray from our thought. The philosophy of the world (διδακτοῖς ἀνθρωπίνης σοφίας λόγοις) cannot provide the language which is needed to carry the thought of the philosophy of God. The Christian is speaking in a different realm and his source is divine, not human, and he needs to couch his thoughts in the heavenly language, by which I do *not* mean autointoxicated gibberish which means nothing and that nobody understands. Paul says that when Christians talk about God's grace they get their words, not from human philosophy, but they speak by means of διδακτοῖς (pedagogic methods) πνεύματος (derived from the Spirit), as they discuss theology with others (circumstantial participle in συγκρίνοντες).

Note that πνευματικά is neuter and that πνευματικοῖς is masculine - "spiritual things with spiritual people." The Oxford Revised Standard Version sees this, but implies that every Christian who possesses the Spirit is thereby to be designated as πνευματικός. It is our view that πνευματικοῖς refers to people who are saved, not to the sphere or framework (context) of the discussion of πνευματικά, but 1 Cor.3:1 forbids the interpretation that all Christians who have the Spirit are also filled with the Spirit.

Paul is talking, not only about *how* we speak, not like unsaved pedants, but like Spirit-filled children of God, but also about our audience, not every

Christian, for some Christians are σαρκίνοις (dominated by the flesh) and must grow beyond the infancy status in Christ before they can participate in the discussion that Paul is talking about.

Of course, when we put spiritual things into spiritual contexts we are doing it for the benefit of spiritual people, so no great damage results from the Oxford RSV when we note the disclaimer of 1 Cor.3:1.

Goodspeed has "giving spiritual truth a spiritual form," which is correct. Weymouth also scores with "adapting spiritual words to spiritual truths." Montgomery comes closer to the distinction between "carnal" and "spiritual" Christians than the RSV with her "interpreting spiritual things to spiritual men."

συγκρίνω (#4111) does not mean "interpret." To discuss God's gifts to us in worldly sophisticated phraseology in an attempt to "convince" the unsaved is to cast pearls before swine and give holy things to dogs" (Mt.7:6). It is the Holy Spirit's job to convince the unsaved (John 16:8). The unsaved are victims of their deep prejudice which grows out of their incurable theophobia. They are already convinced that we are fools. We may as well talk like fools!

Verse 14 - "But the natural man receiveth not the things of the Spirit of God: for they are foolishness unto him: neither can he know them, because they are spiritually discerned."

ψυχικὸς δὲ ἄνθρωπος οὐ δέχεται τὰ τοῦ πνεύματος τοῦ θεοῦ, μωρία γὰρ αὐτῷ ἐστιν, καὶ οὐ δύναται γνῶναι, ὅτι πνευματικῶς ἀνακρίνεται.

"The unspiritual man does not receive the gifts of the Spirit of God, for they are folly to him, and he is not able to understand them because they are spiritually discerned." . . . RSV

#4112 ψυχικὸς (nom.sing.masc.of ψυχιμός, in agreement with ἄνθρωπος).

King James Version

natural - 1 Cor.2:14; 15:44,44; 2 Pet.2:12.
senusal - James 3:15; Jude 19.
that which is natural - 1 Cor.15:46.

Revised Standard Version

unspiritual - 1 Cor.2:14; James 3:15.
physical - 1 Cor.15:44,44,46.
worldly - Jude 19.
instrinct - 2 Pet.2:12.

Meaning: Cf. ψυχή (#233). An adjective describing that which belongs to the ψυχή - animal existence - 2 Pet.2:12. Opposed to πνευματικός (#3791). Characterized in Jude 19 as unregenerate - "having not the Spirit" (Rom.8:9). Unable to accept spiritual things - 1 Cor.2:14; of the human body before the rapture - 1 Cor.15:44,44,46, as opposed to the same body after the rapture - dominated by the Holy Spirit. With reference to unregenerate philosophy - James 3:15.

δὲ (adversative conjunction) 11.

ἄνθρωπος (nom.sing.masc.of ἄνθρωπος, subject of δέχεται) 341.

οὐ (negative particle with the indicative) 130.

δέχεται (3d.per.sing.pres.mid.ind.of δέχομαι, customary) 867.

τὰ (acc.pl.neut.of the article, direct object of δέχεται) 9.

τοῦ (abl.sing.neut.of the article in agreement with πνεύματος) 9.

πνεύματος (abl.sing.neut.of πνεῦμα, source) 83.

τοῦ (gen.sing.masc.of the article in agreement with θεοῦ) 9.

θεοῦ (gen.sing.masc.of θεός, definition) 124.

μωρία (nom.sing.fem.of μωρία, predicate nominative) 4105.

γὰρ (causal conjunction) 105.

αὐτῷ (dat.sing.masc.of αὐτός, personal interest) 16.

ἐστιν (3d.per.sing.pres.ind.of εἰμί, static) 86.

καὶ (continuative conjunction) 14.

οὐ (negative particle with the indicative) 130.

δύναται (3d.per.sing.pres.mid.ind.of δύναμαι, customary) 289.

γνῶναι (aor.inf.of γινώσκω, complementary) 131.

ὅτι (conjunction introducing a subordinate causal clause) 211.

#4113 πνευματικῶς (adverbial).

King James Version

spiritually - 1 Cor.2:14; Rev.11:8.

Revised Standard Version

spiritually - 1 Cor.2:14.
allegorically - Rev.11:8.

Meaning: Cf.πνεῦμα (#83); πνευματικός (#3791); πνέω (#697). In a spiritual manner; by means of the Holy Spirit - 1 Cor.2:14; in a spiritual way in the allegorical sense - Rev.11:8. Opposed to σαρκικός (#4058), σάρκινος (#3924) and ψυχικός (#4112).

ἀνακρίνεται (3d.per.sing.pres.pass.ind.of ἀνακρίνω, static) 2837.

Translation - "But the unregenerate man does not accept the things of the Spirit of God because they are nonesense to him, and he is not able to grasp them because they are known only by spiritual research."

Comment: It is difficult to find an English word to translate ψυχικός. "Soulical" meaning at the animal level comes to mind. "Unspiritual" points up the opposition to πνευματικός. ψυχικός means "unregenerate" only in this context. Paul's meaning is that unsaved people reject the gospel. *cf.* 1 Cor.1:18. γὰρ and the causal clause tells us why. To him the theology of the Spirit of God is nonesense. Not only does he not, but he cannot receive the truth. (2 Cor.4:4). But he could not accept Christ, even if Satan did not blind his eyes, because his philosophy rejects deduction as an approach to truth. He does not believe in faith because he has none (Eph.2:8,9; Rom.10:17; Heb.12:2). The reason for his inability is given in the ὅτι causal clause. Spiritual matters are known only by totally complete, holistic research. *cf.* #2837 to convince yourself that that is the meaning of ἀνακρίνω. Only the Holy Spirit can do that (verses 10,11). The only true closure, so much discussed and sought by gestalt psychologists is in Christ and the revelation of His gifts to us by the Holy Spirit who has researched it all. The irony is that the religious spotlight is trained on modernist preachers who refer to preachers who believe the Bible as theological lightweights. No one has a frame of reference which includes all of the treasures of wisdom and knowledge (Col.2:3) except the regenerated believer. He is in a position to research it all. Unfortunately many Christians are not sufficiently πνευματικός to take full advantage of their intellectual opportunities.

Note the singular verb ἐστιν with the neuter plural subject. This is the classical idiom and reveals Paul's familiarity with it.

Verse 15 - "But he that is spiritual judgeth all things, yet ye himself is judged of no man."

ὁ δὲ πνευματικὸς ἀνακρίνει (τὰ) πάντα, αὐτὸς δὲ ὑπ' οὐδενὸς ἀνακρίνεται.

"The spiritual man judges all things, but is himself to be judged by no one."...

RSV

ὁ (nom.sing.masc.of the article in agreement with πνευματικὸς) 9.

δὲ (adversative conjunction) 11.

πνευματικὸς (nom.sing.masc.of πνευματικός, subject of ἀνακρίνεται) 3791.

ἀνακρίνει (3d.per.sing.pres.act.ind.of ἀνακρίνω, customary) 2837.

(τὰ) (acc.pl.neut.of the article in agreement with πάντα) 9.

πάντα (acc.pl.neut.of πᾶς, direct object of ἀνακρίνει) 67.

αὐτὸς (nom.sing.masc.of αὐτός, subject of ἀνακρίνεται, intensive predicate position) 16.

δὲ (adversative conjunction) 11.

ὑπ' (preposition with the ablative of agent) 117.

οὐδενὸς (abl.sing.masc.of οὐδείς, agent) 446.

ἀνακρίνεται (3d.per.sing.pres.pass.ind.of ἀνακρίνω, static) 2837.

Translation - "But the man who is dominated by the Holy Spirit researches to the depths of everything, but he himself is not evaluated by anyone."

Comment: Here is the goal for every intellectual Christian. The Christian whose life is totally devoted to Christ and who is therefore dominated by the Holy Spirit (πνευματικός) is in a position to research into and come to understand all of reality. He finds it all in Christ (Col.2:3). As a member of the Body of Christ and with the Holy Spirit living in him (1 Cor.6:19,20; John 17:21) he has an eternity in which to find out all that there is to know. Note the eternal durative action in ἀνακρίνει. Research, research, research, hear, hear, hear, discuss, discuss, discuss, grow, grow, grow! Will we ever arrive? (Eph.4:13). Here is Christian idealism in its highest form. This is what Plato dreamed about but never realized. If unreached goals, which nevertheless have a prospect of being

reached are good for personality development the spiritual Christian should
have the most radiant of personalities! That Paul was thinking what we are now -
viz. wondering if the goal which is infinitely ahead of us will ever be reached in all
eternity, is evident in

*Verse 16 - "For who hath known the mind of the Lord, that he may instruct him?
But we have the mind of Christ."*

τίς γὰρ ἔγνω νοῦν κυρίου, ὃς συμβιβάσει αὐτόν; ἡμεῖς δὲ νοῦν Χριστοῦ
ἔχομεν.

*" 'For who has known the mind of the Lord so as to instruct him?' But we have
the mind of Christ." . . . RSV*

τίς (nom.sing.masc.of τίς, interrogative pronoun, subject of ἔγνω) 281.
γὰρ (inferential conjunction) 105.
ἔγνω (3d.per.sing.2d.aor.act.ind.of γινώσκω, constative) 131.
νοῦν (acc.sing.masc.of νοῦς, direct object of ἔγνω) 2928.
κυρίου (gen.sing.masc.of κύριος, possession) 97.
ὃς (nom.sing.masc.of ὅς, relative pronoun, subject of συμβιβάσει) 65.
συμβιβάσει (3d.per.sing.fut.act.ind.of συμβιβάζω, deliberative) 3194.
αὐτόν (acc.sing.masc.of αὐτός, direct object of συμβιβάσει) 16.
ἡμεῖς (nom.pl.masc.of ἐγώ, subject of ἔχομεν) 123.
δὲ (adversative conjunction) 11.
νοῦν (acc.sing.masc.of νοῦς, direct object of ἔχομεν) 2928.
Χριστοῦ (gen.sing.masc.of Χριστός, possession) 4.
ἔχομεν (1st.per.pl.pres.act.ind.of ἔχω aoristic) 82.

*Translation - "So who has known the thinking of the Lord? Who will complete
His education? But we have the mind of Christ."*

Comment: Study carefully #'s 2928 and 3194. νοῦς means the intellectual frame
of reference - the mental model, the schema of one's philosophy. Who thinks like
the Lord thinks? Who thinks so much as He does that he understands the Lord's
model and is thus able to help the Lord "put it all together?" (the basic idea in
συμβιβάζω). Who can help God complete his pattern of thinking? Who, with
God as a thinking partner will help Him achieve closure. These, of course are
rhetorical questions which Isaiah asked 700 years before in that purple passage
of divine sarcasm (Isa.40:12-17). The answer is obvious. No one will ever instruct
God. But the Christian believer at least has Christ's method. We are oriented in
the proper frame of reference . We have the right assumptions. We are headed in
the right direction. It is all a matter of pursuing a goal, reducing the area of our
ignorance and coming closer and closer to closure. Christ has every piece in His
jigsaw puzzle in place. He always has had them all in place. We are working on
ours. Enough of our pieces are in the right places to guide us in where we place
the rest of them. And we have eternity in which to pursue this fascinating game.
Hallelujah!
    Note ὅς, the relative pronoun introducing a consecutive clause. What is the

mind of Christ? Certainly while He is unafraid of the empirical test for truth, He goes much further than to say with the empiricist that only sense perception is the ground for knowledge. His mind bifurcates between subject and object. He believes that man can communicate his thoughts adequately and that knowledge is possible. He believes that there is a basic difference between good and evil. He believes in democracy only if the democrats (small d) are sinless and rational, though, since He was banished from His earth two thousand years ago He has had no particular interest in what particular form of government depraved man tries, since all are destined to fail. Christ's mind also knows that there is meaning in the universe and He is certain that truth, beauty and goodness are greater than error, ugliness and evil. Only those who have the mind of Christ are entitled to share these convictions with Him. These matters do not belong in the frame of reference of the unsaved. Those unregenerates who profess to entertain these convictions, do so only in direct ratio to their ability to be inconsistent.

Another conclusion can be drawn from Paul's argument in 1 Cor.1:18 - 2:16. The term "Christian Education" is redundant. There really is no other kind. State supported education which leaves out Christ and regards His gospel as nonesense is not education at all. It is vocational training.

Fellow Workmen for God

(1 Corinthians 3:1-23)

Chapter 3, Verse 1 - "And I, brethren, could not speak unto you as unto spiritual, but as unto carnal, even as unto babes in Christ."

Κἀγώ, ἀδελφοί, οὐκ ἠδυνήθην λαλῆσαι ὑμῖν ὡς πνευματικοῖς ἀλλ' ὡς σαρκίνοις, ὡς νηπίοις ἐν Χριστῷ.

"But I, brethren, could not address you as spiritual men, but as men of the flesh, as babes in Christ." . . . *RSV*

Κἀγώ (continuative conjunction and ἐγώ, crasis) 178.

ἀδελφοί (voc.pl.masc.of ἀδελφός, address) 15.

οὐκ (negative particle with the indicative) 130.

ἠδυνήθην (1st.per.sing.1st.aor.ind. Attic, constative) 289.

λαλῆσαι (aor.act.inf.of λαλέω, complementary) 815.

ὑμῖν (dat.pl.masc.of σύ, indirect object of λαλῆσαι) 104.

ὡς (particle introducing a comparative clause) 128.

πνευματικοῖς (dat.pl.masc.of πνευματικός, predicate adjective) 3791.

ἀλλ' (alternative conjunction) 342.

ὡς (particle introducing a comparative clause) 128.

σαρκίνοις (dat.pl.masc.of σάρκινος, predicate adjective) 3924.

ὡς (particle introducing a comparative clause) 128.

νηπίοις (dat.pl.masc.of νήπιος, predicate adjective) 951.

ἐν (preposition with the instrumental of association) 80.

Χριστῷ (instru.sing.masc.of Χριστός, association) 4.

Translation - "And I, brethren, was unable to speak to you as though you were spiritfilled, but as you are - motivated by the flesh, as babes in Christ."

Comment: κἀγώ emphasizes the subject, "I" which is in the verb ἠδυνήθην. Note the comparative use of ὡς. Not as if you were πνευματικός but as you are in fact - σαρκίνοις and νηπίοις.

Paul could discuss Christian theology with the mature - τοῖς τελείοις (1 Cor.2:6), but not with the Corinthians, who, though regenerate, were not dominated by the Holy Spirit (πνευματικός). It is significant that Paul does not say that they are ψυχικός, which adjective is reserved for the unsaved (1 Cor.2:14). Thus the Corinthians are never again to be ψυχικός, although they are not yet πνευματικός. The third adjective σάρκινος (#3924) and σαρκικός (#4058) evidently applies to a true regenerate who nevertheless has not grown in grace to the point of victorious and mature Christian living, and thus is still dominated to too great a degree by the flesh, the result of his first physical birth. A babe in Christ, though saved, is undeveloped. *Cf.* Heb.5:11-14 where the writer is saying the same thing to the Hebrew Christians that Paul is saying here to the Corinthians.

The passage divides the human race into two main groups with the second group further subdivided into two component groups.

Group I - They are lost. They are described by the adjective ψυχικός (1 Cor.2:14). Note the use of the word in Jude 19 where it is defined - ψυχικοί, πνεῦμα μὴ ἔχοντες and associate that with Rom.8:9.

Group IIa - These people are regenerate but immature - babes in Christ. Two words describe them - σάρκινος - 1 Cor.3:1 and σαρκικός - 1 Cor.3:3.

Group IIb - These people are also regenerate. They are mature Christians whose lives are dominated by the Holy Spirit. The adjectives which describe them are πνευματικός - 1 Cor.2:15; 3:1 and τέλειος - 1 Cor.2:6.

A Christian who ought to be πνευματικός and τέλειος may backslide and become σαρκικός or σάρκινος, but he will never again be ψυχικός. The student should study thoroughly #'s 4112, 3924, 4058 and 3791.

The σάρκινος Christian presents a problem in spiritual pediatrics to the pastor-teacher who must be, like Paul, adept in the care and feeding of spiritual babies. It is possible to make the mistake of overfeeding the new Christian with a philosophical diet that he is, as yet, unable to take. First he must have the A B C's of the Christian faith.

Verse 2 - "I have fed you with milk, and not with meat; for hitherto ye were not able to bear it, neither now are ye able."

γάλα ὑμᾶς ἐπότισα, οὐ βρῶμα, οὔπω γὰρ ἐδύνασθε, ἀλλ᾽ οὐδὲ ἔτι νῦν δύνασθε.

"I fed you with milk, not solid food; for you were not ready for it; and even yet you are not ready, . . . " . . RSV

#4114 γάλα (acc.sing.neut.of γάλα, direct object of ἐπότισα).

King James Version

1 Cor.3:2; 9:7; Heb.5:12,13; 1 Pet.2:2.

Revised Standard Version

milk - 1 Cor.3:2; 9:7; Heb.5:12,13; 1 Pet.2:2.

Meaning: Milk. Metaphorically of the less complicated and difficult truths of Christian theology, as opposed to βρῶμα, the areas of Christian truth more academically advanced. In this sense in 1 Cor.3:2; Heb.5:12,13; with reference to the Word of God which in the spiritual realm stimulates growth in the new Christian as milk does for the physical baby - 1 Pet.2:2. Properly in 1 Cor.9:7 in an analogy about financial rewards for the minister.

ὑμᾶς (acc.pl.masc.of σύ, direct object of ἐπότισα, double accusative) 104.

ἐπότισα (1st.per.sing.aor.act.ind.of ποτίζω, constative) 900.

οὐ (negative particle with the indicative) 130.

βρῶμα (acc.sing.neut.of βρῶμα, direct object of ἐπότισα) 1118.

οὔπω (temporal adverb) 1198.

γὰρ (causal conjunction) 105.

ἐδύνασθε (2d.per.pl.imp.ind.of δύναμαι, customary) 289.

ἀλλ' (emphatic conjunction) 342.

οὐδὲ (disjunctive particle) 452.

ἔτι (temporal adverb) 448.

νῦν (temporal adverb) 1497.

δύνασθε (2d.per.pl.pres.ind.of δύναμαι, aoristic) 289.

Translation - "*I served milk to you, not solid food because you were not yet ready for it. Nor are you ready for it even now.*"

Comment: Paul's first clause is zeugmatic, joining to the verb ἐπότισα (which means "to give drink") an object, γάλα, which fits the verb but that does not fit the second object βρῶμα. One drinks milk but eats, not drinks, solid food. Note the double accusative after the causative verb, in this case, an accusative of person, ὑμᾶς and two accusatives of the thing γάλα and βρῶμα.

When Paul was in Corinth the first time he preached the gospel simply (1 Cor.2:5), as he should, with the great success we have noted. During the 18 months he remained (Acts 18:11) he fed the new-born flock of God with the simple rudiments of Christian theology. (1 Pet.2:2; Heb.6:1-3). This was proper since they were babes in Christ . οὔτω γὰρ ἐδύνασθε - "because you were not yet able" to understand deep Christian theology. But Paul had every reason to hope that in the meantime they had developed to the point where they could take Paul's theology in all of its depths. Alas it was not true. There is some despair in ἀλλ' οὐδὲ ἔτι νῦν δύνασθε. Paul sighed as he wrote it. "Nor are you ready for it even now." Why the state of arrested spiritual development?

Verse 3 - *"For ye are yet carnal: for whereas there is among you envying, and strife, and divisions, are ye not carnal, and walk as men?"*

ἔτι γὰρ σαρκικοί ἐστε. ὅπου γὰρ ἐν ὑμῖν ζῆλος καὶ ἔρις, οὐχὶ σαρκικοί ἐστε καὶ κατὰ ἄνθρωπον περιπατεῖτε;

"for you are still of the flesh. For while there is jealousy and strife among you, are you not of the flesh, and behaving like ordinary men?" . . . RSV

ἔτι (temporal conjunction) 448.

γὰρ (causal conjunction) 105.

σαρκικοί (nom.pl.masc.of σαρκικός, predicate adjective) 4058.

ἐστε (2d.per.pl.pres.ind.of εἰμί, aoristic) 86.

ὅπου (adverbial - "inasmuch as") 592.

γὰρ (causal conjunction) 105.

ἐν (preposition with the locative with plural pronouns) 80.

ὑμῖν (loc.pl.masc.of σύ, place) 104.

ζῆλος (nom.sing.masc.of ζῆλος, subject of verb understood) 1985.

καὶ (adjunctive conjunction joining nouns) 14.

ἔρις (nom.sing.fem.of ἔρις, subject of verb understood) 3819.

οὐχὶ (negative particle with the indicative in rhetorical question, expecting an affirmative reply) 130.

σαρκικοί (nom.pl.masc.of σαρκικός, predicate adjective) 4058.

ἐστε (2d.per.pl.pres.ind.of εἰμί, rhetorical question) 86.

καὶ (continuative conjunction) 14.

κατὰ (preposition with the accusative, standard) 98.

ἄνθρωπον (acc.sing.masc.of ἄνθρωπος, standard) 341.

περιπατεῖτε (2d.per.pl.pres.act.ind.of περιπατέω, rhetorical question) 384.

Translation - *"Because you are still flesh-oriented; for in view of the fact that there exists among you unwarranted zeal and strife, you are dominated by the flesh, are you not? And do you not conduct yourselves as unsaved men?"*

Comment: ἀλλ' (verse 2) is confirmatory, not adversative, as Paul builds his case against the Corinthians. "Indeed you are not even yet able to assimilate lofty concepts." γὰρ is causal and ὅπου has the force of "in view of the fact that." *Cf.* 2 Peter 2:11 for a similar use of ὅπου. Note that ζῆλος (#1985) is sometimes used in a good ethical sense, but here in an evil sense. Unnecessary zeal, which contributes to fanaticism is a common mark of behavior and attitude of the young Christian who has not yet learned to relax. There is a difference between knowing in one's head that God is on the throne and experiencing this great truth in the heart. Young Christians often think that it is their fight, not God's. God wants witnesses, not defense attorneys. Often young Christians equate their views with God's views and thus tend to denounce as heretics all who differ in the slightest degree. Paul here calls this kind of zeal (ζῆλος) an evidence that such a Christian is still oriented around human psychology. Fanaticism, the strident voiced, glaring eyed, clenched fist defense of God is not a part of Holy Spirit directed behavior. We are to contend for the faith (Jude 3) but we are not to be contentious about the faith.

The aggravated kind of ζῆλος which Paul attacks breeds ἔρις. Both of these are listed in Gal.5:20 as τὰ ἔργα τῆς σαρκός, cf. comment en loc., which supports 1 Cor.3:3. Paul's questions here are rhetorical and they expect "Yes" as the answer. This kind of psychology and the overt behavior which it creates does not result in the loss of salvation, but it can keep the child of God in the state of spiritual infancy. Note that Peter told the saints who had recently become Christians to lay aside their psychological sins, if they expected to develop a desire for the milk of the Word of God (1 Pet.2:1,2). There is nothing more charming than a little baby and nothing more repulsive than a big baby.

κατὰ ἄνθρωπον - an accusative of standard. Paul always means by περιπατέω (#384) the ethical "walk" of Christian behavior. Here he tells the Corinthians that their bickering indicates that they are still behaving like unsaved men. But, though they are acting like unsaved men, he could not address them as such (1 Cor.3:1-3). They will never be ψυχικός again and indeed they may never be πνευματικός until the rapture, although Paul hopes that they will outgrow their infancy to become πνευματικός, like some of the saints in the Galatians churches (Gal.6:1).

Some MSS of early vintage add καὶ διχοστασίαι - "and divisions" after ἔρις, though p11,vid,46 Sinaiticus, B C P Ψ 81 1739 al do not have it. If the words were there originally there was nothing to explain their omission. Hence the textual critics suspect a Western gloss, added perhaps from the list of vices in Gal.5:20. The addition or omission of the words does not affect the exegesis. There is plenty of evidence that the Corinthian saints were spiritually undeveloped infants. Paul gets down to specific evidence in

Verse 4 - "For while one saith, I am of Paul; and another, I am of Apollos; are ye not carnal?"

ὅταν γὰρ λέγῃ τις, Ἐγὼ μέν εἰμι Παύλου, ἕτερος δέ Ἐγὼ Ἀπολλῶ, οὐκ ἄνθρωποί ἐστε;

"For when one says, 'I belong to Paul,' and another, 'I belong to Apollos,' are you not merely men?" . . . RSV

ὅταν (conjunction with the subjunctive in an indefinite temporal clause) 436.
γὰρ (causal conjunction) 105.
λέγῃ (3d.per.sing.pres.act.subj.of λέγω, indefinite temporal clause) 66.
τις (nom.sing.masc.of τις, indefinite pronoun, subject of λέγῃ) 486.
Ἐγὼ (nom.sing.masc.of ἐγώ, subject of εἰμι) 123.
μέν (particle of affirmation) 300.
εἰμι (1st.per.sing.pres.ind.of εἰμί, aoristic) 86.
Παύλου (abl.sing.masc.of Παῦλος, agent) 3284.
ἕτερος (nom.sing.masc.of ἕτερος, subject of λέγῃ) 605.
δὲ (continuative conjunction) 11.

Ἐγώ (nom.sing.masc.of ἐγώ, emphatic, subject of εἰμί) 123.
Ἀπολλῶ (abl.sing.masc.of ἀπολλῶς, agent) 3454.
οὐκ (negative particle with the indicative) 130.
ἄνθρωποι (nom.pl.masc.of ἄνθρωπος, predicate nomintive) 341.
ἐστε (2d.per.pl.pres.ind.of εἰμί, aoristic, rhetorical question) 86.

Translation - *"Because when someone says, 'I, I am of Paul,' but another says, 'I, I am of Apollos' you are acting like mere human beings are you not?"*

Comment: ὅταν, the indefinite temporal introduces the subjunctive in λέγῃ. Paul is not pointing to a definite case, but he is suggesting that the Corinthians had been talking like that and that when they did they indicated that they were still in the infant stage in their development. He is saying that every time, whenever it is and whoever said it, that such a view is expressed it proves his point. This is a common disease in evangelical churches, particularly those who invite a great number of outside evangelists to their pulpits. Radio and Television preachers who pay huge sums for public exposure and who travel about the country holding "rallies" also contribute to this evil, though perhaps in some cases they do not intend to do so. If so the fault is not in them, but in their converts who either are not genuinely regenerated or in such a state of spiritual infancy that they refuse to listen to any preacher except Paul or Apollos, Elmer Gantry or some other, although I am not putting Paul and Apollos in the same category that includes Elmer Gantry. The Elmer Gantry types thrive on this disease among the saints.
    Paul attacks it heartily in

Verse 5 - *"Who then is Paul, and who is Apollos, but ministers by whom ye believed, even as the Lord gave to every man?*

    τί οὖν ἐστιν Ἀπολλῶς; τί δέ ἐστιν Παῦλος; διάκονοι δι' ὧν ἐπιστεύσατε, καὶ ἑκάστῳ ὡς ὁ κύριος ἔδωκεν.

"What then is Apollos? What is Paul? Servants through whom you believed, as the Lord assigned to each." . . . RSV

τί (nom.sing.neut.of τίς, interrogative pronoun, predicate nominative) 281.
οὖν (emphatic conjunction) 68.
ἐστιν (3d.per.sing.pres.ind.of εἰμί, aoristic) 86.
Ἀπολλῶς (nom.sing.masc.of Ἀπολλῶς, subject of ἐστιν) 3454.
τί (nom.sing.neut.of τίς, interrogative pronoun, predicate nominative) 281.
δέ (continuative conjunction) 11.
ἐστιν (3d.per.sing.pres.ind.of εἰμί, aoristic) 86,
Παῦλος (nom.sing.masc.of Παῦλος, subject of ἐστιν) 3284.
διάκονοι (nom.pl.masc.of διάκονος, predicate nominative) 1334.
δι' (preposition with the ablative of agent) 118.
ὧν (abl.pl.masc.of ὅς, relative pronoun, agent) 65.
ἐπιστεύσατε (2d.per.pl.aor.act.ind.of πιστεύω, constative) 734.
καὶ (ascensive conjunction) 14.
ἑκάστῳ (dat.sing.masc.of ἕκαστος, indirect object of ἔδωκεν) 1217.

ὡς (particle introducing a comparative clause) 128.
ὁ (nom.sing.masc.of the article in agreement with κύριος) 9.
κύριος (nom.sing.masc.of κύριος, subject of ἔδωκεν) 97.
ἔδωκεν (3d.per.sing.1st.aor.act.ind.of δίδωμι, constative) 362.

Translation - "Indeed! What is Apollos and what is Paul? Servants through whom you believed, even as the Lord directed each."

Comment: Paul's sarcasm is delightful! οὖν is emphatic. As the Corinthians strutted about boasting of their personal contacts with and allegiance to one preacher or another, Paul says, "Indeed! Big Deal!" Then he does not even dignify himself nor Apollos with the masculine form of the interrogative pronoun. Not "Who" but "What" he asks is Paul and Apollos? It is the contemptuous use of τί. "What are these clowns, Apollos and Paul?"

Then he answers his own question. They are only servants through the agency of whose ministry the Corinthians came to trust Christ, and that only to the extent that the Lord, Who is "head over all things to the church" (Eph.1:22) gave to Paul and/or Apollos the privilege of so serving. ἐκάστῳ refers not to the individual Corinthians but to Paul and Apollos.

No Christian deserves nor can properly be given credit for anything which he may do in the service of the Lord, for the good works which we do are those οἷς προητοίμασεν ὁ θεὸς ἵνα ἐν αὐτοῖς περιπατήσωμεν - "which God has before ordained that we should walk in them" (Eph.2:10). *Cf.* comment *en loc.* The Corinthian Christian who was converted when Apollos preached and who thus feels a special attachment to him - an attachment which, legitimate in itself perhaps, nevertheless leads to a division in the church, should remember that it was the risen Lord who had directed that both he, the sinner and Apollos, the preacher should have been present on the occasion in question. Apollos was only the human agent through whom God did the work.

Thus Paul and Apollos are put in perspective for the Corinthians and God is given all of the credit. Paul continues this line of argument in which he exalts God and denigrates himself and Apollos (as well as all other human agents) through verse 9.

Verse 6 - "I have planted, Apollos watered; but God gave the increase."

ἐγὼ ἐφύτευσα, Ἀπολλῶς ἐπότισεν, ἀλλὰ ὁ θεὸς ηὔξανεν.

"I planted, Apollow watered, but God gave the growth." . . . RSV

ἐγὼ (nom.sing.masc.of ἐγώ, subject of ἐφύτευσα) 123.
ἐφύτευσα (1st.per.sing.aor.act.ind.of φυτεύω, constative) 1154.
Ἀπολλῶς (nom.sing.masc.of Ἀπολλῶς, subject of ἐπότισεν) 3454.
ἐπότισεν (3d.per.sing.aor.act.ind.of ποτίζω, constative) 900.
ἀλλὰ (adversative conjunction) 342.
ὁ (nom.sing.masc.of the article in agreement with θεὸς) 9.
θεὸς (nom.sing.masc.of θεός, subject of ηὔξανεν) 124.
ηὔξανεν (3d.per.sing.imp.act.ind.of αὐξάνω, iterative) 628.

Translation - *"I planted; Apollos watered, but God has been causing the growth."*

Comment: Note the juxtaposition of two aorists with an imperfect. We must not overlook the distinction between the aorist and the imperfect. Robertson says, "Where the aorist and the imperfect occur side by side, it is to be assumed that the change is made on purpose and the difference in idea to be sought. In juxtaposition the aorist lifts the curtain and the imperfect continues the play." (*Grammar*, 838). *Cf.* Mt.25:5; Mk.5:32; 7:35; Mt.4:11.

Paul went to Corinth and planted the seed of the gospel of Christ. *cf.* Mt.13:3, though the word there is σπείρω (#616) not φυτεύω (#1154). It was a completed action in the past, and hence Paul uses the aorist ἐφύτεσα. Apollos followed with further ministry of the Word to the same people. Paul likens this to a gardener who waters the ground where the seed has already been planted. Apollos' work was also complete - hence, another aorist in ἐπότισεν. "But (strong adversative in ἀλλά the increaser is God." Note in verse 7 that the article is joined to the participle αὐξάνων, not to θεός. Paul is emphasizing the fact of the increase. Here is where the supernatural action takes place.

It does not require special intelligence or strength to drop a seed into the soil and cover it. Anyone can plant a seed. Nor is special skill needed to carry a sprinkling can. But germination of the seed, thus planted and watered, involves life and only God, Who is life (Acts 3:15; 5:31) can do that.

In the process it is the Word of God which is sown and watered that God must honor (Isaiah 55:10,11), not the preacher who plants or waters it. Any human being, even an unregenerate, can spread the good news of the gospel of Christ. Witness the evangelist on the American frontier in the 19th century who preached the gospel in the daytime and stole horses at night. Souls were saved in his meetings, no thanks to him.

Thus Paul seeks to correct the Corinthians for "worshipping" the natural gardeners rather than the supernatural life giver .

Verse 7 - *"So then neither is he that planteth anything, neither he that watereth; but God that giveth the increase."*

ὥστε οὔτε ὁ φυτεύων ἐστίν τι οὔτε ὁ ποτίζων, ἀλλ' ὁ αὐξάνων θεός.

"So neither he who plants nor he who waters is anything, but only God who gives the growth." . . . RSV

ὥστε (conjunction with the indicative, actual result) 752.

οὔτε (negative compound correlative) 598.

ὁ (nom.sing.masc.of the article in agreement with φυτεύων) 9.

φυτεύων (pres.act.part.nom.sing.masc.of φυτεύω, substantival, subject of ἐστίν) 1154.

ἐστίν (3d.per.sing.pres.ind.of εἰμί, static) 86.

τι (nom.sing.neut.of τις, indefinite pronoun, predicate nominative) 486.

οὔτε (negative compound correlative) 598.

ὁ (nom.sing.masc.of the article in agreement with ποτίζων) 9.

ποτίζων (pres.act.part.nom.sing.masc.of ποτίζω, substantival, subject of ἐστίν) 900.

ἀλλ' (adversative conjunction) 342.

ὁ (nom.sing.masc.of the article in agreement with αὐξάνων) 9.

αὐξάνων (pres.act.part.nom.sing.masc.of αὐξάνω, substantival, subject of ἐστίν understood) 628.

θεός (nom.sing.masc.of θεός, apposition) 124.

Translation - "Thus we conclude that neither the planter nor the waterer is important, but the one who causes growth - God."

Comment: ὥστε with the indicative is a very rare construction in the New Testament. It speaks of actual, not conceived or intended result. "But actual result may also be expressed by the infinitive with ὥστε. Mt.8:24; 12:22; Lk.5:7." (Mantey, *Manual*, 286). οὔτε . . . οὔτε is a good example of the correlative rather than the disjunctive use. Planter and waterer are in the same unimportant class. But (ἀλλ') God occupies the other class in His role as the One who alone can make the seed grow. This involves life. *Cf.*#628 for growth, both of the Body of Christ (Col.2:19; Eph.2:21; John 3:30), for the spread of Christianity (Acts 6:7; 12:24; 19:20) and in terms of growth in grace for the believer (#628, 5). The argument of verse 7 reinforces that of verse 6. In verses 8 and 9 Paul continues to associate himself with Apollos on the lower level of importance as distinct from God, the prime actor, who deserves the credit. As such he and Apollos are unified in faith and fellowship even though their respective disciples are not. Paul and Apollos had no intention of allowing the dissension among their followers affect their own relationship.

Verse 8 - "Now he that planteth and he that watereth are one: and every man shall receive his own reward according to his own labour."

ὁ φυτεύων δὲ καὶ ὁ ποτίζων ἕν εἰσιν, ἕκαστος δὲ τὸν ἴδιον μισθὸν λήμφεται κατὰ τὸν ἴδιον κόπον.

"He who plants and he who waters are equal, and each shall receive his wages according to his labor." . . . *RSV*

ὁ (nom.sing.masc.of the article in agreement with φυτεύων) 9.

φυτεύων (pres.act.part.nom.sing.masc.of φυτεύω, substantival, subject of εἰσιν) 1154.

δὲ (explanatory conjunction) 11.

καὶ (adjunctive conjunction joining participles) 14.

ὁ (nom.sing.masc.of the article in agreement with ποτίζων) 9.

ποτίζων (pres.act.part.nom.sing.masc.of ποτίζω, substantival, subject of εἰσιν) 900.

ἕν (acc.sing.neut.of εἷς, adverbial) 469.

εἰσιν (3d.per.pl.pres.ind.of εἰμί, static) 86.

ἕκαστος (nom.sing.masc.of ἕκαστος, subject of λήμφεται) 1217.

δὲ (continuative conjunction) 11.

τὸν (acc.sing.masc.of the article in agreement with μισϑὸν) 9.

ἴδιον (acc.sing.masc.of ἴδιος, possessive pronoun, in agreement with μισϑὸν) 778.

μισϑὸν (acc.sing.masc.of μισϑός, direct object of λήμφεται) 441.

λήμφεται (3d.per.sing.fut.mid.ind.of λαμβάνω, predictive) 533.

κατὰ (preposition with the accusative of standard) 98.

τὸν (acc.sing.masc.of the article in agreement with κόπον) 9.

ἴδιον (acc.sing.masc.of ἴδιος, possessive pronoun, in agreement with κόπον) 778.

κόπον (acc.sing.masc.of κόπος, standard) 1565.

Translation - "*Now the planter and he who waters are one, and each man will receive his own reward commensurate with his own labor.*"

Comment: ἕν can be interpreted to mean that there was no personal animosity between Paul and Apollos, despite the fact that their Corinthian followers were at odds. "Why are you fighting among yourselves? Apollos and I are friends." Or we may say that planting and watering are alike in that they are fundamental necessities in agriculture, but also alike in that they are in the natural realm while germination and growth requires supernatural power.

Thus Paul the preacher and Apollos, who followed him to confirm the message, performed human functions and should not therefore be praised.

Or perhaps he meant that he and Apollos had no serious theological differences of opinion, which is a variation of the first possibility (*supra*). All three ideas can be true. They are not mutually exclusive. It is interesting to point out that Paul refrained from telling the Corinthians about Apollos' previous theological error, the sad results of which Paul himself served to correct (Acts 18:24-19:7). Had Paul done so he would have been guilty of a serious breach of professional ethics, which could only have served to exacerbate the unpleasantness which Paul was seeking to alleviate. Paul's restraint in this matter indicates that, in addition to manifesting the high standard of Christian ethics which we would expect from him, he also demonstrated the class we would expect from one of his professional and academic achievement.

The last half of the verse ἕκαστος . . . κόπον lends itself to the view that Paul meant that he and Apollos were only "servants" of God - hired hands, working in the fields "white unto harvest" (John 4:35) and not to be mentioned in the same breath with "the Lord of the harvest" (Mt.9:38), Who would take care to pay both planter and waterer a wage commensurate to his input of pain and inconvenience (*cf.*#1565 for meaning). Thus he is saying, "You need not repay us by posing as our disciples. We will be rewarded by the Lord of the harvest in due time.

Note the accusative of standard or rule in κατὰ τὸν ἴδιον κόπον.

The context begins to suggest that ἕκαστος in verse 10, may refer especially to preachers who are charged with the responsibility of contributing to the superstructure to be built in the Christian life upon the foundation formerly laid.

Verse 9 — "For we are labourers together with God: ye are God's husbandry; ye are God's building."

θεοῦ γάρ ἐσμεν συνεργοί. θεοῦ γεώργιον, θεοῦ οἰκοδομή ἐστε.

"For we are fellow workers for God; you are God's field, God's building." . . . RSV

θεοῦ (gen.sing.masc.of θεός, relationship) 124.

γάρ (causal conjunction) 105.

ἐσμεν (1st.per.pl.pres.ind.of εἰμί, aoristic) 86.

συνεργοί (nom.pl.masc.of συνεργός, predicate nominative) 4066.

θεοῦ (gen.sing.masc.of θεός, possession) 124.

#4115 γεώργιον (nom.sing.neut.of γεώργιον, predicate nominative).

King James Version

husbandry - 1 Cor.3:9.

Revised Standard Version

field - 1 Cor.3:9.

Meaning: Cf. γεωργέομαι (#4966); γεωργός (#1381), *from* γῆ (#157) *and* ἐργάζομαι (#691). A plot of ground under agricultural or horticultural cultivation. A field, farm, garden. Metaphorically, with reference to the saints being cultivated by God to produce fruit - 1 Cor.3:9.

θεοῦ (gen.sing.masc.of θεός, possession) 124.

οἰκοδομή (nom.sing.fem.of οἰκοδομή, predicate nominative) 1481.

ἐστε (2d.per.pl.pres.ind.of εἰμί, static) 86.

Translation - "Because we are fellow workers with God. You are God's garden. You are God's edifice."

Comment: The causal clause naturally follows from verse 8. Apollos and Paul worked together for God, under His supervision, and they looked to Him for reward. What type of work? Agriculture. Where? On God's farm or in His garden. And who is that? The Corinthians, from whom now God expects fruit (Gal.5:22,23).

Suddenly Paul changed the figure, from agriculture to architecture. The Corinthians, thought of in a different way, were God's building. *Cf.*#1481 for all of the references and a great deal of valuable preaching and teaching material. Paul pursues this figure of speech through verse 15.

The γεώργιον figure recalls John 15, where the sequence is "fruit," "more fruit" and "much fruit." (John 15:1,2,5).

The οἰκοδομή figure recalls Ephesians 2:20-22 and Mt.16:18.

Verse 10 - "According to the grace of God which is given unto me, as a wise masterbuilder I have laid the foundation and another buildeth thereon. But let every man take heed how he buildeth thereon."

Κατὰ τὴν χάριν τοῦ θεοῦ τὴν δοθεῖσάν μοι ὡς σοφὸς ἀρχιτέκτων θεμέλιον ἔθηκα, ἄλλος δὲ ἐποικοδομεῖ. ἕκαστος δὲ βλεπέτω πῶς ἐποικοδομεῖ.

"According to the commission of God given to me, like a skilled master builder I laid a foundation, and another man is building upon it. Let each man take care how he builds upon it." . . . RSV

Κατὰ (preposition with the accusative, standard) 98.

τὴν (acc.sing.fem.of the article in agreement with χάριν) 9.

χάριν (acc.sing.fem.of χάρις, standard) 1700.

τοῦ (gen.sing.masc.of the article in agreement with θεοῦ) 9.

θεοῦ (gen.sing.masc.of θεός, description) 124.

τὴν (acc.sing.fem.of the article in agreement with χάριν) 9.

δοθεῖσάν (aor.pass.part.acc.sing.fem.of δίδωμι, adjectival, ascriptive, predicate position in agreement with χάριν) 362.

μοι (dat.sin g.masc .of ἐγώ, indirect object of δοθεῖσάν) 123.

ὡς (particle introducing a comparative clause) 128.

σοφὸς (nom.sing.masc.of σόφος, in agreement with ἀρχιτέκτων) 949.

#4116 ἀρχιτέκτων (nom.sing.masc.of ἀρχιτέκτων, comparative clause).

King James Version

master builder - 1 Cor.3:10.

Revised Standard Version

master builder - 1 Cor.3:10.

Meaning: A combination of ἀρχή (#1285) and τέκτων (#1097). Hence, an architect; a master builder; a supervisor of building construction. Metaphorically - Paul, as a preacher of the gospel working for the Lord in teaching and preaching, in supervision of the building process of the Christian life - 1 Cor.3:10.

θεμέλιον (acc.sing.masc.of θεμέλιος, direct object of ἔθηκα) 2143.

ἔθηκα (1st.per.sing.1st.aor.act.ind.of τίθημι, culminative) 455.

ἄλλος (nom.sing.masc.of ἄλλος, subject of ἐποικοδομεῖ) 198.

δὲ (continuative conjunction) 11.

#4117 ἐποικοδομεῖ (3d.per.sing.pres.act.ind.of ἐποικοδομέω, customary).

King James Version

build thereon - 1 Cor.3:10.
build thereupon - 1 Cor.3:10,14.

build up on - Col.2:7; Jude 20.
build upon - 1 Cor.3:12; Eph.2:20.

Revised Standard Version

build upon - 1 Cor.3:10,10; Eph.2:20.
build on - 1 Cor.3:12,14.
build up - Col.2:7; Jude 20.

Meaning: A combination of ἐπί (#47) and οἰκοδομέω (#694). Hence, to build upon; to place a superstructure on a foundation. Metaphorically, of a Christian, having accepted Christ (θεμέλιος), who now goes on to build a life of ethical achievement; to grow in grace - 1 Cor.3:10,10,12,14; with reference to the body of true believers built up as a building (Christ) in a figure similar to that of a human body (1 Cor.12:12; Rom.12:4) in Eph.2:20. In Col.2:7 there is a double figure of speech - the horticultural and the architechural. In Jude 20, the Christian builds himself up upon the foundation, which is Christ.

ἕκαστος (nom.sing.masc.of ἕκαστος, subject of βλεπέτω) 1217.
δὲ (adversative conjunction) 11.
βλεπέτω (3d.per.sing.pres.act.impv.of βλέπω, command) 499.
πῶς (interrogative adverb) 627.
ἐποικοδομεῖ (3d.per.sing.pres.act.ind.of ἐποικοδομέω, futuristic) 4117.

Translation - "*In keeping with the gift of God which has been given to me, as a wise architect I have laid a foundation; but another is going to erect a superstructure upon it. But let every man be careful how he builds upon it.*"

Comment: κατὰ . . . μοι "In keeping with God's commission to me" (Acts 9:15; Gal.1:15,16). Comparative ὡς as Paul pursues the figure of speech, which began with οἰκοδομή ἐστε of verse 9.

Paul is now a carpenter instead of a planter (verse 6). As such he knows that a good building begins with a foundation. *Cf.* 2 Tim.2:19; Rom.15:20; Eph.2:20; Heb.6:1; Lk.6:48; 1 Tim.6:19. Once the foundation is laid, the superstructure becomes the responsibility of another, who is charged to be careful how he plans to build it.

Some commentators believe that Paul is still talking about another preacher who comes in to teach the recently regenerated child of God and that what follows in verses 11-15 refers to the character of the ministry of the preachers and teachers who follow. Such a view is possible, but the child of God himself, who has accepted Christ, the foundation (verse 11) is basicly responsible for what he does with his life after salvation and before glorification.

The reference to the two workers, working together under God, in planting and watering, ceased with the end of the agricultural analogy in verse 9, clause 2. When Paul changed the figure to architecture in verse 9, clause 3, he speaks only of himself with no further reference to Apollos. ἄλλος refers to the believer, as does ἕκαστος. Paul does not hesitate long to tell us who the foundation of the building represents in the analogy.

Verse 11 - "*For other foundation can no man lay than that is laid, which is Jesus Christ.*"

θεμέλιον γὰρ ἄλλον οὐδεὶς δύναται θεῖναι παρὰ τὸν κείμενον, ὅς ἐστιν Ἰησοῦς Χριστός.

"*For no other foundation can any one lay than that which is laid, which is Jesus Christ.*" . . . RSV

θεμέλιον (acc.sing.masc.of θεμέλιος, direct object of θεῖναι) 2143.

γὰρ (causal conjunction) 105.

ἄλλον (acc.sing.masc.of ἄλλος, in agreement with θεμέλιον) 198.

οὐδεὶς (nom.sing.masc.of οὐδείς, subject of δύναται) 446.

δύναται (3d.per.sing.pres.ind.of δύναμαι, aoristic) 289.

θεῖναι (2d.aor.act.inf.of τίθημι, complementary) 455.

παρὰ (preposition with the accusative, with comparative forms) 154.

τὸν (acc.sing.masc.of the article in agreement with κείμενον) 9.

κείμενον (pres.part.acc.sing.masc.of κεῖμαι, substantival, comparison) 295.

ὅς (nom.sing.masc.of ὅς, relative pronoun, subject of ἐστιν) 65.

ἐστιν (3d.per.sing.pres.ind.of εἰμί, static) 86.

Ἰησοῦς (nom.sing.masc.of Ἰησοῦς, predicate nominative) 3.

Χριστός (nom.sing.masc.of Χριστός, apposition) 4.

Translation - "*Because no one is able to lay another foundation like the one now laid, which is Jesus Christ.*"

Comment: The verse applies especially to the first clause of verse 10. As a wise contractor Paul laid the best possible foundation; in fact it is the only one that will do. No man can devise and lay another that will meet the need. The builder is seeking to build a building that will be viable. No superstructure, however strongly constructed can survive if the foundation upon which it rests is faulty. The foundation which Paul has laid is of sterling quality. It is Jesus Christ. There is none to compare with Him. *Cf.* παρά with the accusative when the context indicates comparison in Heb.1:4; 2:7; 3:3; 9:23; 11:11; 12:24; Lk.13:2,4; 1 Cor.3:11 and Rom.14:5.

The Christian is under great obligation to build the superstructure of his new life in a way commensurate with the quality of the foundation. What we build atop the foundation should match the foundation in quality. Indeed, it can, since the foundation, Who is Jesus Christ, is reproduced by the Holy Spirit in the believer, if only the Holy Spirit is given the opportunity. (Gal.5:16; Eph.4:30; Gal.2:20; 2 Cor.3:18). The foundation is competent to support the house. He is also capable of determining the quality of the building materials and supervising the carpentry by which they are put together. Our Lord is the embodiment of God's revelation to the Old Testament fathers, through the Old Testament prophets (Heb.1:1-3). He is also Ὁ Λόγος by whom God has spoken unto us in the last days. He did not complete the revelation of Himself while He was here, but He promised that the Holy Spirit would complete it and make clear to the Apostles and the early church "all the truth" - ἐν τῇ ἀληθείᾳ πάσῃ (John 16:12-15). This promise was fulfilled as the Holy Spirit directed the writing of the New

Testament in the first century of the Christian era. The revelation became complete as the Apostle John wrote his epistles and his gospel. With a completed revelation gifts of the Holy Spirit that are concerned with imparting special knowledge were no longer needed and were phased out. *cf.* our discussion of this matter in comment upon 1 Cor.13:8. No one since the first century has the supernatural power of the Holy Spirit to "prophesy" or to impart "knowledge" since all of the forthtelling and revelation of knowledge which the Holy Spirit has to give at this time has already been given in the Greek New Testament. Mormons and Pentecostalists who lay claim to special gifts which they call charismatic, presume to occupy the role of special prophets and knowledge dispensers, as though the Holy Spirit had not completed the revelation of Ὁ Λόγος. The prophetic gift and the gift of knowledge have been phased out (1 Cor.13:8). *Cf.* the meaning of καταργέω (#2500) and apply it in all the places where the Holy Spirit has used it.

The rise in the last century of "prophets" and "knowledge dispensers" such as the Millerites, Ellen White, Charles Russell, Mary Baker Eddy, Joseph Smith and the Pentecostal cults, are a threat to New Testament exegesis, for who would wish to spend his time in a painstaking exegesis of a document which is not yet finished? If I were not assured by John 16:12-15 and 1 Cor.13:8 that the Holy Spirit has completed the revelation of Jesus Christ, and that it is contained in full in the Greek New Testament, I would wait until He has written the last word. No serious student of literature attempts to evaluate what is said until he comes to the end of the piece. The Holy Spirit has already revealed all that He has to say and it is all the truth about Jesus Christ that God wants us to know at this time. The sentence is finished and the period is in place at the end. I am not therefore interested in anything that cultists have to say, be it something excavated out of the hills of New York, produced in Brooklyn or translated from the unintelligible mumbo-jumbo of the holy rollers.

There is no promise in the New Testament that the signs which the Holy Spirit gave to the first century Christians would "follow." There is no promise that a Christian can survive snake-bite or that he can drink deadly poison and escape the consequences. There is no statement that water baptism is essential to salvation. Those verses are found in the last twelve verses of Mark's gospel and are clearly not a part of the original text.

The figure which Paul uses here - that of building a superstructure atop a foundation recalls Eph.2:20-22 with its added information that Christ is not only the foundation but He is also the cornerstone. Every good carpenter knows the function of the cornerstone. It dictates the angle at which every other component part of the building is added. This is why the try square is an indispensable part of the builders tool box. *Cf.* comment on Eph.2:20-22.

Cf. comment on Mt.7:24-29. NonChristian institutions are really antiChristian institutions (Mt.12:30), and are destined to fail and fall, despite their protestations with reference to ideals, to which they are not logically entitled. If only our Lord Jesus Christ can undergird a viable superstructure, then the United Nations cannot, nor can any other nonChristian institution. They represent the futile attempts of depraved men to build a peaceful and just world society independent of God. Witness Babel. God indeed has confounded our means of communication. It is with some glee, ill-disguised behind a countenance that tries to effect dismay that the existentialist tells us that no one can communicate anything meaningful to anyone else. Every man is a slave who has been shaped by his own environment, which is different from that of everyone else. Hence his understanding of words, derived as they are from his own set of unique experiences, is not the same as the understanding of the one who is speaking to him. Thus there can be no distinction between subject and object. DesCartes, who thought that he knew what he was talking about, was all wrong.

No matter! In a random universe where there are no absolutes nobody knows what he is talking about anyway so the breakdown of communication is no great loss. One could only wish that since they admit that they are not saying anything, they would stop talking, since the noise pollution problem is getting out of hand.

Faced with the problem of building a superstructure on the only good foundation, the Christian is presented with list of available building materials in

Verse 12 - "Now if any man build upon this foundation gold, silver, precious stones, wood, hay, stubble."

εἰ δέ τις ἐποικοδομεῖ ἐπὶ τὸν θεμέλιον χρυσόν, ἄργυρον, λίθους τιμίους, ξύλα, χόρτον, καλάμην,

"Now if any one builds on the foundation with gold, silver, precious stones, wood, hay, stubble — " . . . RSV

εἰ (conditional particle in a first-class condition) 337.

δέ (explanatory conjunction) 11.

τις (nom.sing.masc.of τις, indefinite pronoun, subject of ἐποικοδομεῖ) 486.

ἐποικοδομεῖ (3d.per.sing.pres.act.ind.of ἐποικοδομέω, first-class condition) 4117.

ἐπὶ (preposition with the accusative of extent) 47,

τὸν (acc.sing.masc.of the article in agreement with θεμέλιον) 9.

θεμέλιον (acc.sing.masc.of θεμέλιος, extent) 2143.

χρυσόν (acc.sing.masc.of χρυσός, direct object of ἐποικοδομεῖ) 192.

ἄργυρον (acc.sing.masc.of ἄργυρος, direct object of ἐποικοδομεῖ) 860.

λίθους (acc.pl.masc.of λίθος, direct object of ἐποικοδομεῖ) 290.

τιμίους (acc.pl.masc.of τίμιος, in agreement with λίθους) 3070.

ξύλα (acc.pl.neut.of ξύλον, direct object of ἐποικοδομεῖ) 1590.

χόρτον (acc.sing.masc.of χόρτος, direct object of ἐποικοδομεῖ) 632.

#4118 καλάμην (acc.sing.fem.of καλάμη, direct object of ἐποικοδομεῖ).

King James Version

stubble - 1 Cor.3:12.

Revised Standard Version

stubble - 1 Cor.3:12.

Meaning: Cf. κάλαμος (#910). The stalk of a flower or plant after the fruit or grain has been harvested. Stubble. Differs from χόρτος (#632) which is the plant as it grows in the field. Highly destructible and hence unacceptable building material - 1 Cor.3:12.

Translation - "Now whether anyone builds upon the foundation gold, silver, precious stones, scrap lumber, hay, stubble . . . "

Comment: δὲ is explanatory. εἰ in the first-class condition has the present indicative in the protasis and the future indicative, in verse 13, in the apodosis. There is uncertainty as to who "any man" is and also as to the building materials which he will choose, but there is no uncertainty that his work will be made manifest in judgment. Whoever it is (which is doubtful) and whatever he chooses, whether good material or bad, (which is also doubtful), the conclusion is not in doubt. The work of every Christian, from the time when he is saved until his death and/or rapture and the judgment seat of Christ, will be made known - a sobering thought to say the least!! In that day the skeletons will come out of their closets.

The six building materials divide naturally into two groups of three each, which differ in terms of intrinsic value and inflammability. Gold, silver and precious stones are relatively costly and fire resistant. Scrap lumber, hay and stubble are relatively worthless and highly inflammable. The context (verses 13-15) places more emphasis upon the latter distinction than upon the former, though the former distinction is there. Paul could have chosen materials that are noninflammable and worthless to replace the gold, silver and precious stones, if he had not wished us to see both distinctions.

Thus two points are made: (1) the fruits of the Spirit, those God inspired activities, are both precious in terms of intrinsic worth, and (2) they are also of a character that will abide the testing fires of a discriminatory God (Heb.12:29).

Another fact is clear: we are about to examine the experiences of two regenerate persons, not a saved man and a lost man. Both of these people have the only permanent foundation Who is Christ (verse 11). They differ in the quality of their superstructures. They are alike in their foundations. Both are saved. One lives a victorious Christian life. The other lives a defeated life. One is πνευματικός (#3791); the other is σαρκικός (#4058). Neither is ψυχικός (#4112). The question of ultimate salvation is not therefore in view. Let the Arminian take note. One will receive a reward in addition to salvation, which is never a reward but the gift of God's grace. The other will suffer the loss of reward, but he too will be saved, since his salvation depends upon God's covenant with Christ and not upon human works, either before or after salvation.

The passage thus forbids two erroneous views - one promoted by Arminians and the other by Antinomians. Antinomians are Calvinists who teach that since salvation is by grace, there is no penalty at the judgment for the carnal (σαρκικός) Christian. This the passage before us denies (verse 15). Arminians teach that salvation is a matter of faith plus good works and thus that Christians, once regenerated, can sin so grievously as to be ultimately lost. This view also the passage denies (verse 15). Thus the middleground truth is that regenerated Christians (really there is no other kind) can never be lost, regardless of the shabby character of their superstructure since at least they have Christ as the foundation, but that God will hold each of us to strict account with regard to how we build upon Christ, and that those who build unwisely are going to suffer grievous loss of reward, though not of salvation. This position is as close as we can bring together the Arminian who rejects the eternal decrees of God and the Antinomian who presumes upon God's grace at the expense of His holiness. Calvinism, which teaches the high desirability of the Spirit-filled life of the believer, fits all of the requirements of the passage before us.

The judgment of believers' works is coming. This is the thought of

Verse 13 - "Every man's work shall be made manifest: for the day shall declare it, because it shall be revealed by fire; and the fire shall try every man's work of what sort it is."

ἑκάστου τὸ ἔργον φανερὸν γενήσεται, ἡ γὰρ ἡμέρα δηλώσει. ὅτι ἐν πυρὶ ἀποκαλύπτεται, καὶ ἑκάστου τὸ ἔργον ὁποῖόν ἐστιν τὸ πῦρ (αὐτὸ) δοκιμάσει.

"each man's work will become manifest; for the Day will disclose it, because it will be revealed with fire, and the fire will test what sort of work each. one has done." . . . RSV

ἑκάστου (gen.sing.masc.of ἕκαστος, possession) 1217.
τὸ (nom.sing.neut.of the article in agreement with ἔργον) 9.
ἔργον (nom.sing.neut.of ἔργον, subject of γενήσεται) 460.
φανερὸν (nom.sing.neut.of φανερός, predicate adjective) 981.
γενήσεται (3d.per.sing.fut.ind.of γίνομαι, predictive) 113.
ἡ (nom.sing.fem.of the article in agreement with ἡμέρα) 9.
γὰρ (causal conjunction) 105.
ἡμέρα (nom.sing.fem.of ἡμέρα, subject of δηλώσει) 135.
δηλώσει (3d.per.sing.fut.act.ind.of δηλόω, predictive) 4102.
ὅτι (conjunction introducing a subordinate causal clause) 211.
ἐν (preposition with the locative, place) 80.
πυρὶ (loc.sing.neut.of πῦρ, place and means) 298.
ἀποκαλύπτεται (3d.per.sing.pres.pass.ind.of ἀποκαλύπτω, predictive) 886.
καὶ (continuative conjunction) 14.
ἑκάστου (gen.sing.masc.of ἕκαστος, possession) 1217.
τὸ (acc.sing.neut.of the article in agreement with ἔργον) 9.
ἔργον (acc.sing.neut.of ἔργον, direct object of δοκιμάσει) 460.
ὁποῖόν (acc.sing.neut.of ὁποῖος, relative qualitative pronoun, in agreement with ἔργον) 3671.
ἐστιν (3d.per.sing.pres.ind.of εἰμί static) 86.
τὸ (nom.sing.neut.of the article in agreement with πῦρ) 9.
πῦρ (nom.sing.neut.of πῦρ, subject of δοκιμάσει) 298.
(αὐτὸ) (nom.sing.neut.of αὐτός, subject of ἐστιν) 16.
δοκιμάσει (3d.per.sing.fut.act.ind.of δοκιμάζω, predictive) 2493.

Translation - "*The work of each will be revealed, because the day will reveal it, because it will be analyzed by fire, and the fire will evaluate the work of each man to ascertain its quality.*"

Comment: Goodspeed, Weymouth and Montgomery construe ἡ ἡμέρα as the subject of ἀποκαλύπτεται. I have taken τὸ ἔργον as the subject, both of ἀποκαλύπτεται and γενήσεται. Thus Goodspeed has ". . . for the day will break in fire." Weymouth - ". . . because that day is to reveal itself in fire" and Montgomery has, ". . . for it dawned in fire." These translations are grammatically possible, but the context seems to me to be against it. It is not the day that is revealed by fire, but the work of the Christian. To be sure the day of the Second Coming of our Lord will be characterized by fire (2 Thess.1:7) but that fire is directed against the unsaved, whereas Paul is speaking here about the fire that is to be used to analyze the quality of the work of the Christian. It will destroy the scrap lumber (plural in ξύλα), hay and stubble, but it will serve to reveal the gold, silver and precious stones which have nothing to fear from its discrimination (2 Cor.5:10; Rev.11:18; Lk.14:14, etc.).

Note that ἀποκαλύπτεται is present tense and represents a general statement that materials such as are described in verse 12 are revealed by means of fire, a fact scarcely to be denied. Paul seems to be explaining the elements in his analogy. If one is in doubt as to whether his superstructure, the product of his service for the Lord, since the day of his conversion, is gold, silver and precious stones, or wood, hay and stubble, the proper test is the attempt to burn it. The fire will seek out and destroy that which can be burned and that which remains will have passed the fiery test. Thus on that day the disclosure will be made, as the fire evaluates (#2493) the work of every Christian as to its quality. ὁποῖόν, the relative pronoun is qualitative, not indefinite (*cf.* #3671).

Note that all of the verbs which relate to the actual qualitative test are future. Only ἀποκαλύπτεται is present. Our superstructure will be made manifest. The day will declare it, not to physical sight but to mental perception (#4102). It will be analyzed by fire. All of this is future. The passage does not say that every Christian at the judgment seat of Christ is to be treated to a vivid visual playback, replete with sound effects, of the sins of every other Christian. What is clear is that on that day each child of God is going to reflect clearly and sadly on the folly of yielding time, talent and strength to the implementation of those desires described as σαρκικός (#4058).

Dr. Will Houghton once wrote, "Teach us the folly of all waste to see." If this prayer is not answered before, it will certainly be answered on that day. Every Christian will see the discriminating fires of God's holiness seek out and destroy the wood, hay and stubble in the superstructure which he built upon the matchless foundation, Christ Jesus.

Some Christians will have the joy of seeing most of their superstructure survive unscathed, since gold, silver and precious stones will not burn. They are described in

Verse 14 - "*If any man's work abide which he hath built thereupon, he shall receive a reward.*"

εἴ τινος τὸ ἔργον μενεῖ ὃ ἐποικοδόμησεν, μισθὸν λήμφεται.

"If the work which any man has built on the foundation survives, he will receive a reward." . . . RSV

εἴ (conditional particle in a first-class condition) 337.
τινος (gen.sing.masc.of τις, indefinite pronoun, possession) 486.
τὸ (nom.sing.neut.of the article in agreement with ἔργον) 9.
ἔργον (nom.sing.neut.of ἔργον, subject of μενεῖ) 460.
μενεῖ (3d.per.sing.pres.act.ind.of μένω, first-class condition) 864.
ὃ (nom.sing.neut.of ὅς, relative pronoun, subject of ἐποικοδόμησεν) 65.
ἐποικοδόμησεν (3d.per.sing.aor.act.ind.of ἐποικοδομέω, culminative) 4117.
μισθὸν (acc.sing.masc.of μισθός, direct object of λήμφεται) 441.
λήμφεται (3d.per.sing.fut.pass.ind.of λαμβάνω, predictive) 533.

Translation - "If the work of any man abides which he has built he will receive a reward."

Comment: εἴ and the indicative in the protasis and the future indicative in the apodosis, indicates a first-class condition. The assumption is that the condition in the protasis is true. Paul is assuming that at least one, or perhaps a few Christians are going to approach the judgment seat of Christ with a record of building out of gold, silver and precious stones.

The verse describes the Christian who lived a victorious life in Christ and built (to carry out the analogy) out of gold, silver and precious stones. The fire will not be able to burn it away. It will stand the test. The result? A reward. Is this reward salvation? By no means. The salvation issue was settled when he got the foundation (verses 10,11). If gold, silver and precious stones merit the reward of salvation, how is the man of verse 15 saved? The reward is a bonus, given over and above salvation. It is contingent upon good works, whereas the salvation is contingent only upon faith. *Cf.*#441 for μισθός in the sense of rewards in heaven to the "over and above" Christian.

Who will receive them? And for what? And when? And from whom? There is much preaching and teaching material here. Note especially Rev.11:18 and Rev.22:12. Note also Luke 14:12-14. *Cf.*#2529.

How can the Christian build only from gold, silver and precious stones? *Cf.* 1 Cor.6:19,20; Phil.1:6; Eph.2:10; Heb.13:20,21; Gal.5:16,22,23; Rom.6:11; Gal.2:20 etc. Only what the Holy Spirit does through the believer will withstand the fiery test. The answer then is in one word - YIELD!

Verse 15, less happily, described the backslidden (σαρκικός) Christian at the judgment seat of Christ.

Verse 15 - "If any man's work shall be burned, he shall suffer loss, but he himself shall be saved; yet so as by fire."

εἴ τινος τὸ ἔργον κατακαήσεται, ζημιωθήσεται, αὐτὸς δὲ σωθήσεται, οὕτως δὲ ὡς διὰ πυρός.

"If any man's work is burned up, he will suffer loss, though he himself will be saved, but only as through fire." . . . RSV

εἰ (conditional particle in a first-class condition) 337.

τινος (gen.sing.masc.of τις, indefinite pronoun, possession) 486.

τὸ (nom.sing.neut.of the article in agreement with ἔργον) 9.

ἔργον (nom.sing.neut.of ἔργον, subject of κατακαήσεται) 460.

κατακαήσεται (3d.per.sing.2d.fut.pass.ind.of κατακαίω, first-class condition) 314.

ζημιωθήσεται (3d.per.sing.fut.pass.ind.of ζημιόω, predictive) 1215.

αὐτὸς (nom.sing.masc.of αὐτός, intensive, predicate position, subject of σωθήσεται) 16.

δὲ (adversative conjunction) 11.

σωθήσεται (3d.per.sing.fut.pass.ind.of σώζω, predictive) 109.

οὕτως (demonstrative adverb) 74.

δὲ (adversative conjunction) 11.

ὡς (particle introducing a comparative clause) 128.

διὰ (preposition with the genitive of description) 118.

πυρός (gen.sing.neut.of πῦρ, description) 298.

Translation - "If the work of any man is burned he will suffer loss, but he himself will be saved, if only as through fire."

Comment: Another first-class condition as in verse 14. The 2d.future passive is of course only a future middle with an aoristic action. The wood, hay and stubble will yield itself (succumb) to the fire and be destroyed. The result is that that Christian will lose the rewards which otherwise he could have had, had he yielded himself to the Holy Spirit.

The cost of spending scarce resources - time, money, strength, talent, technical equiptment - in the service of the flesh is the opportunity cost of foregoing the chance to spend those same resources (which can only be spent once) in the service of the Lord, which service, had it been forthcoming, would have yielded gold, silver and precious stones. The loss suffered is a loss by default.

Example: the nation's economy that operates at a $100 billion contractionary gap, loses by default the $100 billion in goods and services which would have been produced at full employment. Every resource in the life of the child of God spent on wood, hay and stubble could have been spent in activities of gold, silver and precious stones. In that day many of us will reflect upon what we might have done for Christ with those scarce resources which we spent outside the perfect will of God.

There is no Christian whose entire superstructure is all of one or all of the other. No backslidden child of God has been so defeated as to have built only with wood, hay and stubble and with no gold, silver and precious stones. A cup of cold water in Jesus' name is worth something (Mk.9:41). Conversely no victorious Spirit-filled Christian has gone through life sinlessly (1 John 1:8). The entire matter is relative.

But though he suffers grievous loss the carnal Christian will be saved, thanks to his foundation, Christ Jesus. Note that αὐτός in the predicate position, is intensive. "He *himself* will be saved." Note also the adverstive δὲ. οὕτως δὲ ὡς διὰ πυρός - "even though he wades through the fires of God's disapproval upon his works." But God approves of his faith, since it was the basis for his salvation which is God's gift to him (Eph.2:8,9). The Christian of verse 15 lives for Eph.2:8,9, but not for verse 10. The Christian of verse 14 lives for Eph.2:8,9 and 10.

Those who reject what Calvinists call the perseverance (preservation) of the saints, the last point in the TULIP, must rethink their position in the light of this passage. Similarly, Antinomians, who carry Calvinism to presumptuous extremes and look lightly upon sin in the believer, must also rethink their position. God indeed saves those whom he saves eternally, but He will hold all members of His body to strict ethical account of our stewardship. There is no sin in the life of the believer that will not exact a fearful toll. The Calvinist who has been defeated too many times and is bitterly aware of his failure to honor Christ in all that he does will not be inclined to attack the Arminian, who, though he may not understand fully his position in Christ, nevertheless majors on the subjective side of the salvation coin. If salvation is as good as the Calvinists say it is (and it is) it is so good that it cannot make room for the sins of the Antinomians. And if salvation demands my sinless perfection, as some Arminians affirm, then that which demands so much must have a great deal to offer - perhaps more than the Arminian realizes.

The victorious life is not unattainable if the Christian keeps in mind the glorious truth of verse 16 and also the stern warning of verse 17.

Verse 16 - "Know ye not that ye are the temple of God, and that the Spirit of God dwelleth in you?"

οὐκ οἴδατε ὅτι ναὸς θεοῦ ἐστε καὶ τὸ πνεῦμα τοῦ θεοῦ οἰκεῖ ἐν ὑμῖν;

"Do you not know that you are God's temple and that God's Spirit dwells in you?" . . . RSV

οὐκ (negative particle with the indicative in rhetorical question expecting an affirmative reply) 130.

οἴδατε (2d.per.pl.perf.act.ind.of οἶδα, intensive) 144b.

ὅτι (conjunction introducing an object clause in indirect discourse) 211.

ναὸς (nom.sing.masc.of ναός, predicate nominative) 1447.

θεοῦ (gen.sing.masc.of θεός, description) 124.

ἐστε (2d.per.pl.pres.ind.of εἰμί, static) 86.

καὶ (continuative conjunction) 14.

τὸ (nom.sing.neut.of the article in agreement with πνεῦμα) 9.

πνεῦμα (nom.sing.neut.of πνεῦμα, subject of οἰκεῖ) 83.

τοῦ (gen.sing.masc.of the article in agreement with θεοῦ) 9.

θεοῦ (gen.sing.masc.of θεός, description) 124.

οἰκεῖ (3d.per.sing.pres.act.ind.of οἰκέω, static) 3926.

ἐν (preposition with the locative of place with plural pronouns) 80.

ὑμῖν (loc.pl.masc.of σύ, place) 104.

Translation - "You have learned by this time have you not that you are a divine temple and that the Spirit of God is living in you?"

Comment: The question with οὐκ and the indicative is rhetorical and expects "Yes" in reply. The perfect tense in οἴδατε places their understanding of the fact that they were "a divine temple" (ναὸς θεοῦ) in the past. The Corinthians should have learned that long before. Paul may be using a "tongue in cheek" approach. The ὅτι clause is indirect discourse. Note that ναὸς θεοῦ is anarthrous. Hence the translation, "a temple." No Christian is the only temple of God. When the genitive without the article follows a noun it is descriptive, not possessive.

Note that the Holy Spirit, Who is here called "the Spirit of God" - τὸ πνεῦμα τοῦ θεοῦ - is identified as God since He is the One Who lives in the divine temple. His residence in the body of the believer is continuous (present tense in οἰκεῖ). *Cf.* comment on Rom.8:9,11. Paul repeats this in 1 Cor.6:19; 2 Cor.6:16,16, always with the same inferential thrust. In view of the fact that the Holy Spirit, Who is God, Who convicted the believer of sin, righteousness and judgment (John 16:7-11), Who incorporated him into the Body of Christ (1 Cor.12:13), Who leads the believer into all truth (John 16:12-15), Who produces His fruits in the life of the believer (Gal.5:22,23) and Who guarantees the resurrection of the body of the believer (Rom.8:11) is living in the physical body of the believer should motivate the Christian to a life of obedience to the will of God. We can grieve Him, but we cannot grieve Him away (Eph.4:30).

But there is a difference between indwelling and infilling, between resident and regnant, between residing and presiding. He indwells and resides in us and He wants to infill and preside in us. If He directs our walk we will not fulfill the desires of the flesh (Gal.5:16) and there will be little "scrap lumber, hay and stubble" in the superstructure of our Christian life.

An honored guest in one's home is to have every reasonable request granted. The deference which the host pays to his guest is measured in direct ratio to the guest's prestige. The Holy Spirit is God! What greater prestige is there? Should not our divine Guest be allowed to infill, reign and preside over everything in the home? Note the benefits of His residence in Rom.8:9. We sustain a new relationship to God described as being "not in the flesh but in the Spirit" and in Rom.8:11 we have the assurance that God will not allow the residence of the Holy Spirit to be forever defeated in death. Will the Holy Spirit permit the "divine temple" in which He has lived to be forever subject to the biodegradability of the tomb? Μὴ γένοιτο. No way! Thus the resurrection of the physical body is a fruit of the Holy Spirit's residence (1 Cor.15:51,52). It is unthinkable that, with advantages like that, the Christian will prostitute his body to the slavery of the flesh. But we do, but only in times when we forget that our bodies are "divine temples" and that the Holy Spirit of God dwells in us.

The sanctity of the body of the Christian is so important that its defilement may result in its destruction. This is the stern warning of

Verse 17 - "If any man defile the temple of God him shall God destroy: for the temple of God is holy, which temple ye are."

εἴ τις τὸν ναὸν τοῦ θεοῦ φθείρει, φθερεῖ τοῦτον ὁ θεός. ὁ γὰρ ναὸς τοῦ θεοῦ ἅγιος ἐστιν, οἵτινές ἐστε ὑμεῖς.

"*If any one destroys God's temple, God will destroy him. For God's temple is holy, and that temple you are.*" . . . RSV

εἰ (conditional particle in a first-class condition) 337.

τις (nom.sing.masc.of τις, subject of φθείρει) 486.

τὸν (acc.sing.masc.of the article in agreement with ναὸν) 9.

ναὸν (acc.sing.masc.of ναός, direct object of φθείρει) 1447.

τοῦ (gen.sing.masc.of the article in agreement with θεοῦ) 9.

θεοῦ (gen.sing.masc.of θεός, possession) 124.

#4119 φθείρει (3d.per.sing.pres.act.ind.of φθείρω, first-class condition, present progressive).

King James Version

corrupt - 1 Cor.15:33; 2 Cor.7:2; 11:3; Rev.19:2.
defile - 1 Cor.3:17.
destroy - 1 Cor.3:17.
corrupt one's self - Jude 10.
be corrupt - Eph.4:22.
perish - 2 Pet.2:12.

Revised Standard Version

destroy - 1 Cor.3:17,17; Jude 10; 2 Pet.2:12.
ruin - 1 Cor.15:33.
corrupt - 2 Cor.7:2; Rev.19:2.
led astray - 1 Cor.11:3.
corrupt (poet.) - Eph.4:22.

Meaning: To corrupt; destroy. The Jews used the word with reference to the Temple if profaned in any way. Moulton & Milligan, "For the metaph. sense "corrupt," "injure," as in 1 Cor.3:17, *al.*, we may point to the common clause in marriage contracts forbidding the wife φθείρειν τὸν κοινὸν οἶκον (P Tebt I. 104₂₉ (B.C. 92), BGU IV. 1050₂₂ (time of Augustus), P Oxy III. 497₄ (early ii/A.D.), *asl.*): cf. 1 Cor.3:17.

"A literal sense is seen in certain nursing contracts, where provision is made against the nurse's "spoiling" her milk, e.g. BGU IV. 1058₂₉ (B.C.13) μὴ φθίρουσαν τὸ γάλα. In P Strass I. 24₁₅ (A.D. 118) the pass. ἐφθάρη(σ)α(ν) is used of the destruction of cattle. Cf.also P Cairo Zen I. 59037₇ (B.C. 258-7) where a man is described as ἐν Ἀλεξανδρείαι φθειρόμενος, "in Alexandria wasting his time." To expend bodily functions in sin - 1 Cor.3:17a; with reference to physical destruction of the body in divine judgment - 1 Cor.3:17b; 2 Pet.2:12; in an ethical sense - 2 Cor.7:2; with reference to psychological corruption - 2 Cor.11:3; morals - 1 Cor.15:33; of the unregenerate - Eph.4:22; Jude 10; with reference to the corruption of the earth - Rev.19:2.

φθερεῖ (3d.per.sing.fut.act.ind.of φθείρω, predictive) 4119.

τοῦτον (acc.sing.masc.of οὗτος, direct object of φθειρεῖ) 93.

ὁ (nom.sing.masc.of the article in agreement with θεός) 9.

θεός (nom.sing.masc.of θεός, subject of φθειρεῖ) 124.

ὁ (nom.sing.masc.of the article in agreement with ναὸς) 9.

γὰρ (causal conjunction) 105.

ναὸς (nom.sing.masc.of ναός, subject of ἐστιν) 1447.

τοῦ (gen.sing.masc.of the article in agreement with θεοῦ) 9.

θεοῦ (gen.sing.masc.of θεός, possession) 124.

ἅγιος (nom.sing.masc.of ἅγιος, predicate adjective) 84.

ἐστιν (3d.per.sing.pres.ind.of εἰμί, static) 86.

οἵτινες (nom.pl.masc.of ὅστις, predicate nominative) 163.

ἐστε (2d.per.pl.pres.ind.of εἰμί, static) 86.

ὑμεῖς (nom.pl.masc.of σύ, subject of ἐστε) 104.

Translation - "If any man profanes the temple of God, God will destroy it; because the temple of God is holy, which you are."

Comment: Whatever φθείρω (#4119) means, it is used here in two different senses. If the Christian profanes his body and thus destroys its usefulness to the Holy Spirit, Who must live in it, by yielding it to sin (Rom.6:13), which sinful use may lead to an actual physical corruption and disintegration (*e.g.* addiction to alcohol and drugs, illicit sex and venereal disease, *et al.*) God will destroy it. That is, God will complete the destruction which the unfaithful Christian has begun. If God cannot use the Christian's body for His glory, as the Holy Spirit indwells it, as in a temple, He will move to destroy its usefulness to Satan. Sin in the life of the believer profanes the temple of the Holy Spirit. In advanced stages, sin not only profanes, but also corrupts - even to the point of physical disintegration, which is death. The wages of sin is death for the unbeliever in both physical and spiritual senses. For the believer the wages of sin may be physical death.

The antecedent of τοῦτον from a strictly grammatical point of view can be either τις or ναόν, since both are masculine gender and singular number, as is τοῦτον. But other Scriptures forbid the destruction of the soul and personality of the Christian, though other Scriptures teach the destruction of the Christian's body in cases where he continues to refuse to yield it to the Holy Spirit. Thus as an exegete, not as a grammarian, we opt for the view that τοῦτον means the body, not the Christian himself. *Cf.* 1 Cor.5:1-5; 1 John 5:16; Acts 5:1-11, in which latter passage the "corruption" was not physical but psychological. *Cf.* also 2 Cor.7:2; 11:3; 1 Cor.15:33; Eph.4:22; Jude 10; Rev.19:2.

This teaching that when the Christian sins he is in danger of divine judgment which will destroy his body can be pushed too far. Obviously God does not step in to kill the Christian the first time he sins. When God in His wisdom sees that there is nothing further that the Holy Spirit can do in and through the believer, He acts. But only God knows when and under what circumstances this line is crossed. If the believer sins, but repents and forsakes his sin, there is forgiveness (1 John 1:9) and the Holy Spirit may still use him for the glory of God. The

Scriptures abound with examples. God did not kill David when he committed adultery with Uriah's wife and plotted the death of her husband. But He brought the king to repentance and confession (Psalm 51). Had God killed David He could not have fulfilled His covenant promise to the King which He made before the affair with Bathsheba.

Some dramatic chapters in church history could be written about sinning saints whom God killed and about others whom God in His grace and for reasons sufficient unto Himself He chose to spare.

The reason for God's judgmental action is given in the γὰρ clause. If the body of the Christian cannot be kept holy for God's use under the direction of the indwelling Holy Spirit, it has lost its *raison d'etre*. Paul is being argumentative in οἵτινες ἐστε ὑμεῖς - "I mean you."

The Christian who fails and comes to the sad end described in verse 17 does so apparently because he entertains an unwarranted conception of his own understanding of God's ways. The admonition of verse 18, if followed provides insurance against the case of the saved soul and the wasted life.

Verse 18 - "Let no man deceive himself. If any man among you seemeth to be wise in this world, let him become a fool, that he may be wise."

Μηδεὶς ἑαυτὸν ἐξαπατάτω. εἰ τις δοκεῖ σοφὸς εἶναι ἐν ὑμῖν ἐν τῷ αἰῶνι τούτῳ, μωρὸς γενέσθω, ἵνα γένηται σοφός.

"Let no one deceive himself. If any one among you thinks that he is wise in this age, let him become a fool that he may become wise." . . . RSV

Μηδεὶς (nom.sing.masc.of μηδείς, subject of ἐξαπατάτω) 713.

ἑαυτὸν (acc.sing.masc.of ἑαυτοῦ, direct object of ἐξαπατάτω) 288.

ἐξαπατάτω (3d.per.sing.pres.act.impv.of ἐξαπατάω, command) 3922.

εἰ (conditional particle in a first-class condition) 337.

τις (nom.sing.masc.of τις, indefinite pronoun, subject of δοκεῖ in a first-class condition) 486.

δοκεῖ (3d.per.sing.pres.act.ind.of δοκέω, present progressive, in a first-class condition) 287.

σοφὸς (nom.sing.masc.of σοφός, predicate adjective) 949.

εἶναι (pres.inf.of εἰμί, object of δοκεῖ) 86.

ἐν (preposition with the locative, with plural pronouns) 80.

ὑμῖν (loc.pl.masc.of σύ, place) 104.

ἐν (preposition with the locative of sphere) 80.

τῷ (loc.sing.masc.of the article in agreement with αἰῶνι) 9.

αἰῶνι (loc.sing.masc.of αἰών sphere) 1002.

τούτῳ (loc.sing.masc.of οὗτος, in agreement with αἰῶνι) 93.

μωρὸς (nom.sing.masc.of μωρός, predicate nominative) 482.

γενέσθω (3d.per.sing.aor.impv.of γίνομαι, command) 113.

ἵνα (conjunction with the subjunctive in a purpose clause) 114.

γένηται (3d.per.sing.aor.subj.of γίνομαι, purpose clause) 113.

σοφός (nom.sing.masc.of σοφός, predicate adjective) 949.

Translation - *"Let no one fool himself. If any one of your number supposes that he is wise in the thinking of this age, let him become a fool in order that he may be wise."*

Comment: ἐξαπατάτω is an intensified form of the verb (#3922). Some one in Corinth was truly deceived. The context would suggest Antinomianism - the convuluted reasoning that we ought to continue in sin that grace may abound (Rom.6:1), since this attack upon worldly philosophy follows Paul's message on the blessings of the Spirit-filled life and the dangers of the flesh (1 Cor.3:10-17). Perhaps someone in Corinth was teaching that Christians may presume upon the goodness of God without penalty. Paul had dealt with this thoroughly in Romans 6-8. God's true wisdom belongs to him who is willing to take his place before the unsaved world as a fool. The Christian who shuns the world, the flesh and the devil is considered a fool by the pleasure-oriented world of hedonism. To forego the pleasures of sin on the theory that the Spirit of God dwells in us, is a piece of folly to the world. But the "fool for Christ" (1 Cor.4:10) ultimately finds that the Spirit of God gives him a freedom, far in excess to that of the libertine who frets at moral restraint (2 Cor.3:17). Thus divine philosophy (σοφός) is the reward for being a fool (μωρός). *Cf.* Rom.16:18; 2 Thess.2:3.

It is important to note that this passage does not condemn philosophy as such. It is common among Christians who lack formal education in philosophy to denigrate it as something unworthy of the child of God. But Paul warns here, not against σοφός as such but against the σοφός of this world. The true philosopher has thought his way through to the source of all wisdom and knowledge (Col.2:3). In Christ he finds the holism without which there can be no concrescence, consistency, coherence and correspondance to reality. Christians should stop boasting about their ignorance, as though knowledge is something that alienates us from fellowship with Jesus Christ. No one afflicted with leprosy boasts about it. But there are some things worse than leprosy.

Verse 19 - *"For the wisdom of this world is foolishness with God: For it is written, He taketh the wise in their own craftiness."*

ἡ γὰρ σοφία τοῦ κόσμου τούτου μωρία παρὰ τῷ θεῷ ἐστιν. γέγραπται γάρ, Ὁ δρασσόμενος τοὺς σοφοὺς ἐν τῇ πανουργίᾳ αὐτῶν.

"For the wisdom of this world is folly with God. For it is written, 'He catches the wise in their craftiness,' " . . . RSV

ἡ (nom.sing.fem.of the article in agreement with σοφία) 9.
γὰρ (causal conjunction) 105.
σοφία (nom.sing.fem.of σοφία, subject of ἐστιν) 934.
τοῦ (gen.sing.masc.of the article in agreement with κόσμου) 9.
κόσμου (gen.sing.masc.of κόσμος, description) 360.
τούτου (gen.sing.masc.of οὗτος, in agreement with κόσμου) 93.
μωρία (nom.sing.fem.of μωρία, predicate nominative) 4105.
παρὰ (preposition with the locative, with persons) 154.
τῷ (loc.sing.masc.of the article in agreement with θεῷ) 9.

θεῷ (loc.sing.masc.of θεός, place) 124.
ἐστιν (3d.per.sing.pres.ind.of εἰμί, static) 86.
γέγραπται (3d.per.sing.perf.pass.ind.of γράφω, intensive) 156.
γὰρ (inferential conjunction) 105.
Ὁ (nom.sing.masc.of the article in agreement with δρασσόμενος) 9.

#4120 δρασσόμενος (pres.mid.part.nom.sing.masc.of δράσσομαι, substantival, nominative absolute).

King James Version

take - 1 Cor.3:19.

Revised Standard Version

catch - 1 Cor.3:19.

Meaning: To take with the hand; grasp; grab; capture. It is substituted in 1 Cor.3:19 for καταλαμβάνω (#1694) which is used in the quotation in Job 5:13, where we have ὁ καταλαμβάνων σοφοὺς ἐν τῇ φρονήσει. *Cf.* P Oxy X.1298:10 (4th.cent.A.D.) σὲ γὰρ μόνον ἔχω μάρτυρα πῶς ὁ Γοῦνθος δραξάμενός μου ... "laid hands on me." Moulton & Milligan. Hence, in 1 Cor.3:19, to capture and discomfit.

τοὺς (acc.pl.masc.of the article in agreement with σοφοὺς) 9.
σοφοὺς (acc.pl.masc.of σοφός, direct object of δρασσόμενος) 949.
ἐν (preposition with the locative of sphere) 80.
τῇ (loc.sing.fem.of the article in agreement with πανουργίᾳ) 9.
πανουργίᾳ (loc.sing.fem.of πανουργία, sphere) 2693.
αὐτῶν (gen.pl.masc.of αὐτός, possession) 16.

Translation - "Because the philosophy of this world is nonesense to God. So it is written, 'The One who defeats the crafty at their own game.' "

Comment: *Cf.* 1 Cor.1:20. παρὰ τῷ θεῷ - "side by side with God" and in a position where it can be compared. The Job 5:13 passage is parallel to 1 Cor.1:21. God has ordained developments that are ironical. The intellectual craftiness (πανουργία in an evil sense, #2693) of unregenerate philosophers has a way of taking God's truth and twisting it into a cunning perversion. Thus the Antinomians - the gospel is free; salvation is a gift; God is gracious; the truth makes us free. *Ergo*: Let us sin and prostitute God's grace and our bodies which Paul says are the temples of the Holy Spirit. Such philosophy leads the victim into a slavery to sin that is deadly.

The late 20th century situation ethics is an example of the πανουργία of the unsaved.

The views of Paul Tillich provide another example. Salvation is by faith alone. Since the intellectual effort to ascertain what is to be believed is "works" we are not required to make the effort to understand the revealed theology of propositional revelation. Therefore if a man has faith in atheism or any other system of thought that fits his fancy, he is saved, since the Reformation theology bases salvation upon faith alone, not upon the human effort of outlining the theology inherent in faith in the historic Jesus. Thus for Tillich, all men are saved. This is the craftiness of the unsaved which God has determined to use as a means to ensnare them. They will be seen as the authors of their own condemnation. *Cf.* Lk.20:23; 2 Cor.4:2; 11:3; Eph.4:14.

Verse 20 - "And again, the Lord knoweth the thoughts of the wise, that they are vain."

καὶ πάλιν, Κύριος γινώσκει τοὺς διαλογισμοὺς τῶν σοφῶν ὅτι εἰσὶν μάταιοι.

"and again, 'The Lord knows that the thoughts of the wise are futile.'" ...
                                                                          RSV

καὶ (continuative conjunction) 14.

πάλιν (adverbial) 355.

Κύριος (nom.sing.masc.of κύριος, subject of γινώσκει) 97.

γινώσκει (3d.per.sing.pres.act.ind.of γινώσκω, customary) 131.

τοὺς (acc.pl.masc.of the article in agreement with διαλογισμούς) 9.

διαλογισμοὺς (acc.pl.masc.of διαλογισμός, direct object of γινώσκει) 1165.

τῶν (gen.pl.masc.of the article in agreement with σοφῶν) 9.

σοφῶν (gen.pl.masc.of σοφός, possession) 949.

ὅτι (conjunction introducing an object clause in indirect discourse) 211.

εἰσὶν (3d.per.pl.pres.ind.of εἰμί, customary) 86.

μάταιοι (nom.pl.masc.of μάταιος, predicate adjective) 3321.

Translation - "And again, 'The Lord knows the rationale of the philosophers, that they are vapid and vacuous.'"

Comment: The quotation is from Psalm 94:11. *Cf.* Titus 3:9 and 1 Pet.1:18 for the vacuity of the philosophy of the unsaved. *Cf.* #3321 for the meaning of μάταιος. The philosophy of the unsaved, which Paul has discussed at length in 1 Cor.1:18-2:16 is child's play to God. He sees it as the superficial meandering of a blinded and prejudiced child who has a vested interest in maintaining the view, whatever it may be at the moment, to which he is committed. Unbelief is a form of insanity. Augustine understood this when he said, "Thou hast made us for Thyself, and our hearts are restless until the rest in thee." So did Satchel Paige when he said, "the social rumble ain't restful."

The plight of the unsaved is indeed pitiable. Job 8:22; 21:30; Ps.7:11; Prov.11:5 in connection with 1 Cor.3:19; Prov.28:1; Isa.57:20. The sad thing about it is the fact that no one realizes how empty unregenerate thinking is until he himself, by God's sovereign grace, has been supernaturally enabled to see it from Heaven's point of view. Just as the unsaved can see nothing but nonesense in what a Christian recognizes as God's truth and power, so the Christian alone sees through the unregenerate philosophy as a sick, rationalized, self-serving, immature attempt to escape reality.

Verse 21 - "Therefore, let no man glory in men. For all things are yours."

ὥστε μηδεὶς καυχάσθω ἐν ἀνθρώποις, πάντα γὰρ ὑμῶν ἐστιν,

"So let no one boast of men. For all things are yours, . . . RSV

ὥστε (inferential conjunction) 752.

μηδεὶς (nom.sing.masc.of μηδείς, subject of καυχάσθω) 713.

καυχάσθω (3d.per.sing.aor.mid.impv.of καυχάομαι, prohibition) 3847.

ἐν (preposition with the instrumental of cause) 80.

ἀνθρώποις (instru.pl.masc.of ἄνθρωπος, cause) 341.

πάντα (nom.pl.neut.of πᾶς, subject of ἐστιν) 67.

γὰρ (causal conjunction) 105.

ὑμῶν (gen.pl.masc.of σύ, predicate genitive) 104.

ἐστιν (3d.per.sing.pres.ind.of εἰμί, static) 86.

Translation - "So no one should boast about men, for it all belongs to you."

Comment: ὥστε normally introduces a consecutive clause, but not here, where it is inferential. Its force rests upon the foregoing argument which began in 1 Cor.1:18 as the superiority of heavenly philosophy over that of earth is developed. The text has spoken of little else. The world's philosophy is nonesense to God and *vice versa*. Values are the poles apart. Man, outside of Christ, is a fool and destined to a fool's fate and this by sovereign divine decree. There is nothing but bad news for the unsaved after he has ruled against the good news of the gospel of Christ. There is nothing but good news for the elect once they have accepted Christ as Saviour and Lord.

At least two inferences can be drawn from all of this, both of which are grammatically possible. They are also compatible. It is possible to hold both. The first is that the Christian should not be impressed with the approbation which may come his way from the unsaved. If unsaved men are such fools why should Christians seek the headlines? To be praised by an unsaved man is really to be embarrassed before God. If a Christian commends himself to the unsaved, he does no either by talking the world's philosophical nonesense or stepping down to the world's ethical level. If what he thinks, says and does pleases the world, he may well give some thought about how he displeases God and grieves the Holy Spirit, His heavenly Guest (Jam.4:4; Eph.4:30; John 15:18-27). The Christian, no thanks to him, is united with the Godhead (John 17:21) and is therefore in a position infinitely superior to that of the unsaved world, in every way that counts. Yet how often have we, the heirs of God and joint heirs with Christ (Rom.8:17) gone with hat in hand to the unsaved world, with the sycophancy of Uriah Heep, to seek the praise of the world. This is a lesson that one learns, with an assist from experience, only from an intent look in depth at this verse in context.

The other inference that can be drawn is that no Christian should be impressed with what the unsaved world does. Even the world's "successes" in science, art and literature are destined to fail ultimately (verse 19). Of course this statement does not apply to the contributions which Christians themselves have made in creative activity - exploits for which the unsaved world can take no credit. Note the wholesale destruction in Rev.18:1-24; 20:7-15; 2 Pet.3:7,10-12. This is the destiny of the unsaved world, for all of its institutional complexity, scientific achievement and cultural development. Its boast is κόσμος but actually it is chaos. The human drama without Christ will end in catastrophe. Why should the Christian who is marching to a different drum applaud it?

If we take ἐν ἀνϑρώποις as an instrumental of means or cause, our translation and the first interpretation follows. If it is a locative of sphere, then the second interpretation is the point and the translation should be, "No Christian should be proud of accomplishments in the sphere of the unsaved world." Goodspeed has, "So no one should boast about men." It should be repeated that the two interpretations do not clash.

Why this healthy contempt for what the unsaved world has done? The last clause is causal with γάρ. "Everything belongs to the Christian." Would J.Paul Getty envy a bum who had a dime in his pocket? No more shall I the child of God who am a joint heir with Jesus Christ envy the world which cannot appreciate what it has and will discover that it cannot keep what it has.

This fact is inherent in Rom.8:17.

> *My Father is rich in houses and lands,*
> *He holdeth the wealth of the world in His hands.*
> *Of rubies and diamonds, of silver and gold*
> *His coffers are full. He has riches untold.*

And the chorus that follows says, "I am His child."
That Paul makes no exception to this broad statement is clear from

Verse 22 - "Whether Paul, or Apollos, or Cephas, or the world, or life, or death, or things present, or things to come; all are yours."

εἴτε Παῦλος εἴτε Ἀπολλῶς εἴτε Κηφᾶς εἴτε κόσμος εἴτε ζωὴ εἴτε ϑάνατος εἴτε ἐνεστῶτα εἴτε μέλλοντα, πάντα ὑμῶν,

"whether Paul or Apollos or Cephas or the world or life or death or the present or the future, all are yours; ..." ... RSV

εἴτε (disjunctive) 4016.
Παῦλος (nom.sing.masc.of Παῦλος, predicate nominative) 3284.
εἴτε (disjunctive) 4016.
Ἀπολλῶς (nom.sing.masc.of Ἀπολλῶς, predicate nominative) 3454.
εἴτε (disjunctive) 4016.
Κηφᾶς (nom.sing.masc.of Κηφᾶς, predicate nominative) 1964.
εἴτε (disjunctive) 4016.
κόσμος (nom.sing.masc.of κόσμος, predicate nominative) 360.
εἴτε (disjunctive) 4016.
ζωὴ (nom.sing.fem.of ζωή, predicate nominative) 668.
εἴτε (disjunctive) 4016.
ϑάνατος (nom.sing.masc.of ϑάνατος, predicate nominative) 381.
εἴτε (disjunctive) 4016.
ἐνεστῶτα (perf.act.part.nom.pl.neut.of ἐνίστημι, substantival, predicate nominative) 3954.

εἴτε (disjunctive) 4016.

μέλλοντα (pres.act.part.nom.pl.neut.of μέλλω, substantival, predicate nominative) 206.

πάντα (nom.pl.neut.of πᾶς, subject of ἐστί understood) 67.

ὑμῶν (gen.pl.masc.of σύ, predicate genitive) 104.

Translation - "Whether Paul or Apollos or Cephas or the world or life or death or present things or coming things; all things are yours."

Comment: The conditional disjunctives here join substantives, both definite (Παῦλος, 'Απολλῶς, Κηφᾶς) and indefinite, including the two participial substantives, all without the article. *Cf.* Rom.8:38,39. The nouns are all predicate nominatives, as we supply the copulative verb. Note also the ellision of the copula in πάντα ὑμῶν.

Paul got carried away with the glory of the message, as well he might! It is almost irreverent to analyze the statement. The Corinthians were worried about the question of their associations (1 Cor.1:12; 3:4). Paul now tells them that every one of them has all of the others. And then he adds the entire universe (*cf.#360*). So as not to leave out anything he adds life and death, the present and the future. If it is neither alive nor dead, present or future then, pray, what is it? Everything is at the disposal of the child of God, because he is in Christ (John 17:21; Rom.8:17). The reason for all of this wealth is found in 2 Cor.2:14.

Verse 23 - "And ye are Christ's; and Christ is God's."

ὑμεῖς δὲ Χριστοῦ, Χριστὸς δὲ θεοῦ.

"and you are Christ's and Christ is God's." . . . RSV

ὑμεῖς (nom.pl.masc.of σύ, subject of ἐστε understood) 104.
δὲ (continuative conjunction) 11.
Χριστοῦ (gen.sing.masc.of Χριστός, relationship) 4.
Χριστὸς (nom.sing.masc.of Χριστός, subject of ἐστιν understood) 4.
δὲ (continuative conjunction) 11.
θεοῦ (gen.sing.masc.of θεός, relationship) 124.

Translation - "And you belong to Christ and Christ belongs to God."

Comment: The mystic union of the believer with Christ and God is the ground for all identification of the believer with the Godhead. All of the prepositional phrases ἐν Χριστῷ and ἐν κυρίῳ, speak of it. This divine homogeneity of fortune and destiny is the foundation for the New Testament doctrine of soteriology (salvation).

In the light of verses 22 and 23 why should a Christian admire anything the unsaved world has or does and why should he be pleased by anything the unsaved world says in approbation or distressed by anything the world says in ridicule?

But lest this great truth with all of its infinite implications for good seduce us into sinful pride, let it be remembered that we are ἐν Χριστῷ only by divine grace.

> *O to grace how great a debtor Daily I'm constrained to be!*
> *Let The goodness like a fetter, Bind my wandering heart to Thee:*
> *Prone to wander, Lord, I feel it, Prone to leave the God I love;*
> *Here's my heart, O take and seal it. Seal it for Thy courts above.*

The Ministry of the Apostles

(1 Corinthians 4:1-21)

1 Cor.4:1 - "*Let a man so account of us, as of the ministers of Christ, and stewards of the mysteries of God.*"

Οὕτως ἡμᾶς λογιζέσθω ἄνθρωπος ὡς ὑπηρέτας Χριστοῦ καὶ οἰκονόμους μυστηρίων θεοῦ.

"*This is how one should regard us, as servants of Christ and stewards of the mysteries of God.*" . . . RSV

Οὕτως (demonstrative adverb) 74.
ἡμᾶς (acc.pl.masc.of ἐγώ, direct object of λογιζέσθω) 123.
λογιζέσθω (3d.per.sing.pres.mid.impv.of λογίζομαι, command) 2611.
ἄνθρωπος (nom.sing.masc.of ἄνθρωπος, subject of λογιζέσθω) 341.
ὡς (comparative particle) 128.
ὑπηρέτας (acc.pl.masc.of ὑπηρέτης, direct object of λογιζέσθω) 493.
Χριστοῦ (gen.sing.masc.of Χριστός, description) 4.
καὶ (adjunctive conjunction joining nouns) 14.
οἰκονόμους (acc.pl.masc.of οἰκονόμος, direct object of λογιζέσθω) 2488.
μυστηρίων (gen.pl.neut.of μυστήριον, description) 1038.
θεοῦ (gen.sing.masc.of θεός, description) 124.

Translation - "*A man should regard us in this light: as subordinates of Christ and superintendents of the divine mysteries.*"

Comment: Οὕτως, the correlative adverb connects the foregoing with what follows. In the light of the argument of 1 Cor.1:18-3:23, anyone who desires to make an evaluation (#2611) of the Apotles (ἡμᾶς refers to Paul, Apollos, Cephas and any other preachers who may have visited Corinth) should base his opinion upon the fact that they are subordinates (#493) of Christ and as such distributors (#2488) of the revealed truths of Christian theology as having their source in God. οἰκονόμος (#2488) means "steward," "factor," "overseer," "superintendent" or "distributor." The Apostles were responsible to God since they were charged with the task of disseminating the divine message. This message is not of their origin, but has God as its source. They are not responsible for the ultimate truth of it, but only for the fidelity with which they convey it. Paul is saying to the unsaved, "If you do not agree with what I preach, do not blame me. I am only God's messenger. Your quarrel is with God." And to the saints in Corinth he is saying that he and the others included in the plural ἡμᾶς are working under God's direction (1 Cor.3:9) and thus they are not objects of Corinthian worship (1 Cor.3:4), but, though subordinate to God, they are, by virtue of their divine commission, superordinate to the saints. Thus Paul asserts Apostolic authority - a blow directed at the fanatics who were inordinately impressed with the blessings of democracy!

Paul's position as ὑπηρέτης was by divine commission (Acts 26:16). Luke recognized it (Lk.1:2); Jesus extended it to all of His Apostles (Judas was already dead!) (John 18:36). All God-called preachers are stewards or distributors of the truths of the gospel of God (Tit.1:7). Peter extends the privilege to the laity (1 Pet.4:10). The varsity crewmen who are trained to row according to the tempo and rythm of the coxswain will appreciate Paul's position in relation to Christ. The God-called preacher preaches what, when, how and to whom in keeping with God's direction. He does not use a megaphone. He directs by means of the indwelling Holy Spirit and the Old and New Testaments which the Holy Spirit directed the authors to write.

Note the triple accusatives in ἡμᾶς, ὑπηρέτας and οἰκονόμους after λογιζέσθω.

Verse 2 - "Moreover it is required in stewards, that a man be found faithful."

ὧδε λοιπὸν ζητεῖται ἐν τοῖς οἰκονόμοις ἵνα πιστός τις εὑρεθῇ.

"Moreover it is required of stewards that they be found trustworthy." ... RSV

ὧδε (adverbial) 766.
λοιπὸν (acc.sing.neut.of λοιπός, general reference) 1402.
ζητεῖται (3d.per.sing.pres.pass.ind.of ζητέω, customary) 207.
ἐν (preposition with the locative of sphere) 80.
τοῖς (loc.pl.masc.of the article in agreement with οἰκονόμοις) 9.
οἰκονόμοις (loc.pl.masc.of οἰκονόμος, sphere) 2488.
ἵνα (conjunction with the subjunctive in a sub-final clause) 114.
πιστός (nom.sing.masc.of πιστός, predicate adjective) 1522.
τις (nom.sing.masc.of τις, indefinite pronoun, subject of εὑρεθῇ) 486.
εὑρεθῇ (3d.per.sing.1st.aor.pass.subj.of εὑρίσκω, sub-final) 79.

Translation - "Furthermore in the case of stewards, it is always required that a man be found trustworthy."

Comment: After a verb of demanding or beseeching, ἵνα and the subjunctive is sub-final, a cross between pure purpose and pure result, like a ὅτι object clause . The purpose of such a requirement, as well as its practical result, is that a manager, if he is to retain his position, must upon audit be found trustworthy. This is a general statement to support the further argument of verses 3-6, as Paul continues to struggle with the Corinthian problem of undue "worship" of preachers, the sin that created dissension within the church. The οἰκονόμος is held to strict account. By whom and by what standard? The Lord of the steward is the auditor and the judgment is made on the Lord's standards, not on the standards of the world. What is the steward's stock in trade? The divine mysteries. Therefore the question to be answered is, "Has the steward faithfully conveyed the essence of the message given to them? If he has, he is faithful. if not, let him be ἀνάθεμα (Gal.1:8,9). Note that he is not required to be successful. Christ will not say, "Well done, thou good and successful servant." (Mt.25:21).

Since the philosophy of heaven, the message for which the steward is held responsbile, is nonesense to the unsaved world (1 Cor.1:18), the steward is not interested in pleasing the world. In fact he is not concerned in the least with what the world thinks of his stewardship. He must please his Auditor, Who is God. **The Judge of heaven's court measures with a totally different yardstick from that** of the unregenerate judge of earth. This is the truth in

Verse 3 - "But with me it is a very small thing that I should be judged of you, or of any man's judgment: yea, I judge not mine own self."

ἐμοὶ δὲ εἰς ἐλάχιστόν ἐστιν ἵνα ὑφ᾽ ὑμῶν ἀνακριθῶ ἢ ὑπὸ ἀνθρωπίνης ἡμέρας. ἀλλ᾽ οὐδὲ ἐμαυτὸν ἀνακρίνω.

"But with me it is a very small thing that I should be judged by you or by any human court. I do not even judge myself." . . . RSV

ἐμοὶ (loc.sing.masc.of ἐμοῦ, sphere) 1267.
δὲ (adversative conjunction) 11.
εἰς (preposition with the predicate accusative) 140.
ἐλάχιστόν (nom.sing.neut.of ἐλάχιστος, subject of ἐστιν) 159.
ἐστιν (3d.per.sing.pres.ind.of εἰμί, aoristic) 86.
ἵνα (conjunction with the subjunctive in a sub-final clause) 114.
ὑφ᾽ (preposition with the ablative of agent) 117.
ὑμῶν (abl.pl.masc.of σύ, agent) 104.
ἀνακριθῶ (1st.per.sing.1st.aor.pass.subj.of ἀνακρίνω, sub-final) 2837.
ἢ (disjunctive) 465.
ὑπὸ (preposition with the ablative of agent) 117.
ἀνθρωπίνης (abl.sing.fem.of ἀνθρώπινος, in agreement with ἡμέρας) 3415.
ἡμέρας (abl.sing.fem.of ἡμέρα, agent) 135.
ἀλλ᾽ (emphatic alternative conjunction) 342.
οὐδὲ (negative disjunctive particle) 452.
ἐμαυτὸν (acc.sing.masc.of ἐμαυτός, direct object of ἀνακρίνω) 723.
ἀνακρίνω (1st.per.sing.pres.act.ind.of ἀνακρίνω, customary) 2837.

Translation - "But to me it is of very slight concern that I should be examined by you or by the human standard; indeed, I do not even evaluate myself."

Comment: εἰς ἐλάχιστον is a predicate accusative. The superlative ἐλάχιστον has a great deal of elation in it. Our generation would say, "I could not care less."

The ἵνα clause with the subjunctive is sub-final, like an ὅτι object clause - part purpose; part result. It explains that which Paul says is of small concern to him. He is being a little snide with his readers. Neither the opinions of the spiritually underdeveloped saints, nor indeed the opinions of the unsaved world concerned him. Note that he puts the carnal (σαρκικός) Christian in the same category with the natural (ψυχικός) sinner, insofar as ability to make sound judgment as to the quality of his preaching is concerned. Many preachers have had their ministry ruined because they took seriously the criticism which came from backslidden Christians. Paul was totally, even elatedly, indifferent to what the Corinthians thought of him, since they were so underdeveloped as to split into personality cults (1 Cor.1:12; 3:4).

There is warning here also to the carnal (σαρκικός) Christian. If he knows so little about the Spirit-filled life he should know that his opinion as to what constitutes good preaching is worth very little if anything.

Paul even adds that he does not try to evaluate himself - and for the same reason in kind, though perhaps not in degree, - that he recognizes that he is not totally free from the flesh. The preacher who is so certain that he is spiritual (πνευματικός) and thus qualified to give himself an A in exegesis and homiletics, **thinks** of himself "more highly than he ought to think" (Rom.12:3) and is no better qualified to judge himself than the backslidden Christian is to judge him. Paul was not in this category. He recognized that his body was the temple of God and that the Holy Spirit dwelt within him, and he also saw the need for constant filling of the Holy Spirit and the danger of grieving the Holy Spirit (1 Cor.6:19,20; Eph.4:30; 5:18). To be conscious of one's limitations is to be alert to the possibility of being victimized by them.

The King James Version obscures the thought in the penultimate clause with its translation "of man's judgment." The Greek has ἀνθρωπίνης ἡμέρας - "the human day." *Cf.* John 9:4-5 and our comment (*The Renaissance New Testament*, 6, 245-249). "Man's day" resumed when he murdered the "light of the world." It is still "man's day" — a period which God calls night. It contrasts with "the Lord's day" and "the day of Christ." (*Cf.#135*). It is a day in which philosophies, attitudes and judgments are prejudiced against the gospel of Christ. (1 Cor.1:18). It is the day of the great Satanic brainwash (2 Cor.4:4). Paul viewed it with amused contempt. And so should all Christians, especially those who are intellectually capable of thinking the issues down to their roots. Unfortunately, most Christians seek the approval of "man's day," rejoice when they receive it and cringe in despair when they are criticized by it. Paul snapped his fingers at it, and even at the Corinthians saints, who in their backslidden condition had imbibed its spirit. When the "day of Christ"/"day of the Lord" comes, values of divine worth will be admired because philosophies of divine depth will be believed. Meanwhile Paul was only the subordinate of Christ and the steward of God (verse 1) charged with the responsbility of preaching God's gospel which, though it is nonesense to the world, is wisdom to God.

Verse 4 - "For I know nothing by myself; yet am I not hereby justified: but he that judgeth me is the Lord."

οὐδὲν γὰρ ἐμαυτῷ σύνοιδα, ἀλλ᾽ οὐκ ἐν τούτῳ δεδικαίωμαι, ὁ δὲ ἀνακρίνων με κύριός ἐστιν.

"I am not aware of anything against myself, but I am not thereby acquitted. It is the Lord who judges me." . . . RSV

οὐδὲν (acc.sing.neut.of οὐδείς, direct object of σύνοιδα) 446.
γάρ (causal conjunction) 105.
ἐμαυτῷ (dat.sing.masc.of ἐμαυτοῦ, reference) 723.
σύνοιδα (1st.per.sing.perf.ind.of συνεῖδον, intensive) 3052.
ἀλλ᾽ (adversative conjunction) 342.
οὐκ (negative particle with the indicative) 342.
ἐν (preposition with the instrumental, cause) 80.
τούτῳ (instru.sing.neut.of οὗτος, cause) 93.
δεδικαίωμαι (1st.per.sing.perf.pass.ind.of δικαιόω, intensive) 933.
ὁ (nom.sing.masc.of the article in agreement with ἀνακρίνων) 9.
δὲ (adversative conjunction) 11.
ἀνακρίνων (pres.act.part.nom.sing.masc.of ἀνακρίνω, substantival, subject of ἐστιν) 2837.
μέ (acc.sing.masc.of ἐγώ, direct object of ἀνακρίνων) 123.
κύριός (nom.sing.masc.of κύριος, predicate nominative) 97.
ἐστιν (3d.per.sing.pres.ind.of εἰμί, static) 86.

Translation - "Because I am not aware of anything against myself, but this fact does not justify me. The One Who is judging me is the Lord."

Comment: Having totally rejected any criticisms with reference to his ministry that might come, either from the carnal Christians in Corinth or from the unsaved world, and having said that he did not even judge himself (verse 3) he now adds that he is not personally aware of any wrong doing, but he hastens to add that this fact does not constitute vindication. Only when the Lord, Who is the only true Judge (John 5:22) has handed down His decision will any man, saved or unsaved, Spirit-filled or backslidden know the truth.

He then states the conclusion to which these facts lead in

Verse 5 - "Therefore judge nothing before the time, until the Lord come who both will bring to light the hidden things of darkness, and will make manifest the counsels of the hearts: and then shall every man have praise of God."

ὥστε μὴ πρὸ καιροῦ τι κρίνετε, ἕως ἂν ἔλθῃ ὁ κύριος, ὃς καὶ φωτίσει τὰ κρυπτὰ τοῦ σκότους καὶ φανερώσει τὰς βουλὰς τῶν καρδιῶν, καὶ τότε ὁ ἔπαινος γενήσεται ἑκάστῳ ἀπὸ τοῦ θεοῦ.

"Therefore do not pronounce judgment before the time, before the Lord comes, who will bring to light the things now hidden in darkness and will disclose the purposes of the heart. Then every man will receive his commendation from God." . . . RSV

ὥστε (conjunction implying result) 752.

μή (negative particle with the imperative, in a prohibition) 87,

πρό (preposition with the ablative of time separation) 442.

καιροῦ (abl.sing.masc.of καιρός, time separation) 767.

τι (acc.sing.neut.of τις, indefinite pronoun, direct object of κρίνετε) 486.

κρίνετε (2d.per.pl.pres.act.impv.of κρίνω, prohibition) 531.

ἕως (particle introducing the subjunctive with ἄν in an indefinite temporal clause, future reference) 71.

ἄν (particle in an indefinite temporal clause, future reference) 205.

ἔλθῃ (3d.per.sing.aor.subj.of ἔρχομαι, indefinite temporal clause, future reference) 146.

ὁ (nom.sing.masc.of the article in agreement with κύριος) 9.

κύριος (nom.sing.masc.of κύριος, subject of ἔλθῃ) 97.

ὅς (nom.sing.masc.of ὅς, relative pronoun, subject of φωτίσει) 65.

καὶ (adjunctive conjunction joining verbs) 14.

φωτίσει (3d.per.sing.fut.act.ind.of φωτίζω, predictive) 1697.

τὰ (acc.pl.neut.of the article in agreement with κρυπτὰ).

κρυπτὰ (acc.pl.neut.of κρυπτός, direct object of φωτίσει) 565.

τοῦ (gen.sing.masc.of the article in agreement with σκότους) 9.

σκότους (gen.sing.masc.of σκότος, description) 603.

καὶ (adjunctive conjunction joining verbs) 14.

φανερώσει (3d.per.sing.fut.act.ind.of φανερόω, predictive) 1960.

τὰς (acc.pl.fem.of the article in agreement with βουλὰς) 9.

βουλὰς (acc.pl.fem.of βουλή, direct object of φανερώσει) 2163.

τῶν (gen.pl.masc.of the article in agreement with καρδιῶν) 9.

καρδιῶν (gen.pl.fem.of καρδία, description) 432.

καὶ (continuative conjunction) 14.

τότε (temporal adverb) 166.

ὁ (nom.sing.masc.of the article in agreement with ἔπαινος) 9.

ἔπαινος (nom.sing.masc.of ἔπαινος, subject of γενήσεται) 3853.

γενήσεται (3d.per.sing.fut.ind.of γίνομαι, predictive) 113.

ἑκάστῳ (dat.sing.masc.of ἕκαστος, indirect object of γενήσεται) 1217.

ἀπό (preposition with the ablative of source) 70.

τοῦ (abl.sing.masc.of the article in agreement with θεοῦ) 9.

θεοῦ (abl.sing.masc.of θεός, source) 124.

Translation - *"So then you must not judge anything before the time, until such time as the Lord comes, Who also will reveal the hidden things, previously unknown and display the motivations of the hearts. And then the approval from God will be given to each one."*

Comment: ὥστε is almost inferential here. The result of what Paul has said in verses 1-4 leads logically to the injunction of verse 5. "In view of the foregoing, make no premature judgments." Those who do are prejudiced. They assume that they know more than they do and thus they are trying to play God. They are also assuming the role of judge, a position held exclusively by the Lord Jesus Christ (John 5:22). καιροῦ is defined by the indefinite temporal clause with its future reference, ἕως ἄν ἔλθῃ ὁ κύριος. The clause does not doubt that the Lord will come. The doubt involved (with ἄν and the subjunctive in ἔλθῃ) has to do with the precise time when He comes. He is going to come again. No doubt about that. Paul knew that it was in the future, but he did not know the exact time. But "when He comes" there will be a time of judgment (Mt.16:27; Lk.14:12-14; 1 Cor.3:13-15; 2 Cor.5:10; Rev.11:15-19, etc.).

The ὅς relative clause describes the procedure on that day. He will reveal previously hidden facts and explore and publicize motives. We will not only know *what* was done but *why* it was done. These are things that no human court can know fully now, particularly in view of the fact that human courts in "man's day" (1 Cor.4:3) are hopelessly prejudiced against God's philosophy. Motives are important in judicial decisions. No one can judge acts apart from motives. The Heavenly Judge, Who is the only One appointed to the function (John 5:22) knows everything about both acts (τὰ κρυπτὰ τοῦ σκότους) and motives (τὰς βουλὰς τῶν καρδιῶν).

τότε is temporal - "at that time" God's praise, to whatever extent it is deserved, will be given to every Christian. Since only God can assess merit and/or guilt and reward with praise and/or punish with censure, we should leave the judgments up to Him and mind our own business (Mt.7:1).

Verse 6 - "And these things brethren, I have in a figure transferred to myself and to Apollos for your sakes; that ye might learn in us not to think of men above that which is written, that no one of you be puffed up for one against another."

Ταῦτα δέ, ἀδελφοί, μετεσχημάτισα εἰς ἐμαυτὸν καὶ ᾽Απολλῶν δι᾽ ὑμᾶς, ἵνα ἐν ἡμῖν μάθητε τὸ Μὴ ὑπὲρ ἅ γέγραπται, ἵνα μὴ εἰς ὑπὲρ τοῦ ἑνὸς φυσιοῦσθε κατὰ τοῦ ἑτέρου.

"I have applied all this to myself and Apollos for your benefit, brethren, that you may learn by us to live according to scripture, that none of you may be puffed up in favor of one against another." . . . RSV

Ταῦτα (acc.pl.neut.of οὗτος, direct object of μετεσχημάτισα, anaphoric) 93.
δὲ (explanatory conjunction) 11.
ἀδελφοί (voc.pl.masc.of ἀδελφός, address) 15.

#4121 μετεσχημάτισα (1st.per.sing.aor.act.ind.of μετασχηματίζω, culminative).

King James Version

be transformed - 2 Cor.11:13,14,15.
change - Phil.3:21.
transfer in a figure - 1 Cor.4:6.

Revised Standard Version

applied - 1 Cor.4:6.
disguise - 2 Cor.11:13,14,15.
change - Phil.3:21.

Meaning: A combination of μετά (#50) and σχηματίζω - "to assume a certain form." *Cf.* σχῆμα (#4163). Hence to cast something into a form not previously obtaining. To change; to adapt something to something else. To adapt a line of teaching to apply its truths in the solution of a problem - 1 Cor.4:6; to make oneself appear in a false or different light; to disguise for purposes of deception, as did the false teachers who appeared as Apostles - 2 Cor.11:13,15. With reference to Satan - 2 Cor.11:14. With reference to the glorification of the body of the Christian at the resurrection - Phil.3:21.

εἰς (preposition with the predicate accusative) 140.
ἐμαυτὸν (acc.sing.masc.of ἐμαυτοῦ, predicate accusative) 723.
καὶ (adjunctive conjunction joining substantives) 14.
Ἀπολλῶν (acc.sing.masc.of Ἀπολλῶς, predicate accusative) 3454.
δι' (preposition with the accusative, cause) 118.
ὑμᾶς (acc.pl.masc.of σύ, cause) 104.
ἵνα (conjunction with the subjunctive in a purpose clause) 114.
ἐν (preposition with the dative of reference) 80.
ἡμῖν (dat.pl.masc.of ἐγώ, reference) 123.
μάθητε (2d.per.pl.aor.act.subj.of μανθάνω, purpose) 794.
τὸ (acc.sing.neut.of the article, direct object of μάθητε) 9.
Μὴ (negative particle with the infinitive understood) 87.
ὑπὲρ (preposition with the accusative, "beyond") 545.
ἃ (acc.pl.neut.of ὅς, "beyond") 65.
γέγραπται (3d.per.sing.perf.pass.ind.of γράφω, intensive) 156.
ἵνα (conjunction with the subjunctive in a purpose clause) 114.
μὴ (negative particle with the subjunctive in a prohibition) 87.
εἷς (acc.sing.masc.of εἷς, general reference) 469.
ὑπὲρ (preposition with the ablative, comparison) 545.
τοῦ (abl.sing.masc.of the article in agreement with ἑνός) 9.
ἑνὸς (abl.sing.masc.of εἷς, comparison) 469.

#4122 φυσιοῦσθε (2d.per.pl.pres.pass.subj. irreg.for φυσιῶσθε, negative purpose).

    King James Version

puff up - 1 Cor.8:1.
be puffed up - 1 Cor.4:6,18,19; 5:2; 13:4; Col.2:18.

    Revised Standard Version

puff up - 1 Cor.8:1.
puffed up - 1 Cor.4:6; Col.2:18.
arrogant - 1 Cor.4:18,19; 5:2; 13:4.

Meaning: To inflate; blow up; make arrogant; always in an evil psychological sense in the New Testament.

κατὰ (preposition with the ablative of comparison) 98.
τοῦ (abl.sing.masc.of the article in agreement with ἑτέρου) 9.
ἑτέρου (abl.sing.masc.of ἕτερος, comparison) 605.

Translation - *"Now these things, brethren, I have applied to myself and to Apollos, because of you, in order that you may learn not to go beyond that which is written, with reference to us, lest you become arrogant in supposing one is superior in comparison to the other."*

Comment: This is difficult Greek to translate into smooth English. δὲ is explanatory. Ταῦτα is anaphoric, in reference to the material of 1 Cor.4:1-5. Paul's reason for urging upon them the fact that God alone is competent to judge the performance of His servants and that He will reward each one in a manner commensurate with divine justice, is that he is trying to correct the bad attitudes of the Corinthians, with their arrogant opinions as to the superiority of one Apostle above another.

Thus Paul is applying the principle, as an example, to himself and to Apollos. Why? δι' ὑμᾶς - "because of you" and your dissension over who is the better preacher. For what purpose? That you may learn. With reference to what? With reference to us - ἐν ἡμῖν, i.e. Paul and Apollos. Learn what? τὸ introduces the object clause, into which we must inject an infinitive, perhaps νομίζειν - "to think." Paul wants them not to think more (go beyond) than the scripture warrants. Why not? The negative purpose clause follows. That they not be puffed up and that they not show their arrogant attitude by claiming that one is superior to the other. If Paul is greater than Apollos, or Apollos is greater than Paul, that will be up to the Lord to decide when He comes and evaluates the ministry of each. In the meantime it is arrogance for a Christian to assume that he has a seat on a heavenly review board and is charged with the responsibility of grading the performance of God's servants.

If Paul had not explained to them why he included the material of verses 1-5, they might never have got the point.

ἵνα . . . φυσιοῦσθε is possibly a case of ἵνα with the present indicative as in Gal.4:17 - ἵνα ζηλοῦτε, though both are possible subjunctives. But in 1 John 5:20 in ἵνα γινώσκομεν we have the only unquestioned case of ἵνα with the present indicative in the New Testament. It is common in the later patristic writings. Robertson thinks that τοῦ ἑτέρου involves a third person, rather than the second of a pair.If so, Paul is including Cephas (Robertson, *Grammar*, 749).

Paul has just applied the principle of discrimination to himself, Apollos and Peter, and by implication any other preacher. Now he applies the same principle to the Corinthians themselves, in

Verse 7 - *"For who maketh thee to differ from another? And what hast thou that thou didst not receive? Now if thou didst receive it, why dost thou glory, as if thou hadst not received it?"*

τίς γάρ σε διακρίνει; τί δὲ ἔχεις ὃ οὐκ ἔλαβες; εἰ δὲ καὶ ἔλαβες, τί καυχᾶσαι ὡς μὴ λαβών;

"For who sees anything different in you? What have you that you did not receive? If then you received it, why do you boast as if it were not a gift?"... RSV

τίς (nom.sing.masc.of τίς, interrogative pronoun, subject of διακρίνει) 281.

γάρ (explanatory conjunction) 105.

σε (acc.sing.masc.of σύ, direct object of διακρίνει) 104.

διακρίνει (3d.per.sing.pres.act.ind.of διακρίνω, present progressive retroactive, direct question) 1195.

τί (acc.sing.neut.of τίς, interrogative pronoun, direct object of ἔχεις,direct question) 281.

δὲ (adversative conjunction) 11.

ἔχεις (2d.per.sing.pres.act.ind.of ἔχω, aoristic) 82.

ὅ (acc.sing.neut.of ὅς, relative pronoun, direct object of ἔλαβες) 65.

οὐκ (negative particle with the indicative) 130.

ἔλαβες (2d.per.sing.2d.aor.act.ind.of λαμβάνω, culminative) 533.

εἰ (conditional particle in a first-class condition) 337.

δὲ (adversative conjunction) 11.

καὶ (emphatic conjunction) 14.

ἔλαβες (2d.per.sing.2d.aor.act.ind.of λαμβάνω, first-class condition) 533.

τί (acc.sing.neut.of τίς, interrogative pronoun, cause) 281.

καυχᾶσαι (2d.per.sing.pres.act.ind.of καυχάομαι, for καυχῇ, direct question) 3847.

ὡς (particle in a comparative clause) 128.

μὴ (negative particle with the participle) 87.

λαβών (aor.act.part.nom.sing.masc.of λαμβάνω, adverbial, conditional) 533.

Translation - *"Now who regards you as superior? But what do you have that you did not receive? But if in fact you received it as a gift, why are you boasting as if you had not received it as a gift?"*

Comment: There is some asperity in these abrupt questions. Note the three uses of the interrogative pronoun τίς (#281). Who? What? Why? In the third question it is necessary to supply διά - "on account of what?" or "Why?"

The questions need to be faced and honestly answered by all Christians who forget that our exalted position in Christ (John 17:21; Rom.8:14-17; 1 Cor.3:21-23) is not the result of our merit, but of God's grace. These questions also involve the subject of natural intellectual endowment and gifts of personal charm. Apparently those who believe that one preacher is better than another, and who believe it enough to say so, to the glory of one and at the expense of another, also believe that they are intellectually capable of reaching these decisions, and, further that their views are superior to the views of others who disagree with them. It requires some egotism to occupy the judgment throne and hand down a grading scale that makes comparisons. Paul now asks these judges who has assured them that they are more generously endowed than others and thus more qualified to make judgments?

And in the event that some of the Corinthians accepted this challenge and proved to Paul that they were more intelligent than others, he offered his rebuttal. He was willing to grant that some were smarter than others, but his question was whether they gained this superior status by their own efforts, or was it something which was given to them? There is only one answer to that. Superior intelligence and other personal superiorities are inherited not acquired assets, for which those so blessed can take no credit. The last question clinches Paul's argument. It is in the form of a first-class condition. Since in fact it was a gift of God's grace, why were they boasting about it as though it was not?

In verses 8-13 he contrasts the fortunes of the Corinthians with his own.

Verse 8 - "Now ye are full, now ye are rich, ye have reigned as kings without us: and I would to God ye did reign, that we also might reign with you."

ἤδη κεκορεσμένοι ἐστέ. ἤδη ἐπλουτήσατε. χωρὶς ἡμῶν ἐβασιλεύσατε. καὶ ὄφελόν γε ἐβασιλεύσατε, ἵνα καὶ ἡμεῖς ὑμῖν συμβασιλεύσωμεν.

"Already you are filled! Already you have become rich! Without us you have become kings!. And would that you did reign, so that we might share the rule with you!" . . . RSV

ἤδη (temporal adverb) 291.

κεκορεσμένοι (perf.pass.part.nom.pl.masc.of κορέννυμι, perfect periphrastic) 3738.

ἐστέ (2d.per.pl.pres.ind.of εἰμί, perfect periphrastic, intensive) 86.

ἤδη (temporal adverb) 291.

ἐπλουτήσατε (2d.per.pl.aor.act.ind.of πλουτέω, culminative) 1834.

χωρὶς (preposition with the ablative of separation) 1077.

ἡμῶν (abl.pl.masc.of ἐγώ, separation) 123.

ἐβασιλεύσατε (2d.per.pl.aor.act.ind.of βασιλεύω, ingressive) 236.

καὶ (emphatic conjunction) 14.

#4123 ὄφελον (properly a 2d.aor.of ὀφείλω).

King James Version

I would - Gal.5:12; Rev.3:15.
I would to God - 1 Cor.4:8.

Revised Standard Version

wish - Gal.5:12; 2 Cor.11:1.
would - Rev.3:15; 1 Cor.4:8.

Meaning: for ὤφελον with the temporal augment; 2d.aor.of ὀφείλω. In earlier Greek, followed by an infinitive as in ὤφελον θανεῖν - expressing a death wish - "I ought (or I want) to be dead." It became an interjection - "would that" to express a wish that something would happen which had not or would not have happened otherwise. Followed by an imperfect indicative in Rev.3:15; by the future indicative in Gal.5:12; with the imperfect indicative in 2 Cor.11:1 and aorist indicative in 1 Cor.4:8. Used to indicate unattainable wishes.

γε (emphatic particle) 2449.

ἐβασιλεύσατε (2d.per.pl.aor.act.ind.of βασιλεύω, ingressive) 236.

ἵνα (conjunction with the subjunctive in a purpose clause) 114.

καὶ (adjunctive conjunction joining substantives) 14.

ἡμεῖς (nom.pl.masc.of ἐγώ, subject of συμβασιλεύσωμεν) 123.

ὑμῖν (instru.pl.masc.of σύ, with σύν, in composition, association) 104.

#**4124** συμβασιλεύσωμεν (1st.per.pl.aor.act.subj.of συμβασιλεύω, purpose).

King James Version

reign with - 1 Cor.4:8; 2 Tim.2:12.

Revised Standard Version

share the rule - 1 Cor.4:8.
reign with - 2 Tim.2:12.

Meaning: A combination of σύν (#1542) and βασιλεύω (#236). To reign with another; share a throne; to a coregent. With reference to the reign of the saints with Christ in His kingdom - 1 Cor.4:8; 2 Tim.2:12.

Translation - "You have already been fulfilled! You have already become rich! Without us you have begun your reign! Indeed, I wish that you did reign, so that we also might reign with you."

Comment: Here are examples of choice sarcasm. The perfect periphrastic κεκορεσμένοι ἐστέ, indicates a present durative condition due to past completed action - "You became perfect in the past, and as a result you now need nothing!" They had also become rich! Since Paul last saw them and led them out of pagan darkness into Christ they had ascended their thrones and had begun to reign. And this they did without Paul (χωρὶς ἡμῶν). καὶ is emphatic and γε serves to heighten the emphasis, as Paul wishes that indeed the Corinthians did, in fact, reign like kings, since, if that were true, it would be true only because of the return of Christ, in which case Paul also would be reigning with them.

This last wish, as Paul sighs for an end of the Christian warfare and a share in the rewards of victory with Christ, leads him into what may be regarded as a bit of self pity, since he says (verse 14) that he is not writing it to shame the Corinthians into some proper humility.

Verse 9 - "For I think that God hath set forth us the apostles last, as it were appointed to death: for we are made a spectacle unto the world, and to angels, and to men."

δοκῶ γάρ, ὁ θεὸς ἡμᾶς τοὺς ἀποστόλους ἐσχάτους ἀπέδειξεν ὡς ἐπιθανατίους, ὅτι θέατρον ἐγενήθημεν τῷ κόσμῳ καὶ ἀγγέλοις καὶ ἀνθρώποις.

"For I think that God has exhibited us apostles as last of all, like men

sentenced to death; because we have become a spectacle to the world, to angels and to men." . . . *RSV*

δοκῶ (1st.per.sing.pres.act.ind.of δοκέω, aoristic) 287.
γὰρ (causal conjunction) 105.
ὁ (nom.sing.masc.of the article in agreement with θεὸς) 9.
θεὸς (nom.sing.masc.of θεός, subject of ἀπέδειξεν) 124.
ἡμᾶς (acc.pl.masc.of ἐγώ, direct object of ἀπέδειξεν) 123.
τοὺς (acc.pl.masc.of the article in agreement with ἀποστόλους) 9.
ἀποστόλους (acc.pl.masc.of ἀπόστολος, apposition) 844.
ἐσχάτους (acc.pl.masc.of ἔσχατος, predicate adjective) 496.
ἀπέδειξεν (3d.per.sing.aor.act.ind.of ἀποδείκνυμι, culminative) 2989.
ὡς (comparative particle) 128.

#4125 ἐπιθανατίους (acc.pl.masc.of ἐπιθανάτιος, predicate adjective).

King James Version

appointed to death - 1 Cor.4:9.

Revised Standard Version

sentenced to death - 1 Cor.4:9.

Meaning: A combination of ἐπί (#47) and θάνατος (#381). Hence, condemned or doomed to death - 1 Cor.4:9.

ὅτι (conjunction introducing a causal clause) 211.
θέατρον (acc.sing.neut.of θέατρον, direct object of ἐγενήθημεν) 3483.
ἐγενήθημεν (1st.per.pl.aor.pass.ind.of γίνομαι, culminative) 113.
τῷ (dat.sing.masc.of the article in agreement with κόσμῳ) 9.
κόσμῳ (dat.sing.masc.of κόσμος, personal interest) 360.
καὶ (adjunctive conjunction joining nouns) 14.
ἀγγέλοις (dat.pl.masc.of ἄγγελος, personal interest) 96.
καὶ (adjunctive conjunction joining nouns) 14.
ἀνθρώποις (dat.pl.masc.of ἄνθρωπος, personal interest) 341.

Translation - *"Because it seems to me that God has displayed us, the Apostles, last, as marked for death, because we have been made a spectacle before the world and angels and men."*

Comment: Paul explains his desire to see the end of the age with its Messianic reign (verse 8) with the γὰρ causal clause. There are four accusatives joined to ἀπέδειξεν - a pronoun (ἡμᾶς), a noun in apposition (ἀποστόλους) and two predicate adjectives (ἐσχάτους) and, after ὡς in the comparative sense ἐπιθανατίους.

ἐσχάτους may refer to the custom of having the condemned criminals, who were scheduled to die in the arena, march at the end of the procession. Goodspeed translates " . . . God has exhibited us apostles at the very end of the procession, like the men condemned to die in the arena." ὅτι introduces a second causal clause. Note that ἀγγέλοις and ἀνθρώποις are anarthrous while we have τῷ κόσμῳ. Winer thinks that this fact "particularize(s) the τῷ κόσμῳ" (Winer-Thayer, 127, as cited in Robertson, *Grammar*, 788) but Robertson objects that in 1 John 2:16 πᾶν ἐν τῷ κόσμῳ is "particularized" by three words, all of which have the article! (*Ibid.*) The point however is clear. The Apostles had been placed in a position to merit only ridicule in the eyes of the world of men and angels. That he should include ἄγγελοι as contemptuous of him seems to support the view that Paul was a little bit off balance emotionally here, and that he was perhaps unconsciously exaggerating. His disgust with the "babes in Christ" who ought to know better, coupled with his own sufferings, lends itself to his emotion.

That the Holy Spirit, at Whose instigation the New Testament was written, would allow this evidence of Paul's human frailty to creep into the text only enhances the document as genuine. If Paul had been trying to represent himself as sinless he would have edited this passage out of the text.

Verse 10 - "We are fools for Christ's sake, but ye are wise in Christ; we are weak, but ye are strong; ye are honorable, but we are despised."

ἡμεῖς μωροὶ διὰ Χριστόν, ὑμεῖς δὲ φρόνιμοι ἐν Χριστῷ. ἡμεῖς ἀσθενεῖς, ὑμεῖς δὲ ἰσχυροί. ὑμεῖς ἔνδοξοι, ἡμεῖς δὲ ἄτιμοι.

"We are fools for Christ's sake, but you are wise in Christ. We are weak, but you are strong. You are held in honor, but we in disrepute." . . . RSV

ἡμεῖς (nom.pl.masc.of ἐγώ, subject of ἐσμέν understood) 123.
μωροὶ (nom.pl.masc.of μωρός, predicate nominative) 482.
διὰ (preposition with the accusative, cause) 118.
Χριστόν (acc.sing.masc.of Χριστός, cause) 4.
ὑμεῖς (nom.pl.masc.of σύ, subject of ἐστέ understood) 104.
δὲ (adversative conjunction) 11.
φρόνιμοι (nom.pl.masc.of φρόνιμος, predicate adjective) 693.
ἐν (preposition with the instrumental of association) 80.
Χριστῷ (instru.sing.masc.of Χριστός, association) 4.
ἡμεῖς (nom.pl.masc.of ἐγώ, subject of ἐσμέν, understood) 123.
ἀσθενεῖς (nom.pl.masc.of ἀσθενές, predicate adjective) 1551.
ὑμεῖς (nom.pl.masc.of σύ, subject of ἐστέ, understood) 104.
δὲ (adversative conjunction) 11.
ἰσχυροί (nom.pl.masc.of ἰσχυρός, predicate adjective) 303.
ὑμεῖς (nom.pl.masc.of σύ, subject of ἐστέ, understood) 104.
ἔνδοξοι (nom.pl.masc.of ἔνδοξος, predicate adjective) 2160.
ἡμεῖς (nom.pl.masc.of ἐγώ, subject of ἐσμέν understood) 123.
δὲ (adversative conjunction) 11.
ἄτιμοι (nom.pl.masc.of ἄτιμος, predicate adjective) 1102.

Translation - "We are fools because of Christ, but you are wise in association with Him. We are weak, but you are strong. You are highly honored, but we are despised."

Comment: The descriptions of himself are sincere; those of the Corinthians are highly sarcastic. Paul's theology earned him a reputation among the unsaved as a fool, but the Corinthians had twisted Christian logic until, for them, it had become a mark of high philosophical sophistication. Paul's weakness and disgrace was in contrast to their power and prestige. Someone is out of line. The true Christian faith could not react upon Paul and the other Apostles, on the one hand and their converts in Corinth in opposite ways. Actually the Corinthians were not φρόνιμοι, ἰσχυροὶ καὶ ἔνδοξοι in the eyes of the world. They only thought they were. This is the basis for Paul's sarcasm.

Paul was not only an outcast in the philosophical and social worlds. He also suffered from physical and economic ills.

Verse 11 - "Even unto this present hour we both hunger and thirst, and are naked, and are buffeted, and have no certain dwelling place."

ἄχρι τῆς ἄρτι ὥρας καὶ πεινῶμεν καὶ διφῶμεν καὶ γυμνιτεύομεν καὶ κολαφιζόμεθα καὶ ἀστατοῦμεν.

"To the present hour we hunger and thirst, we are ill-clad and buffeted and homeless," . . . RSV

ἄχρι (preposition with the genitive of time description) 1517.
τῆς (gen.sing.fem.of the article in agreement with ὥρας) 9.
ἄρτι (temporal adverb) 320.
ὥρας (gen.sing.fem.of ὥρα, time description) 735.
καὶ (ascensive conjunction) 14.
πεινῶμεν (1st.per.pl.pres.act.ind.of πεινάω, present iterative retroactive) 335.
καὶ (adjunctive conjunction joining verbs) 14.
διφῶμεν (1st.per.pl.pres.act.ind.of διφάω, present iterative retroactive) 427.
καὶ (adjunctive conjunction joining verbs) 14.

#4126 γυμνιτεύομεν (1st.per.pl.pres.act.ind.of γυμνητεύω, for γυμνητεύομεν, present progressive retroactive).

King James Version

be naked - 1 Cor.4:11.

Revised Standard Version

ill-clad - 1 Cor.4:11.

Meaning: lightly clad; ill-clothed. Dressed in clothing that is insufficient, worn and socially unacceptable. With reference to Paul's wardrobe - 1 Cor.4:11. In

Dio Cass. 47,34,2 and Plut. *Aem.* 16, of a lightly armed soldier. Literally it means to be naked. As such it reveals Paul's emotional state, as exaggerative in 1 Cor.4:11.

καὶ (adjunctive conjunction joining verbs) 14.

κολαφιζόμεθα (1st.per.pl.pres.pass.ind.of κολαφίζω, present iterative retroactive) 1607.

καὶ (adjunctive conjunction joining verbs) 14.

#4127 ἀστατοῦμεν (1st.per.pl.pres.act.ind.of ἀστατέω, present iterative retroactive).

King James Version

have no certain dwelling place - 1 Cor.4:11.

Revised Standard Version

homeless - 1 Cor.4:11.

Meaning: cf. ἄστατος - "vagrant." ἀκατάστατος (#5097). It may be formed from α privative plus ἵστημι (#180). Hence, not standing anywhere. Not permanently located; homeless. With reference to Paul's poverty in 1 Cor.4:11.

Translation - "Even until this very hour we have hungered and thirsted and we have been naked and we have been beaten with fists and we have been homeless."

Comment: ἄχρι τῆς ἄρτι ὥρας, coupled with the present retroactives of the tenses involved, either progressive or iterative, indicates that Paul was saying that since the day he began to preach, he and the other Apostles, had been hungry and thirsty, naked, the victims of beatings and homeless. Some of these misfortunes were iterative; other were continuous. It was bad. There is no doubt of that. But it was not that bad. Once again, he is exaggerating, though he denies that he was trying to make the proud Corinthians ashamed (verse 14).

He continues his tale of woe in

Verse 12 - "And labour, working with our own hands: being reviled, we bless; being persecuted, we suffer it."

καὶ κοπιῶμεν ἐργαζόμενοι ταῖς ἰδίαις χερσίν. λοιδορούμενοι εὐλογοῦμεν, διωκόμενοι ἀνεχόμεθα.

"and we labor, working with our own hands. When reviled, we bless; when persecuted, we endure;" . . . RSV

καὶ (adjunctive conjunction joining verbs) 14.

κοπιῶμεν (1st.per.pl.pres.act.ind.of κοπιάω, present iterative retroactive) 629.

ἐργαζόμενοι (pres.mid.part.nom.pl.masc.of ἐργάζομαι, adverbial, modal) 691.

ταῖς (instrumental pl.fem.of the article in agreement with χερσίν) 9.

ἰδίας (instru.pl.fem.of ἴδιος, in agreement with χερσίν) 778.

χερσίν (instr.pl.fem.of χείρ, means) 308.

λοιδορούμενοι (pres.pass.part.nom.pl.masc.of λοιδορέω, adverbial, temporal) 2402.

εὐλογοῦμεν (1st.per.pl.pres.act.ind.of εὐλογέω, present iterative retroactive) 1120.

διωκόμενοι (pres.pass.part.nom.pl.masc.of διώκω, adverbial, temporal) 434.

ἀνεχόμεθα (1st.per.pl.pres.mid.ind.of ἀνέχομαι, present iterative) 1234.

Translation - "And we toil, working with our own hands; when we have been insulted, we have always blessed. In the face of persecution we have always endured it with composure."

Comment: Each of the words used here have interesting connections elsewhere in the New Testament. The student should run the references for inter-scriptural connections that make for good preaching. The use of ἰδίαις, as an attributive adjective with χερσίν is another evidence of Paul's emotional state. With whose hands would he toil (#629) if not with his own?! All that he says is true. The fact that he says it so earnestly is evidence that he felt deeply that the Corinthians were falling short of the apostolic standard, and he intended to make them realize this.

Note carefully the distinction between the progressive present and the iterative present. Paul was not *always* hungry and thirsty in the continuative sense. Had he been he would have died of starvation. But he was *periodically* hungry, thirsty, naked, homeless, etc., in the passages where the iterative applies.

Verse 13 - "Being defamed, we intreat: we are made as the filth of the world, and are the offscouring of all things unto this day."

δυσφημούμενοι παρακαλοῦμεν. ὡς περικαθάρματα τοῦ κόσμου ἐγενήθημεν, πάντων περίψημα, ἕως ἄρτι.

"when slandered, we try to conciliate; we have become, and are now, as the refuse of the world, the offscouring of all things." . . . RSV

#4128 δυσφημούμενοι (pres.pass.part.nom.pl.masc.of δυσφημέω, adverbial, temporal).

King James Version

defame - 1 Cor.4:13.

Revised Standard Version

slander - 1 Cor.4:13.

Meaning: Cf. δυσφημία (#4316). In the passive, to be slandered; to be defamed - 1 Cor.4:13.

παρακαλοῦμεν (1st.per.pl.pres.act.ind.of παρακαλέω, present iterative retroactive) 230.

ὠς (comparative particle) 128.

#4129 περικαϑάρματα (acc.pl.neut.of περικάϑαρμα, direct object of e0genh1uhmen).

King James Version

filth - 1 Cor.4:13.

Revised Standard Version

refuse - 1 Cor.4:13.

Meaning: A combination of περί (#173) and κάϑαρμα - "that which is thrown away in cleansing." *Cf.* περικαϑαίρω - "to cleanse on all sides." To purify completely. Translated "ransom " in Prov.21:18. "The Greeks used to apply the term καϑάρματα to victims sacrificed to make expiation for the people, and even to criminals who were maintained at the public expense, that on the outbreak of a pestilence or other calamity they might be offered as sacrifices to make expiation for the state." (Thayer, 503). Followed by τοῦ κόσμου in 1 Cor.4:13, where Paul means that the world thought that the gods would be pleased if the Apostles were dead.

τοῦ (gen.sing.masc.of the article in agreement with κόσμου) 9.
κόσμου (gen.sing.masc.of κόσμος, description) 360.
ἐγενήϑημεν (1st.per.pl.aor.pass.ind.of γίνομαι, culminative) 113.
πάντων (abl.pl.neut.of πᾶς, comparison) 67.

#4130 περίφημα (acc.sing.neut.of περίφημα, direct object of ἐγενήϑημεν).

King James Version
offscouring - 1 Cor.4:13.

Revised Standard Version

offscouring - 1 Cor.4:13.

Meaning: A combination of περί (#173) and φάω - "to rub off" "to wipe." Hence that which is discarded completely - wiped off all around. *Cf.* #4129. "Suidas and other Greek lexicographers . . . relate that the Athenians, in order to avert public calamities, yearly threw a criminal into the sea as an offering to Poseidon; hence ἀργύριον . . . περίφημα τοῦ παιδίου ἡμῶν γένοιτο, (as if to say) "let it become an expiatory offering, a ransom for our child, *i.e.* in comparison with the saving of our son's life let it be to us a despicable and worthless thing,' Tob. v.18") (Thayer, 507). Paul's statement of the estimate which the world put upon him and the other Apostles - 1 Cor.4:13.

ἕως (preposition with the genitive of time description) 71.
ἄρτι (temporal adverb) 320.

Translation - "When we are slandered we plead for reconciliation. We have come to be regarded as the dregs of society, the scum of the earth, to this moment."

Comment: Study #'s 4129 and 4130 and you have the depths of Paul's meaning. It would be difficult to use figures of speech more degrading. The idea of an expendable sacrifice to the gods, to forestall calamity is in line with the thought for ἐσχάτους in verse 9. Unsaved world society has always looked upon the Christian, who was faithful to the philosophy of the gospel of Christ, as scum, dregs or filth - something to be destroyed for the good of society. *Cf.* Caiphas' attitude toward Jesus in John 11:49-51.

In one last effort to "redeem" world society, Antichrist will murder the Christians in the last half of the tribulation period (Rev.13:6,7; 6:9-11). The world's attitude toward the Christian exactly matches God's attitude toward the sinful world. Each believes that the other must be eliminated so as to bring order in the universe (Rev.20:15-21:1). This mutual rejection is the practical result of their mutual contempt, each for the philosophy of the other (1 Cor.1:18,20). Thus there is no possibility of compromise between the two irreconcilable systems of thought and policy. Thus the question comes down to this: Who is the greater? (1 John 4:4; Mt.28:18; Eph.1:19-23; Phil.2:9-11; Rev.20:10).

But there is one great difference. The Sovereign God, Who is not threatened in His position in the universe by sin, darkness and error, is a God of love Who has determined to redeem some and bring them into total conformity with His will. This He is abundantly able and willing to do.

Verse 14 - "I write not these things to shame you, but as my beloved sons I warn you."

Οὐκ ἐντρέπων ὑμᾶς γράφω ταῦτα, ἀλλ᾽ ὡς τέκνα μου ἀγαπητὰ νουθετῶν.

"I do not write this to make you ashamed, but to admonish you as my beloved children." . . . RSV

Οὐκ (negative particle with the participle) 130.
ἐντρέπων (pres.act.part.nom.sing.masc.of ἐντρέπω, adverbial, telic) 1385.
ὑμᾶς (acc.pl.masc.of σύ, direct object of ἐντρέπων) 104.
γράφω (1st.per.sing.pres.act.ind.of γράφω, aoristic) 156.
ταῦτα (acc.pl.neut.of οὗτος, direct object of γράφω) 93.
ἀλλ᾽ (adversative conjunction) 342.
ὡς (comparative particle) 128.
τέκνα (acc.pl.neut.of τέκνον, direct object of νουθετῶν) 229.
μου (gen.sing.masc.of ἐγώ, relationship) 123.
ἀγαπητὰ (acc.pl.neut.of ἀγαπητός, in agreement with τέκνα) 327.
νουθετῶν (pres.act.part.nom.sing.masc.of νουθετέω, adverbial, telic) 3535.

Translation - "I am writing these things, not to make you ashamed, but in order to remind you, my beloved children."

Comment: Note the epistolary aorist in Philemon 19, 1 Pet.5:12 and 1 John 5:13. Here Paul uses the present tense. Paul is thinking of himself as he writes, not of

the Corinthians as they read. The two participles are telic. Note the rare use of
οὐκ with the participle. This is rare in the New Testament (#130), the usual
negative being μή (#87), but it is not unknown. "In general it may be said of the
κοινή that the presence of οὐ with the participle means that the negative is clear-
cut and decisive." (Robertson, *Grammar*, 1138, 1138).

Paul has gone to great lengths rhetorically to point up the contrast between
the life-style of the Corinthian Christians and his own and that of the other
Apostles. It is a purple passage! We have even suggested elements of self-pity.
Now he says that he is definitely not trying to shame them, but only to order their
thinking (#3535) in a different frame of reference. This is therefore rebuke,
admonition, correction and thought adjustment. They are his converts and as
such he loves them as his spiritual children, begotten in the gospel of Christ. It
makes no difference how many teachers they have had since they were saved,
they cannot forget that it was under Paul's ministry that they first heard the
gospel and came to Christ for salvation. This is the thought in

*Verse 15 - "For though ye have ten thousand instructors in Christ, yet have ye
not many fathers: for in Christ Jesus I have begotten you through the gospel."*

ἐὰν γὰρ μυρίους παιδαγωγοὺς ἔχητε ἐν Χριστῷ, ἀλλ᾽ οὐ πολλοὺς πατέρας,
ἐν γὰρ Χριστῷ Ἰησοῦ διὰ τοῦ εὐαγγελίου ἐγὼ ὑμᾶς ἐγέννησα.

*"For though you have countless guides in Christ, you do not have many
fathers. For I became your father in Christ Jesus through the gospel.". . . RSV*

ἐὰν (conditional particle with the subjunctive in a third-class condition) 363.
γὰρ (causal conjunction) 105.
μυρίους (acc.pl.masc.of μύριοι, in agreement with παιδαγωγοὺς) 1272.

#4131 παιδαγωγοὺς (acc.pl.masc.of παιδαγωγός, direct object of ἔχητε).

    King James Version

instructor - 1 Cor.4:15.
schoolmaster - Gal.3:24,25.

    Revised Standard Version

guides - 1 Cor.4:15.
custodian - Gal.3:24,25.

Meaning: A combination of παιδίον (#174) and ἄγω (#876). Hence, one who
leads or directs a child; in an intellectual way, a teacher, instructor, tutor. Of the
Christian teachers who came to Corinth to teach the Christians after Paul had
led the Corinthians to Christ - 1 Cor.4:15. In a figure, of the Mosaic law, which
sternly reminds the unsaved of his transgressions of its code, thus to awaken him
of his need for Christ. Similarly the Roman slave acted as a tutor to bring up the
son of his master until he reached the age of legal manhood - Gal.3:24,25. *Cf.*
comment, *en loc.*

ἔχητε (2d.per.pl.pres.act.subj.of ἔχω, third-class condition) 82.

ἐν (preposition with the locative of sphere) 80.

Χριστῷ (loc.sing.masc.of Χριστός, sphere) 4.

ἀλλ' (adversative conjunction) 342.

οὐ (negative particle with the indicative understood) 130.

πολλοὺς (acc.pl.masc.of πολύς, in agreement with πατέρας) 228.

πατέρας (acc.pl.masc.of πατήρ, direct object of ἔχετε understood) 238.

ἐν (preposition with the instrumental of association) 80.

γὰρ (causal conjunction) 105.

Χριστῷ (instru.sing.masc.of Χριστός, association) 4.

Ἰησοῦ (instru.sing.masc.of Ἰησοῦς, apposition) 3.

διὰ (preposition with the ablative, intermediate agent) 118.

τοῦ (abl.sing.neut.of the article in agreement with εὐαγγελίου) 9.

εὐαγγελίου (abl.sing.neut.of εὐαγγέλιον, intermediate agent) 405.

ἐγὼ (nom.sing.masc.of ἐγώ, subject of ἐγέννησα) 123.

ὑμᾶς (acc.pl.masc.of σύ, direct object of ἐγέννησα) 104.

ἐγέννησα (1st.per.sing.aor.act.ind.of γεννάω, constative) 8.

Translation - *"Because if you should have had innumerable teachers in the sphere of Christianity, yet you do not have many fathers; because by means of Christ Jesus, through the gospel I fathered you."*

Comment: The third-class condition with ἐὰν and the subjunctive in ἔχητε anticipates the future. There is no certainty as to the number of teachers they had had in the past or how many more they might have in the future - one thing is certain. The Corinthians had only one "father" in the gospel of Christ. That was Paul. It was under his preaching that they were born from above (John 3:3,7) into the Body of Christ (1 Cor.12:13).

Note that Paul defines his preaching ministry carefully. The direct agent of their salvation was Christ Jesus. The indirect agent was the gospel (1 Cor.1:18; 15:1-4), not the wisdom of this world (1 Cor.3:19).

Paul bases his plea of verse 16 upon the fact that he is their spiritual father.

Verse 16 - *"Wherefore I beseech you, be ye followers of me."*
παρακαλῶ οὖν ὑμᾶς, μιμηταί μου γίνεσθε.

"I urge you then, be imitators of me." . . . *RSV*

παρακαλῶ (1st.per.sing.pres.act.ind.of παρακαλῶ, aoristic) 230.

οὖν (inferential conjunction) 68.

ὑμᾶς (acc.pl.masc.of σύ, direct object of παρακαλῶ) 104.

#4132 μιμηταί (nom.pl.masc.of μιμητής, predicate nominative).

    King James Version

follower - 1 Cor.4:16; 11:1; Eph.5:1; 1 Thess.1:6; 2:14; Heb.6:12.

    Revised Standard Version

imitators - 1 Cor.4:16; 11:1; Eph.5:1; 1 Thess.1:6; 2:14; Heb.6:12.

Meaning: An imitator. Followed by an ablative of comparison in 1 Cor.4:16; 11:1 (μου); Eph.5:1 (θεοῦ); 1 Thess.1:6 (ἡμῶν); 2:14 (τῶν ἐκκλησιῶν); Heb.6:12 (τῶν . . . κληρονομούντων).

μου (abl.sing.masc.of ἐγώ, comparison) 123.
γίνεσθε (2d.per.pl.pres.impv.of γίνομαι, command) 113.

Translation - "I beg you then to be my imitators."

Comment: Since Paul was their spiritual father his plea is, "Like father; Like son." He did not hesitate to hold up his own life-style as an example for the saints to follow. *Cf.* Eph.5:1; 1 Cor.11:1; 1 Thess.1:6 in which he adds καὶ τοῦ κυρίου. As Paul followed the Lord he became a safe guide for his own followers. The Christian who says, "Live not by my example but by what I teach" is astray from Paul's philosophy and practise. Paul must beg the Corinthians since to imitate him is to invite his hardships (verses 9-13). The challenge, then and now, is not an easy one, though the Christian is a fool to shrink from it.

In order for the Corinthians to forsake their ways and to return to the paths of Christian obedience which Paul demands, he announces his decision to send Timothy to them, in

Verse 17 - "For this cause have I sent unto you Timotheus, who is my beloved son, and faithful in the Lord, who shall bring you into remembrance of my ways which be in Christ, as I teach everywhere in every church."

δια τοῦτο ἔπεμφα ὑμῖν Τιμόθεον, ὅς ἐστίν μου τέκνον ἀγαπητὸν καὶ πιστὸν ἐν κυρίῳ, ὃς ὑμᾶς ἀναμνήσει τὰς ὁδούς μου τὰς ἐν Χριστῷ (Ἰησοῦ), καθὼς πανταχοῦ ἐν πάσῃ ἐκκλησίᾳ διδάσκω.

"Therefore I sent to you Timothy, my beloved and faithful child in the Lord, to remind you of my ways in Christ, as I teach them everywhere in every church."
                                                    . . . RSV

διὰ (preposition with the accusative, cause) 118.
τοῦτο (acc.sing.neut.of οὗτος, cause) 93.
ἔπεμφα (1st.per.sing.aor.act.ind.of πέμπω, epistolary) 169.
ὑμῖν (dat.pl.masc.of σύ, indirect object of ἔπεμφα) 104.
Τιμόθεον (acc.sing.masc.of Τιμόθεος, direct object of ἔπεμφα) 3354.
ὅς (nom.sing.masc.of ὅς, relative pronoun, subject of ἐστίν) 65.
ἐστίν (3d.per.sing.pres.ind.of εἰμί, static) 86.
μου (gen.sing.masc.of ἐγώ, relationship) 123.
τέκνον (nom.sing.neut.of τέκνον, predicate nominative) 229.
ἀγαπητὸν (nom.sing.masc.of ἀγαπητός, in agreement with τέκνον) 327.
καὶ (adjunctive conjunction joining adjectives) 14.
πιστὸν (nom.sing.neut.of πιστός, in agreement with τέκνον) 1522.
ἐν (preposition with the locative of sphere) 80.

κυρίῳ (loc.sing.masc.of κύριος, sphere) 97.

ὅς (nom.sing.masc.of ὅς, relative pronoun, subject of ἀναμνήσει) 65.

ἀναμνήσει (3d.per.sing.fut.act.ind.of ἀναμιμνήσκω, predictive) 2681.

τὰς (acc.pl.fem.of the article in agreement with ὁδούς) 9.

ὁδούς (acc.pl.fem.of ὁδός, direct object of ἀναμνήσει) 199.

μου (gen.sing.masc.of ἐγώ, possession) 123.

τὰς (acc.pl.fem.of the article in agreement with ὁδούς) 9.

ἐν (preposition with the locative of sphere) 80.

Χριστῷ (loc.sing.masc.of Χριστός, sphere) 4.

(Ἰησοῦ) (loc.sing.masc.of Ἰησοῦς, apposition) 3.

καθώς (compound particle in a comparative clause) 1348.

πανταχοῦ (local adverb) 2062.

ἐν (preposition with the locative of place) 80.

πάσῃ (loc.sing.fem.of πᾶς, in agreement with ἐκκλησίᾳ) 67.

ἐκκλησίᾳ (loc.sing.fem.of ἐκκλησία, place) 1204.

διδάσκω (1st.per.sing.pres.act.ind.of διδάσκω, customary) 403.

Translation - *"That is why I have sent to you Timothy, who is my beloved and faithful son in the Lord, who will review for you my methods in the service of Christ Jesus, just as I teach everywhere in every church."*

Comment: διὰ τοῦτο refers to his plea of verse 16. Timothy's visit will review for them Paul's philosophy and methods in the sphere of God's work. They are the same methods which he has used in every part of the world and in every church. This fact does a great deal to refute the view that a different social milieu demands an adjustment of content and method in preaching. Paul preached the same gospel and followed the same life-style wherever he went without regard to the sociology. Social situations differ in many respects, as they respond to climate, land forms, political structure, cultural background, etc., but they are the same in that the populace is lost in sin and can be saved only through the gospel of Christ.

Paul visited in a large variety of social, economic and political situations. There was little to compare between Athens and the rural regions of Galatia. One thing they had in common. They were blinded by Satan and lost in sin.

Often we hear with referene to some uneducated evangelist, "He can reach a type of person that our church with its ministry cannot reach." This lowers the dignity and power of the gospel of Christ to the Dale Carnegie level. Paul reached all types of people with the same message and the same method - by preaching in the power of the Holy Spirit a message which was nonesense to the audience, whether they were rich or poor, urban or rural, cultured or benighted, wise or unwise.

Timothy is described as Paul's convert, beloved and faithful. Note the two relative pronouns, both of which refer to Timothy. The first relative clause is descriptive. The second expresses purpose. Note that the relative uses the future indicative, in conformity to Attic Greek, though Homer used it with the subjunctive and the optative. That Paul would entrust to Timothy the mission to

Corinth where there were so many spiritual problems is an evidence of Paul's estimate of him.

Verse 18 - "Now some are puffed up, as though I would not come to you."

ὡς μὴ ἐρχομένου δέ μου πρὸς ὑμᾶς ἐφυσιώθησάν τινες.

"Some are arrogant, as though I were not coming to you." . . . RSV

ὡς (particle introducing a genitive absolute in a concessive clause) 128.
μὴ (negative particle with the participle) 87.
ἐρχομένου (pres.mid.part.gen.sing.masc.of ἔρχομαι, genitive absolute in a concessive clause) 146.
δὲ (adversative conjunction) 11.
μου (gen.sing.masc.of ἐγώ, genitive absolute) 123.
πρὸς (preposition with the accusative of extent) 197.
ὑμᾶς (acc.pl.masc.of σύ, extent) 104.
ἐφυσιώθησάν (3d.per.pl.aor.pass.ind.of φυσιόω, constative) 4122.
τινες (nom.pl.masc.of τις, indefinite pronoun, subject of φυσιώθησαν) 486.

Translation - "But some have grown arrogant as though I were not coming to you."

Comment: A genitive absolute in a ὡς clause of concession is rare in the New Testament. He observes that some of the troublemakers at Corinth had grown arrogant and perhaps intended to extend the scope of their influence, since they assumed that Paul would never return to Corinth. This assumption, if they held it, was false as he says in verse 19, where he disabuses them of this fallacious supposition, and he promises that if they do not repent there will be a full display of apostolic authority.

Verse 19 - "But I will come to you shortly, if the Lord will, and will know not the speech of them which are puffed up, but of power."

ἐλεύσομαι δὲ ταχέως πρὸς ὑμᾶς, ἐὰν ὁ κύριος θελήσῃ, καὶ γνώσομαι οὐ τὸν λόγον τῶν πεφυσιωμένων ἀλλὰ τὴν δύναμιν.

"But I will come to you soon, if the Lord wills, and I will find out not the talk of these arrogant people but their power." . . . RSV

ἐλεύσομαι (1st.per.sing.fut.ind.of ἔρχομαι, third-class condition) 146.
δὲ (adversative conjunction) 11.
ταχέως (adverbial) 2531.
πρὸς (preposition with the accusative of extent) 197.
ὑμᾶς (acc.pl.masc.of σύ, extent) 104.
ἐὰν (conditional particle in a third-class condition) 363.
ὁ (nom.sing.masc.of the article in agreement with κύριος) 9.
κύριος (nom.sing.masc.of κύριος, subject of θελήσῃ) 97.
θελήσῃ (3d.per.sing.aor.act.subj.of θέλω, in a third-class condition) 88.

καὶ (continuative conjunction) 14.

γνώσομαι (1st.per.sing.fut.act.ind.of γινώσκω, predictive) 131.

οὐ (negative particle with the indicative) 130.

τὸν (acc.sing.masc.of the article in agreement with λόγον) 9.

λόγον (acc.sing.masc.of λόγος, direct object of γνώσομαι) 510.

τῶν (gen.pl.masc.of the article in agreement with πεφυσιωμένων) 9.

πεφυσιωμένων (perf.pass.part.gen.pl.masc.of φυσιόω, substantival, possession) 4122.

ἀλλὰ (alternative conjunction) 342.

τὴν (acc.sing.fem.of the article in agreement with δύναμιν) 9.

δύναμιν (acc.sing.fem.of δύναμις, direct object of γνώσομαι) 687.

Translation - "But I am going to come to you soon, if the Lord is willing, and I will test, not what these snobs have to say but what they can do."

Comment: Paul has sounded very confident in this context. It is refreshing therefore to see his humble deference to the sovereign God, as he qualifies his promise to return to Corinth with the third-class condition ἐὰν ὁ κύριος θελήσῃ. *Cf.*James 4:13-15. If the Lord would permit him to do so Paul would return to Corinth. The certainty in the third-class condition is in the apodosis, not the protasis. Paul did not know whether the Lord would allow him to go to Corinth or not, but he was certain that if the Lord permitted it, he would return.

The Lord is head over all things to His church (Eph.1:22) and He does not need anyone, not even Paul, to deal with the Corinthian infection. But if the Lord permitted Paul to return and deal with the problem, he was ready to go. When and if he returned he would find out all that the troublemakers were saying. It is probable that he already knew most of this. What they were saying against Paul and against the apostolic authority which he and the other apostles had asserted was not important. The important thing was the degree to which they could make their influence felt within the church and in the city. This Paul intended to test. Paul and the self-appointed leaders of the Corinthian church were on a collision course. A power struggle was in the making and Paul seems eager to begin. He would pit the power of his apostolic authority against the social influence of the enemy, which originated, not in the Holy Spirit and a divine commission, but in their own human wisdom and social and political prestige. Paul reminds them in verse 20 that the divine resources are on his side, not in the eloquence and philosophical profundity of the demagogues.

It is obvious that if Christ could handle the Corinthian problem without Paul (though He always works through some Christian indirect agent) He is not necessarily limited in His efforts in the 20th century to the cooperation of popes, cardinals, bishops, district superintendents, convention presidents or secretaries, denominational editors, association missionaries or deacons. Nothing derogatory is implied about any of these persons, though a common problem in all church bodies is a failure to keep in mind that every Christian is a member of the Body of Christ and has equal access to the Head, through the indwelling Holy Spirit. Every member of the Body of Christ is to refrain from assuming that he has been given a higher position of leadership than that to which the Holy Spirit has appointed him (Rom.12:3).

Verse 20 - "For the kingdom of God is not in word, but in power."

οὐ γὰρ ἐν λόγῳ ἡ βασιλεία τοῦ θεοῦ ἀλλ' ἐν δυνάμει.

"For the kingdom of God does not consist in talk but in power." . . . RSV

οὐ (negative particle with the indicative understood) 130.
γὰρ (causal conjunction) 105.
ἐν (preposition with the locative of sphere) 80.
λόγῳ (loc.sing.masc.of λόγος, sphere) 510.
ἡ (nom.sing.fem.of the article in agreement with βασιλεία) 9.
βασιλεία (nom.sing.fem.of βασιλεία, subject of verb understood) 253.
τοῦ (gen.sing.masc.of the article in agreement with θεοῦ) 9.
θεοῦ (gen.sing.masc.of θεός, description) 124.
ἀλλ' (alternative conjunction) 342.
ἐν (preposition with the instrumental of means) 80.
δυνάμει (instru.sing.fem.of δύναμις, means) 687.

Translation - "Because the kingdom of God does not function in the sphere of words but by means of power."

Comment: It is not always possible to determine what verb should be supplied in an ellision. The context reveals the idea. Paul means that the real work of the Kingdom of God is carried on, not on talk but on performance. Men may say what they like, with or without the approval of the Holy Spirit, but He will do only that which promotes the work of the kingdom. Paul is saying that his critics in Corinth were "talking a good game." He is wondering what, at the end of the ninth inning, their batting average will be. In modern parlance Paul's challenge is "Put up or shut up."

The Holy Spirit will dictate what the policy of the Corinthian church will be. If God wills it, He will use Paul on his next trip to Corinth to implement the will of God. Paul gives them a choice. Do they want a fight when he comes or would they rather settle the matter within the framework of the gifts and fruits of the Holy Spirit?

Verse 21 - "What will ye? Shall I come unto you with a rod, or in love, and in the spirit of meekness?"

τί θέλετε; ἐν ῥάβδῳ ἔλθω πρὸς ὑμᾶς, ἢ ἐν ἀγάπῃ πνεύματί τε πραΰτητος;

"What do you wish? Shall I come to you with a rod, or with love in a spirit of gentleness?" . . . RSV

τί (acc.sing.neut.of τίς, interrogative pronoun, direct object of θέλετε, direct question) 281.
θέλετε (2d.per.pl.pres.act.ind.of θέλω, direct question) 88.
ἐν (preposition with the locative, accompanying circumstance) 80.

ῥάβδῳ (loc.sing.masc.of ῥάβδος, accompanying circumstance) 863.
ἔλθω (1st.per.sing.2d.aor.subj.of ἔρχομαι, deliberative) 146.
πρὸς (preposition with the accusative of extent) 197.
ὑμᾶς (acc.pl.masc.of σύ, extent) 104.
ἤ (disjunctive) 465.
ἐν (preposition with the locative, accompanying circumstance) 80.
ἀγάπῃ (loc.sing.fem.of ἀγάπη, accompanying circumstance) 1490.
πνεύματί (loc.sing.neut.of πνεῦμα, accompanying circumstance) 83.
τε (correlative particle) 1408.

#4133 πραΰτητος (gen.sing.fem.of πραΰτης, description).

King James Version

meekness - 1 Cor.4:21; James 1:21; 3:13; 1 Pet.3:15; 2 Cor.10:1; Gal.5:23; 6:1; Eph.4:2; Col.3:12; 2 Tim.2:25; Tit.3:2.

Revised Standard Version

gentleness - 1 Cor.4:21; 1 Pet.3:15; Gal.5:23; 6:1; 2 Tim.2:25.
meekness - James 1:21; 3:13; 2 Cor.10:1; Eph.4:2; Col.3:12.
courtesy - Tit.3:2.

Meaning: Cf. πραΰς (#425). Gentleness, meekness, mildness. Enjoined upon believers as a true mark of Christian character. The fruit of the Spirit (Gal.5:23). An important attitude to be displayed in diplomatic negotiation.

Translation - "What do you want? Shall I come to you with a rod or in love and in a spirit of gentleness?"

Comment: τί is used here in alternative question. Cf. #281. ἐν ῥάβδῳ here in a figurative sense, though the word is also used literally in some contexts. Cf.#863. Note especially its use in Heb.1:8,8 with its association with authority. Paul was prepared to employ the force of his apostolic authority if necessary, though he preferred to come in love and meekness.

Paul turns now in Chapter 5 to the distinction which the church must make between Christians who commit sin and the unsaved who commit the same sin.

Judgment against Immorality

(1 Corinthians 5:1-13)

1 Cor.5:1 - "It is reported commonly that there is fornication among you, and such fornication as is not so much as named among the Gentiles, that one should have his father's wife."

Ὅλως ἀκούεται ἐν ὑμῖν πορνεία, καὶ τοιαύτη πορνεία ἥτις οὐδὲ ἐν τοῖς ἔθνεσιν, ὥστε γυναῖκά τινα τοῦ πατρὸς ἔχειν.

"It is actually reported that there is immorality among you, and of a kind that is not found even among pagans; for a man is living with his father's wife." ...

RSV

Ὅλως (adverbial) 517.

ἀκούεται (3d.per.sing.pres.pass.ind.of ἀκούω, present iterative retroactive) 148.

ἐν (preposition with the locative, with plural pronouns) 80.

ὑμῖν (loc.pl.masc.of σύ, place) 104.

πορνεία (nom.sing.fem.of πορνεία, subject of ἀκούεται) 511.

καὶ (ascensive conjunction) 14.

τοιαύτη (nom.sing.fem.of τοιοῦτος, in agreement with πορνεία) 785.

πορνεία (nom.sing.fem.of πορνεία, epexegetical) 511.

ἥτις (nom.sing.fem.of ὅστις, subject of verb understood) 163.

οὐδὲ (compound particle, negative, ascensive) 452.

ἐν (preposition with the locative, with plural nouns) 80.

τοῖς (loc.pl.neut.of the article in agreement with ἔθνεσιν) 9.

ἔθνεσιν (loc.pl.neut.of ἔθνος, place) 376.

ὥστε (conjunction with the infinitive, epexegetical) 752.

γυναῖκα (acc.sing.fem.of γυνή, direct object of ἔχειν) 103.

τινα (acc.sing.masc.of τις, indefinite pronoun, general reference) 486.

τοῦ (gen.sing.masc.of the article in agreement with πατρὸς) 9.

πατρὸς (gen.sing.masc.of πατήρ, relationship) 238.

ἔχειν (pres.act.inf.of ἔχω, epexegetical) 82.

Translation - "Illicit sex among you is being reported generally, even such as does not even exist among the pagans - that a certain man has the wife of his father."

Comment: ἀκούεται, a present iterative retroactive, indicates that for some time the rumor was repeated, until it had become general knowledge. This is the force of Ὅλως. τοιαύτη, the correlative demonstrative of quality, is joined by ἥτις, the relative pronoun which is used here in a definite sense. The relative clause is descriptive. The Corinthians were more immoral than the pagans. The ὥστε clause with the infinitive is epexegetical.

There is nothing in the text to assure us that this was incest, though it may have been. Since Paul did not write τὴν μητέρα αὐτοῦ ἔχειν, it may be assumed that the woman involved was the man's stepmother. However καὶ τοιαύτη . . . ἔθνεσιν suggests incest. It is an open question. However the sin was of such a nature as to make mandatory the church action which Paul suggests.

Verse 2 - "And ye are puffed up, and have not rather mourned, that he that hath done this deed might be taken away from among you."

καὶ ὑμεῖς πεφυσιωμένοι ἐστέ, καὶ οὐχὶ μᾶλλον ἐπενθήσατε, ἵνα ἀρθῇ ἐκ μέσου ὑμῶν ὁ τὸ ἔργον τοῦτο ποιήσας;

"And you are arrogant! Ought you not rather to mourn? Let him who has done this be removed from among you." . . . RSV

καὶ (adversative conjunction) 14.

ὑμεῖς (nom.pl.masc.of σύ, subject of ἐστέ) 104.

πεφυσιωμένοι (perf.pass.part.nom.pl.masc.of φυσιόω, perfect periphrastic) 4122.

ἐστέ (2d.per.pl.pres.ind.of εἰμί, perfect periphrastic) 86.

καὶ (adversative conjunction) 14.

οὐχὶ (negative particle in rhetorical question that expects an affirmative reply) 130.

μᾶλλον (adverbial) 619.

πενθήσατε (2d.per.pl.aor.act.impv.of πενθέω, entreaty) 424.

ἵνα (conjunction with the subjunctive, purpose) 114.

ἀρθῇ (3d.per.sing.aor.pass.subj.of αἴρω, purpose) 350.

ἐκ (preposition with the ablative of separation) 19.

μέσου (abl.sing.masc.of μέσος, separation) 873.

ὑμῶν (gen.pl.masc.of σύ, description) 104.

ὁ (nom.sing.masc.of the article in agreement with ποιήσας) 9.

ἔργον (acc.sing.neut.of ἔργον, direct object of ποιήσας) 460.

τοῦτο (acc.sing.neut.of οὗτος, in agreement with ἔργον) 93.

ποιήσας (aor.act.part.nom.sing.masc.of ποιέω, substantival, subject of ἀρθῇ) 127.

Translation - *"But you continue to be unconcerned and have not mourned instead so that the man who did this deed might be removed from your fellowship?"*

Comment: καὶ is adversative. One would normally expect that the sin described in verse 1 would devastate the church. On the contrary, they had become arrogant in the past and they continued in this backslidden state of permissive unconcern to the present. This is the force of the perfect periphrastic. In addition they did not mourn. There had been no contrition in the past, but there was a development of conceit which resulted in the continuing lack of concern. Thus we have the fruits of earthly philosophy among Christians who should know better. The attitude of permissiveness is the result of the secular humanism with its situation ethics and the existentialist view that we live in a random universe where no distinctions between right and wrong can be made.

Paul seemed as concerned about the permissive attitude of the church as he was about the sin of the man in question. Apparently there had been little censure in the church against the life-style of the man, whose sin went further astray in depravity than even the pagans tend to go. A rejection of Christian philosophy can only result in the acceptance of the world's philosophy, for all men have *some* philosophy. The world's philosophy, which is nonesense to God (1 Cor.1:20) breeds the world's indifference to sin and a general attitude of permissiveness toward that which is repulsive to God.

The extreme positions of permissiveness which are evident now by extreme proponents of democracy illustrate the attitude of the Corinthian backslidden saints in this matter.

Existentialists cannot in good logic condemn "sin" since they have no way of distinguishing good from evil. Hence the permissive attitude which is involved in ethical relativism and situation ethics. Pornography, obscenity, smut, violence, drugs, assault in the streets -is all permitted and excused in the name of "freedom."

Paul spoke strongly about apostolic authority in chapter four. Now he introduces some in

Verse 3 - "For I verily, as absent in the body but present in spirit, have judged already, as though I were present, concerning him that hath so done this deed."

ἐγὼ μὲν γάρ, ἀπὼν τῷ σώματι παρὼν δὲ τῷ πνεύματι, ἤδη κέκρικα ὡς παρὼν τὸν οὕτως τοῦτο κατεργασάμενον

"For though absent in body I am present in spirit, and as if present, I have already pronounced judgment" . . . *RSV*

ἐγὼ (nom.sing.masc.of ἐγώ, subject of κέκρικα) 123.
μὲν (particle of affirmation) 300.
γὰρ (inferential conjunction) 105.

#4134 ἀπὼν (pres.part.nom.sing.masc.of ἄπειμι, adverbial, concessive).

King James Version

be absent - 1 Cor.5:3; 2 Cor.10:1,11; 13:2,10; Phil.1:27; Col.2:5.

Revised Standard Version

absent - 1 Cor.5:3; 2 Cor.10:11; 13:2; Phil.1:27; Col.2:5.
be away - 1 Cor.10:1; 13:10.

Meaning: A combination of ἀπό (#70) and εἰμί (#86). To be away from; to be separated from; to be absent. *Cf.* #3394. With reference to Paul's absence from Corinth - 1 Cor.5:3; 2 Cor.10:1,11; 13:2,10. From the Philippians - Phil.1:27; From the Colossians - Col.2:5. Always in the New Testament of physical absence in a geographic sense.

τῷ (loc.sing.neut.of the article in agrement with σώματι) 9.
σώματι (loc.sing.neut.of σῶμα, sphere) 507.
παρὼν (pres.part.nom.sing.masc.of πάρειμι, adverbial, causal) 1592.
δὲ (adversative conjunction) 11.
τῷ (loc.sing.neut.of the article in agreement with πνεύματι) 9.
πνεύματι (loc.sing.neut.of πνεῦμα, sphere) 83.
ἤδη (temporal adverb) 291.
κέκρικα (1st.per.sing.perf.act.ind.of κρίνω, intensive) 531.
ὡς (concessive particle) 128.
παρὼν (pres.part.nom.sing.masc.of πάρειμι, adverbial, conditional) 1592.

τὸν (acc.sing.masc.of the article in agreement with κατεργασάμενον) 9.

οὕτως (demonstrative adverb) 74.

τοῦτο (acc.sing.neut.of οὗτος, direct object of κατεργασάμενον) 93.

κατεργασάμενον (aor.mid.part.acc.sing.masc.of κατεργάζομαι, substantival, direct object of κέκρικα) 3815.

Translation - "So in fact although I am absent in the body, but because I am present in the spirit, I have already reached a conclusion as though I were present about the one who did this."

Comment: ἐγώ is emphatic, and the emphasis is intensified by μὲν,the particle of affirmation, since δὲ is joined to ἀπὼν τῷ σώματι παρὼν δὲ τῷ πνεύματι. The local Corinthians who lived in the same city and met together in the same meetings with the adulterer were not concerned, but Paul, though separated by the miles, was concerned. ἀπὼν is concessive; παρὼν is causal. The second παρὼν is conditional.

The basis for Paul's judgment is the principle which he delineates in verse 6. His judgment is set forth in verses 4 and 5.

Verse 4 - "In the name of our Lord Jesus Christ, when ye are gathered together and my spirit, with the power of our Lord Jesus Christ,"

ἐν τῷ ὀνόματι τοῦ κυρίου (ἡμῶν) Ἰησοῦ, συναχθέντων ὑμῶν καὶ τοῦ ἐμοῦ πνεύματος σὺν τῇ δυνάμει τοῦ κυρίου ἡμῶν Ἰησοῦ,

"in the name of the Lord Jesus on the man who has done such a thing. When you are assembled, and my spirit is present, with the power of our Lord Jesus, . . .
" . . . RSV

ἐν (preposition with the instrumental of association) 80.

τῷ (instru.sing.neut.of the article in agreement with ὀνόματι) 9.

ὀνόματι (instru.sing.neut.of ὄνομα, association) 108.

τοῦ (gen.sing.masc.of the article in agreement with κυρίου) 9.

κυρίου (gen.sing.masc.of κύριος, possession) 97.

(ἡμῶν) (gen.pl.masc.of ἐγώ, relationship) 123.

Ἰησοῦ (gen.sing.masc.of Ἰησοῦς, apposition) 3.

συναχθέντων (aor.pass.part.gen.pl.masc.of συνάγω, genitive absolute, adverbial, temporal) 150.

ὑμῶν (gen.pl.masc.of σύ, genitive absolute) 104.

καὶ (adjunctive conjunction joining substantives) 14.

τοῦ (gen.sing.neut.of the article in agreement with πνεύματος) 9.

ἐμοῦ (gen.sing.neut.of ἐμός, possessive pronoun, in agreement with πνεύματος) 1267.

πνεύματος (gen.sing.neut.of πνεῦμα, genitive absolute) 83.

σὺν (preposition with the instrumental of association) 1542.

τῇ (instru.sing.fem.of the article in agreement with δυνάμει) 9.

δυνάμει (instru.sing.fem.of δύναμις, association) 687.

τοῦ (gen.sing.masc.of the article in agreement with κυρίου) 9.

κυρίου (gen.sing.masc.of κύριος, possession) 97.

ἡμῶν (gen.pl.masc.of ἐγώ, relationship) 123.

Ἰησοῦ (gen.sing.masc.of Ἰησοῦς, apposition) 3.

Translation - ". . . in the name of our Lord Jesus, when you and my spirit have assembled in the power of our Lord Jesus. . . "

Comment: The church must do what it does by Christ's authority (Eph.1:23); they can act only when they are assembled as a church, at which time they are to be guided by what Paul would do if he were present. Their decision, reached under these conditions, has the power of the Lord Jesus behind it. The decision which Paul now dictates is found in the fifth verse.

This passage must be interpreted on *zeitgeist* principles if we are to escape the conclusion that a local church cannot act upon its own authority, without the help of an episcopate. Local church autonomy is not threatened by Paul's apostolic order that dictates in advance what the decision of the Corinthian church must be. Paul was not a member of the Corinthian church (or at least there is nothing in Scripture to say that he was), but even had he been he was only one member and would have had only one vote. But Paul was writing this in the first century before the New Testament literature was complete. He was an Apostle to whom had been given the gifts of prophecy and knowledge (1 Cor.12:8,10; 13:8) on an *ad hoc* basis, in order that the first century churches could have the guidance of the Holy Spirit at a time when they did not have the New Testament available. Paul wrote later in this same epistle (1 Cor.13:8) that when the perfect New Testament revelation was finished, the special gifts of prophecy and knowledge would be phased out. *Cf.* our comment on 1 Cor.13:8. No one since the close of the first century of the Christian era, at which time the Holy Spirit had finished His inspiration of the New Testament literature, has possessed the gifts of prophecy and knowledge that Paul and the other Apostles possessed. There are no prophets, nor those possessed with special knowledge, who are able to give directions on matters not included in the New Testament, nor have there been since the New Testament literature was completed.

The Apostles of whom Paul was one were prophets in this special sense. They also possessed special knowledge. Their gifts are no longer needed because the Holy Spirit has incorporated everything which He wanted the Body of Christ to know in the Greek New Testament - a book that too often lies neglected in the Christian home, and, in some cases, even in the Christian church.

Modern prophets, soothsayers and *Christian* "gurus" whose motivations are various in some respects, but alike in their Satanic origin, ply their trade at the expense of the scholarly hermeneutics which seeks the total message which the Holy Spirit incorporated in the Greek New Testament.

Verse 5 - "To deliver such an one unto Satan for the destruction of the flesh, that the spirit may be saved in the day of the Lord Jesus."

παραδοῦναι τὸν τοιοῦτον τῷ Σατανᾷ εἰς ὄλεθρον τῆς σαρκός, ἵνα τὸ πνεῦμα σωθῇ ἐν τῇ ἡμέρᾳ τοῦ κυρίου.

"*you are to deliver this man to Satan for the destruction of the flesh, that his spirit may be saved in the day of the Lord Jesus.*" . . . RSV

παραδοῦναι (aor.act.inf.of παραδίδωμι, direct object of κέκρικα) 368.
τὸν (acc.sing.masc.of the article in agreement with τοιοῦτον) 9.
τοιοῦτον (acc.sing.masc.of τοιοῦτος, direct object of παραδοῦναι) 785.
τῷ (dat.sing.masc.of the article in agreement with Σατανᾷ) 9.
Σατανᾷ (dat.sing.masc.of Σατανᾶ, indirect object of παραδοῦναι) 365.
εἰς (preposition with the accusative, purpose) 140.

#4135 ὄλεθρον (acc.sing.masc.of ὄλεθρος, purpose).

King James Version

destruction - 1 Cor.5:5; 1 Thess.5:3; 2 Thess.1:9; 1 Tim.6:9.

Revised Standard Version

destruction - 1 Cor.5:5; 1 Thess.5:3; 2 Thess.1:9; 1 Tim.6:9.

Meaning: Cf. ὄλλυμι - "to destroy." Followed by τῆς σαρκός, with adjuncts which indicate that only the flesh, not the spirit, would be destroyed. Hence, physical death of a Christian - 1 Cor.5:5; with reference to the judgment of God on unbelievers at the Second Coming of Christ - 1 Thess.5:3; the everlasting judgment - 2 Thess.1:9. With reference to the general debilitation and ruin caused by sin. The context indicates the type of destruction which is meant - 1 Tim.6:9.

τῆς (gen.sing.fem.of the article in agreement with σαρκός) 9.
σαρκός (gen.sing.fem.of σάρξ, description) 1202.
ἵνα (conjunction with the subjunctive in a purpose clause) 114.
τὸ (nom.sing.neut.of the article in agreement with πνεῦμα) 9.
πνεῦμα (nom.sing.neut.of πνεῦμα, subject of σωθῇ) 83.
σωθῇ (3d.per.sing.aor.pass.subj.of σώζω, purpose) 109.
ἐν (preposition with the locative, time point) 80.
τῇ (loc.sing.fem.of the article in agreement with ἡμέρᾳ) 9.
ἡμέρᾳ (loc.sing.fem.of ἡμέρα, time point) 135.
τοῦ (gen.sing.masc.of the article in agreement with κυρίου) 9.
κυρίου (gen.sing.masc.of κύριος, description) 97.

Translation - ". . . *to surrender this man to Satan that he may die, in order that his spirit may be saved on the day of the Lord.*"

Comment: παραδοῦναι is the object of κέκρικα in verse 3. The predicate use of εἰς and the accusative to introduce purpose is not uncommon in the New Testament. With reference to Paul's judgment of this man *cf.* 1 Tim.1:20. His apostolic authority as here employed included the power to declare certain recalcitrant Christians unfit for further Christian service. Note that the purpose for Paul's decision is to protect the man from a greater loss of reward at the judgment seat of Christ (1 Cor.3:12-15; 2 Cor.5:10; Rev.11:18; Mt.16:18). To have allowed him to go on living in sin was only to result in his piling up "wood, hay and stubble" for the discriminating fires of God's judgment. The question of the man's salvation is not in view. Even if all of his works were scheduled to be burned, he still had the foundation, Christ Jesus (1 Cor.3:11) and he would be saved "yet so as by fire" (1 Cor.3:15).

This is the "sin unto (physical) death" of 1 John 5:16. It is the sin which was committed by Ananias and Sapphira (Acts 5:1-11). Some saints sin as grievously as others, but they repent, ask forgiveness and forsake their sin, and thus live on, by God's grace, to further glorify His name. Their case is not under review here. This is the case of a Christian who goes on sinning without a desire to repent or to seek forgiveness. They will be saved, because Christ's atonement is adequate to justification but their lives are ruined insofar as Christian service is concerned. Paul had the best interests of the man at heart. The kindest thing to do for such a Christian is to pray him into a grave. But Paul was also thinking of the spiritual welfare of the Corinthian church as we see in verse 6.

It is probable that the material in 2 Cor.2:6-11 pertains to this case. If so we shall see that the church took the proper course and the matter was happily resolved.

Paul was thinking, not only of the ultimate good for the man in question. He was thinking also of the spiritual good of the church itself, as we see in

Verse 6 - "Your glorying is not good. Know ye not that a little leaven leaveneth the whole lump?"

Οὐ καλὸν τὸ καύχημα ὑμῶν. οὐκ οἴδατε ὅτι μικρὰ ζύμη ὅλον τὸ φύραμα ζυμοῖ;

"Your boasting is not good. Do you not know that a little leaven leavens the whole lump?" . . . RSV

Οὐ (negative particle with the indicative understood) 130.
καλὸν (acc.sing.neut.of καλός, predicate adjective) 296.
τὸ (nom.sing.neut.of the article in agreement with καύχημα) 9.
καύχημα (nom.sing.neut.of καύχημα, subject of ἐστίν understood) 3881.
ὑμῶν (gen.pl.masc.of σύ, possession) 104.
οὐκ (negative particle with the indicative in rhetorical question which expects an affirmative reply) 130.
οἴδατε (2d.per.pl.perf.act.ind.of οἶδα, intensive, rhetorical question) 144b.
ὅτι (conjunction introducing an object clause in indirect discourse) 211.
μικρὰ (nom.sing.fem.of μικρός, in agreement with ζύμη) 901.
ζύμη (nom.sing.fem.of ζύμη, subject of ζυμοῖ) 1072.
ὅλον (acc.sing.neut.of ὅλος, in agreement with φύραμα) 112.
τὸ (acc.sing.neut.of the article in agreement with φύραμα) 9.
φύραμα (acc.sing.neut.of φύραμα, direct object of ζυμοῖ) 3968.

ζυμοῖ (3d.per.sing.pres.act.ind.of ζυμόω, customary) 1076.

Translation - *"You do not have the proper grounds for boasting. You know, do you not, that a little leaven contaminates the entire lump?"*

Comment: *Cf.*#3881. The word does not mean "a boast" but "the reason for the boast." The Corinthians were not wrong in boasting but they were wrong because they were not boasting about the right thing. Paul's rhetorical question, with οὐκ and the indicative, οἴδατε expects a positive answer. ὅτι introduces the object clause in indirect discourse.

The sociological principle is sound. Cross fertilization of culture occurs when two cultures intermingle. The church of God is holy. Sin is its enemy. To harbor sin in the church is to reap the certain sociological result that sin will first be tolerated, then condoned, then defended and finally accepted and supported. *Cf.* Gal.5:9 where Paul applies the principle to bad theology rather than to bad morals. Thus separation is the rule for God's people. (1 Thess.5:22; 2 Cor.6:14-18).

If the churches through the ages had followed this rule, Satan's philosophy and policies would not have been legally entrenched in the institutional church. The separation is to be implemented by the unleavened saints expelling the leaven, not by the unleavened saints walking out and leaving the old leaven in control of the property. But, however it can be done - either by the Lord's people expelling the world or the Lord's people withdrawing, it must be done, if Christ's pure gospel and the Holy Spirit's ethics are to be maintained upon the earth. Paul's formula is contained in

Verse 7 - *"Purge out therefore the old leaven that ye may be a new lump, as ye are unleavened. For even Christ our passover is sacrificed for us."*

ἐκκαθάρατε τὴν παλαιὰν ζύμην, ἵνα ἦτε νέον φύραμα, καθώς ἐστε ἄζυμοι. καὶ γὰρ τὸ πάσχα ἡμῶν ἐτύθη Χριστός.

"Cleanse out the old leaven that you may be a new lump, as you really are unleavened. For Christ, our paschal lamb, has been sacrificed." . . . RSV

#4136 ἐκκαθάρατε (2d.per.pl.1st.aor.act.impv.of ἐκκαθαίρω, command).

King James Version

purge - 2 Tim.2:21.
purge out - 1 Cor.5:7.

Revised Standard Version

cleanse out - 1 Cor.5:7.
purify - 2 Tim.2:21.

Meaning: A combination of ἐκ (#19) and καθαίρω (#2786). To cleanse; to purge. To remove from something a substance which defiles. With reference to the discipline in the Corinthian church - 1 Cor.5:7. To refrain from contact with that which defiles, followed by ἑαυτὸν ἀπὸ τούτων, a preventive action in 2 Tim.2:21, rather than a corrective one in 1 Cor.5:7.

τὴν (acc.sing.fem.of the article in agreement with ζύμην) 9.

παλαιὰν (acc.sing.fem.of παλαιός, in agreement with ζύμην) 804.

ζύμην (acc.sing.fem.of ζύμη, direct object of ἐκκαθάρατε) 1072.

ἵνα (conjunction with the subjunctive in a purpose clause) 114.

ἦτε (2d.per.pl.pres.subj.of εἰμί, purpose) 86.

νέον (nom.sing.neut.of νέος, in agreement with φύραμα) 809.

φύραμα (nom.sing.neut.of φύραμα, predicate nominative) 3968.

καθώς (demonstrative adverb) 1348.

ἐστε (2d.per.pl.pres.ind.of εἰμί, aoristic) 86.

ἄζυμοι (nom.pl.masc.of ἄζυμος, predicate adjective) 1571.

καὶ (emphatic conjunction) 14.

γὰρ (causal conjunction) 105.

τὸ (nom.sing.neut.of the article in agreement with πάσχα) 9.

πάσχα (nom.sing.neut.of πάσχα, subject of ἐτύθη) 1553.

ἡμῶν (gen.pl.masc.of ἐγω, possession) 123.

ἐτύθη (3d.per.sing.1st.aor.pass.ind.of θύω, constative) 1398.

Χριστός (nom.sing.masc.of Χριστός, apposition) 4.

Translation - *"You must clean out the old leaven so that you may be a fresh lump of dough, just as you are unleavened, because in fact our paschal lamb, Christ was sacrificed."*

Comment: The figure recalls Exodus 12:15-20, which perhaps would be more meaningful to the Hebrew Christians in the Corinthian church than to the Gentiles. The feast of Unleavened Bread portrayed the fact that the Paschal Lamb was without spot or blemish (Exodus 12:3-6; 1 Pet.1:19; Heb.9:14). Since Christ, our Paschal Lamb, is without blemish and now "head over all things to His church" (Eph.1:22,23), the members of His body must also be spotless. Thus Paul orders the church to exterminate the leaven (verse 5) for the purpose of restoring the rest of the body to the newness of a lump of dough, in which the yeast of evil is not at work. καθώς ἐστε ἄζυμοι means "while you are still unleavened yourselves."

The danger was that the little bit of leaven in the church, the adulterous member, would influence others to a similar disgraceful practice (verse 6b). He had already corrupted them to the point that their attitude toward him and his sin was one of permissive complacence (verse 2). What society permits very soon it may indulge in. The church must be unleavened since Christ had already been sacrificed. We mark the fanatical zeal with which the Jewish housewife cleans her home before the Passover meal to remove the tiniest speck of leaven, however minute. We note with regret that the modern church, having already experienced the redemptive benefits of the sacrifice of our spotless Lamb, is so careless about its leavened condition, both in principle and practice. A major reason why the church is so powerless in terms of her influence upon society, is that she has long since abandoned the practice of weeping over the sins of her members and would never think of dismissing a recalcitrant member, much less giving him the treatment suggested in verse 5. *Cf.* Lk.22:1,7 for τὸ πάσχα.

Verse 8 - "Therefore let us keep the feast, not with old leaven, neither with the leaven of malice and wickedness; but with the unleavened bread of sincerity and truth."

ὥστε ἑορτάζωμεν, μὴ ἐν ζύμῃ παλαιᾷ μηδὲ ἐν ζύμῃ κακίας καὶ πονηρίας, ἀλλ' ἐν ἀζύμοις εἰλικρινείας καὶ ἀληθείας.

"Let us, therefore, celebrate the festival, not with the old leaven, the leaven of malice and evil, but with the unleavened bread of sincerity and truth." . . . RSV

ὥστε (conjunction with the subjunctive, result) 752.

#4137 ἑορτάζωμεν (1st.per.pl.pres.act.subj.of ἑορτάζω, hortatory).

King James Version

keep the feast - 1 Cor.5:8.

Revised Standard Version

celebrate the festival - 1 Cor.5:8.

Meaning: Cf. ἑορτή (#1558). To celebrate a feast or festival. With reference to the ordinance of the Lord's Supper - 1 Cor.5:8.

μὴ (negative particle with the subjunctive) 87.
ἐν (preposition with the instrumental of means) 80.
ζύμῃ (instru.sing.fem.of ζύμη, means) 1072.
παλαιᾷ (instru.sing.fem.of παλαιός, in agreement with ζύμῃ) 804.
μηδὲ (negative disjunctive) 612.
ἐν (preposition with the instrumental of means) 80.
ζύμῃ (instru.sing.fem.of ζύμη, means) 1072.
κακίας (gen.sing.fem.of κακία, description) 641.
καὶ (adjunctive conjunction joining nouns) 14.
πονηρίας (gen.sing.fem.of πονηρία, description) 1419.
ἀλλ' (alternative conjunction) 342.
ἐν (preposition with the instrumental of means) 80.
ἀζύοις (instru.pl.masc.of ἄζυμος, means) 1571.

#4138 εἰλικρινείας (gen.sing.fem.of εἰλικρίνεια, description).

King James Version

sincerity - 1 Cor.5:8; 2 Cor.1:12; 2:17.

Revised Standard Version

sincerity - 1 Cor.5:8; 2 Cor.1:12; 2:17.

Meaning: Cf. εἰλικρινής (#4542). From εἴλη - "the heat of the sun" and κρίνω (#531). Thus, that which has been judged by the heat of the sun and found to be genuine. The fraudulent practice of patching cracked pottery with wax, thus to hide imperfection until the sale was consummated, could be prevented by putting the suspected pot in the sun. If wax were present it would melt and reveal the fraud. If there was no fraud, the pot was declared εἰλικρίνεια - "tested by the sun," or, as the Latin has it *sine cera* - "without wax." Cf. the Latin *sinceris*, which in English becomes "sincere" or "without wax." The Greeks meant the same thing when they said εἰλικρίνεια - "tested by the sun." Note its use with ἁπλότητι in 2 Cor.1:12 as opposed to καπηλεύω (#4281) in 2 Cor.2:17 and its association with ἀλήθεια (#1416) in 1 Cor.5:8.

καὶ (adjunctive conjunction joining nouns) 14.
ἀληθείας (gen.sing.fem.of ἀλήθεια, description) 1416.

Translation - "Thus let us observe the Communion feast, not with old leaven, nor with the leaven that grows out of malice and wickedness, but with unleavened sincerity and truth."

Comment: ὥστε often introduces a consecutive (result) idea. If the Corinthians obey the exhortation of verse 7, the result will be a Communion service when Paul arrives in Corinth, such as described in verse 8. But ἑορτάζωμεν is a hortatory subjunctive which makes "with the result that" or "so that let us eat. . . κ.τ.λ." awkward. μή is the negative with the subjunctive and is correlated with μηδὲ - "not with the old leaven of the wickedness of our unregenerate days, nor with the new leaven which has manifested itself in your lives, even though you are Christians, that which comes from κακίας and πονηρίας (either genitives of description or ablatives of source).

Note that the new birth does not remove the possibility of leaven in its evil sense from the Christian life. ἀλλά provides the alternative in contrast. The feast will be celebrated with unleavened sincerity and truth.

Only if the church rids herself of the adulterer and weeps because of her previous arrogance, can she sit down at the Lord's table with sincerity. Cf. #4138.

The cracks of imperfection in the Christian life are often masked with the wax of permissive acquiescence in the sins of the believer. The Corinthians no doubt would have made a great display of piety as they sat down at the feast of unleavened bread with a man who was guilty of a sin that even the pagans were ashamed of. Paul's plea here is for church repentance, a spirit of humility, an act of stern discipline and a prayer for consistency. Note that Paul includes their sins of arrogance, which led some of them to reject his leadership along with the sin of the adulterer, although those who were "puffed up" probably thought of themselves as superior in spiritual development to the man.

Corinth was a city of sin. Only a small portion of her population were Christian. Paul has been dealing with the problem of the Christian's church relationship with an adulterer. Now he introduces the question of the Christians' social relationship with those who are not Christians. The church can rid herself of the corruption within her own ranks. She cannot rid the world of its corrupt life-style.

Verse 9 - "I wrote unto you in an epistle not to company with fornicators."

Ἔγραφα ὑμῖν ἐν τῇ ἐπιστολῇ μὴ συναναμίγνυσθαι πόρνοις,

"I wrote to you in my letter not to associate with immoral men;" . . . RSV

Ἔγραφα (1st.per.sing.aor.act.ind.of γράφω, epistolary) 156.
ὑμῖν (dat.pl.masc.of σύ, indirect object of Ἔγραφα) 104.
ἐν (preposition with the locative of place) 80.
τῇ (loc.sing.fem.of the article in agreement with ἐπιστολῇ) 9.
ἐπιστολῇ (loc.sing.fem.of ἐπιστολή, place) 3180.
μὴ (negative particle with the infinitive, indirect command) 87.

#4139 συναναμίγνυσθαι (pres.mid.inf.of συναναμίγνυμι, indirect command).

King James Version

company with - 1 Cor.5:11.
have company with - 1 Cor.5:9.
keep company - 2 Thess.3:14.

Revised Standard Version

associate - 1 Cor.5:9,11.
have nothing to do with - 2 Thess.3:14.

Meaning: A combination of σύν (#1542), ἀνά (#1059) and μίγνυμι (#1646). Hence, to mix (μίγνυμι) up (ἀνά) together (σύν). In the New Testament with reference to human association. With a fornicator in the church - 1 Cor.5:9,11; with any brother who is disobedient to the Word of God - 2 Thess.3:14.

#4140 πόρνοις (instrumental pl.masc.of πόρνος, association).

King James Version

fornicator - 1 Cor.5:9,11; 6:9; Heb.12:16.
whoremonger - Eph.5:5; 1 Tim.1:10; Heb.13:4; Rev.21:8; 22:15.

Revised Standard Version

immoral men - 1 Cor.5:9,10; 6:9; Eph.5:5.
guilty of immorality - 1 Cor.5:11.
immoral - Heb.12:16; 13:4.
immoral person - 1 Tim.1:10.
fornicator - Rev.21:8; 22:15.

Meaning: Cf. πόρνη (#1374); πορνεία (#511); πορνεύω (#4152). In early Greek, a male prostitute - the masculine form of πόρνη. In the New Testament, a man who is guilty of illicit sex relationships, whether in the church - 1 Cor.5:9,11; Heb.13:4 or in the world - 1 Cor.5:10; 6:9; Heb.12:16; Eph.5:5; 1 Tim.1:10; Rev.21:8; 22:15.

Translation - "I have written to you in the letter ordering you to stop associating with immoral men."

Comment: The article τῇ with ἐπιστολῇ distinguishes this letter from all others which Paul wrote. Some scholars believe that Paul is alluding to another letter which was lost. If so, it does not detract of course from the authority of the two epistles which were not lost. μή with the present middle infinitive is indirect command. Note the present tense - "Do not continue to associate yourselves . . . " or "stop associating yourself with . . . " συναναμίγνυσθαι is a reciprocal middle voice infinitive. This may indicate, if Paul is speaking of a previous letter, that he knew about immorality in the Corinthian church before the present letter was written.

This is a harsh order. Should a Christian shun an erring brother? Not until he has sought to rescue him with the formula of Mt.18:15-17 and in the spirit of Gal.6:1,2.

The fornicating Christian who persists in his sin is here in view. He is a member of the Body of Christ, despite his sin, but he has no right to associate with others who are following the guidance of the Holy Spirit. One of the reasons why sinful saints continue in their sins is that they continue to enjoy the association and even the approbation of the members of their local church.

Paul is teaching what some have called "shunning" but the reason for the break in association which he demands is not for purposes of punishment of the offender, but for the protection of those saints who have not fallen into sin and also for the redemption of the backslider. If the πόρνος is truly regenerate he can not long resist the loving advice and earnest prayer of those who admonish him to turn from his wicked life-style and return to the fellowship of the church. The "shunning" to which most πόρνοι would be subjected in church fellowships who know little of Mt.18:15-17 and Gal.6:1-2, is cruel and would most likely only serve to drive them further from the path of Christian victory. Witness the treatment meted out by the New England "saints" in Nathaniel Hawthorne's *The Scarlet Letter*. This "powerful psychological insight with which he was able to probe guilt and anxiety in the human soul" (Funk & Wagnalls *New Encyclopedia*, 12, 245) reveals the tragedies that could be avoided if Christians would follow the New Testament guidelines for dealing with such problems.

Paul now discusses the position that the Christian should take as he deals with the same problem in the world of the unsaved.

Verse 10 - "Yet not altogether with the fornicators of this world, or with the covetous, or extortioners, or with idolaters: for them must ye needs go out of the world."

οὐ πάντως τοῖς πόρνοις τοῦ κόσμου τούτου ἢ τοῖς πλεονέκταις καὶ ἅρπαξιν ἢ εἰδωλολάτραις, ἐπεὶ ὠφείλετε ἄρα ἐκ τοῦ κόσμου ἐξελθεῖν.

"not at all meaning the immoral of this world, or the greedy or robbers, or idolaters, for then you would need to go out of the world." . . . RSV

οὐ (negative particle with the indicative understood) 130.

πάντως (adverbial) 2029.

τοῖς (instru.pl.masc.of the article in agreement with πόρνοις) 9.

πόρνοις (instru.pl.masc.of πόρνος, association) 4140.

τοῦ (gen.sing.masc.of the article in agreement with κόσμου) 9.

κόσμου (gen.sing.masc.of κόσμος, description) 360.

τούτου (gen.sing.masc.of οὗτος, in agreement with κόσμου) 93.

ἤ (disjunctive) 465.

τοῖς (instru.pl.masc.of the article in agreement with πλεονέκταις) 9.

#4141 πλεονέκταις (instru.pl.masc.of πλεονέκτης, association, after σύν in composition).

King James Version

covetous - 1 Cor.5:10,11; 6:10.
covetous man - Eph.5:5.

Revised Standard Version

greedy - 1 Cor.5:10; 6:10.
guilty of greed - 1 Cor.5:11.
covetous - Eph.5:5.

Meaning: Cf. πλεονάζω (#3907); πλεονεκτέω (#4276); πλεονεξία (#2302) and πλείων (#474). A combination of πλέον and ἔχω (#82). One eager to have more, especially of that belonging to another. Covetous, greedy - 1 Cor.5:10,11; 6:10; Eph.5:5.

καὶ (adjunctive conjunction joining nouns) 14.

ἅρπαξιν (instru.pl.masc.of ἅρπαξ, association, after σύν in composition) 674.

ἤ (disjunctive) 465.

#4142 εἰδωλολάτραις (instru.pl.masc.of εἰδωλολάτρης, association after σύν in composition).

King James Version

idolater - 1 Cor.5:10,11; 6:9; 10:7; Eph.5:5; Rev.21:8; 22:15.

Revised Standard Version

idolater - 1 Cor.5:10,11; 6:9; 10:7; Eph.5:5; Rev.21:8; 22:15.

Meaning: Cf. εἰδωλεῖον (#4172); εἰδωλολατρεία (#4198); εἴδωλον (#3138); εἰδωλόθυτον (#3348). A combination of εἴδωλον and πάτρις - "servant." Hence, one who serves or worships idols. Idolater. Among the unsaved - 1 Cor.5:10; 6:9; Eph.5:5; Rev.21:8; 22:15. In the church - 1 Cor.5:11; 10:7.

ἐπεὶ (subordinating conjunction introducing a causal clause) 1281.

ὠφείλετε (2d.per.pl.imp.act.ind.of ὀφείλω, iterative) 1277.
ἄρα (illative particle) 995.
ἐκ (preposition with the ablative of separation) 19.
τοῦ (abl.sing.masc.of the article in agreement with κόσμου) 9.
κόσμου (abl.sing.masc.of κόσμος, separation) 360.
ἐξελθεῖν (aor.inf.of ἐξέρχομαι, epexegetical) 161.

Translation - "I do not mean at all that you must not associate with the immoral of this world, or the covetous and grasping or idolaters. If I did then you would find it necessary from time to time to leave the world."

Comment: This is a negative explanation of his meaning in verse 9. He does not mean that Christians should shun all associations with the unsaved "porno" or the covetous and greedy exploiters and the idolaters. The rest of the verse is the apodosis of a second-class condition, though the protasis is missing. To supply it, we must say, "If I did mean that you should avoid all sinners such as I have described, outside the church as well as in the church, which I do not mean . . ." - now the apodosis follows with ἐπεὶ and the iterative imperfect in ὀφείλω (a verb of propriety) - "then (or in that case) it would be necessary for you to leave the world again and again." Every time a Christian moved about in the unsaved society all around him, he would be faced with the necessity to repeatedly (iterative imperfect) leave the world. Thus he may as well leave it entirely.

Paul strikes a blow at the anchorite philosophy that teaches that Christians can be victorious only in seclusion. If I may buy my groceries only from merchants who are Christians, then I may indeed starve. There is probably some fornicator in the corporate structure that builds my car. Should I then walk? Paul says, "No." His meaning is in verse 11. In verse 9 he is not speaking of an unsaved fornicator.

With reference to the imperfect tense in ὠφείλετε, referring to present time in a second-class condition, Robertson says, "When a condition is assumed as unreal and refers to present time, the imperfect tense is used both in the protasis and the apodosis in normal constructions. *Cf.* Mt.26:24 and Acts 26:32. In 1 Cor.5:10. . . we have only the apodosis." (Robertson, *Grammar,* 887). Here we have only the "present tense under consideration" (*Ibid.,* 920). The reason that ἐπεὶ seems out of place is only that the apodosis of the second-class condition is present without the protasis, which is implied by the context. (*Ibid.* 963).

Paul's entire thought on the matter is clear as we see in verses 11-13, which complete the unit begun in verse 9.

Verse 11 - "But now I have written unto you not to keep company, if any man that is called a brother be a fornicator, or covetous, or an idolater, or a railer, or a drunkard, or an extortioner, with such an one no not to eat."

νῦν δὲ ἔγραφα ὑμῖν μὴ συναναμίγνυσθαι ἐάν τις ἀδελφὸς ὀνομαζόμενος ᾖ πόρνος ἢ πλεονέκτης ἢ εἰδωλολάτρης ἢ λοίδορος ἢ μέθυσος ἢ ἅρπαξ, τῷ τοιούτῳ μηδὲ συνεσθίειν.

"But rather I wrote to you not to associate with any one who bears the name of

brother if he is guilty of immorality or greed, or is an idolater, reviler, drunkard or robber - not even to eat with such a one." . . . RSV

νῦν (temporal adverb) 1497.

δὲ (adversative conjunction) 11.

ἔγραφα (1st.per.sing.aor.act.ind.of γράφω, epistolary) 156.

ὑμῖν (dat.pl.masc.of σύ, indirect object of ἔγραφα) 104.

μὴ (negative particle with the infinitive in indirect command) 87.

συναναμίγνυσθαι (pres.mid.inf.of συναναμίγνυμι, reciprocal, indirect command) 4139.

ἐάν (conditional particle with the subjunctive, in a third-class condition) 363.

τις (nom.sing.masc.of τις, indefinite pronoun, subject of ᾖ) 486.

ἀδελφὸς (nom.sing.masc.of ἀδελφός, predicate nominative) 15.

ὀνομαζόμενος (pres.pass.part.nom.sing.masc.of ὀνομάζω, present periphrastic) 2115.

ᾖ (3d.per.sing.pres.subj.of εἰμί, third-class condition, present periphrastic) 86.

πόρνος (nom.sing.masc.of πόρνος, predicate nominative) 4140.

ἢ (disjunctive) 465.

πλεονέκτης (nom.sing.masc.of πλεονέκτης, predicate nominative) 4141.

ἢ (disjunctive) 465.

εἰδωλολάτρης (nom.sing.masc.of εἰδωλολάτρης, predicate nominative) 4142.

ἢ (disjunctive) 465.

#4143 λοίδορος (nom.sing.masc.of λοίδορος, predicate nominative).

King James Version

railer - 1 Cor.5:11.
reviler - 1 Cor.6:10.

Revised Standard Version

reviler - 1 Cor.5:11; 6:10.

Meaning: a railer; reviler; one who berates fulminates or indulges in vituperation. An intemperate critic - 1 Cor.5:11; 6:10.

ἢ (disjunctive) 465.

#4144 μέθυσος (nom.sing.masc.of μέθυσος, predicate nominative).

King James Version

drunkard - 1 Cor.5:11; 6:10.

Revised Standard Version

drunkard - 1 Cor.5:11; 6:10.

Meaning: A drunkard. An addict to intemperance. An intoxicated person - 1 Cor.5:11; 6:10.

ἤ (disjunctive) 465.
ἅρπαξ (nom.sing.masc.of ἅρπαξ, predicate nominative) 674.
τῷ (instru.sing.masc.of the article in agreement with τοιούτῳ) 9.
τοιούτῳ (instru.sing.masc.of τοιοῦτος, association) 785.
μηδὲ (negative disjunctive) 612.
συνεσθίειν (pres.act.inf.of συνεσθίω, indirect command) 2539.

Translation - "But now I am writing to you that if any one who is designated as a brother is an immoral person, or a greedy man, or an idolater, or one who berates others, or a drunkard or an extortioner - with a person like that never to eat."

Comment: Note the epistolary aorist in ἔγραφα. What Paul writes now is for the purpose of clarifying what he meant in his previous indirect command (verse 9). Did the Corinthians misinterpret his instruction, in the event that verse 9 refers to a previous letter? Or, if not, did Paul fear that they would misinterpret him? In either case, he did not mean that a Christian cannot have any association with the unsaved world and must live like hermits. What he did mean was that they were not to associate within the fellowship of the church with the immoral types which he mentions.

Note that sins of the flesh are mentioned in the same sentence with psychological sins. *Cf.* Gal.5:19-21; Rom.1:29-32; Mk.7:20-23. With such persons the Christians were forbidden to eat. Does this restriction apply only to the Lord's Table in the Communion Service and Love Feast or does it apply also to meals together outside the formal worship services of the church? Verse 10 would seem to indicate that Paul was not banning non-church associations, although other Scriptures may be cited to govern even these. At the very least, whatever else he may or may not have meant, he meant the Communion Service. This means, of course that such persons should be excluded from the fellowship of the local church body, but only after the efforts to restore them to obedience, described in Mt.18:15-17 and Gal.6:1-2 have failed. This rule, which seems clearly to be Paul's teaching is the Scriptural support for what is commonly referred to as "closed communion" by which is meant that only members of the local congregation should participate in the service. Otherwise the local congregation has no control over the morals of its members. If this rule is followed unworthy Christians are banned from the Lord's table and thus are not in danger of eating and drinking unworthily - a practice which may be fraught with danger (1 Cor.11:29,30). A church that does not follow disciplinary procedures against recalcitrant members of the body, has no logical right to insist upon "closed communion."

It is important to note that exclusion from the membership of the local church membership does not mean the "shunning" of the excluded member in social relationships. On the contrary the spiritual members of the church should redouble their efforts to surround the sinning brother/sister with their love and prayers in order to regain his repentance and return to the Spirit-filled life.

A local police officer in a small midwest city came to the altar at the close of a service. He had been dismissed from the membership of the church for some scriptural reason. He confessed his sin, announced his repentance and asked to be readmiited to the fellowship. His statement was that "it was cold out there" by which he meant that he missed the warmth of the fellowship of Christian love and understanding which the church had provided. There was great rejoicing with many tears of joy among the faithful members who had never shunned him socially and had prayed faithfully that he would forsake his sin and return to the Lord's Table. Apparently this is what the Corinthian church did for the man described in 1 Cor.5:1, if we assume that the passage in 2 Cor.2:6-11 refers to him.

Few churches in recent years, especially those that are institutionally structured, regard these Scriptures seriously, which explains why they have become the objects of contempt among sophisticated unregenerates. There is little pragmatic difference between the church and the world in the late 20th century.

There is another lesson in this passage for those who call themselves "Fundamentalists" who insist upon imposing New Testament doctrines, morals and practices upon the unsaved world while they studiously avoid disciplining their own members within the Body of Christ. They seek through legislation and amendment of the basic law of the land to enlist the legislative, judicial and police power of the secular state to impose Christian morals and doctrine upon the unsaved. There is nothing in the New Testament which enjoins holiness upon the unregenerate. The church's only message to the unsaved is the good news of the gospel and the plea for repentance and commitment to Jesus Christ as Saviour and Lord. Thus as they neglect to exercise discipline upon the saints they expend their energy, time and money in forcing their accepted standards of behavior upon the world. This results in the anomalous situation in which the drunkard and the libertine, under attack for their wicked lifestyles by the preachers who have enlisted the state in alliance, find it necessary to join the church, where they can "enjoy" (!) their lives of sin in peace.

Verse 12 says clearly that Paul did not feel that as long as a man remains outside the Body of Christ, in repudiation and rejection of the person and work of Jesus Christ, his manner of life was any of his business. When the church seeks through political pressure to merge its functions with those of the state we have the formula created by Constantine in A.D.312 when at Pons Mulvius he gained the military victory that led to his Edict of Milan one year later. When the church turns to the state and asks for secular help to conduct the affairs of the Kingdom of God there is nothing left for the Holy Spirit to do, and He may as well bow His way out and seek to do His work through those Christians who still believe that the God of history is still sovereign in this age of the church and will continue to function, despite the wickedness of the state, until the last elect soul for whom Christ died has been called by the Holy Spirit and incorporated into His Body.

Verse 12 - "For what have I to do to judge them also that are without? Do not ye judge them that are within?"

τί γάρ μοι τοὺς ἔξω κρίνειν; οὐχὶ τοὺς ἔσω ὑμεῖς κρίνετε,

"For what have I do to with judging outsiders? Is it not those inside the church whom you are to judge?" . . . RSV

τί (nom.sing.neut.of τίς, interrogative pronoun, pred.nom.) 281.

γάρ (inferential conjunction) 105.

μοι (dat.sing.masc.of ἐγώ, personal interest) 123.

τοὺς (acc.pl.masc.of the article, direct object of κρίνειν) 9.

ἔξω (local adverb) 449.

κρίνειν (pres.act.inf.of κρίνω, noun use, subject of ἐστίν understood) 531.

οὐχὶ (negative particle with the indicative in rhetorical question expecting a positive reply) 130.

τοὺς (acc.pl.masc.of the article, direct object of κρίνετε) 9.

ἔσω (local adverb) 1601.

ὑμεῖς (nom.pl.masc.of σύ, subject of κρίνετε) 104.

κρίνετε (2d.per.pl.pres.act.ind.of κρίνω, rhetorical question) 531.

Translation - "So why should I condemn those outside the church? You are not condemning those inside the church are you?"

Comment: Paul's previous instructions (verse 9) had been interpreted by the Corinthians as a directive for them to avoid association with immoral people outside the church. Thus they became selfrighteous snobs, fellowshipping with a fornicator in the church, while snubbing this sex partner, who presumably was an outsider.

How like the modern church, which develops a public image of being against the sins of outsiders while covering the sins of church members with a mantle of church sanctity. The church applauds an Urban Renewal program, financed by the tax payers, because it eliminates the community house of prostitution, while the minister sits at the Lord's Table with the madam's cash customers. This kind of intellectual and spiritual whoredom revolted Paul as he poured out his sarcasm against it. They applauded what they supposed to be Paul's attack upon the unsaved sinners in Corinth. The truth was that he was talking about the saved sinners in the church. Why should he judge the unsaved sinners who made no pretense of having salvation? If, as they violated God's law, they also violated Roman law, let Caesar judge them. If their violation of God's law did not also involve transgression of the Roman code, they had nothing to fear from Claudius. Nor should they have had anything to fear from the church since they were not members and did not recognize her right to dictate to their lives. Besides if the church did not judge the saved prostitutes in the church, why should the church enlist the help of state to enforce its rules upon those without?

Verse 13 - "But them that are without God judgeth. Therefore put away from among yourselves that wicked person."

τοὺς δὲ ἔξω ὁ θεὸς κρινεῖ. ἐξάρατε τὸν πονηρὸν ἐξ ὑμῶν αὐτῶν.

"God judges those outside. 'Drive out the wicked person from among you.'"..
RSV

τοὺς (acc.pl.masc.of the article, direct object of κρινεῖ) 9.
δὲ (adversative conjunction) 11.
ἔξω (local adverb) 449.
ὁ (nom.sing.masc.of the article in agreement with θεὸς) 9.
θεὸς (nom.sing.masc.of θεός, subject of κρινεῖ) 124.
κρινεῖ (3d.per.sing.fut.act.ind.of κρίνω, predictive) 531.

#4145 ἐξάρατε (2d.per.pl.aor.act.impv.of ἐξαίρω, command).

King James Version

put away - 1 Cor.5:13.

Revised Standard Version

drive out - 1 Cor.5:13.

Meaning: A combination of ἐκ (#19) and αἴρω (#350). To take out; remove;
expel - with reference to dismissing a member from the fellowship of the
Corinthian church - 1 Cor.5:13.

τὸν (acc.sing.masc.of the article in agreement with πονηρὸν) 9.
πονηρὸν (acc.sing.masc.of πονηρός, direct object of ἐξάρατε) 438.
ἐξ (preposition with the ablative of separation) 19.
ὑμῶν (abl.pl.masc.of σύ, separation) 104.
αὐτῶν (abl.pl.masc.of αὐτός, reflexive) 16.

*Translation - "But those without God will judge. You yourselves must dismiss
the evil man from your fellowship."*

Comment: The judgment of the unsaved world is the sole responsibility of the
Son of God (John 5:22). That judgment is a future event (Rev.20:10). *Cf.* Mt.7:1-
5. Our Lord's prerogative as the Judge is vouchsafed unto Him by virtue of the
fact that God raised Him from the dead, after He alone had given His life to save
the lost.(Acts 17:31; Rev.5:9-10). Those who would seek to amass political
power at the polls to force upon the legislative bodies the passage of legislation
designed to enforce Christian morals upon unsaved people, seem to have
forgotten that they have done nothing to redeem the world from sin. Our Lord
alone has paid redemption's price and thus He alone has any moral right to
judge. The Moral Majority leaders of the 1980's seem also to be unaware that
enforced conformity upon the unsaved to standards of Biblical ethics is not the
"birth from above" which is the *sine qua non* of incorporation into the Body of
Christ. The unsaved may obey the Ten Commandments at the point of a
policeman's gun and under threat of imprisonment, but he is not thereby one

428   *The Renaissance New Testament*   1 Cor.5:13-6:1

incorporated by the Holy Spirit into the Body of Christ (1 Cor.12:13). Let us beware lest we "compass sea and land to make one proselyte, and when he is made, (we) make him twofold more the child of hell than (ourselves)" (Mt.23:15).

If the church spent half the time and effort weeping over and condemning her own sins as she does seeking to legislate her moral standards to wipe out the sins in the world of the unsaved, there would be great improvement in her own spiritual condition and the Lord might still use her to bring about a revival. Christians have nothing whatever to do with judging the lives of the unsaved. This is God's prerogative. But the local church has everything to do with the standard of morality of her own membership. She is charged with the responsibility of keeping her local membership free of members whose lives conform only to unregenerate standards. The quotation is from Deut.22:24, which relates to the same sin as the one with which the Corinthians should have been concerned.

Going to Law before Unbelievers

(1 Corinthians 6:1-11)

1 Cor.6:1 - "Dare any of you, having a matter against another, go to law before the unjust, and not before the saints?"

Τολμᾷ τις ὑμῶν πρᾶγμα ἔχων πρὸς τὸν ἕτερον κρίνεσθαι ἐπὶ τῶν ἀδίκων, καὶ οὐχὶ ἐπὶ τῶν ἁγίων;

"When one of you has a grievance against a brother, does he dare go to law before the unrighteous instead of the saints?" . . . RSV

Τολμᾷ (3d.per.sing.pres.act.ind.of τολμάω, aoristic) 1430.
τις (nom.sing.masc.of τις, indefinite pronoun, subject of τολμᾷ) 486.
ὑμῶν (gen.pl.masc.of σύ, partitive genitive) 104.
πρᾶγμα (acc.sing.neut.of πρᾶγμα, direct object of ἔχων) 1266.
ἔχων (pres.act.part.nom.sing.masc.of ἔχω, adverbial, causal) 82.
πρὸς (preposition with the accusative, opposition, with persons) 197.
τὸν (acc.sing.masc.of the article in agreement with ἕτερον) 9.
ἕτερον (acc.sing.masc.of ἕτερος, opposition) 605.
κρίνεσθαι (pres.mid.inf.of κρίνω, complementary) 531.
ἐπὶ (preposition with the genitive of place description) 47.
τῶν (gen.pl.masc.of the article in agreement with ἀδίκων) 9.
ἀδίκων (gen.pl.masc.of ἄδικος place description) 549.
καὶ (adversative conjunction) 14.
οὐχὶ (negative particle with the indicative) 130.
ἐπὶ (preposition with the genitive of place description) 47.
τῶν (gen.pl.masc.of the article in agreement with ἁγίων) 9.
ἁγίων (gen.pl.masc.of ἅγιος, place description) 84.

Translation - "*Does anyone of you, having grounds for suit against the other, dare to litigate before the unrighteous rather than before the saints?*"

Comment: Note the indefinite τις - "anyone of you" in litigation against "the other" - τὸν ἕτερον, where τὸν distinguishes between anyone individual, who is indefinite and another who is specific. ὑμῶν is a partitive genitive. The participle ἔχων is adverbial and can be either temporal, causal or circumstantial. The infinitive complements the verb Τολμᾷ.

Two courts are in contrast. The aggrieved brother can sue his brother in the secular or the church court. If the former he will be before an unsaved judge. If the latter, before a Christian. There were no jury trials under the Roman system of jurisprudence so that is not a consideration, though an application of this principle now would need to take this into consideration.

That Paul should refer to a judge on a Roman bench as ἄδικος (#549), when Rome prided herself on her justice, is a measure of Paul's contempt for the philosophy of the unsaved (1 Cor.1:18-2:16). Paul was not necessarily denigrating the science of jurisprudence *per se* as practised under the Roman system. He himself was a trained legal counsellor (Acts 22:3) and as such he had great respect for the concepts of justice and the legal procedures by which normally evidence was admitted, heard, assessed and upon which decisions were handed down. Paul was comparing the abilities of a trained lawyer, who lacked the wisdom of heaven's philosophy, to those of the most humble Christian with no formal knowledge of the law, but who enjoyed an understanding of heaven's wisdom. A Christian judge trained in the law is a better judge than one not so trained. The Christian who has the mind of Christ has an advantage over an unsaved man whose wisdom is equated with God's "nonesense" however great it may be by earthly standards.

Paul was suprized that the Corinthian Christians, with a church fellowship, best equipped to reach just decisions between litigants should choose to try their cases in pagan courts. Apparently they did not know about their future role in the administration of Messiah's coming kingdom.

Verse 2 - "Do you not know that the saints shall judge the world? And if the world shall be judged by you, are ye unworthy to judge the smallest matters?"

ἢ οὐκ οἴδατε ὅτι οἱ ἅγιοι τὸν κόσμον κρινοῦσιν; καὶ εἰ ἐν ὑμῖν κρίνεται ὁ κόσμος, ἀνάξιοί ἐστε κριτηρίων ἐλαχίστων;

"Do you not know that the saints will judge the world? And if the world is to be judged by you, are you incompetent to try trivial cases?" . . . RSV

ἢ (disjunctive) 465.

οὐκ (negative particle with the indicative in rhetorical question which expects a positive reply) 130.

οἴδατε (2d.per.pl.perf.act.ind.of ὁράω, intensive) 144b.

ὅτι (conjunction introducing an object clause in indirect discourse) 211.

οἱ (nom.pl.masc.of the article in agreement with ἅγιοι) 9.

ἅγιοι (nom.pl.masc.of ἅγιος, subject of κρινοῦσιν) 84.

τὸν (acc.sing.masc.of the article in agreement with κόσμον) 9.

κόσμον (acc.sing.masc.of κόσμος, direct object of κρινοῦσιν) 360.

κρινοῦσιν (3d.per.pl.fut.act.ind.of κρίνω, predictive) 531.

καὶ (continuative conjunction) 14.

εἰ (conditional particle in a first-class condition) 337.

ἐν (preposition with the instrumental of means) 80.

ὑμῖν (instru.pl.masc.of σύ, means) 104.

κρίνεται (3d.per.sing.pres.pass.ind.of κρίνω, futuristic) 531.

ὁ (nom.sing.masc.of the article in agreement with κόσμος) 9.

κόσμος (nom.sing.masc.of κόσμος, subject of κρίνεται) 360.

#4146 ἀνάξιοί (nom.pl.masc.of ἀνάξιος, predicate adjective).

King James Version

unworthy - 1 Cor.6:2.

Revised Standard Version

incompetent - 1 Cor.6:2.

Meaning: α privative plus ἄξιος (#285). Hence, unworthy; unfit; incompetent; not equal to the task - To be a judge - 1 Cor.6:2.

ἐστε (2d.per.pl.pres.ind.of εἰμί, direct question) 86.

#4147 κριτηρίων (abl.pl.neut.of κριτήριον, agent).

King James Version

judgment - 1 Cor.6:4.
judgment seat - James 2:6.
to judge - 1 Cor.6:2.

Revised Standard Version

to try - 1 Cor.6:2.
have cases - 1 Cor.6:4.
court - James 2:6.

Meaning: Criterion; the instrument or means of trying or judging anything. Standard of judgment. Not in this sense in the New Testament. A tribunal; a court; in the plural, a panel of judges or a docket of cases - 1 Cor.6:2,4; James 2:6.

ἐλαχίστων (gen.pl.neut.of ἐλάχιστος, definition, elative) 159.

Translation - "Or do you not know that the saints are going to judge the world? And since the world is to be judged by you, are you incompetent as judges of the most trivial cases?"

Comment: The role of the saints as judges of the world in the kingdom age to come, set forth as grounds for Paul's contention that Christians should never try cases in secular courts, is well supported elsewhere in Scripture. *Cf.* Mt.19:28; Lk.22:30; 1 Cor.4:8; Rev.20:4. The first-class condition with εἰ and the indicative assumes as true the premise in the protasis. "Since the world is scheduled for judgment before the court of the saints, why should any Christian feel incompetent to adjudicate the insignificant trivia of controversy in the Corinthian church?" ἐλαχίστων is elative.

Verse 3 - *"Know ye not that we shall judge angels? How much more things that pertain to this life?"*

οὐκ οἴδατε ὅτι ἀγγέλους κρινοῦμεν, μήτιγε βιωτικά;

"Do you not know that we are to judge angels? How much more, matters pertaining to this life!" . . . *RSV*

οὐκ (negative particle with the indicative in rhetorical question expecting a positive reply) 130.
οἴδατε (2d.per.pl.perf.act.ind. of ὁράω, intensive) 144b.
ὅτι (conjunction introducing an object clause in indirect discourse) 211.
ἀγγέλους (acc.pl.masc. of ἄγγελος, direct object of κρινοῦμεν) 96.
κρινοῦμεν (1st.per.pl.fut.act.ind. of κρίνω, predictive) 531.

#4148 μήτιγε (compound negative).

King James Version

how much more - 1 Cor.6:3.

Revised Standard Version

how much more - 1 Cor.6:3.

Meaning: A combination of μή (#87), τίς (#281) and γε (#2449). Used in a question to intensify the thought - 1 Cor.6:3. γε serves to accenuate the force.

βιωτικά (acc.pl.neut. of βιωτικός, direct object of κρινοῦμεν) 2736.

Translation - *"Do you not know that we are going to judge angels? How much more than matters pertaining only to this life!"*

Comment: *Cf.* Heb.1:4. The angels must give an account of their stewardship. Gal.1:8 pronounces judgment upon an angel who distorts the gospel. Who will judge them? *Cf.* also Jude 6; 2 Pet.2:4. Adjudicators of such weighty and eternal matters should experience no compunctions about sitting in judgment on earthly matters.

Verse 4 - *"If then ye have judgments of things pertaining to this life, set them to judge who are least esteemed in the church."*

βιωτικὰ μὲν οὖν κριτήρια ἐὰν ἔχητε, τοὺς ἐξουθενημένους ἐν τῇ ἐκκλησίᾳ τούτους καθίζετε;

"If then you have such cases, why do you lay them before those who are least esteemed by the church?" . . . RSV

βιωτικὰ (acc.pl.neut.of βιωτικός, in agreement with κριτήρια) 2736.

μὲν (particle of affirmation) 300.

οὖν (inferential conjunction) 68.

κριτήρια (acc.pl.neut.of κριτήριον, direct object of ἔχητε) 4147.

ἐὰν (conditional particle in a third-class condition) 363.

ἔχητε (2d.per.pl.pres.act.subj.of ἔχω, third-class condition) 82.

τοὺς (acc.pl.masc.of the article in agreement with ἐξουθενημένους) 9.

ἐξουθενημένους (perf.pass.part.acc.pl.masc.of ἐξουθενέω, substantival, direct object of καθίζετε) 2628.

ἐν (preposition with the locative of place) 80.

τῇ (loc.sing.fem.of the article in agreement with ἐκκλησίᾳ) 9.

ἐκκλησίᾳ (loc.sing.fem.of ἐκκλησία, place) 1204.

τούτους (acc.pl.masc.of οὗτος, in agreement with ἐξουθενημένους) 93.

καθίζετε (2d.per.pl.pres.act.ind.of καθίζω) 420.

Translation - "Yet if you have cases involving mundane matters you appoint as judges those who have always been regarded in the church as having no prestige!"

Comment: This statement has in it a ring of sarcastic surprise, coming on the heels of verse 3. Since they were told that they would be sitting in judgment in cases in which angels would be the defendants - cases of far greater import than temporal, mundane and relatively insignificant issues, why should they take their cases before unsaved judges, who enjoyed no prestige in the church. If a Christian is going to hear the cases of angels, who kept not their first estate (Jude 6) could he not decide where a property line ran between the real estate holdings of two of the brethren?!

Thus Paul assigns to an ecclesiastical court jurisdiction in all cases in which Christians are litigants. This advice has long since been rejected by most Christians. In the Middle Ages there were no civil courts, nor indeed any canons of civil law beyond the manorial courts. Everything was decided on the basis of canon law in canonical courts, which is not really what Paul meant. He is talking about two Christian brothers, each perhaps so much out of fellowship with Christ, the Head of the Body of which they both are component members, that they feel that they must sue and be sued in order to secure their rights. In such cases it is doubly distressing that they cannot settle their differences within their own local congregation. In fact, two Christians in total fellowship with Christ, through the indwelling Holy Spirit Who indwells each of them, would never have any differences of opinion in the first place.

Had Paul written 1000 years later he probably would have denied jurisdiction to a bishop's court as much as he did to a pagan court in Corinth. The point is that victorious Christians will never find it necessary to litigate. The modern church operates in a pagan democracy under a constitution (or in the case of state jurisdictions, state constitutions), which denies legal jurisdiction (which carries with it the power to enforce decisions) to local church courts. But this does not relieve a Christian of the responsibility of resolving his differences, should they arise between him and another Christian, through Scriptural channels (Mt.5:23-24; 18:15-17; Gal.6:1,2). If the dispute is between a Christian and an unsaved person, the Christian has only one recourse and that is to submit to whatever injustice may be involved (Mt.5:25, 38-48). His reward will be great in heaven (Mt.5:11,12; Rom.8:18).

This is "man's day" (1 Cor.4:3) and no Christian has any scriptural right to expect justice in a civil court, except as the judge/jury happens also to be Christian. Apparently there were no Christian judges in Corinth (1 Cor.1:26).

Verse 5 - "I speak to your shame. Is it so, that there is not a wise man among you? No, not one that shall be able to judge between his brethren?"

πρὸς ἐντροπὴν ὑμῖν λέγω. οὕτως οὐκ ἔνι ἐν ὑμῖν οὐδεὶς σοφὸς ὃς δυνήσεται διακρῖναι ἀνὰ μέσον τοῦ ἀδελφοῦ αὐτοῦ;

"I say this to your shame. Can it be that there is no man among you wise enough to decide between members of the brotherhood, . . . " . . . RSV

πρὸς (preposition with the accusative, result) 197.

#4149 ἐντροπὴν (acc.sing.fem. of ἐντροπή, result).

King James Version

shame - 1 Cor.6:5; 15:34.

Revised Standard Version

shame - 1 Cor.6:15; 15:34.

Meaning: Cf. ἐντρέπω (#1385). A combination of ἐν (#80) and τροπή (#5106). Shame results when one is "turned in" upon himself to see himself as others see him. With reference to Paul's evaluation of the Corinthians who submitted their disputes to an unsaved court - 1 Cor.6:5. With reference to ungodly philosophy and unethical behavior - 1 Cor.15:34.

ὑμῖν (dat.pl.masc.of σύ, indirect object of λέγω) 104.
λέγω (1st.per.sing.pres.act.ind.of λέγω, aoristic) 66.
οὕτως (demonstrative adverb) 74.
οὐκ (negative particle with the indicative) 130.

#4150 ἔνι (3d.per.sing.pres.ind.of ἔνειμι, aoristic).

King James Version

is - 1 Cor.6:5.
there is - Gal.3:28,28,28; Col.3:11; James 1:17.

Revised Standard Version

can it be - 1 Cor.6:5.

there is - Gal.3:28,28,28; James 1:17.
there cannot be - Col.3:11.

Meaning: ἔνι equals ἔνεστι. With οὐκ in a rhetorical question - "is there not?" - 1 Cor.5:6. In a negative assertion - Gal.3:28,28,28; Col.3:11; James 1:17.

ἐν (preposition with the locative of place with plural pronouns) 80.
ὑμῖν (loc.pl.masc.of σύ, place) 104.
οὐδεὶς (nom.sing.masc.of οὐδείς, subject of ἔνι) 446.
σοφὸς (nom.sing.masc.of σοφός, predicate adjective) 949.
ὅς (nom.sing.masc.of ὅς, relative pronoun, subject of δυνήσεται) 65.
δυνήσεται (3d.per.sing.fut.ind.of δύναμαι, deliberative) 289.
διακρῖναι (1st.aor.act.ind.of διακρίνω, epexegetical) 1195.
ἀνὰ (preposition with the accusative, distributive, "between") 1059.
μέσον (acc.sing.neut.of μέσος, distributive, "between" with the genitive) 873.
τοῦ (gen.sing.masc.of the article in agreement with ἀδελφοῦ) 9.
ἀδελφοῦ (gen.sing.masc.of ἀδελφός, description) 15.
αὐτοῦ (gen.sing.masc.of αὐτός, relationship) 16.

Translation - "*I am speaking to you to make you see yourselves in a true light. Is it really true that there is not one wise man among you who is able to judge between two brothers?*"

Comment: The translation is very free in order to bring out the force of πρὸς ἐντροπὴν (#4149).

> *O wad some power the giftie gie us*
> *To see oursels as ithers see us!*
> *It wad frae monie a blunder free us,*
> *an' foolish notion:*
> *What airs in dress and gait wad lae'e us,*
> *An' ev'n devotion!*
>
> Robert Burns, *To a Louse.*

If the Corinthian Christians and Jenny had known the amusement with which they were being observed, they by the Corinthian pagans who witnessed two Christians at law in a pagan court, and she by her Scotch neighbors in the kirk watching the louse on her new hat, they would both have been ashamed.

If we turn our eyes in upon ourselves (#'s 4149, 1385), "It wad frai monie a blunder free us."

In τοῦ ἀδελφοῦ αὐτοῦ we have the collective use of the neuter singular. Another way to write it would be ἀνὰ μέσον τῶν ἀδελφῶν αὐτοῦ or ἀνὰ μέσον ἀδελφοῦ καὶ ἀδελφοῦ. Cf.#1059 for ἀνὰ μέσον followed by the genitive in the sense of "between." Paul's rhetorical question again is sarcasm. Were they really so poverty stricken in personnel in the church, that there was not a single person wise enough to be able to decide between two brothers? Not many wise were called (1 Cor.1:26), but Paul did not say,"Not any." If they were so out of touch with the Holy Spirit and with Christ, the Head, that they were at odds, could they not at least settle the dispute within the church family?

Verse 6 - "But brother goeth to law with brother, and that before the unbelievers."

ἀλλὰ ἀδελφὸς μετὰ ἀδελφοῦ κρίνεται, καὶ τοῦτο ἐπὶ ἀπίστων;

". . . but brother goes to law against brother, and that before unbelievers?" . . .
RSV

ἀλλὰ (adversative conjunction) 342.
ἀδελφὸς (nom.sing.masc.of ἀδελφός, subject of κρίνεται) 15.
μετὰ (preposition with the genitive, opposition) 50.
ἀδελφοῦ (gen.sing.masc.of ἀδελφός, opposition) 15.
κρίνεται (3d.per.sing.pres.mid.ind.of κρίνω, customary) 531.
καὶ (ascensive conjunction) 14.
τοῦτο (nom.sing.neut.of οὗτος, anaphoric, parenthetic nominative) 93.
ἐπὶ (preposition with the genitive of place description) 47.
ἀπίστων (gen.pl.masc.of ἄπιστος, place description) 1231.

Translation - "But one brother is suing another brother - even this before unbelievers!"

Comment: The fact that two Christian brethren are at odds is sad enough. But sadder still (ascensive καὶ) is the fact that when they go to court they choose the jurisdiction of a pagan judge, as though there was no one in the church wise enough to yield a just decision. If this were true, it would mean that everyone in the church was as out of touch with the leading of the Holy Spirit as the two litigants themselves.

The three persons of the triune Godhead are never in disagreement on anything. God cannot contradict Himself. What the Father wants is what the Son and the Holy Spirit also want. In every dispute there is never any doubt about what the right thing to do is and where the total truth lies. The problem lies in the fact that the members of the Body of Christ are not listening to the Holy Spirit Who lives in their bodies (1 Cor.6:19,20). If they did listen and obey Him they would know precisely what the "Head over all things to His church" (Eph.1:22,23) wishes. Thus the victorious life would result in the saving of a great deal of unnecessary legal expense, and the trauma that often follows litigation.

Verse 7 - "Now therefore there is utterly a fault among you, because ye go to law one with another. Why do ye not rather take wrong? Why do ye not rather suffer yourselves to be defrauded?"

ἤδη μὲν (οὖν) ὅλως ἥττημα ὑμῖν ἐστιν ὅτι κρίματα ἔχετε μεθ' ἑαυτῶν. διὰ τί οὐχὶ μᾶλλον ἀδικεῖσθε; διὰ τί οὐχὶ μᾶλλον ἀποστερεῖσθε;

"To have lawsuits at all with one another is defeat for you. Why not rather suffer wrong? Why not rather be defrauded?" . . . RSV

ἤδη (temporal adverb) 291.

μὲν (particle of affirmation) 300.

οὖν (inferential conjunction) 68.

ὅλως (adverbial) 517.

ἥττημα (nom.sing.neut.of ἥττημα, subject of ἐστιν) 3992.

ὑμῖν (dat.pl.masc.of σύ, personal disadvantage) 104.

ἐστιν (3d.per.sing.pres.ind.of εἰμί, static) 86.

ὅτι (conjunction introducing a subordinate causal clause) 211.

κρίματα (acc.pl.neut.of κρίμα, direct object of ἔχετε) 642.

ἔχετε (2d.per.pl.pres.act.ind.of ἔχω, present interative retroactive) 82.

μεθ' (preposition with the genitive, opposition) 50.

ἑαυτῶν (gen.pl.masc.of ἑαυτοῦ, opposition, reciprocally reflexive) 288.

διὰ (preposition with the accusative, cause) 118.

τί (acc.sing.neut.of τίς, interrogative pronoun, direct question, cause) 281.

οὐχὶ (negative particle with the indicative) 130.

μᾶλλον (adverbial) 619.

ἀδικεῖσθε (2d.per.pl.pres.mid.of ἀδικέω, direct question) 1327.

διὰ (preposition with the accusative, cause) 118.

τί (acc.sing.neut.of τίς, interrogative pronoun, cause, direct question) 281.

οὐχὶ (negative particle with the indicative) 130.

μᾶλλον (adverbial) 619.

ἀποστερεῖσθε (2d.per.pl.pres.mid.ind.of ἀποστερέω, present iterative retroactive) 2639.

Translation - *"So in fact you are already incurring a loss because you have been suing one another. Why do you not rather take the loss? Why not permit yourself rather to be cheated?"*

Comment: The Corinthians who sued each other in the secular courts from time to time (present iterative retroactive) were suffering a total loss (#517). What they might gain from each other in financial terms was more than balanced against them by the loss of spiritual power with God, to say nothing of attorneys' fees and court costs, all of which enriched the unsaved and impoverished the saints. Add to this the reputation for hypocrisy which they gained among the unsaved gainsayers in Corinth.

Another possible interpretation, supported by Goodspeed, is that the very fact that they were litigating at all, even in a church court, to say nothing of a suit in a secular court, indicated that they had failed utterly to live the Spirit-filled life. *Cf.* #3992. Goodspeed has, "Having lawsuits with one another at all means your utter failure to begin with."

The ὅτι clause tells us why they were working to their own disadvantage. Would it not be better in every way for them to adopt an alternative policy (μᾶλλον). Should they not suffer injustice? Should they not submit to the fraud, even though it is at your own expense? (Mt.5:25, 38-48). Paul is telling them not to retaliate. Peter had similar advice to give (1 Pet.2:19-25; Rom.12:14). The Christian who moves to protect his rights indicates his own basic insecurity. No

Christian who is victorious in Christ is insecure (2 Tim.1:7). A low level of spirituality in a church is always apparent, made manifest by church quarrels and schisms. It is impossible to hurt a Spirit-filled Christian (Gal.5:22,23). Note the reciprocity in the reflexive pronoun ἑαυτῶν. ἀδικεῖσθε and ἀποστερεῖσθε, are what Robertson calls causative or permissive middles. "Let yourselves be wronged and robbed." (*Grammar*, 808).

Not only were the Corinthians unwilling to suffer injustice at the hands of their marauding brethren - they took the field in counter-offensive.

Verse 8 - *"Nay, ye do wrong, and defraud, and that your brethren."*

ἀλλὰ ὑμεῖς ἀδικεῖτε καὶ ἀποστερεῖτε, καὶ τοῦτο ἀδελφούς.

"But you yourselves wrong and defraud, and that even your own brethren." . .
. RSV

ἀλλὰ (adversative conjunction) 342.
ὑμεῖς (nom.pl.masc.of σύ, subject of ἀδικεῖτε and ἀποστερεῖτε, emphatic) 104
ἀδικεῖτε (2d.per.pl.pres.act.ind.of ἀδικέω, present iterative retroactive) 1327.
καὶ (adjunctive conjunction joining verbs) 14.
ἀποστερεῖτε (2d.per.pl.pres.act.ind.of ἀποστερέω, present iterative retroactive) 2639.
καὶ (ascensive conjunction) 14.
τοῦτο (nom.sing.neut.of οὗτος, parenthetical, nominative absolute) 93.
ἀδελφούς (acc.pl.masc.of ἀδελφός, direct object of ἀποστερεῖτε) 15.

Translation - *"On the contrary you yourselves have been perpetrating injustice and defrauding even your brothers."*

Comment: ἀλλὰ is strongly adversative. The Christian ideal ethic of verse 7 - διὰ τί . . . ἀδικεῖσθε, διὰ τί . . . αποστερεῖσθε is in diametric contrast to their past and current behavior in verse 8. Note again καὶ τοῦτο as in verse 6. They needed the message of Mt.6:19-34, but we must remember that they had no way of knowing at this time what Jesus had said on this subject of avarice.

Verse 9 - *"Know ye not that the unrighteous shall not inherit the kingdom of God? Be not deceived: neither fornicators, nor idolaters, nor adulterers, nor effeminate, nor abusers of themselves with mankind, . . . "*

ἢ οὐκ οἴδατε ὅτι ἄδικοι θεοῦ βασιλείαν οὐ κληρονομήσουσιν; μὴ πλανᾶσθε, οὔτε πόρνοι οὔτε εἰδωλολάτραι οὔτε μοιχοὶ οὔτε μαλακοὶ οὔτε ἀρσενοκοῖται

"Do you not know that the unrighteous will not inherit the kingdom of God? Do not be deceived; neither the immoral, nor idolaters, nor adulterers, nor homosexuals, . . . " . . . RSV

ἢ (disjunctive) 465.
οὐκ (negative particle with the indicative in rhetorical question expecting a positive reply) 130.
οἴδατε (2d.per.pl.perf.act.ind.of ὁράω, intensive) 144b.

ὅτι (conjunction introducing an object clause in indirect discourse) 211.

ἄδικοι (nom.pl.masc.of ἄδικος, subject of κληρονομήσουσιν) 549.

θεοῦ (gen.sing.masc.of θεός, description) 124.

βασιλείαν (acc.sing.fem.of βασιλεία, direct object of κληρονομήσουσιν) 253.

οὐ (negative particle with the indicative) 130.

κληρονομήσουσιν (3d.per.pl.fut.act.ind.of κληρονομέω, predictive) 426.

μὴ (negative particle with the imperative, in a prohibition) 87.

πλανᾶσθε (2d.per.pl.pres.mid.impv.of πλανάω, prohibition) 1257.

οὔτε (negative copulative conjunction) 598.

πόρνοι (nom.pl.masc.of πόρνος, subject of κληρονομήσουσιν) 4140.

οὔτε (negative copulative conjunction) 598.

εἰδωλολάτραι (nom.pl.masc.of εἰδωλολάτρης, subject of κληρονομύσουσιν) 4142.

οὔτε (negative copulative conjunction) 598.

μοιχοὶ (nom.pl.masc.of μοιχός, subject of κληρονομήσουσιν) 2629.

οὔτε (negative copulative conjunction) 598.

μαλακοὶ (nom.pl.masc.of μαλακός, subject of κληρονομήσουσιν) 912.

οὔτε (negative copulative conjunction) 598.

#4151 ἀρσενοκοῖται (nom.pl.masc.of ἀρσενοκοίτης, subject of κληρονομήσουιν).

King James Version

abuser of self with mankind - 1 Cor.6:9.
that defileth self with mankind - 1 Tim.1:10.

Revised Standard Version

homosexual - 1 Cor.6:9.
sodomite - 1 Tim.1:10.

Meaning: A combination of ἄρσην (#1286) and κοίτη (#2448). Hence, a homosexual - 1 Cor.6:9; 1 Tim.1:10.

Translation - "Or are you not aware that the unrighteous will not inherit the kingdom of God? Stop deceiving yourselves. Neither immoral persons, nor idolaters, nor adulterers, nor effeminate males, nor homosexuals . . . "

Comment: The rhetorical question continues through verse 10 to add five other categories of sin. In verse 11 Paul makes clear his entire meaning. Persistent wrong doers indicate that their profession of faith in Christ is not genuine. Paul is not denying that God's elect have eternal salvation. Those who are saved by divine grace are truly regenerate. They will commit sin after they are saved (1 John 1:8), but they do not continue to practice sin (1 John 3:9). They do not "go on sinning." When a pig falls in the mud he lies there and enjoys it to the full. When a sheep falls into the mud he gets out immediately and seeks cleansing. Those who are "born from above" (John 33,7) are sheep, not pigs.

Verse 10 - ". . . nor thieves, nor covetous, nor drunkards, nor revilers, nor extortioners, shall inherit the kingdom of God."

οὔτε κλέπται οὔτε πλεονέκται, οὐ μέθυδοι, οὐ λοίδοροι, οὐχ ἅρπαγες βασιλείαν θεοῦ κληρονομήσουσιν.

". . . nor thieves, nor the greedy, nor drunkards, nor revilers, nor robbers will inherit the kingdom of God." . . . RSV

οὔτε (negative copulative conjunction) 598.

κλέπται (nom.pl.masc.of κλέπτης, subject of κληρονομήσουσιν) 595.

οὔτε (negative copulative conjunction) 598.

πλεονέκται (nom.pl.masc.of πλεονέκτης, subject of κληρονομήσουσιν) 4141.

οὐ (negative particle with the indicative) 130.

μέθυσοι (nom.pl.masc.of μέθυσος, subj.of κληρονομήσουσιν) 4144.

οὐ (negative particle with the indicative) 130.

λοίδοροι (nom.pl.masc.of λοίδορος, subject of κληρονομήσουσιν) 4143.

οὐχ (negative particle with the indicative) 130.

ἅρπαγες (nom.pl.masc.of ἅρπαξ, subject of κληρηνομήσουσιν) 674.

βασιλείαν (acc.sing.fem.of βασιλεία, direct object of κληρονομήσουσιν) 253.

θεοῦ (gen.sing.masc.of θεός, description) 124.

κληρονομήσουσιν (3d.per.pl.fut.act.ind.of κληρονομέω, predictive) 426.

Translation - ". . . nor thieves, nor covetous, not drunkards, not revilers, not extortioners will inherit the kindgom of God."

Comment: Note that he changes from the negative copulative conjunction οὔτε (if it is not a disjunctive) to οὐ and repeats it for rhetorical emphasis.

There are at least three ways to interpret this strong statement of verses 9,10.

Arminians say that here is evidence that true believers may yet lapse into the sins described here and pay the penalty of losing their salvation to spend eternity in hell.

Some premillenialists insist that the rapture of the church at Christ's second coming and the subsequent participation of the raptured saints in the millenial "kingdom of God" is not guaranteed to the elect as is salvation, but a privilege to be earned by victorious Christian living, a privilege which is forfeited by the Christian whose life is here characterized. Under this view the "Kingdom of God" is equated with the millenial reign of Rev.20:4. These people are not eternally lost, in this view, but will be resurrected at the Great White Throne, found to have had their names written in the Book of Life (Rev.20:11-15) and admitted into an eternal heaven. This school of thought points to the resurrection and the rapture as something to be attained and point to Phil.3:10-14, especially verse 11. This view is in harmony with the Calvinistic doctrine of preservation (contra Arminians) and still avoids the antinomian view that there is no penalty for post regeneration sin.

A third view is also Calvinistic, but avoids antinomianism by pointing to these sinners as habitual participants in the sins involved. Thus πόρνοι are people whose life style is adultery. κλέπται are habitual thieves. μέθυσοι are alcoholics, etc. Exponents of this view point to verse 11 for evidence that Paul is not describing the Corinthian saints in their current state, but rather as they lived before they were saved. This does not deny that such persons will forfeit the Kingdom of God, but it implies that the Corinthians were no longer living in sin (1 John 3:9 - "whoever is born of God is not continuing to practice sin.") To say that one lapse by the Christian into any of the sins mentioned forfeits either salvation with the Arminians, or participation in the Kingdom with the selective rapturists is likely to include all regenerate people and mean either "no heaven for anyone" in the Arminian case, or "no kingdom of God" in the case of the partial rapturists.

We therefore identify the phrase "kingdom of God" both with heaven and the millenium and take the view that Paul is simply stressing the fact that the spiritual life in the Kingdom of God is totally out of harmony with the kind of life described in verses 9 and 10, and that Paul is saying to the Corinthians that if their lives are still like that, they were never truly regenerate in the first place. To say that Christians do not on occasion commit adultery, worship idols, fornicate, steal, covet, drink too much, etc. is to oppose both Scripture (1 John 1:8) and experience, though, of course, to admit that they do is not to say that they should. But it can be said that the true Christian does not continue to live like that.

There are many highly respected and sincere students who take a selective rapture position on this passage. It would help if we could be sure what Paul means here by βασιλείαν θεοῦ. Note that the phrase is anarthrous, both in verses 9 and 10.

Verse 11 - "And such were some of you; but ye are washed, but ye are sanctified, but ye are justified in the name of the Lord Jesus, and by the Spirit of our God."

καὶ ταῦτά τινες ἦτε. ἀλλὰ ἀπελούσασθε, ἀλλὰ ἡγιάσθητε, ἀλλὰ ἐδικαιώθητε ἐν τῷ ὀνόματι τοῦ κυρίου Ἰησοῦ Χριστοῦ καὶ ἐν τῷ πνεύματι τοῦ θεοῦ ἡμῶν.

"And such were some of you. But you were washed, you were sanctified, you were justifed in the name of the Lord Jesus Christ and in the Spirit of our God.".
. . RSV

καὶ (continuative conjunction) 14.
ταῦτά (nom.pl.neut.of οὗτος, predicate nominative) 93.
τινες (nom.pl.masc.of τις, indefinite pronoun, subject of ἦτε) 486.
ἦτε (2d.per.pl.imp.ind.of εἰμί, progressive description) 86.
ἀλλὰ (adversative conjunction) 342.
ἀπελούσασθε (2d.per.pl.aor.pass.ind.of ἀπολούω, culminative) 3580.
ἀλλὰ (adversative conjunction) 342.
ἡγιάσθητε (2d.per.pl.aor.pass.ind.of ἁγιάζω, culminative) 576.
ἀλλὰ (adversative conjunction) 342.

ἐδικαιώθητε (2d.per.pl.aor.pass.ind.of δικαιόω, culminative) 933.

ἐν (preposition with the instrumental of association) 80.

τῷ (instru.sing.neut.of the article in agreement with ὀνόματι) 9.

ὀνόματι (instru.sing.neut.of ὄνομα, association) 108.

τοῦ (gen.sing.masc.of the article in agreement with κυρίου) 9.

κυρίου (gen.sing.masc.of κύριος, possession) 97.

Ἰησοῦ (gen.sing.masc.of Ἰησοῦς, apposition) 3.

Χριστοῦ (gen.sing.masc.of Χριστός, apposition) 4.

καὶ (adjunctive conjunction joining prepositional phrases) 14.

ἐν (preposition with the instrumental of means) 80.

τῷ (instru.sing.neut.of the article in agreement with πνεύματι) 9.

πνεύματι (instru.sing.neut.of πνεῦμα, means) 83.

τοῦ (gen.sing.masc.of the article in agreement with θεοῦ) 9.

θεοῦ (gen.sing.masc.of θεός, description) 124.

ἡμῶν (gen.pl.masc.of ἐγώ, relationship) 123.

Translation - *"And some of you were like that, but you have been washed; but you have been set apart for God's service; but you have been declared righteous, in the name of our Lord Jesus Christ, and by the Spirit of our God."*

Comment: ταῦτα in the predicate is much like τοιοῦτοι though more definite and emphatic (Robertson, *Grammar*, 704). The imperfect tense in ἦτε is progressive description, not progressive duration, since the context indicates that the practices had been completed. Paul adds that all of that had been changed. "You were washed" - *cf.* Acts 22:16 and comment which sufficiently answers those who propose baptismal regeneration. They had also been sanctified and declared righteous. Note these culminative aorists. These acts - washing, sanctification and justification, are all divine acts of the Lord Jesus Christ and the Holy Spirit of God. Note that there is no particular order in view. God set them apart for special service (ἡγιάσθητε) and declared them as possessors of Christ's righteousness (ἐδικαιώθητε) and they signified the fact by being immersed in water. These acts of God, and the ceremonial acquiescence by man of God's work put an end to their lives of sin as described in verses 9 and 10 and gave to them a new life of freedom, which carries with it a new dimension of responsibility.

Glorify God in Your Body

(1 Corinthians 6:12-20)

Verse 12 - *"All things are lawful unto me, but all things are not expedient: all things are lawful for me, but I will not be brought under the power of any."*

Πάντα μοι ἔξεστιν, ἀλλ' οὐ πάντα συμφέρει. πάντα μοι ἔξεστιν, ἀλλ' οὐκ ἐγὼ ἐξουσιασθήσομαι ὑπό τινος.

" 'All things are lawful for me,' but not all things are helpful. 'All things are lawful for me,' but I will not be enslaved by anything." . . . RSV

Πάντα (nom.pl.neut.of πᾶς, subject of ἔξεστιν) 67.

μοι (dat.sing.masc.of ἐγώ, personal advantage) 123.

ἔξεστιν (3d.per.sing.pres.ind.of ἔξειμι, static) 966.

ἀλλ' (adversative conjunction) 342.

οὐ (negative particle with the indicative) 130.

πάντα (nom.pl.neut.of πᾶς, subject of συμφέρει) 67.

συμφέρει (3d.per.sing.pres.act.ind.of συμφέρω, static) 505.

πάντα (nom.pl.neut.of πᾶς, subject of ἔξεστιν) 67.

μοι (dat.sing.masc.of ἐγώ, personal advantage) 123.

ἔξεστιν (3d.per.sing.pres.ind.of ἔξειμι, static) 966.

ἀλλ' (adversative conjunction) 342.

οὐκ (negative particle with the indicative) 130.

ἐγώ (nom.sing.masc.of ἐγώ, subject of ἐξουσιασθήσομαι, emphatic) 123.

ἐξουσιασθήσομαι (1st.per.sing.fut.pass.ind.of ἐξουσιάζω, predictive) 2777.

ὑπό (preposition with the ablative of agent) 117.

τινος (abl.sing.masc.of τις, indefinite pronoun, agent) 486.

Translation - "All things are permitted to me but not everything works to my advantage. All things are lawful for me, but I am not going to become enslaved by any of them."

Comment: Paul here seems to be arguing with the antinomians in Corinth (Rom.6:1-3). Their argument went like this: "If salvation is by grace and faith alone, then may we not fornicate, steal, covet, etc. etc.?" Paul replies with devastation. We may indeed do anything we like without prejudice to our salvation, but though all is permitted, not all is good for us. Note οὐκ coming before πάντα and ἐγώ for emphasis and contrast. The distinction must be made between the believer's *standing* in Christ, which is unchanging, and his *state* which fluctuates, depending upon the degree to which he yields to the indwelling Holy Spirit, thus to live the victorious life. Sin in the life of the believer does not negate the atonement which Christ paid for him upon the cross, but it is not smart for the believer to sin. The adulterer is not lost because of his adultery but he is digging his own grave. Paul repeats this argument in 1 Cor.10:23 in a different context. Note the exact force of συμφέρω in #505. If the child of God wants to put it all togehter for the glory of God (Rom.8:28) there are some practices which he must abandon since they exert a disjunctive rather than a conjunctive effect upon his life. The Christian is free (John 8:32,36) and therefore he refuses to allow himself to be enslaved by anything. Idolaters are slaves. The Christian who must smoke, drink, philander, steal, eat too much, etc. is not as free as he ought to be and can be. All that we do involves us in opportunity cost. Paul illustrates in

Verse 13 - "Meats for the belly, and the belly for meats: but God shall destroy both it and them. Now the body is not for fornication, but for the Lord; and the Lord for the body."

τὰ βρώματα τῇ κοιλίᾳ, καὶ ἡ κοιλία τοῖς βρώμασιν ὁ δὲ θεὸς καὶ ταύτην καὶ ταῦτα καταργήσει. τὸ δὲ σῶμα οὐ τῇ πορνείᾳ ἀλλὰ τῷ κυρίῳ, καὶ ὁ κύριος τῷ σώματι.

" 'Food is meant for the stomach and the stomach for food' — and God will destroy both one and the other. The body is not meant for immorality, but for the Lord, and the Lord for the body." . . . RSV

τὰ (nom.pl.neut.of the article in agreement with βρώματα) 9.

βρώματα (nom.pl.neut.of βρῶμα, subject of verb understood) 1118.

τῇ (dat.sing.fem.of the article in agreement with κοιλίᾳ) 9.

κοιλίᾳ (dat.sing.fem.of κοιλία, personal advantage) 1008.

καὶ (continuative conjunction) 14.

ἡ (nom.sing.fem.of the article in agreement with κοιλία) 9.

κοιλία (nom.sing.fem.of κοιλία, subject of verb understood) 1008.

τοῖς (dat.pl.neut.of the article in agreement with βρώμασιν) 9.

βρώμασιν (dat.pl.neut.of βρῶμα, personal advantage) 1118.

ὁ (nom.sing.masc.of the article in agreement with θεὸς) 9.

δὲ (adversative conjunction) 11.

θεὸς (nom.sing.masc.of θεός, subject of καταργήσει) 124.

καὶ (correlative conjunction) 14.

ταύτην (acc.sing.fem.of οὗτος, direct object of καταργήσει, in agreement with κοιλία) 93.

καὶ (correlative adjunctive) 14.

ταῦτα (acc.pl.neut.of οὗτος, direct object of καταργήσει, in agreement with βρώματα) 93.

καταργήσει (3d.per.sing.fut.act.ind.of καταργέω, predictive) 2500.

τὸ (nom.sing.neut.of the article in agreement with σῶμα) 9.

δὲ (adversative conjunction) 11.

σῶμα (nom.sing.neut.of σῶμα, subject of verb understood) 507.

οὐ (negative particle with the indicative) 130.

τῇ (dat.sing.fem.of the article in agreement with πορνείᾳ) 9.

πορνείᾳ (dat.sing.fem.of πορνεία, advantage) 511.

ἀλλὰ (alternative conjunction) 342.

τῷ (dat.sing.masc.of the article in agreement with κυρίῳ) 9.

κυρίῳ (dat.sing.masc.of κύριος, personal advantage) 97.

καὶ (continuative conjunction) 14.

ὁ (nom.sing.masc.of the article in agreement with κύριος) 9.

κύριος (nom.sing.masc.of κύριος, subject of verb understood) 97.

τῷ (dat.sing.neut.of the article in agreement with σώματι) 9.

σώματι (dat.sing.neut.of σῶμα, personal advantage) 507.

Translation - *"The food is for the stomach and the stomach for the food, but God is going to terminate the functions of both stomach and food. But the body is not for the purpose of immorality, but for the Lord, and the Lord is for the body."*

Comment: This verse pursues the thought of verse 12 that though all things are

permitted to the Christian, not all things are good for him. The ethical question -
"What shall I do and what shall I forebear?" - is therefore one of axiology. What
is this or that worth in the long run? Even the legitimate function of eating is of
only short run utility. God made food to be eaten and the digestive tract to
absorb its nourishment and expel the waste, but even such legitimate function as
eating is not to be eternally enjoyed. God will phase out the bodily function.
Here is evidence that the resurrection body will not require food, even though it
will be possible to eat (Luke 24:42,43). *Cf.*#2500 for the basic meaning of
καταργέω. So long as the human body needs nourishment in order to survive it
is legitimate to eat. When the body is glorified at the resurrection/rapture and
there is no further need for food, the ingestive and digestive functions will be
phased out.

The legitimate function of eating food is endowed only with temporal
significance. But Paul flatly states that though God made food to be eaten and
the body to digest it, He did not make the human body for fornication. This
statement denies the assertion often heard that sex, outside of marriage, is
legitimate on the ground that it, like hunger for food, is only a normal and
necessary human drive. This is disproved by the fact that it is impossible to
sublimate the hunger drive and survive. No one ever survived a prolonged fast.
But there are millions of people who have never indulged the sex drive, and who
have not because of this damaged themselves either physically or psychological-
ly. The body can be used for sex, and within the Christian framework, sex
glorifies God, but the body is not for sex in the sense that the stomach is for food.
The body is for the Lord, and reciprocally, the Lord is for the body. The body is
the temple of God and the dwelling place of the Holy Spirit. God will terminate
the function of the alimentary canal but He will never terminate the function of
the body of the Christian. It is scheduled for resurrection (Rom.8:11). *Cf.*
Rom.6:6 where καταργέω (#2500) is used with reference to the body of sin, -τὸ
σῶμα τῆς ἁμαρτίας. Indeed, the body of sin will be destroyed, but the
resurrected body will be like Christ's resurrected body (1 John 3:1-2; Phil.3:21).

That the Lord's interest in our bodies is eternal is clear from

*Verse 14 - "And God hath both raised up the Lord, and will also raise up us by his
own power."*

ὁ δὲ θεὸς καὶ τὸν κύριον ἤγειρεν καὶ ὑμᾶς ἐξεγερεῖ διὰ τῆς δυνάμεως αὐτοῦ.

"And God raised the Lord and will also raise us up by his power." . . . RSV

ὁ (nom.sing.masc.of the article in agreement with θεὸς) 9.
δὲ (continuative conjunction) 11.
θεὸς (nom.sing.masc.of θεός, subject of ἤγειρεν and ἐξεγερεῖ) 124.
καὶ (correlative adjunctive) 14.
τὸν (acc.sing.masc.of the article in agreement with κύριον) 9.
κύριον (acc.sing.masc.of κύριος, direct object of ἤγειρεν) 97.
ἤγειρεν (3d.per.sing.aor.act.ind.of ἐγείρω, constative) 125.
καὶ (correlative adjunctive, joining substantives) 14.

ἡμᾶς (acc.pl.masc.of ἐγώ, direct object of ἐξεγερεῖ) 123.

ἐξεγερεῖ (3d.per.sing.fut.act.ind.of ἐξεγείρω, predictive) 3963.

διὰ (preposition with the ablative of means) 118.

τῆς (abl.sing.fem.of the article in agreement with δυνάμεως) 9.

δυνάμεως (abl.sing.fem.of δύναμις, means) 687.

αὐτοῦ (gen.sing.masc.of αὐτός, possession) 16.

Translation - *"And God has both raised up the Lord, and He will raise us up by His power."*

Comment: The same statement in essence occurs in Romans 8:11. The human body of the believer thus has eternal significance. Throughout the remainder of the chapter Paul builds upon the fact of the dignity of the body of the Christian, his attack upon adultery.

Verse 15 - *"Know ye not that your bodies are the members of Christ? Shall I then take the members of Christ, and make them the members of an harlot? God forbid."*

οὐκ οἴδατε ὅτι τὰ σώματα ὑμῶν μέλη Χριστοῦ ἐστιν; ἄρας οὖν τὰ μέλη τοῦ Χριστοῦ ποιήσω πόρνης μέλη; μὴ γένοιτο.

"Do you not know that your bodies are members of Christ? Shall I therefore take the members of Christ and make them members of a prostitute? Never!" ...
                                                                            RSV

οὐκ (negative particle with the indicative in rhetorical question expecting a positive reply) 130.

οἴδατε (2d.per.pl.perf.act.ind.of ὁράω, intensive, rhetorical question) 144b.

ὅτι (conjunction introducing an object clause in indirect discourse) 211.

τὰ (nom.pl.neut.of the article in agreement with σώματα) 9.

σώματα (nom.pl.neut.of σῶμα, subject of ἐστιν) 507.

ὑμῶν (gen.pl.masc.of σύ, possession) 104.

μέλη (nom.pl.neut.of μέλος, predicate nominative) 506.

Χριστοῦ (gen.sing.masc.of Χριστός, possession) 4.

ἐστιν (3d.per.sing.pres.ind.of εἰμί, static) 86.

ἄρας (aor.act.part.nom.sing.masc.of αἴρω, adverbial, temporal) 350.

οὖν (inferential conjunction) 68.

τὰ (acc.pl.neut.of the article in agreement with μέλη) 9.

μέλη (acc.pl.neut.of μέλος, direct object of ποιήσω) 506.

τοῦ (gen.sing.masc.of the article in agreement with Χριστοῦ) 9.

Χριστοῦ (gen.sing.masc.of Χριστός, possession) 4.

ποιήσω (1st.per.sing.1st.aor.act.subj.of ποιέω, deliberative) 127.

πόρνης (gen.sing.fem.of πόρνη, description) 1374.

μέλη (nom.pl.neut.of μέλος, predicate nominative) 506.

μὴ (negative particle with the optative) 87.

γένοιτο (3d.per.sing.aor.optative of γίνομαι, voluntative) 113.

Translation - "You know, do you not that your bodies are members of Christ? Therefore shall I take the members of Christ's body and make them members of a prostitute? Certainly not!"

Comment: The rhetorical question has the perfect οἴδατε - "Have you not learned previously thus to know now . . . κ.τ.λ."

The material in this object clause is the great mystery which is at the heart of the Christian theology. Jesus Christ now has the same physical body that He had when He died on the cross, in which He suffered. It is the same body that arose from the grave. In that same body He now sits at God's right hand awaiting the hour of His second coming (Psalm 110:1). But Christ, the Head over all things to His church (Eph.1:22,23) also has a spiritual, mystical body made up of the physical bodies of all of the saints (1 Cor.6:15; John 17:21). The σῶμα (physical body) of the Christian is a part (μέλος) of Christ's spiritual body. As such it is also the temple of the Holy Spirit (verse 19). This fact greatly dignifies the body of the Christian and explains why it is scheduled for physical resurrection and transformation (Rom.8:11; Phil.3:20,21; 1 John 3:1-3; 1 Thess.4:13-18; 1 Cor.15:51, etc.)

In some mystical way the Holy Spirit Who dwells in the body of every individual Christian unites all of us into the Body of Christ in such a way that the wishes of Christ the Head are transmitted by the Holy Spirit to each of the members, just as the nervous system of the body transmits messages from the brain to the various parts.

Once this great fact is realized, adultery becomes horrendous beyond expression. For in adultery a Christian is taking his body which is a vital member of the Body of Christ, in whom the Holy Spirit dwells, and associating it with the body of a prostitute. He is forcing the Holy Spirit into a bed of lust.

The deliberative subjunctive asks the incredulous question. (ποιήσω can also be taken as a deliberative future, since the spelling is the same. The exegesis is not affected). μὴ γένοιτο is Paul's strongest language of negation. "God forbid! Never! Certainly not!" Any of these expressions translate it if the reader puts enough revulsion into the negation.

The closest of all intimate relationships is established between the body of the Christian and that of our risen Lord. It still remains to show the intimate relation between the two adulterers. This Paul does in

Verse 16 - "What? Know ye not that he which is joined to an harlot is one body? For two, saith he, shall be one flesh."

(ἤ) οὐκ οἴδατε ὅτι ὁ κολλώμενος τῇ πόρνῃ ἓν σῶμά ἐστιν; Ἔσονται γάρ, φησίν, οἱ δύο εἰς σάρκα μίαν.

"Do you not know that he who joins himself to a prostitute becomes one body with her? For, as it is written, 'The two shall become one.' " . . . RSV

(ἤ) (disjunctive) 465.

οὐκ (negative particle with the indicative in rhetorical question, expecting a positive reply) 130.

οἴδατε (2d.per.pl.perf.act.ind.of ὁράω, intensive) 144b.

ὅτι (conjunction introducing an object clause in indirect discourse) 211.

ὁ (nom.sing.masc.of the article in agreement with κολλώμενος) 9.

κολλώμενος (pres.mid.part.nom.sing.masc.of κολλάομαι, substantival, subject of ἐστιν) 1288.

τῇ (dat.sing.fem.of the article in agreement with πόρνῃ) 9.

ἓν (nom.sing.neut.of εἷς, in agreement with σῶμα) 469.

σῶμά (nom.sing.neut.of σῶμα, predicate nominative) 507.

ἐστιν (3d.per.sing.pres.ind.of εἰμί, static) 86.

ἔσονται (3d.per.pl.fut.ind.of εἰμί, predictive) 86.

γάρ (causal conjunction) 105.

φησίν 93d.per.sing.pres.ind.of φημί, historical) 354.

οἱ (nom.pl.masc.of the article in agreement with δύο) 9.

δύο (nom.pl.masc.of δύο, subject of verb ἔσονται) 385.

εἰς (preposition with the predicate accusative) 140.

σάρκα (acc.sing.fem.of σάρξ, predicate accusative) 1202.

μίαν (acc.sing.fem.of εἷς, in agreement with σάρκα) 469.

Translation - "Or do you not know that the one who is united with the prostitute is one body? Because he said, 'The two shall be one flesh.'"

Comment: ἤ the disjunctive adds the rhetorical question of verse 15 to the one which follows. Both expect positive replies.

In the spiritual realm, the Christian's body is a part of Christ's body. Now it is also true that in the physical realm, sexual intercourse united the parties into one flesh. Paul cites Genesis 2:24, which has reference to the marriage relationship resulting in a child whose flesh is the product of two parental bodies. The enormity of the sin of adultery is seen in verse 17, which clearly involves the Holy Spirit Himself in the believer's sin.

Verse 17 - "But he that is joined unto the Lord is one spirit."

ὁ δὲ κολλώμενος τῷ κυρίῳ ἓν πνεῦμά ἐστιν.

"But he who is united to the Lord becomes one spirit with him." . . . RSV

ὁ (nom.sing.masc.of the article in agreement with κολλώμενος) 9.

δὲ (continuative conjunction) 11.

κολλώμενος (pres.mid.part.nom.sing.masc.of κολλάομαι, substantival, subject of ἐστιν) 1288.

τῷ (dat.sing.masc.of the article in agreement with κυρίῳ) 9.

κυρίῳ (dat.sing.masc.of κύριος, person) 97.

ἓν (nom.sing.neut.of εἷς, in agreement with πνεῦμα) 469.

πνεῦμα (nom.sing.neut.of πνεῦμα, predicate nominative) 83.

ἐστιν (3d.per.sing.pres.ind.of εἰμί, static) 86.

Translation - "And he who is united with the Lord is one spirit."

Comment: Physical union between a Christian and a prostitute joins two fleshly bodies into one. Spiritual union between a Christian and the Lord joins two spirits into one. When a Christian, who is merged with the Lord in spirit, merges his body with a prostitute in the flesh, he thus involves the Lord, Who is the Head of the spiritual Body, and indirectly he also involves all other members of the mystical Body of Christ. The entire Body of Christ is thus sullied by sin! The fact that not all illicit sexual relations result in physical offspring does not lessen the enormity of the sin. Our Lord had His bout with sin at Calvary. Must the saints involve Him again? Due to the peculiar nature of the marriage relationship as a type of the relationship between Christ and His church (Eph.5:22-33), the sin of adultery and fornication is in a class by itself - far worse than other sins.

Verse 18 - "Flee fornication. Every sin that a man doeth is without the body; but he that committeth fornication sinneth against his own body."

φεύγετε τὴν πορνείαν. πᾶν ἁμάρτημα ὃ ἐὰν ποιήσῃ ἄνθρωπος ἐκτὸς τοῦ σώματός ἐστιν, ὁ δὲ πορνεύων εἰς τὸ ἴδιον σῶμα ἁμαρτάνει.

"Shun immorality. Every other sin which a man commits is outside the body; but the immoral man sins against his own body." . . . RSV

φεύγετε (2d.per.pl.pres.act.impv.of φεύγω, command) 202.
τὴν (acc.sing.fem.of the article in agreement with πορνείαν) 9.
πορνείαν (acc.sing.fem.of πορνεία, direct object of φεύγετε) 511.
πᾶν (nom.sing.neut.of πᾶς, in agreement with ἁμάρτημα) 67.
ἁμάρτημα (nom.sing.neut.of ἁμάρτημα, subject of ἐστιν) 2182.
ὃ (acc.sing.neut.of ὅς, direct object of ποιήσῃ) 65.
ἐὰν (conditional conjunction in a third-class condition) 363.
ποιήσῃ (3d.per.sing.aor.act.subj.of ποιέω, third-class condition) 127.
ἄνθρωπος (nom.sing.masc.of ἄνθρωπος, subject of ποιήσῃ) 341.
ἐκτὸς (preposition with the ablative of separation) 1461.
τοῦ (abl.sing.neut.of the article in agreement with σώματος) 9.
σώματός (abl.sing.neut.of σῶμα, separation) 507.
ἐστιν (3d.per.sing.pres.ind.of εἰμί, static) 86.
ὁ (nom.sing.masc.of the article in agreement with πορνεύων) 9.

#4152 πορνεύων (pres.act.part.nom.sing.masc.of πορνεύω, substantival, subject of ἁμαρτάνει).

King James Version

commit fornication - 1 Cor.6:18; 10:8,8; Rev.2:14,20; 17:2; 18:3,9.

Revised Standard Version

the immoral man - 1 Cor.6:18.
indulge in immorality - 1 Cor.10:8,8.
practice immorality - Rev.2:14,20.
commit fornication - Rev.17:2; 18:3,9.

Meaning: Cf. πορνεία (#511); πόρνη (#1374); πόρνος (#4140). To commit fornication - 1 Cor.6:18; 10:8,8; Rev.2:14,20; in a metaphorical sense - Rev.17:2; 18:3,9 of the sins of the city of Babylon which is to be Antichrist's capital city. *Cf.* μοιχεύω (#498).

εἰς (preposition with the accusative, predicate usage, "against") 140.
τὸ (acc.sing.neut.of the article in agreement with σῶμα) 9.
ἴδιον (acc.sing.neut.of ἴδιος, in agreement with σῶμα) 778.
σῶμα (acc.sing.neut.of σῶμα, predicate use, hostility) 507.
ἁμαρτάνει (3d.per.sing.pres.act.ind.of ἁμαρτάνω, aoristic) 1260.

Translation - "Flee fornication. Every sin which a man may commit is separate from the body, but the immoral man is sinning against his own body."

Comment: The Greeks never add the article unless there is a reason. Note τὴν πορνείαν, as Paul makes this particular sin definite. If not reflected in the translation (and it need not always be reflected) it must be alluded to in the comment as we do now. Other sins may or may not pursue, but πορνεία pursues the human race. The sex drive is imperious. Great moral character is required to resist it. Paul advises flight from it. Thus he emphasizes the grave consequences that follow when the Christian commits it. It is different from other sins, which, if committed do not necessarily compromise the body. But πορνεία does. *Cf.* #1260 for the basic concept of "missing the mark."

A Christian who uses his body for fornication misunderstands its divinely appointed purpose. Food is to be eaten; hence we should eat. The stomach is for digestion; hence it can be used for that purpose without sin, during the relatively short time that it is to perform that function. But the physical body of the Christian is for the purpose of coordinating with all of the other bodies in the Body of Christ, and is to serve as the temple of the Holy Spirit, Who has incorporated it into the Body of Christ (1 Cor.12:13). Thus the body has an eternal function, which is spiritual, while the stomach has a temporal function which is physical. We should use what we have for the divinely appointed purpose. This means that our bodies are for Christ's service - Phil.1:6; Eph.2:10; 2 Tim.4:6-8.

Sex within the divinely regulated and appointed marriage relationship, which is a type of Christ and His church, is a proper function, resulting in great physical, psychological and spiritual blessings to the partners, plus the added function of population growth. Thus God has sanctified sex. But sex outside the marriage relationship is a wholesale prostitution of the use of the body, which houses the Holy Spirit and coordinates with all other bodies of regenerates to form the mystical Body of Christ.

Verse 19 - "What? Know ye not that your body is the temple of the Holy Ghost, which is in you, which ye have of God, and ye are not your own?"

ἢ οὐκ οἴδατε ὅτι τὸ σῶμα ὑμῶν ναὸς τοῦ ἐν ὑμῖν ἁγίου πνεύματος ἐστιν, οὗ ἔχετε ἀπὸ θεοῦ, καὶ οὐκ ἐστὲ ἑαυτῶν;

"Do you not know that your body is a temple of the Holy Spirit within you,

which you have from God? You are not your own;" . . . *RSV*

ἤ (disjunctive) 465.

οὐκ (negative particle with the indicative in rhetorical question, expecting a positive reply) 130.

οἴδατε (2d.per.pl.perf.act.ind.of ὁράω, intensive, rhetorical question) 144b.

ὅτι (conjunction introducing an object clause in indirect discourse) 211.

τὸ (nom.sing.neut.of the article in agreement with σῶμα) 9.

σῶμα (nom.sing.neut.of σῶμα, subject of ἐστιν) 507.

ὑμῶν (gen.pl.masc.of σύ, possession) 104.

ναὸς (nom.sing.masc.of ναός, predicate nominative) 1447.

τοῦ (gen.sing.neut.of the article in agreement with πνεύματος) 9.

ἐν (preposition with the locative, with plural pronouns) 80.

ὑμῖν (loc.pl.masc.of σύ, place) 80.

ἁγίου (gen.sing.neut.of ἅγιος, in agreement with πνεύματος) 84.

πνεύματος (gen.sing.neut.of πνεῦμα, description) 83.

ἐστιν (3d.per.sing.pres.ind.of εἰμί, static) 86.

οὗ (gen.sing.neut.of ὅς, attracted to πνεύματος) 65.

ἔχετε (2d.per.pl.pres.act.ind.of ἔχω, present progressive retroactive) 82.

ἀπὸ (preposition with the ablative of source) 70.

θεοῦ (abl.sing.masc.of θεός, source) 124.

καὶ (continuative conjunction) 14.

οὐκ (negative particle with the indicative) 130.

ἐστὲ (2d.per.pl.pres.ind.of εἰμί, aoristic) 86.

ἑαυτῶν (gen.pl.masc.of ἑαυτοῦ, possession) 288.

Translation - *"Or are you not aware that your body is the temple of the indwelling Holy Spirit, whom you have from God, and you are not your own."*

Comment: Note that τὸ σῶμα is singular as Paul calls attention to the individual body, but his question is directed to all of the Corinthians. Hence the plural in ὑμῶν ἐν ὑμῖν and ἑαυτῶν. The Holy Spirit dwells within the body of each Christian individually.

This verse repeats his thought of verse 17. It is because the Holy Spirit indwells the believer that he is "cemented" (#1288) to the Lord. *Cf.* 1 Cor.3:16,17,17; 2 Cor.6:16,16. This is the strongest possible argument for the Spirit-filled life of Christian victory over sin. *Cf.* John 7:38,39; 14:16,17; 16:7-14; Gal.5:16, 22-25. The Christian does not own his body. It belongs to Christ by right of creation and redemption and His promise of resurrection (Rom.8:11; 1 Cor.6:14). And in the meantime, between the time when He incorporated us into the Body of Christ (1 Cor.12:13) and sealed us as God's property (Eph.1:13; 4:30) and the day when we are resurrected, if dead or raptured, if living, we are occupied by the Holy Spirit. How dare we divert God's property to unholy uses?

It is only when the Christian forgets temporarily the intimate relationship which exists between him, the Holy Spirit and the Body of Christ that he yields to the seductions of the flesh.

Verse 20 - "For ye are bought with a price; therefore glorify God in your body, and in your spirit, which are God's."

ἠγοράσθητε γὰρ τιμῆς. δοξάσατε δὴ τὸν θεὸν ἐν τῷ σώματι ὑμῶν.

"you were bought with a price. So glorify God in your body." . . . RSV

ἠγοράσθητε (2d.per.pl.aor.pass.ind.of ἀγοράζω, culminative) 1085.
γὰρ (causal conjunction) 105.
τιμῆς (abl.sing.fem.of τιμή, means) 1619.
δοξάσατε (2d.per.pl.aor.act.impv.of δοξάζω, command) 461.
δὴ (intensive particle) 1053.
τὸν (acc.sing.masc.of the article in agreement with θεὸν) 9.
θεὸν (acc.sing.masc.of θεός, direct object of δοξάσατε) 124.
ἐν (preposition with the locative, place) 80.
τῷ (loc.sing.neut.of the article in agreement with σώματι) 9.
σώματι (loc.sing.neut.of σῶμα, place) 507.
ὑμῶν (gen.pl.masc.of σύ, possession) 104.

Translation - "Because you were bought with a price. So glorify God in your body."

Comment: After a verb of buying or selling we may have the ablative of means. To purchase is to pay a price. *Cf.*#1085 in 1 Cor.7:23; 2 Pet.2:1; Rev.3:18; 5:9; 14:3,4.

The wages of sin is death (Rom.6:23) and the price of redemption is high. But Christ paid it. Hence no Christian owns himself. There is a stern insistence in δὴ after the imperative. Study #1053 to see how this intensive particle is used. We are ordered to glorify God in our bodies. We can do this only by yielding them totally to the Holy Spirit, Who dwells in each of us and Who uses our bodies as His temple (verse 19). When we yield to Him we cannot fulfill the desires of the flesh (Gal.5:16). Instead we use our bodies always as He directs, in perfect coordination with the other body-members of the Body of Christ.

In re the two clauses added by the KJV, Metzger says, "The Textus Receptus, following several of the later uncials and most of the miniscules (C₃ D_c K L P Ψ 1 31 88 915 syr_p.h.) adds after ὑμῶν the words καὶ ἐν τῷ πνεύματι ὑμῶν ἅτινά ἐστι τοῦ θεοῦ. That these words are a gloss with no claim to be original is clear (a) from the decisive testimony of the earliest and best witnesses in support of the shorter text (p₄₆ Sinaiticus A B C* D* F G 33 81 1739* it vg cop_sa bo fay eth Irenaeus_lat Tertullian Origen Cyprian *al*), and (b) from the nature of the addition itself (it is not needed for the argument, which relates to the sanctity of the body, with no mention of the spirit). The words were inserted apparently with a desire to soften Paul's abruptness, and to extend the range of his exhortation." (Bruce M. Metzger, *A Textual Commentary on the Greek New Testament*, 553).

Since 1 Cor.5:1 Paul has had a great deal to say about illicit sex. Naturally the question arises as to the role of sex in the Christian ethic. Is sex ever legitimate and God-glorifying? If so, when and under what conditions? Paul discusses the subject further in chapter 7.

Problems Concerning Marriage

(1 Corinthians 7:1-16)

1 Cor.7:1 - *"Now concerning the things whereof ye wrote unto me: It is good for a man not to touch a woman."*

Περὶ δὲ ὧν ἐγράψατε, καλὸν ἀνθρώπῳ γυναικὸς μὴ ἅπτεσθαι.

"Now concerning the matters about which you wrote. It is well for a man not to touch a woman." . . . RSV

Περὶ (preposition with the genitive of reference) 173.
δὲ (explanatory conjunction) 11.
ὧν (gen.pl.neut.of ὅς, relative pronoun, reference) 65.
ἐγράψατε (2d.per.pl.aor.act.ind.of γράφω, culminative) 156
καλὸν (nom.sing.neut.of καλός, predicate adjective) 296.
ἀνθρώπῳ (dat.sing.masc.of ἄνθρωπος, personal interest) 341.
γυναικὸς (gen.sing.fem.of γυνή, objective genitive) 103.
μὴ (negative particle with the infinitive) 87.
ἅπτεσθαι (pres.mid.inf.of ἅπτω, noun use, subject of ἐστι understood) 711.

Translation - *"Now with reference to those things concerning which you wrote: it is well for a man not to touch a woman."*

Comment: δὲ is explanatory. ὧν, the relative definite pronoun is really attracted to its antecedent τούτων or πραγμάτων, which are to be supplied. That there was a difference of opinion in the Corinthian church with regard to sex is obvious and they had written to Paul for his opinion. It is really pointless to speculate about what the specific issues were, since we do not have the letter which they wrote to Paul.

We have suggested that Paul's attack upon illicit sex (*i.e.* sex outside marriage) in chapter six could be construed as his disapproval of all sex. But this could not be the reaction of the Corinthians since they had not yet seen Paul's first epistle at the time when they wrote to him. Whether there was a Petrine party, who belived in marriage, since Peter was married (Mt.8:14; 1 Cor.9:5), but forbade sex outside marriage, or an ascetic party, who advocated divorce for married Christians, on the ground that all sex is wrong, it is unnecessary to speculate. Nor should we attempt to draw conclusions from what Paul has written about it, as to Paul's own personal views. Some have accused Paul of being a misogynist. That Paul opposed adultery and fornication is clear. That he did not regard sex between husband and wife as sin, even if one partner was unregenerate is also clear. In addition the following inferences seems to be clearly drawn from chapter seven: (1) that Paul recognized the sex drive in the normal human, saved or unsaved, to be strong; (2) that sex hinders fasting and prayer; (3) that he was not assured that his opinions were divinely directed; (4) that Paul was either a bachelor or a widower; (5) that some people who are not married may indulge in sex fantasy; (6) that a wife should not divorce her husband because of her fear that sex is sin; (7) if, however, she does, she must either go back to her husband or remain single; (8) that if either party is married to an unbeliever this fact is not grounds for divorce; (9) that the marriage relationship, even though one party is unsaved, is sanctified, in the sense that children of such a union are not illegitimate; (10) on the other hand, if the unsaved partner wishes to leave the Christian should not oppose it; (11) that the Christian, bereft of a partner as a result of 10 is free to remarry, provided that the new partner is a Christian; (12) that no one should change his social status because he has become a Christian as that status relates to (a) marriage, (b) circumcision or uncircumcision, (c) slavery; (13) that the unmarried should remain so unless he has difficulty remaining continent; (14) that if a virgin marries he/she has not sinned, but (15) his/her marriage obligations *may* hinder Christian service; (16) that Paul's views, which he admits are not necessarily inspired are colored by his belief that the Second Coming of Christ *might* occur in the lifetime of that generation; (17) marriage is permitted under certain guidelines, but celibacy is better; (18) widows and widowers whose mates are dead may remarry "in the Lord" but will probably be happier if they do not, upon which point Paul felt surer than upon some of the other points.

Paul's grammar in verse 1 is good classic Greek. μὴ ἅπτεσθαι is the subject infinitive of ἐστιν understood. γυναικός, the objective genitive is the object of the infinitive. Note that the infinitive is in the middle voice - "That a woman should not have the experience of having a man touch her . . . is good." Yet ἀνθρώπῳ is a dative, rather than an accusative of general reference, normally used with an infinitive, since the infinitive, not being a finite verb, cannot have a subject. We cannot translate "A woman should not be touched by a man" for the same grammatical reason. Paul's message however is clear. He is saying that it is a good thing for men and women to refrain from sex. However, he qualifies his statement in

Verse 2 - "Nevertheless, to avoid fornication let every man have his own wife, and let every woman have her own husband."

διὰ δὲ τὰς πορνείας ἕκαστος τὴν ἑαυτοῦ γυναῖκα ἐχέτω, καὶ ἑκάστη τὸν ἴδιον ἄνδρα ἐχέτω.

"But because of the temptation to immorality, each man should have his own wife and each woman her own husband." . . . RSV

διὰ (preposition with the accusative, cause) 118.
δὲ (adversative conjunction) 11.
τὰς (acc.pl.fem.of the article in agreement with πορνείας) 9.
πορνείας (acc.pl.fem.of πορνεία, cause) 511.
ἕκαστος (nom.sing.masc.of ἕκαστος, subject of ἐχέτω) 1217.
τὴν (acc.sing.fem.of the article in agreement with γυναῖκα) 9.
ἑαυτοῦ (gen.sing.masc.of ἑαυτοῦ, possessive pronoun) 288.
γυναῖκα (acc.sing.fem.of γυνή, direct object of ἐχέτω) 103.

ἐχέτω (3d.per.sing.pres.act.impv.of ἔχω, command) 82.
καὶ (continuative conjunction) 14.
ἑκάστη (nom.sing.fem.of ἕκαστος, subject of ἐχέτω) 1217.
τὸν (acc.sing.masc.of the article in agreement with ἄνδρα) 9.
ἴδιον (acc.sing.masc.of ἴδιος, in agreement with ἄνδρα) 778.
ἄνδρα (acc.sing.masc.of ἀνήρ, direct object of ἐχέτω) 63.
ἐχέτω (3d.per.sing.pres.act.impv.of ἔχω, command) 82.

Translation - *"But due to the prevalence of illicit sex let each man have his own wife, and each woman have her own husband."*

Comment: διὰ with the accusative is causal. δὲ is adversative as Paul prepares to qualify what he said in verse 1 about the blessings of total abstinence. τὰς πορνείας is an example of the abstract substantive which often occurs in the plural in the New Testament. Robertson cites Mk.7:22; James 2:1; Mt.15:19 and adds that this "does indeed lay stress on the separate acts." (*Grammar*, 408). Thus we have a clue that there was some immorality in the Corinthian church, as the expression of Christian love escalated to unscriptural and unholy out-of-bounds extent. As a preventive measure Paul advocated marriage for every man and woman who was having difficulty. Note Paul's use of ἑαυτοῦ and ἴδιον, each in the attributive position and apparently carrying the same idea.

In order that this monogamous arrangement might serve to solve the problem he adds in verse 3 that neither husband nor wife should withhold participation in sex with the marriage partner. The presence of ἑαυτοῦ and ἴδιον rules out concubinage, polygamy and other liaisons.

For those who wish to read into verse two the idea that Paul thought of marriage only as an expedient to avoid immorality, and thus that Paul really had a low opinion of marriage, we must point out that (1) Paul is the one who shows the typical significance of marriage in relation to the unity of the believer in Christ (Eph.5:32) and (2) Paul believed that the Second Coming of Christ was imminent.

Verse 3 - *"Let the husband render unto the wife due benevolence; and likewise also the wife unto the husband."*

τῇ γυναικὶ ὁ ἀνὴρ τὴν ὀφειλὴν ἀποδιδότω, ὁμοίως δὲ καὶ ἡ γυνὴ τῷ ἀνδρί.

"The husband should give to his wife her conjugal rights, and likewise the wife to her husband." . . . RSV

τῇ (dat.sing.fem.of the article in agreement with γυναικὶ) 9.
γυναικὶ (dat.sing.fem.of γυνή, indirect object of ἀποδιδότω) 103.
ὁ (nom.sing.masc.of the article in agreement with ἀνὴρ) 9.
ἀνὴρ (nom.sing.masc.of ἀνήρ, subject of ἀποδιδότω) 63.
τὴν (acc.sing.fem.of the article in agreement with ὀφειλὴν) 9.
ὀφειλὴν (acc.sing.fem.of ὀφειλή, direct object of ἀποδιδότω) 1280.
ἀποδιδότω (3d.per.sing.pres.act.impv.of ἀποδίδωμι, command) 495.
ὁμοίως (adverbial) 1425.
δὲ (continuative conjunction) 11.

καὶ (adjunctive conjunction joining nouns) 14.

ἡ (nom.sing.fem.of the article in agreement with γυνή) 9.

γυνή (nom.sing.fem.of γυνή, subject of ἀποδιδότω, understood) 103.

τῷ (dat.sing.masc.of the article in agreement with ἀνδρί) 9.

ἀνδρί (dat.sing.masc.of ἀνήρ, indirect object of ἀποδιδότω) 63.

Translation - "*The husband will fulfill his sex obligation to his wife and likewise the wife to her husband.*"

Comment: The context of verses 1-5 is one regarding sex. Hence τὴν ὀφειλὴν ἀποδιδότω here refers to a command, not a permissive suggestion by Paul that each party respond upon the occasion of the other's advances. Otherwise monogamy, as a social institution, cannot prevent immorality. Behind all of Paul's instructions there can be detected his awareness that the sex drive is an imperious demand of the flesh. Perhaps this, in part, explains his anguished cry of Romans 7:24, though he could also have had other temptations in mind. Even the most Spirit-filled Christian will at times find the desire for sexual gratification demanding. If either husband or wife is frigid and unwilling or unresponding to the advances of the other, adultery may result. Thus Paul felt it necessary, not only to command marriage (verse 2) but also to command compatability as an obligation of the marriage contract.

It is important to note that the verbs in verses 2,3 are imperatives. Paul is not making diplomatic suggestions. He is laying down rules. He reinforces his point in verses 4 and 5.

Verse 4 - "*The wife hath not power of her own body but the husband; and likewise the husband hath not power of his own body, but the wife.*"

ἡ γυνὴ τοῦ ἰδίου σώματος οὐκ ἐξουσιάζει ἀλλὰ ὁ ἀνήρ, ὁμοίως δὲ καὶ ὁ ἀνὴρ τοῦ ἰδίου σώματος οὐκ ἐξουσιάζει ἀλλὰ ἡ γυνή.

"*For the wife does not rule over her own body, but the husband does; likewise the husband does not rule over his own body, but the wife does.*" . . . RSV

ἡ (nom.sing.fem.of the article in agreement with γυνή) 9.

γυνή (nom.sing.fem.of γυνή, subject of ἐξουσιάζει) 103.

τοῦ (gen.sing.neut.of the article in agreement with σώματος) 9.

ἰδίου (gen.sing.neut.of ἴδιος, in agreement with σώματος) 778.

σώματος (gen.sing.neut.of σῶμα, reference) 507.

οὐκ (negative particle with the indicative) 130.

ἐξουσιάζει (3d.per.sing.pres.act.ind.of ἐξουσιάζω, static) 2777.

ἀλλὰ (adversative conjunction) 342.

ὁ (nom.sing.masc.of the article in agreement with ἀνήρ) 9.

ἀνήρ (nom.sing.masc.of ἀνήρ, subject of verb understood) 63.

ὁμοίως (adverbial) 1425.

δὲ (continuative conjunction) 11.

καὶ (adjunctive conjunction joining nouns) 14.

ὁ (nom.sing.masc.of the article in agreement with ἀνήρ) 9.

ἀνήρ (nom.sing.masc.of ἀνήρ, subject of ἐξουσιάζει) 63.

τοῦ (gen.sing.neut.of the article in agreement with σώματος) 9.

ἰδίου (gen.sing.neut.of ἴδιος, in agreement with σώματος) 778.

σώματος (gen.sing.neut.of σῶμα, reference) 507.

οὐκ (negative particle with the indicative) 130.

ἐξουσιάζει (3d.per.sing.pres.act.ind.of ἐξουσιάζω, static) 2777.

ἀλλά (adversative conjunction) 342.

ἡ (nom.sing.fem.of the article in agreement with γυνή) 9.

γυνή (nom.sing.fem.of γυνή, subject of verb understood) 103.

Translation - "The wife does not possess sole authority with reference to her own body, but the husband does: and in the same way also the husband does not possess sole authority with reference to his own body, but his wife does."

Comment: Here is a formula for conjugal reciprocity which results in compatability and prevents extra-marital immorality. There is no superior authority of either partner over the other.

The current women's liberation movement frequently charges that women have traditionally been subordinated to the wishes of their husbands (a fact that unfortunately has been true), their own wishes to the contrary notwithstanding. They get no comfort here. Husbands are as subject to the wishes of their wives as wives are to the wishes of their husbands. Paul's instruction here assumes compatability. His teaching is also consistent with modern sex theory that a desire for sex is easily aroused between cooperating partners. The sin which Paul forbids is the rebuff which either partner might wish to impose upon the other. If Paul's advice were heeded it is likely that there would be fewer broken marriages.

In Ephesians 5:22-25 Paul orders wives to be subject to their husbands, but balances the emphasis by ordering husbands to love their wives as Christ loved the church. The wife who is fortunate enough to have a husband who loves her with the sacrificial love that is like that of Christ and His love for His church, will lose nothing by being subject to him. Unfaithful husbands have frequently quoted Eph.5:22, but neglected to note Eph.5:25, while dictatorial wives in their struggle for something which they call their "rights" point to Eph.5:25 and ignore Eph.5:22.

Verse 5 - "Defraud ye not one the other except it be with consent for a time, that ye may give yourselves to fasting and prayer, and come together again, that Satan tempt you not for your incontinency."

μὴ ἀποστερεῖτε ἀλλήλους, εἰ μήτι ἂν ἐκ συμφώνου πρὸς καιρὸν ἵνα σχολάσητε τῇ προσευχῇ καὶ πάλιν ἐπὶ τὸ αὐτὸ ἦτε, ἵνα μὴ πειράζῃ ὑμᾶς ὁ Σατανᾶς διὰ τὴν ἀκρασίαν ὑμῶν.

"Do not refuse one another except perhaps by agreement for a season, that you may devote yourselves to prayer; but then come together again, lest Satan tempt you through lack of self-control." . . . RSV

μὴ (negative particle with the imperative in a prohibition) 87.

ἀποστερεῖτε (2d.per.pl.pres.act.impv.of ἀποστερέω, prohibition) 2639.
ἀλλήλους (acc.pl.masc.of ἀλλήλων, direct object of ἀποστερεῖτε) 1487.
εἰ (conditional particle in an elliptical condition) 337.
μήτι (negative conditional conjunction) 676.
ἄν (contingent particle) 205.
ἐκ (preposition with the ablative of source) 19.

#4153 συμφώνου (abl.sing.masc.of σύμφωνος, source).

   King James Version

consent - 1 Cor.7:5.

   Revised Standard Version

agreement - 1 Cor.7:5.

Meaning: A combination of σύν (#1542) and φωνή (#222). Hence, mutual consent; agreement. *cf.* συμφωνέω (#1265); συμφώνησις (#4320) and συμφωνία (#2557). With reference to an agreement between husband and wife - 1 Cor.7:5.

πρὸς (preposition with the accusative in a time expression) 197.
καιρὸν (acc.sing.masc.of καιρός, time extent) 767.
ἵνα (conjunction introducing the subjunctive in a purpose clause) 114.
σχολάσητε (2d.per.pl.aor.act.subj.of σχολάζω, purpose) 1021.
τῇ (loc.sing.fem.of the article in agreement with προσευχῇ) 9.
προσευχῇ (loc.sing.fem.of προσευχή, sphere) 1238.
καὶ (adversative conjunction) 14.
πάλιν (adverbial) 355.
ἐπὶ(preposition with the accusative of extent) 47.
τὸ (acc.sing.neut.of the article in agreement with αὐτὸ) 9.
αὐτὸ (acc.sing.neut.of αὐτός, extent) 16.
ἦτε (2d.per.pl.pres.subj.of εἰμί, purpose) 86.
ἵνα (conjunction with the subjunctive, negative purpose) 114.
μὴ (negative particle with the subjunctive) 87.
πειράζῃ (3d.per.sing.pres.act.subj.of πειράζω, negative purpose) 330.
ὑμᾶς (acc.pl.masc.of σύ, direct object of πειράζῃ) 104.
ὁ (nom.sing.masc.of the article in agreement with Σατανᾶς) 9.
Σατανᾶς (nom.sing.masc.of Σατανᾶς, subject of πειράξῃ) 365.
διὰ (preposition with the accusative, cause) 118.
τὴν (acc.sing.fem.of the article in agreement with ἀκρασίαν) 9.
ἀκρασίαν (acc.sing.fem.of ἀκρασία, cause) 1459.
ὑμῶν (gen.pl.masc.of σύ, possession) 104.

Translation - "*Do not continue to deprive each other, except possibly out of mutual agreement for a short time, in order that you may concentrate your energies in prayer, but resume the same relationship lest Satan tempt you because of your lack of self-control.*"

Comment: μή with the present imperative means, "Stop depriving each other...
" which hints at the possibility that one reason for their immorality was the
incompatability that prevented a normal sex life between husband and wife. The
reason why they were abstaining is not given. It is possible that the inchoate
development of Gnosticism, with its implied need for asceticism, is the reason.

Paul qualifies his order with εἰ μήτι ἀν ... τῇ προσευχῇ - "except possibly for
a time for prayer." Their temporary abstinence will grow out of a mutual
agreement - ἐκ συμφώνου. That it is temporary is clear from πρὸς καιρόν. Why?
The ἵνα clause suggests that the energy normally devoted to sex should be
devoted to prayer. *Cf.* #1021 for meaning. Paul tells them to pour all of their
energy into prayer. "Empty yourself by giving all of your power to prayer." This
supports Paul's statement in verse 28 that the obligations of married life compete
for the uses of scarce physical and mental resources with the obligations of
spiritual life. Sex between husband and wife is not immoral, but it hinders a total
commitment to prayer. Thus during periods of great spiritual concentration sex
should be foregone. However, though temporarily suspended, it cannot be
totally denied. Hence, Paul adds καὶ (adversative) πάλιν ἐπὶ τὸ αὐτὸ ἦτε - which
can be translated like the military order, "As you were." *Cf.* Acts 2:44,47; 4:26 -
"Be at the same place" or "Come together." The reason for the resumption of the
normal married relationship is given in the negative purpose clause with ἵνα μὴ
πειράζῃ ... ὑμῶν - "Lest Satan tempt you because of your lack of self-control."

That Paul understood that celibacy was not the normal order is clear from this
verse. He balances the need for sex against the need to devote all of our energy to
prayer. The order is "Enjoy sex... forego sex... pray... resume sex activity, lest
unfulfilled sex desire drive you to immorality. All prayer and celibacy may lead
to aberration. The history of monasticism tends to support this, in some cases.
Not all celibates are perverts. The opposite extreme - all sex and no prayer, is
unworthy of the Christian life.

Thus Paul occupies a moderate position, that is neither ascetic nor hedonistic.
It is difficult to charge him with being a misogynist.

Verse 6 - "But I speak this by permission and not by commandment."

τοῦτο δὲ λέγω κατὰ συγγνώμην, οὐ κατ' ἐπιταγήν.

"I say this by way of concession, not of command." ... RSV

τοῦτο (acc.sing.neut.of οὗτος, direct object of λέγω, anaphoric) 93.
δὲ (adversative conjunction) 11.
λέγω (1st.per.sing.pres.act.ind.of λέγω, aoristic) 66.
κατὰ (preposition with the accusative, standard) 98.

#4154 συγγνώμην (acc.sing.fem.of συγγνώμη, standard).

King James Version

permission - 1 Cor.7:6.

Revised Standard Version

concession - 1 Cor.7:6.

Meaning: A combination of σύν (#1542) and γινώσκω (#131). Concession; permissive suggestion. Opposed to ἐπιταγή (#4099) in 1 Cor.7:6.

οὐ (negative particle with the indicative) 130.
κατ' (preposition with the accusative, standard) 98.
ἐπιταγήν (acc.sing.fem.of ἐπιταγή, standard) 4099.

Translation - "But I am saying this by way of concession - not as an order."

Comment: Paul has made concessions to sex that he did not like to make, since, although he recognized the necessity for sex expression and believed that marriage was a divine institution and that in its proper function a deterrent to immorality, yet, in view of his belief that Christ would soon return, he thought that, under these conditions, celibacy was better. Thus he warns his readers that verses 2 - 5 were not to be considered as a divine mandamus, but rather a reluctant concession to the practical need for sex expression. His real feeling is found in the first clause of verse 7.

It is not at all unreasonable to say that Christians at the end of the church age, who will know that Christ will return within the next seven years or less, will be well advised to devote all of their energies to witnessing the message of the gospel of Christ and to prayer for the salvation of the lost.

Verse 7 - "For I would that all men were even as I myself. But every man hath his proper gift of God, one after this manner, and another after that."

θέλω δὲ πάντας ἀνθρώπους εἶναι ὡς καὶ ἐμαυτόν, ἀλλὰ ἕκαστος ἴδιον ἔχει χάρισμα ἐκ θεοῦ, ὁ μὲν οὕτως, ὁ δὲ οὕτως.

"I wish that all were as I myself am. But each has his own special gift from God, one of one kind and one of another." . . . RSV

θέλω (1st.per.sing.pres.act.ind.of θέλω, aoristic) 88.
δὲ (adversative conjunction) 11.
πάντας (acc.pl.masc.of πᾶς, in agreement with ἀνθρώπους) 67.
ἀνθρώπους (acc.pl.masc.of ἄνθρωπος, general reference) 341.
εἶναι (pres.inf.of εἰμί, noun use, direct object of θέλω) 86.
ὡς (particle in a comparative clause) 128.
καὶ (adjunctive conjunction joining substantives) 14.
ἐμαυτόν (acc.sing.masc.of ἐμαυτοῦ, general reference) 723.
ἀλλὰ (adversative conjunction) 342.
ἕκαστος (nom.sing.masc.of ἕκαστος, subject of ἔχει) 1217.
ἴδιον (acc.sing.neut.of ἴδιος, in agreement with χάρισμα) 778.
ἔχει (3d.per.sing.pres.act.ind.of ἔχω, static) 82.
χάρισμα (acc.sing.neut.of χάρισμα, direct object of ἔχει) 3790.
ἐκ (preposition with the ablative of source) 19.

θεοῦ (abl.sing.masc.of θεός, source) 124.

ὁ (nom.sing.masc.of the article, nominative absolute) 9.

μὲν (correlative particle of affirmation) 300.

οὕτως (demonstrative adverb) 74.

ὁ (nom.sing.masc.of the article nominative absolute) 9.

δὲ (correlative adversative conjunction) 11.

οὕτως (demonstrative adverb) 74.

Translation - *"But I wish that all men were as I myself also am, though each man has his own gift from God, one in one way and another in a different way."*

Comment: πάντας ἀνθρώπους εἶναι is the object infinitive of θέλω. The predicate is ὡς καὶ ἐμαυτόν, in agreement in case with ἀνθρώπους in general reference. καὶ is redundant.

Paul apparently was able to sublimate his sex drive and devote all of his energy to the spiritual demands of his ministry and he could wish that all men could do the same. Yet he concedes that such is not the case. God has not made every man alike. The Holy Spirit has distributed His gifts to various people and in various ways "as He chose" (1 Cor.12:11). Paul is trying to be tolerant toward other Christians who are married.

This recognition of the dignity of every member of the Body of Christ, whose life style may be different from one's own is a fruit of Christian love.

Verse 8 and 9 restate the case, again putting Paul's first choice in prominence.

Verse 8 - *"I say therefore to the unmarried and widows, It is good for them if they abide even as I."*

Λέγω δὲ τοῖς ἀγάμοις καὶ ταῖς χήραις, καλὸν αὐτοῖς ἐὰν μείνωσιν ὡς κἀγώ.

"To the unmarried and the widows I say that it is well for them to remain single as I do." . . . RSV

Λέγω (1st.per.sing.pres.act.ind.of λέγω, aoristic) 66.

δὲ (adversative conjunction) 11.

τοῖς (dat.pl.masc.of the article in agreement with ἀγάμοις) 9.

#4155 ἀγάμοις (dat.pl.masc.of ἄγαμος, indirect object of λέγω).

    King James Version

unmarried - 1 Cor.7:8,11,32,34.

    Revised Standard Version

unmarried - 1 Cor.7:8,32,34.
single - 1 Cor.7:11.

Meaning: α privative plus γάμος (#1394). Unmarried. With reference to men - 1 Cor.7:8,32; with reference to women - 1 Cor.7:11,34. the Greeks usually used the word ἄνανδρος.

καὶ (adjunctive conjunction joining nouns) 14.

ταῖς (dat.pl.fem.of the article in agreement with χήραις) 9.

χήραις (dat.pl.fem.of χήρα, indirect object of λέγω) 1910.

καλὸν (acc.sing.neut.of καλός, predicate adjective) 296.

αὐτοῖς (dat.pl.masc.of αὐτός, personal advantage) 16.

ἐὰν (conditional particle in a third-class condition) 363.

μείνωσιν (3d.per.pl.aor.act.subj.of μένω, third-class condition) 864.

ὡς (particle in a comparative clause) 128.

κἀγώ (adjunctive and first personal pronoun, crasis) 178.

Translation - *"But to the unmarried and the widows I say that it is good for them if they remain single as I am."*

Comment: Thus Paul returns to his thought of verses 1-7a, although he concedes the other side of the question in

Verse 9 - *"But if they cannot contain, let them marry: for it is better to marry than to burn."*

εἰ δὲ οὐκ ἐγκρατεύονται γαμησάτωσαν, κρεῖττον γάρ ἐστιν γαμῆσαι ἢ πυροῦσθαι.

"But if they cannot exercise self-control, they should marry. For it is better to marry than to be aflame with passion." . . . *RSV*

εἰ (conditional particle in a first-class condition) 337.

δὲ (adversative conjunction) 11.

οὐκ (negative particle with the indicative) 130.

#4156 ἐγκρατεύονται (3d.per.pl.pres.ind.of ἐγκρατεύομαι, first-class condition).

King James Version

be temperate - 1 Cor.9:25.

can contain - 1 Cor.7:9.

Revised Standard Version

exercise self-control - 1 Cor.7:9; 9:25.

Meaning: Cf.ἐγκρατής (#4881), ἐγκράτεια (#3630). To exercise self-control. With reference to sex - 1 Cor.7:9; in the discipline of training for an athletic event - 1 Cor.9:25.

γαμησάτωσαν (3d.per.pl.aor.act.impv.of γαμέω, command) 512.

#4157 κρεῖττον (acc.sing.neut.of κρείττων, predicate adjective).

King James Version

The Renaissance New Testament   1 Cor.7:9

best - 1 Cor.12:31.
better - 1 Cor.7:9,38; 11:17; Phil.1:23; Heb.1:4; 7:7,19,22; 8:6,6; 9:23; 10:34; 11:16,35; 1 Pet.3:17; 2 Pet.2:21.
better country - Heb.11:16.
better thing - Heb.6:9.
better - Heb.11:40; 12:24.

Revised Standard Version

higher - 1 Cor.12:31.
better - 1 Cor.7:9,38; 11:17; Phil.1:23; Heb.7:19,22; 9:23; 10:34; 11:35; 1 Pet.3:17; 2 Pet.2:21; Heb.11:16,40; 6:9.
superior to - Heb.1:4; 7:7.
more excellent - Heb.8:6,6.
more graciously - Heb.12:24.

Meaning: Better. Predicate adjective with an infinitive - 1 Cor.7:9. An adjective with the substantive missing to be supplied from the context - 1 Cor.11:17; Heb.7:7; 6:9; 11:16; 12:24. An adjective in the attributive position - Heb.7:9,22; 8:6,6; 9:23; 10:34; 11:35,40. Adverbial in 1 Cor.7:38; Phil.1:23; Heb.1:4; 1 Pet.3:17; 2:21. The text or context shows that the following is better - a better policy - 1 Cor.7:9,38; 1 Pet.3:17; 2:21; spiritual condition in the church - 1 Cor.11:17; a better situation for Paul - Phil.1:23; superior standing - Heb.1:4; 7:7; hope, Heb.7:19; covenant, Heb.7:22; ministry, Heb.8:6; sacrifice, Heb.9:23; 12:24; reward in heaven, Heb.10:34; resurrection, Heb.11:35; behavior, Heb.6:9; country, Heb.11:16; a better destiny for New Testament saints - Heb.11:40.

γάρ (causal conjunction) 105.
ἐστιν (3d.per.sing.pres.ind.of εἰμί, static) 86.
γαμῆσαι (aor.act.inf.of γαμέω, noun use, subject of ἐστιν) 512.
ἤ (disjunctive) 465.

#4158 πυροῦσθαι (pres.pass.inf.of πυρόω, noun use, subject of verb understood).

King James Version

be on fire - 2 Pet.3:12.
be tried - Rev.3:18.
burn - 1 Cor.7:9; 2 Cor.11:29; Rev.1:15.
fiery - Eph.6:16.

Revised Standard Version

be aflame with passion - 1 Cor.7:9.
indignant - 2 Cor.11:29.
flaming - Eph.6:16.
be kindled - 2 Pet.3:12.
refined - Rev.1:15; 3:18.

Meaning: Cf. πῦρ (#298); πυρά (#3757); πυρέσσω (#737); πυρετός (#738); πύρινος (#5375); πυῤῥάζω (#1191) and πυῤῥός (#5350). Properly, to set afire; to kindle - 2 Pet.3:12; in a metaphorical sense, of the fiery darts of Satan - Eph.6:16; of the feet of our Lord at His second coming, of brass refined in a furnace to eliminate dross - Rev.1:15; 3:18. Trop.of aroused emotion - 2 Cor.11:29; intense sex drive - 1 Cor.7:9.

Translation - "But if they cannot exercise self-control they should marry, because to marry is better than to be consumed with lust."

Comment: εἰ introduces a first-class condition which assumes that the premise in the protasis is correct. Paul is not saying that he knows that those in question cannot control their desires. He does not know whether they can or not. Some can; other cannot. He is saying that in those cases where immorality is certain to result if they do not marry, they should marry. The ideal for those persons discussed in verse 8 may be unattainable. If so the next best policy is marriage. γάρ is causal to show why. Marriage is not a sin (verse 28), but the experience of being inflamed with unfulfilled sex drive is intolerable. Thus for Paul the order of policy preference for the single person is (1) celibacy and no sex problems, (2) marriage, (3) immorality or sex frustration. The context indicates that πυροῦσθαι refers to passion, not fire. Also note that πυροῦσθαι is present passive and cannot refer to 1 Cor.3:15 where the word is κατακαίω (#314). However we can also say that marriage, if it is the only way to avoid immorality, is better than the future experience at the judgment seat of Christ of having one's life of wood, hay and stubble burned away because of uncontrollable sex drive. This indeed is true but it is not what 1 Cor.7:9 says.

Ideally the mature Spirit-filled Christian will never yield to the desires of the flesh whether he is married or not. No doubt there are many celibates who are aware of inclinations to enjoy sexual fulfillment who sublimate these drives by yielding to the Holy Spirit and who do not suffer psychic trauma. Their lives manifest the glory of the Lord in an extraordinary way. They prove every day that it is possible to "walk in the Spirit" and thus to reject the demands of the flesh (Gal.5:16).

Paul was not a Gnostic and he rejected the asceticism that teaches that all expressions of the flesh are evil and therefore that Christians who wish to live the victorious life must be divorced. This is the thought in

Verse 10 - "And unto the married I command, yet not I, but the Lord, Let not the wife depart from her husband."

τοῖς δὲ γεγαμηκόσιν παραγγέλλω, οὐκ ἐγὼ ἀλλὰ ὁ κύριος, γυναῖκα ἀπὸ ἀνδρὸς μὴ χωρισθῆναι

"To the married I give charge, not I but the Lord, that the wife should not separate from her husband. . ." . . . RSV

τοῖς (dat.pl.masc.of the article in agreement with γεγαμηκόσιν) 9.
δὲ (continuative conjunction) 11.

γεγαμηκόσιν (perf.act.part.dat.pl.masc.of γαμέω, substantival, indirect object of παραγγέλλω) 512.

παραγγέλλω (1st.per.sing.pres.act.ind.of παραγγέλλω, aoristic) 855.

οὐκ (negative particle with the indicative) 130.

ἐγώ (nom.sing.masc.of ἐγώ, subject of verb understood) 123.

ἀλλά (alternative conjunction) 342.

ὁ (nom.sing.masc.of the article in agreement with κύριος) 9.

κύριος (nom.sing.masc.of κύριος, subject of παραγγέλλει understood) 97.

γυναῖκα (acc.sing.fem.of γυνή, general reference) 103.

ἀπὸ (preposition with the ablative of separation) 70.

ἀνδρὸς (abl.sing.masc.of ἀνήρ, separation) 63.

μὴ (negative particle with the infinitive) 87.

χωρισθῆναι (aor.pass.inf.of χωρίζω, noun use, direct object of παραγγέλλω) 1291.

Translation - *"But to those who are married, it is not I but the Lord who orders a wife not to separate from her husband."*

Comment: Both γυναῖκα and ἀνδρός are anarthrous, not by omission but by design. This is a reference, not to a specific individual but to a class of persons who are married. The infinitive is the object of παραγγέλλω. Paul attaches more authority to this directive than to the one which he introduces in verse 12. See also verse 25. The distinction which he makes between his own opinions and those for which he claims divine authority only strengthens the inspiration of the passage. If Paul were trying to deceive us he would not call attention to the fact that there could be a difference between his own views and those dictated by the Holy Spirit.

Verse 11 makes it clear that Paul means that a wife should not leave her husband in order to enter into a sex intrigue with another man. That she might leave him on other grounds may be implied, but if so, the rule of verse 11 is to apply.

Verse 11 - *"But and if she depart, let her remain unmarried, or be reconciled to her husband: and let not the husband put away his wife."*

—ἐὰν δὲ καὶ χωρισθῇ, μενέτω ἄγαμος ἢ τῷ ἀνδρὶ καταλλαγήτω — καὶ ἄνδρα γυναῖκα μὴ ἀφιέναι.

ἐὰν (conditional particle in a third-class condition) 363.

δὲ (adversative conjunction) 11.

καὶ (emphatic conjunction) 14.

χωρισθῇ (3d.per.sing.aor.pass.subj.of χωρίζω, third-class condition) 1291.

μενέτω (3d.per.sing.pres.act.impv.of μένω, command) 864.

ἄγαμος (nom.sing.masc.of ἄγαμος, predicate adjective) 4155.

ἢ (disjunctive) 465.

τῷ (dat.sing.masc.of the article in agreement with ἀνδρὶ) 9.

ἀνδρὶ (dat.sing.masc.of ἀνήρ, person) 63.

καταλλαγήτω (3d.per.sing.2d.aor.pass.impv.of καταλλάσσω, command) 3899.

καὶ (continuative conjunction) 14.

ἄνδρα (acc.sing.masc.of ἀνήρ, general reference) 63.

γυναῖκα (acc.sing.fem.of γυνή, direct object of ἀφιέναι) 103.

μὴ (negative particle with the infinitive) 87.

ἀφιέναι (pres.act.inf.of ἀφίημι, noun use, direct object of παραγέλλω understood) 319.

Translation - "... but if in fact she is now separated, let her remain unmarried or let her be reconciled to her husband. And I forbid a husband to leave his wife."

Comment: Adversative δὲ with emphatic καὶ and the effective aorist subjunctive with ἐὰν and the third-class condition. Paul had no way of knowing whether any of the women in the church were separated from their husbands. Thus the third-class condition. But if, in fact, she was ... the order in the imperative was to be obeyed. Such a woman had two choices open to her. She could either remain single or go back to her husband. Thus, while Paul does not forbid a wife to leave her husband on other grounds, he does forbid her to leave him in order to live with another man. The same principle also applies to the husband.

Now Paul turns to another problem in verses 12-16 where he does not claim supernatural direction.

Verse 12 - "But to the rest speak I, not the Lord: If any brother hath a wife that believeth not, and she be pleased to dwell with him, let him not put her away."

Τοῖς δὲ λοιποῖς λέγω ἐγώ, οὐχ ὁ κύριος. εἴ τις ἀδελφὸς γυναῖκα ἔχει ἄπιστον, καὶ αὕτη συνευδοκεῖ οἰκεῖν μετ' αὐτοῦ, μὴ ἀφιέτω αὐτήν.

"To the rest I say, not the Lord, that if any brother has a wife who is an unbeliever, and she consents to live with him, he should not divorce her." ...

RSV

Τοῖς (dat.pl.masc.of the article in agreement with λοιποῖς) 9.

δὲ (adversative conjunction) 11.

λοιποῖς (dat.pl.masc.of λοιπός, indirect object of λέγω) 1402.

λέγω (1st.per.sing.pres.act.ind.of λέγω, aoristic) 66.

ἐγώ (nom.sing.masc.of ἐγώ, subject of λέγω, emphatic) 123.

οὐχ (negative particle with the indicative) 130.

ὁ (nom.sing.masc.of the article in agreement with κύριος) 9.

κύριος (nom.sing.masc.of κύριος, subject of λέγει understood) 97.

εἴ (condition particle in a first-class condition) 337.

τις (nom.sing.masc.of τις, indefinite pronoun in agreement with ἀδελφὸς) 486.

ἀδελφὸς (nom.sing.masc.of ἀδελφός, subject of ἔχει) 15.

γυναῖκα (acc.sing.fem.of γυνή, direct object of ἔχει) 103.

ἔχει (3d.per.sing.pres.act.ind.of ἔχω, present progressive retroactive) 82.

ἄπιστον (acc.sing.fem.of ἄπιστος, predicate adjective) 1231.

καί (adversative conjunction) 14.

αὕτη (nom.sing.fem.of οὗτος, subject of συνευδοκεῖ) 93.

συνευδοκεῖ (3d.per.sing.pres.act.ind.of συνευδοκέω, present progressive retroactive) 2468.

οἰκεῖν (pres.act.inf.of οἰκέω, epexegetical) 3926.

μετ᾽ (preposition with the genitive, accompaniment) 50.

αὐτοῦ (gen.sing.masc.of αὐτός, accompaniment) 16.

μή (negative particle with the imperative in a prohibition) 87.

ἀφιέτω (3d.per.sing.aor.act.impv.of ἀφίημι, prohibition) 319.

αὐτήν (acc.sing.fem.of αὐτός, direct object of ἀφιέτω) 16.

Translation - "*But to the rest of you I am speaking, not the Lord. If any brother has an unbelieving wife, but she wants to live with him, he must not divorce her.*"

Comment: When Paul spoke on his own authority he said so — a fact which heightens the fact that at other times he was speaking by divine inspiration. *Cf.* comment on 2 Tim.3:16,17.

Again, as in verse 9, we have εἰ and a first-class condition. Paul is making a hypothetical case. He is saying, "There may or may not be in Corinth a Christian man or woman married to an unbeliever." There probably were many such cases, as Paul's revival during his first visit to Corinth brought one member of a family to Christ and not the other. In such a case what policy should be followed? It is contingent upon the wishes of the unsaved wife. She has no spiritual fellowship with her husband. Her condition is described in Eph.2:1-3; 2 Cor.4:3,4; 1 Cor.1:18, while his is described in 1 Cor.6:19,20; Rom.8:14-17; John 17:21. They march to drums of opposing and conflicting tempo and rhythm. Yet she may love him and find in his human fellowship a better psychological, sociological and economic milieu than she could find elsewhere. If she wishes to maintain their relationship, despite the fact that he has been saved and marches to a different drum, he should not cast her out. There is a chance that his influence as a Christian will be used of the Holy Spirit to lead her to Christ (verse 16).

Verse 13 states the same proposition except that in this case the wife is saved and her husband is lost.

Verse 13 - "*And the woman which hath an husband that believeth not, and if he be pleased to dwell with her, let her not leave him.*"

καὶ γυνὴ εἰ τις ἔχει ἄνδρα ἄπιστον, καὶ οὗτος συνευδοκεῖ οἰκεῖν μετ᾽ αὐτῆς, μὴ ἀφιέτω τὸν ἄνδρα.

"*If any woman has a husband who is an unbeliever, and he consents to live with her, she should not divorce him.*" . . . RSV

καί (continuative conjunction) 14.

γυνή (nom.sing.fem.of γυνή, subject of ἔχει) 103.

εἰ (conditional particle in a first-class condition) 337.

τις (nom.sing.fem.of τις, indefinite pronoun, in agreement with γυνή) 486.

ἔχει (3d.per.sing.pres.act.ind.of ἔχω, present progressive retroactive) 82.

ἄνδρα (acc.sing.masc.of ἀνήρ, direct object of ἔχει) 63.
ἄπιστον (acc.sing.masc.of ἄπιστος, in agreement with ἄνδρα) 1231.
καὶ (adversative conjunction) 14.
οὗτος (nom.sing.masc.of οὗτος, subject of συνευδοκεῖ) 93.
συνευδοκεῖ (3d.per.sing.pres.act.ind.of συνευδοκέω, present progressive retroactive) 2468.
οἰκεῖν (pres.act.inf.of οἰκέω, epexegetical) 3926.
μετ' (preposition with the genitive of accompaniment) 50.
αὐτῆς (gen.sing.fem.of αὐτός, accompaniment) 16.
μὴ (negative particle with the imperative in a prohibition) 87.
ἀφιέτω (3d.per.sing.aor.act.impv.of ἀφίημι, prohibition) 319.
τὸν (acc.sing.masc.of the article in agreement with ἄνδρα) 9.
ἄνδρα (acc.sing.masc.of ἀνήρ, direct object of ἀφιέτω) 63.

Translation - "And if any woman has an unbelieving husband, but if he wishes to continue to live with her, she must not divorce him."

Comment: There is large support for ἥτις, the indefinite relative pronoun instead of εἴ τις which the United Bible Societies' Committee has chosen. "Partly because of a slight preponderance of weight of the external evidence (p46 Sinaiticus D* G P*al* it vg cop*sa*) and partly because of parallelism with the previous clause (ver.12), the Committee preferred the reading of εἴ τις" (Metzger, *A Textual Commentary on the Greek New Testament*, 554). In any case the exegesis is the same.

The cases referred to in verses 12 and 13 probably resulted from the conversion to Christ of one of a pair of unbelievers, since Paul advises against marriage between Christians and unbelievers (2 Cor.6:14-18).

Verse 14 - "For the unbelieving husband is sanctified by the wife, and the unbelieving wife is sanctified by the husband: else were your children unclean, but now they are holy."

ἡγίασται γὰρ ὁ ἀνὴρ ὁ ἄπιστος ἐν τῇ γυναικί, καὶ ἡγίασται ἡ γυνὴ ἡ ἄπιστος ἐν τῷ ἀδελφῷ. ἐπεὶ ἄρα τὰ τέκνα ὑμῶν ἀκάθαρτά ἐστιν, νῦν δὲ ἅγια ἐστιν.

"For the unbelieving husband is consecrated through his wife, and the unbelieving wife is consecrated through her husband. Otherwise, your children would be unclean, but as it is they are holy." . . . RSV

ἡγίασται (3d.per.sing.perf.pass.ind.of ἁγιάζω, intensive) 576.
γὰρ (causal conjunction) 105.
ὁ (nom.sing.masc.of the article in agreement with ἀνήρ) 9.
ἀνὴρ (nom.sing.masc.of ἀνήρ, subject of ἡγίασται) 63.
ὁ (nom.sing.masc.of the article in agreement with ἄπιστος) 9.
ἄπιστος (nom.sing.masc.of ἄπιστος, in agreement with ἀνὴρ) 1231.
ἐν (preposition with the instrumental of means) 80.

τῇ (instru.sing.fem.of the article in agreement with γυναικί) 9.

γυναικί (instru.sing.fem.of γυνή, means) 103.

καί (continuative conjunction) 14.

ἡγίασται (3d.per.sing.perf.pass.ind.of ἁγιάζω, intensive) 576.

ἡ (nom.sing.fem.of the article in agreement with γυνή) 9.

γυνή (nom.sing.fem.of γυνή, subject of ἡγίασται) 103.

ἡ (nom.sing.fem.of the article in agreement with γυνή) 9.

ἄπιστος (nom.sing.fem.of ἄπιστος, in agreement with γυνή) 1231.

ἐν (preposition with the instrumental, means) 80.

τῷ (instru.sing.masc.of the article in agreement with ἀδελφῷ) 9.

ἀδελφῷ (instru.sing.masc.of ἀδελφός, means) 15.

ἐπεί (compound conditional particle in an elliptical condition) 1281.

ἄρα (illative particle) 995.

τά (nom.pl.neut.of the article in agreement with τέκνα) 9.

τέκνα (nom.pl.neut.of τέκνον, subject of ἐστιν) 229.

ὑμῶν (gen.pl.masc.of σύ, relationship) 104.

ἀκάθαρτά (nom.pl.neut.of ἀκάθαρτος, predicate adjective, in agreement with τέκνα) 843.

ἐστιν (3d.per.sing.pres.ind.of εἰμί, present progressive retroactive) 86.

νῦν (temporal adverb) 1497.

δέ (adversative conjunction) 11.

ἅγια (nom.pl.neut.of ἅγιος, predicate adjective, in agreement with τέκνα) 84.

ἐστιν (3d.per.sing.pres.ind.of εἰμί, present progressive retroactive) 86.

Translation - "*Because the husband who is an unbeliever has been consecrated through union with his wife, and the woman who is an unbeliever also has been consecrated through union with her husband. Otherwise your children would be unclean, but now they are holy.*"

Comment: The causal clause with γάρ depends upon the directives of verses 12 and 13. Unsaved wives and husbands who wish to continue living with their Christian mates, should be allowed to do so "because . . . " They are set apart. Note the effective force of the perfect tense. Having been married in the past the union is now socially sanctioned. In this sense the unbeliever is "sanctified" as the legitimate mate of his/her Christian wife/husband. This is social, not theological sanctification. Paul is not saying that unsaved husbands or wives are saved by virtue of their marriage to Christians. Our Lord has no brother/sister-in-laws.

If this were not true the children born to such unions would be illegitimate, which is not the case. On the contrary the children also are set apart as legitimate children of a legitimate union.

Paul is saying that the coming of Christianity to Corinth, which, in some cases, resulted in Christians and non-Christians living together by virtue of the conversion of one but not yet the other, did not upset the social mores of the city. Or at least, it need not, if the unbeliever is willing to go on living with the Christian. On the other hand, if the unbeliever wishes to sever the relationship he should be allowed to do so.

Verse 15 - "But if the unbelieving depart, let him depart. A brother or a sister is not under bondage in such cases; but God hath called us to peace."

εἰ δὲ ὁ ἄπιστος χωρίζεται, χωριζέσθω. οὐ δεδούλωται ὁ ἀδεφλὸς ἢ ἡ ἀδελφὴ ἐν τοῖς τοιούτοις. ἐν δὲ εἰρήνη κέκληκεν ὑμᾶς ὁ θεός.

"But if the unbelieving partner desires to separate, let it be so; in such a case the brother or sister is not bound. For God has called us to peace." . . . RSV

εἰ (conditional particle in a first-class condition) 337.
δὲ (adversative conjunction) 11.
ὁ (nom.sing.masc.of the article in agreement with ἄπιστος) 9.
ἄπιστος (nom.sing.masc.of ἄπιστος, subject of χωρίζεται) 1231.
χωρίζεται (3d.per.sing.pres.mid.ind.of χωρίζω, aoristic) 1291.
χαριζέσθω (3d.per.sing.pres.mid.impv.of χωρίζω, command) 1291.
οὐ (negative particle with the indicative) 130.
δεδούλωται (3d.per.sing.perf.pass.ind.of δουλόω, intensive) 3103.
ὁ (nom.sing.masc.of the article in agreement with ἀδελφὸς) 9.
ἀδελφὸς (nom.sing.masc.of ἀδελφός, subject of δεδούλωται) 15.
ἢ (disjunctive) 465.
ἡ (nom.sing.fem.of the article in agreement with ἀδελφή) 9.
ἀδελφὴ (nom.sing.fem.of ἀδελφή, subject of δεδούλωται) 1025.
ἐν (preposition with the locative of accompanying circumstance) 80.
τοῖς (loc.pl.neut.of the article in agreement with τοιούτοις) 9.
τοιούτοις (loc.pl.neut.of τοιοῦτος, accompanying circumstance) 785.
ἐν (preposition with the locative of sphere) 80.
δὲ (adversative conjunction) 11.
εἰρήνη (loc.sing.fem.of εἰρήνη, sphere) 865.
κέκληκεν (3d.per.sing.perf.act.ind.of καλέω, intensive) 107.
ὑμᾶς (acc.pl.masc.of σύ, direct object of κέκληκεν) 104.
ὁ (nom.sing.masc.of the article in agreement with θεός) 9.
θεός (nom.sing.masc.of θεός, subject of κέκληκεν) 124.

Translation - "But if the unbeliever leaves, let him leave. The brother or the sister is not under obligation under these circumstances. But God has called us to get along with others."

Comment: εἰ introduces the first-class condition. There is no certainty that the unsaved partner will leave, but if he does, his Christian spouse is to let him go. χωριζέσθω is a permissive imperative.

Under these circumstances the Christian man or woman has no further obligation to the one who departed. The nature of this obligation is not set forth in the text. Does Paul mean that he/she is permitted to remarry, provided, of course that the new partner is a Christian? He has already suggested that it is better for the unmarried to remain so, if possible. However the last sentence indicates that the Christian is under obligation to his unsaved mate to live with him so peaceably that he will not wish to leave. The Christian may even bring about the regeneration of the unsaved spouse. The inference that the deserted Christian may remarry does not conflict with Mt.5:32 since Christ was not talking about mixed marriages.

The hint that the unsaved spouse who chose to leave did so because of the obnoxious behavior of the Christian is supported by Paul's suggestion in

Verse 16 - "For what knowest thou, O wife, whether thou shalt save thy husband? Or how knowest thou, O man, whether thou shalt save thy wife?"

τί γὰρ οἶδας, γύναι, εἰ τὸν ἄνδρα σώσεις; ἢ τί οἶδας, ἄνερ, εἰ τὴν γυναῖκα σώσεις;

"Wife, how do you know whether you will save your husband? Husband, how do you know whether you will save your wife?" . . . *RSV*

τί (acc.sing.neut.of τίς, interrogative pronoun, direct object of οἶδας) 281.
γὰρ (causal conjunction) 105.
οἶδας (2d.per.sing.perf.act.ind.of ὁράω, intensive) 144b.
γύναι (voc.sing.fem.of γυνή, address) 103.
εἰ (particle with the future in deliberative question) 337.
τὸν (acc.sing.masc.of the article in agreement with ἄνδρα) 9.
ἄνδρα (acc.sing.masc.of ἀνήρ, direct object of σώσεις) 63.
σώσεις (2d.per.sing.fut.act.ind.of σώζω, deliberative question) 109.
ἢ (disjunctive) 465.
τί (acc.sing.neut.of τίς, interrogative pronoun, direct object of οἶδας) 281.
οἶδας (2d.per.sing.perf.act.ind.of ὁράω, intensive) 144b.
ἄνερ (voc.sing.masc.of ἀνήρ, address) 63.
εἰ (particle introducing the future in deliberative question) 337.
τὴν (acc.sing.fem.of the article in agreement with γυναῖκα) 9.
γυναῖκα (acc.sing.fem.of γυνή, direct object of σώσεις) 103.
σώσεις (2d.per.sing.fut.act.ind.of σώζω, deliberative question) 109.

Translation - "Because how do you know, wife, whether or not you will save your husband? Or how do you know, man, whether or not you will save your wife?"

Comment: εἰ here introduces the future in deliberative question. *Cf.* #337 for other such examples. Since the Christian husband or wife has no way of knowing whether or not his/her influence will be used by the Holy Spirit to call the unsaved spouse to salvation, the Christian should not initiate separation proceedings. The Christian is in a better position to keep the relationship amicable than the unsaved spouse. If it is kept in mind that Christians are called to be peacemakers, the marriage may be saved. It is possible that the unsaved partner is partially justified in taking offense in certain situations. Undue zeal without knowledge on the part of the Christian may be unreasonable. A Christian woman was determined that a prayer of thanksgiving to God would be prayed before every meal, despite the strenuous objections of her husband. She misinterpreted her selfish stubbornness and her natural penchant for nagging her husband as the leading of the Holy Spirit. She was determined in the name of the Lord to make him thank God for his food or else. Her pastor suggested that if she wanted to keep her husband she had better desist. After all he was joint owner of the house, the table, the silverware and napkins and he worked hard for the money which bought the food. This added up to the view that her husband had some rights which included eating his food without going through a ceremony which to him was without point. Her pastor added that if she wanted to thank God for the food she should do so silently before she announced that dinner was served. She took her pastor's advice, stopped trying to sell Christianity like a television used car salesman and began to pray that he might be saved. He was. After that they returned thanks at the table without a family fight.

The Life Which the Lord Has Assigned

(1 Corinthians 7:17-24)

Verse 17 - "But as God hath distributed to every man, as the Lord hath called every one, so let him walk. And so ordain I in all churches."

Εἰ μὴ ἑκάστῳ ὡς ἐμέρισεν ὁ κύριος, ἕκαστον ὡς κέκληκεν ὁ θεός, οὕτως περιπατείτω. καὶ οὕτως ἐν ταῖς ἐκκλησίαις πάσαις διατάσσομαι.

"Only, let every one lead the life which the Lord has assigned to him, and in which God has called him. This is my rule in all the churches." . . . RSV

Εἰ (conditional particle in an elliptical conditional clause) 337.
μὴ (negative particle, *cf.* comment *infra*) 87.
ἑκάστῳ (dat.sing.masc.of ἕκαστος, indirect object of ἐμέρισεν) 1217.
ὡς (comparative particle) 128.
ἐμέρισεν (3d.per.sing.aor.act.ind.of μερίζω, constative) 993.
ὁ (nom.sing.masc.of the article in agreement with κύριος) 9.
κύριος (nom.sing.masc.of κύριος, subject of ἐμέρισεν) 97.
ἕκαστον (acc.sing.masc.of ἕκαστος, direct object of κέκληκεν) 1217.
ὡς (comparative particle) 128.
κέκληκεν (3d.per.sing.perf.act.ind.of καλέω, intensive) 107.
ὁ (nom.sing.masc.of the article in agreement with θεός) 9.
θεός (nom.sing.masc.of θεός, subject of κέκληκεν) 124.
οὕτως (demonstrative adverb) 74.
περιπατείτω (3d.per.sing.pres.act.impv.of περιπατέω, command) 384.
καὶ (continuative conjunction) 14.
οὕτως (demonstrative adverb) 74.
ἐν (preposition with the locative of place) 80.
ταῖς (loc.pl.fem.of the article in agreement with ἐκκλησίαις) 9.
ἐκκλησίαις (loc.pl.fem.of ἐκκλησία, place) 1204.

πάσαις (loc.pl.fem.of πᾶς, in agreement with ἐκκλησίαις) 67.

διατάσσομαι (1st.per.sing.pres.mid.ind.of διατάσσω, present iterative retroactive) 904.

Translation - *"Only, as the Lord assigned to each one when he called him, so let him walk. And this is what I have commanded in all the churches."*

Comment: Εἰ μή - "only". It is not construed as belonging to περιπατείτω. "The protasis itself is sometimes abbreviated almost to the vanishing point, as in εἰ μή without a verb, in the sense of "except" (Mt.5:13). Here εἰ and μή seem to coalesce into one word like πλήν. Cf.11:27, οὐδεὶς ἐπιγινώσκει τὸν υἱὸν εἰ μὴ ὁ πατήρ. This is very common as in classic Greek. Sometimes we have εἰ μὴ μόνον as in Mt.21:19. The origin of this use of εἰ μή was the fact that the verb was identical with the preceding one in the apodosis and so was not repeated. From this ellipsis the usage spread to mere exceptions to the previous statement, a limitation simply. Εἰ μή may make exception to a preceding negative as in Gal.1:19, ἕτερον δὲ τῶν ἀποστόλων οὐκ εἶδον εἰ μὴ Ἰάκωβον τὸν ἀδελφόν. The effect here is to make εἰ μή seem adversative instead of exceptive. Cf.Mt.12:4. . . . In 1 Cor.7:17 εἰμή has the sense of 'only' and is not to be construed with περιπατείτω." (Robertson, *Grammar,* 1024, 1025). Here the protasis is abbravinated by omitting the verb.

Paul's thought is that the Lord has assigned to each Christian a lot in life, and that that lot is the one in which he finds himself when God calls him to salvation. His command is that the elect shall not change this lot. He develops this thought through verse 28, though he admits in verse 25 that he has no direct communication from the Lord on the subject of marraige after salvation. The reason for this teaching against "revolution" is, not that Christians should not seek to change bad situations, but rather that the time for the second coming of Christ was at hand (verse 29). All of Paul's thought in this passage is colored by that conviction.

Back of all of this advice about submitting to the *status quo* was Paul's deep conviction that the sovereign God, the Author of the history designed to glorify His name, knows about the status of each of His children and that He will reward amply every Christian who carries his cross without complaint during the relatively short period of time which remains until the second coming. It should be added that efforts to change some of the situations which the Christian found to be unacceptable in the first century would have been futile in any case due to the dictatorship of the Roman government.

Verse 18 - *"Is any man called being circumcised? Let him not become uncircumcised. Is any called in uncircumcision? Let him not be circumcised."*

περιτετμημένος τις ἐκλήθη; μὴ ἐπισπάσθω. ἐν ἀκροβυστίᾳ κέκληταί τις; μὴ περιτεμνέσθω.

"Was any one at the time of his call already circumcised: Let him not seek to remove the marks of circumcision. Was any one at the time of his call

uncircumcised? Let him not seek circumcision." . . . *RSV*

περιτετμημένος (perf.pass.part.nom.sing.masc.of περιτέμνω, adverbial, circumstantial) 1842.

τις (nom.sing.masc.of τις, indefinite pronoun, subject of ἐκλήθη) 486.

ἐκλήθη (3d.per.sing.aor.pass.ind.of καλέω, constative) 107.

μή (negative particle with the imperative in a prohibition) 87.

#4159 ἐπισπάσθω (2d.per.sing.pres.mid.impv.of ἐπισπάω, prohibition).

King James Version

become uncircumcised - 1 Cor.7:18.

Revised Standard Version

seek to remove the marks of circumcision - 1 Cor.7:18.

Meaning: A combination of ἐπί (#47) and σπάω (#2802) - "to draw out" or "to draw upon." "From the days of Antiochus Epiphanes (B.C.175-164) down, there had been Jews who in order to conceal from heathen persecutors or scoffers the external sign of their nationality, sought artificially to compel nature to reproduce the prepuce, by extending or drawing forward with an iron instrument the remnant of it still left, so as to cover the *glaus*." (Thayer, 243). Thus in 1 Cor.7:18 μή ἐπισπάσθω - "let him not try to conceal the fact that he was circumcised."

ἐν (preposition with the locative of accompanying circumstance) 80.

ἀκροβυστίᾳ (loc.sing.fem.of ἀκροβυστία, accompanying circumstance) 3236.

κέκληται (3d.per.sing.perf.pass.ind.of καλέω, intensive) 107.

τις (nom.sing.masc.of τις, indefinite pronoun, subject of κέκληται) 486.

μή (negative particle with the imperative, in a prohibition) 87.

περιτεμνέσθω (3d.per.sing.pres.pass.impv.of περιτέμνω, prohibition) 1842.

Translation - "Was any one called having already been circumcised? Let him not seek to conceal the fact. Was any one called when he was uncircumcised? Let him not be circumcised."

Comment: The perfect circumstantial participle indicates a present state as a result of a previous operation. This clause applies to the Hebrew Christians at Corinth. Circumcised as Jewish infants they were later called to Christianity. *Cf*.#4159. This operation was very painful. James A. Michener has a passage describing it in *The Source*.

The last clause refers to the other Christians in Corinth who were Gentiles. Note the accompanying circumstance in ἐν ἀκροβυστίᾳ. Whether circumcised or uncircumcised at the time that they were called to Christ, no change was necessary. The fact that Paul includes this order indicates that there were questions in the Corinthian church about the relative merits or demerits of

Judaism and Christianity. Hebrew Christians may have suggested to their Gentile brothers that they were better because of their membership in a chosen nation, while Gentile Christians may have criticized their Jewish brethren for their circumcision which has nothing to do with salvation.

Why was no change necessary? And why was neither circumcision nor the lack of it a mark of superiority?

Verse 19 - "Circumcision is nothing, and uncircumcision is nothing, but the keeping of the commandments of God."

ἡ περιτομὴ οὐδέν ἐστιν, καὶ ἡ ἀκροβυστία οὐδέν ἐστιν, ἀλλὰ τήρησις ἐντολῶν θεοῦ.

"For neither circumcision counts for anything nor uncircumcision, but keeping the commandments of God." . . . RSV

ἡ (nom.sing.fem.of the article in agreement with περιτομή) 9.
περιτομή (nom.sing.fem.of περιτομή, subject of ἐστιν) 2368.
οὐδέν (nom.sing.neut.of οὐδείς, predicate nominative) 446.
ἐστιν (3d.per.sing.pres.ind.of εἰμί, static) 86.
καὶ (continuative conjunction) 14.
ἡ (nom.sing.fem.of the article in agreement with ἀκροβυστία) 9.
ἀκροβυστία (nom.sing.fem.of ἀκροβυστία, subject of ἐστιν) 3236.
οὐδέν (nom.sing.neut.of οὐδείς, predicate nominative) 446.
ἐστιν (3d.per.sing.pres.ind.of εἰμί, static) 86.
ἀλλὰ (alternative conjunction) 342.
τήρησις (nom.sing.fem.of τήρησις, predicate nominative) 3026.
ἐντολῶν (gen.pl.fem.of ἐντολή, description) 472.
θεοῦ (gen.sing.masc.of θεός, description) 124.

Translation - "Circumcision is nothing and uncircumcision is nothing, but compliance with a divine command is everything."

Comment: ἀλλὰ here does not mean "except." That is expressed by εἰ μή. Paul means that compliance with a divine command is everything in contrast to either circumcision or the lack of it. The Hebrew Christian's pride in his circumcision was not justified. First of all it happened when he was a baby and his decision was not involved. It marked his position as a member of God's chosen race of people whose function was to produce the Messiah. Now that Messiah had come and redeemed the elect, of which favored group he was one, he was marked with a more significant circumcision that gave him membership in the Body of Christ (Rom.2:28,29). But the Gentile Christians also had that circumcision of the heart and were also sealed as God's special property (Eph.1:13; 4:30). Thus there was no reason for the Hebrew Christian to be unduly aware of a superior status.

The Gentile Christian, on the other hand, need not feel inferior, because he was never commanded by the Lord to be circumcised. As a member of an outcaste race (as compared with Israel) he had nevertheless been chosen as a member of the Body of Christ and in regeneration had received the circumcision of the heart (Rom.2:28,29), just as had his Hebrew Christian brother in Christ.

Paul was concerned about their compliance with God's ethical, not his formal demands. He had spoken of little else than the commands which they had broken - dissension in the church over the personalities of various leaders, adultery, other illicit sex relations, litigation in secular courts, fraud, etc. Obedience in these areas was of far greater importance than outward observances that go back to pre-Christian Judaism. It is the "gnat straining, camel swallowing" syndrome. They were so concerned about circumcision, either to practice it or to hide it that they were neglecting weightier matters (Mt.23:23).

Verse 20 - "Let every man abide in the same calling wherein he was called."

ἕκαστος ἐν τῇ κλήσει ᾗ ἐκλήθη ἐν ταύτῃ μενέτω.

"Every one should remain in the state in which he was called." . . . *RSV*

ἕκαστος (nom.sing.masc.of ἕκαστος, subject of μενέτω) 1217.
ἐν (preposition with the locative of sphere) 80.
τῇ (loc.sing.fem.of the article in agreement with κλήσει) 9.
κλήσει (loc.sing.fem.of κλῆσις, sphere) 4003.
ᾗ (loc.sing.fem.of ὅς, relative pronoun, sphere) 65.
ἐκλήθη (3d.per.sing.aor.pass.ind.of καλέω, constative) 107.
ἐν (preposition with the locative of sphere) 80.
ταύτῃ (loc.sing.fem.of οὗτος, sphere, anaphoric) 93.
μενέτω (3d.per.sing.pres.act.impv.of μένω, command) 864.

Translation - "Every one must continue in the same calling in which he was called."

Comment: Note ᾗ, which would have been ἥν, the cognate accusative, except for the attraction to κλήσει, the locative of sphere. ταύτῃ is anaphoric, in reference to τῇ κλήσει. Whatever the calling in life the man had when he was called by God's grace to salvation - in that same calling he was ordered to continue in Christ (verse 17).

Having already applied the principle to circumcision and uncircumcision (verses 18,19), he procedes to apply it to human slavery (verses 21-23). But he is not sure about the marriage relationship (verse 25).

These passages should not be stretched to support a view that Paul had no interest in allowing the ethics of the regenerated Christian life to impact upon social conditions in this life. There is a place for the social application of the ethics of the gospel (which is not the same as the social gospel) in society. Paul, however, was of the opinion that his generation would witness the second coming of Messiah and thus that the church's only interest should be the evangelistic call to the elect who were as yet unsaved.

On the day that Daniel 9:27a is fulfilled, the day which will mark the beginning of the period covered by the Revelation, it will be the true teaching of the New Testament that no Christian should seek to alter in any way his social, economic or political status. That day at this writing (7 August 1982) has not yet come and today there is no way to determine when it will. Hence, it is proper for the Christian to try to change society, even though we know full well that in the long run, man's day will bring society crashing down in total confusion before the second coming of Messiah.

Verse 21 - "Art thou called being a servant? Care not for it; but if thou mayest be made free, use it rather."

δοῦλος ἐκλήθης; μή σοι μελέτω. ἀλλ' εἰ καὶ δύνασαι ἐλεύθερος γενέσθαι, μᾶλλον χρῆσαι.

"Were you a slave when called? Never mind. But if you can gain your freedom, avail yourself of the opportunity." . . . RSV

δοῦλος (nom.sing.masc.of δοῦλος, predicate nominative) 725.
ἐκλήθης (2d.per.sing.aor.pass.ind.of καλέω, constative, direct question) 107.
μή (negative particle with the imperative) 87.
σοι (dat.sing.masc.of σύ, personal interest) 104.
μελέτω (2d.per.sing.pres.act.impv.of μέλω, command) 1417.
ἀλλ' (alternative conjunction) 342.
εἰ (conditional particle in a first-class condition) 337.
καὶ (emphatic conjunction) 14.
δύνασαι (2d.per.sing.pres.ind.of δύναμαι, aoristic) 289.
ἐλεύθερος (nom.sing.masc.of ἐλεύθερος, predicate adjective) 1245.
γενέσθαι (aor.inf.of γίνομαι, epexegetical) 113.
μᾶλλον (adverbial) 619.
χρῆσαι (2d.per.sing.1st.aor.act.impv.of χράω, command) 2447.

Translation - "Were you a slave when you were called? Do not let it worry you. On the other hand, if you can in fact gain your freedom, take advantage of the opportunity."

Comment: A social and political slave who is called to salvation gains his spiritual freedom (John 8:32,36). Therefore he should not be too concerned about the fact that, though he is now spiritually free, having been called by God's grace to salvation, he remains a slave to another man. Thus Paul admonishes against political revolutions by Christians who seek to ameliorate social injustice. "The servant of the Lord must not strive" (2 Tim.2:24).

This is not to say that Paul approved of slavery. He did not, but a violent *coup d'etat* is an evil that should never be used by a Christian to correct another evil. It is better for the Christian slave to absorb the social wrong and console himself with the fact that he is freer than his unsaved master. On the other hand (ἀλλά) if he is in fact (emphatic καὶ) permitted to be free, he should accept his political freedom and use its privileges to better serve the Lord. He may gain political freedom on earth, but the Christian will never escape his bondage to Christ. Who wants to?

Verse 22 - "For he that is called in the Lord, being a servant, is the Lord's freeman likewise also he that is called, being free, is Christ's servant."

ὁ γὰρ ἐν κυρίῳ κληθεὶς δοῦλος ἀπελεύθερος κυρίου ἐστίν. ὁμοίως ὁ ἐλεύθερος κληθεὶς δοῦλός ἐστιν Χριστοῦ.

"For he who was called in the Lord as a slave is a freedman of the Lord. Likewise he who was free when called is a slave of Christ." . . . RSV

ὁ (nom.sing.masc.of the article in agreement with κληθεὶς) 9.

γὰρ (causal conjunction) 105.

ἐν (preposition with the instrumental, association) 80.

κυρίῳ (instru.sing.masc.of κύριος, association) 97.

κληθεὶς (aor.pass.part.nom.sing.masc.of καλέω, substantival, subject of ἐστίν) 107.

δοῦλος (nom.sing.masc.of δοῦλος, apposition) 725.

#4160 ἀπελεύθερος (nom.sing.masc.of ἀπελεύθερος, predicate nominative).

King James Version

freeman - 1 Cor.7:22.

Revised Standard Version

freedman - 1 Cor.7:22.

Meaning: A combination of ἀπό (#70) and ἐλεύθερος (#1245). A freedman; a manumitted slave. Followed by a genitive of possession, κυρίου. Hence, a Christian, saved from sin and hence free from its slavery - 1 Cor.7:22.

κυρίου (gen.sing.masc.of κύριος, possession) 97.

ἐστίν (3d.per.sing.pres.ind.of εἰμί, aoristic) 86.

ὁμοίως (adverbial) 1425.

ὁ (nom.sing.masc.of the article in agreement with ἐλεύθερος) 9.

ἐλεύθερος (nom.sing.masc.of ἐλεύθερος, apposition) 1245.

κληθεὶς (aor.pass.part.nom.sing.masc.of καλέω, substantival, subject of ἐστίν) 107.

δοῦλός (nom.sing.masc.of δοῦλος, predicate nominative) 725.

ἐστιν (3d.per.sing.pres.ind.of εἰμί, static) 86.

Χριστοῦ (gen.sing.masc.of Χριστός, possession) 4.

Translation - "*Because the one who was called by the Lord when he was a slave is the Lord's freedman; similarly the one who was called when he was free is the slave of Christ.*"

Comment: Paul explains why he gave the advice of verse 21, that one's political and social freedom, while a blessing, is not as important as one's spiritual freedom in Christ. Therefore the political slavery of the Christian is not important enough to him, relatively speaking, to merit violent revolution.

In verse 22 he discusses the terms δοῦλος and ἐλεύθερος in a wholly different sphere. The saved slave on earth is in bondage to his master but he is spiritually free from the law of sin and death (Rom.8:2). However he has a new slave obligation to Christ (Rom.1:1). The lost slave is in bondage in both senses, but he owes no spiritual obligation to Christ. He is free from Christ, but he is a slave both to his earthly master and to the law of sin and death. The lost master is free politically but in slavery to sin, death and Satan. If he were called to salvation he would become the Lord's freedman, — freed from the law of sin and death, but now a slave of Jesus Christ. Being in bondage to the law of Christ Who has manumitted him from the law of sin and death (Rom.8:1-3) he may or may not understand his Christian obligation to end his political domination over his slaves, although he should. Thus a lost master is in more slavery than a saved slave, who is in bondage to his master on earth and to Christ, spiritually, but is free from the law of sin and death. The relative positions of a lost master and a saved slave are thus seen to put the Christian slave in an infinitely better position than his unfortunate master. Why then should a saved slave seek his political freedom? We remind the reader again that Paul's advice is colored by his belief that Messiah's coming was imminent (verse 29). Indeed a Christian slave might gain his freedom and was advised by Paul to do so if it could be done without violence and in an thoroughly honorable arrangement.

In addition to the Christian principle of non-violence which is the chief motivation for Paul's advice, it is possible that he also was thinking of the practical problem that would face slaves who revolted against imperial Rome. Less than one hundred years before Spartacus and his gladiator associates had led an army of slaves in a campaign for freedom that overran southern Italy, defeated five Roman armies and reached Cisalpine Gaul, only to be defeated by the Roman commander Marcus Licinius Crassus in 71 B.C. Spartacus was killed in battle and the remainder of his army died by crucifixion. (Funk & Wagnalls, *New Encyclopedia*, 22, 133).

One wonders if those Christian moralists who assume that they belong to the majority in democratic America are aware of the Spartacus story. The effort to enforce Christian morality upon the unsaved, at the behest of the secular legislature, in compliance with a court order and at the point of a policeman's gun is an exercise in futility. We applaud Spartacus' desire to be free, but cannot commend him for his naive thought that he and his fellow gladiators could gain their freedom on the field of battle with the imperial Roman legions.

Should not Christians be more concerned with the victorious prayer and triumphant proclamation of the good news of the gospel of Christ? If so, perhaps the Holy Spirit would do with His regenerating power in the lives of sinners what the police cannot enforce with the threat of punishment. The best way to stop crime in the streets is to pray that the Holy Spirit will call the criminal to salvation.

Verse 23 - "Ye are bought with a price; be not ye the servants of men."

τιμῆς ἠγοράσθητε. μὴ γίνεσθε δοῦλοι ἀνθρώπων.

"You were bought with a price; do not become slaves of men." . . . RSV

τιμῆς (abl.sing.fem.of τιμή, means) 1619.

ἠγοράσθητε (2d.per.pl.aor.pass.ind.of ἀγοράζω, culminative) 1085.

μή (negative particle with the imperative in a prohibition) 87.

γίνεσθε (2d.per.pl.pres.impv.of γίνομαι, prohibition) 113.

δοῦλοι (nom.pl.masc.of δοῦλος, predicate nominative) 725.

ἀνθρώπων (gen.pl.masc.of ἄνθρωπος, description) 341.

Translation - "You have been bought with a price. Do not become human slaves."

Comment: *Cf.* 1 Cor.6:20 where the inference drawn from the fact of redemption is that we must not become slaves to human passions. Here he repeats the redemptive fact and adds that, now that we are purchased with the redemptive blood of Christ (2 Pet.2:1; Rev.5:9; 14:3,4), we should not become slaves to sinful men. This does not conflict with verse 21 or Eph.6:5 in which passages Paul is speaking to Christians who were already slaves — possibly slaves before they became Christians, or perhaps enslaved since. Here he is speaking to Christians who are not slaves and suggests that they should remain free from the bonds of political slavery. The passage can also be construed to mean that a Christian slave should not obey his master who ordered him to commit an act in violation to the will of Christ, his spiritual Master.

Verse 24 - "Brethren, let every man, wherein he is called, therein abide with God."

ἕκαστος ἐν ᾧ ἐκλήθη, ἀδελφοί, ἐν τούτῳ μενέτω παρὰ θεῷ.

"So, brethren, in whatever state each was called, there let him remain with God." . . . RSV

ἕκαστος (nom.sing.masc.of ἕκαστος, subject of μενέτω) 1217.

ἐν (preposition with the locative of sphere) 80.

ᾧ (loc.sing.masc.of ὅς, relative pronoun, sphere) 65.

ἐκλήθη (3d.per.sing.aor.pass.ind.of καλέω, constative) 107.

ἀδελφοί (voc.pl.masc.of ἀδελφός, address) 15.

ἐν (preposition with the locative of sphere) 80.

τούτῳ (loc.sing.neut.of οὗτος, sphere, anaphoric) 93.

μενέτω (2d.per.sing.pres.act.impv.of μένω, command) 864.

παρά (preposition with the locative, with persons) 154.

θεῷ (loc.sing.masc.of θεός, place, with persons) 124.

Translation - "Brethren each man must continue in fellowship with God in the same calling in which he was called."

Comment: There is no antecedent for the relative pronoun ᾧ. We supply ἐν κλήσει. In the calling in which each man was at the time that God called him to salvation - in that calling (ἐν τούτῳ) let him remain παρὰ θεῷ - "side by side with God in close association." This verse supports Paul's suggestion of verse 23 that a free man who was free when he became a Christian should resist being enslaved, just as a slave, who is a Christian, should not seek to be liberated.

Paul's emphasis upon this principle is lessened somewhat in verse 25 as he disclaims divine inspiration for his advice to virgins.

The Unmarried and Widows

(1 Corinthians 7:25-40)

Verse 25 - "Now concerning virgins I have no commandment of the Lord; yet I give my judgment as one that hath obtained mercy of the Lord to be faithful."

Περὶ δὲ τῶν παρθένων ἐπιταγὴν κυρίου οὐκ ἔχω, γνώμην δὲ δίδωμι ὡς ἠλεημένος ὑπὸ κυρίου πιστὸς εἶναι.

"Now concerning the unmarried, I have no command of the Lord, but I give my opinion as one who by the Lord's mercy is trustworthy." . . . RSV

Περὶ (preposition with the genitive of reference) 173.

δὲ (explanatory conjunction) 11.

τῶν (gen.pl.masc.of the article in agreement with παρθένων) 9.

παρθένων (gen.pl.masc.of παρθένος, reference) 120.

ἐπιταγὴν (acc.sing.fem.of ἐπιταγή, direct object of ἔχω) 4099.

κυρίου (gen.sing.masc.of κύριος, description) 97.

οὐκ (negative particle with the indicative) 130.

ἔχω (1st.per.sing.pres.act.ind.of ἔχω, aoristic) 82.

γνώμην (acc.sing.fem.of γνώμη, direct object of δίδωμι) 3499.

δὲ (adversative conjunction) 11.

δίδωμι (1st.per.sing.pres.act.ind.of δίδωμι, aoristic) 362.

ὡς (comparative particle) 128.

ἠλεημένος (perf.pass.part.nom.sing.masc.of ἐλεέω, substantival) 430.

ὑπὸ (preposition with the ablative of source) 117.

κυρίου (abl.sing.masc.of κύριος, source) 97.

πιστὸς (nom.sing.masc.of πιστός, predicte adjective) 1522.

εἶναι (pres.act.inf.of εἰμί, purpose) 86.

Translation - "Now with reference to those who have never married, I do not have a divine directive, but I give my opinion as one who has always received mercy from the Lord in order to be faithful."

Comment: Paul's advice which follows in verses 26-28 is offered, not with the authority of divine inspiration, but it is put forward as good advice, since Paul is offering to others a policy which, by God's grace, he has been able to follow with consistency. He is about to suggest total abstinence with reference to sex, because he views the world as in imminent danger of collapse (verse 29). He is not asking others to forego sex while he indulges in it. He speaks as one who has obtained mercy from the Lord to be faithful to Christ in this matter, though a bachelor. Because Paul had been a victorious celibate he dares to suggest celibacy to others.

Verse 26 - "I suppose therefore that this is good for the present distress, I say, that it is good for a man so to be."

Νομίζω οὖν τοῦτο καλὸν ὑπάρχειν διὰ τὴν ἐνεστῶσαν ανάγκην, ὅτι καλὸν ἀνθρώπῳ τὸ οὕτως εἶναι.

"I think that in view of the impending distress it is well for a person to remain as he is." . . . RSV

Νομίζω (1st.per.sing.pres.act.ind.of νομίζω, aoristic) 462.

οὖν (inferential conjunction) 68.

τοῦτο (acc.sing.neut.of οὗτος, general reference) 93.

καλὸν (acc.sing.neut.of καλός, predicate adjective) 296.

ὑπάρχειν (pres.inf.of ὑπάρχω, noun use, direct object of νομίζω) 1303.

διὰ (preposition with the accusative, cause) 118.

τὴν (acc.sing.fem.of the article in agreement with ἀνάγκην) 9.

ἐνεστῶσαν (perf.act.part.acc.sing.fem.of ἐνίστημι, adjectival, attributive position, ascriptive, in agreement with ἀνάγκην) 3954.

ἀνάγκην (acc.sing.fem.of ἀνάγκη, cause) 1254.

ὅτι (conjunction introducing the infinitive in indirect declaration) 211.

καλὸν (acc.sing.neut.of καλός, predicate adjective) 296.

ἀνθρώπῳ (dat.sing.masc.of ἄνθρωπος, personal advantage) 341.

τὸ (acc.sing.neut.of the article in agreement with εἶναι, in indirect declaration).

οὕτως (demonstrative adverb) 74.

εἶναι (pres.inf.of εἰμί, acc.sing.neut., indirect declaration) 86.

Translation - "I think then that in view of the current difficulty a man ought to remain as he is."

Comment: We have the infinitive ὑπάρχειν as a substantive in the accusative case, the object of the finite verb νομίζω. εἶναι is the present infinitive in indirect declaration. The causal phrase διὰ τὴν ...ἀνάγκην is joined to the verb νομίζω. Why did Paul think as he did? "Because of the current problem." What did he think? "That it is good for a man to be as he is." The participle ἐνεστῶσαν is adjectival. Note that it is in the perfect tense. The difficulty which the Corinthians had had developed in the past and it was still with them. This is the force of the intensive perfect.

Paul's feeling was that the age was coming to a close with the approaching appearance of Messiah. In view of that fact he felt that if one is a Christian there is nothing to be gained by changing one's status in life, either in terms of marriage, slavery or anything else.

Verse 27 - "Art thou bound unto a wife? Seek not to be loosed. Art thou loosed from a wife? Seek not a wife."

δέδεσαι γυναικί; μὴ ζήτει λύσιν. λέλυσαι ἀπὸ γυναικός; μὴ ζήτει γυναῖκα.

"Are you bound to a wife? Do not seek to be free. Are you free from a wife? Do not seek marriage." . . . RSV

δέδεσαι (2d.per.sing.perf.pass.ind.of δέω, intensive) 998.
γυναικί (instru.sing.fem.of γυνή, association) 103.
μὴ (negative particle with the imperative, in a prohibition) 87.
ζήτει (2d.per.sing.pres.act.impv.of ζητέω, prohibition) 207.

#4161 λύσιν (acc.sing.fem.of λῦσις, direct object of ζήτει).

King James Version

to be loosed - 1 Cor.7:27.

Revised Standard Version

to be free - 1 Cor.7:27.

Meaning: Cf. λύω (#471); a loosing; severance from whatever bonds the context indicates. With reference to the marriage vow - 1 Cor.7:27.

λέλυσαι (2d.per.sing.perf.pass.ind.of λύω, intensive) 471.
ἀπὸ (preposition with the ablative of separation) 70.
γυναικός (abl.sing.fem.of γυνή, separation) 103.
μὴ (negative particle with the imperative in a prohibition) 87.
ζήτει (2d.per.sing.pres.act.impv.of ζητέω, prohibition) 207.
γυναῖκα (acc.sing.fem.of γυνή, direct object of ζήτει) 103.

Translation - "Are you now bound to a wife? Stop seeking a divorce. Are you now free from a wife? Stop looking for a wife."

Comment: The perfect tenses in δέδεσαι and λέλυσαι speak of present conditions resulting from past completed actions. They are effective, *i.e.* the emphasis is upon the result of a previous action. "Were you once married and hence are now bound to a wife?" "Were you once set free (by death or divorce) and hence are now single?" ζήτει is a present tense imperative - "Do not continue to seek freedom . . . . . do not continue to seek a wife." Stop trying to change the present situation, whether you are married or single. (Phil.4:11).

Verse 28 - "But and if thou marry, thou hast not sinned: and if a virgin marry, she hath not sinned. Nevertheless such shall have trouble in the flesh: but I spare you."

ἐὰν δὲ καὶ γαμήσῃς, οὐχ ἥμαρτες. καὶ ἐὰν γήμῃ ἡ παρθένος, οὐχ ἥμαρτεν. θλῖψιν δὲ τῇ σαρκὶ ἕξουσιν οἱ τοιοῦτοι, ἐγὼ δὲ ὑμῶν φείδομαι.

"But if you marry, you do not sin, and if a girl marries she does not sin. Yet those who marry will have worldly troubles, and I would spare you that." . . .
RSV

ἐὰν (conditional particle in a third-class condition) 363.

δέ (adversative conjunction) 11.

καὶ (emphatic conjunction) 14.

γαμήσῃς (2d.per.sing.aor.act.subj.of γαμέω, third-class condition) 512.

οὐχ (negative particle with the indicative) 130.

ἥμαρτες (2d.per.sing.2d.aor.act.ind.of ἁμαρτάνω, constative) 1260.

καὶ (continuative conjunction) 14.

ἐὰν (conditional particle in a third-class condition) 363.

γήμῃ (3d.per.sing.aor.act.subj.of γαμέω, third-class condition) 512.

ἡ (nom.sing.fem.of the article in agreement with παρθένος) 9.

παρθένος (nom.sing.fem.of παρθένος, subject of γήμῃ) 120.

οὐχ (negative particle with the indicative) 130.

ἥμαρτεν (3d.per.sing.aor.act.ind.of ἁμαρτάνω, constative) 1260.

θλῖψιν (acc.sing.fem.of θλῖψις, direct object of ἕξουσιν) 1046.

δέ (adversative conjunction) 11.

τῇ (loc.sing.fem.of the article in agreement with σαρκὶ) 9.

σαρκὶ (loc.sing.fem.of σάρξ, sphere) 1202.

ἕξουσιν (3d.per.pl.fut.act.ind.of ἔχω, predictive) 82.

οἱ (nom.pl.masc.of the article in agreement with τοιοῦτοι) 9.

τοιοῦτοι (nom.pl.masc.of τοιοῦτος, subject of ἕξουσιν) 785.

ἐγὼ (nom.sing.masc.of ἐγώ, subject of φείδομαι) 123.

δέ (continuative conjunction) 11.

ὑμῶν (gen.pl.masc.of σύ, objective genitive) 104.

φείδομαι (1st.per.sing.pres.mid.ind.of φείδομαι, aoristic) 3533.

Translation - "*But if in fact you marry you have not sinned; and if a virgin marries she has not sinned; but such persons will experience conflicting desires in the flesh, and I want to help you to avoid this.*"

Comment: The ἐὰν clauses with the subjunctive are third-class conditions. Paul does not know whether the persons involved will marry or not. His positive statement is in the apodosis in each case. There is no sin involved. The widower who remarries does not thereby transgress God's law. Nor does the virgin who marries for the first time. But such persons will be putting themselves under pressure (θλῖψις, #1046) because of their desires for sex expression and a possible conflict between the obligations of married life and the obligations to serve the Lord. A concentrated Christian wishes to devote his energy to the promotion of the spiritual goals of the gospel of Christ. This calls at times for fasting, prayer, sacrificial giving of time, talents and money. All of this involved self-denial. One cannot promote the Spirit and the flesh at the same time (Gal.5:16,17). Thus, such a Christian who is married finds himself pressured in opposite directions. By warning the virgin that this situation would develop, Paul is not saying that sex within Christian marriage is wrong. Indeed he explicitly states the contrary. But he does imply that an unmarried Christian, who, by God's grace, has no domineering compulsion for sex (verse 25) is in a better position to devote all of his energies for Christ than one who is married.

We have already stated that Paul's views are influenced by his conviction that Christ's return to earth was to be momentarily expected. His views cannot therefore be said to support permanent celibacy.

It is significant that Bible students who with Paul have been mistaken about the second coming have also tended to be celibate, *e.g.* the Shakers. Paul attacked celibacy as a heresy in 1 Tim.4:1-5. A comparative study of both these passages will put Paul's true views in perspective.

Verse 29 - "But this I say, brethren, the time is short: it remaineth that both they that have wives be as though they had none."

τοῦτο δέ φημι, ἀδελφοί, ὁ καιρὸς συνεσταλμένος ἐστίν. τὸ λοιπὸν ἵνα καὶ οἱ ἔχοντες γυναῖκας ὡς μὴ ἔχοντες ὦσιν,

"I mean, brethren, the appointed time has grown very short; from now on, let those who have wives live as though they had none," . . . RSV

τοῦτο (acc.sing.neut.of οὗτος, direct object of φημι) 93.

δὲ (adversative conjunction) 11.

φημι (1st.per.sing.pres.act.ind.of φημι, aoristic) 354.

ἀδελφοί (voc.pl.masc.of ἀδελφός, address) 15.

ὁ (nom.sing.masc.of the article in agreement with καιρὸς) 9.

καιρὸς (nom.sing.masc.of καιρός, subject of ἐστίν) 767.

συνεσταλμένος (perf.pass.part.nom.sing.masc.of συστέλλω, perfect periphrastic) 3053.

ἐστίν (3d.per.sing.pres.ind.of εἰμί, perfect periphrastic) 86.

τὸ (acc.sing.neut.of the article in agreement with λοιπὸν) 9.

λοιπὸν (acc.sing.neut.of λοιπός, adverbial) 1402.

ἵνα (conjunction with the subjunctive, elliptical imperative) 114.

καὶ (inferential conjunction) 14.

οἱ (nom.pl.masc.of the article in agreement with ἔχοντες) 9.

ἔχοντες (pres.act.part.nom.pl.masc.of ἔχω, substantival, subject of ὦσιν) 82.

γυναῖκας (acc.pl.fem.of γυνή, direct object of ἔχοντες) 103.

ὡς (comparative particle) 128.

μὴ (negative particle with the participle) 87.

ἔχοντες (pres.act.part.nom.pl.masc.of ἔχω, substantival, predicate nominative) 82.

ὦσιν (3d.per.pl.pres.subj.of εἰμί, elliptical imperative) 86.

Translation - "But I say this, brothers, the appointed event is approaching. With reference to the remaining time, therefore those who have wives must continue as though they had none."

Comment: τοῦτο δὲ φημι indicates that Paul has one more thing to say beyond his statement of verse 28. καιρός does not mean "time" in the sense of χρόνος (*cf.*#767 with #168). It means "an occasion" and normally would be followed by a descriptive genitive - *e.g.* Christmas time; the time of the wedding; graduation time etc. Paul here is speaking of the occasion of the second coming of our Lord, which he said was approaching (the perfect periphrastic in συνεσταλμένος ἐστίν). Of course, since the time (καιρός) is approaching, the time (χρόνος) that remains between the time (καιρός) when Paul wrote this and the time (occasion καιρός) of the second coming of Christ was growing shorter. That statement can be made about any moment in historic time (χρόνος). Since the second coming is future all occasions in history, as they occur have less time (χρόνος) remaining until the time (καιρός) of our Lord's appearing.

Paul's error, commonly held by first century Christians, was in his estimation of how much time (χρόνος) remained until the time (καιρός) of the second coming. His point will become valid during the seven year tribulation period covered by Revelation (Daniel 9:27).

τό λοιπόν is an adverbial accusative - "as for the remaining time," or "from henceforth," or "from this moment on."

The ἵνα clause with the subjunctive has the imperative upon which it depends missing. Moulton says, "An innovation in Hellenistic is ἵνα with the subjunctive in commands, which takes the place of the classic ὅπως with the future indicative." (Moulton, *Prol.,* 178, as cited in Robertson, *Grammar,* 994). Robertson adds, " . . . this elliptical imperative is undoubted in the N.T." (*Ibid.*). I do not construe καί here as joined with the καί . . . καί . . . καί . . . καί sequences of verses 30,31. Here it is inferential as introducing the logical inference of his statement which precedes it.

On the basis of his belief that the second coming was soon to occur (*i.e.* within the lifetime of those then living) he lists the activities which Christians should forego. Marriage for virgins, sex within the marriage relationship, weeping, rejoicing and the institution of private ownership and the profit motive are all to be forgotten in the closing days of the "last days" (Heb.1:2)

Verse 30 - "And they that weep, as though they wept not; and they that rejoice, as though they rejoiced not; and they that buy, as though they possessed not."

καί οἱ κλαίοντες ὡς μή κλαίοντες, καί οἱ χαίροντες ὡς μή χαίροντες, καί οἱ ἀγοράζοντες ὡς μή κατέχοντες,

"*. . . and those who mourn as though they were not mourning, and those who rejoice as though they were not rejoicing, and those who buy as though they had no goods, . . . "* . . . RSV

καί (adjunctive conjunction joining participles) 14.
οἱ (nom.pl.masc.of the article in agreement with κλαίοντες) 9.
κλαίοντες (pres.act.part.nom.pl.masc.of κλαίω, substantival, subject of ὦσιν understood) 225.
ὡς (comparative particle) 128.
μή (negative particle with the participle) 87.
κλαίοντες (pres.act.part.nom.pl.masc.of κλαίω, substantival, predicate nominative) 225.
καί (adjunctive conjunction joining participles) 14.
οἱ (nom.pl.masc.of the article in agreement with χαίροντες) 9.
χαίροντες (pres.act.part.nom.pl.masc.of χαίρω, substantival, subject of ὦσιν understood) 182.

ὡς (comparative particle) 128.

μὴ (negative particle with the participle) 87.

χαίροντες (pres.act.part.nom.pl.masc.of χαίρω, substantival, predicate nominative) 182.

καὶ (adjunctive conjunction joining participles) 14.

οἱ (nom.pl.masc.of the article in agreement with ἀγοράζοντες) 9.

ἀγοράζοντες (pres.act.part.nom.pl.masc.of ἀγοράζω, substantival, subject of ὦσιν understood) 1085.

ὡς (comparative particle) 128.

μὴ (negative particle wih the participle) 87.

κατέχοντες (pres.act.part.nom.pl.masc.of κατέχω, substantival, predicate nominative) 2071.

Translation - "... *and those who weep as though they were not weeping, and those who are rejoicing as though they were not rejoicing, and the buyers as though they owned nothing.*"

Comment: This verse continues the sentence begun in verse 29. All are participial substantives. Those who have wives, who weep, who rejoice, who buy, who own property or (verse 31) who operate within the world system in any way, should now and until Christ comes again cease all of the activities connected with these functions and devote all of their energies to the gospel cause. Nothing else in those closing days and hours will be important. The tragedy that brings tears or the good fortune that brings joy, or the commercial transaction that shows a profit or the business administration of one's property or any other activity in which the Christian functions as a unit of world society is only temporary. Messiah's coming will bring a totally new and superior world order. The Christian's viewpoint should thus shift from the temporal to the eternal; from the mundane to the supernal; from the earthly to the heavenly.

The normal human reaction to any event of whatever nature, when the Christian assumes that time will go on and on, is opposite to his reaction when he knows that time is short. It is a difference between a long run and a short run analysis. Paul is ordering here an attitude of the short run.

For example: If the reader inherited a fortune six weeks before the second coming of Christ would he rejoice? Or if he lost a fortune at that time would he be too distressed? If he thought that the Lord's coming was scheduled for next week would he play the stock market? Or if his house burned down would it make much difference?

Verse 31 - "And they that use this world, as not abusing it: for the fashion of this world passeth away."

καὶ οἱ χρώμενοι τὸν κόσμον ὡς μὴ καταχρώμενοι. παράγει γὰρ τὸ σχῆμα τοῦ κόσμου τούτου.

"... *and those who deal with the world as though they had no dealings with it. For the form of this world is passing away.*" ... RSV καὶ (adjunctive conjunction joining participles) 14.

οἱ (nom.pl.masc.of the article in agreement with χρώμενοι) 9.

χρώμενοι (pres.mid.part.nom.pl.masc.of χράομαι, substantival, subject of ὦσιν understood) 2447.

τὸν (acc.sing.masc.of the article in agreement with κόσμον) 9.

κόσμον (acc.sing.masc.of κόσμος, direct object of χρώμενοι) 360.

ὡς (comparative particle) 128.

μὴ (negative particle with the participle) 87.

#4162 καταχρώμενοι (pres.mid.part.nom.pl.masc.of καταχράομαι, predicate nominative).

King James Version

abuse - 1 Cor.7:31; 9:18.

Revised Standard Version

have dealings with - 1 Cor.7:31.
make full use of - 1 Cor.9:18.

Meaning: A combination of κατά (#98) and χράομαι (#2447). Hence, to use up; to exhaust a supply by use; to exploit; to use excessively with damaging effect. κατά intensifies the meaning of χράομαι. In Paul's admonition to the Corinthians not to exploit the institutions of the world to the fullest extent in pursuit of personal gain - 1 Cor.7:31. With reference to the practice of preaching the gospel for financial gain - 1 Cor.9:18.

παράγει (3d.per.sing.pres.act.ind.of παράγω, present progressive retroactive) 786.

γὰρ (causal conjunction) 105.

τὸ (nom.sing.neut.of the article in agreement with σχῆμα) 9.

#4163 σχῆμα (nom.sing.neut.of σχῆμα, subject of παράγει).

King James Version

fashion - 1 Cor.7:31; Phil.2:8.

Revised Standard Version

form - 1 Cor.7:31; Phil.2:8.

Meaning: A combination of ἔχω (#82) and σχεῖν. That which something has. *cf.* English be-havior from "have." The substance of this world, *i.e.* its *modus operandi*. Its form, since form relates to function. 1 Cor.7:31. Whatever in a person that appeals to the senses - the figure, bearing, discourse, action, manner of life - With reference to Jesus who became a man and so appeared - Phil.2:8.

τοῦ (gen.sing.masc.of the article in agreement with κόσμου) 9.

κόσμου (gen.sing.masc.of κόσμος, description) 360.

τούτου (gen.sing.masc.of οὗτος, in agreement with κόσμου) 93.

Translation - ". . . and they who deal with the world as not exploiting it, because this world in its present mode of operation is passing away."

Comment: The sentence begun in verse 29 ends here. Christians who are engaged in business and as such are involved in the commercial and financial institutions of the world must indeed be absorbed in their fortunes to some extent. It is impossible to live a Christian life in the world and not be involved in it to some extent (1 Cor.5:9,10). But Paul warns that such Christians should not get so thoroughly involved in the world system as to exploit it, in a frantic effort to maximize profits, as though the world system, in which we have so much invested, would exist forever and thus be their only source of support and well being. He adds that the world system of human institutions - social, political and economic which exists upon earth, which is guided by unregenerate philosophy, is scheduled to come to an end. *Cf.* 1 John 2:16,17, where John makes the same point and for the same reason.

The Christian is a corporate member of the Body of Christ and, as such is guided by the philosophy of Christ and geared to His eternal program which is being worked out in human history. Christ is the Head of the Body (Eph.1:22,23) and the Christian is inextricably, if inexplicably united to the Head. He thus is destined to share in the fortunes of the Lord Jesus Christ.

The entire thrust of the passage beginning in verse 29 is that a Christian should never become *thoroughly* involved with his earthly and worldly milieu, whether his involvement is marriage, sex and reproduction of the next generation, weeping with the sad, rejoicing with the glad, buying in the market place or investing in the world system with a view to cornering the market. The multinational corporations whose operations transcend national boundary lines to monopolize strategic raw materials, exploit native populations and control world markets at administered prices will discover to their great disappointment that the world system which they have succeeded in controlling is due to pass away. The Christian has his roots in eternity past and a stake in eternity future.

The transitory nature of the first century world was heightened by Paul's belief that Messiah would soon reappear. But the fact that Christ did not return in the first century of the Christian era, and that indeed He still tarries in the twentieth century, does nothing to lessen the truth that Paul is teaching. For though Messiah may not come soon, it cannot be denied that He will come on some future day (Acts 17:31; Heb.10:35-37). When He comes this present world system will be destroyed. Hence the ethical point which Paul is making is a good one. Christians are pilgrims and strangers in a foreign land (Heb.11:13; 1 Pet.2:11). We are God's soldiers in enemy territory (Eph.6:12-17) and we should not get involved any more than is necessary.

Verse 32 - "But I would have you without carefulness. He that is unmarried careth for the things that belong to the Lord, how he may please the Lord."

θέλω δὲ ὑμᾶς ἀμερίμνους εἶναι. ὁ ἄγαμος μεριμνᾷ τὰ τοῦ κυρίου, πῶς ἀρέσῃ τῷ κυρίῳ.

"*I want you to be free from anxieties. The unmarried man is anxious about the affairs of the Lord, how to please the Lord;*" . . . RSV

θέλω (1st.per.sing.pres.act.ind.of θέλω, present progressive retroactive) 88.
δὲ (adversative conjunction) 11.
ὑμᾶς (acc.pl.masc.of σύ, general reference) 104.
ἀμερίμνους (acc.pl.masc.of ἀμέριμνος, predicate adjective) 1692.
εἶναι (pres.inf.of εἰμί, noun use, direct object of θέλω) 86.
ὁ (nom.sing.masc.of the article in agreement with ἄγαμος) 9.
ἄγαμος (nom.sing.masc.of ἄγαμος, subject of μεριμνᾷ) 4155.
μεριμνᾷ (3d.per.sing.pres.act.ind.of μεριμνάω, customary) 609.
τὰ (acc.pl.neut.of the article, direct object of μεριμνᾷ) 9.
τοῦ (gen.sing.masc.of the article in agreement with κυρίου) 9.
κυρίου (gen.sing.masc.of κύριος, possession) 97.
πῶς (adverbial) 627.
ἀρέσῃ (3d.per.sing.aor.act.subj.of ἀρέσκω, deliberative) 1110.
τῷ (dat.sing.masc.of the article in agreement with κυρίῳ) 9.
κυρίῳ (dat.sing.masc.of κύριος, personal advantage) 97.

Translation - "*But I want you to be carefree. The unmarried man is always concerned about the things of the Lord, how he can please the Lord.*"

Comment: That Paul has the subject of marriage and sex on his mind more than any other subject (though the spiritual principle from which the argument procedes applies to all other earthly matters) is clear from the fact that he returns to the subject again in verse 32 and continues the same line of thought through verse 40.

For the faithful Christian who is married and who also wishes to serve the Lord, the problem of the division of resources between his family and the Lord is always present. This is a problem that Paul did not face and he hoped that he might save others from the necessity of facing it.

Verse 33 - "*But he that is married careth for the things that are of the world, how he may please his wife.*"

ὁ δὲ γαμήσας μεριμνᾷ τὰ τοῦ κόσμου, πῶς ἀρέσῃ τῇ γυναικί.

"*. . . but the married man is anxious about worldly affairs, how to please his wife,. . .*" . . . RSV

ὁ (nom.sing.masc.of the article in agreement with γαμήσας) 9.
δὲ (adversative conjunction) 11.
γαμήσας (aor.act.part.nom.sing.masc.of γαμέω, substantival, subject of μεριμνᾷ) 512.
μεριμνᾷ (3d.per.sing.pres.act.ind.of μεριμνάω, customary) 609.
τὰ (acc.pl.neut.of the article, direct object of μεριμνᾷ) 9.
τοῦ (gen.sing.masc.of the article in agreement with κόσμου) 9.
κόσμου (gen.sing.masc.of κόσμος, description) 360.

πῶς (adverbial) 627.

ἀρέσῃ (3d.per.sing.aor.act.subj.of ἀρέσκω, deliberative) 1110.

τῇ (dat.sing.fem.of the article in agreement with γυναικί) 9.

γυναικί (dat.sing.fem.of γυνή, personal advantage) 103.

Translation - "But the married man is always concerned about the affairs of the world, how he can please his wife."

Comment: Note the article τά followed by the descriptive genitive in τοῦ κόσμου. We have the same grammatical pattern here as in verse 32. The married man is under conflicting pressures. Should he serve the Lord? Or his wife? Paul seems to imply that the sociological pull is stronger than the spiritual.

I feel impelled to say a word here in defense of the Christian wives whose love for the Lord and devotion to His cause is so great that for years they have sacrificed their right to demand their legitimate rights, both for themselves and for their children, in order that their husbands might be free to serve the Lord as he chose. We must not read into this passage the idea that every woman who is married to a Christian man is a selfish tyrant who will not permit her husband to serve the Lord. Paul's point still stands however, if we do not read into it more than he intended. A Christian with no obligations to wife or children is certain to be more able to serve the Lord than the Christian who does have such legitimate obligations. Paul is not telling Christian husbands to abandon their wives and family if they believe that the Lord will return in their lifetime. He is telling those who are not married not to assume obligations now that will hinder their service for the Lord.

Just as there is no necessary accusation that wives, as such, are hindrances to the Christian service of their husbands, so there is no such accusation in the verse which follows that husbands hinder their wives who wish to serve the Lord.

Verse 34 - "There is a difference between a wife and a virgin. The unmarried woman careth for the things of the Lord, that she may be holy both in body and in spirit: but she that is married careth for the things of the world, how she may please her husband."

καὶ μεμέρισται. καὶ ἡ γυνὴ ἡ ἄγαμος καὶ ἡ παρθένος μεριμνᾷ τὰ τοῦ κυρίου, ἵνα ἦ ἀγία (καὶ) τῷ σώματι καὶ τῷ πνεύματι. ἡ δὲ γαμήσασα μεριμνᾷ τὰ τοῦ κόσμου, πῶς ἀρέσῃ τῷ ἀνδρί.

". . . and his interests are divided. And the unmarried woman or girl is anxious about the affairs of the Lord, how to be holy in body and spirit; but the married woman is anxious about worldly affairs, how to please her husband." . . . RSV

καὶ (inferential conjunction) 14.

μεμέρισται (3d.per.sing.perf.pass.ind.of μερίζω, intensive) 993.

καὶ (adversative conjunction) 14.

ἡ (nom.sing.fem.of the article in agreement with γυνή) 9.

γυνὴ (nom.sing.fem.of γυνή, subject of μεριμνᾷ) 103.

ἡ (nom.sing.fem.of the article in agreement with ἄγαμος) 9.

ἄγαμος (nom.sing.fem.of ἄγαμος, in agreement with γυνή) 4155.

καὶ (adjunctive conjunction joining nouns) 14.

ἡ (nom.sing.fem.of the article in agreement with παρϑένος) 9.

παρϑένος (nom.sing.fem.of παρϑένος, subject of μεριμνᾷ) 120.

μεριμνᾷ (3d.per.sing.pres.act.ind.of μεριμνάω, customary) 609.

τὰ (acc.pl.neut.of the article, direct object of μεριμνᾷ) 9.

τοῦ (gen.sing.masc.of the article in agreement with κυρίου) 9.

κυρίου (gen.sing.masc.of κύριος, possession) 97.

ἵνα (conjunction with the subjunctive, purpose clause) 114.

ᾖ (3d.per.sing.pres.subj.of εἰμί, purpose) 86.

ἁγία (nom.sing.fem.of ἅγιος, predicate adjective) 84.

καὶ (correlative conjunction) 14.

τῷ (loc.sing.neut.of the article in agreement with σώματι) 9.

σώματι (loc.sing.neut.of σῶμα, sphere) 507.

καὶ (adjunctive conjunction joining nouns) 14.

τῷ (loc.sing.neut.of the article in agreement with πνεύματι) 9.

πνεύματι (loc.sing.neut.of πνεῦμα, sphere) 83.

ἡ (nom.sing.fem.of the article in agreement with γαμήσασα) 9.

δὲ (adversative conjunction) 11.

γαμήσασα (aor.act.part.nom.sing.fem.of γαμέω, subject of μεριμνᾷ) 512.

μεριμνᾷ (3d.per.sing.pres.act.ind.of μεριμνάω, customary) 609.

τὰ (acc.pl.neut.of the article, direct object of μεριμνᾷ) 9.

τοῦ (gen.sing.masc.of the article in agreement with κόσμου) 9.

κόσμου (gen.sing.masc.of κόσμος, possession) 360.

πῶς (adverbial) 627.

ἀρέσῃ (3d.per.sing.aor.act.subj.of ἀρέσκω, deliberative) 1110.

τῷ (dat.sing.masc.of the article in agreement with ἀνδρί) 9.

ἀνδρί (dat.sing.masc.of ἀνήρ, personal advantage) 63.

Translation - "*So he is frustrated. But the woman who is not married and the virgin are concerned about the affairs of the Lord in order that they may be holy, both in body and in spirit. But the married woman is concerned for the things of the world, how she can please her husband.*"

Comment: καὶ μεμέρισται belongs to the thought of verse 33, a point which the KJV misses completely. Goodspeed, speaking of the married man of verse 33 has "and so his interests are divided." The Christian husband is drawn in opposite directions. The Spirit dictates a concern for the Lord; the flesh is concerned only about pleasing his wife. For Paul it was impossible to please both at the same time.

He then applies the same thought to the women. Widows and virgins are women of single purpose. They are unhindered in their attempt to be holy, both in the sphere of the physical and in the sphere of the spiritual. *Contra* the married woman whose dilemma is like that of the married man of verse 33. It seems obvious that Paul is thinking of Christian men and women who are married to unsaved partners. There should be no problem for Christians who marry each other, since both are interested in the things of the Lord.

Verse 35 - "And this I speak for your own profit; not that I may cast a snare upon you, but for that, which is comely, and that ye may attend upon the Lord without distraction."

τοῦτο δὲ πρὸς τὸ ὑμῶν αὐτῶν σύμφορον λέγω, οὐχ ἵνα βρόχον ὑμῖν ἐπιβάλω, ἀλλὰ πρὸς τὸ εὔσχημον καὶ εὐπάρεδρον τῷ κυρίῳ ἀπερισπάστως.

"I say this for your own benefit, not to lay any restraint upon you, but to promote good order and to secure your undivided devotion to the Lord." ...

RSV

τοῦτο (acc.sing.neut.of οὗτος, direct object of λέγω) 93.
δὲ (adversative conjunction) 11.
πρὸς (preposition with the accusative, purpose) 197.
τὸ (acc.sing.neut.of the article in agreement with σύμφορον) 9.
ὑμῶν (gen.pl.masc.of σύ, possession) 104.
αὐτῶν (gen.pl.masc.of αὐτός, intensive) 16.

#4164 σύμφορον (acc.sing.neut.of σύμφορος, purpose).

King James Version

profit - 1 Cor.7:35; 10:33.

Revised Standard Version

benefit - 1 Cor.7:35.
advantage - 1 Cor.10:33.

Meaning: Cf. συμφέρω (#505). Profit, advantage, benefit. With reference to the victorious Christian life - 1 Cor.7:35; in terms of personal popularity and any benefits that might result therefrom - 1 Cor.10:33.

λέγω (1st.per.sing.pres.act.ind.of λέγω, aoristic) 66.
οὐχ (negative particle with the indicative) 130.
ἵνα (conjunction with the subjunctive, purpose) 114.

#4165 βρόχον (acc.sing.masc.of βρόχος, direct object of ἐπιβάλω).

King James Version

snare - 1 Cor.7:35.

Revised Standard Version

restraint - 1 Cor.7:35.

Meaning: A noose; slipknot, by which a person, animal or object is caught and restrained. A figurative expression borrowed from war or from the hunt. A device to hold another in restraint, as on a leash. With reference to Paul's advice about marriage - 1 Cor.7:35.

ὑμῖν (dat.pl.masc.of σύ, indirect object of ἐπιβάλω) 104.
ἐπιβάλω (1st.per.sing.2d.aor.act.subj.of ἐπιβάλλω, purpose) 800.
ἀλλά (alternative conjunction) 342.
πρὸς (preposition with the accusative, purpose) 197.
τὸ (acc.sing.neut.of the article in agreement with εὔσχημον) 9.
εὔσχημον (acc.sing.neut.of εὐσχήμων, purpose) 2872.
καὶ (adjunctive conjunction joining nouns) 14.

#4166 εὐπάρεδρον (acc.sing.neut.of εὐπάρεδρος, purpose).

King James Version

that you may attend - 1 Cor.7:35.

Revised Standard Version

to secure your undivided devotion - 1 Cor.7:35.

Meaning: A combination of εὐ (#1536) and πάρεδρος, which is from παρά (#154) and ἕδρος - "sitting beside." Hence assiduous devotion to something; careful attention; undivided attention. With reference to Paul's attempt to persuade the Corinthians to concentrate upon the Lord's work - 1 Cor.7:35.

τῷ (dat.sing.masc.of the article in agreement with κυρίῳ) 9.
κυρίῳ (dat.sing.masc.of κύριος, personal advantage) 97.

#4167 ἀπερισπάστως (adverbial).

King James Version

without distraction - 1 Cor.7:35.

Revised Standard Version

to secure your undivided devotion - 1 Cor.7:35. (Joined with #4166 to translate as shown).

Meaning: A combination of α privative and περισπάω (#2441). An adverb - without distraction; without interference or hindrance. With reference to the legitimate demands of married life which inhibit one's devotion to the Lord's service - 1 Cor.7:35.

Translation - "But I am saying this for your own good, not to put a noose around your neck, but that you may do your best and that you may give assiduous attention to the Lord with no distractions."

Comment: The two πρὸς phrases with the articular neuter substantives, τὸ σύμφορον, τὸ εὔσχημον καὶ εὐπάρεδρον are purpose constructions. Paul has spoken thus in order to secure certain desired results: (1) their own benefit. (It is debatable whether αὐτῶν is intensive or reflexive); (2) their proper performance as Christians, and (3) their undivided attention to the work of the Lord. These goals can be attained only if there are no distractions, a thought added by the adverb ἀπερισπάστως. Parenthetically Paul denies that he desired to "cast a halter around their necks." If a Corinthian Christian who was unmarried and faced with the problem of a persistent sex drive which he could not sublimate, wished to marry he was free to do so without sin. But this admission is wrung from Paul's pen with reluctance. He much preferred that they forget about sex and "sit beside the Lord's work for good" (#4166), without dividing their resources (#4167).

Verse 36 - "But if any man think that he behaveth himself uncomely toward his virgin, if she pass the flower of her age, and need so require, let him do what he will, he sinneth not; let them marry."

Εἰ δέ τις ἀσχημονεῖν ἐπὶ τὴν παρθένον αὐτοῦ νομίζει ἐὰν ᾖ ὑπέρακμος, καὶ οὕτως ὀφείλει γίνεσθαι, ὃ θέλει ποιείτω. οὐχ ἁμαρτάνει. γαμείτωσαν.

"If any one thinks that he is not behaving properly toward his betrothed, if his passions are strong, and it has to be, let him do as he wishes: let them marry — it is no sin." . . . RSV

Εἰ (conditional particle in a first-class condition) 337.
δέ (adversative conjunction) 11.
τις (nom.sing.masc.of τις, indefinite pronoun, subject of νομίζει) 486.

#4168 ἀσχημονεῖν (pres.act.inf.of ἀσχημονέω, noun use, direct object of νομίζει).

King James Version

behave self uncomely - 1 Cor.7:36.
behave self unseemly - 1 Cor.13:5.

Revised Standard Version

not behaving properly - 1 Cor.7:36.
is not arrogant or rude - 1 Cor.13:5.

Meaning: Cf. ἀσχήμων (#4218); ἀσχημοσύνη (#3814) ἀσχήμων - "deformed." Cf. τὴν κεφαλὴν ἀσχημονεῖν - "a bald head," Ael. v.h. 11,4. Followed by ἐπὶ τὴν παρθένον αὐτοῦ, *i.e.* to disgrace her. 1 Cor.7:36. To behave in a rude and wholly improper manner - 1 Cor.13:5.

ἐπὶ (preposition with the accusative of extent) 47.
τὴν (acc.sing.fem.of the article in agreement with παρθένον) 9.
παρθένον (acc.sing.fem.of παρθένος, extent) 120.
αὐτοῦ (gen.sing.masc.of αὐτός, possession) 16.
νομίζει (3d.per.sing.pres.act.ind.of νομίζω, first-class condition) 462.
ἐὰν (conditional particle with the subjunctive in a third-class condition) 363.
ᾖ (3d.per.sing.pres.subj.of εἰμί, third-class condition) 86.

#4169 ὑπέρακμος (nom.sing.masc.of ὑπέρακμος, predicate adjective).

pass the flower of age - 1 Cor.7:36.

Revised Standard Version

his passions are strong - 1 Cor.7:36.

Meaning: A combination of ὑπέρ (#545) and ἀκμή - "bloom." Hence, beyond the bloom of life. Overripe. Fully developed sexually and hence with a compelling sex drive - 1 Cor.7:36.

καὶ (continuative conjunction) 14.
οὕτως (demonstrative adverb) 74.
ὀφείλει (3d.per.sing.pres.act.ind.of ὀφείλω, aoristic) 1277.
γίνεσθαι (pres.inf.of γίνομαι, complementary) 113.
ὃ (acc.sing.neut.of ὅς, relative pronoun, direct object of ποιείτω) 65.
θέλει (3d.per.sing.pres.act.ind.of θέλω, aoristic) 88.
ποιείτω (3d.per.sing.pres.act.impv.of ποιέω, permission) 127.
οὐχ (negative particle with the indicative) 130.
ἁμαρτάνει (3d.per.sing.pres.act.ind.of ἁμαρτάνω, aoristic) 1260.
γαμείτωσαν (3d.per.pl.pres.act.impv.of γαμέω, permission) 512.

Translation - "But if any man thinks that he is conducting himself improperly with his fiancee, if he is oversexed and the case requires it, let him do what he wishes. He is not sinning. Let them marry."

Comment: We have no choice except to translate literally what is here, without regard to the sanctions of society. There is no way to tell whether τις means the father of his virgin daughter or her fiance. Nor does the word παρθένος reveal the relationship between her and τις. The relationship between τις and παρθένον, whether father-daughter or fiance-fiancee is not clear. If Paul meant that τις was the father he could have said that παρθένον was his daughter. The passage must be interpreted on the basis of the anwer to this question. Similarly θέλει can mean what the father wants or what the girl and/or her sweetheart wants. Similarly ἢ can refer either to the young man or the young woman. It could hardly apply to the father of the girl, but even this is based upon contextual considertions, not upon grammar. Who is the subject of ὀφείλει? Father, daughter or suitor? The passage only suggests the answers to these questions. It seems to say that when two young people are deeply in love and greatly desirous of the sex experience, they should not be forbidden to marry because of anything Paul has said against marriage. He concedes that marriage between Christians is not wrong under these circumstances. He is not suggesting his approval of pre-marital sex. "Let him do what he pleases" means that if he marries her he has not sinned. To involve the father of the girl in verses 37 and 38 is pure eisegesis.

We cannot be sure how involved the marriage ceremony was in Corinth. We can be sure that in some way at least the Christian community was made aware of the decision of the parties to live together and that this announcement preceded the consummation of their union.

Verse 37 - *"Nevertheless he that standeth stedfast in his heart, having no necessity, but hath power over his own will, and hath so decreed in his heart that he will keep his virgin, doeth well."*

ὃς δὲ ἕστηκεν ἐν τῇ καρδίᾳ αὐτοῦ ἑδραῖος, μὴ ἔχων ἀνάγκην, ἐξουσίαν δὲ ἔχει περὶ τοῦ ἰδίου θελήματος, καὶ τοῦτο κέκρικεν ἐν τῇ ἰδίᾳ καρδίᾳ, τηρεῖν τὴν ἑαυτοῦ παρθένον, καλῶς ποιήσει.

"But whoever is firmly established in his heart, being under no necessity but having his desire under control, and has determined this in his heart, to keep her as his betrothed, he will do well." . . . RSV

ὃς (nom.sing.masc.of ὅς, relative pronoun, subject of ἕστηκεν, ἔχει, κέκρικεν and ποιήσει) 65.
δὲ (adversative conjunction) 11.
ἕστηκεν (3d.per.sing.perf.act.ind.of ἵστημι, intensive) 180.
ἐν (preposition with the locative of sphere) 80.
τῇ (loc.sing.fem.of the article in agreement with καρδίᾳ) 9.
καρδίᾳ (loc.sing.fem.of καρδία, sphere) 432.
αὐτοῦ (gen.sing.masc.of αὐτός, possession) 16.

#4170 ἑδραῖος (nom.sing.masc.of ἑδραῖος, predicate adjective).

King James Version

settled - Col.1:23.
steadfast - 1 Cor.7:37; 15:58.

Revised Standard Version

firmly established - 1 Cor.7:37.
steadfast - 1 Cor.15:58; Col.1:23.

Meaning: Cf. ἑδραίωμα (#4742). ἑδραιόω - "to make stable; settle firmly." Hence, firm, immovable, steadfast, fixed in purpose. With reference to the decision to remain celibate - 1 Cor.7:37; to continue in Christian service generally in 1 Cor.15:58; Col.1:23.

μὴ (negative particle with the participle) 87.
ἔχων (pres.act.part.nom.sing.masc.of ἔχω, adverbial, causal) 82.
ἀνάγκην (acc.sing.fem.of ἀνάγκη, direct object of ἔχων) 1254.
ἐξουσίαν (acc.sing.fem.of ἐξουσία, direct object of ἔχει) 707.
δὲ (adversative conjunction) 11.
ἔχει (3d.per.sing.pres.act.ind.of ἔχω, aoristic) 82.
περὶ (preposition with the genitive of reference) 173.
τοῦ (gen.sing.neut.of the article in agreement with θελήματος) 9.
ἰδίου (gen.sing.neut.of ἴδιος, possessive pronoun, in agreement with θελήματος) 778.

θελήματος (gen.sing.neut.of θέλημα, reference) 577.

καὶ (adjunctive conjunction joining verbs) 14.

τοῦτο (acc.sing.neut.of οὗτος, direct object of κέκρικεν) 93.

κέκρικεν (3d.per.sing.perf.act.ind.of κρίνω, intensive) 531.

ἐν (preposition with the locative of place, metaphorical) 80.

τῇ (loc.sing.fem.of the article in agreement with καρδίᾳ) 9.

ἰδίᾳ (loc.sing.fem.of ἴδιος, possessive pronoun, in agreement with καρδίᾳ) 778.

καρδίᾳ (loc.sing.fem.of καρδία, place, metaphorical) 432.

τηρεῖν (pres.act.inf.of τηρέω, epexegetical) 1297.

τὴν (acc.sing.fem.of the article in agreement with παρθένον) 9.

ἑαυτοῦ (gen.sing.masc.of ἑαυτοῦ, in agreement with παρθένον) 288.

παρθένον (acc.sing.fem.of παρθένος, direct object of τηρεῖν) 120.

καλῶς (adverbial) 977.

ποιήσει (3d.per.sing.fut.act.ind.of ποιέω, predictive) 127.

Translation - "However the man who is standing steadfast in his heart, because he is not under pressure, but has control over his own will and has determined this in his heart - to keep his own fiancee a virgin - he will be doing well."

Comment: The relative ὅς is subject of all of the verbs in the sentence. He who stands steadfast, has control and has reached a decision will do well. That Paul should have broken the pattern with the causal participle μὴ ἔχων constitutes an anacoluthon (a break in an otherwise smooth syntax). But this is nothing new for Paul. His meaning is very clear. He is talking about a hypothetical case in which a young man who, though in love with his fiancee, is not under unbearable physical pressure to marry her. He has determined in his heart to persist in his decision not to marry her. He has power over his own will. He will forego marriage in order to devote all of his energies to Christian service. Paul applauds the decision of such a man. Taken by itself, the statement implies that if he marries her, he does not do well. But Paul is not willing to go that far. To do so is to say that the marriage relationship is evil. Paul has already indicated otherwise (verse 36). The matter is relative, and he puts it in perspective in

Verse 38 - "So then he that giveth her in marriage doeth well; but he that giveth her not in marriage doeth better."

ὥστε καὶ ὁ γαμίζων τὴν ἑαυτοῦ παρθένον καλῶς ποιεῖ, καὶ ὁ μὴ γαμίζων κρεῖσσον ποιήσει.

"So that he who marries his betrothed does well; and he who refrains from marriage will do better." . . . RSV

ὥστε (conjunction with the indicative in a result clause) 752.

καὶ (inferential conjunction) 14.

ὁ (nom.sing.masc.of the article in agreement with γαμίζων) 9.

γαμίζων (pres.act.part.nom.sing.masc.of γαμίζω, substantival, subject of ποιεῖ) 1426.

τὴν (acc.sing.fem.of the article in agreement with παρθένον) 9.
ἑαυτοῦ (gen.sing.masc.of ἑαυτοῦ, possession) 288.
παρθένον (acc.sing.fem.of παρθένος, direct object of γαμίζων) 120.
καλῶς (adverbial) 977.
ποιεῖ (3d.per.sing.pres.act.ind.of ποιέω, present progressive) 127.
καὶ (adversative conjunction) 14.
ὁ (nom.sing.masc.of the article in agreement with γαμίζων) 9.
μὴ (negative particle with the participle) 87.
γαμίζων (pres.act.part.nom.sing.masc.of γαμίζω, substantival, subject of ποιήσει) 1426.
κρεῖσσον (acc.sing.neut.of κρείσσων, predicate adverb) 4157.
ποιήσει (3d.per.sing.fut.act.ind.of ποιέω, predictive) 127.

Translation - "*Therefore it comes down to this: the man who marries his own fiancee does well, but the one who does not will do better.*"

Comment: We have a rare use of ὥστε with the indicative in a result clause. *Cf.* John 3:16 for another example. καὶ is inferential - "So the result is this . . . " It is good to get married; it is better to remain single. In verses 39 and 40 he applies the same principle to a widow. Once again we point out that Paul was writing this advice with the assumption that the coming of the Lord Jesus Christ was very near.

Verse 39 - "*The wife is bound by the law as long as her husband liveth; but if her husband be dead she is at liberty to be married to whom she will; only in the Lord.*"

Γυνὴ δέδεται ἐφ' ὅσον χρόνον ζῇ ὁ ἀνὴρ αὐτῆς. ἐὰν δὲ κοιμηθῇ ὁ ἀνήρ, ἐλευθέρα ἐστὶν ᾧ θέλει γαμηθῆναι, μόνον ἐν κυρίῳ.

"*A wife is bound to her husband as long as he lives. If the husband dies, she is free to be married to whom she wishes, only in the Lord.*" . . . RSV

Γυνὴ (nom.sing.fem.of γυνή, subject of δέδεται) 103.
δέδεται (3d.per.sing.perf.pass.ind.of δέω, intensive) 998.
ἐφ' (preposition with the accusative, time extent) 47.
ὅσον (acc.sing.masc.of ὅσος, in agreement with χρόνον) 660.
χρόνον (acc.sing.masc.of χρόνος, time extent) 168.
ζῇ (3d.per.sing.pres.act.ind.of ζάω, present progressive) 340.
ὁ (nom.sing.masc.of the article in agreement with ἀνὴρ) 9.
ἀνὴρ (nom.sing.masc.of ἀνήρ, subject of ζῇ) 63.
αὐτῆς (gen.sing.fem.of αὐτός, relationship) 16.
ἐὰν (conditional particle in a third-class condition) 363.
δὲ (adversative conjunction) 11.
κοιμηθῇ (3d.per.sing.1st.aor.pass.subj.of κοιμάω, third-class condition) 1664.
ὁ (nom.sing.masc.of the article in agreement with ἀνήρ) 9.
ἀνήρ (nom.sing.masc.of ἀνήρ, subject of κοιμηθῇ) 63.

ἐλευθέρα (nom.sing.fem.of ἐλεύθερος, predicate adjective) 1245.

ἐστὶν (3d.per.sing.pres.ind.of εἰμί, third-class condition) 86.

ᾧ (dat.sing.masc.of ὅς, dative of person) 65.

θέλει (3d.per.sing.pres.act.ind.of θέλω, aoristic) 88.

γαμηθῆναι (aor.pass.inf.of γαμέω, complementary) 512.

μόνον (acc.sing.neut.of μόνος, adverbial) 339.

ἐν (preposition with the instrumental, association) 80.

κυρίῳ (instru.sing.masc.of κύριος, association) 97.

Translation - *"A woman continues to be bound for such time as her husband is alive, but if her husband dies she is free to be married to whom she wishes, subject only to the Lord's will."*

Comment: δέδεται is effective. The emphasis is upon the resultant condition which flows from her past marriage. The marriage bond is inviolate and can be broken only by the death of one of the parties. Note ἐφ' ὅσον χρόνον in a relative time expression. ἐάν and the subjunctive introduces a third-class condition. If he dies (nothing dogmatic about whether he will or not) she is free to be married again if she wishes and to whom she wishes, subject only to one restriction - her decision to remarry must be consistent with the Lord's will. This, at least, means that her new husband must be a Christian, and it can mean more than that.

Thus Paul applies the permissive principle to the widow as he had previously applied it to the virgin. But he cannot refrain from closing this long treatment of sex and marriage with an expression of his own, admittedly uninspired views.

Verse 40 - "But she is happier if she so abide, after my judgment: and I think also that I have the Spirit of God."

μακαριωτέρα δὲ ἐστιν ἐὰν οὕτως μείνῃ, κατὰ τὴν ἐμὴν γνώμην, δοκῶ δὲ κἀγὼ πνεῦμα θεοῦ ἔχειν.

"But in my judgment she is happier if she remains as she is. And I think that I have the Spirit of God" . . . RSV

μακαριωτέρα (nom.sing.fem.comp.of μακάριος, predicate adjective) 422.

δὲ (adversative conjunction) 11.

ἐστιν (3d.per.sing.pres.ind.of εἰμί, present progressive) 86.

ἐὰν (conditional particle in a third-class condition) 363.

οὕτως (demonstrative adverb) 74.

μείνῃ (3d.per.sing.aor.act.subj.of μένω, third-class condition) 864.

κατὰ (preposition with the accusative, standard) 98.

τὴν (acc.sing.fem.of the article in agreement with γνώμην) 9.

ἐμὴν (acc.sing.fem.of ἐμός, in agreement with γνώμην) 1267.

γνώμην (acc.sing.fem.of γνώμη, standard) 3499.

δοκῶ (1st.per.sing.pres.act.ind.of δοκέω, aoristic) 287.

δὲ (continuative conjunction) 11.

κἀγὼ (emphatic conjunction and first personal pronoun, crasis) 178.

πνεῦμα (acc.sing.neut.of πνεῦμα, direct object of ἔχειν) 83.

θεοῦ (gen.sing.masc.of θεός, description) 124.

ἔχειν (pres.act.inf.of ἔχω, noun use, direct object of δοκῶ) 82.

Translation - "But she is happier if she remains free, according to my opinion, and I think in fact that I have the divine Spirit."

Comment: The apodosis of the third-class condition precedes the protasis. If the widow remains a widow after her husband dies, she will be happier than if she remarries, even though her second marriage is within the sphere of the Lord's will. This is Paul's opinion, but he adds that he thinks that it is also God's view of the matter.

Thus the long discussion about marriage comes to a close. The final thrust of Paul's teaching is that while marriage among Christians is not a sin, on the other hand, in view of Messiah's soon appearing, celibacy is better, since it allows the child of God to devote all of his energy to the service of Christ.

It is important to note that Paul is not discussing the social institution of marriage among unbelievers, but only as it relates to members of the Body of Christ.

Food Offered to Idols

(1 Corinthians 8:1-13)

1 Cor.8:1 - "Now as touching things offered unto idols, we know that we all have knowledge. Knowledge puffeth up, but charity edifieth."

Περὶ δὲ τῶν εἰδωλοθύτων, οἴδαμεν ὅτι πάντες γνῶσιν ἔχομεν. ἡ γνῶσις φυσιοῖ, ἡ δὲ ἀγάπη οἰκοδομεῖ.

"Now concerning food offered to idols: we know that 'all of us possess knowledge.' 'Knowledge' puffs up, but love builds up." . . . RSV

Περὶ (preposition with the genitive of reference) 173.
δὲ (explanatory conjunction) 11.
τῶν (gen.pl.neut.of the article in agreement with εἰδωλοθύτων) 9.
εἰδωλοθύτων (gen.pl.neut.of εἰδολόθυτον, reference) 3348.
οἴδαμεν (1st.per.pl.perf.act.ind.of ὁράω, intensive) 144b.
ὅτι (conjunction introducing an object clause in indirect discourse) 211.
πάντες (nom.pl.masc.of πᾶς, subject of ἔχομεν) 67.
γνῶσιν (acc.sing.fem.of γνῶσις, direct object of φυσιοῖ) 1856.
ἔχομεν (1st.per.pl.pres.act.ind.of ἔχω, static) 82.
ἡ (nom.sing.fem.of the article in agreement with γνῶσις) 9.
γνῶσις (nom.sing.fem.of γνῶσις, subject of φυσιοῖ) 4122.
φυσιοῖ (3d.per.sing.pres.act.ind.of φυσιόω, customary) 4122.
ἡ (nom.sing.fem.of the article in agreement with ἀγάπη) 9.
δὲ (adversative conjunction) 11.
ἀγάπη (nom.sing.fem.of ἀγάπη, subject of οἰκοδομεῖ) 1490.
οἰκοδομεῖ (3d.per.sing.pres.act.ind.of οἰκοδομέω, customary) 694.

Translation - *"Now with reference to those things which are offered to idols, we are all aware that all that knowlege! Knowledge inflates the ego, but love edifies."*

Comment: δὲ is explanatory as Paul finally terminates his discussion of sex and turns to another matter - apparently one about which the Corinthians had asked him. περὶ with the genitive of reference is often found in the New Testament. ὅτι introduces the object clause in indirect discourse after οἴδαμεν. The second δὲ is adversative. γνῶσις acts upon the Christian in one way; ἀγάπη in the opposite way. γνῶσις blows up; ἀγάπη builds up.

The Revised Standard Version seems to sense Paul's mood. Note the quotation marks in their translation. I have tried to indicate the same thing with the exclamation mark. It is a good guess that the letter from Corinth to Paul, to which his letter is the reply had referred to some in the church who seemed to have more "knowledge" than others. Thus the controversy over food offered to idols arose. Paul had seen these self-appointed pseudosophisticated sophomores before, and he was stimulated to amused contempt. Everyone had an opinion about the propriety of eating meat which had previously been offered to an idol. *Cf.*#3348. Some believed that if they ate that meat they were tacitly compromising with idolatry. Thus it was a sin. Others took the more advanced view that the fact that the animal had been slaughtered before an idol altar by a pagan priest had nothing to do with the quality of the meat which was later placed on sale in the open market. After all, the idol could not eat it and there was no good reason to throw it away. As a matter of fact, it was probably true that such meat was of a better quality because of its having been chosen to offer to the god.

Paul's personal opinion was on the side of those who could with a clear conscience eat such meat and he reasons his position quite well in the verses which follow. But there was a more important consideration. Everyone had his own view of the matter, and it was quite natural that each man should think that his reasoning was superior to that of those who disagreed with him. Thus he was in danger of suffering from ego-inflation. Paul warns that knowledge, once we begin to reflect, not upon how little of it we have, but upon how much we have, is certain to give us an exaggerated estimate of our own importance. Thus we violate Paul's warning in Romans 12:3. The Christian who falls into that trap needs the tolerance which love produces.

Knowledge (γνῶσις, #1856) is used here in a special technical sense, not common to its use elsewhere. Here Paul is being sarcastic, as he uses the word to denote some special "illumination" which an opinionated dogmatist might think that he possessed that made him right and all who disagreed with him wrong. Such a man does not know as much as he thinks he knows nor as much as he ought to know. Knowledge in this sense is bad and the disease can be mitigated only with Christian love, which develops tolerance for other views and a proper humility.

Verse 2 - *"And if any man think that he knoweth anything, he knoweth nothing yet as he ought to know."*

εἴ τις δοκεῖ ἐγνωκέναι τι, οὔπω ἔγνω καθὼς δεῖ γνῶναι.

"If any one imagines that he knows something, he does not yet know as he ought to know." . . . RSV

εἴ (conditional particle in a first-class condition) 337.
τις (nom.sing.masc.of τις, indefinite pronoun, subject of δοκεῖ) 486.
δοκεῖ (3d.per.sing.pres.act.ind.of δοκέω, present progressive) 287.
ἐγνωκέναι (perf.act.inf.of γινώσκω, noun use, direct object of δοκεῖ) 131.
τι (acc.sing.neut.of τις, indefinite pronoun, direct object of ἐγνωκέναι) 486.
οὔπω (temporal adverb) 1198.
ἔγνω (3d.per.sing.2d.aor.act.ind.of γινώσκω, constative) 131.
καθὼς (compound comparative adverb) 1348.
δεῖ (3d.per.sing.pres.impersonal) 1207.
γνῶναι (2d.aor.act.inf.of γινώσκω, complementary) 131.

Translation - "If any one thinks that he has learned something, still he did not learn what he ought to know."

Comment: Human thought processes are unreliable and lead us to conclusions that are likely to be either totally or partially invalid. It is easy to assume that a learning experience in the past (perfect infinitive in ἐγνωκέναι) has led us to hold a valid position in the present. We suppose that we learned what we think we know correctly, and therefore that our present views are correct. Paul challanges this in the apodosis of the first-class condition. He insists that there is a possibility that we did not learn it as we should have learned it. The superficial thinker builds upon incomplete investigation of the facts and thus comes to a false conclusion. Example: the view that all Indians walk in single file based upon the fact that a man saw two Indians walking down the street in tandem!

True learning is facilitated by the love of God (verse 3). How tragic to find the dogmatic views of Christians who are too sure of the validity of their present positions to rethink the processes by which they arrived at them. One often hears in strident voice, "But my Bible says . . . !" If indeed the Bible says what they say it does, they are to be congratulated for their steadfastness, but does the Bible say what they think it does?

Everyone in Corinth had his view about the propriety of eating meat which had previously been slaughtered before a pagan altar. Some were unwilling to question their views. As a result the church was split.

Verse 3 - "But if any man love God, the same is known of him."

εἰ δὲ τις ἀγαπᾷ τὸν θεόν, οὗτος ἔγνωσται ὑπ' αὐτοῦ.

"But if one loves God, one is known by him." . . . RSV

εἰ (conditional particle in a first-class condition) 337.
δὲ (adversative conjunction) 11.
τις (nom.sing.masc.of τις, indefinite pronoun, subject of ἀγαπᾷ) 486.

ἀγαπᾷ (3d.per.sing.pres.act.ind.of ἀγαπάω, first-class condition) 540.

τὸν (acc.sing.masc.of the article in agreement with θεόν) 9.

θεόν (acc.sing.masc.of θεός, direct object of ἀγαπᾷ) 124.

οὗτος (nom.sing.masc.of οὗτος, subject of ἔγνωσται, deictic) 93.

ἔγνωσται (3d.per.sing.perf.pass.ind.of γινώσκω, consummative) 131.

ὑπ' (preposition with the ablative of agent) 117.

αὐτοῦ (abl.sing.masc.of αὐτός, agent) 16.

Translation - "But if any one loves God (it is because) that one has been previously known (and is therefore now known) by Him."

Comment: In my view Goodspeed has missed the point with his translation, "But if a man loves God, God is known by him." Williams sides with Goodspeed, with an added footnote in which he says that οὗτος refers to τὸν θεόν (God), not to τις (any one). The fact that οὗτος is nominative is due to its position as the subject of ἔγνωσται, and does not prove from a grammatical standpoint that it refers to τις. The question is, "Who is it who has been known in the past as a result of which God is now loved?" Who was known and who did the knowing? The Goodspeed/Williams translations say that the man came to know God in the past and that they now love Him. My translation says that the man was known by God in the past and that now the man loves God, as a result. The loving is in the present tense; the having been known is in the perfect tense and points to the consummation of an act of knowing in the past which leads now to an ongoing result. The verb of knowing is not a culminative aorist, but a consummative perfect. Mantey well remarked that "Whatever difference there is between the consummative perfect and the culminative aorist consists in the reference to the results of the action. The culminative aorist sees the fact that the act has been consummated; the perfect sees the existence of the consummated act. We might make a graphical distinction thus: culminative aorist, presenting the fact that the process has been completed, —————————*; consummative perfect, presenting the completed process, ——————————*..........; intensive perfect, presenting the results of the completed process, ...*—————————————. These distinctions are of course theoretical, but they constitute the basis of practice as we find it in the actual text of the Greek. The English student finds diffculty here because all three of these points of view are included in the present-perfect in English." (Mantey, *Manual*, 203).

The context is the final arbiter in this case. If a Christian is loving God at present he is one who, prior to the present, had been known and is therefore correctly known by God. God's previous knowledge of the man, which extends into the durative present (consumamtive perfect in ἔγνωσται) is the reason for the man's present durative love for God. Thus God is the source of the Christian's love for Him. Is He also not the source of our knowledge of everything, including the proper attitude toward idol foods? Should not we, if we love God, ask Him for wisdom on all of these controversial points rather than assuming that our views are correct. Paul's point seems to be that if it were not for the fact that God knew us in the past we would not love God now. Certainly that can be clearly established by other Scripture, whether this passage teaches it or not. Thus Paul associates right thinking with love for God since God is the source of our Christian experience. He is trying to instill into the fractious Corinthians a little intellectual humility by telling them that if it had not been for the fact that God knew them before they were born, loved them enough to die for them and then called them to Himself after they were born, they would not love God now and it would not make any difference whether they ate meat offered to idols or not. Since he showed some contempt for their supposed "knowledge" in verse 1 it would seem that the thrust of his effort now, before he discusses the question of meat offered to idols, is to deflate their inflated egos. Goodspeed and Williams have translated to say that the Corinthians know God and His ways because they loved Him. How does this contribute to their intellectual humility? Just as they were not able to know God in the first place and therefore are unable to love God now, neither are they erudite enough to think through the question about meat offered to idols to the point where they can be certain that they are correct.

Verse 4 - "As concerning therefore the eating of those things that are offered in sacrifice unto idols, we know that an idol is nothing in the world, and that there is none other God but one."

Περὶ τῆς βρώσεως οὖν τῶν εἰδωλοθύτων οἴδαμεν ὅτι οὐδὲν εἴδωλον ἐν κόσμῳ, καὶ ὅτι οὐδεὶς θεὸς εἰ μὴ εἷς.

"Hence, as to the eating of food offered to idols, we know that 'an idol has no real existence,' and that 'there is no God but one.' " . . . RSV

Περὶ (preposition with the genitive of reference) 173.
τῆς (gen.sing.fem.of the article in agreement with βρῶσις) 9.
βρῶσις (gen.sing.fem.of βρῶσις, reference) 594.
οὖν (inferential conjunction) 68.
τῶν (gen.pl.neut.of the article in agreement with εἰδωλοθύτων) 9.
εἰδωλοθύτων (gen.pl.neut.of εἰδωλόθυτον, description) 3348.
οἴδαμεν (1st.per.pl.perf.act.ind.of ὁράω, intensive) 144b.
ὅτι (conjunction introducing an object clause in indirect discourse) 211.
οὐδὲν (nom.sing.neut.of οὐδείς, predicate nominative) 446.
εἴδωλον (nom.sing.neut.of εἴδωλον, subject of ἐστιν understood) 3138.
ἐν (preposition with the locative of place) 80.
κόσμῳ (loc.sing.masc.of κόσμος, place) 360.
καὶ (adjunctive conjunction joining object clauses) 14.
ὅτι (conjunction introducing an object clause in indirect discourse) 211.
οὐδεὶς (nom.sing.masc.of οὐδείς, in agreement with θεὸς) 446.
θεὸς (nom.sing.masc.of θεός, subject of ἐστιν understood) 124.
εἰ (conditional particle in an elliptical condition) 337.
μὴ (negative particle in an elliptical condition) 87.
εἷς (nom.sing.masc.of εἷς, predicate nominative) 469.

Translation - "Therefore with reference to the food of the idols, we know that an

1 Cor.8:4,5   *The Renaissance New Testament*   505gment>

idol is nothing in the world, and that if God is not the One then there is no God."

Comment: We have two object clauses following οἴδαμεν ὅτι, both in indirect discourse. Two things we know: (1) An idol in the world is nothing. So why get excited about it? (2) If the God of the Judeo-Christian tradition does not exist, then no God exists. And if no God exists why bother about ethics? What difference does it make what you eat? But since the Corinthians had a commitment to the God of the Bible and therefore gave no status to other gods, it follows that the worship of another 'god" is an empty exercise in futility. Why give it status? If one does not believe in something, why should he spend his time opposing it? Witness the atheist who spent his life fighting against the God that did not exist! Thus Paul will say that he had no problem about eating meat previously offered to a idol. But he will also recognize the fact that some of the Christians in Corinth, who were not thinking as carefully about it as he, did have the problem and he will urge those on each side of the question to be tolerant about the views of the other side.

Verse 5 - "For though there be that are called gods, whether in heaven or in earth (as there be gods many, and lords many),"

καὶ γὰρ εἴπερ εἰσὶν λεγόμενοι θεοὶ εἴτε ἐν οὐρανῷ εἴτε ἐπὶ γῆς, ὥσπερ εἰσὶν θεοὶ πολλοὶ καὶ κύριοι πολλοί,

"For although there may be so-called gods in heaven or on earth - as indeed there are many 'gods' and many 'lords' — " . . . RSV

καὶ (ascensive conjunction) 14.
γὰρ (causal conjunction) 105.
εἴπερ (intensive conditional particle) 3879.
εἰσὶν (3rd.per.pl.pres.ind.of εἰμί, present periphrastic) 86.
λεγόμενοι (pres.pass.part.nom.pl.masc.of λέγω, present periphastic) 66.
θεοὶ (nom.pl.masc.of θεός, subject of εἰσὶν) 124.
εἴτε (conditional particle) 4016.
ἐν (preposition with the locative, place) 80.
οὐρανῷ (loc.sing.masc.of οὐρανός, place) 254.
εἴτε (conditional particle) 4016.
ἐπὶ (preposition with the genitive of place description) 47.
γῆς (gen.sing.fem.of γῆ, place description) 157.
ὥσπερ (intensive particle introducing a comparative clause) 560.
εἰσὶν (3d.per.pl.pres.ind.of εἰμί, aoristic) 86.
θεοὶ (nom.pl.masc.of θεός, subject of εἰσὶν) 124.
πολλοὶ (nom.pl.masc.of πολύς, in agreement with θεοὶ) 228.
καὶ (adjunctive conjunction joining nouns) 14.
κύριοι (nom.pl.masc.of κύριος, subject of εἰσὶν) 97.
πολλοί (nom.pl.masc.of πολύς, in agreement with κύριοι) 228.

Translation - "Because despite the fact that there are many that are called gods, whether in heaven or upon earth, precisely as there are many gods and many lords. . . "

Comment: καὶ . . . εἴπερ is an intensified ascensive with causal γὰρ. "Because even if . . . κ.τ.λ. or "Because, despite the fact that. . . κ.τ.λ." εἴτε introduces the first-class condition. There are no gods in the world except the God of the Bible, but there are "so-called" gods. Hence the first-class condition. These "so-called" gods are allegedly scattered throughout heaven and earth, just as (ὥσπερ) there are many gods and lords, human and divine and many of them alleged to be divine. The sentence goes on in

Verse 6 - "But to us there is but one God, the Father, of whom are all things, and we in him; and one Lord Jesus Christ, by whom are all things, and we by him."

ἀλλ' ἡμῖν εἷς θεὸς ὁ πατήρ, ἐξ οὗ τὰ πάντα καὶ ἡμεῖς εἰς αὐτόν, καὶ εἷς κύριος Ἰησοῦς Χριστός, δι' οὗ τὰ πάντα καὶ ἡμεῖς δι' αὐτοῦ.

"yet for us there is one God, the Father, from whom are all things and for whom we exist, and one Lord, Jesus Christ, through whom are all things and through whom we exist." . . . RSV

ἀλλ' (adversative conjunction) 342.
ἡμῖν (dat.pl.masc.of ἐγώ, personal advantage) 123.
εἷς (nom.sing.masc.of εἷς, in agreement with θεὸς) 469.
θεὸς (nom.sing.masc.of θεός, subject of ἐστιν understood) 124.
ὁ (nom.sing.masc.of the article in agreement with πατήρ) 9.
πατήρ (nom.sing.masc.of πατήρ, apposition) 238.
ἐξ (preposition with the ablative of source) 19.
οὗ (abl.sing.masc.of ὅς, relative pronoun, source) 65.
τὰ (nom.pl.neut.of the article in agreement with πάντα) 9.
πάντα (nom.pl.neut.of πᾶς, subject of verb understood) 67.
καὶ (continuative conjunction) 14.
ἡμεῖς (nom.pl.masc.of ἐγώ, subject of verb understood) 123.
εἰς (preposition with the accusative, original static use) 140.
αὐτόν (acc.sing.masc.of αὐτός, static use) 16.
καὶ (continuative conjunction) 14.
εἷς (nom.sing.masc.of εἷς, in agreement with κύριος) 469.
κύριος (nom.sing.masc.of κύριος, subject of verb understood) 97.
Ἰησοῦς (nom.sing.masc.of Ἰησοῦς, apposition) 3.
Χριστός (nom.sing.masc.of Χριστός, apposition) 4.
δι' (preposition with the ablative, indirect agent) 118.
οὗ (abl.sing.masc.of ὅς, relative pronoun, indirect agent) 65.
τὰ (nom.pl.neut.of the article in agreement with πάντα) 9.
πάντα (nom.pl.neut.of πᾶς, subject of verb understood) 67.
καὶ (continuative conjunction) 14.
ἡμεῖς (nom.pl.masc.of ἐγώ, subject of verb understood) 123.
δι' (preposition with the ablative of indirect agent) 118.
αὐτοῦ (abl.sing.masc.of αὐτός, indirect agent) 16.

Translation - "But in our view there is one God, the Father, from whom are all things, and we in Him, and one Lord, Jesus Christ, through whom are all things and we by Him."

Comment: Verse 5 describes the pagan world's idea of God or gods. In verse 6 Paul states the Christian position. He has omitted all of the copulative verbs. God the Father is the source of all things - ἐξ οὗ, an ablative of source. καὶ ἡμεῖς εἰς αὐτόν equals the thought of Acts 17:28.

The question of idol offerings involved some of the Corinthians in what they thought was a compromise with idolatry, - a compromise which no Christian can afford, since all of our fortunes, past, present and future are in the one true God Who will have no competitors (Ex.20:3-6). The direct agent is God the Father and the intermediate agent is the Lord Jesus Christ, through Whose agency (δι' οὗ) all things were created (John 1:3) and by Whose resurrection life Christians live (Gal.2:20).

Thus Paul sets forth the theism of the Christian faith, which involves Father and Son as Co-creators and Jesus Christ as the Sustainer of the universe. He adds that the fortunes of the Christian are tied to the Father and His Son, Jesus Christ. The phrases εἰς αὐτόν and δι' αὐτοῦ express our relationship respectively with the Father and the Son. This is basic Christian theology, though Paul has said nothing here about the Executive of the Godhead, the Holy Spirit.

There is a hint in the language that speaks of God as the source of all things that those Corinthians who had scruples about eating meat offered to idols were being influenced by Gnosticism, with its view that evil is coeternal and coequal with good and that matter, the resident source of evil is coeval with God. This view, which became widespread at the close of the first century of the Christian era leads to asceticism, and one who is influenced by it might think of the pagan gods, which were material creations of the hands of men, as inherently evil. Thus that the animal sacrifices offered to them were tainted and should be avoided.

Though Paul will restate his view that matter is not evil *per se* and therefore that the mature Christian will have no scruples about the meat in question, he recognizes that not all Christians are able to think with him on this level.

Verse 7 - "Howbeit there is not in every man that knowledge: for some with conscience of the idol unto this hour eat it as a thing offered unto an idol; and their conscience being weak is defiled."

Ἀλλ' οὐκ ἐν πᾶσιν ἡ γνῶσις. τινὲς δὲ τῇ συνηθείᾳ ἕως ἄρτι τοῦ εἰδώλου ὡς εἰδωλόθυτον ἐσθίουσιν, καὶ ἡ συνείδησις αὐτῶν ἀσθενὴς οὖσα μολύνεται.

"However, not all possess this knowledge. But some, through being hitherto accustomed to idols, eat food as really offered to an idol; and their conscience being weak, is defiled." . . . RSV

ἀλλ' (adversative conjunction) 342
οὐκ (negative particle with the indicative) 130.
ἐν (preposition with the locative of place) 80.

πᾶσιν (loc.pl.masc.of πᾶς, place) 67.
ἡ (nom.sing.fem.of the article in agreement with γνῶσις) 9.
γνῶσις (nom.sing.fem.of γνῶσις, subject of verb understood) 1856.
τινὲς (nom.pl.masc.of τις, indefinite pronoun, subject of ἐσθίουσιν) 486.
δὲ (adversative conjunction) 11.
τῇ (instru.sing.fem.of the article in agreement with συνηθείᾳ) 9.
συνηθείᾳ (instru.sing.fem.of συνήθεια, cause) 2843.
ἕως (preposition with the genitive in a time expression) 71.
ἄρτι (temporal adverb) 320.
τοῦ (gen.sing.neut.of the article in agreement with εἰδώλου) 9.
εἰδώλου (gen.sing.neut.of εἴδωλον, reference) 3138.
ὡς (comparative particle) 128.
εἰδωλόθυτον (acc.sing.neut.of εἰδωλόθυτον, direct object of ἐσθίουσιν) 3348.
ἐσθίουσιν (3d.per.pl.pres.act.ind.of ἐσθίω, present progessive retroactive) 610.
καὶ (continuative conjunction) 14.
ἡ (nom.sing.fem.of the article in agreement with συνείδησις) 9.
συνείδησις (nom.sing.fem.of συνείδησις, subj.of μολύνεται) 3590.
αὐτῶν (gen.pl.masc.of αὐτός, possession) 16.
ἀσθενὴ (nom.sing.fem.of ἀσθενής, predicate adjective) 1551.
οὖσα (pres.act.part.nom.sing.fem.of εἰμί, adverbial, causal) 86.

#4171 μολύνεται (3d.per.sing.pres.pass.ind.of μολύνω, present progressive).

King James Version

defile - 1 Cor.8:7; Rev.3:4; 14:4.

Revised Standard Version

defile - 1 Cor.8:7; Rev.14:4.
soil - Rev.3:4.

Meaning: pollute, stain, contaminate, soil, defile. Used only figuratively in the New Testament. With reference to the compromise of conscience by engaging in eating meat previously offered to an idol - 1 Cor.8:7. Of participation in sinful practices - Rev.3:4; with special reference to adultery - Rev.14:4.

Translation - "But not everyone understands this. For some who in the past have been in the habit of worshipping the idol are now eating as though the food was offered to an idol, and because their conscience is weak they are being troubled."

Comment: ἕως ἄρτι refers to the past when some of the Corinthians were conditioned to believe that the meat they offered to the idol was eaten by the god. That this was not true is clear from verse 6. But not all of the Corinthians understood this. Although they believed that the Christian God was superior to all others, they continued to look upon the idol as a competing deity. This in fact was also false since there is no such thing as a real idol (verses 4,5). They had not yet realized that there was no moral question involved in eating such food, because idols do not really exist in the world insofar as the Christian is concerned. Thus, since their conscience was weak (causal participle in ἀσθενὴς οὖσα) due to their lack of sophistication, when they ate their consciences were troubled. The weakness of their faith was due to their lack of understanding of the truth. That is why the Great Commission orders Christian Education immediately after immersion, in order to strengthen the weak faith of the babe in Christ.

Verse 8 - "But meat commendeth us not to God:for neither, if we eat, are we the better; neither, if we eat not, are we the worse."

βρῶμα δὲ ὑμᾶς οὐ παραστήσει τῷ θεῷ. οὔτε ἐὰν μὴ φάγωμεν ὑστερούμεθα, οὔτε ἐὰν φάγωμεν περισσεύομεν.

"Food will not commend us to God. We are no worse off if we do not eat, and no better off if we do." . . . RSV

βρῶμα (nom.sing.neut.of βρῶμα, subject of παραστήσει) 1118.
δὲ (adversative conjunction) 11.
ἡμᾶς (acc.pl.masc.of ἐγώ, direct object of παραστήσει) 123.
παραστήσει (3d.per.sing.fut.act.ind.of παρίστημι, predictive) 1596.
τῳ (loc.sing.masc.of the article in agreement with θεῷ) 9.
θεῷ (loc.sing.masc.of θεῷ, with persons, after παρά in composition) 124.
οὔτε (negative copulative conjunction) 598.
ἐὰν (conditional particle with the subjunctive in a third-class condition) 363.
μὴ (negative particle with the subjunctive) 87.
φάγωμεν (1st.per.pl.aor.act.subj.of ἐσθίω, third-class condition) 610.
ὑστερούμεθα (1st.per.pl.pres.mid.ind.of ὑστερέω, third-class condition) 1302.
οὔτε (negative copulative conjunction) 598.
ἐὰν (conditional particle in a third-class condition) 363.
φάγωμεν (1st.per.pl.aor.act.subj.of ἐσθίω, third-class condition) 610.
περισσεύομεν (1st.per.pl.pres.act.ind.of περισσεύω, third-class condition) 473.

Translation - "But meat does not commend us to God. We are neither made worse if we do not eat, nor are we better if we do."

Comment: The logic of this statement follows from verses 4 and 5. There is no moral question involved one way or the other. Neither side of the dispute could claim advantage with God on the basis of his position. The eaters were no better because they ate and could not therefore claim moral superiority over their brethren. The abstainers were no worse for their abstinence. But indirectly, there is a moral question involved in the problem, which Paul explains in verse 9-13. Though he thought the abstainers were the weaker of the two groups, he warned those who ate that in the exercise of their Christian liberty they might offend their weaker brethren and cause their spiritual downfall.

Verse 9 - "But take heed lest by any means this liberty of yours become a stumbling block to them that are weak."

βλέπετε δὲ μή πως ἡ ἐξουσία ὑμῶν αὕτη πρόσκομμα γένηται τοῖς ἀσθενέσιν.

"Only take care lest this liberty of yours somehow become a stumbling block to the weak." . . . RSV

βλέπετε (2d.per.pl.pres.act.impv.of βλέπω, command) 499.
δὲ (adversative conjunction) 11.
μή (negative particle with the subjunctive in a negative sub-final clause) 87.
πως (particle with μή and the subjunctive in a negative sub-final clause) 3700.
ἡ (nom.sing.fem.of the article in agreement with ἐξουσία) 9.
ἐξουσία (nom.sing.fem.of ἐξουσία, subject of γένηται) 707.
ὑμῶν (gen.pl.masc.of σύ, possession) 104.
αὕτη (nom.sing.fem.of οὗτος, reflexive) 93.
πρόσκομμα (nom.sing.neut.of πρόσκομμα, predicate nominative) 3974.
γένηται (3d.per.sing.aor.subj.of γίνομαι, negative sub-final clause) 113.
τοῖς (dat.pl.masc.of the article in agreement with ἀσθενέσιν) 9.
ἀσθενέσιν (dat.pl.masc.of ἀσθενής, personal disadvantage) 1551.

Translation - "But be careful lest by some chance your liberty itself becomes a stumbling block to the weak."

Comment: μή πως (in some manuscripts written μήπως) after βλέπετε, the imperative, introduces the aorist subjunctive in a negative sub-final clause (purpose/result). *Cf.* 2 Cor.11:3. Paul made the same point in Romans 14:13,20. Obedience to this precept is an exercise of Christian charity in its highest expression. It calls for a Christian of superior intelligence and spiritual development to give up pleasures that do not involve him in compromise with the moral standards of the gospel of Christ in order to prevent his participation in them to become the cause for a less enlightened Christian to fall by the wayside.

There was no possible reason why a Christian should not eat meat, regardless of its previous history in participation in heathen religious exercises, since the heathen worship was an exercise in futility. Yet, because some other Christian, due to an aberrated outlook, thought it was wrong, and would stumble over what to him was inconsistency and perhaps be dragged down to deeper sin, the more enlightened saint surrenders his liberty.

The error of the weak is that he is giving status to an idol which deserves no status. The error of the strong Christian is his inability or unwillingness to recognize the problem of his weaker brother and his decision to exercise his liberty in Christ regardless of the consequences to his brother.

A pastor gave up golf, a favorite form of relaxation on his day off, because a troublesome woman in his church, a true Christian, no doubt, but one with an exaggerated conception of her own spirituality, objected to the game. The question arises as to what that pastor should have done if she realized that in the exercise of this ploy she could make even more unreasonable and arrogant demands upon his life. Suppose that she objected to the color of his necktie? Or suppose that she owned stock in General Motors and therefore objected because he drove a Ford? Can not this principle, which is a sound one when it is put in practice because of the sincere convictions of the babe in Christ, be carried to extremes? Babes in Christ should not exercise dictatorial power over more mature saints. What obligation does the Christian who can eat meat, or play golf or wear a necktie without self-condemnation owe to the babe in Christ who thinks that those things are wrong?

Verse 10 - "For if any man see thee which has knowledge sit at meat in the idol's temple, shall not the conscience of him who is weak be emboldened to eat those things which are offered to idols;"

ἐὰν γάρ τις ἴδῃ σὲ τὸν ἔχοντα γνῶσιν ἐν εἰδωλείῳ κατακείμενον, οὐχὶ ἡ συνείδησις αὐτοῦ ἀσθενοῦς ὄντος οἰκοδομηθήσεται εἰς τὸ τὰ εἰδωλόθυτα ἐσθίειν;

ἐὰν (conditional particle with the subjunctive in a third-class condition) 363.
γάρ (inferential conjunction) 105.
τις (nom.sing.masc.of τις, indefinite pronoun, subject of ἴδῃ) 486.
ἴδῃ (3d.per.sing.2d.aor.act.subj.of ὁράω, third-class condition) 144.
σε (acc.sing.masc.of σύ, direct object of ἴδῃ) 104.
τὸν (acc.sing.masc.of the article in agreement with ἔχοντα) 9.
ἔχοντα (pres.act.part.acc.sing.masc.of ἔχω, substantival, in apposition) 82.
γνῶσιν (acc.sing.fem.of γνῶσις, direct object of ἔχοντα) 1856.
ἐν (preposition with the locative of place) 80.

#4172 εἰδωλείῳ (loc.sing.neut.of εἰδωλεῖον, place).

King James Version

idol's temple - 1 Cor.8:10.

Revised Standard Version

idol's temple - 1 Cor.8:10.

Meaning: A temple consecrated to idols. In Corinth - 1 Cor.8:10.

κατακείμενον (pres.mid.part.acc.sing.masc.of κατάκειμαι, adverbial, circumstantial) 2065.
οὐχὶ (negative particle with the indicative in rhetorical question, which expects a positive reply) 130.
ἡ (nom.sing.masc.of the article in agreement with συνείδησις) 9.
συνείδησις (nom.sing.fem.of συνείδησις, subject of οἰκοδομηθήσεται) 3590.
αὐτοῦ (gen.sing.masc.of αὐτός, possession) 16.
ἀσθενοῦς (gen.sing.masc.of ἀσθενής, predicate adjective in a genitive absolute) 1551.

ὄντος (pres.part.gen.sing.masc.of εἰμί, genitive absoulte, adverbial, causal) 86.

οἰκοδομηθήσεται (3d.per.sing.fut.pass.ind.of οἰκοδομέω, deliberative) 694.

εἰς (preposition with the accusative, result) 140.

τὸ (acc.sing.neut.of the article in agreement with ἐσθίειν, result) 9.

τὰ (acc.pl.neut.of the article in agreement with εἰδωλόθυτα) 9.

εἰδωλόθυτα (acc.pl.neut.of εἰδωλόθυτα, direct object of ἐσθίειν) 3348.

ἐσθίειν (pres.act.inf.of ἐσθίω, verbal use, accusative of result) 610.

Translation - "For if any one sees you, the one who has understanding, sitting down in an idol's temple will not his conscience, since it is weak, be emboldened to eat the things offered to idols?"

Comment: γάρ is inferential, as Paul moves on to his conclusion. ἐὰν . . . ἴδῃ is a third-class condition with a rhetorical question in the apodosis which expects a positive reply. Note τὸν ἔχοντα γνῶσιν, the substantival participle (serving as a noun) in apposition to the second personal pronoun σε - an interesting construction since it is not often found in the New Testament. But it is excellent Greek. Who is this Christian whom somebody (τις) sees? He is one who has knowledge. What is he doing when he is observed? The circumstantial participle κατακείμενον tells us that he was seen reclining (sitting down) in an idol's temple. All of that is the object of ἴδῃ. If such occurs it is logical to ask the rhetorical question in the apodosis. And it expects one to reply by saying, "Yes." Note the deliberative future in οἰκοδομηθήσεται. Will not his conscience be built up with the result that he will eat things offered to an idol? We have an interesting genitive absolute with the adverbial causal participle in ἀσθενοῦς ὄντος. Why will the young Christian be seduced to violate his conscience? Because he is weak. And what will be the result? He will do that which he believes is wrong. The infinitive in the accusative case is introduced by εἰς and it speaks of the result. Stephen used this same construction (εἰς and the accusative verbal infinitive) to speak of result in Acts 7:19. The result of the Egyptian order to throw the boy babies into the Nile River was that they died. Here the result that follows when a weak Christian sees a strong one eating in an idol's temple is that he too will do so. For the strong Christian there is no problem of conscience. For the weak Christian there is. The mature Christian has a sophisticated understanding of the situation. He is not there to worship the idol. He knows that the idol is nothing but sticks and stones. He worships only God the Father, God the Son, Jesus Christ and God the Holy Spirit. So why is he there? To eat a steak! Prime quality because that is the only quality that the pagans would dare offer to the idol? The Greek and Roman deities demanded the best. Zeus and Jupiter would settle for nothing less.

But if the weak Christian, encouraged by what he sees, goes in and eats he is sinning, not because of what he eats or where he eats it, but because he doubts when he eats (Rom.14:22,23). Thus the exercise of Christian liberty, which does not involve one personally in sin, is the sociological cause of involving the weaker Christian in behavior which, for him, is sin. Thus indirectly one is militating against the spiritual development of the weaker brother. And this is sin. God has other places for the mature Christian (Gal.6:2). If he wants to eat the superior steak let him buy it, take it home and eat it.

Verse 11 - "And through thy knowledge shall the weak brother perish, for whom Christ died?"

ἀπόλλυται γὰρ ὁ ἀσθενῶν ἐν τῇ σῇ γνώσει, ὁ ἀδελφὸς δι' ὃν Χριστὸς ἀπέθανεν;

"And so by your knowledge this weak man is destroyed, the brother for whom Christ died." . . . RSV

ἀπόλλυται (3d.per.sing.pres.ind.pass.of ἀπόλλυμι, deliberative) 208.

γὰρ (inferential conjunction) 105.

ὁ (nom.sing.masc.of the article in agreement with ἀσθενῶν) 9.

ἀσθενῶν (pres.part.nom.sing.masc.of ἀσθενέω, substantival, subject of ἀπόλλυται) 857.

ἐν (preposition with the instrumental of cause) 80.

τῇ (instru.sing.fem.of the article in agreement with γνώσει) 9.

σῇ (instru.sing.fem.of σός, possessive pronoun, in agreement with γνώσει) 646.

γνώσει (instru.sing.fem.of γνῶσις, cause) 1856.

ὁ (nom.sing.masc.of the article in agreement with ἀδελφὸς) 9.

ἀδελφὸς (nom.sing.masc.of ἀδελφός, apposition) 15.

δι' (preposition with the accusative, cause) 118.

ὃν (acc.sing.masc.of ὅς, relative pronoun, cause, "if behalf of") 65.

Χριστὸς (nom.sing.masc.of Χριστός, subject of ἀπέθανεν) 4.

ἀπέθανεν (3d.per.sing.aor.act.ind.of ἀποθνήσκω, constative) 774.

Translation - "Thus the weak man is destroyed, because of your knowledge - the brother for whom Christ died."

Comment: γὰρ is inferential and the context points the result back to verse 10. So we translate, "Thus." ὁ ἀδελφὸς is in apposition to the participial substantive ὁ ἀσθενῶν. The student should examine #208 and run all of the references where this verb occurs. Note that the context dictates the sense in which the word is used. Note our comment on other passages where ἀπόλλυμι occurs. The context here makes it clear that Paul does not mean that the weak brother's soul is lost, but that his growth in grace is arrested and his life of Christian usefulness is brought to an end. As long as he thinks that eating meat in the temple of an idol is sin, then for him, indeed it is sin (Rom.14:22,23). The weak unsophisticated Christian is the type who would say, "If he may eat meat, so may I." The proper course for the knowledgeable Christian is to refrain from eating meat until he has carried on a course in Christian education with the weak brother. The order of the Great Commission is "disciple, . . . immerse in water, . . . teach" (Mt.28:18-20). Then when the weak brother has grown up they both can enjoy liberty in Christ. Meanwhile the mature Christian has no choice but to make the sacrifice. He must remember that he is a member of the Body of Christ of which his weak brother is also a member. The eye of the body does not strengthen the body by causing damage to the little fingernail.

Verse 12 - "But when ye sin so against the brethren, and wound their weak conscience, ye sin against Christ."

οὕτως δὲ ἁμαρτάνοντες εἰς τοὺς ἀδελφοὺς καὶ τύπτοντες αὐτῶν τὴν συνείδησιν ἀσθενοῦσαν εἰς Χριστὸν ἁμαρτάνετε.

"Thus, sinning against your brethren and wounding their conscience when it is weak, you sin against Christ."

οὕτως (demonstrative adverb) 74.

δὲ (adversative conjunction) 11.

ἁμαρτάνοντες (pres.act.part.nom.pl.masc.of ἁμαρτάνω, adverbial, temporal, modal) 1260.

εἰς (preposition with the accusative, opposition) 140.

τοὺς (acc.pl.masc.of the article in agreement with ἀδελφοὺς) 9.

ἀδελφοὺς (acc.pl.masc.of ἀδελφός, opposition) 15.

καὶ (adjunctive conjunction joining participles) 14.

τύπτοντες (pres.act.part.nom.pl.masc.of τύπτω, adverbial, temporal, modal) 1526.

αὐτῶν (gen.pl.masc.of αὐτός, possession) 16.

τὴν (acc.sing.fem.of the article in agreement with συνείδησιν) 9.

συνείδησιν (acc.sing.fem.of συνείδησις, direct object of τύπτοντες) 3590.

ἀσθενοῦσαν (pres.act.part.acc.sing.fem.of ἀσθενέω, adjectival, predicate position, restrictive, in agreement with συνείδησιν) 857.

εἰς (preposition with the accusative, opposition) 140.

Χριστὸν (acc.sing.masc.of Χριστός, opposition) 4.

ἁμαρτάνετε (2d.per.pl.pres.act.ind.of ἁμαρτάνω, present progressive) 1260.

Translation - "But when you sin against your brothers like this and confuse their conscience which is already weak, you are sinning against Christ."

Comment: οὕτως goes back to verse 10 for explanation. The participles ἁμαρτάνοντες and τύπτοντες are adverbial, both temporal and modal. When and by means of sinning against the brethren and wounding their conscience, the mature Christian is sinning against Christ. Note the adjectival participle ἀσθενοῦσαν which modifies συνείδησιν. The conscience of the babe in Christ is already weak, since he has been saved only a short time. We can also think of the other participles as causal - when, by means of and because . . . .

When one eats meat in the idol's temple, even though for him no sin is involved, he is sinning against Christ because, when and by means of his act he is sinning against his weaker brother and wounding his weak conscience. His conscience is weak because he fails to understand Paul's philosophy in verses 4 and 5. (Mt.25:40,45; Rom.12:4,5; 1 Cor.6:15; 12:12ff). Paul concludes this section with

Verse 13 - "Wherefore, if meat make my brother to offend, I will eat no flesh

while the world standeth, lest I make my brother to offend."

διόπερ εἰ βρῶμα σκανδαλίζει τὸν ἀδελφόν μου, οὐ μὴ φάγω κρέα εἰς τὸν αἰῶνα, ἵνα μὴ τὸν ἀδελφόν μου σκανδαλίσω.

"Therefore, if food is a cause of my brother's falling, I will never eat meat, lest I cause my brother to fall." . . . RSV

#4173 διόπερ (intensive inferential conjunction).

King James Version

wherefore - 1 Cor.8:13; 10:14; 14:13.

Revised Standard Version

therefore - 1 Cor.8:13; 10:14; 14:13.

Meaning: A combination of διό (#1622) and intensive περ. An enclitic particle of strong inference. It introduces a conclusion where the certainty of the result is especially to be emphasized. A stronger word than διό- 1 Cor.8:13; 10:14; 14:13.

εἰ (conditional particle in a first-class condition) 337.
βρῶμα (nom.sing.neut.of βρῶμα, subject of σκανδαλίζει) 1118.
σκανδαλίζει (3d.per.sing.pres.act.ind.of σκανδαλίζω, customary) 503.
τὸν (acc.sing.masc.of the article in agreement with ἀδελφόν) 9.
ἀδελφόν (acc.sing.masc.of ἀδελφός, direct object of σκανδαλίζει) 15.
μου (gen.sing.masc.of ἐγώ, relationship) 123.
οὐ (negative particle with μὴ and the subjunctive in emphatic negation) 130.
μὴ (negative particle with οὐ and the subjunctive in emphatic negation) 87.
φάγω (1st.per.sing.2d.aor.act.subj.of ἐσθίω, emphatic negation) 610.
κρέα (acc.sing.neut.of κρέας, direct object of φάγω) 4043.
εἰς (preposition with the accusative, time extent) 140.
τὸν (acc.sing.masc.of the article in agreement with αἰών, time extent) 1002.
αἰῶνα (acc.sing.masc.of αἰών, time extent) 1002.
ἵνα (conjunction with the subjunctive in a negative purpose clause) 114.
μὴ (negative particle with the subjunctive in a negative purpose clause) 87.
τὸν (acc.sing.masc.of the article in agreement with ἀδελφόν) 9.
ἀδελφόν (acc.sing.masc.of ἀδελφός, direct object of σκανδαλίσω) 15.
μου (gen.sing.masc.of ἐγώ, relationship) 123.
σκανδαλίσω (1st.per.sing.aor.act.subj.of σκανδαλίζω, negative purpose) 503.

Translation - "Therefore if meat is offending my brother I will never again eat flesh sacrificed to idols until eternity, lest I offend my brother."

Comment: Paul is not saying that he is sure that his meat will offend his brother, but the first-class condition assumes for the sake of the argument that the premise in the protasis is true. It may or may not be true, but if in fact it is true then Paul's conclusion in the apodosis is emphatic. οὐ μὴ φάγω εἰς τὸν αἰῶνα is emphatic negation with an infinite time extent. After all, is it too much to ask that we give up meat, in order to edify the Body of Christ of which we ourselves are also a living member? On the other hand the overscrupulous and hypersensitive saint would help to edify the Body of Christ if he would dedicate his mind to Christ as well as his body and grow up to the point where he would determine to grow in grace regardless of what other Chrisians do or refrain from doing.

Thus far in 1 Corinthians Paul has dealt with the carnality of the Corinthians as revealed in their hero worship, immorality in the church and their unconcern for it, their practice of submitting legal disputes to the secular courts, instructions with reference to marriage and sex and advice about eating food previously offered to idols. In chapter 9 he answers critics in the church who apparently had challenged his standing as an Apostle, asserts his right to marry, though he was not married and claims the right to accept money in return for his ministry although he boasts that he has never taken money for himself from them.

The Rights of an Apostle

(1 Corinthians 9:1-27)

1 Cor.9:1 - "Am I not an apostle? Am I not free? Have I not seen Jesus Christ our Lord? Are not ye my work in the Lord?"

Οὐκ εἰμὶ ἐλεύθερος; οὐκ εἰμὶ ἀπόστολος; οὐχὶ Ἰησοῦν τὸν κύριον ἡμῶν ἑώρακα; οὐ τὸ ἔργον μου ὑμεῖς ἐστε ἐν κυρίῳ;

"Am I not free? Am I not an apostle? Have I not seen Jesus our Lord? Are not you my workmanship in the Lord?"

Οὐκ (negative particle with the indicative in rhetorical question expecting a positive reply) 130.

εἰμὶ (1st.per.sing.pres.ind.of εἰμί, aoristic) 86.

ἐλεύθερος (nom.sing.masc.of ἐλεύθερος, predicate adjective) 1245.

οὐκ (negative particle with the indicative in rhetorical question expecting a positive reply) 130.

εἰμὶ (1st.per.sing.pres.ind.of εἰμί, aoristic) 86.

ἀπόστολος (nom.sing.masc.of ἀπόστολος, predicate nominative) 844.

οὐχὶ (negative particle with the indicative in rhetorical question expecting a positive reply) 130.

Ἰησοῦν (acc.sing.masc.of Ἰησοῦς, direct object of ἑώρακα) 3.

τὸν (acc.sing.masc.of the article in agreement with κύριον) 9.

κύριον (acc.sing.masc.of κύριος, direct object of ἑώρακα) 97.

ἡμῶν (gen.pl.masc.of ἐγώ, relationship) 123.

ἑώρακα (1st.per.sing.perf.act.ind.of ὁράω, consummative) 144.

οὐ (negative particle with the indicative in rhetorical question expecting a positive reply) 130.

τὸ (nom.sing.neut.of the article in agreement with ἔργον) 9.

ἔργον (nom.sing.neut.of ἔργον, predicate nominative) 460.

μου (gen.sing.masc.of ἐγώ, possession) 123.

ὑμεῖς (nom.pl.masc.of σύ, subject of ἐστε) 104.

ἐστε (2d.per.pl.pres.ind.of εἰμί, present progressive retroactive) 86.

ἐν (preposition with the locative of sphere) 80.

κυρίῳ (loc.sing.masc .of κύριος, sphere) 97.

Translation - "I am free am I not? I am an Apostle am I not? Have I not seen Jesus our Lord? You have been (and are) my work in the Lord have you not?"

Comment: These four questions are rhetorical and may be answered either with "Yes" or "No" but the anticipated answer is "Yes." Paul was so sure of his ground that he knew that the Corinthians would not dare to deny what he says. Thus the rhetorical question is a literary form of strong affirmation.

Apparently the Corinthians who had asked him about sex and marriage, adjudication in secular courts and eating meat offered to idols, had also raised some questions about Paul's authority to preach as did the other Apostles. The fact that he was not one of the original twelve chosen by Jesus (Mt.10:1-5) and that he had not been with Jesus, nor even had seen Him before the ascension, was also alluded to. Paul now writes to defend his position as an Apostle of Jesus Christ, who, as such was charged with the responsibility of setting local church policy in the period before the New Testament literature was written. Did he possess the gifts of knowledge and prophecy (1 Cor.13:8) which were so necessary before the New Testament was finished and due to be withdrawn when it was finished?

He was free. He was an Apostle (Acts 9:15; 22:14,15; 26:15-19). He had indeed seen the Lord, though he does not reveal the details of the story to them until he wrote the second Corinthian letter (2 Cor.12:1-5).

Furthermore the very existence of the Corinthian church, made up of Christians, most of whom were saved under his ministry (Acts 18:1-11) was evidence that God had endowed Paul with Apostolic power and authority. We can construe ἐν κυρίῳ, either in the sense of mystical association with the Lord or as a locative of sphere. Paul's connection with the Corinthians was in the sphere of their Christian experience, though he could have established connections with them in other spheres - tent making or lectures in Roman and Jewish law, fields in which he was competent.

His point in the last clause of verse 1 is reemphasized in verse 2.

Verse 2 - "If I be not an apostle unto others yet doubtless I am to you: for the seal of mine apostleship are ye in the Lord."

εἰ ἄλλοις οὐκ εἰμὶ ἀπόστολος, ἀλλά γε ὑμῖν εἰμι. ἡ γὰρ σφραγίς μου τῆς ἀποστολῆς ὑμεῖς ἐστε ἐν κυρίῳ.

"If to others I am not an apostle, at least I am to you; for you are the seal of my apostleship in the Lord." . . . RSV

εἰ (conditional particle in a first-class condition) 337.

ἄλλοις (dat.pl.masc.of ἄλλος, personal advantage) 198.

οὐκ (negative particle with the indicative) 130.

εἰμὶ (1st.per.sing.pres.ind.of εἰμί, present progressive retroactive) 86.

ἀπόστολος (nom.sing.masc.of ἀπόστολος, predicate nominative) 844.

ἀλλὰ (adversative conjunction) 342.

γε (intensive particle) 2449.

ὑμῖν (dat.pl.masc.of σύ, personal advantage) 104.

εἰμι (1st.per.sing.pres.ind.of εἰμί, present progressive retroactive) 86.

ἡ (nom.sing.fem.of the article in agreement with σφραγίς) 9.

σφραγίς (nom.sing.fem.of σφραγίς, predicate nominative) 3886.

μου (gen.sing.masc.of ἐγώ, possession) 123.

τῆς (gen.sing.fem.of the article in agreement with ἀποστολῆς) 9.

ἀποστολῆς (gen.sing.fem.of ἀποστολή, definition) 2954.

ὑμεῖς (nom.pl.masc.of σύ, subject of ἐστε) 104.

ἐστε (2d.per.pl.pres.ind.of εἰμί, present progressive retroactive) 86.

ἐν (preposition with the instrumental, association) 80.

κυρίῳ (instru.sing.masc.of κύριος, association) 97.

Translation - *"If I am not an Apostle for others, in fact, I am for you, because you are the seal of my apostleship in the Lord."*

Comment: Paul's critics in Corinth might have made out a more plausible case against him if they had cited his ministry in Athens. The evidence for his divine appointment was probably more abundant in Corinth than in any other place. The Corinthians themselves were his proof.

Verse 3 - "Mine answer to them that do examine me is this,"

Ἡ ἐμὴ ἀπολογία τοῖς ἐμὲ ἀνακρίνουσίν ἐστιν αὕτη,

"This is my defense to those who would examine me." . . . RSV

Ἡ (nom.sing.fem.of the article in agreement with ἀπολογία) 9.

ἐμὴ (nom.sing.fem.of ἐμός, in agreement with ἀπολογία) 1267.

ἀπολογία (nom.sing.fem.of ἀπολογία, subject of ἐστιν) 3573.

τοῖς (dat.pl.masc.of the article in agreement with ἀνακρίνουσίν) 9.

ἐμὲ (acc.sing.masc.of ἐμός, direct object of ἀνακρίνουσίν) 1267.

ἀνακρίνουσίν (pres.act.part.dat.pl.masc.of ἀνακρίνω, substantival, indirect object) 2837.

ἐστιν (3d.per.sing.pres.ind.of εἰμί, aoristic) 86.

αὕτη (nom.sing.fem.of οὗτος, predicate nominative) 93.

Translation - *"My answer to those who are investigating me is this . . ."*

Comment: Since ἀνακρίνω (#2837) means "to do research," "conduct an inquiry," the word "defense" for ἀπολογία (#3573) is too strong. No one in Corinth (at least not according to the text) was attacking Paul. Some however who had more confidence in Apollos or Cephas (1 Cor.1:12,13) were investigating him. To them he offers his rationale, designed to prove that he did indeed have Christ's commission to carry on his ministry as an Apostle.

This problem of authentication of an Apostle's authority disappeared when the canon of New Testament scripture became complete at the end of the first century. The last of the Apostles was John, the author of the Revelation, the Gospel and his three Epistles. There was no further need for Apostles after that. There are no Apostles now, nor has there been since those whom Jesus chose died. Jesus chose thirteen - one a devil "in order that the Scriptures might be fulfilled" (John 6:70,71; 13:18,19; 17:12). Saul of Tarsus was the last Apostle called, the divine choice to fill the position vacated by Judas Iscariot. *Cf.* our comment on Acts 1:15-26.

To these twelve men - Paul and the eleven who remained at the Last Supper after Judas left - the Holy Spirit gave special gifts and authority, in order that they might guide the church in its inchoate stage, until they had written the New Testament. Then (after the New Testament was complete) the gifts of prophecy and knowledge, the sources of necessary enlightenement and guidance were phased out (1 Cor.13:8-11 on which see comment). The Apostles were all-important as long as they were needed. Their ability to guide the early churches was indispensable. Then their function as Apostles was terminated so far as the church age is concerned. In the kingdom age they will serve in judiciary capacities (Mt.19:28; Lk.22:30). When the Apostles had finished their courses (2 Tim.4:6-7; Eph.2:10; Phil.1:6) they died. But during the Apostolic age, it was important for the churches to know who was and who was not an Apostle. Thus God vindicated them in the eyes of the churches.

Vindication of apostleship in the first century was far more important than ordination since. The Holy Spirit gives specific gifts to all saints (1 Cor.12:1-11; Rom.12:6-8), and formal ordination as carried on by the modern church confers no powers not possessed by the laity as a whole. Ordination to the gospel ministry is a function of the local church (or in the case of the episcopacies, of a more prestigious church council) which presumably certifies that the candidate under examination has demonstrated adequate proof of conversion, call to the ministry and some knowledge of Christian theology. Dwight L. Moody was never formally ordained to the ministry, nor was Charles Haddon Spurgeon. The laity is free to study the completed canon of Scripture under the guidance of the Holy Spirit and witness to the grace of God as revealed in the gospel of Christ. An unhealthy exaltation of the ordained clergy can result in an equally unhealthy reduction in the dignity and prestige of the laity - an unfortunate chain of events which results in the reduction of efficiency of both the unduly exalted preacher and the unduly suppressed lay person. Lay people who do not understand this are induced to neglect Bible study on the ground that that is the exclusive function of the preacher. Thus he believes only what his pastor tells him is the truth and spends no time investigating for himself. Thus he becomes the intellectual slave of his pastor. This is not what the Bereans did (Acts 17:11). When a backslidden and/or deistic body of deacons/preachers lay their empty hands on the empty head of a deist who wishes to pose as a Christian minister, they have conferred upon him and he has received no special powers. But it is likely that a diabolical inflation of egos has been experienced by all hands on board.

Verse 4 - "Have we not power to eat and to drink?"

μὴ οὐκ ἔχομεν ἐξουσίαν φαγεῖν καὶ πεῖν;

"Do we not have the right to our food and drink?" . . . RSV

μὴ (negative particle with the sentence) 87.
οὐκ (negative particle with the verb, indicative, in rhetorical question expecting a positive reply) 130.
ἔχομεν (1st.per.pl.pres.act.ind.of ἔχω, rhetorical question) 82.
ἐξουσίαν (acc.sing.fem.of ἐξουσία, direct object of ἔχομεν) 707.
φαγεῖν (aor.act.inf.of ἐσθίω, noun use, in apposition with ἐξουσίαν) 610.
καὶ (adjunctive conjunction joining infinitives) 14.
πεῖν (aor.act.inf.of πίνω, noun use, in apposition with ἐξουσίαν) 611.

Translation - "Do we not have a right to eat and to drink?"

Comment: μὴ is the interrogative particle of the sentence. οὐκ is joined to the verb ἔχομεν. The question expects a positive reply. "But in interrogative (independent) sentences οὐ always expects an answer 'yes.' The Greek here draws a distinction between οὐ and μή that is rather difficult to reproduce in English. The use of a negative in the question seems naturally to expect the answer 'yes,' since the negative is challenged by the question. This applies to οὐ. . . . Οὐ in questions corresponds to the Latin *nonne*. Cf. Mt.7:22, οὐ τῷ σῷ ὀνόματι ἐπροφητεύσαν κτλ., where οὐ is the negative of the whole long question, and is not repeated with the other verbs. . . . In Lu.18:7, οὐ μὴ ποιήσῃ —καὶ μακροθυμεῖ ἐπ' αὐτοῖς we come near having οὐ μή in a question with the present indicative as well as with the aorist subjunctive. In a question like μὴ οὐκ ἔχομεν (1 Cor.9:4) οὐ is the negative of the verb, while μή is the negative of the sentence. Cf. Ro.10:18,19." (Robertson, *Grammar*, 1157, 1158). Note that we have ellided parts of the Robertson statement which are not directly pertinent to 1 Cor.9:4. The student may wish to follow Robertson's discussion in depth.

Apparently Paul is defending his right to accept at least enough financial remuneration from his ministry to pay for his food and drink. It should be obvious that no one was challenging his right to eat and drink. He also asserts his right to marry in the event that he should choose to do so, in

Verse 5 - "Have we not power to lead about a sister a wife, as well as other apostles, and as the brethren of the Lord, and Cephas?"

μὴ οὐκ ἔχομεν ἐξουσίαν ἀδελφὴν γυναῖκα περιάγειν, ὡς καὶ οἱ λοιποὶ ἀπόστολοι καὶ οἱ αδελφοὶ τοῦ κυρίου καὶ Κηφᾶς;

"Do we not have the right to be accompanied by a wife, as the other apostles and the brothers of the Lord and Cephas?" . . . RSV

μή (negative particle with the sentence) 87.

οὐκ (negative particle with the indicative in rhetorical question expecting a positive reply) 130.

ἔχομεν (1st.per.pl.pres.act.ind.of ἔχω, present progressive retroactive, rhetorical question) 82.

ἐξουσίαν (acc.sing.fem.of ἐξουσία, direct object of ἔχομεν) 707.

ἀδελφήν (acc.sing.fem.of ἀδελφή, direct object of περιάγειν) 1025.

γυναῖκα (acc.sing.fem.of γυνή, apposition) 103.

περιάγειν (pres.act.inf.of περιάγω, noun use, in apposition with ἐξουσίαν) 402.

ὡς (comparative particle) 128.

καί (adjunctive conjunction joining substantives) 14.

οἱ (nom.pl.masc.of the article in agreement with ἀπόστολοι) 9.

λοιποί (nom.pl.masc.of λοιπός, in agreement with ἀπόστολοι) 1402.

ἀπόστολοι (nom.pl.masc.of ἀπόστολος, subject of ἔχουσιν understood) 844.

καί (adjunctive conjunction joining nouns) 14.

οἱ (nom.pl.masc.of the article in agreement with ἀδελφοί) 9.

ἀδελφοί (nom.pl.masc.of ἀδελφός, subject of ἔχουσιν understood) 15.

τοῦ (gen.sing.masc.of the article in agreement with κυρίου) 9.

κυρίου (gen.sing.masc.of κύριος, relationship) 97.

καί (adjunctive conjunction joining nouns) 14.

Κηφᾶς (nom.sing.masc.of Κηφᾶς, subject of ἔχει understood) 1964.

Translation - "Do we not have a right to escort a Christian wife as do the other Apostles and the brothers of our Lord and Cephas?"

Comment: μή οὐκ again as in verse 4. Apparently someone in Corinth had pointed to the fact that although Peter, the other Apostles and the half-brothers of Jesus were married, Paul was not and had raised the question as to why this should be so, as if there was something in Paul's background that prevented him from getting married. Though he had written an entire chapter to show that he was a better servant of the Lord as a bachelor, he now defends his right to marry if he chose to do so, subject only to the restriction that his wife, if he took one, should be a Christian (ἀδελφήν). That ἀδελφήν here means a Christian sister in the Lord and not a sibling is obvious. Otherwise Paul would be defending his right to live in incest.

It should be pointed out that, at least in Cephas' case, we have evidence that he was probably married before he became a Christian (Mt.8:14,15).

He next defends his right and that of Barnabas to quit his job and live off of the love gifts which came to them as preachers of the gospel.

Verse 6 - "Or I only and Barnabas, have not we power to forebear working?"

ἢ μόνος ἐγὼ καὶ Βαρναβᾶς οὐκ ἔχομεν ἐξουσίαν μὴ ἐργάζεσθαι;

"Or is it only Barnabas and I who have no right to refrain from working for a living?" . . . RSV

ἤ (disjunctive) 465.

μόνος (nom.sing.masc.of μόνος, adverbial) 339.

ἐγώ (nom.sing.masc.of ἐγώ, nominative absolute) 123.

καί (adjunctive conjunction joining substantives) 14.

Βαρναβᾶς (nom.sing.masc.of Βαρναβᾶς, nominative absolute) 3047.

οὐκ (negative particle with the indicative in rhetorical question expecting a positive reply) 130.

ἔχομεν (1st.per.pl.pres.act.ind.of ἔχω, present progressive retroactive, rhetorical question) 82.

ἐξουσίαν (acc.sing.fem.of ἐξουσία, direct object of ἔχομεν) 707.

μή (negative particle with the infinitive) 87.

ἐργάζεσθαι (pres.mid.inf.of ἐργάζομαι, in apposition with ἐξουσίαν) 691.

Translation - "Or is it only Barnabas and I that have no right to give up working for a living?"

Comment: The question is sarcasm as Paul expects the Corinthians to say, "Yes." Apparently the other Apostles and the half-brothers of Jesus accepted love gifts of money and hospitality in exchange for their ministry of preaching and teaching the Word. Paul devotes verses 7 - 15 to an exposition of his attitude toward the question, although he also boasted that he had chosen not to take money (Acts 20:33-35).

Verse 7 - "Who goeth a warfare any time at his own charges? Who planteth a vineyard, and eateth not of the fruit thereof? Or who feedeth a flock, and eateth not of the milk of the flock?"

τίς στρατεύεται ἰδίοις ὀφωνίοις ποτέ; τίς φυτεύει ἀμπελῶνα καὶ τὸν καρπὸν αὐτοῦ οὐκ ἐσθίει; ἢ τίς ποιμαίνει καὶ ἐκ τοῦ γάλακτος τῆς ποίμνης οὐκ ἐσθίει;

"Who serves as a soldier at his own expense? Who plants a vineyard without eating of its fruit? Who tends a flock without getting some of the milk?" ... *RSV*

τίς (nom.sing.masc.of τίς, interrogative pronoun, direct question) 281.

στρατεύεται (3d.per.sing.pres.mid.ind.of στρατεύω, customary) 1944.

ἰδίοις (loc.pl.neut.of ἴδιος, accompanying circumstance) 778.

ὀφωνίοις (loc.pl.neut.of ὀφώνιον, accompanying circumstance) 1947.

ποτέ (enclitic temporal particle) 2399.

τίς (nom.sing.masc.of τίς, interrogative pronoun, subject of φυτεύει, direct question) 281.

φυτεύει (3d.per.sing.pres.act.ind.of φυτεύω, customary) 1154.

ἀμπελῶνα (acc.sing.masc.of ἀμπελών, direct object of φυτεύει) 1316.

καί (adversative conjunction) 14.

τόν (acc.sing.masc.of the article in agreement with καρπόν) 9.

καρπόν (acc.sing.masc.of καρπός, direct object of ἐσθίει) 284.

αὐτοῦ (gen.sing.masc.of αὐτός, possession) 16.

οὐκ (negative particle with the indicative) 130.

ἐσθίει (3d.per.sing.pres.act.ind.of ἐσθίω, customary) 610.

ἤ (disjunctive) 465.

τίς (nom.sing.masc.of τίς, interrogative pronoun, direct question) 281.

ποιμαίνει (3d.per.sing.pres.act.ind.of ποιμαίνω, customary) 164.

ποίμνων (acc.sing.fem.of ποίμην, direct object of ποιμαίνει) 1580.

καὶ (adversative conjunction) 14.

ἐκ (preposition with the ablative of source) 19.

τοῦ (abl.sing.neut.of the article in agreement with γάλακτος) 9.

γάλακτος (abl.sing.neut.of γάλα, source) 4114.

τῆς (gen.sing.fem.of the article in agreement with ποίμνης) 9.

ποίμνης (gen.sing.fem.of ποίμνη, description) 1580.

οὐκ (negative particle with the indicative) 130.

ἐσθίει (3d.per.sing.pres.act.ind.of ἐσθίω, customary) 610.

Translation - *"Who ever goes into battle carrying rations which he bought for himself? Who plants a vineyard but does not eat of its fruit? Or who shepherds a flock but does not drink some of the milk?"*

Comment: These are rhetorical questions, the answer to each of which is "No one." *Cf.* #1947 for our justification for the translation. "At his own expense" is general and true to Paul's point, but our translation is closer to the original Greek. The verbs are customary presents. It is customary for the government to feed the soldiers and for the farmer and the shepherd to eat the fruit and drink the milk. Note the cognate accusative in ποιμαίνει ποίμνην. The antecedent of αὐτοῦ may be ἀμπελῶνα or it may be possessive with reference to the farmer who planted the vineyard. In either case the thought is the same.

Paul is defending the right of a preacher to derive a living wage from his ministry. He presses the point through verse 15. *Cf.* 2 Cor.10:3 and 1 Tim.1:18 where στρατεύω (#1944) refers to the spiritual warfare that the Christian wages against Satan. Thus Paul's analogy is apt. *Cf.* 2 Cor.11:8 for ὀφώνιον (#1947) in this sense. One of those churches was Philippi (Phil.4:8). The vineyard analogy is supported by 1 Cor.3:6,7,8 where φυτεύω (#1154) occurs in the sense of preaching the Word of God. For the shepherd analogy *cf.* Luke 17:7-9 where ποιμαίνω (#164) occurs. That shepherd was compelled to eat at the second table, but at least he got to eat. Most evangelists in modern times are happy to eat at the second or indeed at any table.

Verse 8 - *"Say I these things as a man? Or saith not the law the same also?"*

Μὴ κατὰ ἄνθρωπον ταῦτα λαλῶ, ἤ καὶ ὁ νόμος ταῦτα οὐ λέγει;

"Do I say this on human authority? Does not the law say the same?" ... *RSV*

Μὴ (negative particle with the indicative, rhetorical question, expecting a negative reply) 87.

κατὰ (preposition with the accusative, standard) 98.

ἄνθρωπον (acc.sing.masc.of ἄνθρωπος, standard) 341.

ταῦτα (acc.pl.neut.of οὗτος, direct object of λαλῶ) 93.

λαλῶ (1st.per.sing.pres.act.ind.of λαλέω, aoristic) 815.
ἤ (disjunctive) 465.
καὶ (adjunctive conjunction joining substantives) 14.
ὁ (nom.sing.masc.of the article in agreement with νόμος) 9.
νόμος (nom.sing.masc.of νόμος, subject of λέγει) 464.
ταῦτα (acc.pl.neut.of οὗτος, direct object of λέγει) 93.
οὐ (negative particle with the indicative in rhetorical question expecting a positive reply) 130.
λέγει (3d.per.sing.pres.act.ind.of λέγω, present progressive retroactive) 66.

Translation - "I am not saying these things on human authority am I? Because is it not true that the law also says these things?"

Comment: Paul is asking alternative rhetorical questions. The first one with μή expects "No" for an answer; the second with οὐ expects "Yes." κατά and the accusative of standard or rule. Paul did not expect his readers to accept what he said solely on his own authority. Note that ἄνθρωπον is anarthrous. No reference to a specific man, but to the human race in general as opposed to the Divine authority as expressed on ὁ νόμος. The context allows "because" although ἤ does not mean "because." The negative answer to the first question is demanded because of the positive answer to the second.

If Paul had been unable to point to Deut.25:4 in verse 9 it would be debatable whether or not his argument was self-serving. How often preachers have hesitated to preach about money lest they be accused of being mercenary! Even Paul (verse 12b).

Verse 9 - "For it is written in the law of Moses, Thou shalt not muzzle the ox that treadeth out the corn. Doth God take care for oxen?"

ἐν γὰρ τῷ Μωϋσέως νόμῳ γέγραπται, Οὐ κημώσεις βοῦν ἀλοῶντα. μὴ τῶν βοῶν μέλει τῷ θεῷ;

"For it is written in the law of Moses, 'You shall not muzzle an ox when it is treading out the grain.' Is it for oxen that God is concerned?" . . . RSV

ἐν (preposition with the locative of place) 80.
γὰρ (causal conjunction) 105.
τῷ (loc.sing.masc.of the article in agreement with νόμῳ) 9.
Μωϋσέως (gen.sing.masc.of Μωϋσέως, description) 715.
νόμῳ (loc.sing.masc.of νόμος, place) 464.
γέγραπται (3d.per.sing.perf.pass.ind.of γράφω,intensive) 156.
Οὐ (negative particle with the future in a prohibition) 130.

#4174 κημώσεις (2d.per.sing.fut.act.ind.of κημόω, prohibition).

King James Version

muzzle - 1 Cor.9:9.

Revised Standard Version

muzzle - 1 Cor.9:9.

Meaning: Cf. κημός - "a muzzle. Hence to put a muzzle over the mouth to prevent biting, or in the case of 1 Cor.9:9, eating.

βοῦν (acc.sing.masc.of βοῦς, direct object of κημώσεις) 1978.

#4175 ἀλοῶντα (pres.act.part.acc.sing.masc.of ἀλοάω, adjectival, predicate position, restrictive, in agreement with βοῦν).

King James Version

thresh - 1 Cor.9:10.
tread out the corn - 1 Cor.9:9; 1 Tim.5:18.

Revised Standard Version

tread out the grain - 1 Cor.9:9; 1 Tim.5:18.
thresher - 1 Cor.9:10.

Meaning: Cf. ἡ ἅλως (#310) or ἀλωή - "threshing floor." To tread out the grain. An ancient method of threshing grain was employed by which oxen were driven over the grain spread upon the floor. The chaff was blown away and the grain collected. Used of the oxen properly in 1 Cor.9:9 and 1 Thess.5:18. Metaphorically of a preacher in 1 Cor.9:10.

μή (negative particle with the indicative in rhetorical question expecting a negative reply) 87.
τῶν (gen.pl.masc.of the article in agreement with βοῶν) 9.
βοῶν (gen.pl.masc.of βοῦς, objective genitive) 1978.
μέλει (3d.per.sing.pres.act.ind.of μέλω, aoristic) 1417.
τῷ (dat.sing.masc.of the article in agreement with θεῷ) 9
θεῷ (dat.sing.masc.of θεός, personal interest) 124.

Translation - "Because it is written in the law of Moses, 'You shall not muzzle the threshing ox.' God's concern is not for the oxen is it?"

Comment: γάρ is causal as Paul demonstrates the truth of verse 8b. The quotation is from Deut.25:4 and is quoted again in 1 Tim.5:18. The genitive with a verb of emotion is common. God was indeed concerned about the oxen, but Pauls' point is that God was not concerned *solely* for the oxen, but intended that the principle involved could and should be applied also to preachers who are preaching His Word. Note the imperative future tense with οὐ. "This idiom as it occurs in the New Testament shows clearly the influence of the Septuagint. It occurs most frequently in prohibitions, its negative being, as also commonly in classical Greek, not μή, but οὐ." (Burton, *Moods and Tenses*, 35, as cited in Mantey, *Manual*, 192). But we should be careful not to take this idiom as a Hebraism, for it is of frequent occurrence in Attic Greek; e.g. Euripides: *Medea,* λέγ' εἴ τι βούλει . χειρὶ δ' οὐ φαύσεις ποτέ.

Say whatever you wish; you shall by no means touch my hand.

Examples are plentiful. . . . It is just another case where parallel idioms appear in both languages, it being, therefore, the frequency and not the fact of the idiom in the New Testament which shows Septuagint influence." (Mantey, *Ibid., 192, 193).*

The other part of the alternative question is in

Verse 10 - "Or saith he it altogether for our sakes? For our sakes, no doubt, this is written: that he that ploweth should plow in hope; and that he that thresheth in hope should be partaker of his hope."

ἢ δι' ἡμᾶς πάντως λέγει; δι' ἡμᾶς γὰρ ἐγράφη, ὅτι ὀφείλει ἐπ' ἐλπίδι ὁ ἀροτριῶν ἀροτριᾶν, καὶ ὁ ἀλοῶν ἐπ' ἐλπίδι τοῦ μετέχειν.

"Does he not speak entirely for our sake? It was written for our sake, because the plowman should plow in hope and the thresher thresh in hope of a share in the crop." . . . RSV

ἢ (disjunctive) 465.
δι' (preposition with the accusative, cause) 118.
ἡμᾶς (acc.pl.masc.of ἐγώ, causal) 123.
πάντως (adverbial) 2029.
λέγει (3d.per.sing.pres.act.ind.of λέγω, aoristic) 66.
δι' (preposition with the accusative, cause) 118.
ἡμᾶς (acc.pl.masc.of ἐγώ, cause) 123.
γὰρ (emphatic conjunction) 105.
ἐγράφη (3d.per.sing.aor.pass.ind.of γράφω, culminative) 156.
ὅτι (conjunction introducing an object clause in indirect discourse) 211.
ὀφείλει (3d.per.sing.pres.act.ind.of ὀφείλω, aoristic) 1277.
ἐπ' (preposition with the locative, basis) 47.
ἐλπίδι (loc.sing.fem.of ἐλπίς, basis) 2994.
ὁ (nom.sing.masc.of the article in agreement with ἀροτριῶν) 9.
ἀροτριῶν (pres.act.part.nom.sing.masc.of ἀροτριάω, substantival, subject of ὀφείλει) 2594.
ἀροτριᾶν (pres.act.inf.of ἀροτριάω, epexegetical) 2594.
καὶ (continuative conjunction) 14.
ὁ (nom.sing.masc.of the article in agreement with ἀλοῶν) 9.
ἀλοῶν (pres.act.part.nom.sing.masc.of ἀλοάω, substantival, subject of ὀφείλει) 4175.
ἐπ' (preposition with the locative, basis) 47.
ἐλπίδι (loc.sing.fem.of ἐλπίς, basis) 2994.
τοῦ (gen.sing.neut.of the article in agreement with μετέχειν) 9.

#4176 μετέχειν (pres.act.inf.of μετέχω, adnominal).

King James Version

be partaker - 1 Cor.9:10,12; 10:17,21,30.
pertain to - Heb.7:13.
take part of - Heb.2:14.
use - Heb.5:13

Revised Standard Version

share in the crop - 1 Cor.9:10.
share this claim - 1 Cor.9:12.
partake - 1 Cor.10:17,21,30; Heb.2:14.
live on - Heb.5:13.
belong - Heb.7:13.

Meaning: A combination of μετά (#50) and ἔχω (#82). To have with or together; to share; to have a part in; to be a co-partaker of. With reference to a grain harvest - 1 Cor.9:10; to be paid money for preaching - 1 Cor.9:12; to share the communion elements - 1 Cor.10:17,21; with reference to meat offered to idols - 1 Cor.10:30; of Jesus' participation in flesh and blood in the incarnation - Heb.2:14; of milk, *i.e.* of superficial theological teaching - Heb.5:13; of membership in the tribe of Judah - Heb.7:13.

Translation - "Or does He in fact say it about us? Indeed it was written for our sakes that the plowman ought to plow in hope and the thresher ought to thresh in hope that he will share in the crop."

Comment: ἤ again divides the alternative questions. πάντως here does not mean "solely" but "by all means" or "certainly." γὰρ, in line with the force of πάντως is emphatic. It was written that the plowman and the thresher should do their work on the basis of the fact that they expected to share in the rewards when the work was finished. The genitive articular infinitive τοῦ μετέχειν is adnominal. *Cf.* others in Rom.15:23; 1 Cor.16:4; 2 Cor.8:11; Phil.3:21. The adnominal infinitive is used with an adnoun (a noun with an adjectival use). Here it explains what the thresher hoped - he hoped to share in the harvest.

If an ox is fed a part of the grain which he threshes, should not a preacher expect to get paid? Paul bridges across from the agricultural analogy to the spiritual lesson in

Verse 11 - "If we have sown unto you spiritual things, is it a great thing if we shall reap your carnal things?"

εἰ ἡμεῖς ὑμῖν τὰ πνευματικὰ ἐσπείραμεν, μέγα εἰ ἡμεῖς ὑμῶν τὰ σαρκικὰ θερίσομεν;

"If we have sown spiritual good among you, is it too much if we reap your material benefits?" . . . RSV

εἰ (conditional particle in a first-class condition) 337.
ἡμεῖς (nom.pl.masc.of ἐγώ, subject of ἐσπείραμεν) 123.
ὑμῖν (dat.pl.masc.of σύ, personal advantage) 104.

τὰ (acc.pl.neut.of the article in agreement with πνευματικὰ) 9.

πνευματικὰ (acc.pl.neut.of πνευματικός, direct object of ἐσπείραμεν) 3791.

ἐσπείραμεν (1st.per.pl.aor.act.ind.of σπείρω, culminative, first-class condition) 616.

μέγα (nom.sing.neut.of μέγας, predicate nominative) 184.

εἰ (conditional particle with a first-class condition) 337.

ἡμεῖς (nom.pl.masc.of ἐγώ, subject of θερίσομεν) 123.

ὑμῶν (gen.pl.masc.of σύ, possession) 104.

τὰ (acc.pl.neut.of the article in agreement with σαρκικὰ) 9.

σαρκικὰ (acc.pl.neut.of σαρκικός, direct object of θερίσομεν) 4058.

θερίσομεν (1st.per.pl.fut.act.ind.of θερίζω, first-class condition) 617.

Translation - "Since we have sowed for your benefit the spiritual truths, is it something unreasonable if we reap your material wealth?"

Comment: We have a first-class condition with a double protasis. Both the εἰ clauses are first-class, the first with the aorist and the second with the future indicative. Paul was certain that the first was true. He had indeed sowed the seed of spiritual truth for the benefit of the saints in Corinth. That is how they became Christians. Paul is not certain that the condition of the second protasis will be met, but his assumption is that it will. His question is, "Is the fact that you will give me some money any great thing?" In modern parlance Paul might have shrugged his shoulders and asked, "Are you going to pay me? Big deal!" Note that he was so emotional about it that he omitted the verb in the apodosis!

The spiritual truths of the gospel and the eternal results for good in the lives of the Corinthians are in contrast with the financial resources which Paul might receive. He had been the instrument through whom God had saved them eternally from the consequences of their sin. Should they consider it unreasonable if they delivered him temporarily from his financial distress? He had given them something that they could never lose. They should give him something which they could not keep in any case.

He returns to this subject in his second epistle (2 Cor.9:6,6). Note μέγα in the same sense in 2 Cor.11:15. Note the same point in Romans 15:27.

The assurance of salvation from sin is a far greater gift to a lost sinner than any size check in a love offering. Not that Paul gave them their salvation. That could only come from God, but Paul was the messenger whom God used to bring them the good news.

He hastens to assure the Corinthians that his motives for this line of thought are not mercenary. His whole point is the vindication of his apostleship — on a par with the other Apostles. Note the emphatic position of ὑμῶν.

Verse 12 - "If others be partakers of this power over you, are not we rather? Nevertheless, we have not used this power; but suffer all things, lest we should hinder the gospel of Christ."

εἰ ἄλλοι τῆς ὑμῶν ἐξουσίας μετέχουσιν, οὐ μᾶλλον ἡμεῖς; Ἀλλ' οὐκ ἐχρησάμεθα τῇ ἐξουσίᾳ ταύτῃ, ἀλλὰ πάντα στέγομεν ἵνα μή τινα ἐγκοπὴν δῶμεν τῷ εὐαγγελίῳ τοῦ Χριστοῦ.

"If others share this rightful claim upon you, do not we still more? Nevertheless, we have not made use of this right, but we endure anything rather than put an obstacle in the way of the gospel of Christ." . . . RSV

εἰ (conditional particle in a first-class condition) 337.

ἄλλοι (nom.pl.masc.of ἄλλος, subject of μετέχουσιν) 198.

τῆς (gen.sing.fem.of the article in agreement with ἐξουσίας) 9.

ὑμῶν (gen.pl.masc.of σύ, objective genitive) 104.

ἐξουσίας (gen.sing.fem.of ἐξουσία, objective genitive) 707.

μετέχουσιν (3d.per.pl.pres.act.ind.of μετέχω, first-class condition) 4176.

οὐ (negative particle with the indicative understood, in rhetorical question expecting a positive reply) 130.

μᾶλλον (adverbial) 619.

ἡμεῖς (nom.pl.masc.of ἐγώ, subject of verb understood, in rhetorical question) 123.

’Αλλ’ (adversative conjunction) 342.

οὐκ (negative particle with the indicative) 130.

ἐχρησάμεθα (1st.per.pl.aor.mid.ind.of χράω, culminative) 2447.

τῇ (instru.sing.fem.of the article in agreement with ἐξουσίᾳ) 9.

ἐξουσίᾳ (instru.sing.fem.of ἐξουσία, means) 707.

ταύτῃ (instru.sing.fem.of οὗτος, in agreement with ἐξουσίᾳ) 93.

ἀλλὰ (alternative conjunction) 342.

πάντα (acc.pl.neut.of πᾶς, direct object of στέγομεν) 67.

#4177 στέγομεν (1st.per.pl.pres.act.ind.of στέγω, present progressive retroactive).

King James Version

bear - 1 Cor.13:7.
can forbear - 1 Thess.3:1,5.
suffer - 1 Cor.9:12.

Revised Standard Version

endure - 1 Cor.9:12; 13:7.
bear - 1 Thess.3:1,5.

Meaning: Cf. στέγη (#720). Hence to cover over with silence; to overlook; to endure a wrong without protest. Paul absorbed the wrongs inflicted upon him by the Corinthians in silence - 1 Cor.9:12. Love absorbs all wrongs in silence - 1 Cor.13:7; Paul tried to endure in silence his lack of news about the Thessalonians, but could not; hence he sent Timothy to Thessalonica - 1 Thess.3:1,5.

ἵνα (conjunction with the subjunctive in a negative sub-final clause) 114.

μή (negative particle with the subjunctive in a negative sub-final clause) 87.

τινα (acc.sing.fem.of τις, indefinite pronoun in agreement with ἐγκοπὴν) 486.

#4178 ἐγκοπὴν (acc.sing.fem.of ἐγκοπή, direct object of δῶμεν).

King James Version

hinder - 1 Cor.9:12.

Revised Standard Version

put an obstacle in the way of - 1 Cor.9:12.

Meaning: Cf. ἐγκόπτω (#3617). Literally a cutting made in the road to hinder the progress of an enemy. Hence, a hindrance; any impediment to progress - 1 Cor.9:12.

δῶμεν (1st.per.pl.aor.act.subj.of δίδωμι, negative sub-final clause) 362.
τῷ (dat.sing.neut.of the article in agreement with εὐαγγελίῳ) 9.
εὐαγγελίῳ (dat.sing.neut.of εὐαγγέλιον, personal disadvantage) 405.
τοῦ (gen.sing.masc.of the article in agreement with Χριστοῦ) 9.
Χριστοῦ (gen.sing.masc.of Χριστός, description) 4.

Translation - "If others are exercising authority over you may we not even more? But we did not supply our own needs by means of this authority; instead we have been paying our own way lest we hinder the progress of the gospel of Christ."

Comment: Other preachers apparently had preached in Corinth and taken an offering for their needs. Paul does not deny their right to do so. He only asks if he has not had even a greater right. He expects the answer to his question to be affirmative, since he was the one who first carried the good news of the gospel to Corinth. Despite that fact he says that he had never taken money from them, but had always been silent about money (present progressive retroactive in στέγομεν). The middle voice in ἐχρησάμεθα translates "serve our own needs." But Paul had absorbed all of the costs connected with his ministry. We have an excellent example of ἀλλά, first as an adversative and then as an alternative conjunction. Why did Paul choose not to exercise his rights as an Apostle? The negative sub-final clause with ἵνα μή and the subjunctive tells us. To have insisted on his right to be paid for his services might have impeded the progress of the gospel of Christ. Paul seems to be fighting the battle for social security for all other preachers while insisting that he would rather not take money for preaching.

Having appealed to social custom to prove his point in verse 10, he now appeals to the law of the Mosaic tabernacle in

Verse 13 - "Do ye not know that they which minister about holy things live of the things of the temple? And they which wait at the altar are partakers with the altar?"

οὐκ οἴδατε ὅτι οἱ τὰ ἱερὰ ἐργαζόμενοι (τὰ) ἐκ τοῦ ἱεροῦ ἐσθίουσιν, οἱ τῷ θυσιαστηρίῳ παρεδρεύοντες τῷ θυσιαστηρίῳ συμμερίζονται;

"Do you not know that those who are employed in the temple service get their food from the temple, and those who serve at the altar share in the sacrificial offerings?" . . . RSV

οὐκ (negative particle with the indicative in rhetorical question expecting a positive reply) 130.

οἴδατε (2d.per.pl.perf.act.ind.of ὁράω, intensive) 144b.

ὅτι (conjunction introducing an object clause in indirect discourse) 211.

οἱ (nom.pl.masc.of the article in agreement with ἐργαζόμενοι) 9.

τὰ (acc.pl.neut.of the article in agreement with ἱερὰ) 9.

#4179 ἱερὰ (acc.pl.neut.of ἱερός, direct object of ἐργαζόμενοι).

King James Version

holy - 2 Tim.3:15.
holy things - 1 Cor.9:13.

Revised Standard Version

temple service - 1 Cor.9:13.
sacred - 2 Tim.3:15.

Meaning: Cf. ἱερατεία (#1789); ἱεράτευμα (#5176); ἱερατεύω (#1785); ἱερεύς (#714); ἱερόν (#346); ἱεροπρεπής (#4889); ἱεροσυλέω (#3850); ἱερόσυλος (#3494); ἱερωσύνη (#4986) and ἱερουργέω (#4051). "Primary sense is thought to be mighty" (Thayer, 299). Therefore mighty in the sense of authoritative, because connected with the temple of God. Thus the words in ἱερ . . . pertain to the temple, the priesthood, holy things, holy temple service, etc. The temple service - 1 Cor.9:13; the holy writings - 2 Tim.3:15.

ἐργαζόμενοι (pres.mid.part.nom.pl.masc.of ἐργάζομαι, substantival, subject of ἐσθίουσιν) 691.

(τὰ) (acc.pl.neut.of the article direct object of ἐσθίουσιν) 9.

ἐκ (preposition with the ablative of source) 19.

τοῦ (abl.sing.neut.of the article in agreement with ἱεροῦ) 9.

ἱεροῦ (abl.sing.neut.of ἱερόν, source) 346.

ἐσθίουσιν (3d.per.pl.pres.act.ind.of ἐσθίω, customary) 610.

οἱ (nom.pl.masc.of the article in agreement with παρεδρεύοντες) 9.

τῷ (dat.sing.neut.of the article in agreement with θυσιαστηρίῳ) 9.

θυσιαστηρίῳ (dat.sing.neut.of θυσιαστήριον, advantage) 484.

#4180 παρεδρεύοντες (pres.act.part.nom.pl.masc.of παρεδρεύω, substantival, subject of συμμερίζονται).

King James Version

wait at - 1 Cor.9:13.

Revised Standard Version

serve at - 1 Cor.9:13.

Meaning: A combination of παρά (#154) and ἑδρεύω - "to sit" - from παρεδρός -

"a sitting beside." Hence, to serve or attend. Joined with θυσιαστηρίῳ - "to serve at the altar." Thus to perform service in the Levitical tabernacle/temple - 1 Cor.9:13.

τῷ (instru.sing.neut.of the article in agreement with θυσιαστηρίῳ) 9.
θυσιαστηρίῳ (instru.sing.neut.of θυσιαστήριον, association) 484.

#4181 συμμερίζονται (3d.per.pl.pres.mid.ind.of συμμερίζω, customary).

King James Version

be partakers with - 1 Cor.9:13.

Revised Standard Version

share in - 1 Cor.9:13.

Meaning: A combination of σύν (#1542) and μερίζω (#993); to divide with; to share. The Levitical priests of the temple shared personally in the offerings of the temple (Lev.6:16,26; Num.18:8,31; Deut.18:1-3) - 1 Cor.9:13.

Translation - "You are aware, are you not, that the administrators of the temple service eat the offerings of the temple? They who serve at the altar share with the altar."

Comment: The rhetorical question which expects a positive reply is followed by a statement. ὅτι introduces the indirect discourse. Paul reference is to the passages listed under #4181. His argument is that the concept of a paid ministry is not new. The Levitical law forbade the priests to own real estate but, in recompense provided that they should eat a part of the sacrifices brought to the Lord. Thus it is not wrong for some of the Lord's money to be appropriated for living expenses for the preacher. This is Paul's conclusion in

Verse 14 - "Even so hath the Lord ordained that they which preach the gospel should live of the gospel."

οὕτως καὶ ὁ κύριος διέταξεν τοῖς τὸ εὐαγγέλιον καταγγέλλουσιν ἐκ τοῦ εὐαγγελίου ζῆν.

"In the same way, the Lord commanded that those who proclaim the gospel should get their living by the gospel." . . . RSV

οὕτως (demonstrative adverb) 74.
καὶ (adjunctive conjunction) 14.
ὁ (nom.sing.masc.of the article in agreement with κύριος) 9.
κύριος (nom.sing.masc.of κύριος, subject of διέταξεν) 97.
διέταξεν (3d.per.sing.aor.act.ind.of διατάσσω, constative) 904.
τοῖς (dat.pl.masc.of the article in agreement with καταγγέλλουσιν) 9.
τὸ (acc.sing.neut.of the article in agreement with εὐαγγέλιον) 9.
εὐαγγέλιον (acc.sing.neut.of εὐαγγέλιον, direct object of καταγγέλλουσιν) 405.

καταγγέλλουσιν (pres.act.part.dat.pl.masc.of καταγγέλλω, substantival, indirect object of διέταξεν) 3023.

ἐκ (preposition with the ablative of source) 19.

τοῦ (abl.sing.neut.of the article in agreement with εὐαγγελίου) 9.

εὐαγγελίου (abl.sing.neut.of εὐαγγέλιον, source) 405.

ζῆν (pres.act.inf.of ζάω, epexegetical) 340.

Translation - "In the same way also the Lord has ordered those who are preaching the gospel to live of the gospel."

Comment: οὕτως depends upon verse 13. As it was in the Levitical tabernacle or temple so it shall be also in the Christian churches. The participial substantive in the dative case is the indirect object of διέταξεν. Note the epexegetical infinitive ζῆν. Cf.#904 for other orders God has given.

Was Paul, who refused to take money for his services, disobeying God's order? Like all concepts which the Scripture puts into tension, the truth emerges in a moderate position that avoids the extremes. Preachers are entitled to a living so that they can devote all of their time and energy to the study of the Word and prayer, but no preacher has a moral right to exploit the gospel to make vast sums of money. Paul took no money from any of the churches except the church in Philippi (Phil.4:10-19).

Verse 15 - "But I have used none of these things: neither have I written these things, that it should be so done unto me: for it were better for me to die, than that any man should make my glorying void."

ἐγὼ δὲ οὐ κέχρημαι οὐδενὶ τούτων. οὐκ ἔγραφα δὲ ταῦτα ἵνα οὕτως γένηται ἐν ἐμοί, καλὸν γάρ μοι μᾶλλον ἀποθανεῖν ἤ — καύχημά μου οὐδεὶς κενώσει.

"But I have made no use of these rights, nor am I writing this to secure any such provision. For I would rather die than have any one deprive me of my ground for boasting." . . . RSV

ἐγὼ (nom.sing.masc.of ἐγώ, subject of κέχρημαι) 123.

δὲ (adversative conjunction) 11.

οὐ (negative particle with the indicative) 130.

κέχρημαι (1st.per.sing.perf.mid.ind.of χράω, consummative) 2447.

οὐδενὶ (acc.sing.neut.of οὐδείς, direct object of κέχρημαι) 446.

τούτων (gen.pl.neut.of οὗτος, partitive genitive) 93.

οὐκ (negative particle with the indicative) 130.

ἔγραφα (1st.per.sing.aor.act.ind.of γράφω, epistolary) 156.

δὲ (continuative conjunction) 11.

ταῦτα (acc.pl.neut.of οὗτος, direct object of ἔγραφα) 93.

ἵνα (conjunction with the subjunctive in a purpose clause) 114.

οὕτως (demonstrative adverb) 74.

γένηται (3d.per.sing.aor.subj.of γίνομαι, purpose) 113.

ἐν (preposition with the locative of sphere) 80.

ἐμοί (loc.sing.masc.of ἐμός, sphere) 1267.

καλὸν (acc.sing.neut.of καλός, adverbial accusative) 296.

γάρ (causal conjunction) 105.

μοι (dat.sing.masc.of ἐγώ, personal interest) 123.

μᾶλλον (adverbial) 619.

ἀποθανεῖν (aor.inf.of ἀποθνήσκω, subject of verb understood) 774.

ἤ (disjunctive) 465.

τὸ acc.sing.neut.of the article in agreement with καύχημά) 9.

καύχημά (acc.sing.neut.of καύχημα, direct object of κενώσει) 3881.

μου (gen.sing.masc.of ἐγώ, possession) 123.

οὐδεὶς (nom.sing.masc.of οὐδείς, subject of κενώσει) 446.

κενώσει (3d.per.sing.fut.act.ind.of κενόω, gnomic) 3888.

Translation - "But I have not turned a single one of these things to my advantage. Nor have I written these things in order that it may be done thus for me, because I would rather die than for one man to take away my ground for boasting."

Comment: The first δὲ is adversative; the second continuative. Note the perfect middle in κέχρημαι. Paul had not used the philosophy of verses 6-14 for himself. Note the epistolary aorist in ἔγραφα. "A Greek writer would sometimes place himself at the viewpoint of his reader or readers, and use an aorist indicative in stating an act or event which was present or future to him." (Mantey, *Manual*, 198). "This idiom is merely a matter of standpoint. The writer looks at his letter as the recipient will" (Robertson, *Grammar*, 845). It is a case where the writer "puts himself in the place of his reader and describes as past that which is to himself present, but which will be past to his reader." (Burton, *Moods and Tenses*, 21). The epistolary aorist occurs in Latin and is of very frequent occurrence in the papyri. "There is therefore no adequate reason for denying its presence in the New Testament" (Robertson, *Ibid.*, 846). Paul is not referring to a previous letter but to the foregoing verses in this letter.

There are variant readings for οὐθεὶς κενώσει. A has οὐθεὶς μὴ κενώσῃ; G has τίς κενώσει; Κ Ψ and other mss. have ἵνα τις κενώσῃ. Also ἵνα τις μὴ κενώσει and ἵνα τις οὐ μὴ κενώσῃ. The text accepted by the United Bible Societies' Committee results in a broken sentence, but in any case Paul's meaning is clear. He would rather have died than have a single man able to say that he had been inconsistent in this philosophy. This statement implies that since Paul received no money for his preaching he intended to ground his boast upon the fact that he preached at personal sacrifice for nothing. But he deserved no praise for his preaching.

Verse 16 - "For though I preach the gospel, I have nothing to glory of: for necessity is laid upon me; yea, woe is unto me, if I preach not the gospel."

ἐὰν γὰρ εὐαγγελίζωμαι, οὐκ ἔστιν μοι καύχημα. ἀνάγκη γάρ μοι ἐπίκειται. οὐαὶ γάρ μοί ἐστιν ἐὰν μὴ εὐαγγελίσωμαι.

"For if I preach the gospel, that gives me no ground for boasting. For necessity is laid upon me. Woe to me if I do not preach the gospel!" . . . RSV

ἐὰν (conditional particle in a third-class condition) 363.

γὰρ (concessive conjunction) 105.

εὐαγγελίζωμαι (1st.per.sing.pres.mid.subj.of εὐαγγελίζω, third-class condition) 909.

οὐκ (negative particle with the indicative) 130.

ἔστιν (3d.per.sing.pres.ind.of εἰμί, aoristic) 86.

μοι (dat.sing.masc.of ἐγώ, personal interest) 123.

καύχημα (nom.sing.neut.of καύχημα, subject of ἔστιν) 3881.

ἀνάγκη (nom.sing.fem.of ἀνάγκη, subject of ἐπίκειται) 1254.

γάρ (causal conjunction) 105.

μοι (dat.sing.masc.of ἐγώ, person) 123.

ἐπίκειται (3d.per.sing.pres.pass.ind.of ἐπίκειμαι, present progressive retroactive) 2040.

οὐαί (exclamation) 936.

γάρ (emphatic conjunction) 105.

μοί (dat.sing.masc.of ἐγώ, personal disadvantage) 123.

ἔστιν (3d.per.sing.pres.ind.of εἰμί, aoristic) 86.

ἐὰν (conditional particle in a third-class condition) 363.

μὴ (negative particle with the subjunctive) 87.

εὐαγγελίσωμαι (1st.per.sing.aor.mid.subj.of εὐαγγελίζω, third-class condition) 909.

Translation - "Although if I preach the gospel there is no ground for boasting, because I am under a great compulsion. In fact, woe is me if I do not preach the gospel."

Comment: γὰρ is concessive. *Cf.* comment on verse 15. ἐὰν and the subjunctive in εὐαγγελίζωμαι in a third-class condition. The apodosis has the present indicative. Paul is correcting what otherwise might have been a false impression. He will take no money lest he be deprived of the right to boast about his preaching. But even though he preaches (concessive γὰρ) he cannot boast about it since (causal γάρ) he cannot refrain from preaching due to the great compulsion to tell the good news of the gospel of Christ. In fact (emphatic γάρ) he will be miserable if he does not preach the gospel. Note that in the second third-class condition Paul puts the apodosis ahead of the protasis. *Cf.* Jer.20:9.

Verse 17 - "For if I do this thing willingly, I have a reward: but if against my will, a dispensation of the gospel is committed unto me."

εἰ γὰρ ἑκὼν τοῦτο πράσσω, μισθὸν ἔχω. εἰ δὲ ἄκων, οἰκονομίαν πεπίστευμαι.

"For if I do this of my own will, I have a reward; but if not of my own will, I am entrusted with a commission." . . . RSV

εἰ (conditional particle in a first-class condition) 337.

γὰρ (causal conjunction) 105.

ἑκὼν (pres.act.part.nom.sing.masc.of ἕκω, adverbial, causal) 3941.

τοῦτο (acc.sing.neut.of οὗτος, direct object of πράσσω) 93.

πράσσω (1st.per.sing.pres.act.ind.of πράσσω, first-class condition) 1943.

μισθὸν (acc.sing.masc.of μισθός , direct object of ἔχω) 441.
ἔχω (1st.per.sing.pres.act.ind.of ἔχω, futuristic) 82.
εἰ (conditional particle in a first-class condition) 337.
δὲ (adversative conjunction) 11.

#4182 ἄκων (adverbial).

King James Version

against my will - 1 Cor.9:17.

Revised Standard Version

not of my own will - 1 Cor.9:17.

Meaning: A contraction from ἀέκων - α privative and ἕκων (#3941). Hence, unwillingly; not of one's own will - 1 Cor.9:17.

οἰκονομίαν (acc.sing.fem.of οἰκονομία, direct object of πεπίστευμαι) 2560.
πεπίστευμαι (1st.per.sing.perf.pass.ind.of πιστεύω, intensive) 734.

Translation - "Because if I do this willingly I will have a reward, but if unwillingly I have a commission entrusted to me."

Comment: The εἰ clauses are first-class conditions. But there is nothing in the grammar of a first-class condition to tell us whether the premise in the protasis is true or whether it is only considered to be true for the sake of the argument. Did Paul preach the gospel willingly or not? One's general impression, gathered from the entire history of his ministry is that he did - that he was delighted to preach the gospel. What did he mean in verse 16? He said that he was under compulsion, but the compulsion is not defined. Did he mean that he found so much joy in preaching the good news that he was miserable when he was not preaching? Or did he mean that if he did not preach he would be punished for being unfaithful to his commission? We opt for the former interpretation. Thus the first clause of verse 17 can be translated "*Since* I am doing this willingly. . . κ.τ.λ." That being true he could look forward to a future reward (futuristic present in ἔχω). By the same reasoning the second first-class condition should be translated "*If* unwillingly . . . κ.τ.λ." If Paul had ever gone out to preach the gospel although he was really unwilling to preach it he would be faced with the necessity to explain at the judgment seat of Christ why he, who was given a special commission to preach (Acts 9:15; Eph.3:1-11) the gospel to the Gentiles, should have been unwilling to fulfill his ministry. The answer to this problem rests in how we interpret the last clause of verse 16. If he preached joyously because he wanted to preach then his reward was immediate, for it is rewarding to do what one wishes to do. But his reward is also forthcoming at the judgment seat of Christ. Conversely if he preached unwillingly his "woe" (οὐαί) was also immediate, since it is annoying to do what one wishes not to do, and also forthcoming at the judgment seat of Christ.

Paul was always under the obligation to preach the gospel until he had preached the last sermon and given the last witness which had been specifically assigned to him by our Lord Who is Head over all things to His church (Eph.1:22,23; 2:10; 2 Tim.4:6-7). Paul went to his death with a clear conscience. He had told the good news on the occasion of his last divinely assigned appointment. That is why he looked forward to the crown of righteousness which was his reward. Whether he preached joyously or under duress he was fulfilling his commission (Eph.3:2; Col.1:25).

Verse 18 - "What is my reward then? Verily that, when I preach the gospel, I may make the gospel of Christ without charge, that I abuse not my power in the gospel."

τίς οὖν μού ἐστιν ὁ μισθός; ἵνα εὐαγγελιζόμενος ἀδάπανον θήσω τὸ εὐαγγέλιον, εἰς τὸ μὴ καταχρήσασθαι τῇ ἐξουσίᾳ μου ἐν τῷ εὐαγγελίῳ.

"What then is my reward? Just this: that in my preaching I may make the gospel free of charge, not making full use of my right in the gospel." . . . RSV

τίς (nom.sing.masc.of τίς, interrogative pronoun, predicate nominative, direct question) 281.

οὖν (inferential conjunction) 68.

μού (gen.sing.masc.of ἐγώ, possession) 123.

ἐστιν (3d.per.sing.pres.ind.of εἰμί, futuristic) 86.

ὁ (nom.sing.masc.of the article in agreement with μισθός) 9.

μισθός (nom.sing.masc.of μισθός, subject of ἐστιν) 441.

ἵνα (conjunction with the subjunctive in a sub-final clause) 114.

εὐαγγελιζόμενος (pres.mid.part.nom.sing.masc.of εὐαγγελίζομαι, adverbial, temporal, modal) 909.

#4183 ἀδάπανον (acc.sing.neut.of ἀδάπανος, adverbial).

King James Version

without charge - 1 Cor.9:18.

Revised Standard Version

free of charge - 1 Cor.9:18.

Meaning: α privative and δαπάνη (#2533). Hence without cost; free. *Cf.* δαπανάω (#2238). With reference to the service of preaching the gospel - 1 Cor.9:18.

θήσω (1st.per.sing.1st.aor.act.subj.of τίθημι, sub-final) 455.

τὸ (acc.sing.neut.of the article in agreement with εὐαγγέλιον) 9.

εὐαγγέλιον (acc.sing.neut.of εὐαγγέλιον, direct object of θήσω) 405.

εἰς (preposition with the articular infinitive in the accusative, purpose) 140.

τὸ (acc.sing.neut.of the article in agreement with καταχρήσασθαι, purpose) 9.

μή (negative particle with the infinitive in a negative purpose clause) 87.

καταχρήσασθαι (aor.mid.inf.of καταχρήάομαι, negative purpose) 4162.

τῇ (instru.sing.fem.of the article in agreement with ἐξουσίᾳ) 9.

ἐξουσίᾳ (instru.sing.fem.of ἐξουσία, means) 707.

μου (gen.sing.masc.of ἐγώ, possession) 123.

ἐν (preposition with the locative of sphere) 80.

τῷ (loc.sing.neut.of the article in agreement with εὐαγγελίῳ) 9.

εὐαγγελίῳ (loc.sing.neut.of εὐαγγέλιον, sphere) 405.

Translation - "What then is my reward? That when I preach the gospel and by making it free of charge, I am not exploitative of my authority in the gospel ministry."

Comment: Verse 18 intensifies the point in verse 17, in which he said that whether he preached willingly or under the compulsion of faithful fulfillment of a divine commision, he had psychic income. In the former case he found joy in doing what he wanted to do anyway. In the latter case, even if he did what he did not enjoy, he had the satisfaction of knowing that he was a faithful steward.

Now, if he took money for his preaching the financial gain would put in jeopardy the validity of his claim to the other rewards. He would never know precisely why he preached if both psychic income and money were forthcoming. But in Paul's case there would be no money. Hence this is his reward.

The ἵνα **clause** is sub-final (purpose/result). εὐαγγελιζόμενος is adverbial, both temporal and modal. When he preached, by making it gratuitous he gained the result which he purposed. In εἰς τὸ μή καταχρήσασθαι we have a rare use of εἰς with the articular infinitive in the accusative case to denote purpose. We also have πρός in this construction. For εἰς see Romans 1:11. For πρός see Mt.5:28. ὥστε and ὡς with the infinitive also rarely speak of purpose, but without the article. For ὥστε see Mt.27:1 and for ὡς Luke 9:52. *Cf.* also Mt.6:1; Lk.4:29; Heb.7:9. This research reveals the flexibility of the κοινή in passages in which the context makes the meaning clear. No other language medium has this kind of flexibility without also clouding the meaning.

Paul had the authority to exploit the right to preach the gospel to the fullest extent. It was his divinely appointed occupation. If God has ordained that a Christian spend his life as a merchant God has willed that the merchant make a profit from his business. Thus Paul had a right to ask for an honorarium for his services as a preacher. He could have exploited this right to the fullest extent. But had he done so it would have destroyed his higher purpose. By giving up his right he gained an additional reward, both in time as a result of his psychic benefit and in the future at the judgment seat of Christ (2 Cor.5:10; 1 Cor.3:11-15).

It is interesting that only as a preacher did Paul take this magnanimous attitude toward money. When he made tents he charged all that the market would permit. He maximized profits in tent-making so that he could maximize psychic income in the sphere of the gospel. If he had not made tents for a living he would have been forced to depend upon love gifts and if they were not forthcoming he would have starved to death.

Verse 19 - "For though I be free from all men, yet have I made myself servant unto all, that I might gain the more."

Ἐλεύθερος γὰρ ὢν ἐκ πάντων πᾶσιν ἐμαυτὸν ἐδούλωσα, ἵνα τοὺς πλείονας κερδήσω.

"For though I am free from all men, I have made myself a slave to all, that I might win the more." . . . RSV

Ἐλεύθερος (nom.sing.masc.of ἐλεύθερος, predicate adjective) 1245.
γὰρ (inferential conjunction) 105.
ὢν (pres.part.nom.sing.masc.of εἰμί, adverbial, concessive) 86.
ἐκ (preposition with the ablative of separation) 19.
πάντων (abl.pl.masc.of πᾶς, separation) 67.
πᾶσιν (dat.pl.masc.of πᾶς, personal advantage) 67.
ἐμαυτὸν (acc.sing.masc.of ἐμαυτοῦ, direct object of ἐδούλωσα) 723.
ἐδούλωσα (1st.per.sing.aor.act.ind.of δουλόω, culminative) 3103.
ἵνα (conjunction with the subjunctive in a purpose clause) 114.
τοὺς (acc.pl.masc.of the article in agreement with πλείονας) 9.
πλείονας (acc.pl.masc.of πλείων, direct object of κερδήσω) 474.
κερδήσω (1st.per.sing.aor.act.subj.of κερδαίνω, purpose) 1214.

Translation - "So, despite the fact that I am free from all men, I have made myself a slave to all, in order that I may win a greater number."

Comment: In what sense Paul is under no obligation to anyone may be inferred from the previous verses. He had no obligation to preach the gospel at all to anybody since he had refused all cash payments and had provided for his own food and lodging (Acts 20:33,34). If someone had paid him in advance for a preaching mission and he had not delivered the service he would have been under obligation. Of course he is speaking now about his financial obligations, if any, to any man, not about his spiritual obligation to God to fulfill the ministry of his commission. Note the concessive adverbial participle ὢν.

Paul's personal slavery which he has imposed upon himself (reflexive ἐμαυτόν) is for a purpose, introduced by the final clause with ἵνα and the subjunctive κερδήσω. He considered himself in debt to every man, woman and child - a debt which he could pay only by telling them the good news that Jesus Christ died for them and rose again according to the Scriptures (Acts 20:26). So for the sake of winning the greatest possible number of souls to Christ he was willing to give up all of his financial rights and assume total spiritual obligation to all men. This is "the last full measure of devotion" to the cause of Christ (Abraham Lincoln, *Gettysburg Address*). Paul could do no more to call the elect to Christ than the soldiers buried at Gettysburg did to preserve the Union, and he dared not do less.

He specifies these obligations in verses 20-22.

Verse 20 "And unto the Jews I became as a Jew that I might gain the Jews; to them that are under the law, as under the law, that I might gain them that are under the law."

καὶ ἐγενόμην τοῖς Ἰουδαίοις ὡς Ἰουδαῖος, ἵνα Ἰουδαίους κερδήσω τοῖς ὑπὸ νόμον ὡς ὑπὸ νόμον, μὴ ὢν αὐτὸς ὑπὸ νόμον, ἵνα τοὺς ὑπὸ νόμον κερδήσω.

*"To the Jews I became as a Jew, in order to win Jews; to those under the law —
though not being myself under the law — that I might win those under the law.".*

. . RSV

καὶ (continuative conjunction) 14.
ἐγενόμην (1st.per.sing.aor.ind.of γίνομαι, constative) 113.
τοῖς (dat.pl.masc.of the article in agreement with Ἰουδαίοις) 9.
Ἰουδαίοις (dat.pl.masc.of Ἰουδαῖος, personal interest) 143.
ὡς (comparative particle) 128.
Ἰουδαῖος (nom.sing.masc.of Ἰουδαῖος, predicate nominative) 143.
ἵνα (conjunction with the subjunctive in a purpose clause) 114.
κερδήσω (1st.per.sing.aor.act.subj.of κερδαίνω, purpose) 1214.
τοῖς (dat.pl.masc.of the article, personal interest) 9.
ὑπὸ (preposition with the accusative, rest) 117.
νόμον (acc.sing.masc.of νόμος, rest) 464.
ὡς (comparative particle) 128.
ὑπὸ (preposition with the accusative, rest) 117.
νόμον (acc.sing.masc.of νόμος, rest) 464.
μὴ (negative particle with the participle) 87.
ὢν (pres.part.nom.sing.masc.of εἰμί, adverbial, concessive) 86.
αὐτὸς (nom.sing.masc.of αὐτός, intensive) 16.
ὑπὸ (preposition with the accusative, rest) 117.
νόμον (acc.sing.masc.of νόμος, rest) 464.
ἵνα (conjunction with the subjunctive in a purpose clause) 114.
τοὺς (acc.pl.masc.of the article, direct object of κερδήσω) 9.
ὑπὸ (preposition with the accusative, rest) 117.
νόμον (acc.sing.masc.of νόμος, rest) 464.
κερδήσω (1st.per.sing.aor.act.subj.of κερδαίνω, purpose) 1214.

*Translation - "And to the Jews I acted like a Jew in order to win Jews; to those
under law as under law, although I am not under law myself, that I might win
those under law."*

Comment: Paul uses the dramatic aorist ἐγενόμην to indicate something in the
past the effect of which is still in the present - "I became . . . and I still am." For
the sake of Jews and those under the law Paul acted like a Jew as though he was
under the law, though (concessive ὢν) he tells us parenthetically that he was not
under the law. Why did Paul behave like this? The purpose clause with ἵνα
follows - "in order to win them." Paul would do anything legitimate in order to
win the lost. His motivation was the same as that which prompted him to refuse
money for his preaching. He was trying to employ every possible psychological
strategy to commend himself to his prospects. κοινωνία (#3001) is fellowship
between persons who have a common ground of interest. Social or political
κοινωνία opens the door of opportunity for witnessing for Christ which may

result in spiritual κοινωνία. Paul's interest was not in social camaraderie as such. Rather it was his means to an end - the salvation of the prospect. *Cf.* Acts 21:20-27.

Dᶜ K Ψ and some miniscules omit the parenthesis.

Verse 21 - "To them that are without law, as without law (being not without law to God, but under the law of Christ,) that I might gain them that are without law."

τοῖς ἀνόμοις ὡς ἄνομος, μὴ ὢν ἄνομος θεοῦ ἀλλ' ἔννομος Χριστοῦ, ἵνα κερδάνω τοὺς ἀνόμους.

"To those outside the law I became as one outside the law — not being without law toward God but under the law of Christ — that I might win those outside the law." . . . RSV

τοῖς (dat.pl.masc.of the article in agreement with ἀνόμοις) 9.

ἀνόμοις (dat.pl.masc.of ἄνομος, personal interest) 2772.

ὡς (comparative particle) 128.

ἄνομος (nom.sing.masc.of ἄνομος, predicate adjective) 2772.

μὴ (negative particle with the participle) 87.

ὢν (pres.part.nom.sing.masc.of εἰμί, adverbial, concessive) 86.

ἄνομος (nom.sing.masc.of ἄνομος, predicate adjective) 2772.

θεοῦ (gen.sing.masc.of θεός, description) 124.

ἀλλ' (alternative conjunction) 342.

ἔννομος (nom.sing.masc.of ἔννομος, predicate adjective) 3496.

Χριστοῦ (gen.sing.masc.of Χριστός, description) 4.

ἵνα (conjunction with the subjunctive, in a purpose clause) 114.

κερδάνω (1st.per.sing.1st.aor.act.subj.of κερδαίνω, purpose) 1214.

τοὺς (acc.pl.masc.of the article in agreement with ἀνόμους) 9.

ἀνόμους (acc.pl.masc.of ἄνομος, direct object of κερδάνω) 2772.

Translation - "To those not subject to law as not subject to law, although not being without divine law, but obligated by the law of Christ, in order that I might win those without law."

Comment: The same grammatical pattern prevails as in verse 20. Note the alternative spelling of the aorist active subjunctive κερδάνω (#1214). Paul's obligation to divine law is his obligation to the law of Christ, which is the law of love. Note that the word is not ἀνομία (#692) - "lawlessness" but ἄνομος - "under no obligation to a set of rules."

Paul goes on in this vein in

Verse 22 - "To the weak became I as weak, that I might gain the weak; I am made all things to all men, that I might by all means save some."

ἐγενόμην τοῖς ἀσθενέσιν ἀσθενής, ἵνα τοὺς ἀσθενεῖς κερδήσω. τοῖς πᾶσιν γέγονα πάντα, ἵνα πάντως τινὰς σώσω.

"To the weak I became weak, that I might win the weak. I have become all things to all men, that I might by all means save some." . . . RSV

ἐγενόμην (1st.per.sing.aor.ind.of γίνομαι, dramatic) 113.
τοῖς (dat.pl.masc.of the article in agreement with ἀσθενέσιν) 9.
ἀσθενέσιν (dat.pl.masc.of ἀσθενής, personal interest) 1551.
ἀσθενής (nom.sing.masc.of ἀνθενής, predicate adjective) 1551.
ἵνα (conjunction with the subjunctive in a purpose clause) 114.
τοὺς (acc.pl.masc.of the article in agreement with ἀσθενεῖς) 9.
ἀσθενεῖς (acc.pl.masc.of ἀσθενής, direct object of κερδήσω) 1551.
κερδήσω (1st.per.sing.aor.act.subj.of κερδαίνω, purpose) 1214.
τοῖς (dat.pl.masc.of the article in agreement with πᾶσιν) 9.
πᾶσιν (dat.pl.masc.of πᾶς, personal interest) 67.
γέγονα (1st.per.sing.perf.ind.of γίνομαι, dramatic) 113.
πάντα (acc.pl.neut.of πᾶς, direct object of γέγονα) 67.
ἵνα (conjunction with the subjunctive in a purpose clause) 114.
πάντως (adverbial) 2029.
τινὰς (acc.pl.masc.of τις, indefinite pronoun, direct object of σώσω) 486.
σώσω (1st.per.sing.1st.aor.act.subj.of σώζω, purpose) 109.

Translation - *"I became weak for the weak, in order the gain the weak. I have been made everything for the benefit of everybody that by one means or another I might save some."*

Comment: "There was never a more nimble mind than that of Paul, and he knew how to adapt himself to every mood of his readers or hearers without any sacrifice of principle. It was no declaimer's tricks, but love for the souls of men that made him become all things to all men (1 Cor.9:22)" (Robertson, *Grammar*, 1199). We can only add that preachers have gone astray on both sides of Paul's policy. Some, with an unnecessary application of principle which they regarded as Puritanical, have been aloof and unapproachable, with the result that they have acquired a reputation for a "holier than thou" attitude. Thus their influence has been truncated. Others have become everything to everyone, even when to do so meant a blatant disregard for principle. Thus though they won all men they did not win them to anything. How to compromise the non-essentials in order to preserve the essentials of the gospel is a problem to be solved only by a constant communication with the indwelling Holy Spirit. Paul was not a "Holy Joe" but his unsaved friends were not afraid to associate with him and they respected him for his convictions and were interested in the gospel which he preached.

Verse 23 - *"And this I do for the gospel's sake, that I might be partaker thereof with you."*

πάντα δὲ ποιῶ διὰ τὸ εὐαγγέλιον, ἵνα συγκοινωνὸς αὐτοῦ γένωμαι.

"I do it all for the sake of the gospel, that I may share in its blessings." ... RSV

πάντα (acc.pl.neut.of πᾶς, direct object of ποιῶ) 67.
δὲ (continuative conjunction) 11.

ποιῶ (1st.per.sing.pres.act.ind.of ποιέω, customary) 127.

διὰ (preposition with the accusative, cause) 118.

τὸ (acc.sing.neut.of the article in agreement with εὐαγγέλιον) 9.

εὐαγγέλιον (acc.sing.neut.of εὐαγγέλιον, cause) 405.

ἵνα (conjunction with the subjunctive in a purpose clause) 114.

συγκοινωνὸς (nom.sing.masc.of συγκοινωνός, predicate nominative) 3997.

αὐτοῦ (gen.sing.masc.of αὐτός, description) 16.

γένωμαι (1st.per.sing.aor.subj.of γίνομαι, purpose) 113.

Translation - "And I do all these things to promote the gospel, in order that I may be a participant in it."

Comment: If Paul thought that his policy as described in verses 19 - 22 would be regarded by his critics as shocking or extreme, he may have used δὲ here in the adversative sense, in order to counter their criticism by showing why he pursued this policy. Otherwise it is only continuative. He wanted to promote the claims of the gospel in as many lives as possible. He wanted to be a soul winner - to participate in the glories of the gospel ministry. Goodspeed has, ". . . so that I may share in its blessings along with the rest."

The Pauline theology, in perfect conformity with that of our Lord as expressed in John 6, is in modern terms referred to correctly as Augustinian and/or Calvinistic. The elect members of the Body of Christ were specifically foreknown and predestinated from before the foundation of the world, but their identities and the time and place of their birth and rebirth are known but to God, Who has not chosen to reveal to His messengers who is and who is not elect. Thus the Great Commission of our Lord commanded that the gospel be preached to everyone. When the gospel of Christ is preached in the power of the Holy Spirit the work of God is going on - work which eventually results in the salvation of the elect. Paul preached the good news to every person he met and took care to make his presentation of it as attractive as possible. Not everyone who heard Paul preach was saved. Some may have heard him preach who came to Christ at some later time as the result of having heard another messenger of the cross. But Paul got some people saved. The preacher who wants only to do the will of God and who yields himself to the Holy Spirit need not be concerned with the statistics. God is a good record keeper. He said, "Well done thou good and faithful (not successful) servant."

A preacher in southern Illinois announced that he had preached for forty years without evidence that a single soul had been saved as a result of his ministry. He further announced that he would never preach the gospel again. A man arose to say that thirty years before he had heard the preacher preach and that shortly after the preacher left the community he had come to Christ. He concluded that if the downhearted man of God had led no one else to Christ, he had led him to Christ. The preacher arose and said, "Here goes for another forty years!"

Verse 24 - "Know ye not that they which run in a race run all, but one receiveth the prize? So run, that ye may obtain."

Οὐκ οἴδατε ὅτι οἱ ἐν σταδίῳ τρέχοντες πάντες μὲν τρέχουσιν, εἶς δὲ λαμβάνει τὸ βραβεῖον; οὕτως τρέχετε ἵνα καταλάβητε.

"Do you not know that in a race all the runners compete, but only one receives the prize? So run that you may obtain it." . . . RSV

Οὐκ (negative particle with the indicative in rhetorical question expecting a positive reply) 130.

οἴδατε (2d.per.pl.perf.act.ind.of ὁράω, intensive) 144b.

ὅτι (conjunction introducing an object clause in indirect discourse) 211.

οἱ (nom.pl.masc.of the article in agreement with τρέχοντες) 9.

ἐν (preposition with the locative of place) 80.

#4184 σταδίῳ (loc.sing.neut.of στάδιον, place).

     King James Version

race - 1 Cor.9:24.

     Revised Standard Version

race - 1 Cor.9:24.

Meaning: Cf. #1127, which is a measure of distance. τὸ στάδιον was a race course, like the one at Olympia. Such tracks were 600 Greek feet in length. *Cf.*#1127 for comparative distances in Roman and English metric systems. Whereas #1127 refers to the measurement στάδιον refers to the foot race event that went that distance. It equals 202.25 English yards - 1 Cor.9:24.

τρέχοντες (pres.act.part.nom.pl.masc. of τρέχω, substantival, subject of τρέχουσιν) 1655.

πάντες (nom.pl.masc.of πᾶς, in agreement with τρέχοντες) 67.

μὲν (particle of affirmation) 300.

τρέχουσιν (3d.per.pl.pres.act.ind.of τρέχω, customary) 1655.

εἶς (nom.sing.masc.of εἶς, subject of λαμβάνει) 469.

δὲ (adversative conjunction) 11.

λαμβάνει (3d.per.sing.pres.act.ind.of λαμβάνω, customary) 533.

τὸ (acc.sing.neut.of the article in agreement with βραβεῖον) 9.

#4185 βραβεῖον (acc.sing.neut.of βραβεῖον, direct object of λαμβάνει).

     King James Version

prize - 1 Cor.9:24; Phil.3:14.

     Revised Standard Version

prize - 1 Cor.9:24; Phil.3:14.

Meaning: Cf. βραβεύω (#4634). *Cf.* also βραβεύς for βραβευτής - the director, referee, umpire of an athletic contest who awards the prize. Hence βραβεῖον is the prize itself. Properly in 1 Cor.9:24. Metaphorically of an award given to the victorious Christian over and above salvation which is not awarded on merit, but on grace. *Cf.* comment on Phil.3:14.

οὕτως (demonstrative adverb) 74.

τρέχετε (2d.per.pl.pres.act.impv.of τρέχω, command) 1655.

ἵνα (conjunction with the subjunctive in a purpose clause) 114.

καταλάβητε (2d.per.pl.2d.aor.act.subj.of καταλαμβάνω, purpose) 1694.

Translation - "You know, do you not, that all the runners in a race do in fact compete, but one receives the prize? Run in such a way that you may capture the prize."

Comment: In the previous verses Paul has been discussing the intense effort and sacrificial costs of the Christian life. Now he illustrates with something that the Corinthians, as indeed all of the Greeks, understood well. The question is rhetorical and expects "Yes" in reply. Of course the Corinthians knew. Many of them had watched the foot races in the arena many times. All of the runners indeed run, but only one runner wins. μὲν intensifies the point and underlies our word "really" in the translation. δὲ is adversative. All the runners run but not all of the runners win. Only one does. This does not deny that the losers exerted themselves with intensity, but the winner was more intense than the others.

Οὕτως transfers the point to the spiritual realm. *Cf.#*74. The Christian is admonished to concentrate on Christian application of effort as hard as the athletes do on the field events in the Olympics.

Note the basic meaning of καταλαμβάνω (#1694) - "to take down," or "to capture." - "To catch and grasp firmly." Paul alludes to the prize - τὸ βραβεῖον (#4185) also in Phil.3:14. He also uses καταλαμβάνω in that same context (Phil.3:12,13).

He is not talking about winning the race in order to gain salvation, but about the intense effort after salvation has been granted as a gift, to gain a reward, over and above salvation. Salvation is not a prize to be won by a strong contender, but a gift of God's grace given to the helpless. If salvation were in view here (which it is not) then only one person would be saved. There is only one winner in this race. Many are called (Mt.20:16) and hence many are justified (Rom.8:30), and of the many who are saved, some (certainly more than one) will receive a reward for superior Christian effort after salvation.

The analogy to the race cannot be pushed in all of its details. Paul's point is that there is a reward for superior effort in the service of Christ after salvation by grace is bestowed (2 Tim.4:6-8; Heb.11:35; Phil.3:10-14).

Pursuant to the analogy to athletics, Paul next stresses the austerity of the sacrificial training program in which the athlete must engage before the intense effort of the race itself.

Verse 25 - "And every man that striveth for the mastery is temperate in all things. Now they do it to obtain a corruptible crown; but we an incorruptible."

πᾶς δὲ ὁ ἀγωνιζόμενος πάντα ἐγκρατεύεται, ἐκεῖνοι μὲν οὖν ἵνα φθαρτὸν στέφανον λάβωσιν, ἡμεῖς δὲ ἄφθαρτον.

"*Every athlete exercises self-control in all things. They do it to receive a perishable wreath, but we an imperishable.*" . . . RSV

πᾶς (nom.sing.masc.of πᾶς in agreement with ἀγωνιζόμενος) 67.

δὲ (explanatory conjunction) 11.

ὁ (nom.sing.masc.of the article in agreement with ἀγωνιζόμενος) 9.

ἀγωνιζόμενος (pres.mid.part.nom.sing.masc.of ἀγωνίζομαι, substantival, subject of ἐγκρατεύεται) 2511.

πάντα (acc.pl.neut.of πᾶς, cognate accusative, inner content) 67.

ἐγκρατεύεται (3d.per.sing.pres.mid.ind.of ἐγκρατεύομαι, aoristic) 4156.

ἐκεῖνοι (nom.pl.masc.of ἐκεῖνος, subject of verb understood) 246.

μὲν (particle of affirmation) 300.

οὖν (explanatory conjunction) 68.

ἵνα (conjunction with the subjunctive in a purpose clause) 114.

φθαρτὸν (acc.sing.masc.of φθαρτός, in agreement with στέφανον) 3804.

στέφανον (acc.sing.masc.of στέφανος, direct object of λάβωσιν) 1640.

λάβωσιν (3d.per.pl.aor.act.subj.of λαμβάνω, purpose) 533.

ἡμεῖς (nom.pl.masc.of ἐγώ, subject of verb understood) 123.

δὲ (adversative conjunction) 11.

ἄφθαρτον (acc.sing.masc.of ἄφθαρτος, in agreement with στέφανον, direct object of λάβωμεν understood) 3802.

Translation - "*Now everyone who trains hard exercises moderation in everything. These indeed then (do it) in order that they may receive a crown that will soon wilt, but we one which will always retain its beauty.*"

Comment: δὲ is explanatory as Paul pursues the spiritual application of the analogy. *Cf.*#2511 for the other uses of ἀγωνίζομαι. There is much valuable preaching material here - 1 Tim.6:12; 4:7; Col.1:29; 4:12. Some Calvinists perhaps have become infected with an antinomian complacancy because of their secure faith (which is well founded) in the ultimate victory of God. God's victory indeed is certain, but that every elect Christian will share in the rewards is not certain. The crown belongs to those who agonize.

Note that the emphasis is upon temperance, not upon total abstinence (2 Pet.1:6; Gal.5:23). The demand for total abstinence is a result of the Gnostic view that material things are inherently evil. Thus for the Gnostic, Jesus was not God because He had a material human body, or that if He was God He did not have a material human body. The Christian view is that God created all things (John 1:3; Col.1:16; Heb.1:2) and that everything is for the use of the child of God (1 Cor.3:21-23). The Christian's obligation is to know how much of anything he should have. This is Aristotle's "golden mean" written into the New Testament.

Note the μὲν . . . δὲ sequence. The athletes in the Olympic games strive for one thing, but we Christians for a better thing.

The athlete's crown was a sprig of olive which was tied around his head. It had beauty only for the moment, since it was destined soon to wilt. The Christian's crown, if he wins it, retains its beauty forever. What a prize to win in order to cast it at His feet (Rev.4:10). Although the four and twenty elders are not redeemed saints, yet, by implication, if they should cast their crowns before the throne, should Christians do less?

The material in the New Testament about crowns (#1640) provides a solid basis for preaching about the victorious life of the believer.

Modern athletes who win gold medals at the Olympic Games are in the media spot-light for a short time and then forgotten. Some of them parlay their temporary fame into lucrative contracts to endorse products, write books, give lectures or make movies. Their rewards then are a bit more lasting than the olive branch of the Greek winner in Paul's day, but Paul's point still stands. The rewards of the temporary winner are not to be compared with the eternal crown of glory which belonged to the Apostle Paul (2 Tim.4:6-8) and to other Christians who pay the price now in order to be a winner at the judgment seat of Christ.

Verse 26 - "I therefore so run, not as uncertainly; so fight I, not as one that beateth the air:"

ἐγὼ τοίνυν οὕτως τρέχω ὡς οὐκ ἀδήλως, οὕτως πυκτεύω ὡς οὐκ ἀέρα δέρων.

"Well, I do not run aimlessly, I do not box as one beating the air;" . . . RSV

ἐγώ (nom.sing.masc.of ἐγώ, subject of τρέχω) 123.

τοίνυν (inferential compound conjunction) 2694.

οὕτως (demonstrative adverb) 74.

τρέχω (1st.per.sing.pres.act.ind.of τρέχω, present progressive retroactive) 1655.

ὡς (comparative particle) 128.

οὐκ (negative particle with the indicative) 130.

#4186 ἀδήλως (adverbial).

King James Version

uncertainly - 1 Cor.9:26.

Revised Standard Version

aimlessly - 1 Cor.9:26.

Meaning: α privative plus δῆλος (#1612). *Cf.*ἄδηλος (#2465); ἀδηλότης (#4791). An adverb - uncertainly; aimlessly; at random. With οὐκ - thus to run a race with a definite plan designed to reach a definite goal - 1 Cor.9:26.

οὕτως (demonstrative adverb) 74.

#4187 πυκτεύω (1st.per.sing.pres.act.ind.of πυκτεύω, present progressive retroactive.

King James Version

fight - 1 Cor.9:26.

Revised Standard Version

box - 1 Cor.9:26.

Meaning: Cf. πύκτης - "a boxer." "a pugilist." *Cf.* πυγμή (#2296). Hence to engage in fisticuffs; to box; to fight with fists in a ring. Metaphorically, to engage in spiritual warfare - 1 Cor.9:26.

ὡς (comparative adverb) 74.

οὐκ (negative particle with the indicative) 130.

ἀέρα (acc.sing.masc.of ἀήρ, direct object of δέρων) 3584.

δέρων (pres.act.part.nom.sing.masc.of δέρω, substantival, subject of verb understood in the comparative clause) 1383.

Translation - "So that is how I have always run; not without a goal. I have always fought in the same way; not by pummelling the air."

Comment: postpositive τοίνυν (#2694) is used like γάρ, inferentially. οὗτως in both instances refers to verse 25. Paul's training in order to be the best possible servant of Christ was always in terms of temperance. Note that the two verbs are present progressive retroactives. They describe Paul's past policies of Christian service as well as those of the present. He had been running in the race, or, to change the figure of speech, boxing in the ring, temperately - that is to say intelligently. Intemperance is the result of stupidity. A stupid runner in a long race runs intemperately and wears himself out before he has covered half the distance. A well-coached runner has a race plan. He conserves his strength for his best effort in the sprint, when he gets up on his toes as he sees the tape. Track coaches time sections of the race, allotting so many seconds for the first quarter, so many for the half, etc. The unwise runner sprints away at the start and has nothing left at the finish. This is intemperance and it results in failure.

A boxer also has a technique. Aimless flailing about with the fists succeeds only in beating the air. A hard punch that misses the opponent's jaw is much more taxing of one's strength than one that lands solidly. An amateur fights intemperately. A professional, like Paul, fights with a plan. Many Christian workers are amateurs. They waste energy on inconsequential issues. They fire valuable gospel ammunition at unworthy targets. They major on minors. They use fifty pound sledge hammers to drive ten penny nails. The evangelist who wastes thirty minutes of valuable pulpit time preaching "Mickey Mouse" morals is beating the air. This is what Paul had in mind when he told Timothy to ignore fables (1 Tim.1:4) and to shun "profane and babblings" (2 Tim.2:16). A successful evangelist was preaching on the street corner when a heckler approached with a stupid question, only to be told, "I do not waste good gospel ammunition on doodle bugs!" Nor did Paul. He describes his own training and discipline in

Verse 27 - "But I keep under my body, and bring it into subjection; lest that by any means, when I have preached to others, I myself should be a castaway."

ἀλλὰ ὑπωπιάζω μου τὸ σῶμα καὶ δουλαγωγῶ, μή πως ἄλλοις κηρύξας αὐτὸς ἀδόκιμος γένωμαι.

"but I pommel my body and subdue it, lest after preaching to others I myself should be disqualified." . . . RSV

ἀλλὰ (alternative conjunction) 342.

ὑπωπιάζω (1st.per.sing.pres.act.ind.of ὑπωπιάζω, present progressive retroactive) 2624.

μου (gen.sing.masc.of ἐγώ, possession) 123.

τὸ (acc.sing.neut.of the article in agreement with σῶμα) 9.

σῶμα (acc.sing.neut.of σῶμα, direct object of ὑπωπιάζω) 507.

καὶ (adjunctive conjunction joining verbs) 14.

#4188 δουλαγωγῶ (1st.per.sing.pres.act.ind.of δουλαγωγέω, present progressive retroactive).

King James Version

bring into subjection - 1 Cor.9:27.

Revised Standard Version

subdue - 1 Cor.9:27.

Meaning: Cf. δουλάγωγος and παιδαγωγός (#4131). To enslave; to lead away into slavery; to claim as one's slave. To treat with stern discipline. With reference to Paul's treatment of his own body in his effort to serve Christ - 1 Cor.9:27.

μή (negative particle with the subjunctive in a negative purpose clause) 87.

πως (adverbial) 3700.

ἄλλοις (dat.pl.masc.of ἄλλος, indirect object of κηρύξας) 198.

κηρύξας (aor.act.part.nom.sing.masc.of κηρύσσω, adverbial, temporal) 249.

αὐτὸς (nom.sing.masc.of αὐτός, intensive, predicate position) 16.

ἀδόκιμος (nom.sing.masc.of ἀδόκιμος, predicate adjective) 3818.

γένωμαι (1st.pers.sing.2d.aor.subj.of γίνομαι, negative purpose clause) 113.

Translation - "But I have kept on hitting myself under the eye and I have kept my body under control, for fear that, after I have preached to others, I myself should have already been disqualified."

Comment: I have chosen to translate ὑπωπιάζω literally. Cf.#2624, though of course one cannot keep himself from sin by physical self-punishment. The verse contains no support for asceticism. Paul means that he has been (present progressive retroactive) very severe with himself in view of the struggle between the flesh and the spirit, which he describes in Romans 7:21-24. Rather than be enslaved by sin (Romans 6:6; Titus 3:3) Paul has enslaved his body by rigid discipline.

This is a far cry from the psychology that looks upon every bodily drive as normal and needful, which, if suppressed and denied, results in personality disequilibrium. The behaviorist may say that a little sin is good for the soul, but Paul is saying here that sin will disqualify him in the Christian race for the prize, despite the fact that he may have been a successful preacher to others. The passage clearly says that rigid self-discipline, stern denial of the call of the flesh and diligent training for the Christian race is essential to the prize. *Cf.* Phil.3:11-14. *Cf.*#3818 for the meaning of ἀδόκιμος.

The Arminian view that the passages teaches the possible loss of salvation overlooks the context. Paul is not talking about salvation, but about rewards (verses 19-27). The housewife in Pompeii who wrote ἀδόκιμος on a teacup which, though cracked and useless, was nevertheless placed upon a cupboard shelf and treasured for sentimental reasons, expressed Paul's meaning. *Cf.* our comment on Hebrews 5:11-6:12, with special attention to Heb.6:8, where ἀδόκιμος is found and the same thought is taught.

God will never throw away one of His elect for whom Christ died, even though they become useless to Him. This loss of utility for his Lord, because of his own lack of self-discipline and the consequent loss of the race for the prize is what Paul feared, not the loss of his salvation. For if that occurred the loss would be, not only that of Paul, but also that of Christ, Who paid the price (John 17:12). *Cf.* also 2 Cor.13:5,6,7.

Warning Against Idolatry

(1 Corinthians 10:1-22)

1 Cor.10:1 - "Moreover, brethren, I would not that ye should be ignorant how that all our fathers were under the cloud, and all passed through the sea."

Οὐ θέλω γὰρ ὑμᾶς ἀγνοεῖν, ἀδελφοί, ὅτι οἱ πατέρες ἡμῶν πάντες ὑπὸ τὴν νεφέλην ἦσαν καὶ πάντες διὰ τῆς θαλάσσης διῆλθον,

"I want you to know, brethren, that our fathers were all under the cloud, and all passed through the sea, . . . " . . . RSV

Οὐ (negative particle with the indicative) 130.

θέλω (1st.per.sing.pres.act.ind.of θέλω, aoristic) 88.

γὰρ (explanatory conjunction) 105.

ὑμᾶς (acc.pl.masc.of σύ, general reference) 104.

ἀγνοεῖν (pres.act.inf.of ἀγνοέω, direct object of θέλω) 2345.

ἀδελφοί (voc.pl.masc.of ἀδελφός, address) 15.

ὅτι (conjunction introducing an object clause in indirect discourse) 211.

οἱ (nom.pl.masc.of the article in agreement with πατέρες) 9.

πατέρες (nom.pl.masc.of πατήρ, subject of ἦσαν) 238.

ἡμῶν (gen.pl.masc.of ἐγώ, relationship) 123.

πάντες (nom.pl.masc.of πᾶς, in agreement with πατέρες) 67.

ὑπὸ (preposition with the accusative of extent) 117.

τὴν (acc.sing.fem.of the article in agreement with νεφέλην) 9.

νεφέλην (acc.sing.fem.of νεφέλη, place) 1225.

ἦσαν (3d.per.pl.imp.act.ind.of εἰμί, progressive description) 86.

καὶ (continuative conjunction) 14.

πάντες (nom.pl.masc.of πᾶς, subject of διῆλθον) 67.

διὰ (preposition with the genitive of place description) 118.

τῆς (gen.sing.fem.of the article in agreement with θαλάσσης) 9.

θαλάσσης (gen.sing.fem.of θάλασσα, physically through) 374.

διῆλθον (3d.per.pl.aor.ind.of διέρχομαι, constative) 1017.

Translation - "Now, brethren, I do not want you to be unaware of the fact that all our ancestors were under the cloud, and all passed through the sea."

Comment: γὰρ is explanatory as Paul prepares to show how Israel's experience demonstrates the point which he has just made in chapter 9, *viz.* that the children of the covenant, though saved, can sin and lose their reward. He has just expressed a fear that he might disqualify himself in the race for rewards, after leading the field. The expression of his concern indicates that he believed that such loss was indeed possible, if not probable.

We have already seen that the loss involved is not a loss of salvation but of reward. *Cf.* comment on 1 Cor.9:27. Now he wants to tell the Corinthians, some of whom were Hebrew Christians who already knew the story, but many of whom were Gentiles who had never heard it, about Israel's sad experience in the wilderness. The story will be an illustrative warning to them to forestall their own backsliding. The infinitive ἀγνοεῖν is the object of θέλω and is followed by ὅτι and the object clause in indirect discourse.

Note that ἦσαν is imperfect tense, indicating an extended period during which the children of Israel had the protection of the Cloud (Exodus 13:21,22), while διῆλθον is a constative aorist, since they had only one Red Sea passage (Exodus 14:22-29).

The picture is one of grace and salvation. God led them by the pillars of fire and cloud by night and day for forty years. The cloud went before them for guidance and stood behind them for protection from Pharaoh and his onrushing forces. They were children of Abraham, Isaac and Jacob, with all of whom God had unconditional covenant relations. They were indeed a chosen and redeemed people, redeemed both by blood and by power. Their Red Sea deliverance was a notable miracle.

The first four verses reinforce the point that Israel was God's nation in full possession of a covenant of salvation by grace. Yet as the story unfolds it reveals a sad picture of sin, unbelief, ingratitude, immorality and idolatry, which resulted, not in a loss of personal salvation but with the loss of the privilege of entrance into the Promised Lord and participation in its ownership.

Just as the Jews in the story, though saved - under the blood of the Paschal Lamb and thus untouched by the visit of the death angel in Egypt, and rescued by the power which held back the Red Sea for their safe passage, nevertheless sinned and fell in the wilderness, short of Canaan, so a Christian can be saved, but, through unbelief and sin, lose his reward in the coming Messianic kingdom. Paul will tell us in verse 11 that the Jews in the wilderness are examples unto us.

Verse 2 - "And were all baptized unto Moses in the cloud and in the sea."

καί πάντες εἰς τὸν Μωϋσῆν ἐβαπτίσαντο ἐν τῇ νεφέλῃ καὶ ἐν τῇ θαλάσσῃ,

"*. . . and all were baptized into Moses in the cloud and in the sea, . . .*" *. . . RSV*

καὶ (continuative conjunction) 14.
πάντες (nom.pl.masc.of πᾶς, subject of ἐβαπτίσαντο) 67.
εἰς (preposition with the accusative of general reference) 140.
τὸν (acc.sing.masc.of the article in agreement with Μωϋσῆν) 9.
Μωϋσῆν (acc.sing.masc.of Μωϋσῆς, general reference) 715.
ἐβαπτίσαντο (3d.per.pl.aor.mid.ind.of βαπτίζω, constative) 273.
ἐν (preposition with the locative of place) 80.
τῇ (loc.sing.fem.of the article in agreement with νεφέλῃ) 9.
νεφέλῃ (loc.sing.fem.of νεφέλη, place) 1225.
καὶ (adjunctive conjunction joining prepositional phrases) 14.
ἐν (preposition with the locative of place) 80.
τῇ (loc.sing.fem.of the article in agreement with θαλάσσῃ) 9.
θαλάσσῃ (loc.sing.fem.of θάλασσα, place) 374.

Translation - "And all got themselves overwhelmed as they followed Moses in the cloud and in the sea."

Comment: The basic meaning of βαπτίζω (#273) is the experience of being engulfed, covered, overwhelmed, totally surrounded - in whatever medium the context indicates. The form is a constative aorist in the middle voice. They submitted themselves to the experience of being engulfed as they followed Moses (εἰς τὸν Μωϋσῆν). There were two baptisms, in the first of which there were two media - the Shekinah cloud of glory by day and the fire of the divine presence at night. These clouds enveloped (*i.e.* totally surrounded) them. The Sea was also around them on both sides. This is an accommodated usage since the water was neither beneath nor above the people. This willingness to follow Moses, who had promised them deliverance from bondage, was Israel's commitment to him, analogous to the submission of the Corinthian Christians to immersion in water. The thrust of the passage is the fact that Israel made a commitment to Moses.

Having been delivered with redemption, both by blood and by fire, and having seen both the guidance of God and His protection from their enemies, they also were sustained in the wilderness with the heavenly food. This is the thought of

Verse 3 - "And did all eat the same spiritual meat."

καὶ πάντες τὸ αὐτὸ πνευματικὸν βρῶμα ἔφαγον,

"*. . . and all ate the same supernatural food . . .*" *. . . RSV*

καὶ (continuative conjunction) 14.

πάντες (nom.pl.masc.of πᾶς, subject of ἔφαγον) 67.

τὸ (acc.sing.neut.of the article in agreement with βρῶμα) 9.

αὐτὸ (acc.sing.neut.of αὐτός, intensive, in agreement with βρῶμα) 16.

πνευματικὸν (acc.sing.neut.of πνευματικός, in agreement with βρῶμα) 3791.

βρῶμα (acc.sing.neut.of βρῶμα, direct object of ἔφαγον) 1118.

ἔφαγον (3d.per.pl.aor.act.ind.of ἐσθίω, constative) 610.

Translation - *"And everyone ate the same spiritual food."*

Comment: The reference is to Exodus 16:4,35; Deut.8:3; Psalm 78:24-29. Paul's use of the constative aorist in ἔφαγον "contemplates the action in its entirety. It takes an occurrence and, regardless of the extent of duration, gathers it into a single whole. We have here the basal, unmodified force of the aorist tense" (Mantey, *Manual*, 196). A look at the record in the Old Testament references reveals that they ate the manna every day except the Sabbath for almost forty years. The intensive force of αὐτὸ (in the attributive position) means that it was the same food every day for forty years. God did not bother to vary the diet in view of the heavenly character of the food. It was spiritual food, but this does not mean that it was not also material, for πνευματικός is never an antonym for the material. It was divinely supplied, supernaturally nutritious and of unknown chemical composition. That is why they called it Manna (Exod.16:15) for manna means "What is it?" "They called it 'what is it?' for they knew not what it was." Moses told them that it was the bread which the Lord had given them to eat.

Paul is building up his case that Israel was the object of God's supernatural love, grace, power and care in order, in contrast, to show the enormity of their wickedness as they turned against Him (verses 5-12).

Only the biblically uninitiated will need to be told to connect our verse about the food from heaven with John 6:31-51.

Verse 4 - *"And did all drink of the same spiritual drink: for they drank of that spiritual Rock that followed them: and that Rock was Christ."*

καὶ πάντες τὸ αὐτὸ πνευματικὸν ἔπιον πόμα. ἔπινον γὰρ ἐκ πνευματικῆς ἀκολουθούσης πέτρας. ἡ πέτρα δὲ ἦν ὁ Χριστός.

". . . and all drank the same supernatural drink. For they drank from the supernatural Rock which followed them, and the Rock was Christ." . . . RSV

καὶ (continuative conjunction) 14.

πάντες (nom.pl.masc.of πᾶς, subject of ἔπιον) 67.

τὸ (acc.sing.neut.of the article in agreement with πόμα) 9.

αὐτὸ (acc.sing.neut.of αὐτός, intensive, attributive position, in agreement with πόμα) 16.

πνευματικὸν (acc.sing.neut.of πνευματικός, in agreement with πόμα) 3791.

ἔπιον (3d.per.pl.2d.aor.act.ind.of πίνω, constative) 611.

#4189 πόμα (acc.sing.neut.of πόμα, direct object of ἔπιον).

King James Version

drink - 1 Cor.10:4; Heb.9:10.

Revised Standard Version

drink - 1 Cor.10:4; Heb.9:10.

Meaning: drink. Water from the rock of Horeb - 1 Cor.10:4; in the Levitical services - Heb.9:10.

ἔπινον (3d.per.pl.imp.act.ind.of πίνω, iterative) 611.
γὰρ (causal conjunction) 105.
ἐκ (preposition with the ablative of source) 19.
πνευματικῆς (abl.sing.fem.of πνευματικός, in agreement with πέτρας) 3791.
ἀκολουθούσης (pres.act.part.abl.sing.fem.of ἀκολουθέω, adjectival, ascriptive, in agreement with πέτρας) 394.
πέτρας (abl.sing.fem.of πέτρα, source) 695.
ἡ (nom.sing.fem.of the article in agreement with πέτρα) 9.
πέτρα (nom.sing.fem.of πέτρα, subject of ἦν) 695.
δὲ (continuative conjunction) 11.
ἦν (3d.per.sing.imp.ind.of εἰμί, progressive description) 86.
ὁ (nom.sing.masc.of the article in agreement with Χριστός) 9.
Χριστός (nom.sing.masc.of Χριστός, predicate nominative) 4.

Translation - "*And everyone drank the same spiritual drink because they drank again of the spiritual Rock which was following them; and the Rock was Christ.*"

Comment: The second aorist in ἔπιον is constative as in the case of ἔφαγον in verse 3. But note that the verb is repeated in the next clause with ἔπινον which is the iterative imperfect, not the aorist. For they drank from the rock in Horeb twice. The first time, shortly after the Red Sea escape is recorded in Exodus 17:1-7. Thirty-eight years later they drank again from the same Rock (Numbers 20:1-13). *Cf.* Psalm 78:15. Thus πόμα refers to the literal water which quenched their physical thirst. On the first occasion Moses was commanded to smite the rock. On the second occasion the command was to speak to it. Moses, in angry impatience with the people (who can blame him?) smote the rock the second time and thus destroyed a beautiful type which our Lord had planned for us, a mistake for which Moses paid dearly, as he was not permitted to enter Canaan, but had to settle for a premature grave on Mount Nebo. (Numbers 20:1-13; Deut.34:1-4).

Paul continues to stress the supernatural provision for physical needs which God in grace provided for an unworthy people, who, though unworthy were the children of Abraham unto whom God was obligated with the solemn obligation of his unconditional covenant. He had given them protection and guidance in the Shekinah cloud, safe passage through the Red Sea and the manna in the wilderness. Now he provides them with water from the rock. Paul could have added shoes that wore like iron and stood the test of 38 years of desert wandering
In the second clause the emphasis shifts from the physical to the spiritual. God

had provided for their physical thirst (1st.clause) by supernatural means (πνευμακικὸν πόμα) and they did indeed believe upon Him for a spiritual drink as well as a physical drink. They drank repeatedly (iterative imperfect in ἔπινον) of the spiritual water of everlasting life from the Rock, Who is Christ, Who followed them in a way that a stationary rock in Horeb could not. The aorist ἔπιον and the imperfect ἔπινον are not interchangeable. There is great significance in the fact that Paul used both in juxtaposition which the exegete must not overlook. They drank and drank again as thirsty people do from the physical water at Horeb, both at the beginning of their wilderness wanderings and at the end (Exod.17; Numbers 20). They also drank, as do all believers, continuously (with no intervening lapses) of the spiritual water of everlasting life (John 4:13-14; 7:37-39). It is clear therefore that the children of Israel were regenerated people and thus that the thrust of the passage is not salvation but rewards and their possible forfeiture, which are available to the saints after they are saved.

Note that we said *supra* that Moses' sin at Horeb the second time destroyed God's type. The Rock, once smitten (Exod.17:6) needs only to be spoken to (Num.20:7-13). Moses destroyed the picture and paid a stiff penalty. That Rock is a type of Christ, Who was smitten on the cross in order that we may drink the water of everlasting life. Once smitten at Calvary, He need never be smitten again. "Christ being raised from the dead, dieth no more. Death hath no more dominion over Him. For in that He died, He died unto sin once, and in that He liveth He liveth unto God" (Rom.6:9,10). When we want another refreshing drink we do not smite Him. We only speak to Him.

Despite all of God's care for His people, many of them did not respond in faith. This is the thought of

Verse 5 - "But with many of them God was not well pleased: for they were overthrown in the wilderness."

ἀλλ' οὐκ ἐν τοῖς πλείοσιν αὐτῶν εὐδόκησεν ὁ θεός, κατεστρώθησαν γὰρ ἐν τῇ ἐρήμῳ.

"Nevertheless with most of them God was not well pleased; for they were overthrown in the wilderness." . . . RSV

ἀλλ' (adversative conjunction) 342.
οὐκ (negative particle with the indicative) 130.
ἐν (preposition with the locative with plural pronouns) 80.
τοῖς (loc.pl.masc.of the article in agreement with πλείοσιν) 9.
πλείοσιν (loc.pl.masc.of πλείων) 474.
αὐτῶν (gen.pl.masc.of αὐτός, partitive genitive) 16.
εὐδόκησεν (3d.per.sing.aor.act.ind.of εὐδοκέω, constative) 328.
ὁ (nom.sing.masc.of the article in agreement with θεός) 9.
θεός (nom.sing.masc.of θεός, subject of εὐδόκησεν) 124.

#4190 κατεστρώθησαν (3d.per.pl.aor.pass.ind.of καταστρώννυμι, constative).

King James Version

overthrow - 1 Cor.10:5.

Revised Standard Version

overthrow - 1 Cor.10:5.

Meaning: A combination of κατά (#98) and στρώννυμι (#1351). To scatter thoroughly and indiscriminately. κατά adds the distributive idea. With reference to the dead bodies of the backslidden Jews who died in the wilderness and were scattered all along the trail followed by Israel in the years of wandering (Numbers 33:1-49) - 1 Cor.10:5.

γὰρ (inferential conjunction) 105.
ἐν (preposition with the locative of place) 80.
τῇ (loc.sing.fem.of the article in agreement with ἐρήμῳ) 9.
ἐρήμῳ (loc.sing.fem.of ἔρημος, place) 250.

Translation - "But God was not pleased with the most of them; therefore they were scattered about in the desert."

Comment: Note that οὐκ is out of place for emphasis. The main point now is that, despite the fact that the children of Israel were the recipients of God's grace (verses 1-4) God was displeased with most of them. ἐν with the locative case with plural nouns or pronouns. κατά in composition is distributive.

Those who disbelieved God at Kadesh-Barnea (Numbers 14:26-39) did not lose their salvation, but they were condemned to physical death along the wilderness trail and thus they were deprived of the privilege of entering the Promised Land. Caleb and Joshua, the two spies who brought in the minority report to the effect that God would deliver the inhabitants of Canaan into their hands were the only two persons in Israel who were over twenty years of age, thirty-eight years before, who were permitted to cross the Jordan and take possession of the land. In recognition of this fact Paul says that God was displeased with "most of them."

The defeated Christian will not be lost (1 Cor.3:15) but he will lose his chance to be rewarded in the kingdom reign of the Messiah (*Cf.* comment on Romans 8:21; Phil.3:10-14).

The Arminian view that salvation begun by faith is completed by the Christian's merit is wrong, but the Holiness emphasis that Christians must live victorious lives for which they will receive bonus rewards, which rewards are forfeited if holy living is not forthcoming is correct . The disagreement between Arminians and Calvinists, while going much deeper than the point here, is on the nature of the loss to the backslidden Christian. His loss is not salvation, but rewards. He is typified by those Jews who died in the desert and were buried by the trail.

Verse 6 - "Now these things were our examples, to the intent we should not lust after evil things, as they also lusted."

ταῦτα δέ τύποι ἡμῶν ἐγενήθησαν, εἰς τὸ μὴ εἶναι ἡμᾶς ἐπιθυμητὰς κακῶν, καθὼς κἀκεῖνοι ἐπεθύμησαν.

"Now these things are warnings for us, not to desire evil as they did." ... RSV

ταῦτα (nom.pl.neut.of οὗτος, subject of ἐγενήθησαν) 93.

δὲ (explanatory conjunction) 11.

τύποι (nom.pl.masc.of τύπος, predicate nominative) 2917.

ἡμῶν (gen.pl.masc.of ἐγώ, reference) 123.

ἐγενήθησαν (3d.per.pl.aor.pass.ind.of γίνομαι, ingressive) 113.

εἰς (preposition with the articular infinitive in a negative purpose clause) 140.

τὸ (acc.sing.neut.of the article, in agreement with εἶναι) 9.

μὴ (negative particle with the infinitive) 87.

εἶναι (pres.inf.of εἰμί, accusative case, negative purpose) 86.

ἡμᾶς (acc.pl.masc.of ἐγώ, general reference) 123.

#4191 ἐπιθυμητὰς (acc.pl.masc.of ἐπιθυμητής, predicate accusative).

    King James Version

lust after - 1 Cor. 10:6.

    Revised Standard Version

desire - 1 Cor. 10:6.

Meaning: A combination of ἐπί (#47) and θυμός (#2034). *Cf.* also ἐπιθυμέω (#500). One who lusts after or covets something. One who strongly desires - followed by κακῶν in 1 Cor. 10:6.

κακῶν (gen.pl.neut.of κακός, objective genitive) 1388.

καθὼς (compound comparative adverb) 1348.

κἀκεῖνοι (nom.pl.masc.of κἀκεῖνος, subject of ἐπεθύμησαν) 1164.

ἐπεθύμησαν (3d.per.pl.aor.act.ind.of ἐπιθυμέω, constative) 500.

Translation - "Now these things became illustrations for us in order that we will not lust after that which is evil as they did."

Comment: δὲ is explanatory. ταῦτα is anaphoric referring to Israel's sad experiences of sin and judgment in verse 5. The picture is clear. A chosen nation, in possession of a clear-cut unconditional covenant promise from God, given to their forefathers that they were to possess the land of Canaan, but who also rashly accepted another conditional covenant at Mount Sinai, failed the conditions of the law covenant and died in the wilderness. God had kept His bargain with Abraham, Isaac and Jacob by redeeming His people by blood (Exodus 12) and by power (Exodus 14). He had provided guidance, protection, food, water and sustenance. Despite the fact that they were saved people, they rebelled against and disbelieved God's promises and paid a fearful price for their backsliding. All who disbelieved God at Kadesh-Barnea, except the chidlren who were less than twenty years old, died at some point along the trail of the 38 year trek through a desert that covered only a few counties of average size. The student who wishes to research this point should trace their itinerary (Numbers 33) on a map which has all of the place names. They moved 42 times in 40 years and crossed and recrossed their path again and again. Yet during all of this long period they ate the manna from heaven and were otherwise sustained. This continued until the last adult Jew who criticized God at Kadesh-Barnea was dead and buried beside the trail, the last of whom was Moses who got close enough to see across the Jordan but could not enter the promised land.

Paul tells this story to warn Christians not to take God's grace and mercy for granted. Note the negative final clause with εἰς and the articular infinitive in the accusative case. - "Lest we should lust after evil as they did."

Antinomian and careless Calvinism, with its complacent presumption upon God's grace will get no comfort here. Arminians are supported in their pleas for the victorious life but rebuked for their view that the Jews who died in the wilderness were lost eternally . God is angry with sin, especially when He finds it in the lives of His children who ought to know better. Sin in the Christian's life does not short-circuit his justification, but it denies to him his status as an overcomer and results in his loss of reward at the judgment seat of Christ (1 Cor.3:15). Though the passage generally is a warning against all sin in the life of the believer, in verses 7-10 Paul mentions specifically four sins which the Jews committed which called down the wrath of God upon them.

Verse 7 - "Neither be ye idolaters, as were some of them; as it is written, The people sat down to eat and drink and rose up to play."

μηδὲ εἰδωλολάτραι γίνεσθε, καθώς τινες αὐτῶν. ὥσπερ γέγραπται, Ἐκάθισεν ὁ λαὸς φαγεῖν καὶ πεῖν, καὶ ἀνέστησαν παίζειν.

"Do not be idolaters as some of them were; as it is written, 'The people sat down to eat and drink and rose up to dance.' " . . . RSV

μηδὲ (negative continuative conjunction with the imperative) 612.
εἰδωλολάτραι (nom.pl.masc.of εἰδωλολάτρης, predicate nominative) 4142.
γίνεσθε (2d.per.pl.pres.impv.of γίνομαι, prohibition) 113.
καθώς (compound comparative particle) 1348.
τινες (nom.pl.masc.of τις, indefinite pronoun, subject of ἦσαν understood) 486.
αὐτῶν (gen.pl.masc.of αὐτός, partitive genitive) 16.
ὥσπερ (intensive comparative particle) 560.
γέγραπται (3d.per.sing.perf.pass.ind.of γράφω, intensive) 156.
Ἐκάθισεν (3d.per.sing.aor.act.ind.of καθίζω, constative) 420.
ὁ (nom.sing.masc.of the article in agreement with λαὸς) 9.
λαὸς (nom.sing.masc.of λαός, subject of ἐκάθισεν and ἀνέστησαν) 110.
φαγεῖν (aor.act.inf.of ἐσθίω, purpose) 610.

καὶ (adjunctive conjunction joining infinitives) 14.
πεῖν (aor.act.inf.of πίνω, purpose) 611.
καὶ (adjunctive conjunction joining verbs) 14.
ἀνέστησαν (3d.per.pl.aor.act.ind.of ἀνίστημι, constative) 789.

#4192 παίζειν (pres.act.inf.of παίζω, purpose).

King James Version

play - 1 Cor.10:7.

Revised Standard Version

dance - 1 Cor.10:7.

Meaning: To play like a child; play, sport, jest, give way to hilarity, with singing and dancing. Equal to the Hebrew in Ex.32:6; Gen.21:9; 26:8; Judges 16:25. *Cf.* ἐμπαίζω (#212). With reference to the activity of Israel at Sinai - 1 Cor.10:7.

Translation - "Neither be idolaters as some of them were, as it stands written, 'The people sat down to eat and to drink and they stood up to dance."

Comment: Note the μὴ . . . μηδὲ . . . . μηδὲ . . . . μηδὲ . . . . μηδὲ sequence in verses 6 - 10. Do not lust, worship idols, fornicate, tempt the Lord nor complain. All of these sins Israel committed for which they paid dearly. The quotation is from Exodus 32:6. παίζω (#4192) means more than innocent play, jesting or artistic dancing. It involved illicit sex (Exodus 32:25). The irony is that the party at the foot of Mount Sinai was going on at the precise time that Moses was in the mountain receiving the law which they had presumptuously declared their intention and ability to keep. The golden calf and Aaron's lame excuse for its existence (Exodus 32:24) is evidence that "when the commandment came, sin revived and I died." (Rom.7:9).

Verse 8 - "Neither let us commit fornication, as some of them committed, and fell in one day three and twenty thousand."

μηδὲ πορνεύωμεν, καθώς τινες αὐτῶν ἐπόρνευσαν, καὶ ἔπεσαν μιᾷ ἡμέρᾳ εἴκοσι τρεῖς χιλιάδες.

"We must not indulge in immorality as some of them did, and twenty-three thousand fell in a single day." . . . RSV

μηδὲ (negative continuative conjunction with the hortatory subjunctive) 612.
πορνεύωμεν (1st.per.pl.pres.act.subj.of πορνεύω, hortatory) 4152.
καθώς (compound comparative particle) 1348.
τινες (nom.pl.masc.of τις, indefinite pronoun, subject of ἐπόρνευσαν) 486.
αὐτῶν (gen.pl.masc.of αὐτός, partitive genitive) 16.
ἐπόρνευσαν (3d.per.pl.aor.act.ind.of πορνεύω,constative) 4152.
καὶ (adjunctive conjunction joining verbs) 14.
ἔπεσαν (3d.per.pl.aor.act.ind.of πίπτω, constative) 187.

μιᾷ (loc.sing.fem.of εἷς, in agreement with ἡμέρᾳ) 469.

ἡμέρᾳ (loc.sing.fem.of ἡμέρα, time point) 135.

εἴκοσι (numeral) 2283.

τρεῖς (numeral) 1010.

χιλιάδες (nom.pl.of χιλιας, subject of ἔπεσαν) 2536.

Translation - "Nor let us indulge in immorality as some of them did and twenty-three thousand fell in one day."

Comment: *Cf.* Numbers 25:1-9. Paul adds a detail not given by Moses. The total dead was twenty-four thousand, twenty-three thousand of whom died in a single day. Note that Satan used sex as the bait to lead the children of Israel to idolatry.

Verse 9 - "Neither let us tempt Christ, as some of them also tempted, and were destroyed of serpents."

μηδὲ ἐκπειράζωμεν τὸν κύριον, καθώς τινες αὐτῶν ἐξεπείρασαν, καὶ ὑπὸ τῶν ὄφεων ἀπώλλυντο.

"We must not put the Lord to the test, as some of them did and were destroyed by serpents;" . . . RSV

μηδὲ (negative continuative conjunction with the hortatory subjunctive) 612.

ἐκπειράζωμεν (1st.per.pl.pres.act.subj.of ἐκπειράζω, hortatory) 356.

τὸν (acc.sing.masc.of the article in agreement with κύριον) 9.

κύριον (acc.sing.masc.of κύριος, direct object of ἐκπειράζωμεν) 97.

καθώς (compound comparative particle) 1348.

τινες (nom.pl.masc.of τις, indefinite pronoun, subject of ἐξεπείρασαν) 486.

αὐτῶν (gen.pl.masc.of αὐτός, partitive genitive) 16.

ἐξεπείρασαν (3d.per.pl.aor.act.ind.of ἐκπειράζω, constative) 356.

καὶ (continuative conjunction) 14.

ὑπὸ (preposition with the ablative of agent) 117.

τῶν (abl.pl.masc.of the article in agreement with ὄφεων) 9.

ὄφεων (abl.pl.masc.of ὄφις, agent) 658.

ἀπώλλυντο (3d.per.pl.imp.mid.ind.of ἀπόλλυμι, iterative) 208.

Translation - "Neither let us try the Lord's patience as some of them tempted Him and they were being killed by the serpents."

Comment: ἐκπειράζω (#356) - "to try the Lord's patience." To presume upon His goodness. Some mss. have Χριστόν or θεόν, instead of κύριον. Miniscule 1985 omits τὸν κύριον. Metzger defends the reading by saying, "Paul's reference to Christ here is analogous to that in verse 4." (Metzger, *A Textual Commentary on the Greek New Testament*, 560). The story is found in Numbers 21:5-6. Israel complained about her treatment from the Lord and the invasion of the snakes was God's answer. Note the imperfect in ἀπώλλυντο, since as some died, others repented and looked to the uplifted serpent of brass to live. *Cf.* our comment on John 3:14,15.

Verse 10 - "Neither murmer ye, as some of them also murmered, and were destroyed of the destroyer."

μηδὲ γογγύζετε, καθάπερ τινὲς αὐτῶν ἐγόγγυσαν, καὶ ἀπώλοντο ὑπὸ τοῦ ὀλοθρευτοῦ.

". . .nor grumble, as some of them did and were destroyed by the Destroyer."..

. RSV

μηδὲ (negative continuative conjunction with the imperative) 612.
γογγύζετε (2d.per.pl.pres.act.impv.of γογγύζω, command) 1322.
καθάπερ (intensive comparative particle) 3883.
τινὲς (nom.pl.masc.of τις, indefinite pronoun, subject of ἐγόγγυσαν) 486.
αὐτῶν (gen.pl.masc.of αὐτός, partitive genitive) 16.
ἐγόγγυσαν (3d.per.pl.aor.act.ind.of γογγύζω, constative) 1322.
καὶ (adjunctive conjunction joining verbs) 14.
ἀπώλοντο (3d.per.pl.2d.aor.mid.ind.of ἀπόλλυμι, constative) 208.
ὑπὸ (preposition with the ablative of agent) 117.
τοῦ (abl.sing.masc.of the article in agreement with ὀλοθρευτοῦ) 9.

#4193 ὀλοθρευτοῦ (abl.sing.masc.of ὀλοθρευτής, agent).

King James Version

destroyer - 1 Cor.10:10.

Revised Standard Version

Destroyer - 1 Cor.10:10.

Meaning: Cf. ὀλοθρεύω (#5038); ὄλεθρος (#4135). Destroyer - 1 Cor.10:10.

Translation - "Neither continue to complain exactly like they complained, and were destroyed by the Destroyer."

Comment: Paul here finishes his list of injunctions which began in verse 6. Paul's philosophy of history included his view that a knowledge of the past would enable him to make value judgments about certain things and thus provide a warning not to repeat certain evil acts or attitudes. This is not the historicism of the existentialist who professes a profound ignorance of the past and hence disclaims any ability to draw ethical lessons from it. On the contrary Paul was telling the Corinthian Christians to study the history of Israel from the Passover to their entry into Canaan in order to understand their errors and the misfortunes that resulted, and thus avoid committing the same sins.

He closes this section with the admonitions of verses 11,12. To events to which he alludes here are recorded in Numbers 14:2,36; 16:41-49; Ps.106:25-27; Heb.3:11,17.

Verse 11 - "Now all these things happened unto them for ensamples; and they are written for our admonition, upon whom the ends of the world are come."

ταῦτα δὲ τυπικῶς συνέβαινεν ἐκείνοις, ἐγράφη δὲ πρὸς νουθεσίαν ἡμῶν, εἰς οὕς τὰ τέλη τῶν αἰώνων κατήντηκεν.

"Now these things happened to them as a warning, but they were written down for our instruction, upon whom the end of the ages has come." . . . RSV

ταῦτα (nom.pl.neut.of οὗτος, subject of συνέβαινεν) 93.
δὲ (explanatory conjunction) 11.

#4194 τυπικῶς (adverbial).

King James Version

for ensamples - 1 Cor.10:11.

Revised Standard Version

as a warning - 1 Cor.10:11.

Meaning: By way of example. *Cf.* #2917. Prefiguratively. Typically - 1 Cor.10:11.

συνέβαινεν (3d.per.sing.imp.act.ind.of συμβαίνω, iterative) 2642.
ἐκείνοις (dat.pl.masc.of ἐκεῖνος, personal interest) 246.
ἐγράφη (3d.per.sing.2d.aor.pass.ind.of γράφω, constative) 156.
δὲ (continuative conjunction) 11.
πρὸς (preposition with the accusative, purpose) 197.

#4195 νουθεσίαν (acc.sing.fem.of νουθεσία, purpose).

King James Version

admonition - 1 Cor.10:11; Eph.6:4; Titus 3:10.

Revised Standard Version

instruction - 1 Cor.10:11; Eph.6:4.
admonish - Titus 3:10.

Meaning: A combination of νοῦς (#2928) and τίθημι (#455). *Cf.* νουθετέω (#3535). Hence, a placing of the mind; an intellectual adjustment to bring one's thinking to a desired position. Admonition, instruction, warning - 1 Cor.10:11; Eph.6:4; Titus 3:10.

ἡμῶν (gen.pl.masc.of ἐγώ, possession) 123.
εἰς (preposition with the accusative of extent) 140.
οὕς (acc.pl.masc.of ὅς, relative pronoun, extent) 65.
τὰ (nom.pl.neut.of the article in agreement with τέλη) 9.
τέλη (nom.pl.neut.of τέλος, subject of καθήντηκεν) 881.
τῶν (gen.pl.masc.of the article in agreement with αἰώνων) 9.
αἰώνων (gen.pl.masc.of αἰών, description) 1002.
κατήντηκεν (3d.per.sing.perf.act.ind.of κατεντάω, intensive) 3353.

Translation - *"Now these things were happening to them for purposes of illustration, and they were written for our admonition, unto whom the ends of the ages have come."*

Comment: Paul repeats the statement of verse 6. God had a double purpose for punishing Israel. His reaction to their crimes was an intended lesson for them and also a warning for Christians.

Paul clearly reveals here that he thought that his generation would live to see the second coming of Messiah. For him, entrance into the spiritual Canaan (the Messianic Kingdom Age) was at hand, but he feared that some of the Corinthian saints who had their problems might be left out of it, just as unworthy Jews died in the wilderness and were denied entrance into Canaan.

Will all of the members of the Body of Christ be raptured when He comes? Is Revelation 20:6 an implication that not all of the saints will take part in the first resurrection? Is this what Phil.3:14 means? And Heb.11:35? The reader will note that I am asking questions, not giving answers! The reward that victorious Christians will receive and that other saints, justified to be sure, but having lived defeated lives will forfeit could be awarded or withheld in the Kingdom Age, after the rapture of the entire Body of Christ. Thus it is possible to reconcile total rapture with the teaching here in regard to punishment for the Christian's sin. Those students who insist that "Partial Rapture is Rupture" may have a convincing point. One thing is certain — no one be he justified saint or condemned sinner can violate the law of God without incurring His displeasure and must pay for his indiscretion one way or the other. Economists speak of the TINSTAAFL principle by which they mean "There is no such thing as a free lunch." Members of the Body of Christ do not forfeit their position in the Body as punishment for the sins, but there is a loss of reward at some future time. This loss is assessed at the judgment seat of Christ (2 Cor.5:10,11). After that in some way and at some time every child of God will pay for his failure to have lived his Christian life in keeping with the will of God and in compliance with the leading of the Holy Spirit.

Verse 12 - *"Wherefore let him that thinketh he standeth take heed lest he fall."*

ὥστε ὁ δοκῶν ἑστάναι βλετέτω μὴ πέσῃ.

"Therefore let any one who thinks that he stands take heed lest he fall." . . .
                                                                              RSV

ὥστε (inferential conjunction) 752.

ὁ (nom.sing.masc.of the article in agreement with δοκῶν) 9.

δοκῶν (pres.act.part.nom.sing.masc.of δοκέω, substantival, subject of βλεπέτω) 287.

ἑστάναι (2d.perf.act.inf.of ἵστημι, object of δοκῶν) 180.

βλεπέτω (3d.per.sing.pres.act.impv.of βλέπω, command) 499.

μὴ (negative particle with the subjunctive in a negative purpose clause) 87.

πέσῃ (3d.per.sing.2d.aor.act.subj.of πίπτω, negative purpose) 187.

Translation - "Therefore let him who thinks he is standing take care lest he fall."

Comment: ὥστε here is used inferentially like οὖν. Robertson says, "Of the 95 instances (Yeager's count is 90) of ὥστε in the N.T. probably 30 do not come up for discussion under either final or consecutive clauses. The word in these examples is merely an introductory inferential particle like οὖν. The structure is wholly paratactic. In this sense of 'therefore' the particle occurs with the ind. nineteen times. Cf.Mt.12:12; ὥστε ἔξεστιν. Once the subj. appears, 1 Cor.5:8, ὥστε ἑορτάζωμεν. . . . The other eleven instances have the imper. (pres.). Cf.ὥστε βλεπέτω (1 Cor.10:12). See 1 Cor.3:21; 11:33, etc." (*Grammar*, 999, 1000). *Cf.*#752. Thus the logical result of what Paul has said in verses 5-11 follows in verse 12. Note that ἑστάναι is a second perfect infinitive. How often we see some "mature" Christian, living in the past (*contra* Phil.3:13), boasting of a long record of Christian living and drawing the unwarranted conclusion that since he has been "standing" so long he is secure now. That kind of thinking is fraught with danger. "The past is" not necessarily "prologue."

The thought here is "Take care. You are saved and have a good record - up to this point. But you can lose it all except your salvation" (Heb.6:4-6).

It is therefore quite fitting for Paul to introduce verse 13 with its formula by which we can withstand temptation.

Verse 13 - "There hath no temptation taken you but such as is common to man: but God is faithful, who will not suffer you to be tempted above that ye are able; but will with the temptation also make a way to escape, that ye may be able to bear it."

πειρασμὸς ὑμᾶς οὐκ εἴληφεν εἰ μὴ ἀνθρώπινος. πιστὸς δὲ ὁ θεός, ὃς οὐκ ἐάσει ὑμᾶς πειρασθῆναι ὑπὲρ ὃ δύνασθε, ἀλλὰ ποιήσει σὺν τῷ πειρασμῷ καὶ τὴν ἔκβασιν τοῦ δύνασθαι ὑπενεγκεῖν.

"No temptation has overtaken you that is not common to man. God is faithful, and he will not let you be tempted beyond your strength, but with the temptation will also provide the way to escape, that you may be able to endure it." . . . RSV

πειρασμὸς (nom.sing.masc.of πειρασμός, subject of εἴληφεν) 583.

ὑμᾶς (acc.pl.masc.of σύ, direct object of εἴληφεν) 104.

οὐκ (negative particle with the indicative) 130.

εἴληφεν (3d.per.sing.perf.act.ind.of λαμβάνω, iterative) 533.

εἰ (conditional particle in an elliptical condition) 337.

μὴ (negative particle in an elliptical condition) 87.

ἀνθρώπινος (nom.sing.masc.of ἀνθρώπινος, predicate adjective) 3415.

πιστὸς (nom.sing.masc.of πιστός, predicate adjective) 1522.

δὲ (adversative conjunction) 11.

ὁ (nom.sing.masc.of the article in agreement with θεός) 9.

θεός (nom.sing.masc.of θεός, subject of ἐστίν understood) 124.

ὃς (nom.sing.masc.of ὅς, relative pronoun, subject of ἐάσει, adjectival) 65.

οὐκ (negative particle with the indicative) 130.
ἐάσει (3d.per.sing.fut.act.ind.of ἐάω, predictive) 1521.
ὑμᾶς (acc.pl.masc.of σύ, general reference) 104.
πειρασθῆναι (aor.pass.inf.of πειράζω, direct object of ἐάσει) 330.
ὑπέρ (preposition with the accusative of extent - "beyond" or "more than") 545.
ὅ (acc.sing.neut.of ὅς, relative pronoun, adjectival) 65.
δύνασθε (2d.per.pl.pres.mid.ind.of δύναμαι, aoristic) 289.
ἀλλά (alternative conjunction) 342.
ποιήσει (3d.per.sing.fut.act.ind.of ποιέω, predictive) 127.
σὺν (preposition with the locative of accompanying circumstance) 1542.
τῷ (loc.sing.masc.of the article in agreement with πειρασμῷ) 9.
πειρασμῷ (loc.sing.masc.of πειρασμός, accompanying circumstance) 583.
καὶ (adjunctive conjunction joining verbs) 14.
τὴν (acc.sing.fem.of the article in agreement with ἔκβασιν) 9.

#4196 ἔκβασιν (acc.sing.fem.of ἔκβασις, direct object of ποιήσει).

King James Version

way to escape - 1 Cor.10:13.
end - Heb.13:7.

Revised Standard Version

way of escape - 1 Cor.10:13.
outcome - Heb.13:7.

Meaning: Cf. ἐκβαίνω (#5031). Hence, the way out. A combination of ἐκ (#19) and βαίνω - "to go." egress. Metaphorically, with reference to a way to escape temptation - a solution - 1 Cor.10:13. In Heb.13:7 with reference to the manner in which one approaches and experiences the end of his life. The attitude that a good man or woman has about physical death as expressed in his view of death.

τοῦ (gen.sing.neut.of the article, purpose) 9.
δύνασθαι (pres.mid.inf.of δύναμαι, purpose) 289.

#4197 ὑπενεγκεῖν (2d.aor.act.inf.of ὑποφέρω, epexegetical).

King James Version

bear - 1 Cor.10:13.
endure - 2 Tim.3:11; 1 Pet.2:19.

Revised Standard Version

endure - 1 Cor.10:13; 2 Tim.3:11; 1 Pet.2:19.

Meaning: A combination of ὑπό (#117) and φέρω (#683). To endure or bear by carrying from beneath. To bear up; to carry. Metaphorically, to endure temptation without yielding to it - 1 Cor.10:13; with reference to persecutions - 2

Tim.3:11 (without retaliation); grief - 1 Pet.2:19, without collapse.

Translation - "No temptation has ever seized upon you except one which all men experience. But God is faithful, Who will not permit you to be tempted beyond your ability to withstand, but He will also provide with the temptation the way out in order that you will be able to endure it."

Comment: The geographic position of Corinth in the Mediterranean world was such that a great many visitors came there for commercial and other purposes. The result was that it was a wicked city. The Corinthian Christians may have thought themselves beset with temptations which were more imperious than most. Paul assures them that such is not the case. It is as difficult to live the Christian life in the rural areas as in the city. It is also as easy to live for Christ when we remember that wherever we live the Holy Spirit is using our body as His temple and He is always available for help.

The 2d.perfect εἴληφεν covers the past and the present. Note that it is an iterative perfect, an infrequent construction in the New Testament. *Cf.* John 1:18; 5:37; 2 Cor.12:17. Theirs was not a continuous inducement to evil, without intervening lapses, but again and again in the past they had been induced to commit sin. The Corinthians were not the only Christians with this problem. It is charactertistic of the experience of all human beings.

Note the adjectival relative clause which modifies ὁ θεός. What kind of a God is He? One Who will not permit us to be tempted beyond our ability to resist.

When the inducement to evil comes God makes a way for us to escape it. The articular infinitive τοῦ δύνασθαι is telic and is followed by another which is epexegetical. "In order that we will be able to do what?" To escape the temptation. There is always a way out (τὴν ἔκβασιν.).

God has not chosen to rapture us into glory at the moment of our regeneration. His purpose that we should remain in the world to witness to His grace before the unsaved would thus be frustrated. Nor did He grant us glorification at the same time that He gave us justification, although we are certain to be glorified when we see Him (1 John 3:1,2; Phil.3:20,21). Thus we live in a social environment that makes strong appeals to the flesh in fleshly bodies that are nothing loathe to yield to them. But this does not mean that the Christian must live a defeated life. He cannot rationalize his downfall by saying that the inducement to evil was too great. This verse denies that. God wants us to withstand temptation and He is aware when we are tempted. The way to escape is always there. Our task is to seek, find and utilize it. Some may not look for the way out. Others may look and not find it. Still others may find but not take advantage of it. This is because we are lusting after evil (verse 6). Doolittle, the London bum of *My Fair Lady* sang about his experience when temptation came - "With a little bit of luck you give right in."

The Christian who fears and hates sin can always escape.

Verse 14 - "Wherefore, my dearly beloved, flee from idolatry."

Διόπερ, αγαπητοί μου, φεύγετε απὸ τῆς εἰδωλολατρίας.

"Therefore, my beloved, shun the worship of idols." . . . RSV

Διόπερ (intensive inferential particle) 4173.
αγαπητοί (voc.pl.masc.of αγαπητός, address) 327.
μου (gen.sing.masc.of εγώ, relationship) 123.
φεύγετε (2d.per.pl.pres.act.impv.of φεύγω,command) 202.
απὸ (preposition with the ablative of separation) 70.
τῆς (abl.sing.fem.of the article in agreement with εἰδωλολατρίας) 9.

#4198 εἰδωλολατρίας (abl.sing.fem.of εἰδωλολατρεία, separation).

King James Version

idolatry - 1 Cor.10:14; Gal.5:20; Col.3:5; 1 Pet.4:3.

Revised Standard Version

worship of idols - 1 Cor.10:14.
idolatry - Gal.5:20; Col.3:5; 1 Pet.4:3.

Meaning: Cf. εἰδωλεῖον (#4172); εἰδωλολάτρης (#4142); εἴδωλον (#3138); εἰδωλόθυτον (#3348). Hence idolatry - the worship of idols and pagan deities. One of τὰ ἔργα τῆς σαρκός Gal.5:20; 1 Cor.10:14; 1 Pet.4:3. Associated with τὴν πλεονεξίαν in Col.3:5.

Translation - "I conclude of course, my beloved ones, that you flee from idol worship."

Comment: The translation must reflect the intensity of the inferential conjunction. Διόπερ (#4173) is stronger than διό (#1622) or γάρ (#105). "Wherefore" or "Therefore" is not enough. Paul urges upon his readers the conclusion that flows from verse 13. An idol cannot rescue the devotee from temptation. *Au contraire* idol worship has always been connected with and contributory to the grossest of sins. Idol worship tempts. God rescues from temptation. The idol is faithless. God is faithful. "Therefore (Διόπερ) always flee from idol worship." The idol is an insult to God and the ethics of idolatry is an insult to human decency and dignity. Note that the Ten Commandments swing full circle as they begin and end with a ban on idolatry (Col.3:5).

Verse 15 - "I speak as to wise men; judge ye what I say."

ὡς φρονίμοις λέγω. κρίνατε ὑμεῖς δ φημι.

"I speak as to sensible men; judge for yourselves what I say." . . . RSV

ὡς (comparative particle) 128.
φρονίμοις (dat.pl.masc.of φρόνιμος, indirect object of λέγω) 693.
λέγω (1st.per.sing.pres.act.ind.of λέγω, aoristic) 66.

κρίνατε (2d.per.pl.1st.aor.act.impv.of κρίνω, command) 531.
ὑμεῖς (nom.pl.masc.of σύ, subject of κρίνατε) 104.
ὅ (acc.sing.neut.of ὅς, relative pronoun, direct object of κρίνατε) 65.
φημι (1st.per.sing.pres.act.ind.of φημί, aoristic) 354.

Translation - "I am speaking to men who can think. You must evaluate what I am saying."

Comment: The intellectual approach, so unsuccessful when employed in speaking to an unsaved audience (Acts 17:22-34; 18:1; 1 Cor.2:1-5) is proper when used upon the saints (1 Cor.2:6). Paul is saying here, "Use your head."

Paul now returns for the remainder of the chapter to a more involved discussion of the problem of eating food previously offered to idols in an idol's temple.

Verse 16 - "The cup of blessing which we bless, is it not the communion of the blood of Christ? The bread which we break, is it not the communion of the body of Christ?"

τὸ ποτήριον τῆς εὐλογίας ὅ εὐλογοῦμεν, οὐχὶ κοινωνία ἐστὶν τοῦ αἵματος τοῦ Χριστοῦ; τὸν ἄρτον ὅν κλῶμεν, οὐχὶ κοινωνία τοῦ σώματος τοῦ Χριστοῦ ἐστιν;

"The cup of blessing which we bless, is it not a participation in the blood of Christ? The bread which we break, is it not a participation in the body of Christ?.
. . *RSV*

τὸ (nom.sing.neut.of the article in agreement with ποτήριον) 9.
ποτήριον (nom.sing.neut.of ποτήριον, subject of ἐστὶν) 902.
τῆς (gen.sing.fem.of the article in agreement with εὐλογίας) 9.
εὐλογίας (gen.sing.fem.of εὐλογία, description) 4060.
ὅ (acc.sing.neut.of ὅς, relative pronoun, adjectival, in agreement with ποτήριον) 65.
εὐλογοῦμεν (1st.per.pl.pres.act.ind.of εὐλογέω, customary) 1120.
οὐχὶ (negative particle with the indicative) 130.
κοινωνία (nom.sing.fem.of κοινωνία, predicate nominative) 3001.
ἐστὶ (3d.per.sing.pres.ind.of εἰμί, present progressive retroactive) 86.
τοῦ (gen.sing.neut.of the article in agreement with αἵματος) 9.
αἵματος (gen.sing.neut.of αἷμα, description) 1203.
του (gen.sing.masc.of the article in agreement with Χριστοῦ) 9.
Χριστοῦ (gen.sing.masc.of Χριστός, possession) 4.
τὸν (acc.sing.masc .of the article in agreement with ἄρτον) 9.
ἄρτον (acc.sing.masc.of ἄρτος, subject of ἐστιν, attracted to ὅν) 338.
ὅν (acc.sing.masc.of ὅς, relative pronoun, adjectival, object of κλῶμεν) 65.
κλῶμεν (1st.per.pl.pres.act.ind.of κλάω customary) 1121.
οὐχὶ (negative particle with the indicative) 130.
κοινωνία (nom.sing.fem.of κοινωνία, predicate nominative) 3001.

τοῦ (gen.sing.neut.of the article in agreement with σώματος) 9.

σώματος (gen.sing.neut.of σῶμα, description) 507.

τοῦ (gen.sing.masc.of the article in agreement with Χριστοῦ) 9.

Χριστοῦ (gen.sing.masc.of Χριστός, possession) 4.

ἐστιν (3d.per.sing.pres.ind.of εἰμί, present progressive retroactive) 86.

Translation - "Has not the cup of blessing which we bless always been the fellowship of the blood of Christ? Has not the bread which we break always been the fellowship of the body of Christ?"

Comment: The two rhetorical questions expect positive replies. Paul is reminding the Corinthians of the spiritual significance of eating and drinking the elements at the Supper. Note the customary present tenses in εὐλογοῦμεν and κλῶμεν and the present progressive retroactive force of the copulas.

The word "participation" in the Revised Standard Version is too close to sacerdotalism. That the communion is not sacerdotal is clear from the fact that the physical body and blood of our Lord are not present at the table, since He is sitting at the right hand of God (Psalm 110:1; Heb.1:3; Col.3:1). Paul's meaning is in the symbolism of the cup and the bread. When we pray over the cup and break the bread we do so in contemplation of the fact that just as the elements are eaten to sustain us physically, so our risen Lord sustains us spiritually. The elements participate in (become part and parcel of) our bodies. So we have been incorporated into the Body of Christ by the baptism of the Holy Spirit (1 Cor.12:13) and are part and parcel of His Body.

The Christian communion service therefore is unique in its significance since it sets forth in symbol the unique sacrifice of the unique Son of God in His unique incarnation.

Note the rare case of the antecedent τὸν ἄρτον, the subject of ἐστίν, and, as such, normally in the nominative case, attracted to the accusative case of its relative ὅν, which is accusative by virtue of its use in its own clause as object of κλῶμεν.

Paul is setting the stage for an argument against idolatry which follows.

Verse 17 - "For we being many are one bread, and one body; for we are all partakers of that one bread."

ὅτι εἷς ἄρτος, ἓν σῶμα οἱ πολλοί ἐσμεν, οἱ γὰρ πάντες ἐκ τοῦ ἑνὸς ἄρτου μετέχομεν.

"Because there is one bread, we who are many are one body, for we all partake of the one bread." . . . RSV

ὅτι (conjunction in a causal clause) 211.

εἷς (nom.sing.masc.of εἷς, in agreement with ἄρτος) 469.

ἄρτος (nom.sing.masc.of ἄρτος, predicate nominative) 338.

ἓν (nom.sing.neut.of εἷς, in agreement with σῶμα) 469.

σῶμα (nom.sing.neut.of σῶμα, predicate nominative) 507.

οἱ (nom.pl.masc.of the article in agreement with πολλοί) 9.

πολλοί (nom.pl.masc.of πολύς, subject of ἐσμεν) 228.

ἐσμεν (1st.per.pl.pres.ind.of εἰμί, present progressive retroactive) 86.

οἱ (nom.pl.masc.of the article in agreement with πάντες) 9.

γὰρ (causal conjunction) 105.

πάντες (nom.pl.masc.of πᾶς, subject of μετέχομεν) 67.

ἐκ (preposition with the ablative of source) 19.

τοῦ (abl.sing.masc.of the article in agreement with ἄρτου) 9.

ἑνὸς (abl.sing.masc.of εἷς, in agreement with ἄρτου) 469.

ἄρτου (abl.sing.masc.of ἄρτος, source) 338.

μετέχομεν (1st.per.pl.pres.act.ind.of μετέχω, aoristic) 4176.

Translation - *"Because the many are one bread, one body because we all are partaking of the one bread."*

Comment: Note that ὅτι and γὰρ, both causal, are used together. Individual Christians are "the many" but when viewed corporately we are "the all." As such, since each of us individually and all of us collectively partake of the one bread (John 6:48-58; 17:21; Rom.12:4,5). Paul is uniting all the believers who participate in the communion into one spiritual body of Christ, but he is also uniting each individual believer with the bread which he eats and the cup which he drinks. The total identification of the Christian with the bread and with all other Christians who are also identified with the bread is the point - a point which he pursues in

Verse 18 - *"Behold Israel after the flesh: are not they which eat of the sacrifices partakers of the altar?"*

βλέπετε τὸν Ἰσραὴλ κατὰ σάρκα. οὐχ οἱ ἐσθίοντες τὰς θυσίας κοινωνοὶ τοῦ θυσιαστηρίου εἰσίν;

"Consider the practice of Israel; are not those who eat the sacrifices partners in the altar?" . . . RSV

βλέπετε (2d.per.pl.pres.act.impv.of βλέπω, command) 499.

τὸν (acc.sing.masc.of the article in agreement with Ἰσραὴλ) 9.

Ἰσραὴλ (acc.sing.masc.of Ἰσραὴλ, direct object of βλέπετε) 165.

κατὰ (preposition with the accusative, standard) 98.

σάρκα (acc.sing.fem.of σάρξ, standard) 1202.

οὐχ (negative particle with the indicative in rhetorical question expecting a postive reply) 130.

οἱ (nom.pl.masc.of the article in agreement with ἐσθίοντες) 9.

ἐσθίοντες (pres.act.part.nom.pl.masc.of ἐσθίω, substantival, subject of εἰσίν) 610.

τὰς (acc.pl.fem.of the article in agreement with θυσίας) 9.

θυσίας (acc.pl.fem.of θυσία, direct object of ἐσθίοντες) 796.

κοινωνοὶ (nom.pl.masc.of κοινωνός, predicate nominative) 1470.

τοῦ (gen.sing.neut.of the article in agreement with θυσιαστηρίου) 9.

θυσιαστηρίου (gen.sing.neut.of θυσιαστήριον, description) 484.

εἰσίν (3d.per.pl.pres.ind.of εἰμί, customary) 86.

Translation - *"Consider the nation Israel from a natural point of view. Is it not true that those who eat the physical sacrifices are partakers of the spiritual significance of the altar?"*

Comment: βλέπετε in the sense of "consider." *Cf.*#499 for other examples. Paul is about to draw a lesson from the physical and historical practice of Israel. The rhetorical question expects a positive response. The priests who derived their living from a portion of the animal sacrifices brought to the Tabernacle were obviously in agreement with the institution of the Levitical priesthood and thus morally identified with it. To attend the altar, carry on its functions and eat its offerings was to become involved in all that the altar represented..

Verse 19 - *"What say I then? That the idol is nothing, or that which is offered in sacrifice to idols is anything?"*

τί οὖν φημι; ὅτι εἰδωλόθυτόν τί ἐστιν; ἤ ὅτι εἴδωλόν τί ἐστιν;

"What do I imply then? That food offered to idols is anything, or that an idol is anything?" . . . RSV

τί (acc.sing.neut.of τίς, interrogative pronoun, direct object of φημι) 281.
οὖν (inferential conjunction) 68.
φημι (1st.per.sing.pres.act.ind.of φημί, aoristic) 354.
ὅτι (conjunction introducing an object clause in indirect discourse) 211.
εἰδωλόθυτόν (nom.sing.neut.of εἰδωλόθυτον, subject of ἐστιν) 3348.
τί (nom.sing.neut.of τις, indefinite pronoun, predicate nominative) 486.
ἐστιν (3d.per.sing.pres.ind.of εἰμί, present progressive retroactive) 86.
ἤ (disjunctive) 465.
ὅτι (conjunction introducing an object clause in indirect discourse) 211.
εἴδωλόν (nom.sing.neut.of εἴδωλον, subject of ἐστιν) 3138.
τί (nom.sing.neut.of τις, indefinite pronoun, predicate nominative) 486.
ἐστιν (3d.per.sing.pres.ind.of εἰμί, present progressive retroactive) 86.

Translation - *"So what am I saying? That that which is offered to idols is anything? Or that an idol is anything?"*

Comment: The point that Paul wishes to make is in danger of being misunderstood. In verses 16 and 17 he spoke of the mystic union of the believer with Christ as a result of birth from above (John 3:3,7) and the baptism of the Holy Spirit (1 Cor.12:13). Customarily we symbolize this glorious fact when we sit in communion at the Lord's table. Then he pointed out in verse 18 that the priests at the Levitical altar who ate of its proceeds were in sympathy with the spirit of the altar service. The Corinthians were likely to say therefore that when they ate at an idol's altar they became mystically united with the pagan god. Would not the identification of the worshipper with the god of the altar be the same - whether it was a Christian at the Lord's table, a Jewish priest in the

Levitical tabernacle, or indeed a pagan before an idol? The God of the Levitical tabernacle is the God Whom the Christian worships, as the Epistle to the Hebrews was to make clear, but it does not follow that an idol is anything or that the offering to the idol has any significance. Paul has a different point to make in

Verse 20 - "But I say, that the things which the Gentiles sacrifice, they sacrifice to devils, and not to God: and I would not that ye should have fellowship with devils."

ἀλλ' ὅτι ἃ θύουσιν (τὰ ἔθνη), δαιμονίοις καὶ οὐ θεῷ θύουσιν, οὐ θέλω δὲ ὑμᾶς κοινωνοὺς τῶν διαμονίων γίνεσθαι.

"No, I imply that what pagans sacrifice they offer to demons and not to God. I do not want you to be partners with demons." . . . RSV

ἀλλ' (alternative conjunction) 342.
ὅτι (conjunction introducing an object clause in indirect discourse) 211.
ἃ (acc.pl.neut.of ὅς, relative pronoun, direct object of θύουσιν) 65.
θύουσιν (3d.per.pl.pres.act.ind.of θύω, customary) 1398.
(τὰ (nom.pl.neut.of the article in agreement with ἔθνη) 9.
ἔθνη) (nom.pl.neut.of ἔθνος, subject of θύουσιν) 376.
διαμονίοις (dat.pl.neut.of δαιμόνιον, indirect object of θύουσιν) 686.
καὶ (adversative conjunction) 14.
οὐ (negative particle with the indicative) 130.
θεῷ (dat.sing.masc.of θεός, indirect object of θύουσιν) 124.
θύουσιν (3d.per.pl.pres.act.ind.of θύω, customary) 1398.
οὐ (negative particle with the indicative) 130.
θέλω (1st.per.sing.pres.act.ind.of θέλω, aoristic) 88.
δὲ (continuative conjunction) 11.
ὑμᾶς (acc.pl.masc.of σύ, general reference) 104.
κοινωνοὺς (acc.pl.masc.of κοινωνός, predicate accusative) 1470.
τῶν (gen.pl.neut.of the article in agreement with δαιμονίων) 9.
δαιμονίων (gen.pl.neut.of δαιμόνιον, description) 686.
γίνεσθαι (pres.mid.inf.of γίνομαι, direct object of θέλω) 113.

Translation - "On the contrary I am saying that the things which the Gentiles sacrifice, they sacrifice to demons and not to God; and I do not want you to be associated with the demons."

Comment: The alternative conjunction ἀλλ' indicates what Paul is saying. It is not what they supposed he meant by verse 19. Neither idols nor that which is offered to them has any real significance, but pagans who worship idols are worshipping demons. So when a Christian goes into an idol temple and eats the meat from an animal which was previously offered to an idol he seems to be in fellowship with the demons, just as he is in fellowship with Christ at the Christian Communion table (verse 17) and as a Jewish priest is in fellowship with God in a Levitical temple (verse 18). The idol is nothing but the Christian is lending his personal support to that which is designed to commune with demons. This Paul does not wish for the Corinthians. The appearance is real even though there is no substance to the idol worship. There is nothing either good or evil about the idol or the temple. They are only stone and timber. But the demons at the behest of Satan engineered the carving of the idol and the construction of the temple. And they motivate the worshipper to worship, after which the flesh of the worshipper, already totally fallen produces its activities (Gal.5:19-21).

Verse 21 - "Ye cannot drink the cup of the Lord, and the cup of devils: ye cannot be partakers of the Lord's table, and of the table of devils."

οὐ δύνασθε ποτήριον κυρίου πίνειν καὶ ποτήριον δαιμονίων. οὐ δύνασθε τραπέζης κυρίου μετέχειν καὶ τραπέζης δαιμονίων.

"You cannot drink the cup of the Lord and the cup of demons. You cannot partake of the table of the Lord and the table of demons." . . . RSV

οὐ (negative particle with the indicative) 130.
δύνασθε (2d.per.pl.pres.mid.ind.of δύναμαι, aoristic) 289.
ποτήριον (acc.sing.neut.of ποτήριον, direct object of πίνειν) 902.
κυρίου (gen.sing.masc.of κύριος, description) 97.
πίνειν (pres.act.inf.of πίνω, epexegetical) 611.
καὶ (adjunctive conjunction joining nouns) 14.
ποτήριον (acc.sing.neut.of ποτήριον, direct object of πίνειν) 902.
δαιμονίων (gen.pl.neut.of δαιμόνιον, description) 686.
οὐ (negative particle with the indicative) 130.
δύνασθε (2d.per.pl.pres.mid.ind.of δύναμαι, aoristic) 289.
τραπέζης (gen.sing.fem.of τράπεζα, fellowship) 1176.
κυρίου (gen.sing.masc.of κύριος, description) 97.
μετέχειν (pres.act.inf.of μετέχω, epexegetical) 4176.
καὶ (adjunctive conjunction joining nouns) 14.
τραπέζης (gen.sing.fem.of τράπεζα, fellowship) 1176.
δαιμονίων (gen.pl.neut.of δαιμόνιον, description) 686.

Translation - "You cannot drink a divine cup and a demonic cup. You cannot eat at a divine table and a demonic table."

Comment: οὐ and καί are in contrast. Not one and the other. If one, then not the other. Note that both κυρίου and δαιμονίων are anarthrous, but the context makes clear what Paul means. The Christian communion table is divine; the pagan idol temple is demonic. It is impossible to relate both to Christ and to demons. μετέχειν is a verb of sharing. At the Lord's table we share with others the symbols of the body and blood of Christ and, in a deeper sense, we share participation in the Body of Christ. How then can the Christian also share with pagans in a service that is dedicated to the worship of Satan? There is diametric polarization in the universe between God and Satan. Detente is impossible. Christians have chosen God; pagans have chosen Satan. No basis for fellowship between them exists. *Cf.* 2 Cor.6:14-18.

One wonders how far we can go in applying this principle to the problem of membership in a local church which has not disciplined and excluded those who reject theism? Peripheral differences of opinion with reference to doctrine and practice among those who agree on focal theological questions can be tolerated. The freedom which one demands for himself to study the Word and come to his own conclusions cannot be denied to others. Thus the premillenialist and the amillenialist can share at the Lord's table because each is committed to the Lord Jesus Christ as Head over all things to His church and each is an incorporated member of His body through birth from above. But the eschatological question which divides them does not strike at the focal message of Christian theology. So also Christians with varying views about the ordinances, church government and the place of women in the church can fellowship without destroying the unity of the faith. But what about a trinitarian who belongs to a church where the pastor openly denies the deity of Christ, His incarnation, virgin birth, blood atonement, bodily resurrection and high priestly ministry at the right hand of God?

Verse 22 - "Do we provoke the Lord to jealousy? Are we stronger than he?"

ἢ παραζηλοῦμεν τὸν κύριον; μὴ ἰσχυρότεροι αὐτοῦ ἐσμεν;

"Shall we provoke the Lord to jealousy? Are we stronger than he?" . . . *RSV*

ἢ (disjunctive) 465.

παραζηλοῦμεν (1st.per.pl.pres.act.ind.of παραζηλόω, futuristic) 3976.

τὸν (acc.sing.masc.of the article in agreement with κύριον) 9.

κύριον (acc.sing.masc.of κύριος, direct object of παραζηλοῦμεν) 97.

μὴ (negative particle with the indicative in rhetorical question expecting a negative response) 87.

ἰσχυρότεροι (nom.pl.masc.of ἰσχυρότερος, predicate adjective) 303.

αὐτοῦ (abl.sing.masc.of αὐτός, comparison) 16.

ἐσμεν (1st.per.pl.pres.ind.of εἰμί, rhetorical question) 86.

Translation - "Or are we going to provoke the Lord to jealousy? We are not stronger than He are we?"

Comment: Paul asks a direct question in the first clause and follows with an incredulous rhetorical question in the second. To sit at meat in an idol temple is a bush-league insult to God. Are the Corinthians going to continue to do this? This is a direct question. Paul is asking for information, not expressing his disgust. The second question demands "No" for an answer. Can Christians do what God Himself cannot do? The idol is our Lord's competitor, albeit ultimately destined to lose out in the competition. Satan bruised the heel of the Seed of the woman (Gen.3:15). The children of the devil (John 8:44) crucified Christ, as the demons stirred up to populace to laugh at Him while He suffered. The question is not a question of salvation. The compromising Christian does not lose his salvation. It is a moral question. That which is expedient is not necessarily moral. This is Paul's point in

Do All to the Glory of God

(1 Corinthians 10:23-33)

Verse 23 - "All things are lawful for me, but all things are not expedient: all things are lawful for me, but all things edify not."

Πάντα ἔξεστιν, ἀλλ' οὐ πάντα συμφέρει. πάντα ἔξεστιν, ἀλλ' οὐ πάντα οἰκοδομεῖ.

" 'All things are lawful,' but not all things are helpful. 'All things are lawful,' but not all things build up." . . . RSV

Πάντα (nom.pl.neut.of πᾶς, subject of ἔξεστιν) 67.
ἔξεστιν (3d.per.sing.pres.ind.of ἔξεστι, static) 966.
ἀλλ' (adversative conjunction) 342.
οὐ (negative particle with the indicative) 130.
πάντα (nom.pl.neut.of πᾶς, subject of συμφέρει) 67.
συμφέρει (3d.per.sing.pres.act.ind.of συμφέρω, customary) 505.
πάντα (nom.pl.neut.of πᾶς, subject of ἔξεστιν) 67.
ἔξεστιν (3d.per.sing.pres.ind.of ἔξεστι, static) 966.
ἀλλ' (adversative conjunction) 342.
οὐ (negative conjunction with the indicative) 130.
πάντα (nom.pl.neut.of πᾶς, subject of οἰκοδομεῖ) 67.
οἰκοδομεῖ (3d.per.sing.pres.act.ind.of οἰκοδομέω, customary) 694.

Translation - "Everything is legal but not everything is to my advantage; everything is permitted, but not everything is contributing to Christian development."

Comment: *Cf.* comment on 1 Cor.6:12. Grace indeed liberates from legalistic rules, but grace also calls us to the highest possible achievement in Christian ethics. To break God's laws and contribute to our own downfall is not Christian wisdom. What we do should work for our own long-run advantage. The Christian who prays for "My Utmost for His Highest" will always think and act in the long-run. Note συνεργέω (#2931) in Rom.8:28 and συμφέρω (#505) here. The child of God needs edification, not disintegration.

In the previous discussion about idolatry in chapter 8, Paul's emphasis was upon the Christian's obligation to avoid becoming a stumbling block to a weaker Christian. Now he is discussing what compromise with idolatry does to hinder, not our brother's/sister's growth but our own.

Verse 24 - "Let no man seek his own, but every man another's wealth."

μηδεὶς τὸ ἑαυτοῦ ζητείτω ἀλλὰ τὸ τοῦ ἑτέρου.

"Let no one seek his own good, but the good of his neighbor." . . . RSV

μηδεὶς (nom.sing.masc.of μηδείς, subject of ζητείτω) 713.
τὸ (acc.sing.neut.of the article, direct object of ζητείτω) 9.
ἑαυτοῦ (gen.sing.masc.of ἑαυτοῦ, possession) 288.
ζητείτω (3d.per.sing.pres.act.impv.of ζητέω, command) 207.
ἀλλὰ (alternative conjunction) 342.
τὸ (acc.sing.neut.of the article, direct object of ζητείτω) 9.
τοῦ (gen.sing.masc.of the article in agreement with ἑτέρου) 9.
ἑτέρου (gen.sing.masc.of ἕτερος, possession) 605.

Translation - *"No one must seek his own advantage but that of others."*

Comment: The affirmative may be inferred from the negative μηδεὶς
(Robertson, *Grammar*, 394). Everyone is ordered to be always looking after the
best interests of someone other than himself (present continuous action in
ζητείτω). Note τοῦ with ἑτέρου which makes the substantive specific. We must
note the specificity; we need not translate it, but the Greek never uses the article
without a reason. Paul is pointing here specifically to the fortunes of others, not
to our own fortunes. The KJV misleads the thought of the context by supplying
the word "wealth," which can leave the impression that Paul is talking only
about money. Indeed the KJV has led some misguided souls to say that Paul is
ordering theft!

Christians must seek to promote the best interests of others, whether these
concerns involve spiritual or material benefits.

The connection with the foregoing is this: When a Christian indulges in
something which, though lawful (verse 23) is not constructive, he may be seeking
a short-run advantage for himself (the thrill of the moment) but he is
contributing to the downfall of others, and in the long-run analysis he is also
destroying himself. The selfish motive then, as well as the social motive, should
cause us to sort out from all lawful things those things which are and are not
constructive and developmental to our highest good in the light of eternity -
which is a very long run.

This issue may involve the Christian in social situations in which the only
question is that of good manners. Verses 25-27 describe one situation and offer
Paul's advice. Verses 28 describes a different situation and offers his advice.

Verse 25 - *"Whatsoever is sold in the shambles, that eat, asking no question for
conscience sake."*

Πᾶν τὸ ἐν μακέλλῳ πωλούμενον ἐσθίετε μηδὲν ἀνακρίνοντες διὰ τὴν
συνείδησιν,

*"Eat whatever is sold in the meat market without raising any question on the
ground of conscience."* . . . *RSV*

Πᾶν (acc.sing.neut.of πᾶς, in agreement with πωλούμενον) 67.
τὸ (acc.sing.neut.of the article in agreement with πωλούμενον) 9.
ἐν (preposition with the locative of place) 80.

#4199 μακέλλῳ (loc.sing.masc.of μάκελλον, place).

King James Version

shambles - 1 Cor.10:25.

Revised Standard Version

meat market - 1 Cor.10:25.

Meaning: Liddell & Scott list a neuter noun, τὸ μάκελλον, which means an enclosure. Also ὁ μάκελλος, which corresponds to the Latin *macellum*, a market place where various items, including meat and other foods were sold. A shopping center offering a variety of items for sale - 1 Cor.10:25.

πωλούμενον (pres.pass.part.acc.sing.neut. of πωλέω, substantival, direct object of ἐσθίετε) 892.

ἐσθίετε (2d.per.pl.pres.act.impv. of ἐσθίω, command) 610.

μηδὲν (acc.sing.neut. of μηδείς, direct object of ἀνακρίνοντες) 713.

ἀνακρίνοντες (pres.act.part.nom.pl.masc. of ἀνακρίνω, adverbial, circumstantial) 2837.

διὰ (preposition with the accusative, cause) 118.

τὴν (acc.sing.fem. of the article in agreement with συνείδησιν) 9.

συνείδησιν (acc.sing.fem. of συνείδησις, cause) 3590.

Translation - "Eat whatever is sold in the grocery store and ask no questions because of your conscience."

Comment: We have translated διὰ τὴν συνείδησιν literally - "because of your conscience." Some overscrupulous Christian who thought it sin to eat meat previously involved in idol worship might wish to enquire about a particular cut of meat for sale - "Has this meat been offered to an idol?" This investigation would be necessary if the Christian wished to be certain that he was avoiding compromise. Paul says, "Don't do it." Buy the meat, take it home, cook and eat it and ask no questions. A similar situation exists today because an orthodox Jew cannot be sure that a given steak offered in the store is kosher (*i.e.* sanctioned by Jewish law). The teetotalist should never embarrass the hostess at a dinner party by asking if the meat has been marinated in alcohol, or if cooking sherry was used in any of the food. Some Christians are such fanatics that they do not know how to behave in polite society, and they do the cause of Christ more harm with their intolerance than good with their consistency. A case in point: a university dean and his wife refused to eat the meat served at a dinner party given in his honor by the young wife of one of his new professors, because she had marinated it. The young hostess went to the kitchen and wept. Her husband resigned his position at the close of his contract year. The dean did not apologize! No sin is involved if one inadvertantly compromises a position which may or may not be good ethics in the first place. Why? Because of what Paul says in

Verse 26 - "For the earth is the Lord's and the fulness thereof."

τοῦ κυρίου γὰρ ἡ γῆ καὶ τὸ πλήρωμα αὐτῆς.

"For 'the earth is the Lord's and everything in it.' " . . . RSV

τοῦ (gen.sing.masc.of the article in agreement with κυρίου) 9.
κυρίου (gen.sing.masc.of κύριος, possession) 97.
γὰρ (causal conjunction) 105.
ἡ (nom.sing.fem.of the article in agreement with γῆ) 9.
γῆ (nom.sing.fem.of γῆ, subject of ἐστιν understood) 157.
καὶ (adjunctive conjunction joining nouns) 14.
τὸ (nom.sing.neut.of the article in agreement with πλήρωμα) 9.
πλήρωμα (nom.sing.neut.of πλήρωμα, subject of ἐστιν understood) 805.
αὐτῆς (gen.sing.fem.of αὐτός, possession) 16.

Translation - "Because the earth and everything in it is the Lord's."

Comment: The quotation if from Psalm 24:1. His by right of creation (John 1:3; Heb.1:2; Col.1:16) Hence everything is of divine origin and is good. To say that some things are *always* evil is to propagate the dualistic Manichean heresy which leads to asceticism. The mature Christian rule is not abstinence but temperance and proper use. The teetotalist is really saying that God made some things so evil that He will not touch them and has forbidden His children to touch them, which really says that some Christians have higher standards then God possesses!

Verse 27 - "If any of them that believe not bid you to a feast, and ye be disposed to go, whatsoever is set before you, eat, asking no question for conscience sake."

εἰ τις καλεῖ ὑμᾶς τῶν ἀπίστων καὶ θέλετε πορεύεσθαι, πᾶν τὸ παρατιθέμενον ὑμῖν ἐσθίετε μηδὲν ἀνακρίνοντες διὰ τὴν συνείδησιν.

"If one of the unbelievers invites you to dinner and you are disposed to go, eat whatever is set before you without raising any question on the ground of conscience." . . . RSV

εἰ (conditional particle in a first-class condition) 337.
τις (nom.sing.masc.of τις, indefinite pronoun, subject of καλεῖ) 486.
καλεῖ (3d.per.sing.pres.act.ind.of καλέω, first-class condition) 107.
ἡμᾶς (acc.pl.masc.of σύ, direct object of καλεῖ) 104.
τῶν (gen.pl.masc.of the article in agreement with ἀπίστων) 9.
ἀπίστων (gen.pl.masc.of ἄπιστος, partitive genitive) 1231.
καὶ (continuative conjunction) 14.
θέλετε (2d.per.pl.pres.act.ind.of θέλω, first-class condition) 88.
πορεύεσθαι (pres.mid.inf.of πορεύομαι, epexegetical) 170.
πᾶν (acc.sing.neut.of πᾶς in agreement with παρατιθέμενον) 67.
τὸ (acc.sing.neut.of the article in agreement with παρατιθέμενον) 9.
παρατιθέμενον (pres.pass.part.acc.sing.neut.of παρατίθημι, substantival, direct object of ἐσθίετε) 1055.
ὑμῖν (loc.pl.masc.of σύ, place)

ἐσθίετε (2d.per.pl.pres.act.impv.of ἐσθίω, command) 610.

μηδὲν (acc.sing.neut.of μηδείς, direct object of ἀνακρίνοντες) 713.

ἀνακρίνοντες (pres.act.part.nom.pl.masc.of ἀνακρίνω, adverbial, circumstantial) 2837.

διὰ (preposition with the accusative, cause) 118.

τὴν (acc.sing.fem.of the article in agreement with συνείδησιν) 9.

συνείδησιν (acc.sing.fem.of συνείδησις, cause) 3590.

Translation - "If any of the unbelievers invite you to a dinner and you want to go, eat all that is placed before you, asking no question because of your conscience."

Comment: Here we have a first-class condition with some uncertainty about whether or not the conditions in the protasis will ever happen. Paul was not certain that a Christian would ever be invited to a dinner party given by an unbeliever. There is a second condition. The Christian may or may not wish to accept the invitation. But, if and when the invitation is forthcoming and if and when the Christian chooses to accept it, his course is clear. The apodosis has the imperative. He is to eat all that his host serves, with the added circumstantial condition - he is to raise no question which might arise because of his conscience. He is to make no inquiries about the food. It is the same point as that of verse 25. In comment there we also discussed the situation of verse 27. The two situations are slightly different. In verse 25 we have the Christian shopper in the grocery store. In verse 27 we have the Christian as a guest in the home of an unbeliever. In neither case should the Christian make a scene by pursuing his own particular point in ethics. He should eat what is offered without implying that his own standards of ethics are higher than those of his host.

The alternative would be to say, "I am a Christian. Take this away. It is not fit to eat!"

Protestations of this sort often reveal that the Christian is insecure and makes the protest in order to gain attention. A young evangelist and the pastor of the church in which he was preaching were guests in the home of one of the members. The hostess asked him if he wanted a cup of coffee, to which he replied, "No, I am a Christian. I do not drink coffee." The implication was, either that he was the only Christian present, or that others were not living the victorious life. The pastor rescued the situation by saying gruffly, "I am a Christian too, but I am not a fool about it. I would like a cup of coffee, please, thank you."

In verse 28 we have another different situation.

Verse 28 - "But if any man say unto you, This is offered in sacrifice unto idols, eat not for his sake that shewed it, and for conscience sake: for the earth is the Lord's, and the fulness thereof."

ἐὰν δέ τις ὑμῖν εἴπῃ, Τοῦτο ἱερόθυτόν ἐστιν, μὴ ἐσθίετε δι' ἐκεῖνον τὸν μηνύσαντα καὶ τὴν συνείδησιν —

("But if some one says to you, 'This has been offered in sacrifice,' then out of consideration for the man who informed you, and for conscience' sake —" . . .
RSV

ἐάν (conditional particle in a third-class condition) 363.
δέ (adversative conjunction) 11.
τις (nom.sing.masc.of τις, indefinite pronoun, subject of εἴπῃ) 486.
ὑμῖν (dat.pl.masc.of σύ, indirect object of εἴπῃ) 104.
εἴπῃ (3d.per.sing.aor.act.subj.of εἶπον, third-class condition) 155.
Τοῦτο (nom.sing.neut.of οὗτος, subject of ἐστιν) 93.

#4200 ἱερόθυτόν (nom.sing.neut.of ἱερόθυτός, predicate nominative).

King James Version

offered in sacrifice in sacrifice unto idols - 1 Cor.10:28.

Revised Standard Version

offered in sacrifice unto idols - 1 Cor.10:28.

Meaning: A combination of ἱερός (#4179) and θύω (#1398). Hence, something offered in sacrifice - to idols as the context indicates - 1 Cor.10:28.

ἐστιν (3d.per.sing.pres.ind.of εἰμί, present progressive retroactive) 86.
μή (negative particle with the imperative in a prohibition) 87.
ἐσθίετε (2d.per.pl.pres.act.impv.of ἐσθίω, prohibition) 610.
δι' (preposition with the accusative, cause) 118.
ἐκεῖνον (acc.sing.masc.of ἐκεῖνος, in agreement with μηνύσαντα) 246.
τόν acc.sing.masc.of the article in agreement with μηνύσαντα) 9.
μηνύσαντα (aor.act.part.acc.sing.masc.of μηνύω, substantival, cause) 2666.
καί (adjunctive conjunction joining substantives) 14.
τήν (acc.sing.fem.of the article in agreement with συνείδησιν) 9.
συνείδησιν (acc.sing.fem.of συνείδησις, cause) 3590.

Translation - "But should anyone say to you, 'This has been sacrificed to idols,' eat no more of it, because of the one who told you and his conscience."

Comment: Note the first-class condition with εἰ . . . καλεῖ in verse 27 and the third-class condition with ἐάν . . . εἴπῃ in verse 28. There is more doubt that the condition of verse 28 should occur than that of verse 27. The Christian may or may not be invited to dinner by an unbeliever, and, if so, he may or may not wish to go. But if he goes, it is possible (not probable) that another weaker Christian will also be present, who will ignore Paul's instruction of verse 27. If the weaker Christian makes a scene with his remark about the food, a new situation arises which calls for a different ethical decision. The choice is to insult the unsaved host or become a "trap-stick" (#1082) to the over scrupulous brother. The chance of the former is less than the latter since one has already begun to eat the meat in question without inquiry as to its history. The host will have noticed the courtesy of the mature Christian and also the rude behavior of the fanatic. The host will also understand the dilemma in which his courteous Christian guest is now placed by the impertinent criticism of the boor. On the other hand the critic has already demonstrated his immaturity and will doubtless be more offended if the mature Christian continues to eat. Hence Paul's instruction - "Stop eating" (μή with the present imperative in ἐσθίετε - "Do not continue to eat.") Why? For the sake of your informant and his conscience. The Greek in verse 28 does not say "his" conscience, but Paul add that in verse 29. The spiritual development of the weak brother has priority over the social amenities due an unregenerate host however gracious he may be.

"The Textus Receptus, following a few later uncials (Hc K L Ψ) and most minuscules, adds τοῦ γὰρ κυρίου ἡ γῆ καὶ τὸ πλήρωμα αὐτῆς. That this is a gloss derived from ver.26 is clear from (a) the decisive evidence supporting the shorter text (Sinaiticus A B C D F G H* P 33 81 181 1739 it vg syrₚ copₛₐ,bo arm eth al), and (b) the lack of any good reason to account for deletion of the words,had they been in the text originally." (Metzger, *A Textual Commentary on the Greek New Testament*, 561).

Verse 29 - "Conscience, I say, not thine own, but of the other: for why is my liberty judged of another man's conscience?"

συνείδησιν δὲ λέγω οὐχὶ τὴν ἑαυτοῦ ἀλλὰ τὴν τοῦ ἑτέρου. ἱνατι γὰρ ἡ ἐλευθερία μου κρίνεται ὑπὸ ἄλλης συνειδήσεως;

"I mean his conscience, not yours — do not eat it.— For why should my liberty be determined by another man's scruples?" . . . RSV

συνείδησιν (acc.sing.fem.of συνείδησις, direct object of λέγω) 3590.
δὲ (adversative conjunction) 11.
λέγω (1st.per.sing.pres.act.ind.of λέγω, aoristic) 66.
οὐχὶ (negative particle with the indicative) 130.
τὴν (acc.sing.fem.of the article, direct object of λέγω) 9.
ἑαυτοῦ (gen.sing.masc.of ἑαυτοῦ, possession) 288.
ἀλλὰ (alternative conjunction) 342.
τοῦ (gen.sing.masc.of the article in agreement with ἑτέρου) 9.
ἑτέρου (gen.sing.masc.of ἕτερος, possession) 605.
ἱνατί (Crasis - ἵνα plus τί, in direct question) 3039.
γὰρ (adversative conjunction) 105.
ἡ (nom.sing.fem.of the article in agreement with ἐλευθερία) 9.
ἐλευθερία (nom.sing.fem.of ἐλευθερία, subject of κρίνεται) 3943.
μου (gen.sing.masc.of ἐγώ, possession) 123.
κρίνεται (3d.per.sing.pres.pass.ind.of κρίνω, direct question) 531.
ὑπὸ (preposition with the ablative of agent) 118.
ἄλλης (gen.sing.fem.of ἄλλος, possession) 198.
συνειδήσεως (abl.sing.fem.of συνείδησις, agent) 3590.

Translation - "But I am not speaking of one's own conscience, but of that of the other man. But under what situation should my freedom be judged on the basis of another man's conscience?"

Comment: Paul hastens to clarify his statement about conscience. He means the conscience of the weak brother, not that of the mature Christian who was behaving properly in keeping with verse 27. ἑαυτοῦ is an indirect reflexive. τὴν in τὴν τοῦ ἑτέρου is demonstrative. The τί in ἱνατί is the nom.sing.neut.of the interrogative τίς (#281) and is the subject of γένηται which is ellided. "What happens that makes my freedom of action to eat what I please subject to scrutiny on the basis of the scruples of someone else?" It seems clear that γάρ may be adversative here, since the question naturally arises in rebuttal to Paul's directive of verse 28- μὴ ἐσθίετε - "do not continue to eat." This seems unfair on the surface. *Cf.*#105 for other adversative uses of γάρ, though few grammarians have noted them. Why should a mature Christian be forced into a position that he does not espouse because someone else is less enlightened?

Verse 30 - "For if I by grace be a partaker, why am I evil spoken of for that for which I give thanks?"

εἰ ἐγὼ χάριτι μετέχω, τί βλασφημοῦμαι ὑπὲρ οὗ ἐγὼ εὐχαριστῶ;

"If I partake with thankfulness, why am I denounced because of that for which I give thanks?" . . . RSV

εἰ (conditional particle in a first-class condition) 337.
ἐγὼ (nom.sing.masc.of ἐγώ, subject of μετέχω) 123.
χάριτι (instru.sing.fem.of χάρις, manner) 1700
μετέχω (1st.per.sing.pres.act.ind.of μετέχω, customary) 4176.
τί (acc.sing.neut.of τίς, interrogative pronoun, cause) 281.
βλασφημοῦμαι (1st.per.sing.pres.pass.ind.of βλασφημέω, aoristic) 781.
ὑπὲρ (preposition with the genitive of reference) 545.
οὗ (gen.sing.neut.of ὅς, relative pronoun, reference) 65.
ἐγὼ (nom.sing.masc.of ἐγώ, subject of εὐχαριστῶ) 123.
εὐχαριστῶ (1st.per.sing.pres.act.ind.of εὐχαριστέω, customary) 1185.

Translation - "Since I eat with thanksgiving, why am I being maligned about something for which I am giving thanks?"

Comment: The εἰ clause is a first-class condition. A Christian may partake of everything which God has created (1 Cor.3:21-23). This is because by grace we have been saved (Eph.2:8,9) and we enjoy total liberty as children of God. Since therefore everything we do is by grace and we are mature enough to appreciate our liberty in Christ, why (τί without διά) should a Christian be criticized or denounced for eating something for which he has just sincerely thanked God? The fact that before it was placed upon the table to be eaten it was offered to an idol, which is nothing but a piece of wood, stone or metal (1 Cor.8:4) is of no concern to the mature Christian. This is not the same situation as described in verses 14-22, in which case Christians were eating meat in an idol's temple. This argument in verse 30 reinforces the objection of the last half of verse 29. This is a strong argument, advanced on good theological grounds. Paul does not deny its validity, but answers it in terms of sociology in verses 31-33.

Verse 31 - "Whether therefore ye eat, or drink or whatsoever ye do, do all to the glory of God."

εἴτε οὖν ἐσθίετε εἴτε πίνετε εἴτε τι ποιεῖτε, πάντα εἰς δόξαν θεοῦ ποιεῖτε.

"So, whether you eat or drink, or whatever you do, do all to the glory of God."

             ... RSV

εἴτε (conditional disjunctive) 4016.

οὖν (causal responsive conjunction) 68.

ἐσθίετε (2d.per.pl.pres.act.ind.of ἐσθίω, first-class condition) 610.

εἴτε (conditional disjunctive) 4016.

πίνετε (2d.per.pl.pres.act.ind.of πίνω, first-class condition) 611.

εἴτε (conditional disjunctive) 4016.

τι (acc.sing.neut.of τις, indefinite pronoun, direct object of ποιεῖτε) 486.

ποιεῖτε (2d.per.pl.pres.act.ind.of ποιέω, aoristic) 127.

πάντα (acc.pl.neut.of πᾶς, direct object οι ποιειτε) 67.

εἰς (preposition with the accusative, purpose) 140.

δόξαν (acc.sing.fem.of δόξα, purpose) 361.

θεοῦ (gen.sing.masc.of θεός, description) 124.

ποιεῖτε (2d.per.pl.pres.act.impv.command) 127.

Translation - "So whether you are eating or drinking, or whatever you are doing, do everything for the divine glory."

Comment: Remember that verse 30 poses a question that demands an answer. It is therefore contextually inappropriate to take οὖν here as inferential. Nor should we take it as transitional, emphatic, intensive or adversative. None of these ideas fit the context. Mantey speaks of a responsive use, by which he means that " . . . it is used to introduce a new speaker who responds to what another person has just said." (Julius R. Mantey, *The Meaning of οὖν* in John's Writings, Chapter V, page 1. Unpublished Th.D. dissertation, Southern Baptist Theological Seminary, Louisville, Kentucky). He finds this use only in John's gospel. When the question to which the statement is a response is "Why?" responsive οὖν is also causal as in 1 Cor.10:31. "Why should a Christian be condemned for exercising his liberty?" The answer (responsive οὖν) is "Because (causal οὖν) a Christian is supposed to be promoting the divine glory in everything he does, whether it is eating or drinking or anything else." We do not promote God's glory by behaving in a way that causes our weak brethren to be ensnared (#1082). Note the conditional particle in sequence. εἰς with the accusative is purpose. Anarthrous θεοῦ is descriptive - the glory of a divine essence.

Verse 31 is the positive reply to the question of verse 30. The negative reply is found in

Verse 32 - "Give none offence, neither to the Jews, nor to the Gentiles, nor to the church of God."

ἀπρόσκοποι καὶ Ἰουδαίοις γίνεσθε καὶ Ἕλλησιν καὶ τῇ ἐκκλησίᾳ τοῦ θεοῦ.

"Give no offense to Jews or to Greeks or to the church of God," . . . RSV

ἀπρόσκοποι (nom.pl.masc.of ἀπρόσκοπος, predicate adjective) 3626.
καὶ (correlative conjunction) 14.
Ἰουδαίοις (dat.pl.masc.of Ἰουδαῖος, personal advantage) 143.
γίνεσθε (2d.per.pl.pres.mid.impv.of γίνομαι, command) 113.
καὶ (adjunctive conjunction joining nouns) 14.
Ἕλλησιν (dat.pl.masc.of Ἕλλήν, personal advantage) 2373.
καὶ (adjunctive conjunction joining nouns) 14.
τῇ (dat.sing.fem.of the article in agreement with ἐκκλησίᾳ) 9.
ἐκκλησίᾳ (dat.sing.fem.of ἐκκλησία, personal advantage) 1204.
τοῦ (gen.sing.masc.of the article in agreement with θεοῦ) 9.
θεοῦ (gen.sing.masc.of θεός, possession) 124.

Translation - "Always be inoffensive both to Jews and Greeks and to the church of God."

Comment: *Cf.*#3626. *Cf.* Acts 24:16; Phil.1:10.
The nature of the advice here is negative but the form is positive. We are always to be inoffensive. A Christian is never justified in giving offense, however powerfully we may be motivated. Note that Paul divides the world into three categories: unsaved Jews, unsaved Gentiles and saints, who may be either Jews or Gentiles. The Christian should offend none of them.

Note that θεοῦ was anarthrous in verse 31 but has the article in verse 32. Without the article the idea is definition or essence. With the article it is possession. Since a full exercise of Christian liberty of action would offend the unsaved and the babes in Christ in the church, we have Paul's reply to the question of verse 30. If we are going to be without offense to all men, Jew and Gentile, saved and unsaved, we must be prepared to exercise the highest right we possess - the right to give up our rights. We have a magnificant example to guide us. Our Lord gave up His rights at Calvary. His imperative - "This is my commandment, That ye love one another. . . " is based upon His indicative - ". . . as I have loved you."

Society in the late twentieth century is falling into chaotic collapse. One major cause is the strident demand that our rights be made secure. The idea that if the general welfare of society is to be secured we must give up our rights finds few proponents. Labor and management each insist upon their rights. Women dedicated to "Women's Liberation" demand their rights. Pregnant women with unwanted babies demand their rights over their bodies, which in some way they imagine they will secure if they are permitted to abort their unborn child. Few in society, not even those in the Christian community, are willing to give up their rights. Most Christians will eat whatever they like even if others are destroyed.

Verse 33 - "Even as I please all men in all things, not seeking mine own profit, but the profit of many, that they may be saved."

καθὼς κἀγὼ πάντα ἀρέσκω, μὴ ζητῶν τὸ ἐμαυτοῦ σύμφορον ἀλλὰ τὸ τῶν πολλῶν, ἵνα σωθῶσιν.

"Just as I try to please all men in everything I do, not seeking my own advantage, but that of many, that they may be saved." . . . RSV

καθὼς (complound comparative particle) 1348.

κἀγὼ (adjunctive conjunction and first personal pronoun, crasis) 178.

πάντα (acc.pl.masc.of πᾶς, direct object of ἀρέσκω) 67.

πᾶσιν (dat.pl.neut.of πᾶς, reference) 67.

ἀρέσκω (1st.per.sing.pres.act.ind.of ἀρέσκω, present progressive retroactive) 1110.

μὴ (negative particle with the participle) 87.

ζητῶν (pres.act.part.nom.sing.masc.of ζητέω, adverbial, modal) 207.

τὸ (acc.sing.neut.of the article in agreement with σύμφορον) 9.

ἐμαυτοῦ (gen.sing.masc.of ἐμαυτοῦ, possession) 723.

σύμφορον (acc.sing.neut.of σύμφορος, direct object of ζητῶν) 4164.

ἀλλὰ (alternative conjunction) 342.

τὸ (acc.sing.neut.of the article, direct object of ζητῶν) 9.

τῶν (gen.pl.masc.of the article in agreement with πολλῶν) 9.

πολλῶν (gen.pl.masc.of πολύς, possession) 228.

ἵνα (conjunction with the subjunctive, purpose) 114.

σωθῶσιν (3d.per.pl.pres.act.subj.of σώζω, purpose) 109.

Translation - "Just as I also always please all men in every situation, by not seeking my own advantage, but that of the others, so that they may be saved."

Comment: Paul sets himself forth as an example of the ethics of verses 31 and 32. Paul tried to please everyone with respect to everything that he did. How did he go about to do this? The modal adverbial participle tells us how. "By never seeking my own advantage." What alternative policy did he follow? "By always seeking the advantage of the others." Why did he do this? The purpose clause with ἵνα σωθῶσιν tells us - "In order that they might be saved."

If Paul could travel, preach, make tents to pay his own bills, get thrown into a Philippian jail and beaten, get stoned until his enemies thought he was dead, narrowly escape drowning at sea, survive snake bite and finally lose his head in a Roman arena, surely a Corinthian Christian could forego the pleasure of a bite of meat in order to help a weak brother. This statement of self-denial is the essence of Christian love. Nothing in history and upon this earth is as important as the salvation of one otherwise lost soul.

The King James Version places the next verse in the next chapter, although it obviously belongs in chapter ten. We will reserve its exegesis for the next chapter and the next volume.

INDEX